AF328414

BRITISH WILDLIFE

PHOTOGRAPHY AWARDS 12

British Wildlife Photography Awards 12
Published in Great Britain in 2024 by Bird Eye Books,
an imprint of Graffeg Limited.

Text and photographs by British Wildlife Photography
Awards copyright © 2024. Designed and produced
by Graffeg Limited copyright © 2024.

Graffeg Limited, 24 Stradey Park Business Centre,
Mwrwg Road, Llangennech, Llanelli, Carmarthenshire,
SA14 8YP, Wales, UK. www.graffeg.com.

British Wildlife Photography Awards is hereby identified as
the author of this work in accordance with section 77 of
the Copyright, Designs and Patents Act 1988.

A CIP Catalogue record for this book is available
from the British Library.

The publisher gratefully acknowledges the financial
support of this book by the Books Council of Wales.
www.gwales.com.

ISBN 9781802586206

1 2 3 4 5 6 7 8 9

Cover image: *Three's a Crowd*,
Hidden Britain Winner by Ross Hoddinott.

BRITISH WILDLIFE

PHOTOGRAPHY AWARDS **12**

FOREWORD BY
STEVE BACKSHALL

EDITED BY
WILL NICHOLLS

BIRD EYE BOOKS

CATEGORIES AND AWARDS

Animal Behaviour – Images that convey wildlife behaviour and action.

Animal Portrait – Images that capture the beauty and 'character' of the subject, often showcasing the 'personality' of an animal.

Botanical Britain – Images of trees, plants, flowers, fungi and algae that showcase the diversity of the botanical world.

Black & White – Images of British wildlife or landscapes that use this medium creatively, such as highlighting texture and tone.

Coast & Marine – Images showcasing nature beneath the waves.

Habitat – Images that portray the relationship between an environment and the animals that live there.

Hidden Britain – Images that show the life of invertebrates on a small scale.

Urban Wildlife – Images showing wild animals or plants within an urban environment.

Wild Woods – Images that celebrate the beauty and sheer splendour of British woodlands and their residents.

SPECIAL AWARDS

British Seasons – A sequence of four images that show British wildlife at its best across all four seasons.

Documentary Series – A sequence of up to six images of any British wildlife, habitat or landscape conservation issue.

RSPB Young British Wildlife Photographer of the Year – Celebrating the talent of photographers under the age of 18, this award is split into three age groups:
11 and under
12-14 years
15-17 years

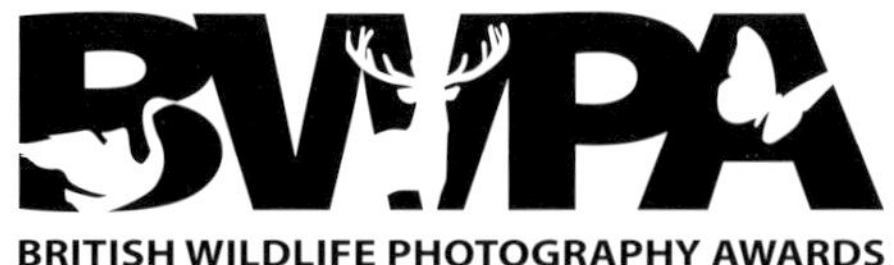

For further information about the annual competition and touring exhibition please visit:
www.bwpawards.org

CONTENTS

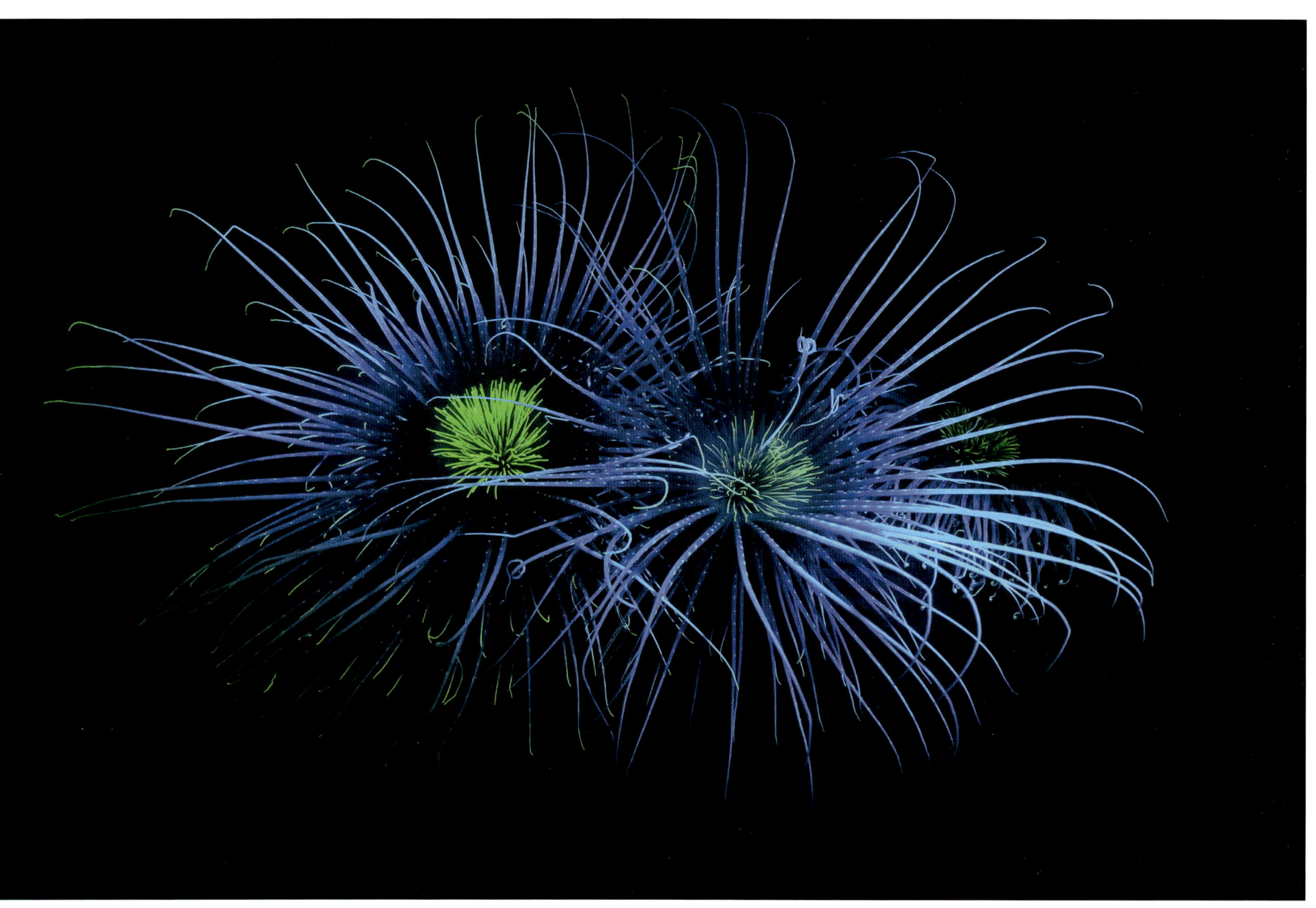

Fire in the Night
Dan Bolt
Page 22

FOREWORD

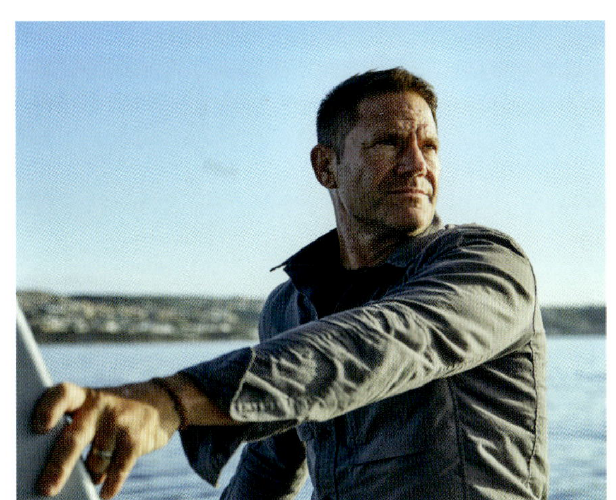

Image from Sky Original *Shark* with Steve Backshall.
Photo © Sky UK Limited & True to Nature.

The greatest joy of wildlife photography is to offer a different perspective on the wild world, to make you think, or see beauty as if for the first time. The British Wildlife Photography Awards is the most perfect example of this, offering either a sharp focus or distorting lens on the natural world that has been my home, my backyard, my escape and my solace since I was a boy, sifting through the manure heap in the search for grass snakes. I feel I know this place well, yet flip through these pages and see familiar things as if I'm an alien visiting the planet for the first time!

There are images that force me to reimagine the British countryside and its fauna, captured by naturalists prepared to look in new ways. That could be through technology, like the fireworks anemones in Loch Fyne shot using filters our eyes simply don't have to create aquatic neon wonderment. It could be with composition, such as the glorious sea hare shot by Shannon Moran off the Falmouth coast, seeming to be riding on a magic carpet of kelp. The gifted picture painter can freeze a moment in time, turning a long-tailed tit with its wings spread into the angel Gabriel, or arresting red squirrels mid-leap so they take on the appeal of hyper-real taxidermy. The best wildlife photography can blow up the microscopic, turning slime moulds into a fairground balloon display, or it can watch from a respectful distance, spying in as frogs in amplexus cavort in courtship embrace.

Wildlife photographers tend to make the best naturalists (and vice versa). To capture the perfect shot you need to get into that animal's head, and I see that process on every page of this beautiful book. Tireless work has allowed these genius frame-snatchers to figure out how an animal is going to behave so they can anticipate their movements and be primed and ready when they step out onto their natural stage. Often, that can be within our towns and cities, with the wild and the urban juxtaposed in often jarring ways.

Every time I see a book like this, I'm inspired to pick up my own camera and make my own history of the world outside my window. Truth is, my bigger duty right now is to bring my three small children to the natural world, hence every wildlife photo I take is now with at least one small human hanging around my neck! But I have so much respect for the photographers receiving this accolade, and such envy for your commitment to process and artistry. You have recorded a snapshot of our nation's nature in time, and our world is a little more beautiful because of it.

Steve Backshall

THE BRITISH WILDLIFE PHOTOGRAPHY AWARDS

Once again, the British Wildlife Photography Awards (BWPA) brings to light the spectacular tapestry of Britain's natural heritage. This year, as we turn the pages of our annual competition book, we unfold a narrative of nature's raw beauty and diversity, showcasing enchanting scenes from British woodlands, wetlands and wildlife.

With over 13,000 entries, each photograph is a tribute to the extraordinary resilience of nature, an echo of the strength and persistence that define it.

The photographers whose works grace these pages have been chosen for their exceptional skill and artistic vision, as well as fieldcraft and understanding of the natural world.

This collection is more than just a gallery of images; it is a celebration, a reminder of the enduring beauty of British wildlife and a call to preserve the natural spaces that we are so fortunate to have in Britain. It is an invitation to pause, to appreciate and to be inspired by the wild, majestic and beautifully untamed spirit of Britain's nature.

Take this inspiration beyond these pages. Engage with local conservation efforts, visit natural reserves and learn about the wildlife that shares our countryside and urban spaces. Your actions, no matter how small, can contribute to a larger impact in protecting and nurturing Britain's natural legacy.

Will Nicholls, Director

Stag in Snow ▶
Animal Portraits

Peter Whitehead
Red deer (*Cervus elaphus*)
Upper Spey Valley, Scotland

Canon EOS 7D Mark II with 150-600mm F5-6.3 lens. 374mm; 1/500th second; f/6.3; ISO 640.

During harsh winters, deer will come down from the high tops of Scotland's mountains and congregate in the headwaters of river valleys. Here, they can find more shelter and easier access to food. This image was taken in the Upper Spey valley. I watched as a snow shower came in and wanted an image that showed the severe conditions these animals face. I was able to get down low and frame the stag against a faint background of woodland and the meagre vegetation these animals rely on during the winter months.

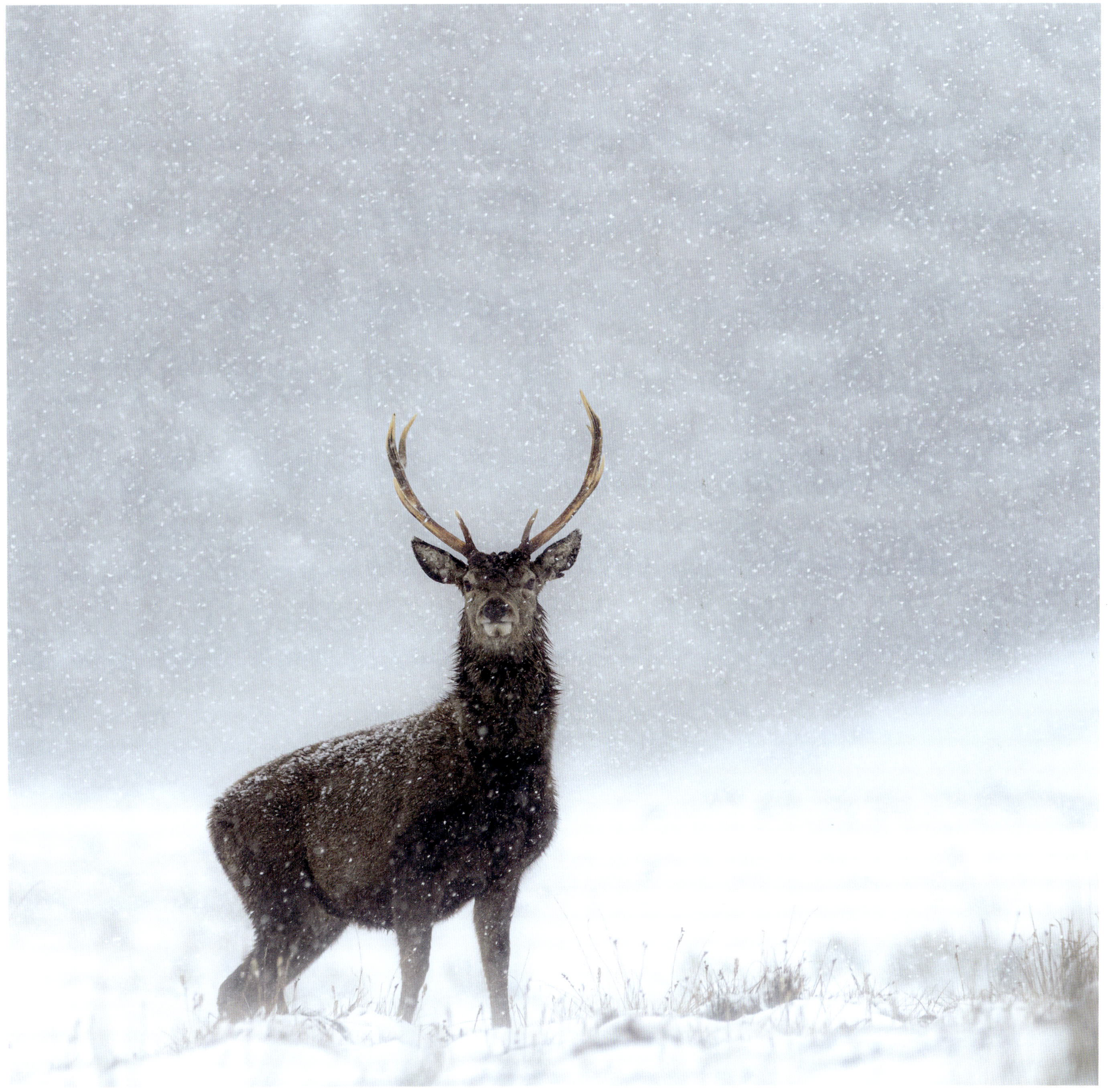

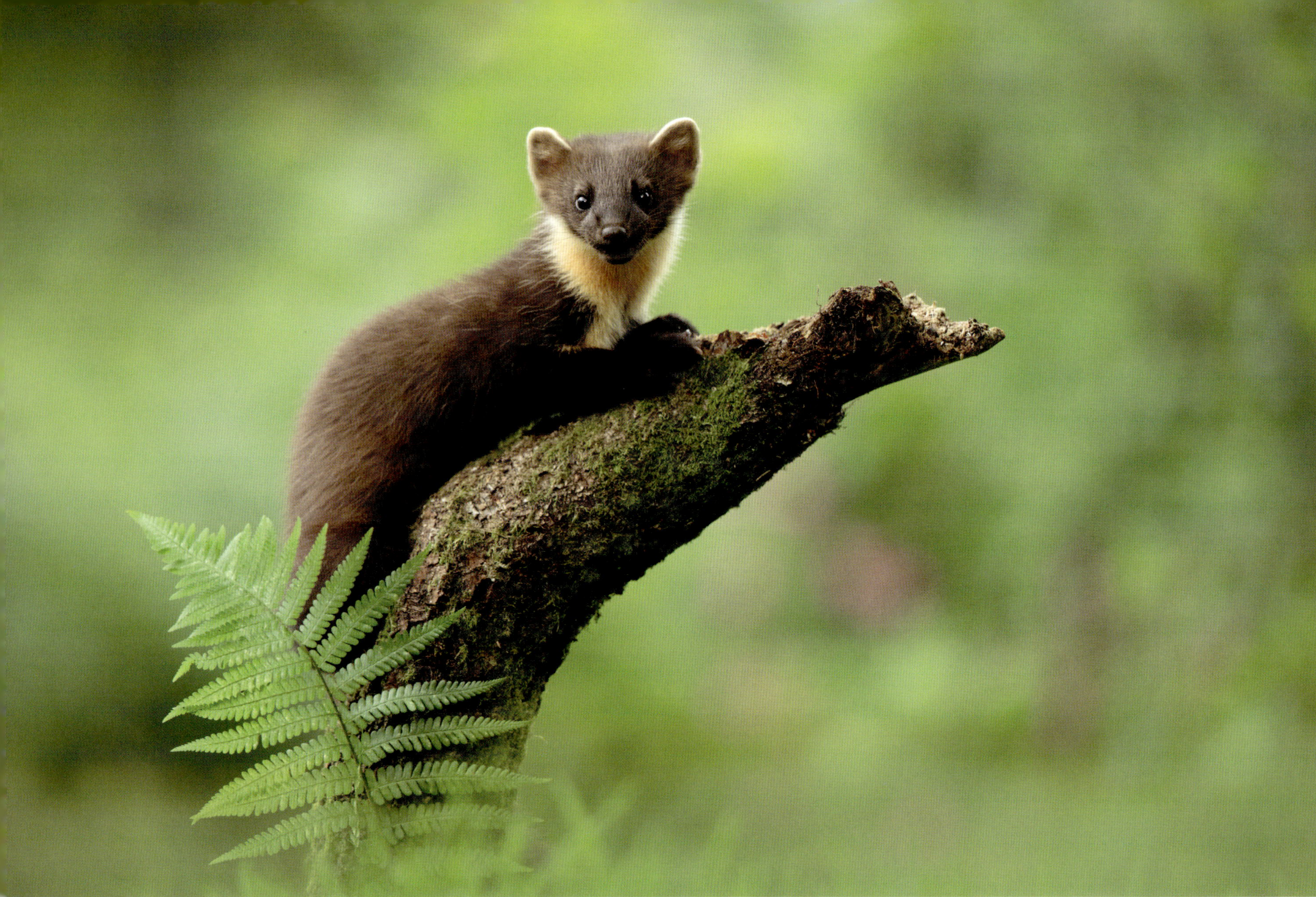

Cute Killer
Animal Portraits

Daniel Trim
Pine marten (*Martes martes*)
Ardnamurchan, Scotland

Canon 5DS with 500mm f/4 II lens. 500mm;
1/250th second; f/4; ISO 1000.

While staying in a remote cottage in western
Scotland, we were blessed with nightly visits from
a pine marten mother and her two kits. This is one
of the kits. It looks quite adult-like, but that cuter
face and those big paws reveal its age! I was hiding
behind some scrim netting and accidentally dragged
my foot on the ground. Instantly, I was under
investigation!

JUDGES

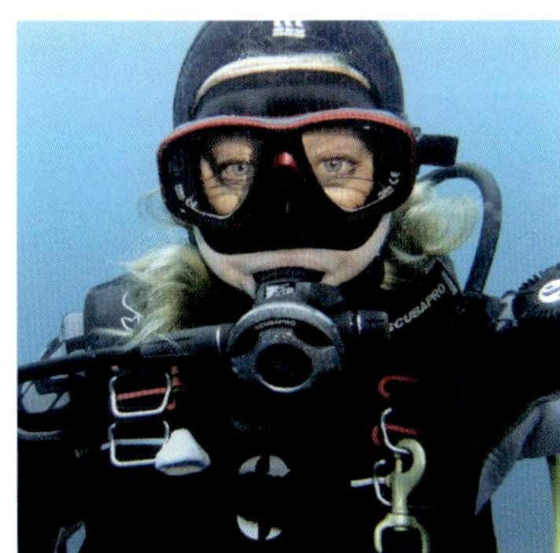

Jane Morgan
An underwater photojournalist with a passion for all creatures great and small, Jane loves the adventure of travelling but is also crazy about the marine life at home in the UK. She is currently working as Dive Safety Officer at Falmouth University, where she shares her love of the marine environment.

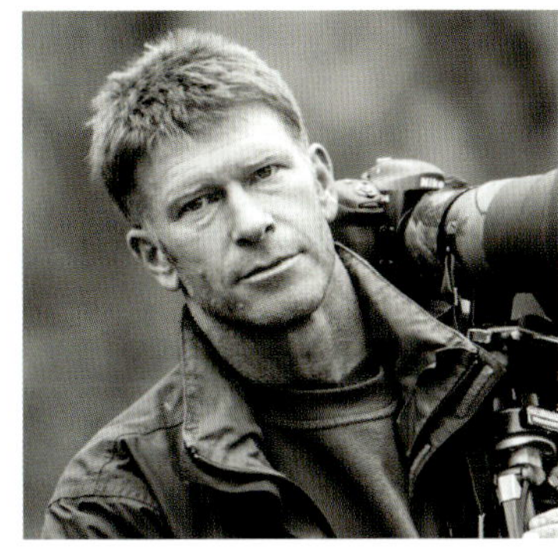

David Plummer
David is a wildlife photographer and conservationist. He also guides, is a wildlife consultant for many international television crews and films for BBC *Springwatch*. David's best-selling book, *7 years of Camera Shake*, was published in 2017.

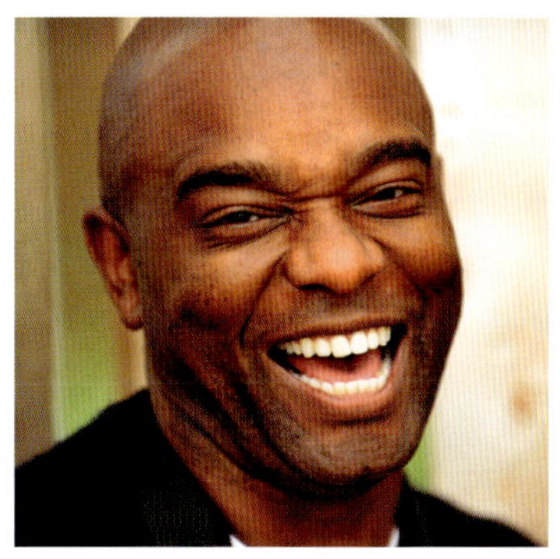

David Lindo
David Lindo is The Urban Birder – broadcaster, writer, speaker, educator and bird tour leader. His mission is to engage city folk around the world with the environment through birds.

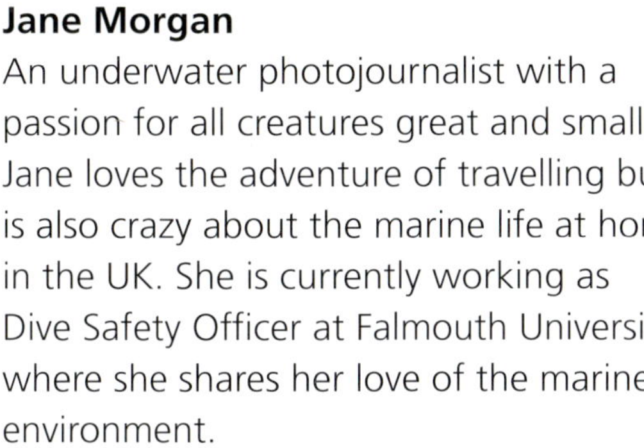

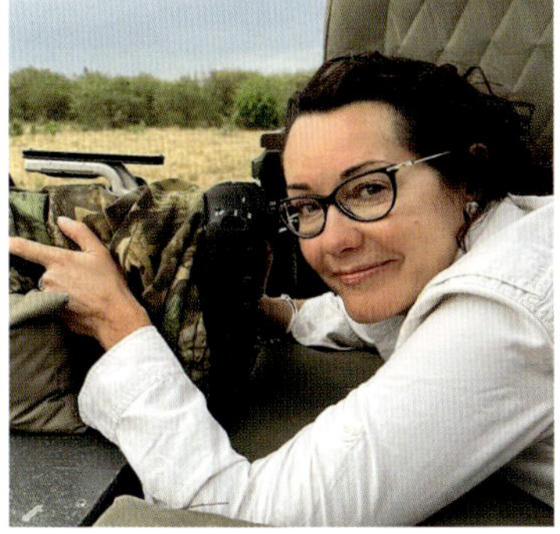

Ellie Rothnie
Best known for bird and mammal portraiture, professional photographer Ellie has been awarded in international competitions and exhibited overseas. She photographs across Europe, USA and Africa.

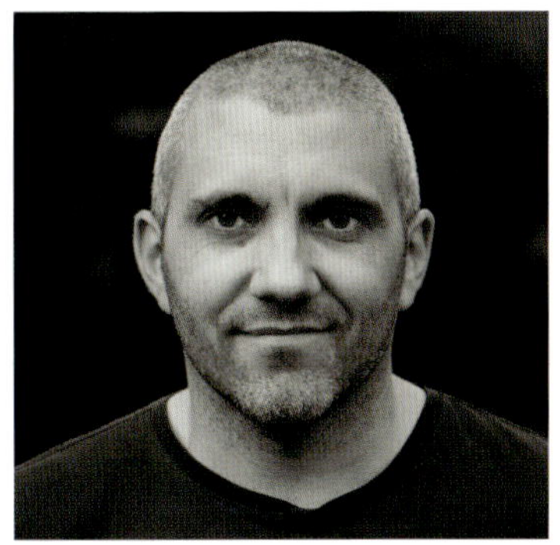

Richard Peters
Richard is a wildlife photographer, speaker and author, with a style that favours light over subject. His work has received international acclaim and he regularly works with brands such as Nikon and Datacolor as an ambassador.

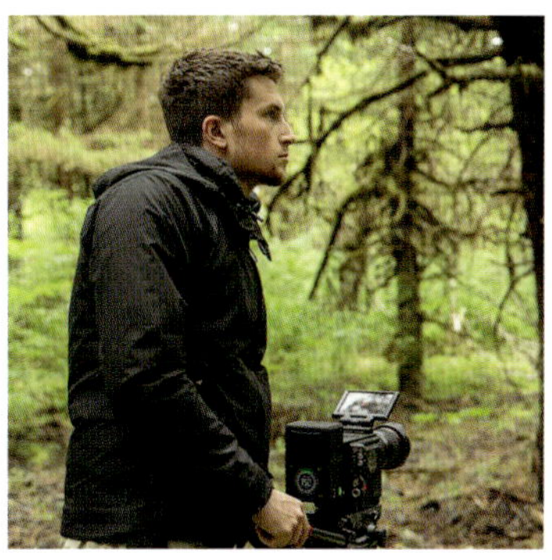

Will Nicholls
Will is the director of BWPA. He is also a wildlife cameraman working in natural history television for major broadcasters including Netflix, Disney, and Apple TV+. He has been a stills photographer since 2007.

SPONSORS

Canon is dedicated to helping people reimagine and push the boundaries of what is possible through imaging, helping to see our world in ways we never have before. www.canon.co.uk.

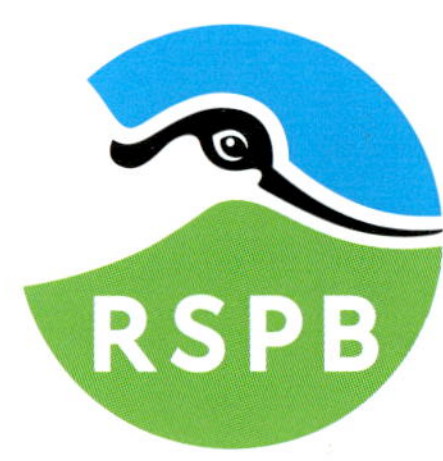

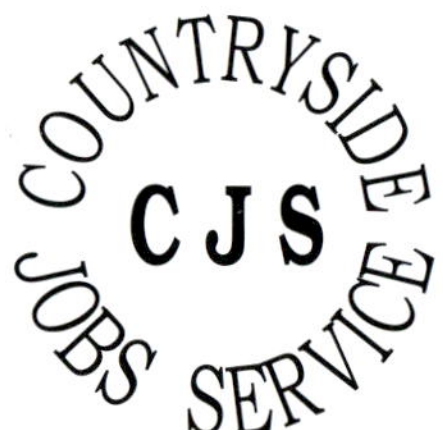

The RSPB – protecting habitats, saving species and helping to end the nature and climate emergency. Nature is in crisis, together we can save it. www.rspb.org.uk.

CJS is an ethical business working in harmony with environmental professionals to conserve the British countryside and natural world. Motivated by conservation success, not profits. www.countryside-jobs.com.

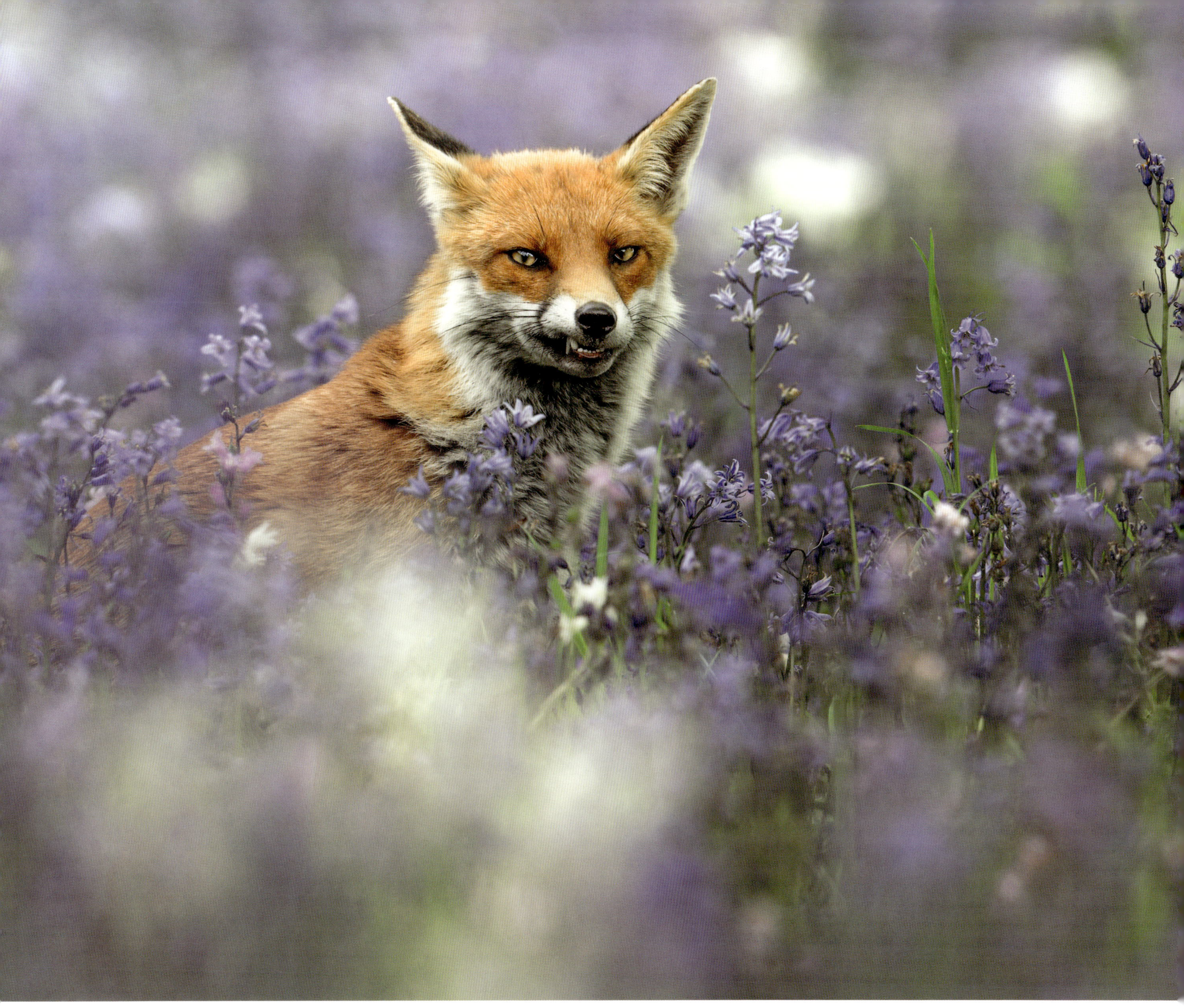

A Fox in the Bluebells
Victor Soares
Page 82

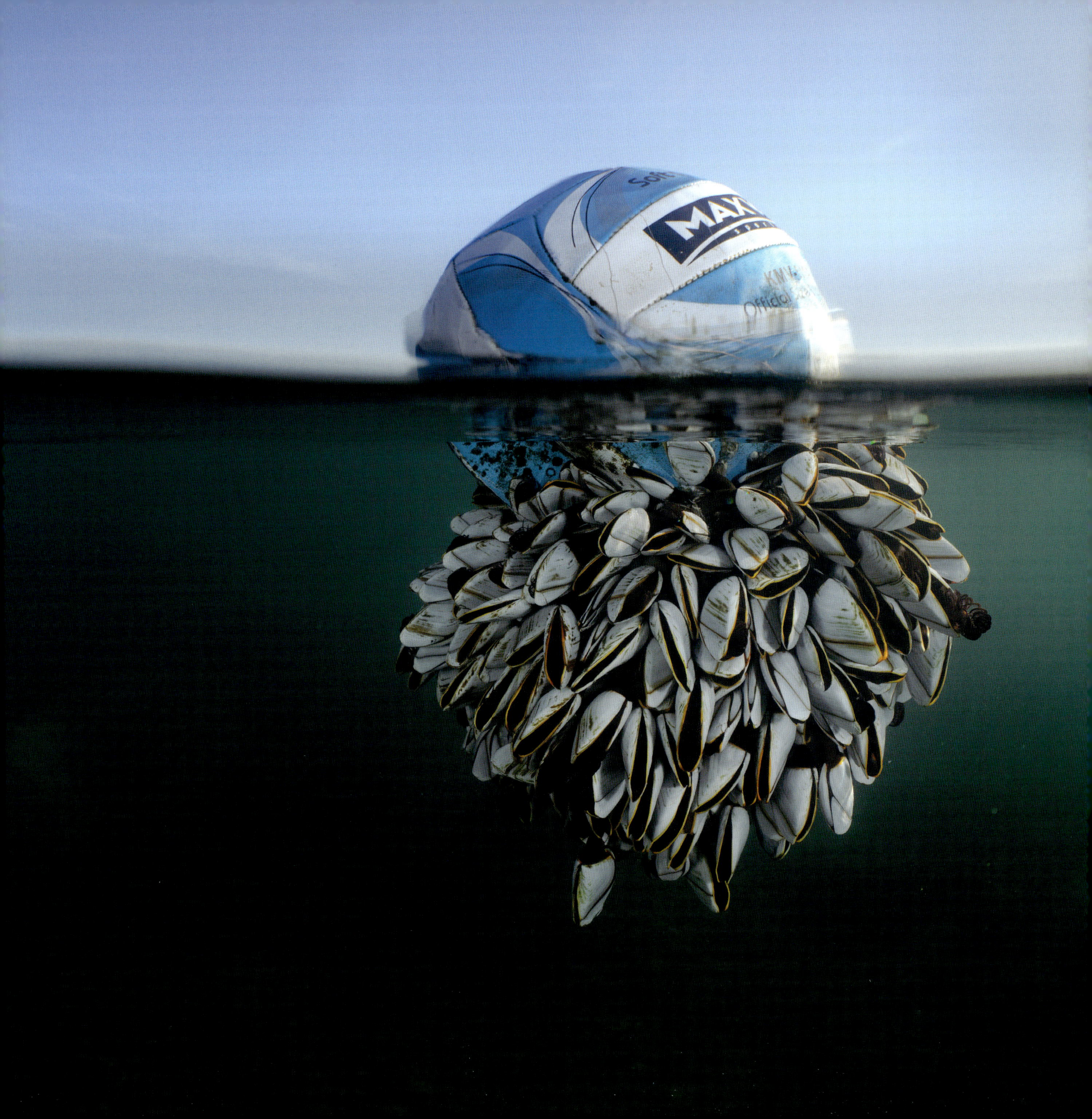
Soft
MAX
KML
Official

OVERALL WINNER

Ocean Drifter
British Wildlife Photographer of the Year 2024
and Winner of Coast & Marine

Ryan Stalker
Goose barnacles (Thoracica)
Portland, Dorset, England

Sony A7R IV with Sony 28-60mm f/4-5.6 lens. 29mm; 1/200th second;
f/7.1; ISO 80.

Ocean Drifter is a photo of a football that is covered in goose barnacles
below the waterline. Above the water is just a football. But below the
waterline is a colony of creatures. The football was washed up in Dorset
after making a huge ocean journey across the Atlantic and then returned
to the sea for the photo to be taken.

Goose barnacles are not native to the UK but can wash up on our shores
during powerful Atlantic storms. Although the ball is waste and should
not be in the sea, I do wonder about the journey the ball has been on.
From initially being lost, then spending time in the tropics where the
barnacles are native and perhaps years in the open ocean before arriving
in Dorset.

However, this waste can also bring creatures that may survive in UK
waters and could become invasive species. More human waste in the sea
could increase the risk of more creatures making it to our shores.

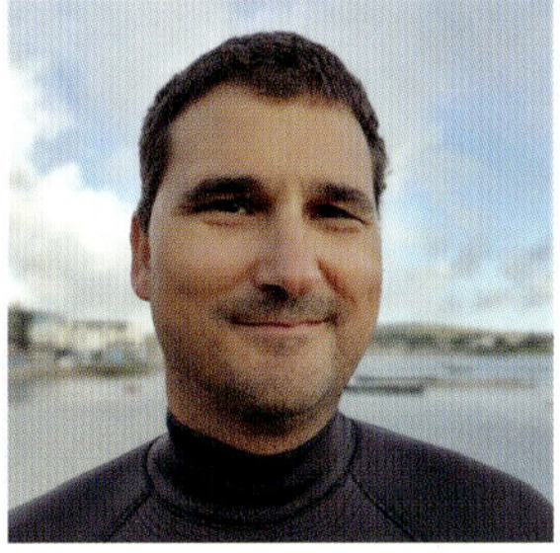

Ryan Stalker
Ryan grew up on Portland along the beautiful Dorset coastline. At a
young age he became fascinated with the sea and the creatures that
live within it, wanting to see and learn more about them. He began his
diving adventures at the age of 16 and has spent almost all his spare time
in the sea since then, exploring the Dorset coastline as well as some more
tropical places. He first became interested in underwater photography
to show people the amazing variety of life around our coastline. This has
since led to him being awarded in UK and international competitions and
has driven a passion to develop further as an underwater photographer
and capture amazing moments beneath or above the waves.

Checking the Wind
Animal Behaviour

Tony Moss
Badger (*Meles meles*)
New Forest, Hampshire, England

Nikon Z6 II with Nikon 500mm f/4 lens.
500mm; 1/500th second; f/5; ISO 1,800.

Having photographed badgers for many years,
I am still occasionally surprised by just how much
noise they make and how often they scare one
another while going about their daily business.
On this occasion, two cubs were crashing about in
the nearby bracken when this adult emerged from
the sett. On hearing all the noise, it immediately
froze. For a brief moment, it raised its head and
tested the air for danger. Once satisfied that all
was well, it soon continued foraging.

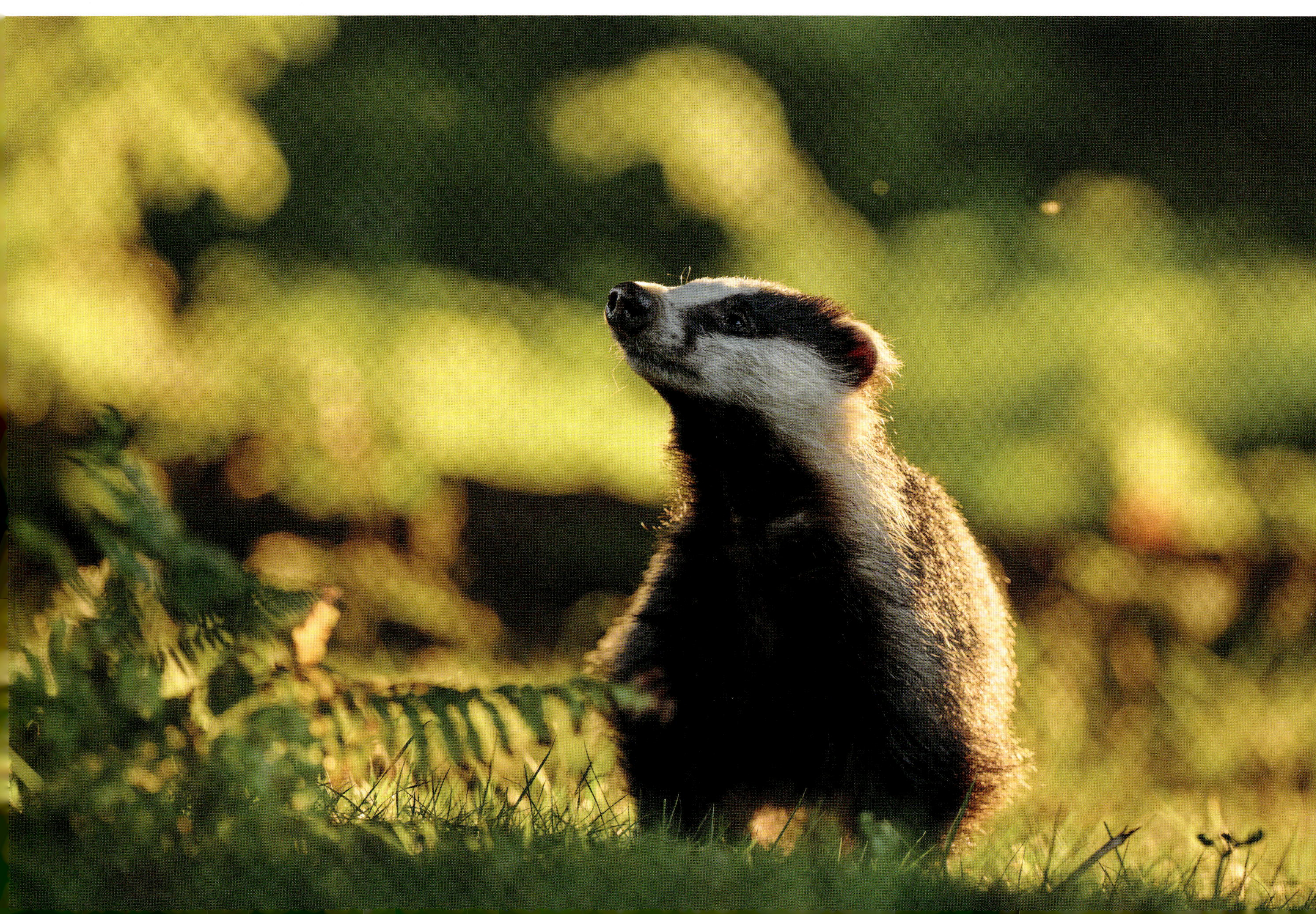

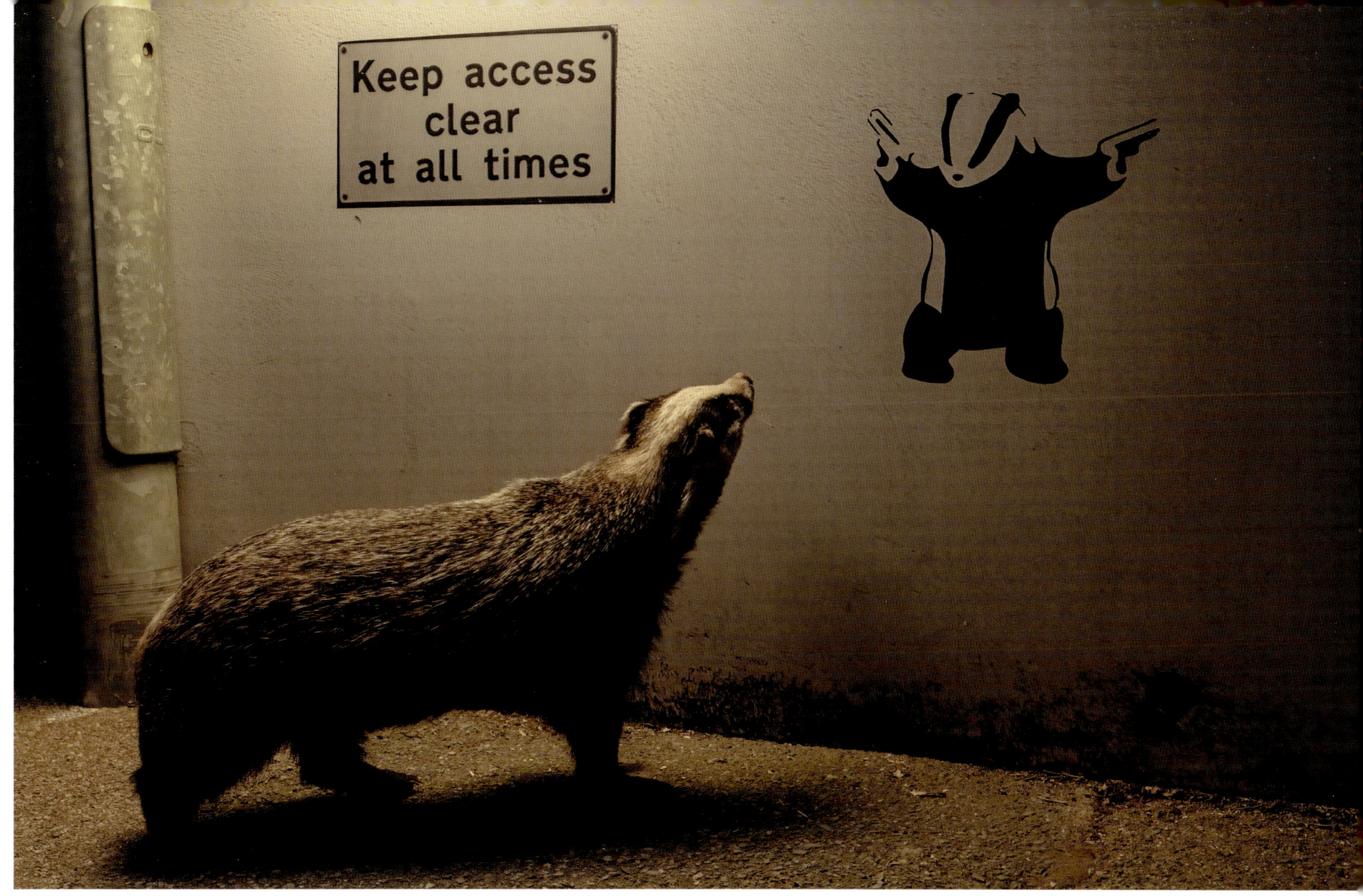

No Access
Urban Wildlife | Highly Commended

Ian Wood
Badger (*Meles meles*)
St Leonards-on-Sea, East Sussex, England

Nikon D500 with Nikon 18-35mm F3.5/4.5 lens.
31mm; 1/100th second; f/9; ISO 2500.

It took about 18 months from seeing this image when returning home late one night to being able to capture it. I lurked in a pop-up hide in the road quite a bit and started to get the odd shot of a badger walking past, but I wanted to try and capture one looking up at the graffiti. Badgers have an incredible sense of smell, so in the end putting a small amount of wet cat food on the wall did the trick, and I was thrilled when, for a brief second, it sniffed the air.

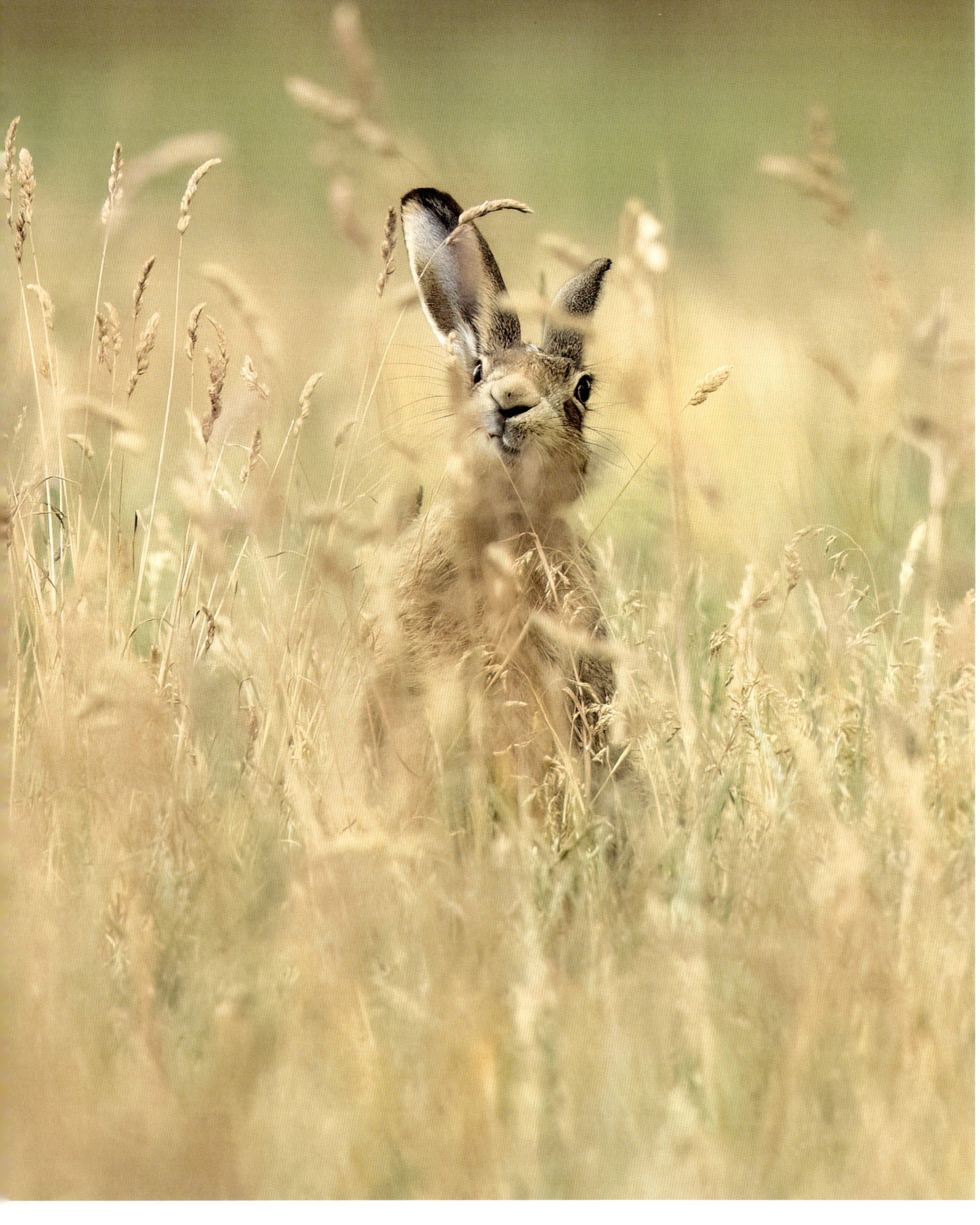

Jonathan Gaunt
Brown hare (*Lepus europaeus*)
North Northumberland, England

Canon EOS R5 with Canon RF 100-
500mm f/4.5-7.1 lens. 1/400th second;
f/7.1; ISO 2,500.

This brown hare was being very selective
in choosing and nibbling off the grass
seed heads it wanted to eat.

Mountain Hare
Animal Portraits | Highly Commended

Danny Green
Mountain hare (*Lepus timidus*)
Cairngorms National Park, Scotland

Canon EOS 1D X II with Canon 500mm
f/4 lens & 1.4x teleconverter. 700mm;
1/250th second; f/5.6; ISO 400.

I took this image in the Cairngorms
National Park. I was actually looking for
ptarmigan, but found this mountain
hare along the way. It was very relaxed
with my presence, and I spent most of
the day with him.

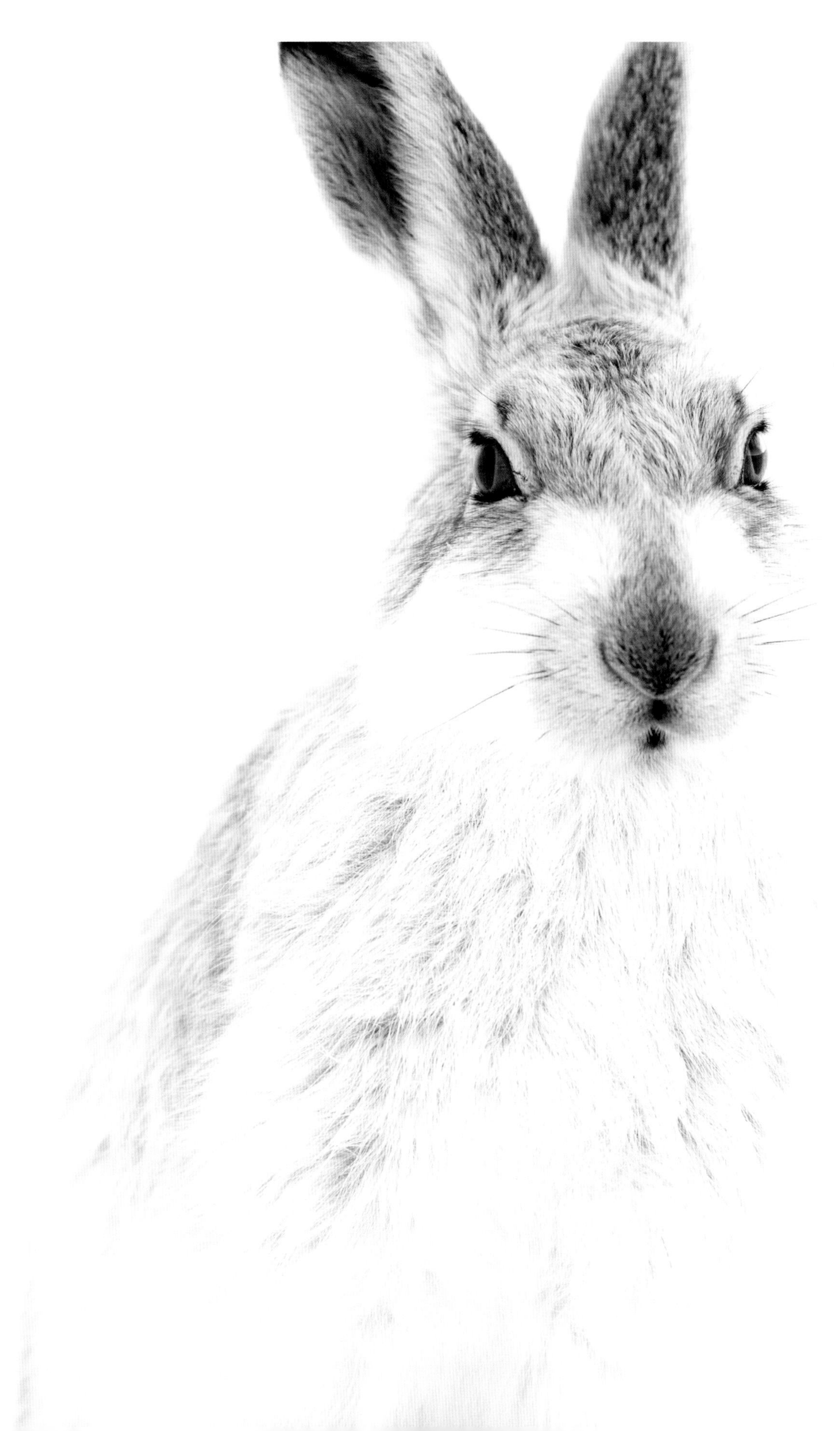

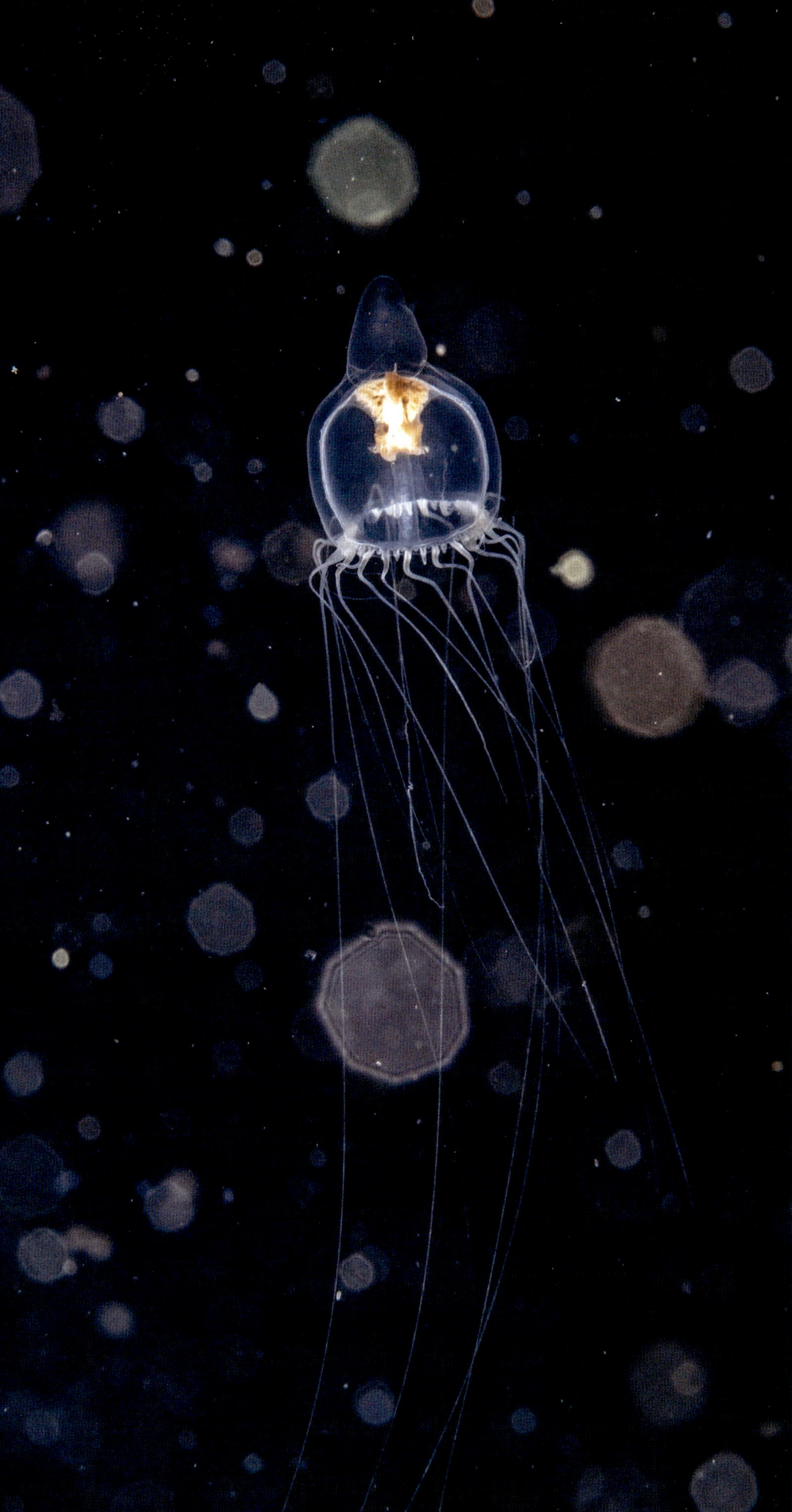

Bloomin'
Coast & Marine

Billy Arthur
Hydrozoa
Boddam, Shetland Islands, Scotland

Sony A7R III with Sony 90mm f/2.8 lens. 90mm; 1/125th second; f/18; ISO 640.

This small jellyfish was swimming through the twilight sea during the spring bloom. I tried to light the shot to give it a space-like feeling, as I love the way these tiny jellyfish remind me of spacecraft cruising through a galaxy of backscattered stars. Usually, backscatter is the enemy in underwater photography, but in some cases it can positively add to the image. It's always a challenge to nail the focus on these types of shots, as the camera, cameraman and subject are all moving, not to mention the tiny subject and shooting in the dark.

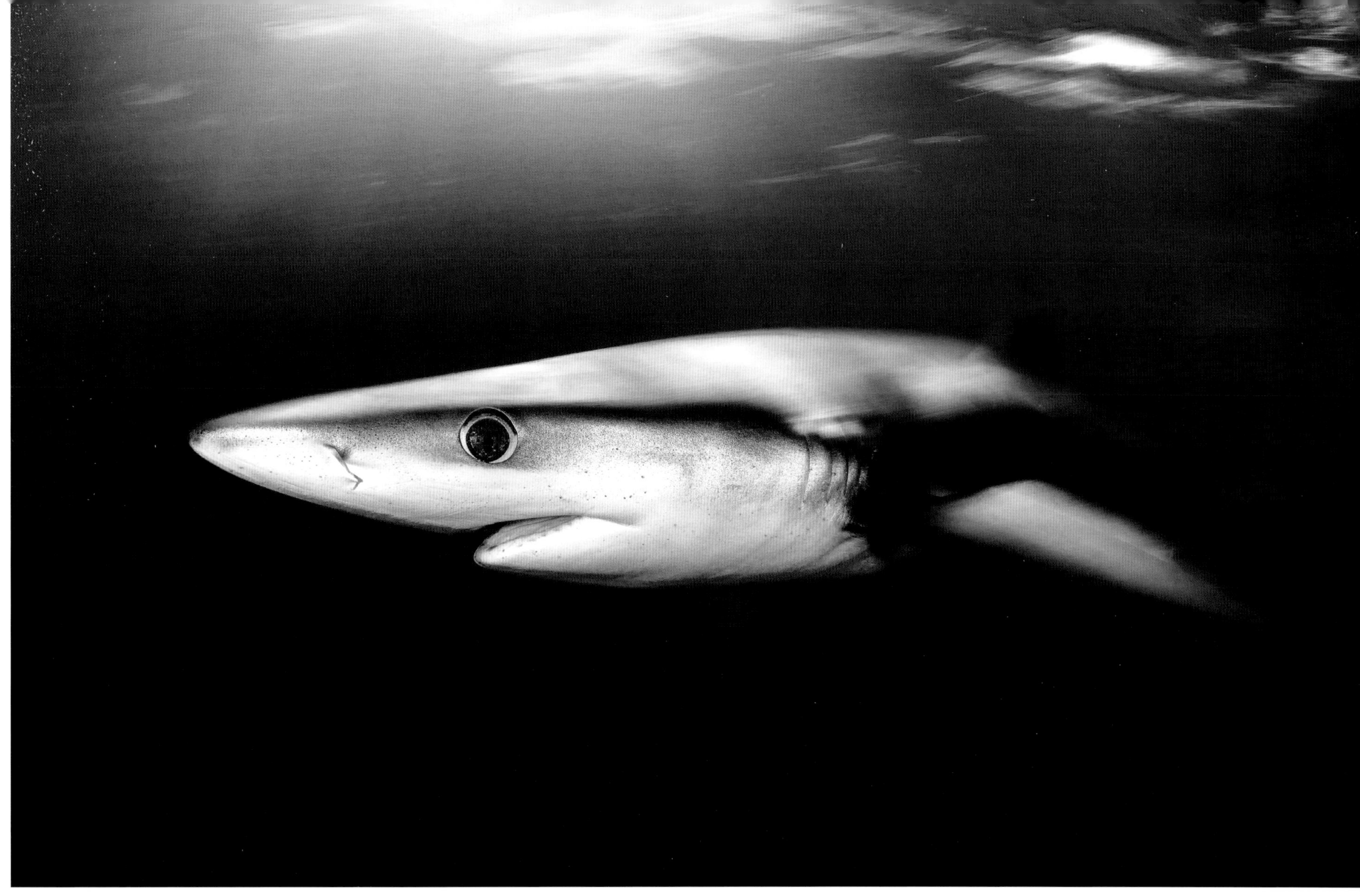

Black and Blue

Black & White | Highly Commended

Kirsty Andrews

Blue shark (*Prionace glauca*)
Offshore from Penzance, Cornwall, England

Nikon D500 with Tokina 10-17mm lens.
10mm; 1/13th second; f/22; ISO 100.

Swimming with blue sharks is one of the most wonderful wildlife activities I have experienced in UK waters. Often, offshore waters are crystal clear, but on this day there were clouds and slightly murkier water, providing an opportunity to use slow shutter speeds. I used a panning technique to accentuate the languid movement of the shark, while my flash highlighted the beautiful detail in the shark's body, even more starkly in monochrome. For example, you can clearly see the ampullae of Lorenzini, sensors that allow the shark to detect the electric fields created by its prey.

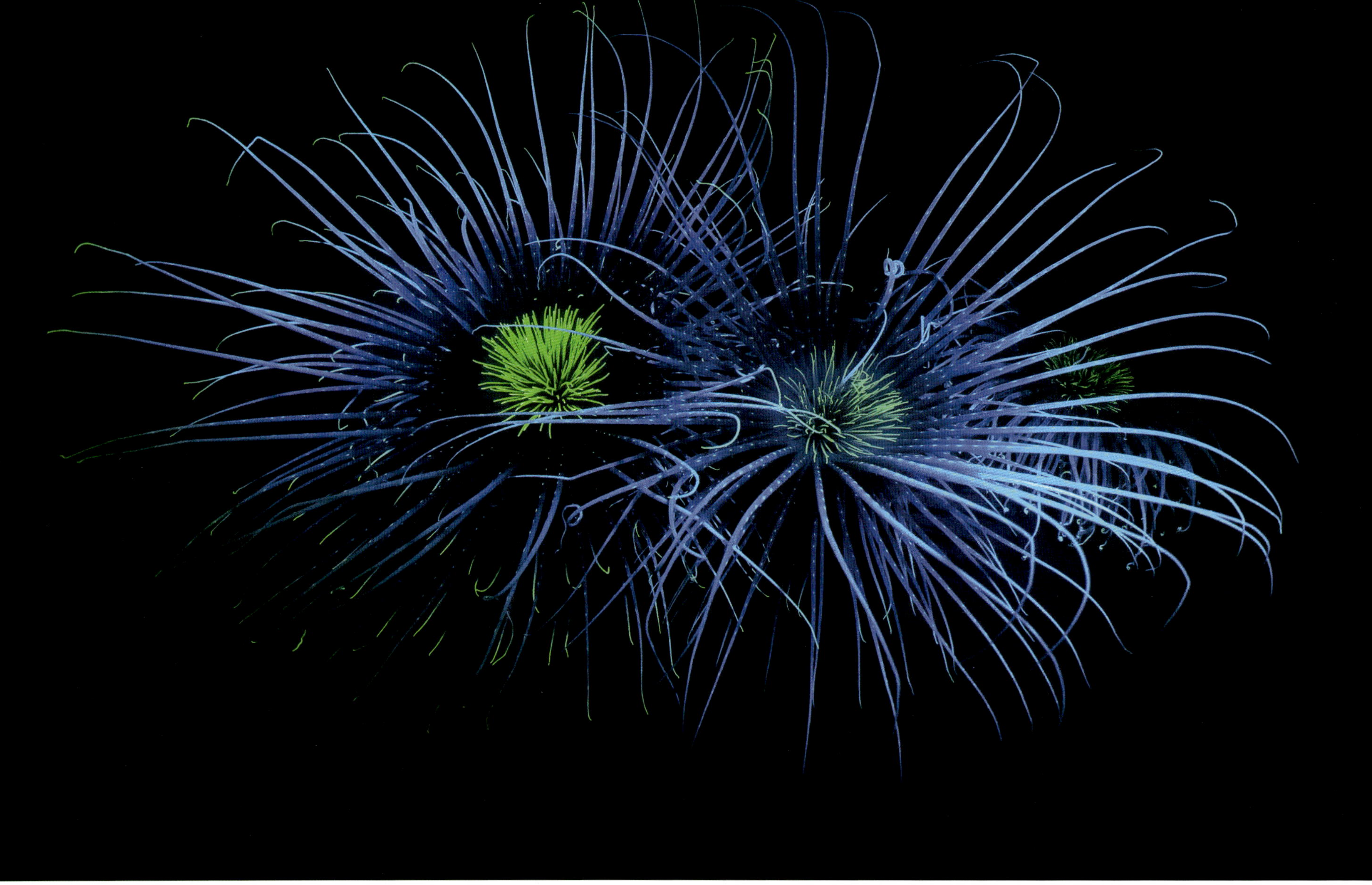

Fire in the Night
Coast & Marine | Runner-up

Dan Bolt
Fireworks anemone (*Pachycerianthus multiplicatus*)
Loch Fyne, Scotland

Olympus E-M1 with Olympus 18-42mm lens. 14mm;
1/320th second; f/5.6; ISO 1,000.

Fluorescence photography requires specialist filters:
one 'exciter' filter on your white-light source to create
the blue light and another 'barrier' filter in front of
your lens to reduce the ambient light reaching your
sensor. These dual filters mean that high ISOs and
open apertures are very much required in order to
capture the excited, or fluoresced, light. The subject
requires a careful approach too; these anemones live
in very still water and are sensitive to the slightest
movement. If disturbed, they will retract in mere
seconds.

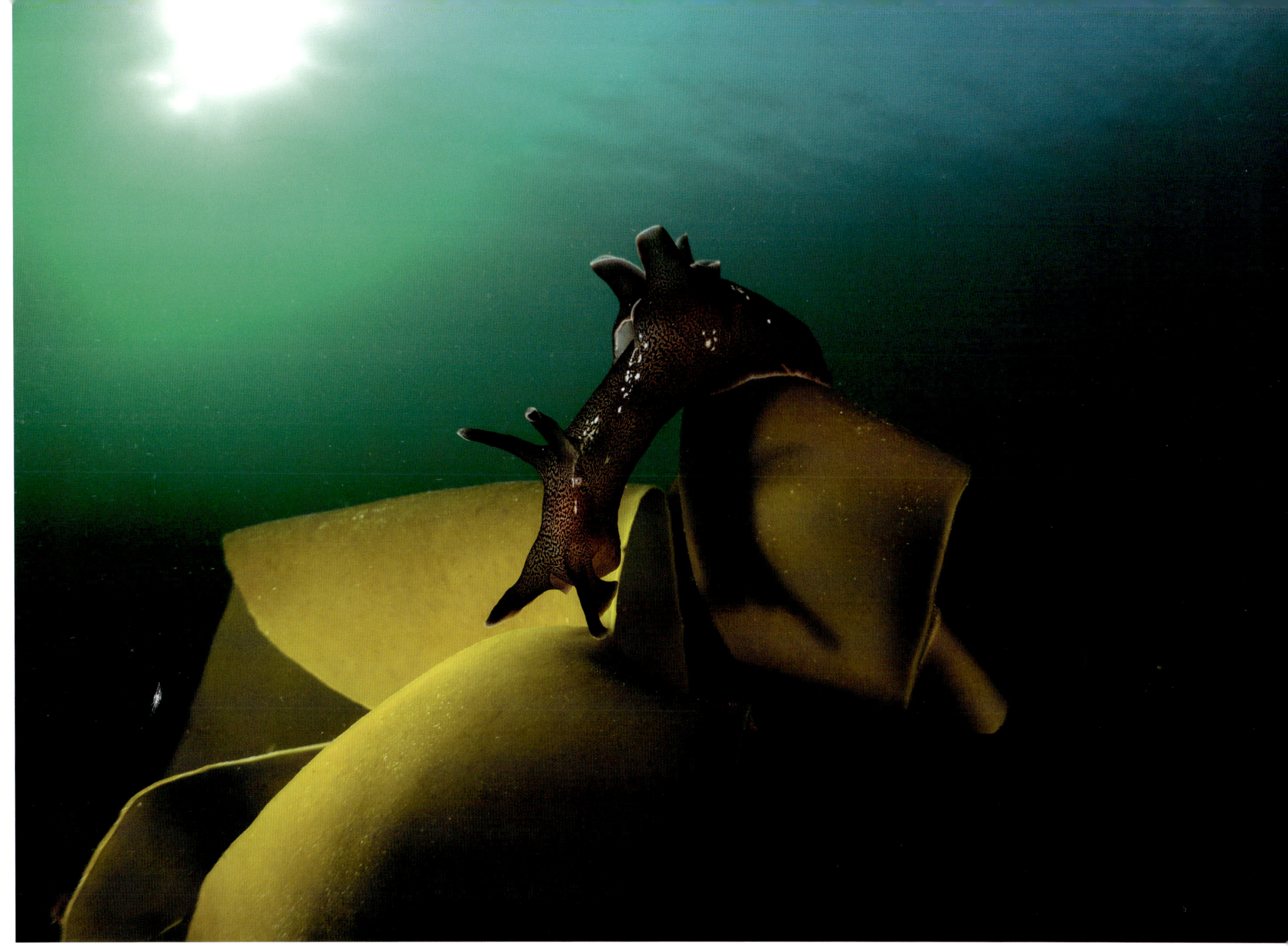

Sea Hare
Coast & Marine

Shannon Moran
Sea hare (*Aplysia punctata*) and
Golden kelp (*Laminaria ochroleuca*)
Falmouth, Cornwall, England

Olympus EM1 II with Lumix 8mm Fisheye lens.
8mm; 1/160th second; f/6.3; ISO 320.

A rather large sea hare perched on top of a piece of
golden kelp. After searching around for the first part
of the dive for a well-placed subject where the green,
algae-filled waters ended and the clearer blue water
of the shallows merged, I finally found this individual
atop the kelp with a beautiful turquoise background,
reaching out for the sky as it slowly moved along
the kelp.

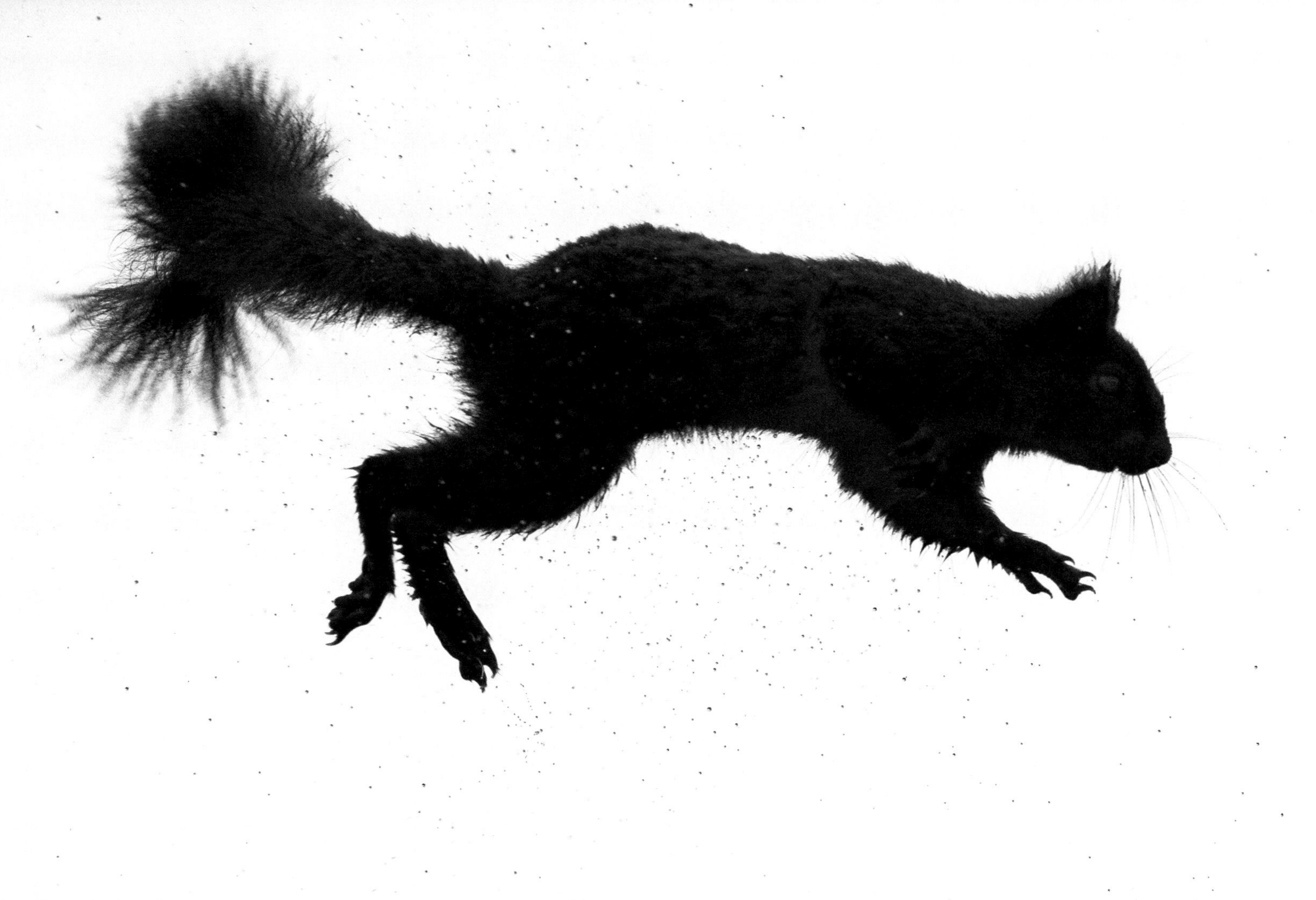

Squirrel Silhouette
Black & White | Runner-up

Rosamund Macfarlane
Red squirrel (*Sciurus vulgaris*)
Cumbria, England

Canon EOS R6 with Canon 100-400mm f/4.5-5.6 II lens. 400mm; 1/5,000th second; f/8; ISO 1,600.

Red squirrels are native and cherished in Cumbria, although they face competition and disease from grey squirrels. These charming creatures visit our garden daily for hazelnuts, and I can capture their antics without causing disturbance. During winter, when food is scarce, providing for them feels like helping our native population. This spring, young kits joined the adults for breakfast, and capturing their dynamic movements against the sky was a fascinating challenge.

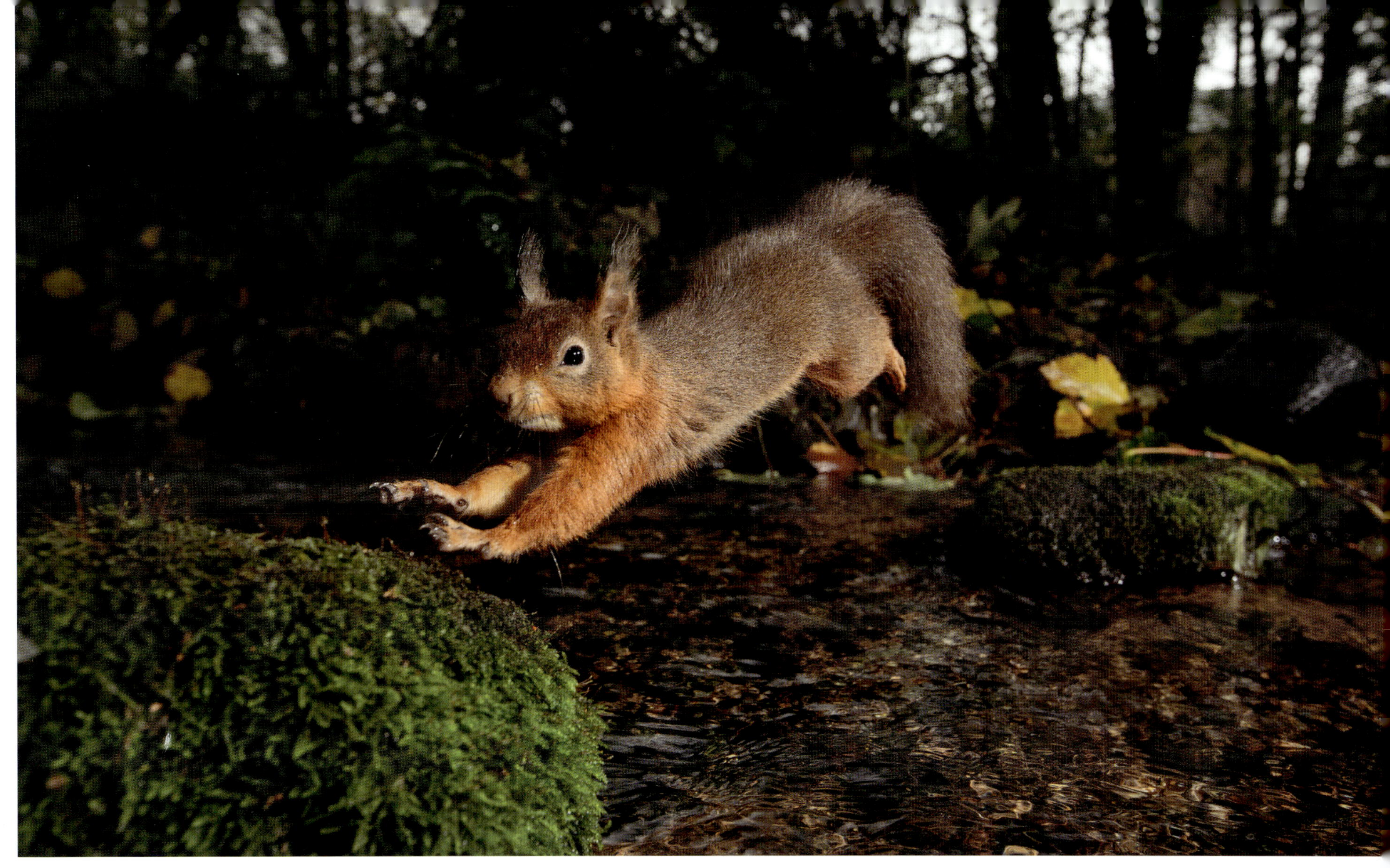

The Great Leap
Animal Behaviour | Highly Commended

Alastair Marsh
Red squirrel (*Sciurus vulgaris*)
Cumbria, England

Canon EOS 5D Mark IV with Canon 16-35mm f/2.8 II lens. 29mm; 1/50th second; f/8; ISO 500.

Each autumn and winter, I spend as much time as possible in the company of a red squirrel population in Cumbria. Thanks to a good friend who lives nearby, I've gotten to know the landowner, who does an awful lot to save the species in the area. Hazelnuts are put in squirrel feeders in the area to provide them with a reliable food source. There's a small stream that runs through the woodland they call home, and they use rocks to hop across, as you can see here.

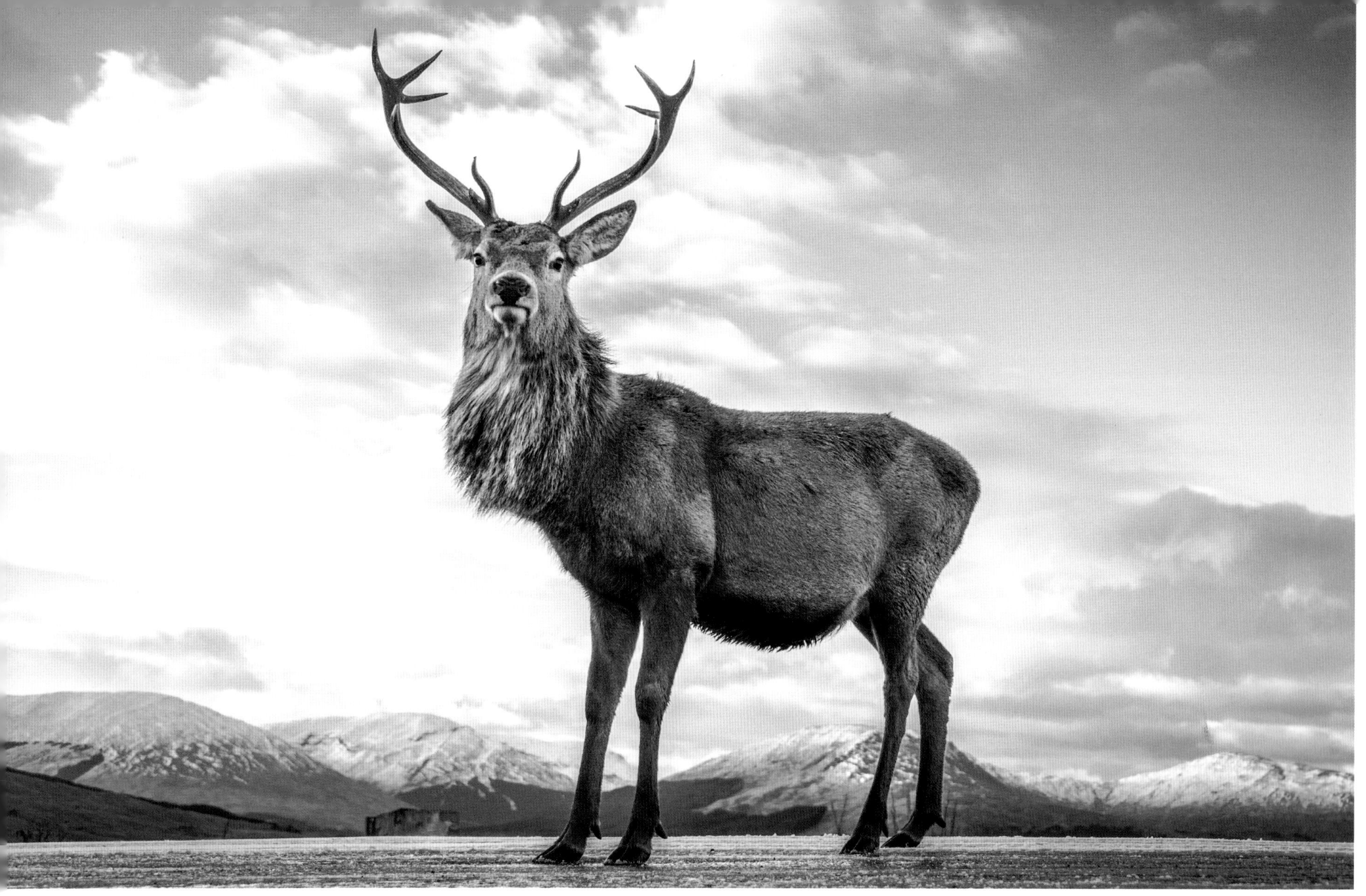

Stag Portrait
Habitat | Highly Commended

Graham Niven
Red deer (*Cervus elaphus*)
Black Mount, Western Highlands of Scotland

Nikon D850 with Nikon 28-300mm f/3.5-5.6 lens.
40mm; 1/125th second; f/5.6; ISO 64.

Cutting a striking figure against a winter sky, encounters with one of our most iconic mammals are often not quite as wild as we might wish – the tarmac under his hooves did not take away from the magnificence of his stature, however; it was made more prominent by the low-angle composition and monochrome tone.

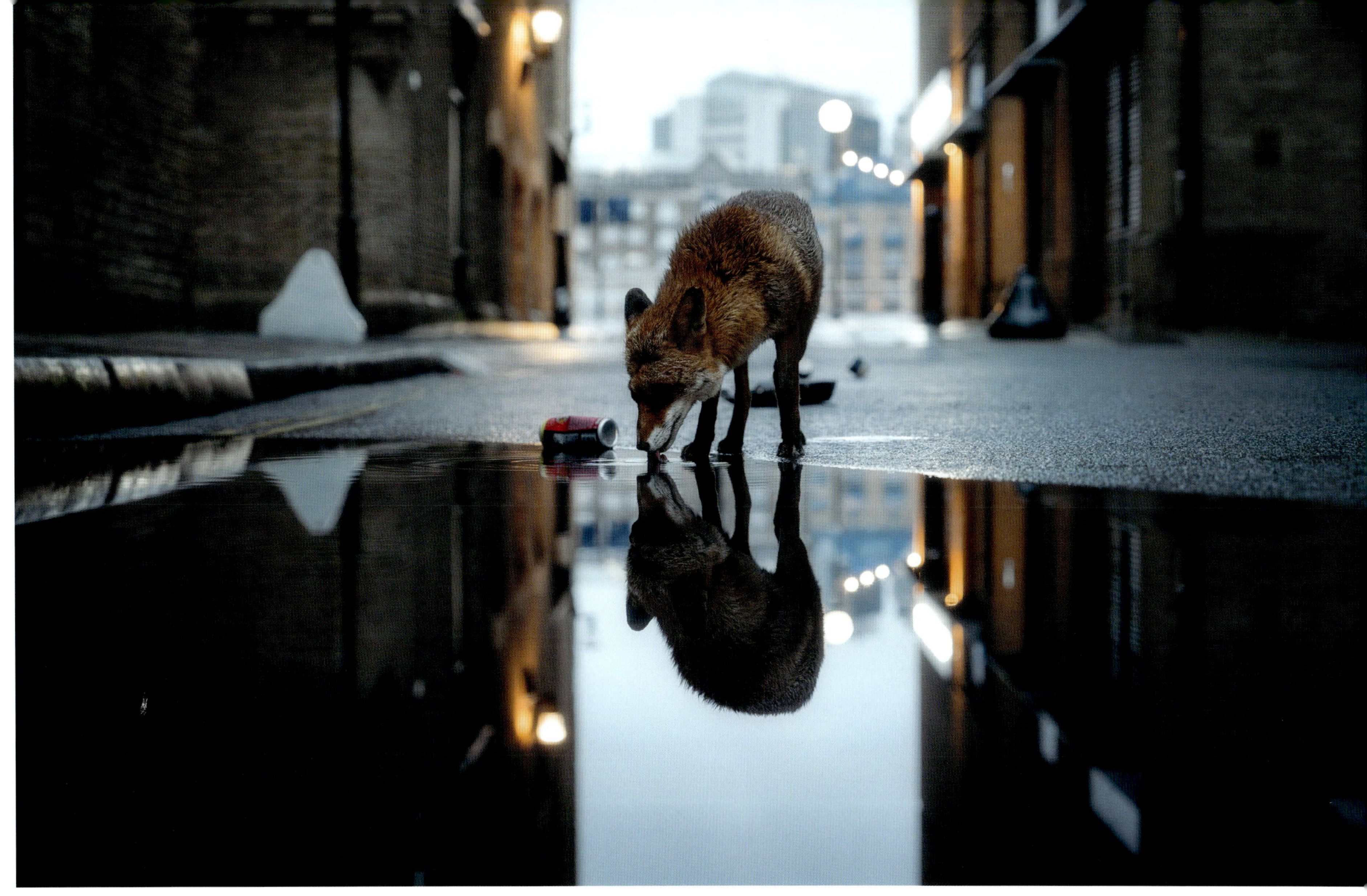

Urban Oasis
Urban Wildlife | Highly Commended

Oscar Lindsey
Red fox (*Vulpes vulpes*)
Shad Thames, London, England

Sony A7 III with Sony 24-70mm f/2.8 II lens.
63mm; 1/80th second; f/2.8; ISO 2,500.

As an urban photographer, rain is something that I frequently seek because it brings reflections that can completely transform an image. I was eager to combine my urban photography knowledge with the city wildlife and went out to explore the morning after a heavy night of downpour. It appeared the stars had aligned, and I caught this fox tucking into the scraps left behind by a rubbish truck that had swept down the street moments before. This image highlights how much wild foxes have mirrored human activities to enable their survival, while the same activities have proven to be fatal to other wildlife.

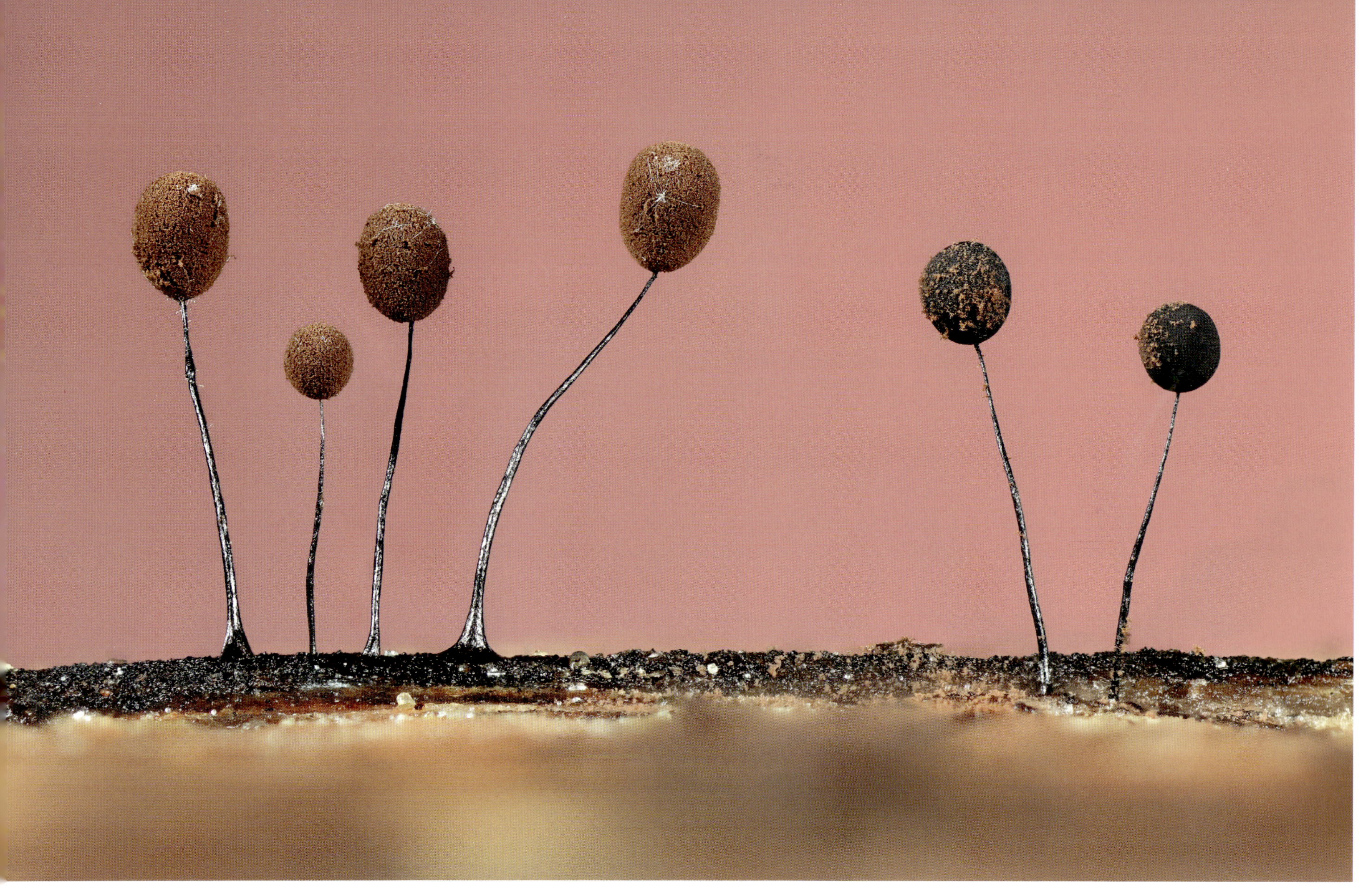

Tiny Forest Balloons
Botanical Britain | Winner

Jason McCombe
Slime mould (*Comatricha nigra*)
Essex, England

Canon EOS R7 with Canon 100mm f/2.8 lens & Kenko extension tubes.

The world of slime moulds is fascinating. They're neither plants nor fungi. I had never noticed them before, but when I set out to find some to photograph, I discovered that, if conditions are right, they're everywhere! They're just so small that if you are not looking for them you will simply overlook them. Each head on these fruiting bodies is approximately 1mm wide, and the depth of field when shooting at such high magnification is so shallow that focus stacking is required. This image was made using 160 images, each focused on a different area of the scene, then stacked together to create one highly detailed image.

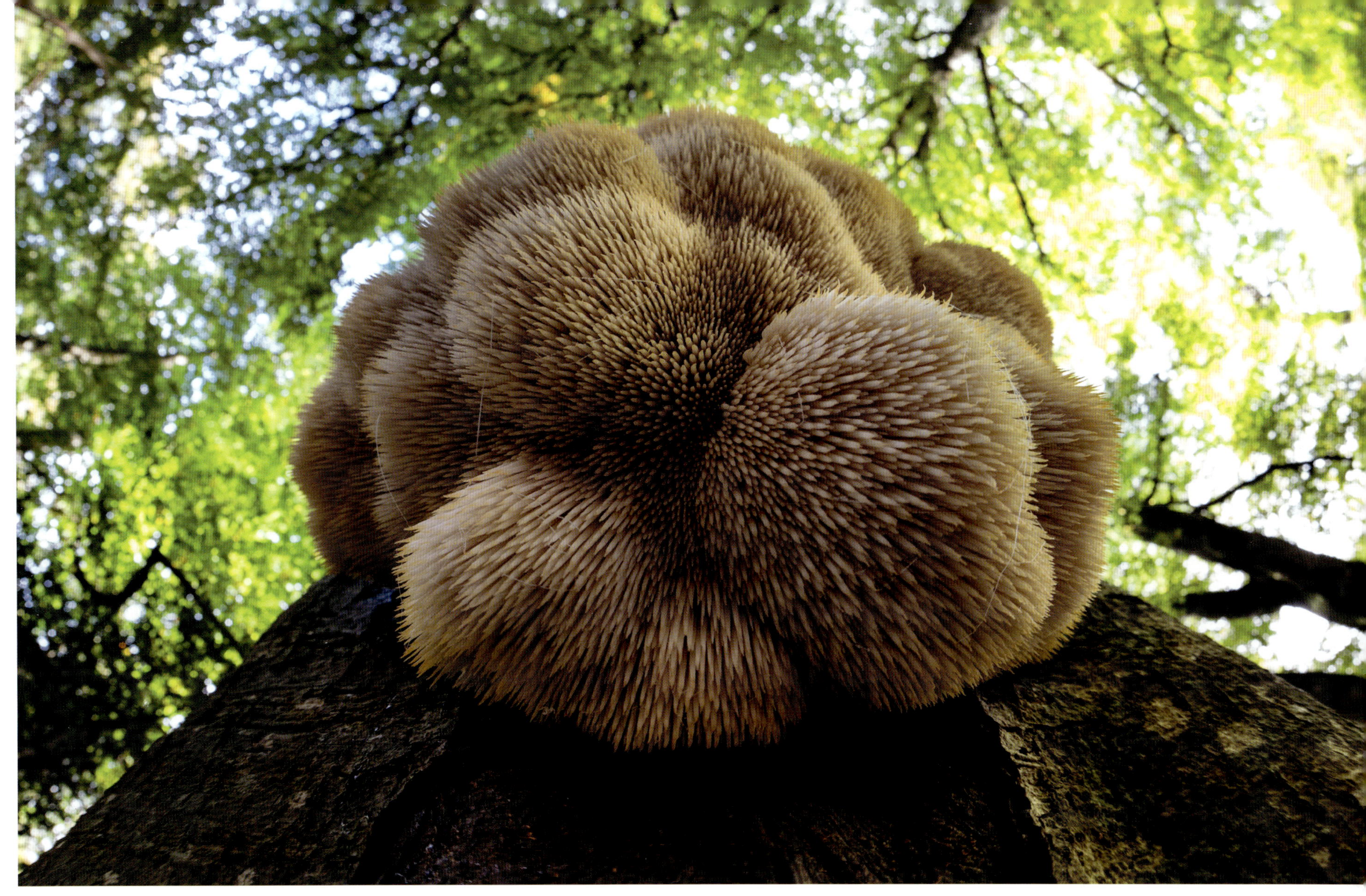

Treebeard
Botanical Britain | Highly Commended

David Pressland
Bearded tooth (*Hericium erinaceus*)
Undisclosed location in the New Forest,
Hampshire, England

Nikon D750 with Sigma 15mm Fisheye lens.
15mm; 1/13th second; f/8; ISO 400.

Seen here growing on the trunk of a beech tree, its preferred host, the rare bearded tooth fungus is a protected species listed on Schedule 8 of the Wildlife and Countryside Act. It is also on England's list of rare and most threatened species.

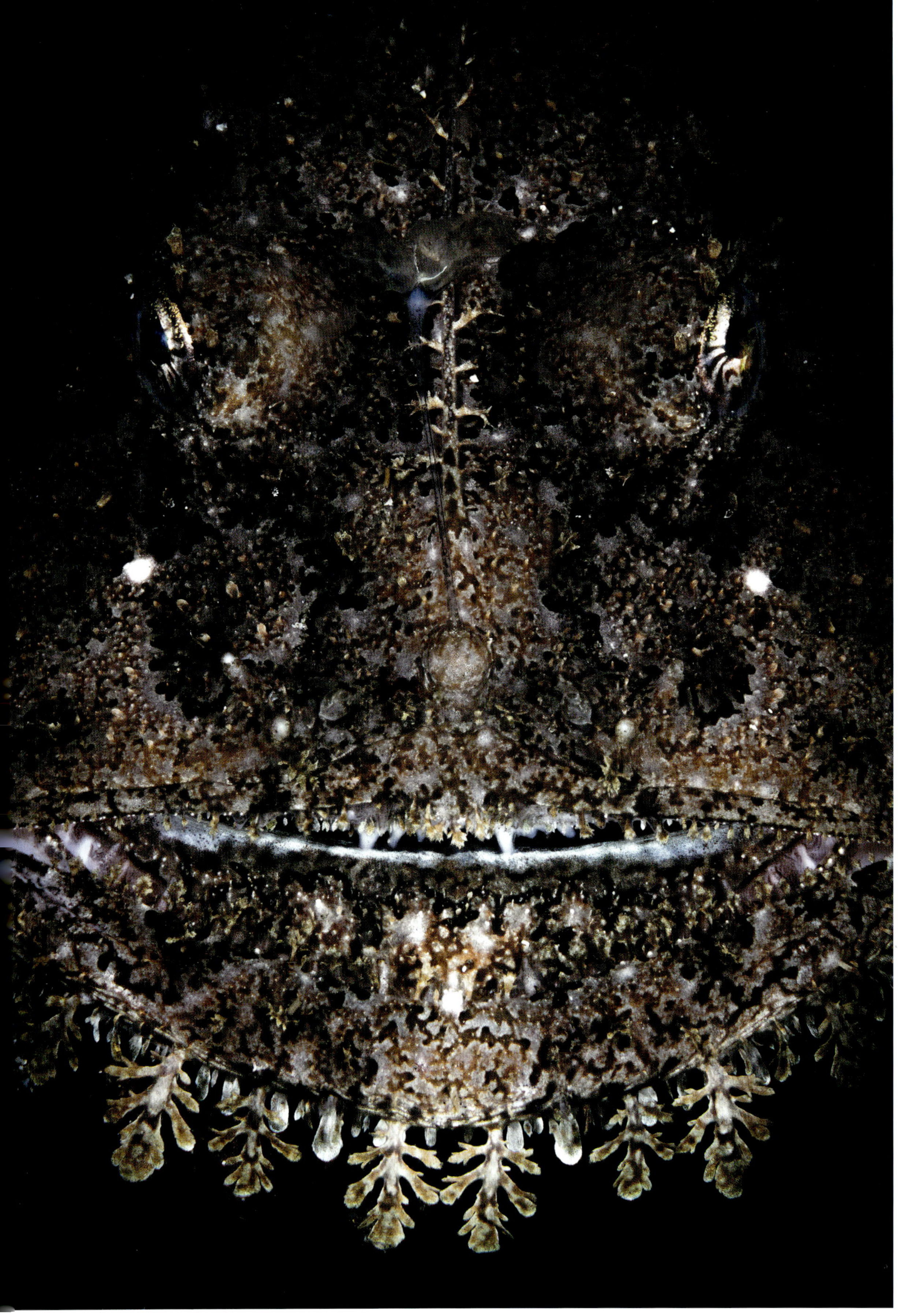

Angry Angler
Animal Portraits

Billy Arthur
Anglerfish (*Lophius piscatorious*)
Willie's Hole, Levenwick, Shetland Islands, Scotland

Sony A7R III with Sony 90mm f/2.8 lens. 90mm; 1/160th second; f/22; ISO 250.

Portrait of a juvenile anglerfish. A relatively rare sighting, I was happy that the subject wasn't disturbed by my presence, and I was able to compose the shot and then leave the anglerfish in peace. Ensuring that I had both eyes in focus helps to draw the viewer's attention in.

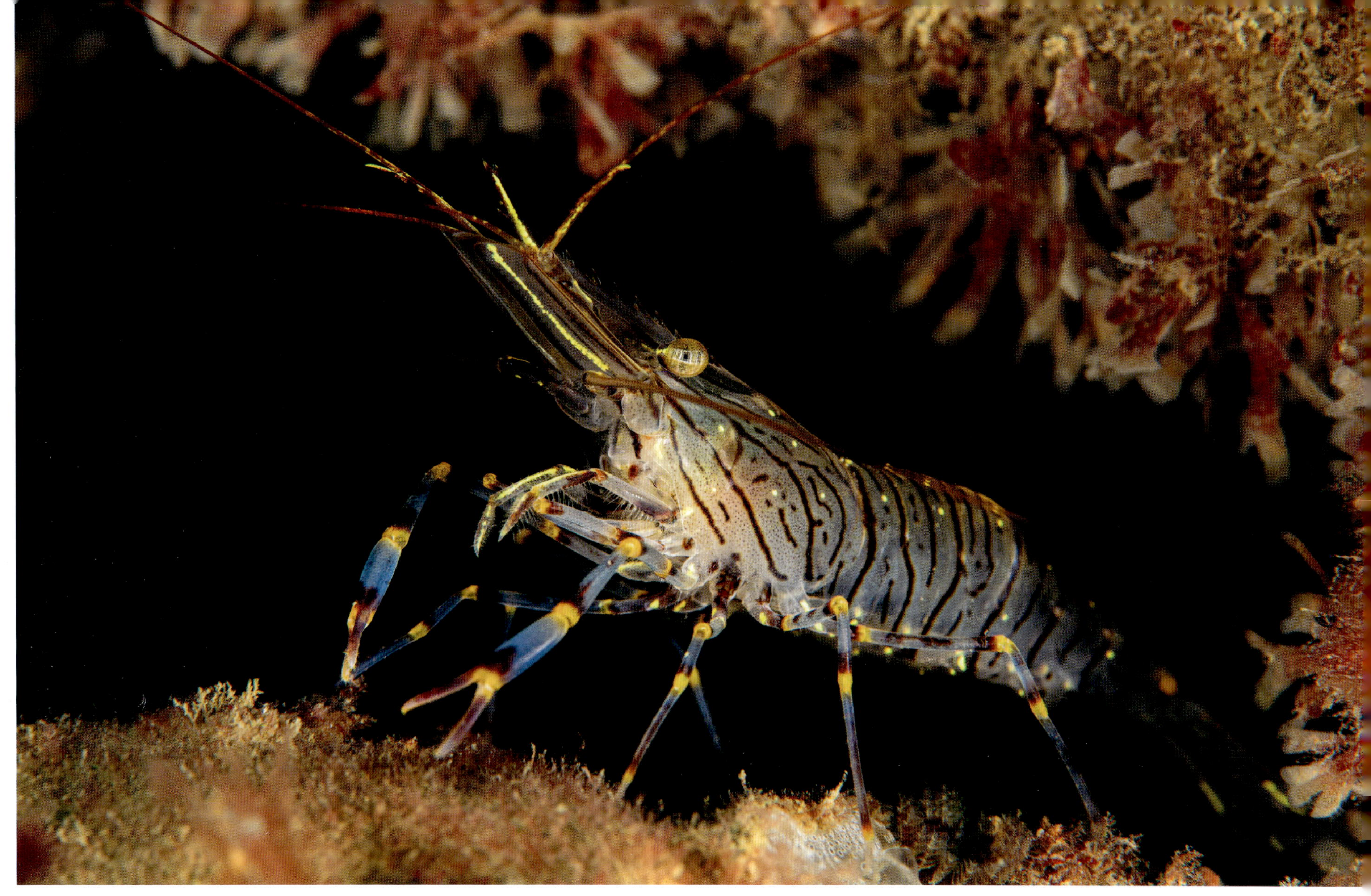

Alien Invasion
Coast & Marine

Martyn Guess
Common prawn (*Palaemon serratus*)
Fleur de Lys wreck, Swanage, Dorset, England

Nikon D5 with Nikon 105mm Macro lens.
105mm; 1/40th second; f/18; ISO 400.

A common prawn in its weedy habitat, taken in Swanage Harbour while diving on the wreck of the French trawler *Fleur de Lys*. Although mainly lying broken up, there are many of these prawns, but they are usually difficult to photograph due to their shyness – they tend to hide deep inside pieces of the wreck, which can be hard to access. I captured this particular subject as it was sitting relatively exposed. The image was lit with a single strobe light fitted with a snoot, narrowing the beam and enabling me to bring out the intricate colours and textures of the subject.

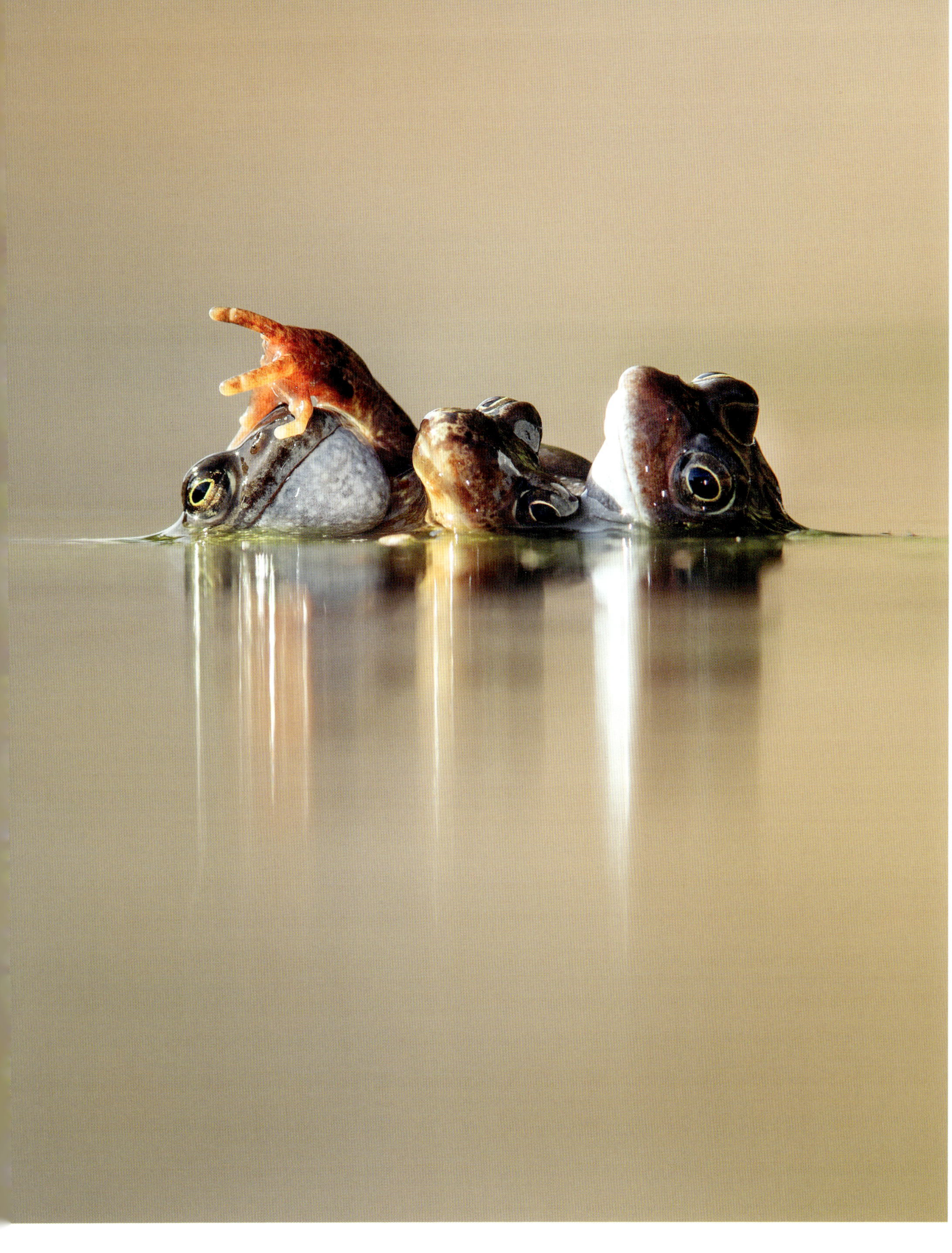

Three Frogs in Amplexus
Animal Behaviour | Winner

Ian Mason
Common frog (*Rana temporaria*)
Perthshire, Scotland

Canon EOS 1D X with Canon 300mm f/4 lens and 1.4x teleconverter. 420mm; 1/160th second; f/10; ISO 800.

Every March, our garden ponds suddenly come alive with hundreds of frogs that seem to appear overnight from nowhere. I have been photographing them for many years, and I am always fascinated and amused by their antics. Here, there has been a competition to mate with a female. For a lot of the time there is a frenzy of activity, but sometimes they freeze long enough to get a shot. The image is taken with the lens at water level, and the background is a distant larch tree.

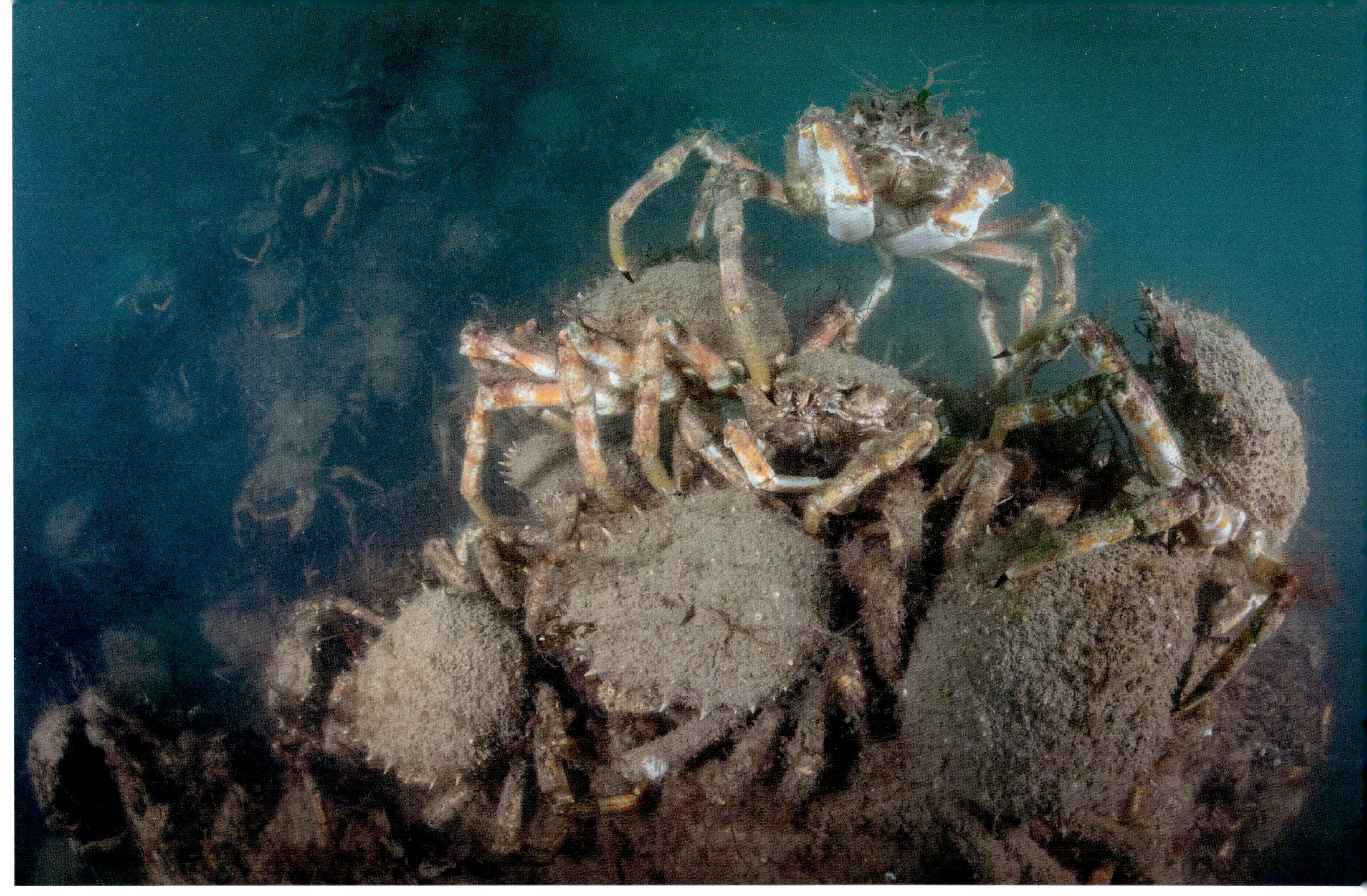

Spider Crabs Assemble!
Animal Behaviour

Kirsty Andrews
Spiny spider crab (*Maja squinado*)
Babbacombe beach, Torquay, England

Nikon D500 with Tokina 10-17mm lens. 10mm; 1/30th second; f/14; ISO 800.

In summer, just off many UK beaches, spiny spider crabs gather in large numbers. They do this as they are getting ready to moult, shedding their hard, spiny exoskeletons to reveal a new, larger body underneath. The crabs come together for safety during this vulnerable stage because, until the new shell hardens, they are at the mercy of predators.

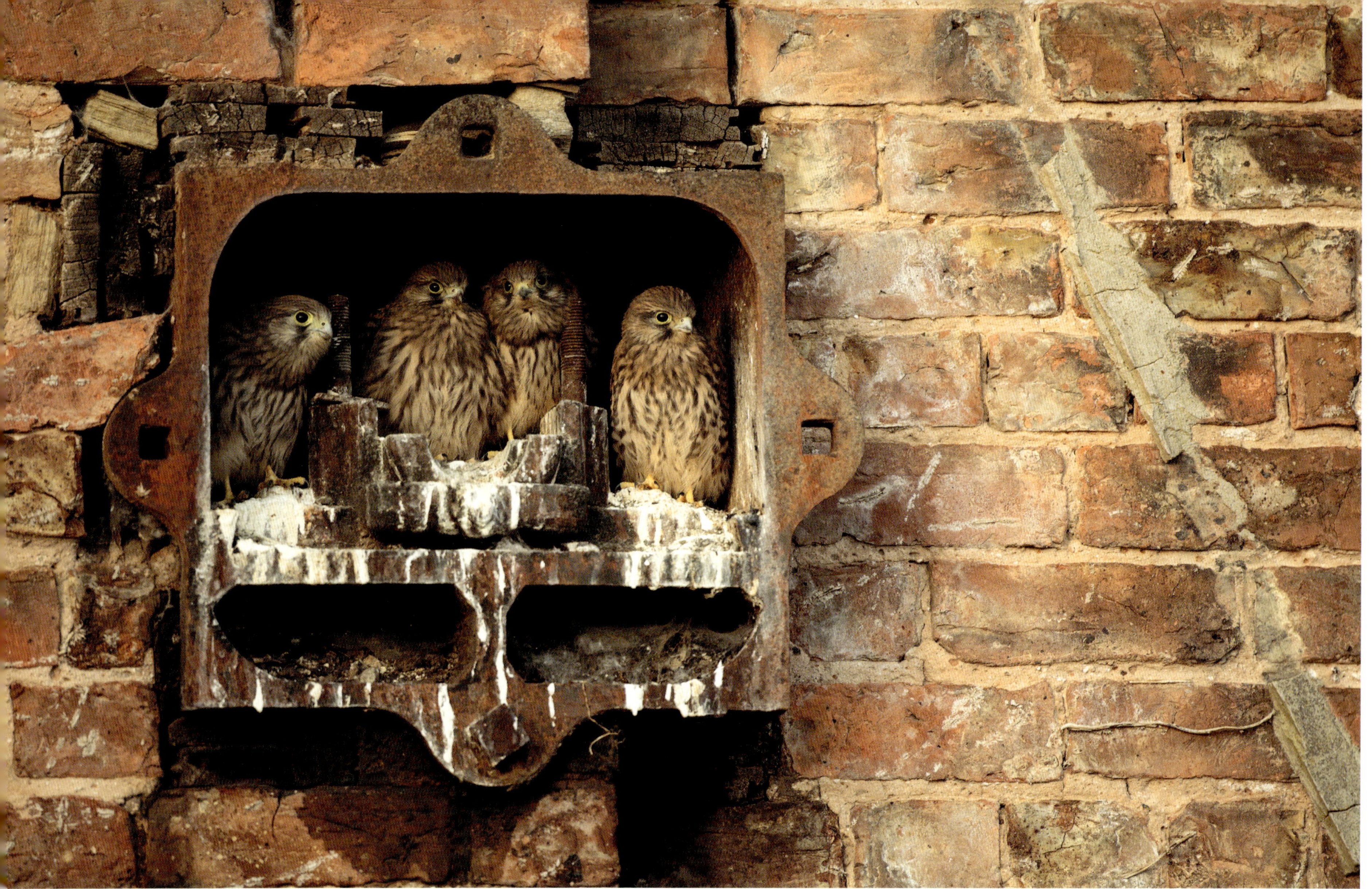

Industrial Home
Urban Wildlife | Highly Commended

Ben Andrew
Kestrel (*Falco tinnunculus*)
Yorkshire, England

Canon EOS 5D Mark IV with Canon 500mm f/4 lens.
500mm; 1/320th second; f/4; ISO 500.

This image shows four young kestrel chicks that were just days away from fully fledging this industrial nest, which was in an old and unused building on an industrial site. The rest of the site had a constant flow of people traffic, but the birds didn't seem to mind! The chicks would wait patiently at the nest entrance for a returning adult.

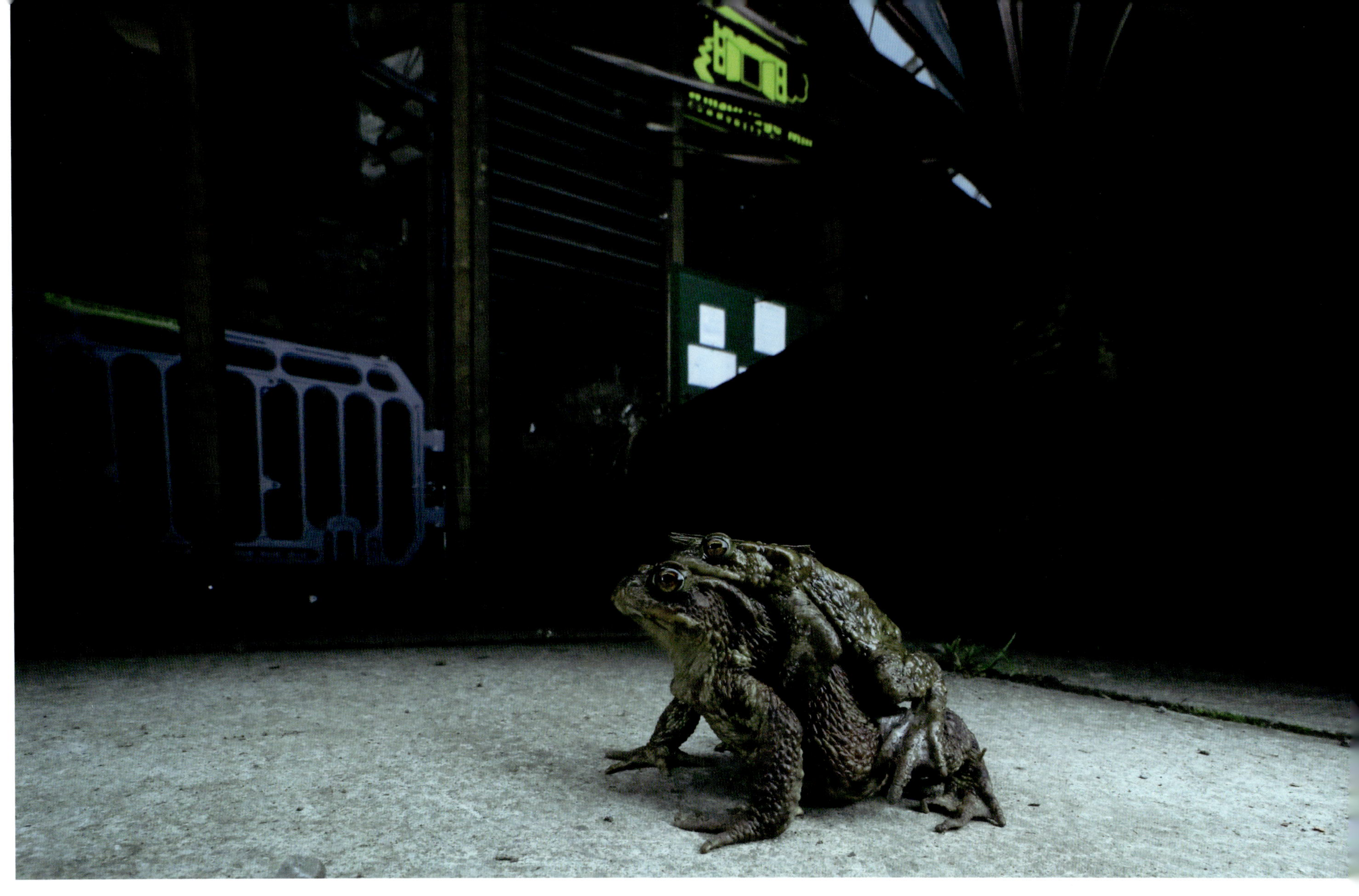

Romancing Toads
Urban Wildlife

Ian Wade
Common toad (*Bufo bufo*)
Bristol, England

Canon EOS 5D III with Laowa 15mm f/4 lens.
15mm; 13 seconds; f/8; ISO 4,000.

The springtime migration of common toads is one of nature's great events. These amphibians embark on a journey of up to four miles to reach their ancestral breeding ponds. Along the way, they face many challenges, including predators, traffic and the urban environment. This photograph captures a pair of common toads in amplexus, a mating behaviour. The female is carrying the smaller male on her back, which is a testament to her strength and endurance. The toads are illuminated by man-made light sources, which is a reminder that this migration is taking place in an urban environment.

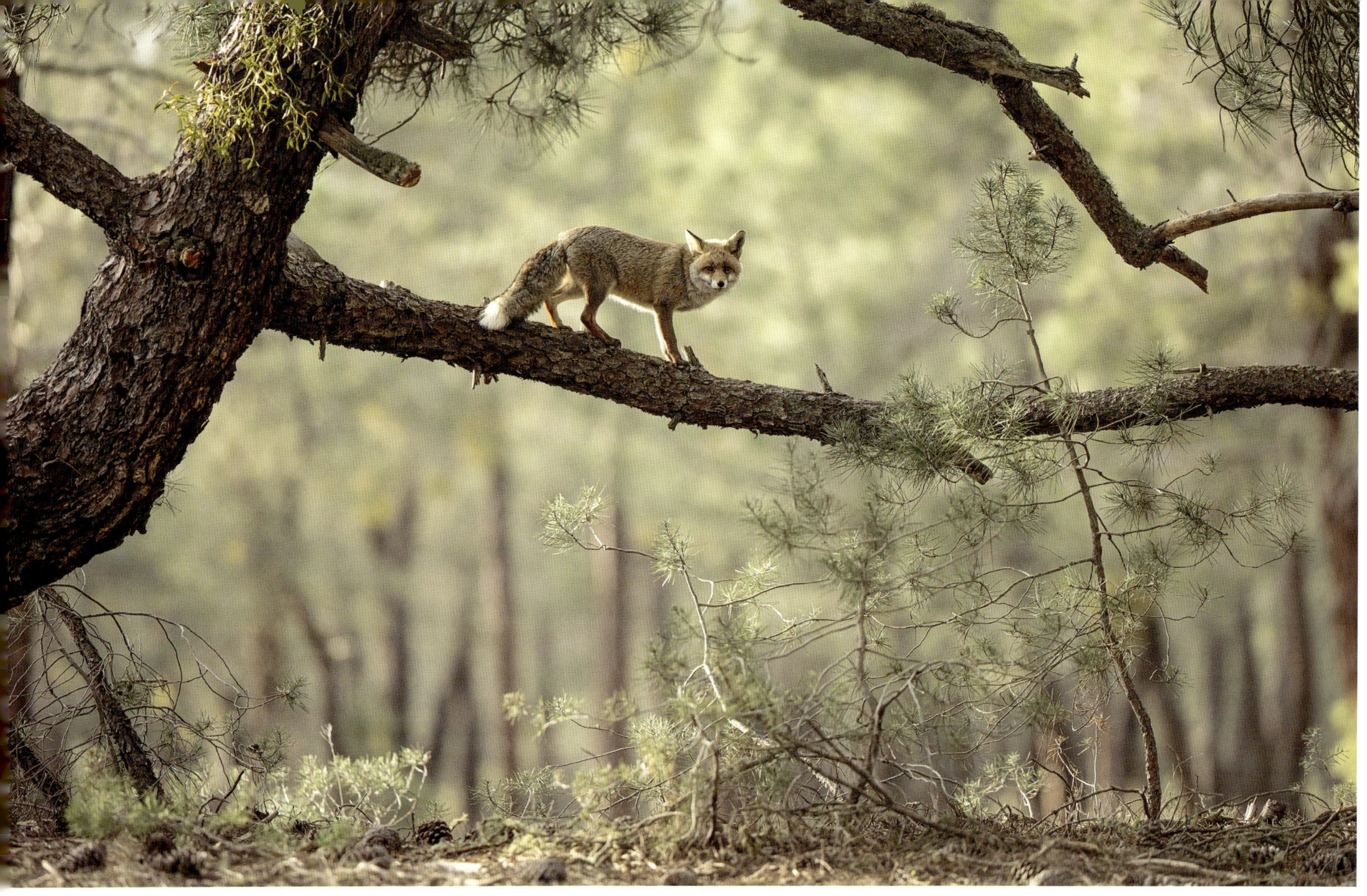

The Tightrope Walker
Habitat | Winner

Daniel Valverde Fernandez
Red fox (*Vulpes vulpes*)
Sherwood Pines Forest Park, Nottinghamshire, England

Canon EOS R3 with Canon 300mm f/2.8 II lens. 300mm; 1/5,000th second; f/2.8; ISO 3,200.

In this image, you can see a red fox walking along a tree branch at a considerable height from the ground, demonstrating that these animals are true tightrope walkers of nature. The fox is perfectly framed between the branches and its silhouette is subtly highlighted by the sun's rays falling on it.

Day Walker
Urban Wildlife | Winner

Simon Withyman
Red fox (*Vulpes vulpes*)
Bristol, England

Canon EOS R5 with Canon 24-80mm f/2.8 II lens.
41mm; 1/1,000th second; f/2.8; ISO 100.

This vixen had taken up residence in an electricity
substation after being pushed out of her parental
territory. The fenced-off area provided her with a
quiet place to rest away from the busy city. She
would often walk along this wall, and I was able to
capture this photo through the gaps in the metal
fencing, while making the most of some striking
lens flare.

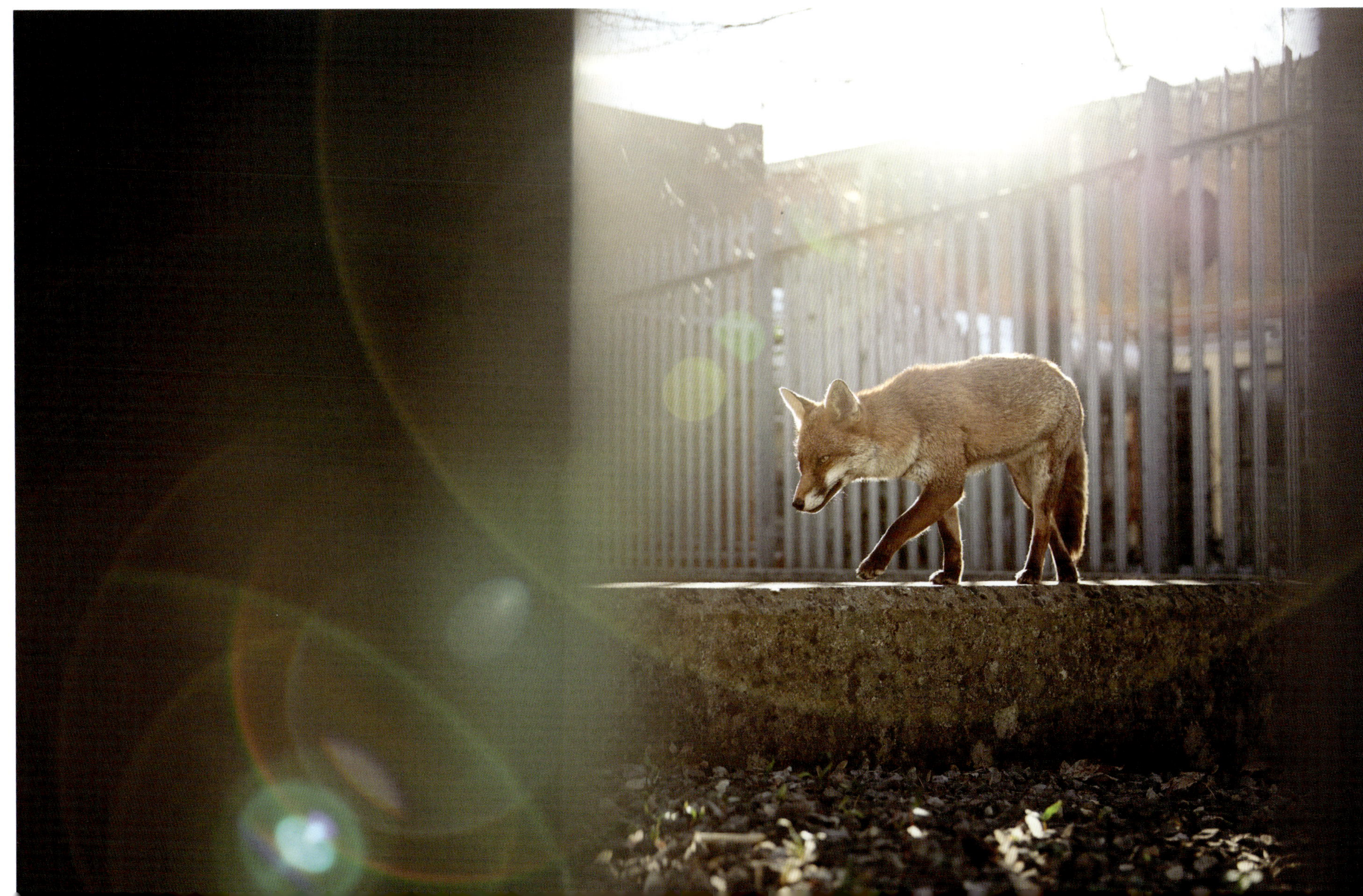

Cemetery Badger
Urban Wildlife

Sam Rowley
Badger (*Meles meles*)
Bristol, England

Nikon D500 with Sigma 10-20mm f/3.5 lens.
17mm; 1/100th second; f/10; ISO 1,600.

A badger emerges from the graves in a forgotten Bristol cemetery. The tombstones provide a perfect habitat for the animals – they can dig underneath them as they would tree roots. The badgers are still extremely shy of people, despite their city home. They only venture out when it's completely dark, so the only way to photograph them is using camera traps. Using trail cams, I figured out their nocturnal passages around the cemetery, informing me of the position to set up my camera trap. I was delighted to find this shot the next morning of a very happy-looking badger!

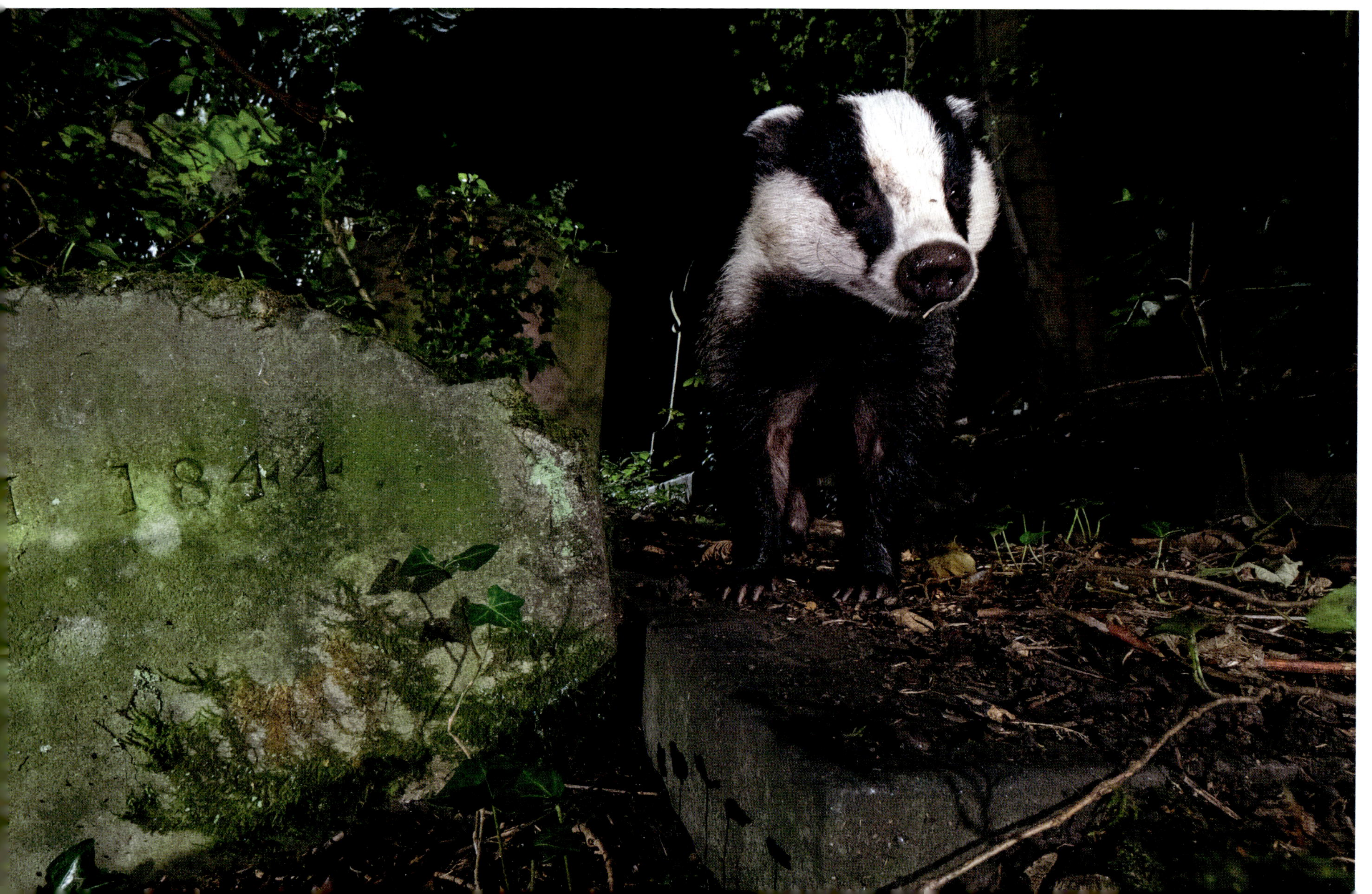

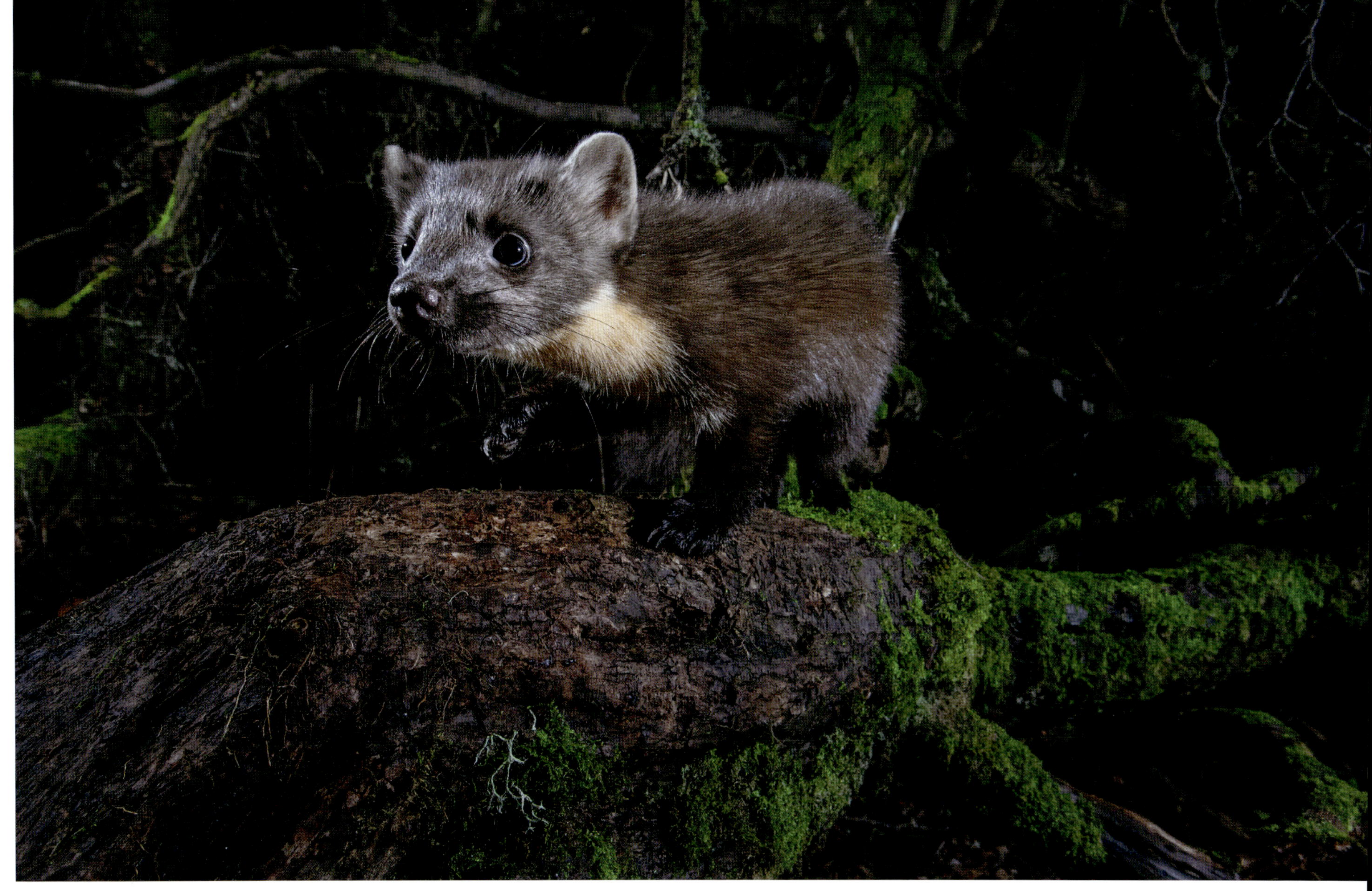

Pine Marten on the Prowl
Wild Woods | Highly Commended

James Roddie
Pine marten (*Martes martes*)
The Black Isle, near Inverness, Scotland

Nikon D610 with Nikon 16-35mm f/4.
16mm; 1/100th second; f/11; ISO 3,200.

Pine martens are nocturnal hunters. To capture their essence in their nighttime habitat, I carefully positioned camera traps without overusing flash. After experimenting with flashgun placement near a fallen tree where I had drizzled some honey, I placed the lens inches away from where I wanted the animal to appear, and this was the result after a few nights.

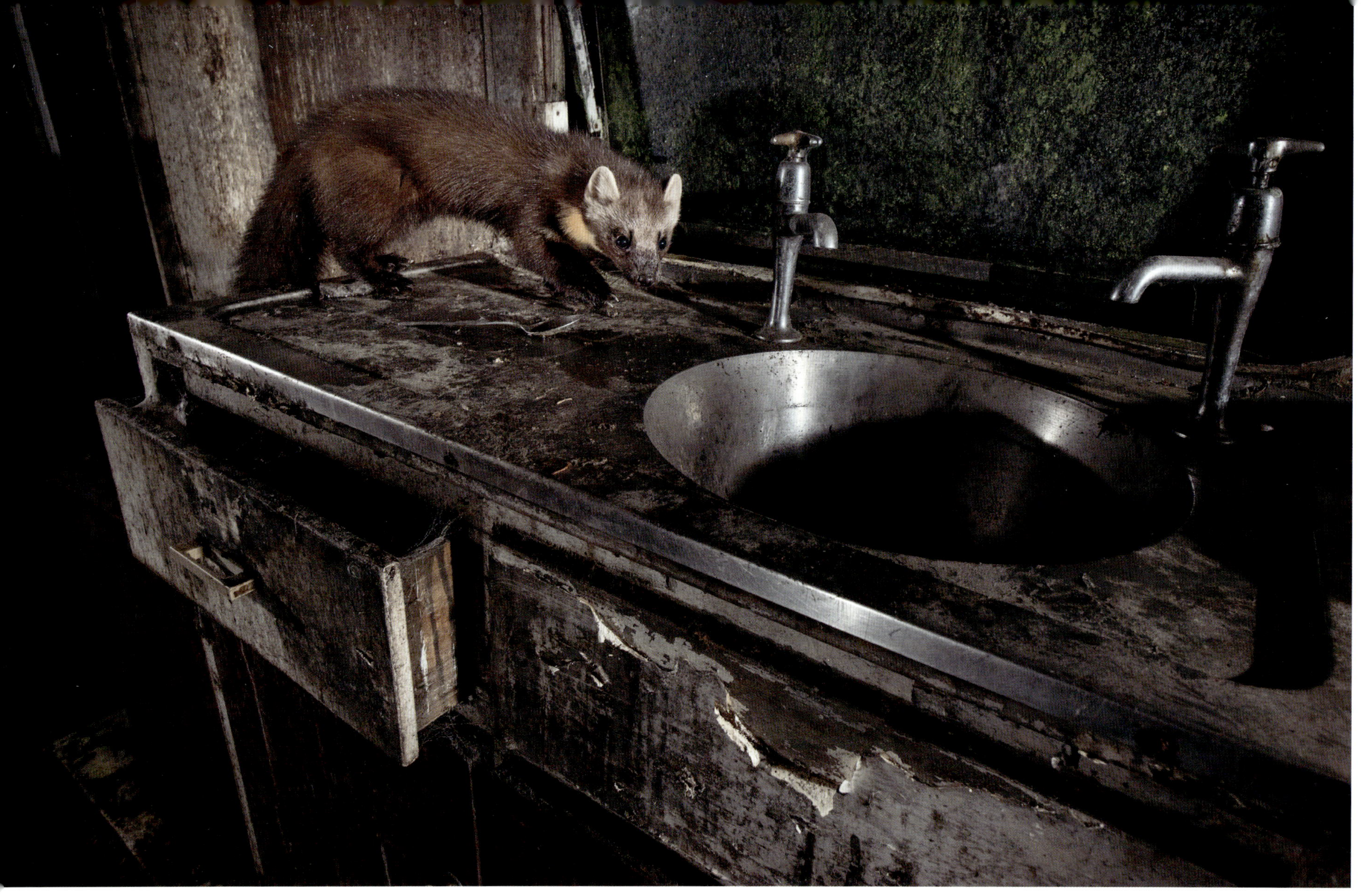

Pine Marten in an Abandoned House
Urban Wildlife

James Roddie
Pine marten (*Martes martes*)
Near Inverness, Scotland

Nikon D750 with Nikon 20mm f/1.8 lens.
20mm; 1/30th second; f/13; ISO 2,000.

After discovering signs of pine martens outside an old abandoned house in the woods, I placed a trail camera to see if I could capture any footage. The pine martens did not have a den in the cottage but were sporadically visiting, perhaps to hunt the numerous mice living there. I deployed a DSLR camera trap in the cottage for three months and managed to capture several images. It was a project with numerous challenges. I was glad I had persisted, as not long afterwards the abandoned house was demolished.

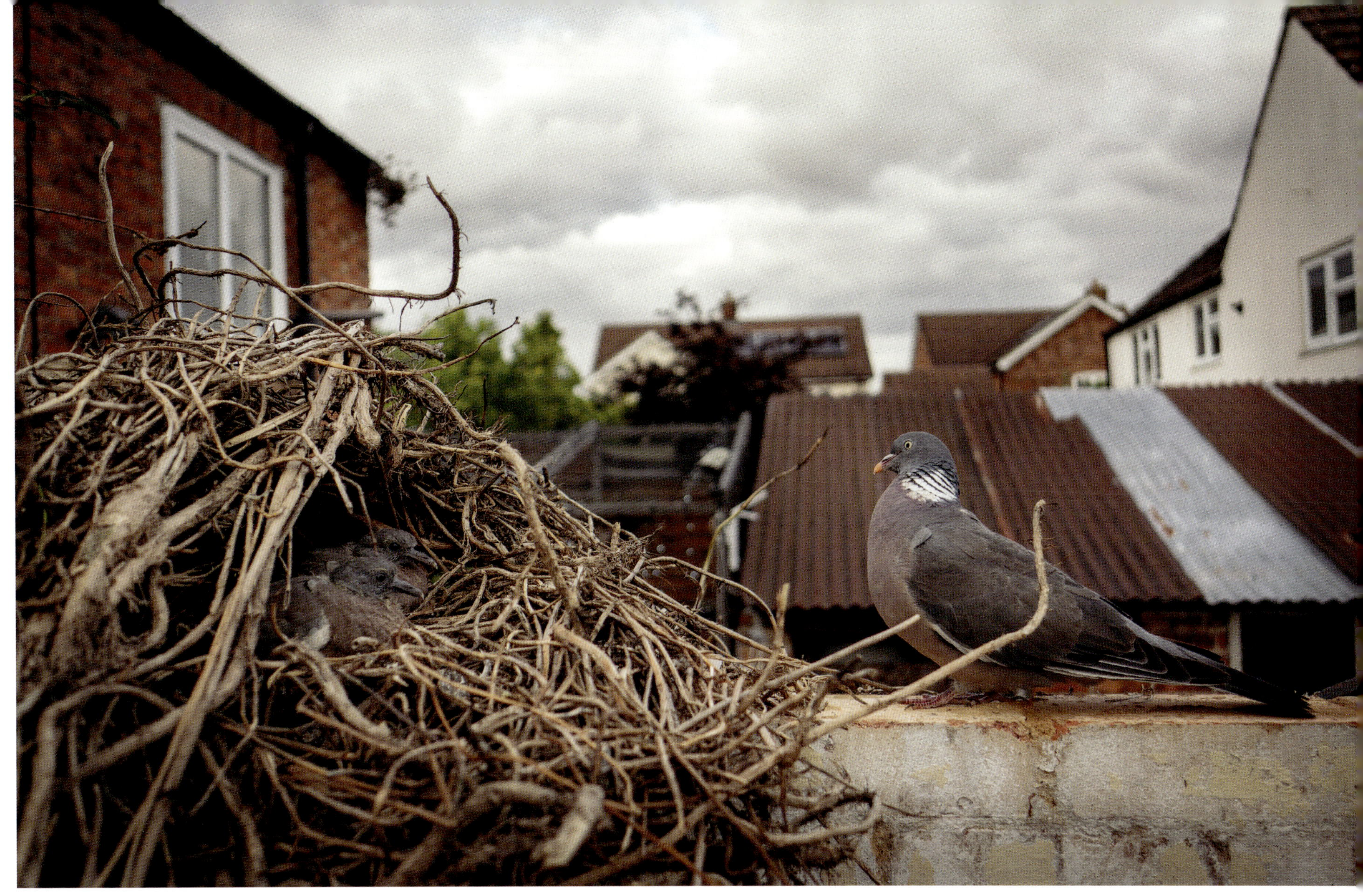

Dome Nest
Urban Wildlife

Jamie Peters
Wood pigeon (*Columba palumbus*)
Milton Keynes, Buckinghamshire, England

Sony A9 II with 24mm f/2.8 lens. 24mm;
1/800th second; f/2.8; ISO 200.

The landlord removed a large ivy bush from an outbuilding late in the season, not expecting any nesting birds. During the removal, two squabs were found. As a wildlife enthusiast, he sought my advice, and I recommended creating a makeshift platform for the squabs. The nest was near my kitchen, allowing me to regularly observe an adult feeding them. To protect them from the rain, I placed a dome of ivy roots over the nest. Setting up a camera on a tripod and connecting it to my smartphone, I captured the parents feeding the squabs. A week later, the squabs fledged but continued visiting the garden to eat birdseed.

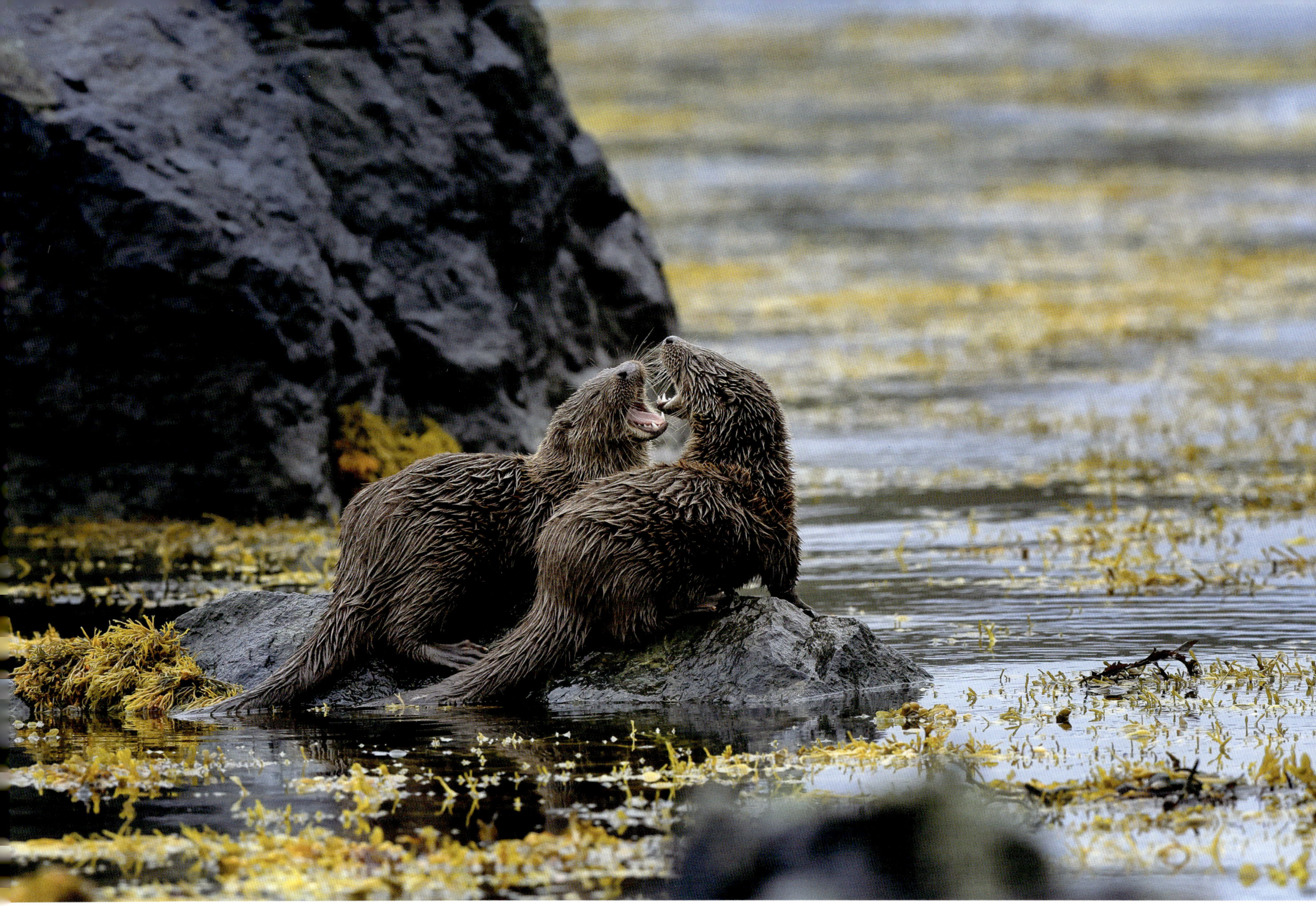

Sitting on the Rock of a Bay
Habitat

Edwin De A Godinho
Common otter (*Lutra lutra*)
Isle of Mull, Scotland

Canon EOS R3 with Canon 400mm f/2.8 II lens
& 1.4 teleconverter. 560mm; 1/500th second;
f/8; ISO 1,000.

We arrived at the loch one early morning, just as the
first light broke. The tide line looked perfect for fishing
otters. We saw a ripple along the edge of the water
near the rocks. It was a mother with two kits, out
fishing. We picked our spot and waited for them to
come towards us. And they did, giving us half an hour
of pure bliss watching them do their own thing. This
image captures two kits having a sibling conversation
on a rock while mum was out hunting. It shows the
habitat as well, with seaweeds and rocks.

Grey Wagtail Gathering Insects
Habitat

Dick Hawkes
Grey wagtail (*Motacilla cinerea*)
River Avon, Woodford Valley, England

Olympus OM-1 M1 with Olympus M. Zuiko 300mm
F/4 lens. 300mm; 1/2500th second; f/4; ISO 800.

I stood, several times, watching, fascinated by the skill of the grey wagtail catching insects in mid-flight at a hatchpool on the River Avon in the Woodford Valley. The recently cut weed was a haven for a variety of insects. It took several round trips of 120 miles to get an image with the catch in the bird's beak and the swirling water of the hatchpool in the background.

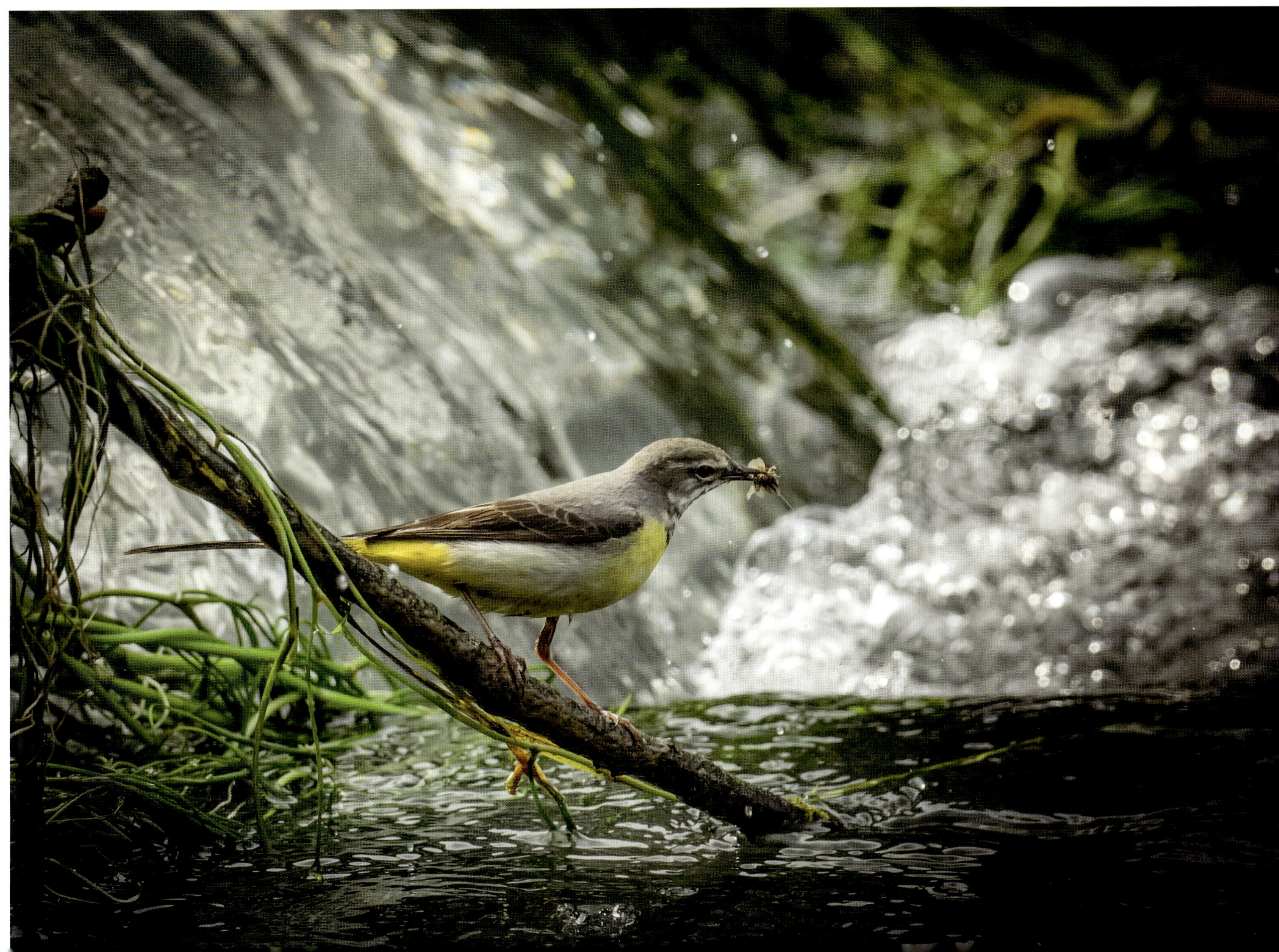

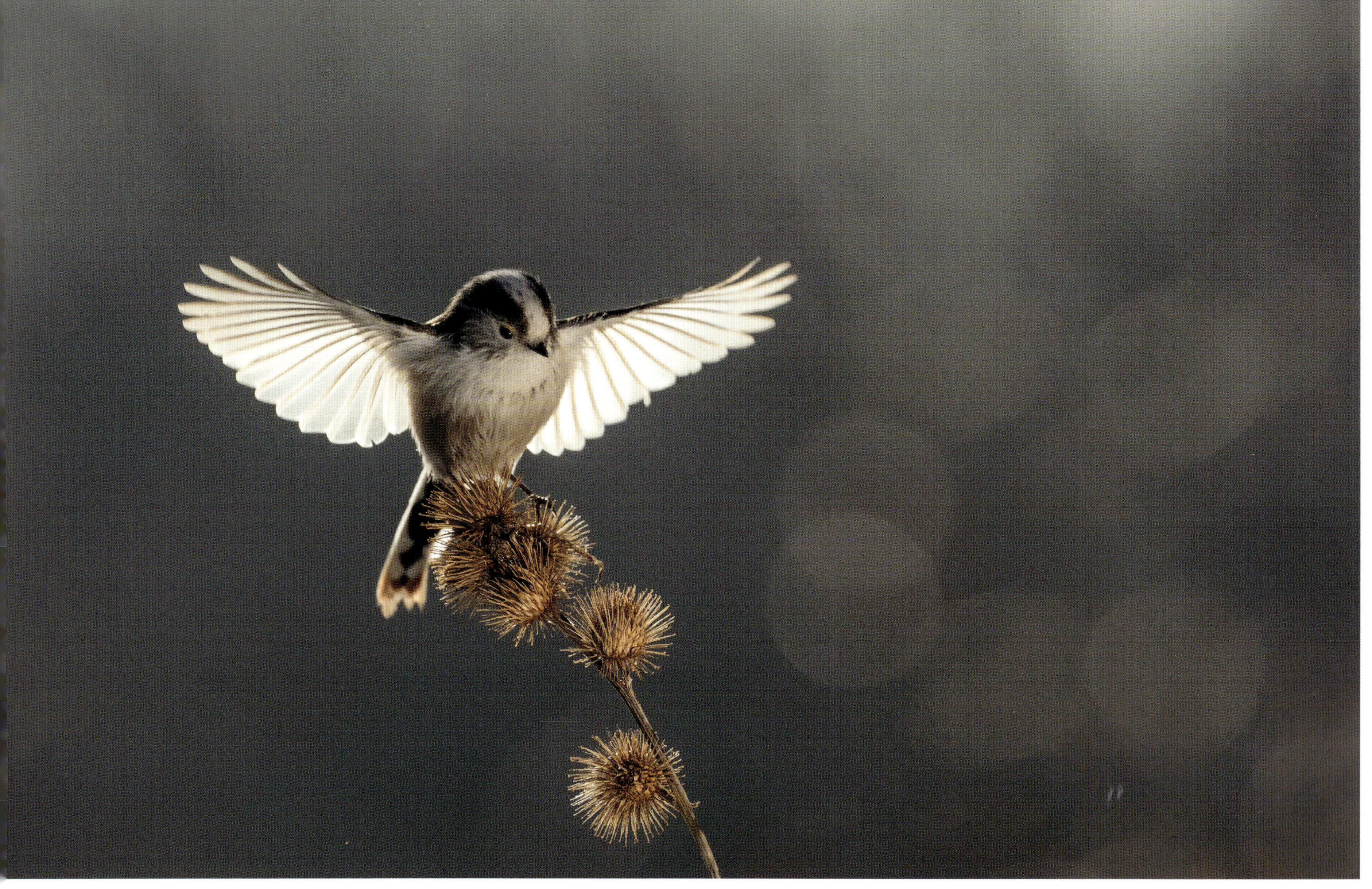

Angel Wings
Animal Portraits | Highly Commended

Lee O'Dwyer
Long-tailed tit (*Aegithalos caudatus*)
Lancashire, England

Sony A9 with Sony 200-600mm f/5.6-6.3 lens.
600mm; 1/3,200th second; f/9; ISO 2,500.

This image was created at my garden feeders. The long-tailed tits breed close by, and every year I get the whole family coming to feed at my feeders.
I place various things in strategic places for them to perch on while they wait their turn to feed. I have about a one-hour window when the light is perfect for backlighting the feathers, so I set the camera up on a tripod on the decking and sit in the kitchen with a remote shutter release, waiting for the action. It involves much trial and error, but occasionally patience is rewarded!

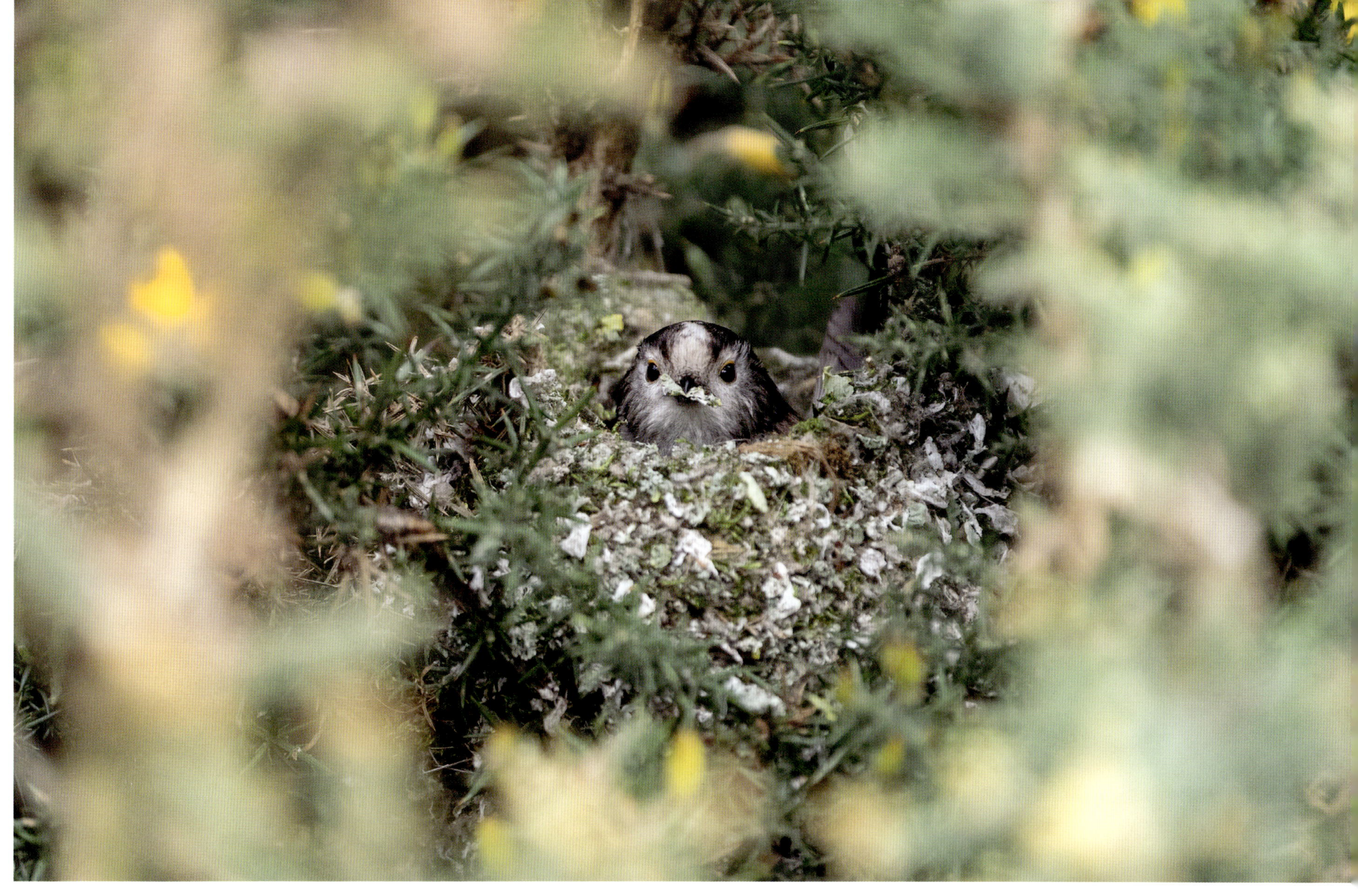

Houseproud
Animal Behaviour | Highly Commended

Takaki Nemoto
Long-tailed tit (*Aegithalos caudatus*)
London, England

Sony A9II with FE200-600mm f/5.6-6.3 lens.
600mm; 1/1600th second; f/6.3; ISO 4000.

One day in March, I noticed a pair of long-tailed tits with nesting materials in their beaks pausing momentarily before cautiously flying into a gap in a gorse bush nearby. My heart skipped a beat immediately. They were building a nest! Each of them tirelessly returned with more lichens and moss, delicately sewing each piece with cobwebs until they ended up with what looked like a beanie hat. This was the moment when one of the pair, disliking where the piece was placed by the partner, picked it up and pondered where it should be placed instead.

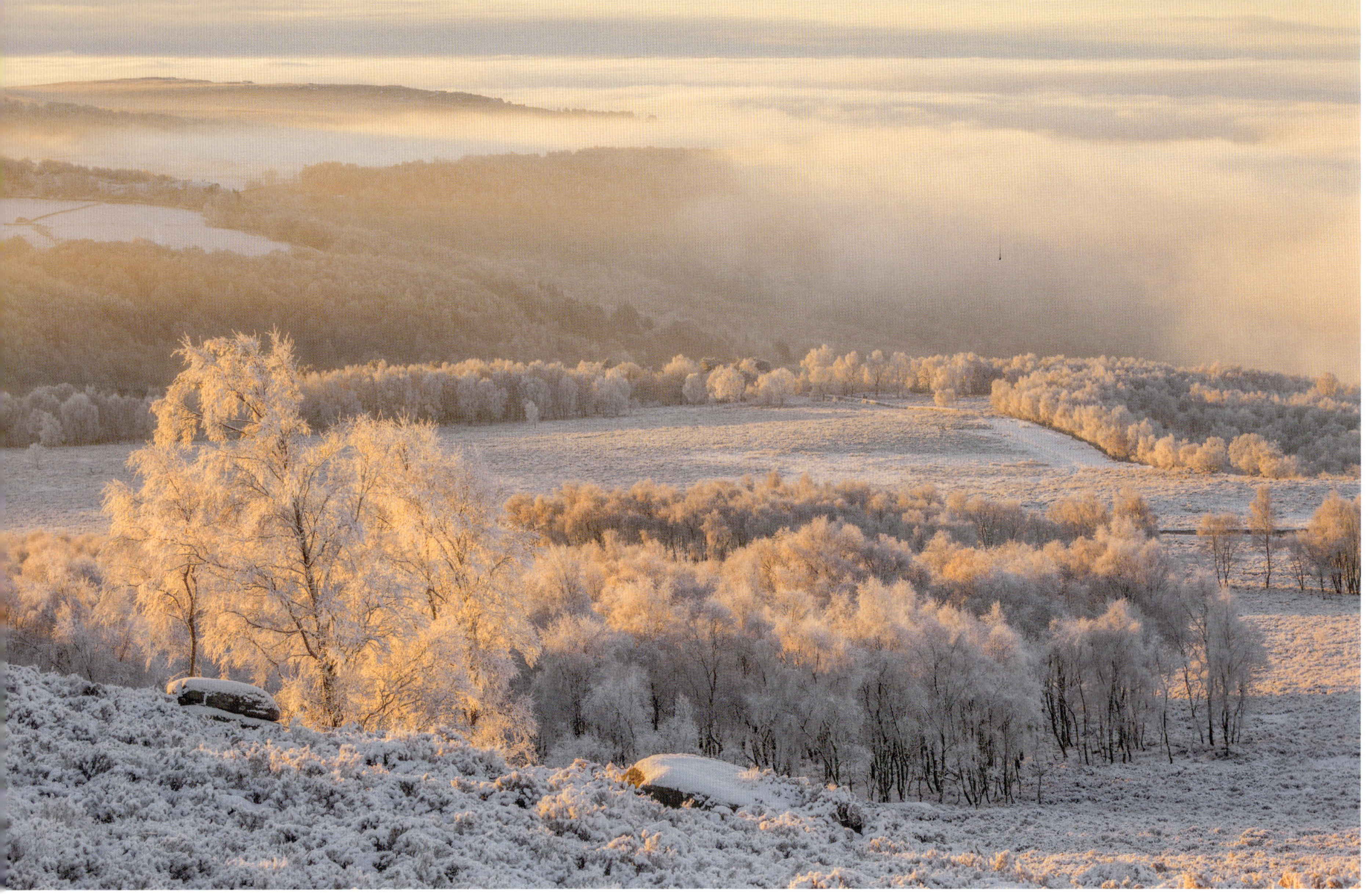

Surprise Ice
Wild Woods

Verity Milligan
Surprise View, Peak District, England

Canon EOS R5 with Canon 70-200mm f/2.8 II lens.
100mm; 1/13th second; f/13; ISO 100.

It was early December in 2022, and the UK experienced one of the coldest snaps in the last five years. I took a trip up to the Peak District and found the roads to be clear, but the woodland around Surprise View was covered in snow and hoar frost. I seemed to be the only person around, and I was treated to the most amazing mist and light. Looking down from Millstone Edge to Padley Gorge, the whole woodland had transformed into a winter wonderland, and I captured it as the morning light caught the tops of the frozen trees.

Twig, Bluebells and Beech
Wild Woods

Matthew Cattell
Bluebell (*Hyacinthoides non-scripta*) and
Beech tree (*Fagus* sp.)
Chiltern Hills, Oxfordshire, England

Nikon D850 with Nikon 24-70mm f/2.8 lens.
50mm; 5 seconds; f/8; ISO 64.

There is no experience quite like a woodland on a
spring morning – the riot of colours, the sweet scent
of wildflowers and the calls of the dawn chorus.
The beech woodlands of the Chiltern Hills have
become a sanctuary, and I visit frequently to witness
the seasons change. On this particularly foggy
morning, I spent several hours exploring an area of
ancient beech, seeking out a strong composition.
I settled on this simple arrangement that combined
the delicate carpets of bluebells with the fresh
explosions of lime-green beech leaves.

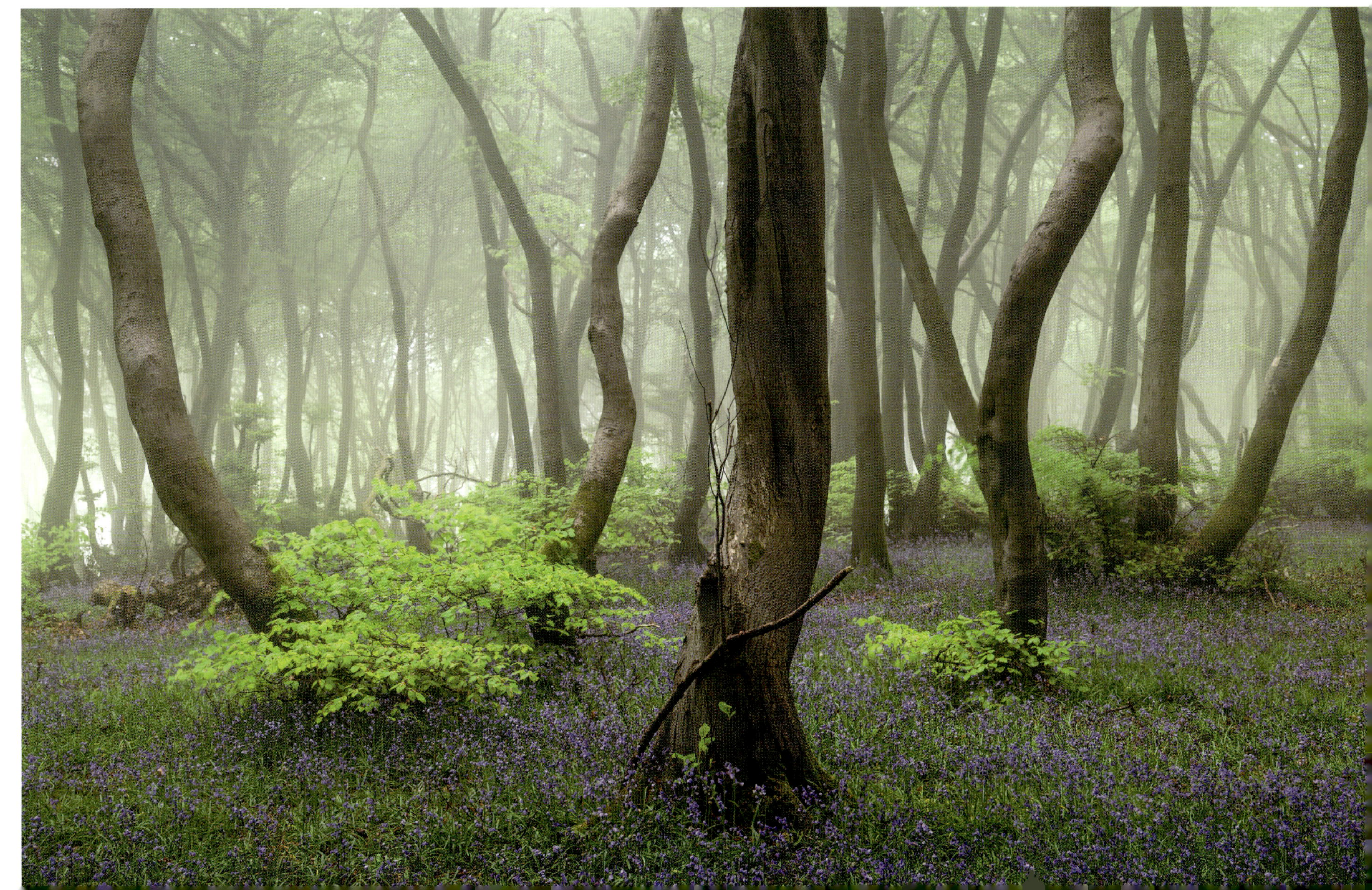

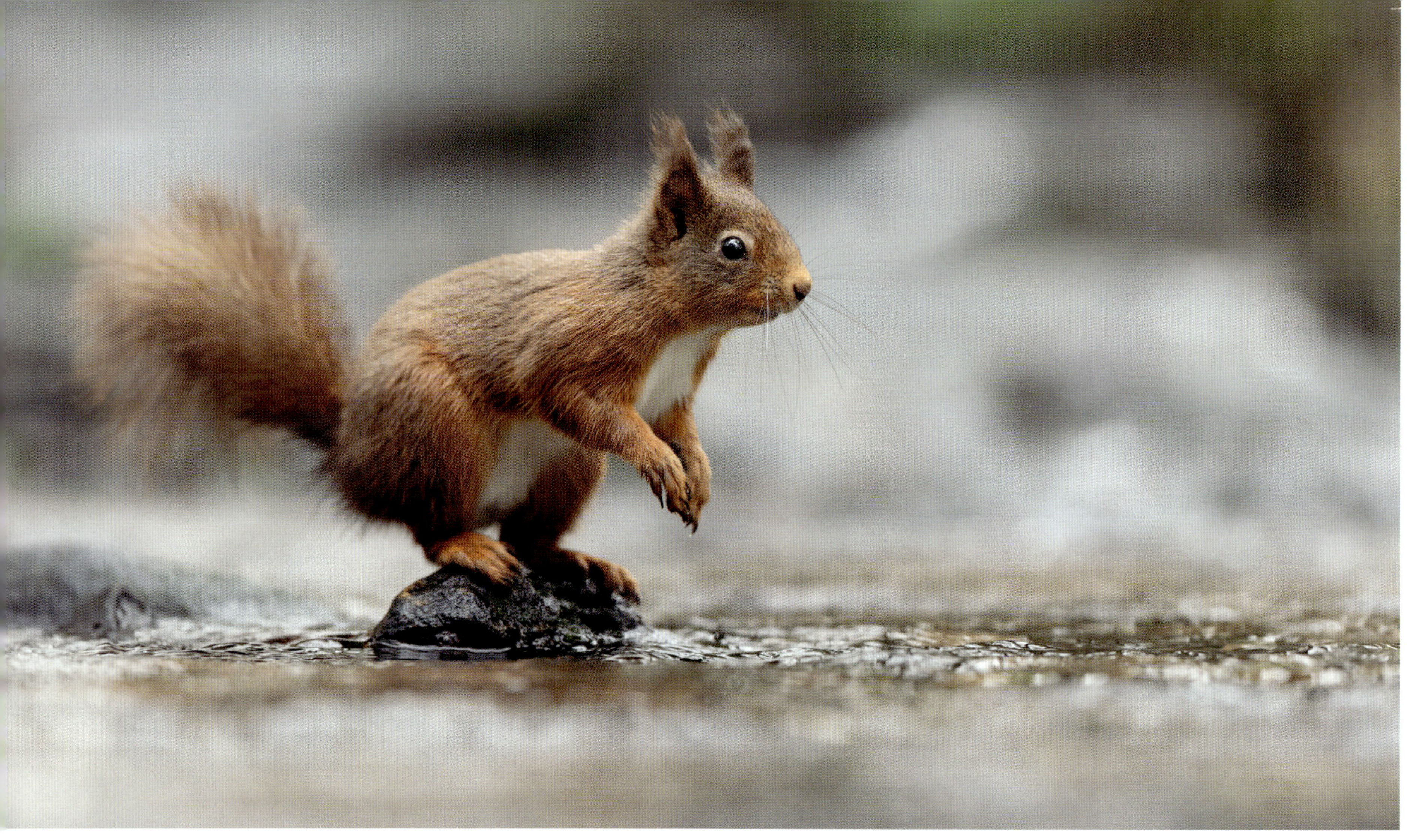

A Precarious Pose
Animal Portraits | Highly Commended

Alastair Marsh
Red squirrel (*Sciurus vulgaris*)
Cumbria, England

Canon EOS R3 with Canon 300mm f/2.8 lens.
300mm; 1/320th second; f/3.5; ISO 1,600.

Each autumn and winter, I spend as much time as
possible in the company of a red squirrel population
in Cumbria. Thanks to a good friend who lives
nearby, I've gotten to know the landowner, who does
an awful lot to save the species in the area. Hazelnuts
are put in squirrel feeders in the area to provide them
with a reliable food source. There's a small stream
that runs through the woodland they call home, and
they use rocks to hop across, as you can see here.

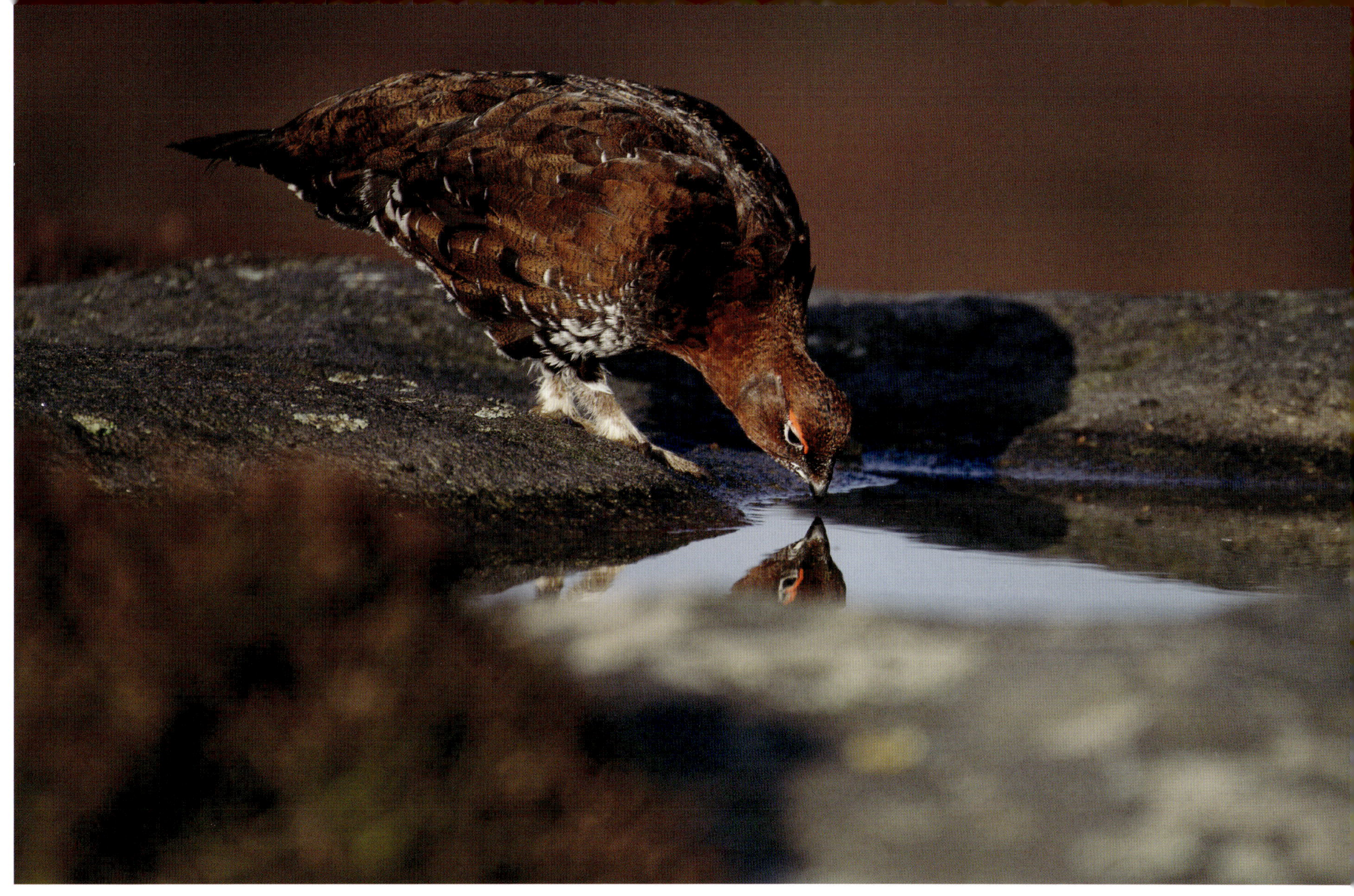

At the Watering Hole
Animal Portraits

Mary Michael Patterson
Red grouse (*Lagopus lagopus scotica*)
Peak District, England

Nikon D850 with Nikon 180-400mm f/4.0 lens.
400mm; 1/1,000th second; f/5.6; ISO 320.

High up on the top of a rocky plateau in the Peak District, there are large gritstone rock formations that have been shaped by wind and rain over millions of years. I had been to this area several times and noticed more wildlife activity on one particular rock formation than on others. A pair of sheep climbing up on the rock alerted me that this was an important site for the local wildlife to find rainwater in the natural rock pool. It took several attempts to get the image I wanted, but as luck would have it, a male red grouse walked slowly to the water, paused for a moment of reflection, drank the water and flew off.

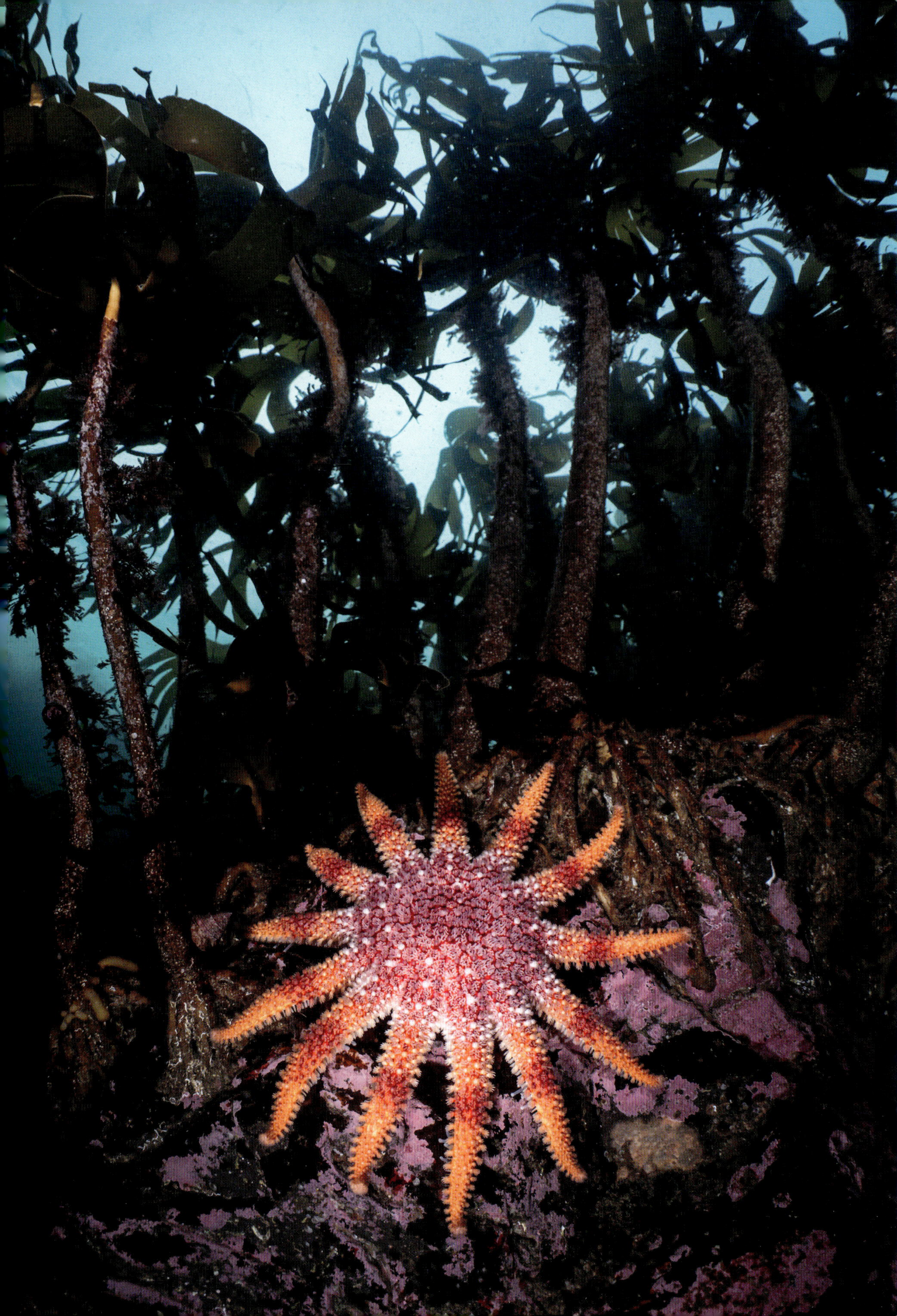

Star Beneath the Canopy
Coast & Marine

Billy Arthur
Common sunstar (*Crossaster papposus*)
and Cuvie kelp (*Laminaria hyperborea*)
Levenwick, Shetland Islands, Scotland

Sony A7R III with Sony 28-60mm f/4-
5.6 lens. 29mm; 1/160th second; f/10;
ISO 500.

A typical rocky reef scene around
the shores of Shetland. Beneath the
kelp forest, this common sunstar was
lurking. These shots can often be hard
to compose because I need to be so
close to the bottom. Shooting from
the hip, checking the image and then
recomposing if needed can often help
in this situation when there is limited
space between the camera and the
seabed.

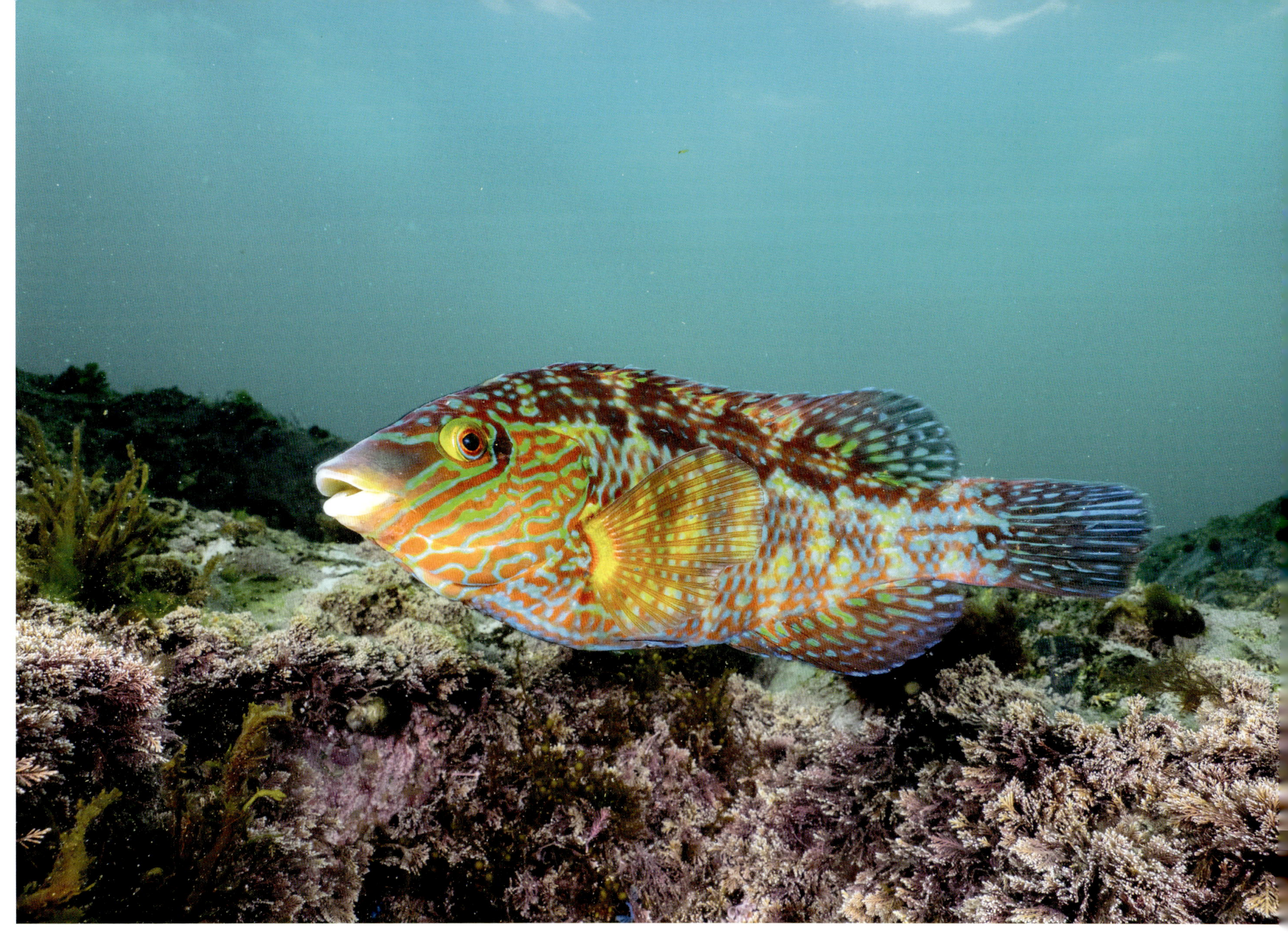

Magnificent Wrasse
Coast & Marine

Martin Stevens
Corkwing wrasse (*Symphodus melops*)
Falmouth, Cornwall, England

Olympus EM5 III with Olympus 7-14mm f/2.8 lens.
14mm; 1/60th second; f/11; ISO 500.

Few fish are as stunning as a male corkwing wrasse, especially during the breeding season. This common fish builds nests lined with seaweed along the rocky shore. The wrasse here was busily collecting material and putting it in his nest, which was just below the bottom of the photo, paying little attention to me most of the time. Taken in Falmouth, Cornwall, with a wide-angle zoom lens.

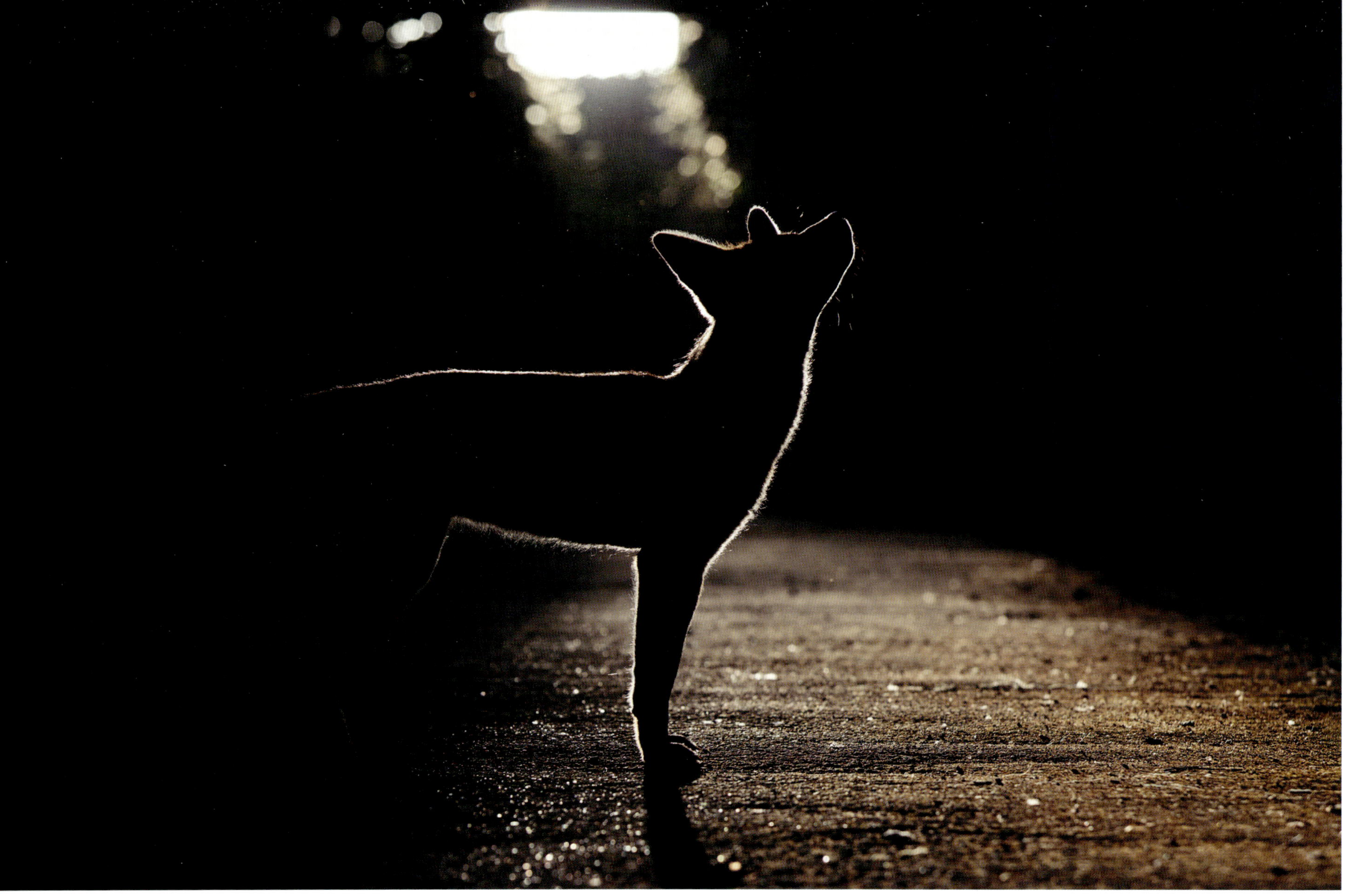

Back Street Fox
Urban Wildlife

Simon Withyman
Red fox (*Vulpes vulpes*)
Bristol, England

Canon EOS R5 with Canon 70-200mm f/2.8 lens.
120mm; 1/500th second; f/5.6; ISO 400.

For just a few weeks of the year, the light would
shine down this small back street near my home,
creating a magical lighting effect. My furry subject
paused briefly while she stood perfectly in a pool of
light, checking out herring gulls calling from a nearby
rooftop.

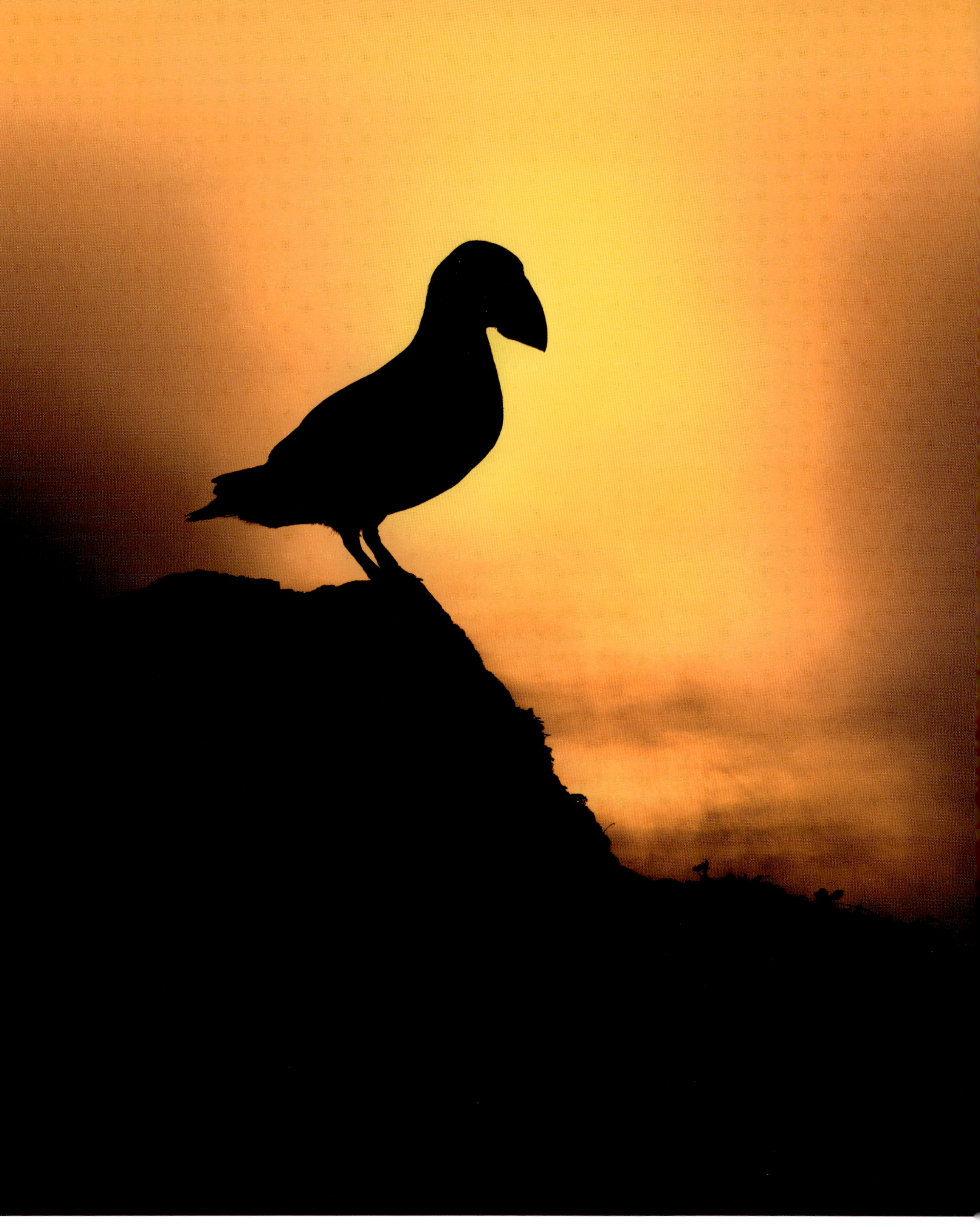

Skomer Silhouette
Animal Portraits

Drew Buckley
Atlantic puffin (*Fratercula arctica*)
Skomer Island,
Pembrokeshire, Wales

Canon EOS R5 with Canon 500mm f/4 II lens. 500mm; 1/2,500th second; f/5.6; ISO 800.

A puffin stood on rocks on Skomer, silhouetted in front of the sunset. Even after visiting the island many times every year for the last decade, we could probably count on one hand when we've had perfect conditions for this type of image. After many years of trying and not forgetting, we finally saw the birds in the right place with the right pose! Underexposing and shooting into the sunset, the birds are silhouetted against a vivid orange backdrop.

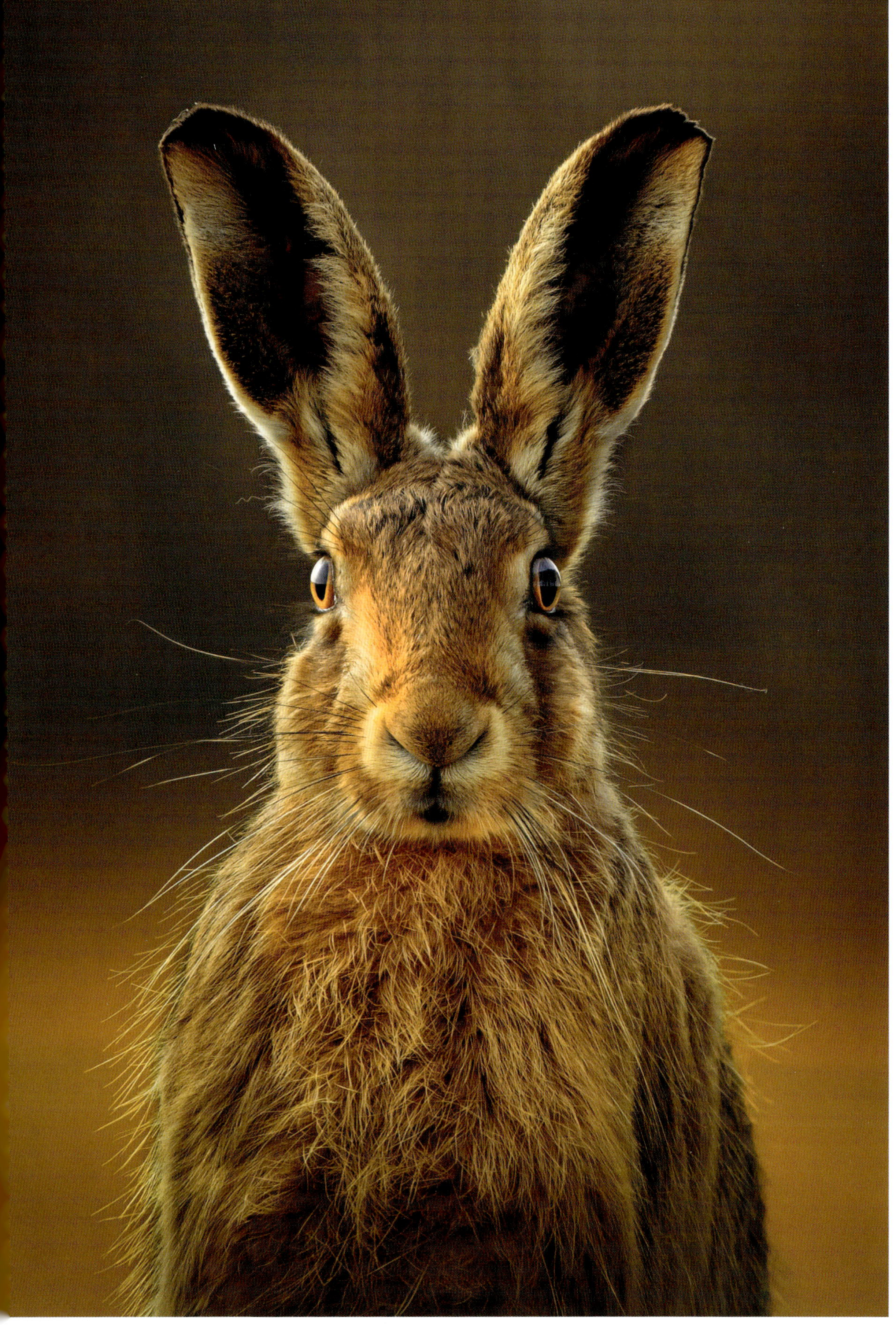

Hare
Animal Portraits

Weng Lee
Brown hare (*Lepus europaeus*)
Hibaldstow, Lincolnshire, England

Sony A9 II with Sony 200-600mm f/5.6-6.3 lens. 600mm; 1/1,250th second; f/7.1; ISO 1,250.

I lay in the field, patiently waiting for a hare. March is their season, but sighting them up close isn't always guaranteed. For several hours, I remained still, nestled among the grass. Then, as if by a stroke of luck, a hare decided to wander in my direction. I seized the opportunity and managed to capture a few shots of it.

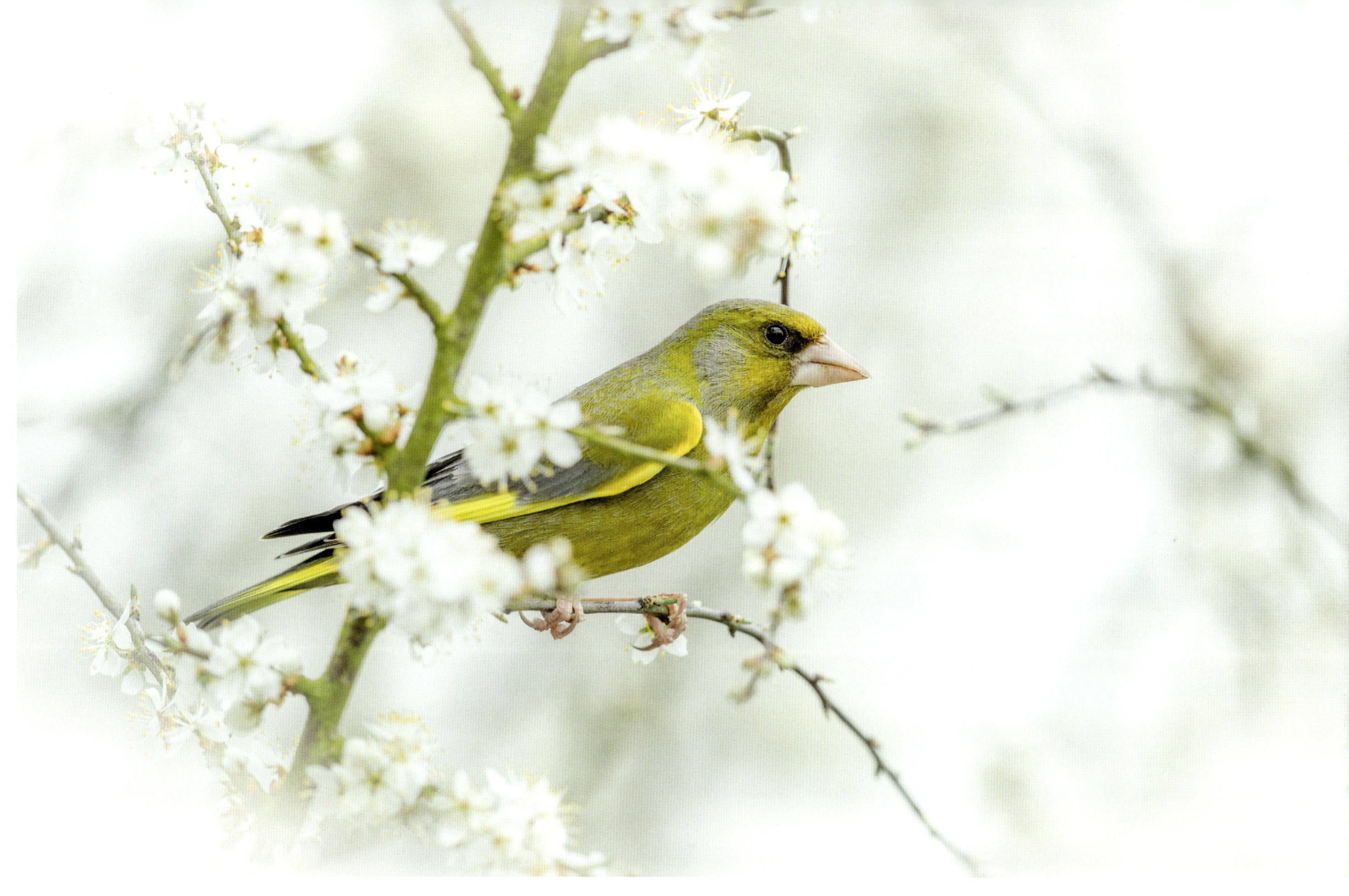

Blackthorn Beauty
Animal Portraits

Philip Male
Greenfinch (*Chloris chloris*)
Broad Town, Wiltshire, England

Canon 1DX MII with Canon 600mm f/4 lens.
600mm; 1/1000th second; f/5; ISO 500.

I always think greenfinches look pretty, but perched in a sea of white they really do shine. In the spring, the hedgerow by our house is covered in blackthorn blossom, and I was fortunate enough to capture this one with the whole flower-covered hedgerow behind. It's so good to see them making a comeback after the hard time with trichomonosis.

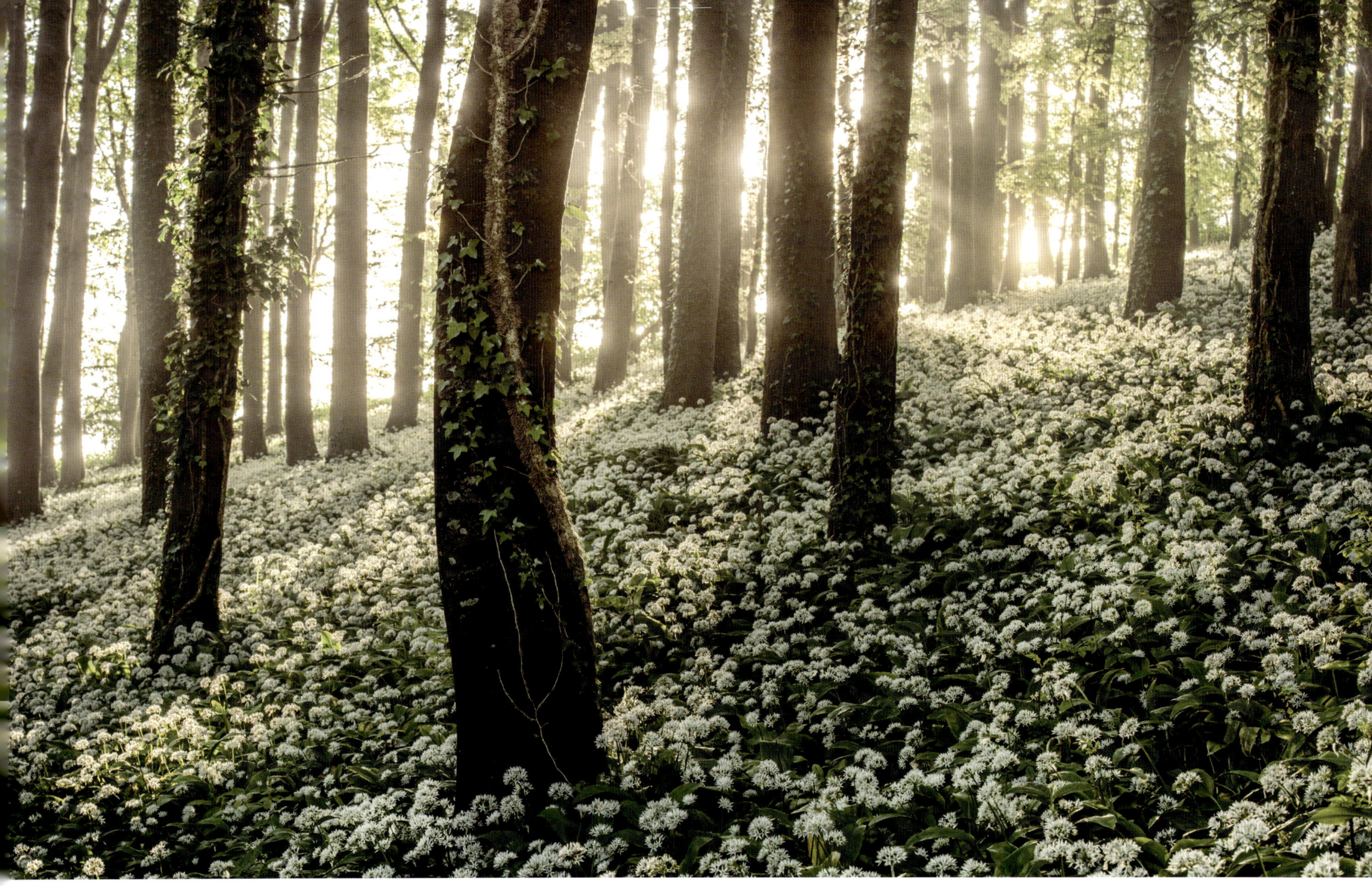

Ethereal Garlic
Wild Woods

Robin Goodlad
Ramson, Dorset, England

Nikon D800 with Nikon 70-200mm f/2.8 lens. 70mm;
1/3rd second; f/16; ISO 100.

After photographing the sunrise in the wild garlic
woods, I was drawn to the light at the edge of the
wood, which was very bright but suggested another
world beyond.

Snakeshead Fritillaries Dew Dance
Botanical Britain

Stephen Davis
Snake's-head fritillary (*Fritillaria meleagris*)
Upper Waterway, Wiltshire, England

Canon EOS 5D IV with Canon 70-300mm f/4-5.6 lens. 269mm; 1/320th second; f/5.6; ISO 200.

The snake's-head fritillary is a native plant of the rare habitat Flood Plain Meadows, with only 30 such meadows in Britain, six of which occur in Wiltshire. In only one, at Upper Waterhay, the predominant form is white (as opposed to the normal red), which makes up 80% of the population and occurs in its thousands. This small meadow is a fragment of the formerly much more extensive floodplain meadow habitat that occurs in the Thames Valley floodplain, vulnerable to gravel extraction and development. This image was taken shortly after sunrise with the camera mounted low to the ground on a tripod, shooting through the dew-laden grass to a group of fritillary flowers. I chose a wide aperture on a long zoom lens deliberately to create the foreground bokeh and soft background.

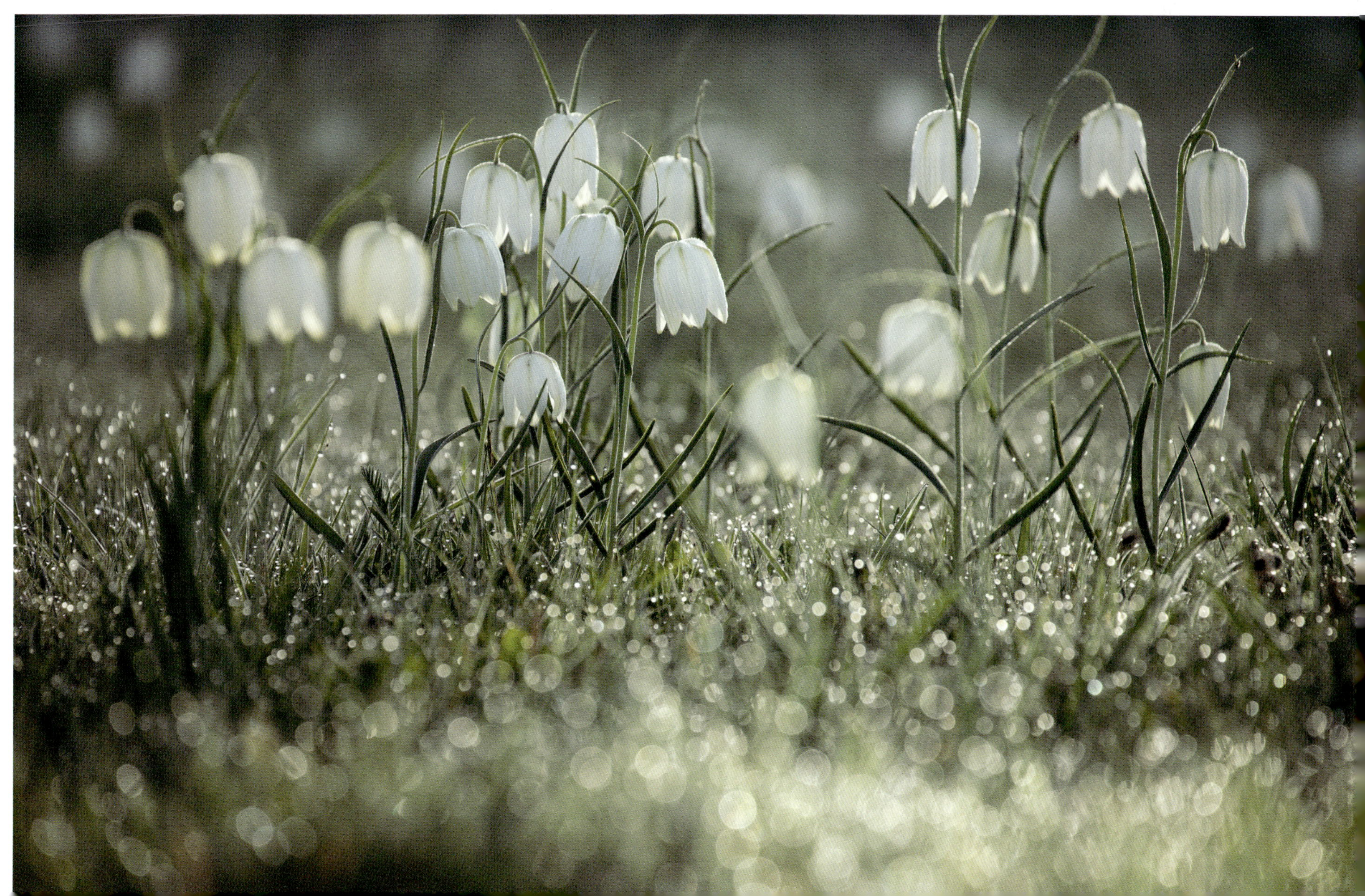

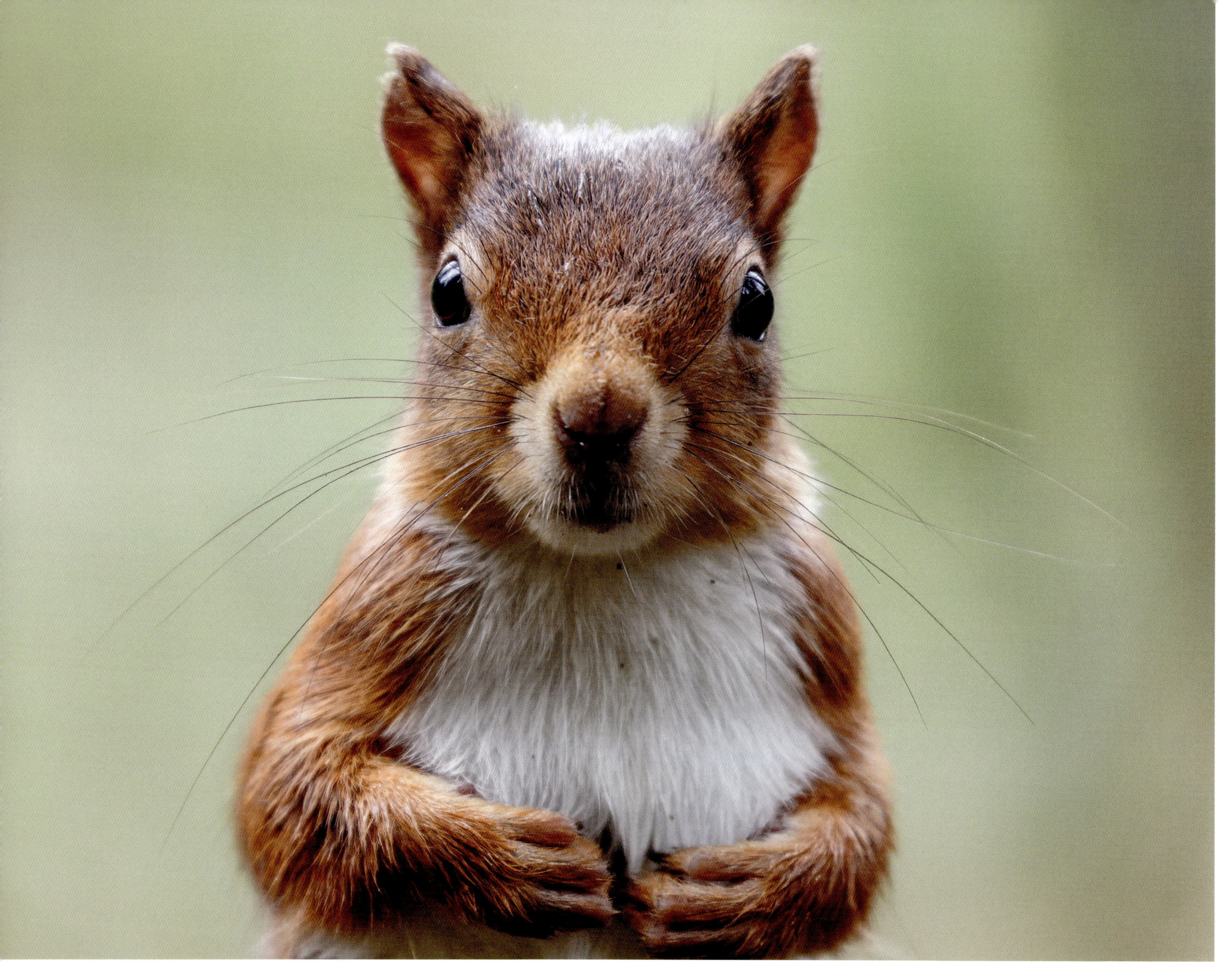

Who, Me?
Animal Portraits

Andy Nayler
Red squirrel (*Sciurus vulgaris*)
Yorkshire Dales, England

Canon 7D II with Canon 100-400mm f/4.5-5.6 II lens.
400mm; 1/250th second; f/5.6; ISO 1,600.

Heading out for a walk in the Yorkshire Dales, I hadn't planned it to be a photography trip, so just took a camera and one zoom lens. The dull, overcast weather made the light levels under the trees low, but I set the ISO to 1600 and trusted the image stabilisation. The feeders at the viewing area had been recently filled, and up to five squirrels helped themselves to the nuts and chased each other through the woods. Some came very close, and one sat up perfectly and stared into the camera, probably wondering why my shutter was so loud.

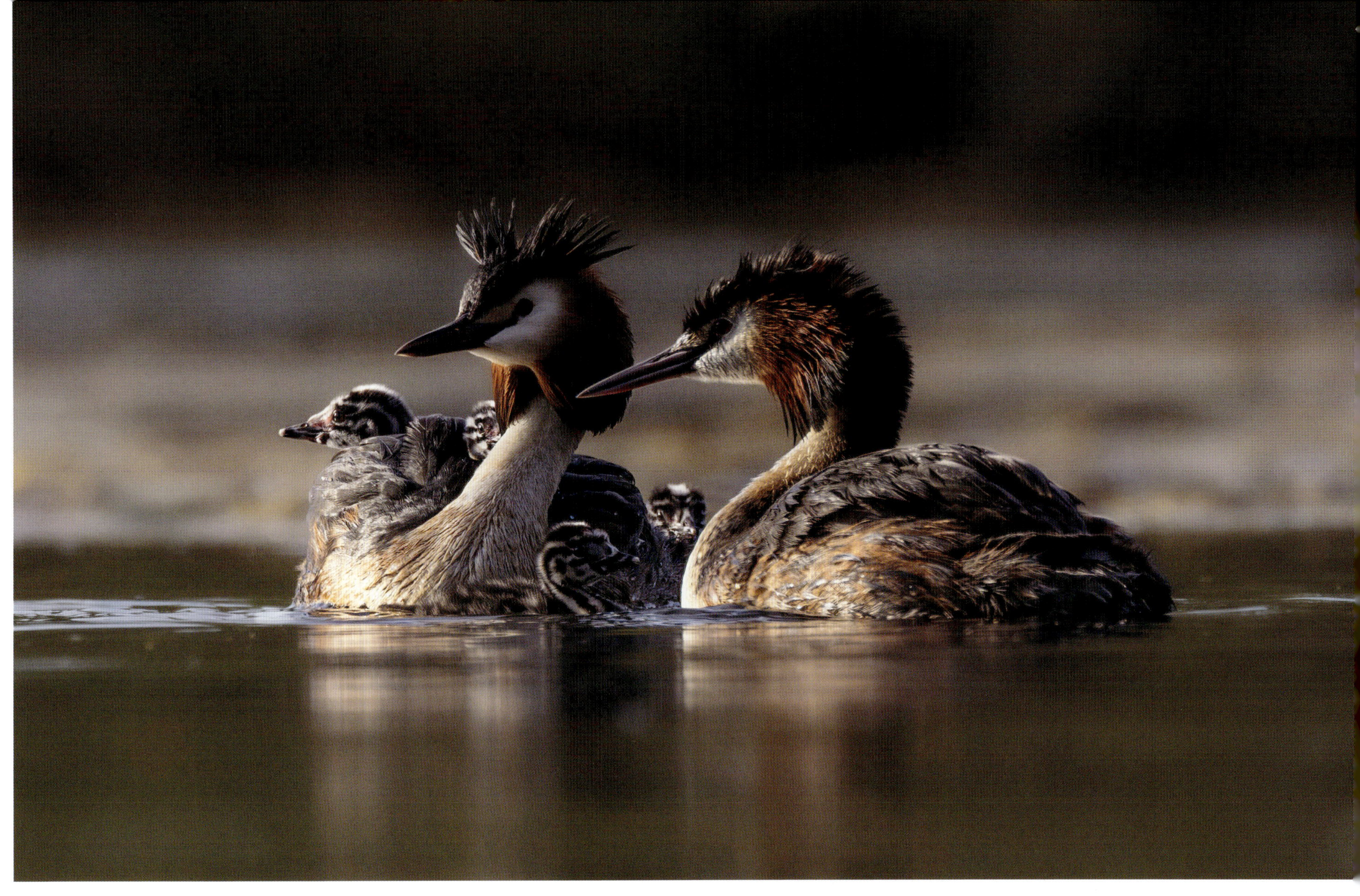

Teamwork Makes the Dream Work
Animal Behaviour

Nathan Martin
Great crested grebe (*Podiceps cristatus*)
Country Park, Essex, England

Canon R5 with Canon RF100-500mm F4.5-7.1 lens.
500mm; 1/2500th second; f/7.1; ISO 1,600.

Last year, I witnessed these two grebes preparing their nest, ready for their chicks, of which they successfully raised three. It was amazing to witness, but I never really captured them as I'd hoped. Thankfully, this year, the same pair had built their nest in the same spot, this time hatching four little humbugs. Watching their heads pop out as they ride on their parents' backs is one of the sweetest sights in nature. Coupled with the dedication of the parents, forever off gathering little fish for their young to eat, it really is a privilege to witness.

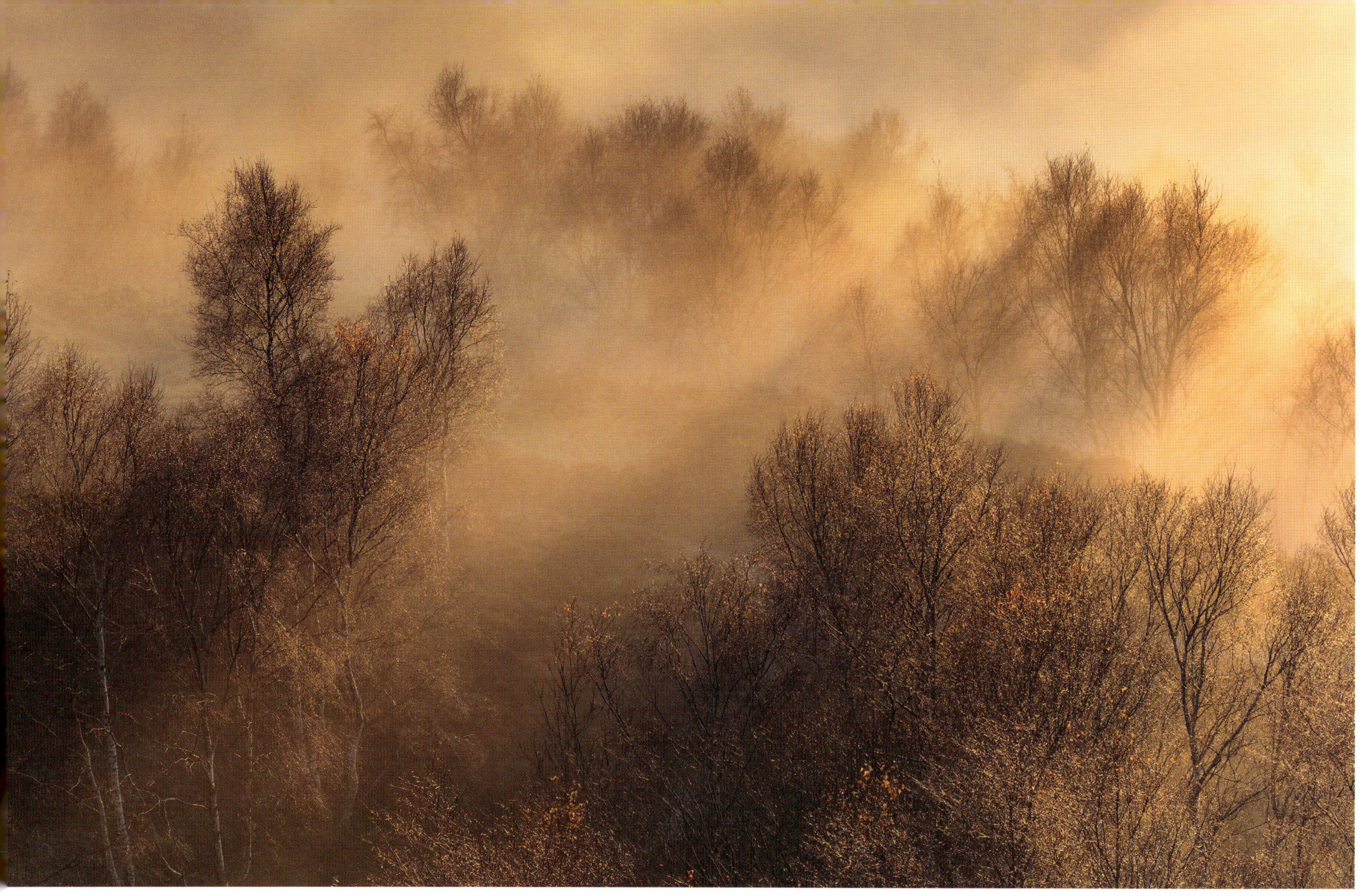

Cloud Inversion at Sunset
Wild Woods

Verity Milligan
Surprise View, Peak District, England

Fujifilm X-T2 with Fujifilm 50-140mm f/2.8 II lens. 70mm; 1/30th second; f/13; ISO 320.

On a late November day, the whole of the Peak District was shrouded in fog for the whole day. After wandering through the endless woodland of Surprise View and Padley Gorge, the fog started to dip into the Hope Valley and reveal the sun. It's the only cloud inversion I've ever experienced at sunset, with the light breaking through the fog and illuminating the birch of Bolehill Quarry below. It was an evening I'll never forget.

Into the Light
Wild Woods

Pete Humphry
Rhinefield Ornamental Drive, Brockenhurst,
Hampshire, England

Nikon D7200 with Sigma 17-70mm f/2.8-4 lens.
70mm; 1/6,400th second; f/4; ISO 500.

The New Forest is such a beautiful part of England
regardless of the weather, but this morning was
nothing short of spectacular. An hour after sunrise,
light was bursting through the trees, illuminating
the forest with incredible scenes around every
corner. Time was of the essence, so before the light
disappeared, I found somewhere to park, rushed to
get into position to capture the side-lit trees, set the
camera up and just enjoyed the moment.
A combination of light, mist and beautiful scenery
made this no ordinary drive into work.

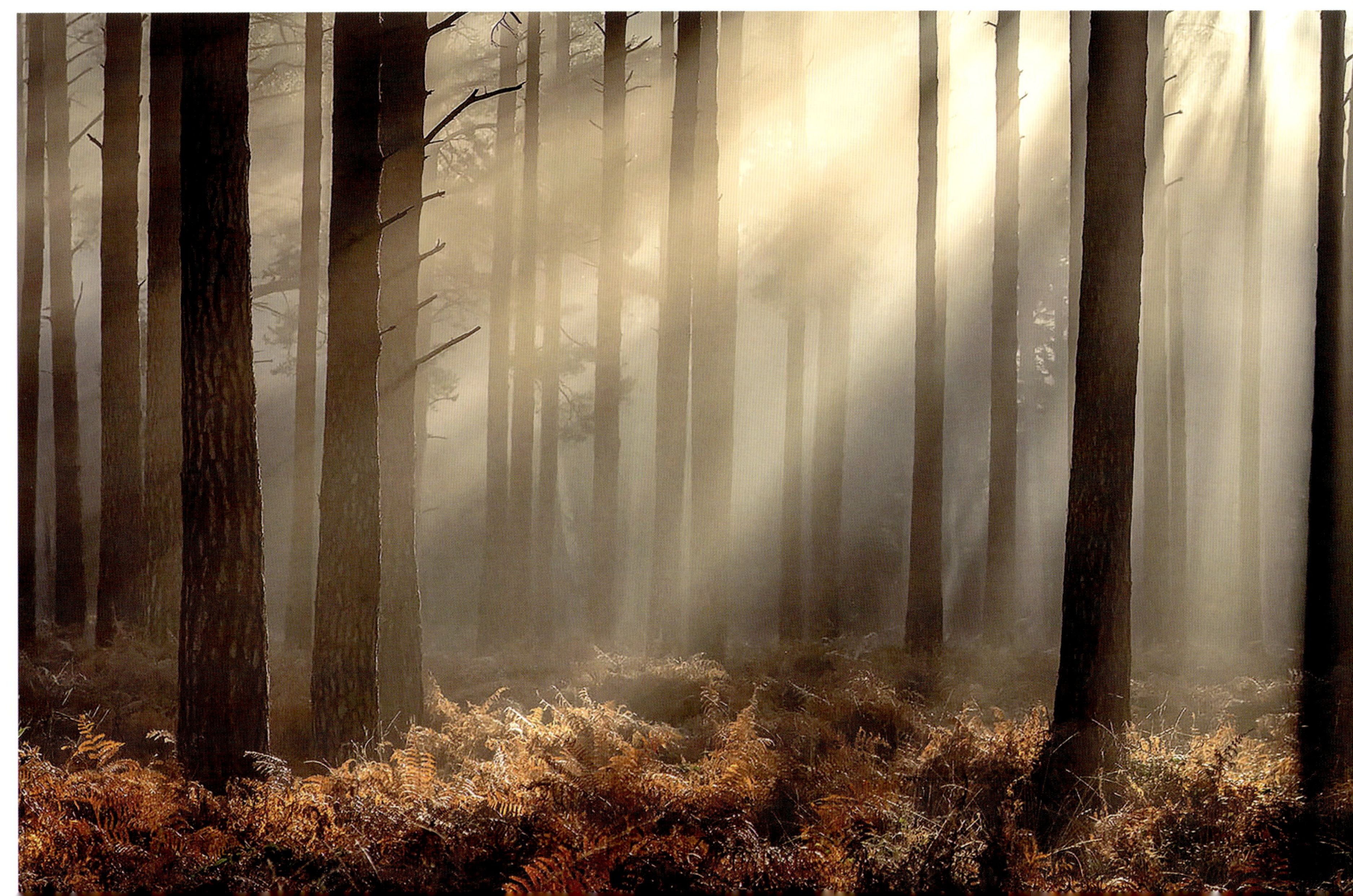

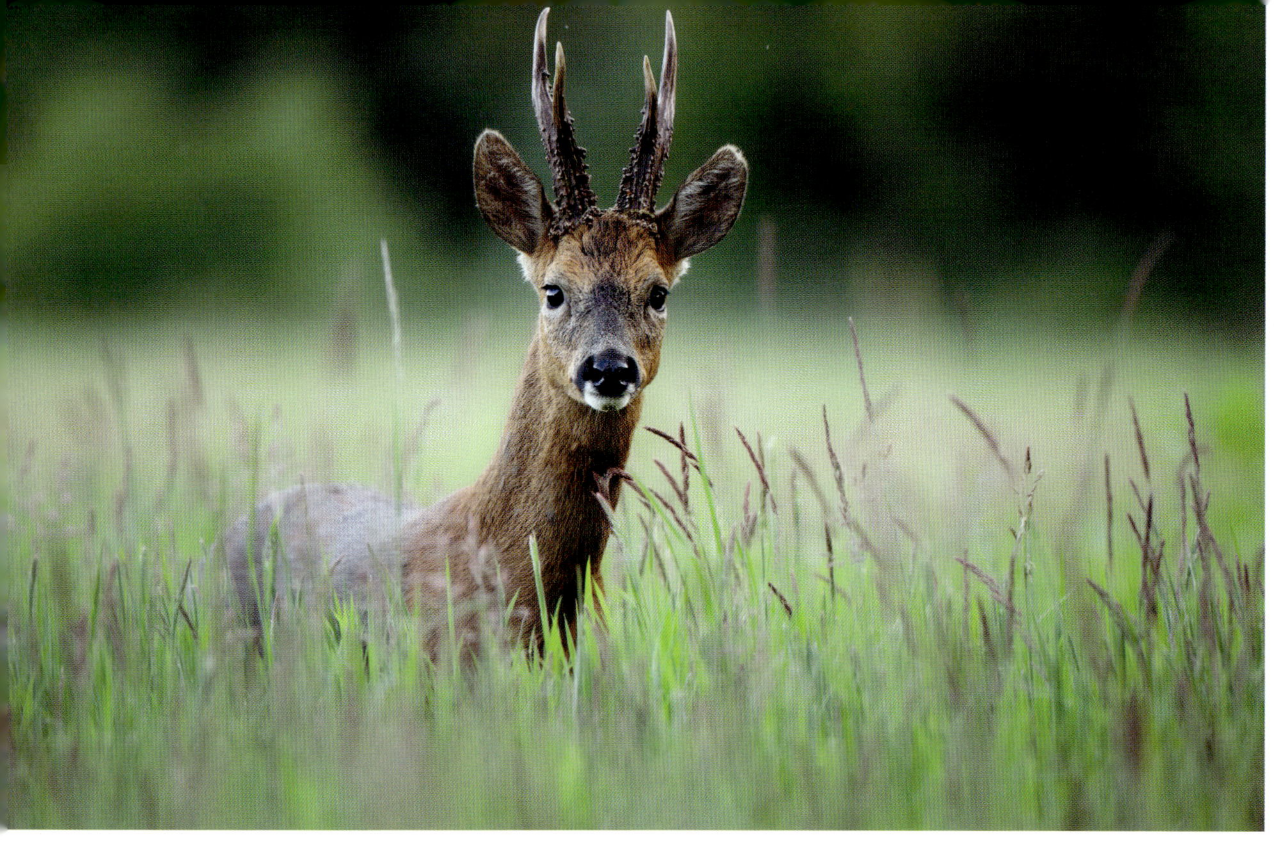

Big Buck
Animal Portraits

Alex Witt
Roe deer (*Capreolus capreolus*)
Surrey, England

Nikon D7200 with Sigma 17-70mm f/2.8-4 lens. 70mm; 1/6,400th second; f/4; ISO 500.

This buck is probably the most impressive I have ever come across in terms of the thickness of the antlers. He could often be found in the same field every evening, and with a barbed wire fence between us, he was extremely calm and relaxed. He would even often approach me out of curiosity, showing no signs of fear. On the couple of occasions I encountered him outside of this safe space, it was like encountering a completely different buck, and his behaviour was extremely timid. The physical boundary of the barbed wire fence was enough for him to feel completely safe.

Winter Fairytale
Animal Portraits

Dovydas Vicius
Chinese water deer (*Hydropotes inermis*)
Sewell, Bedfordshire, England

Sony A1 with Sony 600mm f/4 lens. 600mm; 1/1,600th second; f/4; ISO 1250.

After a chilly winter morning successfully photographing Chinese water deer in the fields, I returned to my backpack, which I had left behind in the tall grass along the canal, needing a cup of hot tea to warm up. Before I could even taste a sip of the tea, a water deer doe suddenly rose from the grass, maybe 50 metres away, and headed straight towards me. I carefully put down the cup and grabbed a camera. The result was an unrepeatable experience.

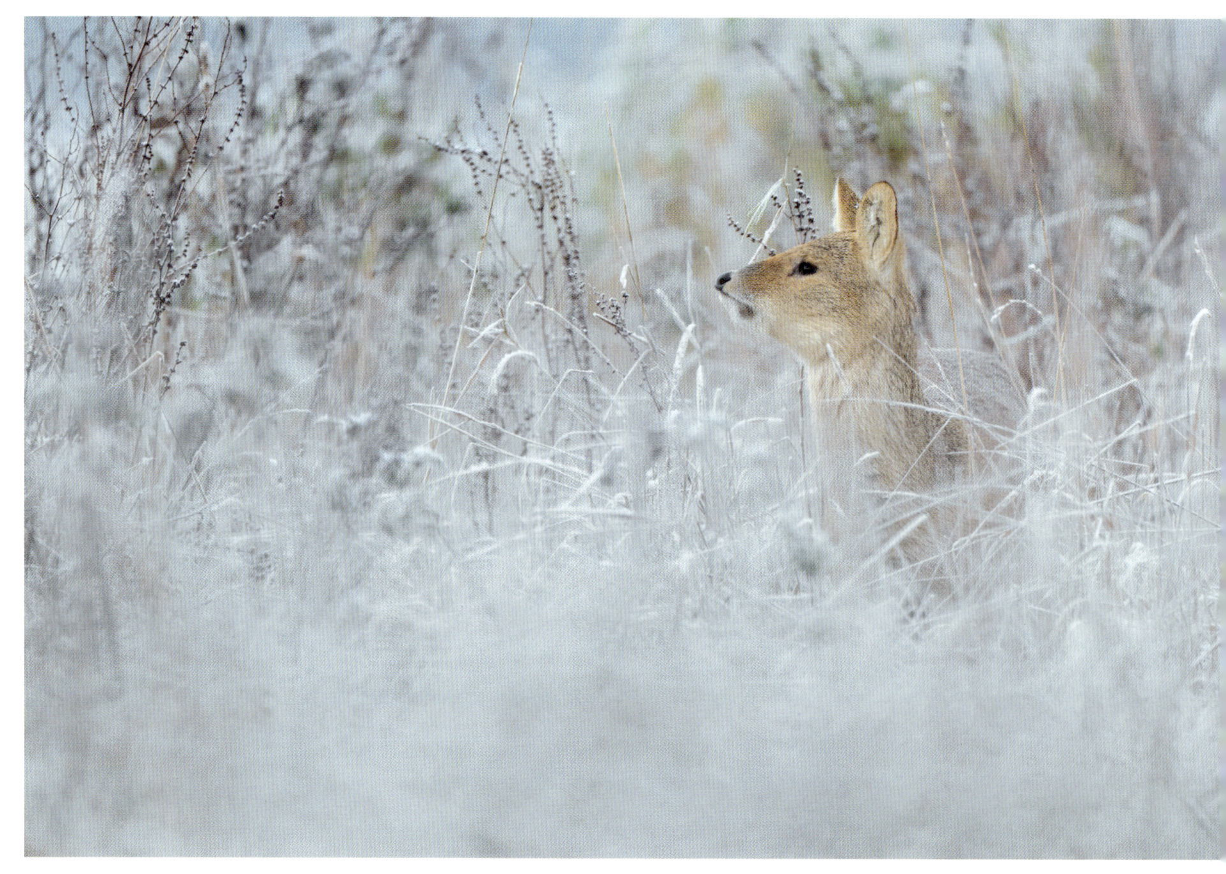

From Dawn to Dusk
Animal Portraits

Lawrie Brailey
Red deer (*Cervus elaphus*)
Richmond, London, England

Nikon D4 with Nikon 300mm f/2.8 lens. 300mm; 1/1,600th second; f/2.8, ISO 1,600.

When it comes to UK wildlife, I'm not sure there's a more distinctive silhouette than a red deer stag in the middle of the rut. This particular male had seen a lot of success and was diligently defending his large harem of females. With the sun setting, he was proudly asserting his dominance while patrolling his 'patch'. After noticing how much time he spent on the bank next to a shallow riverbed, I lay down in the water and waited for him to return. Not only did he eventually return, but he also stopped and bellowed in exactly the right spot!

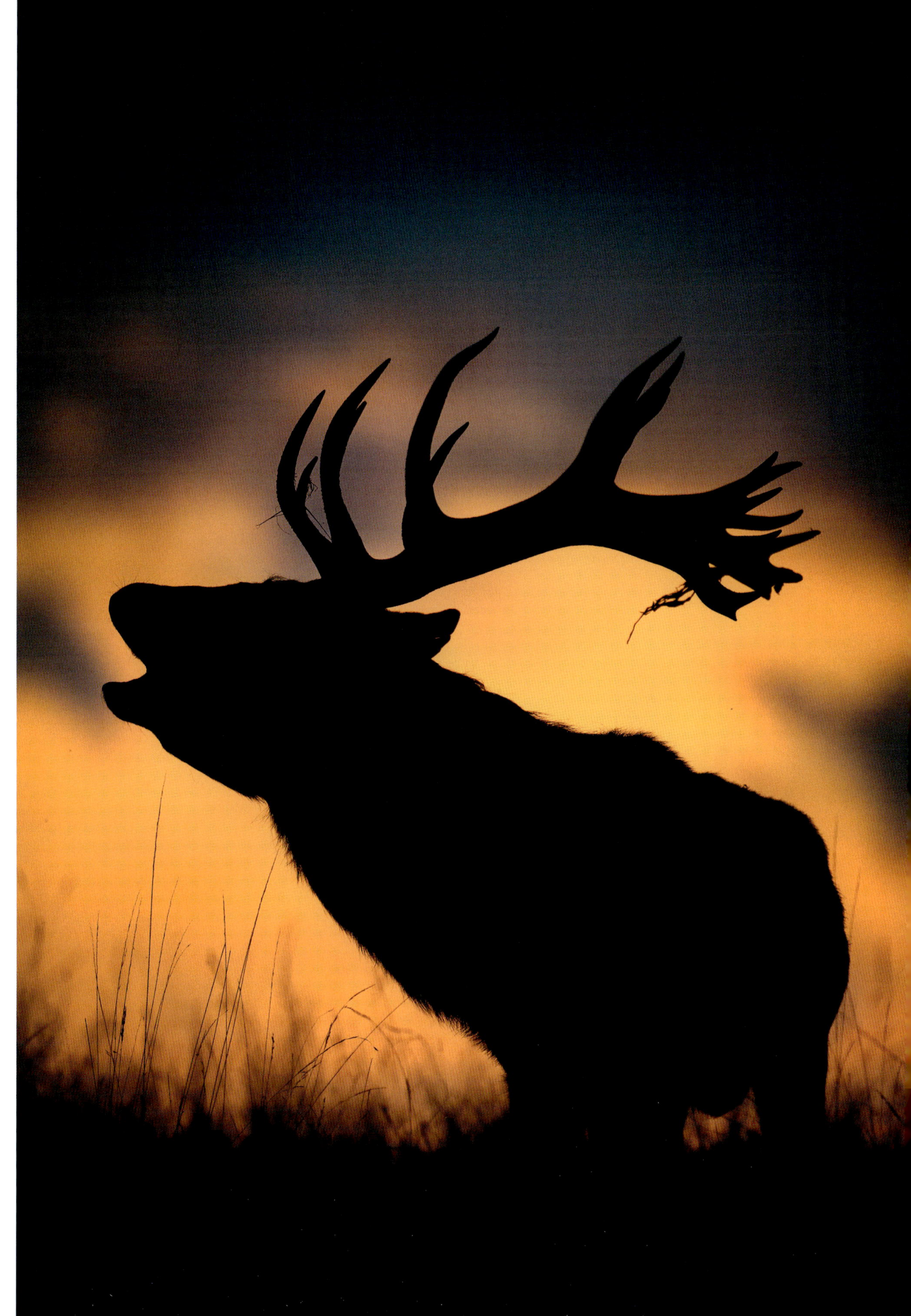

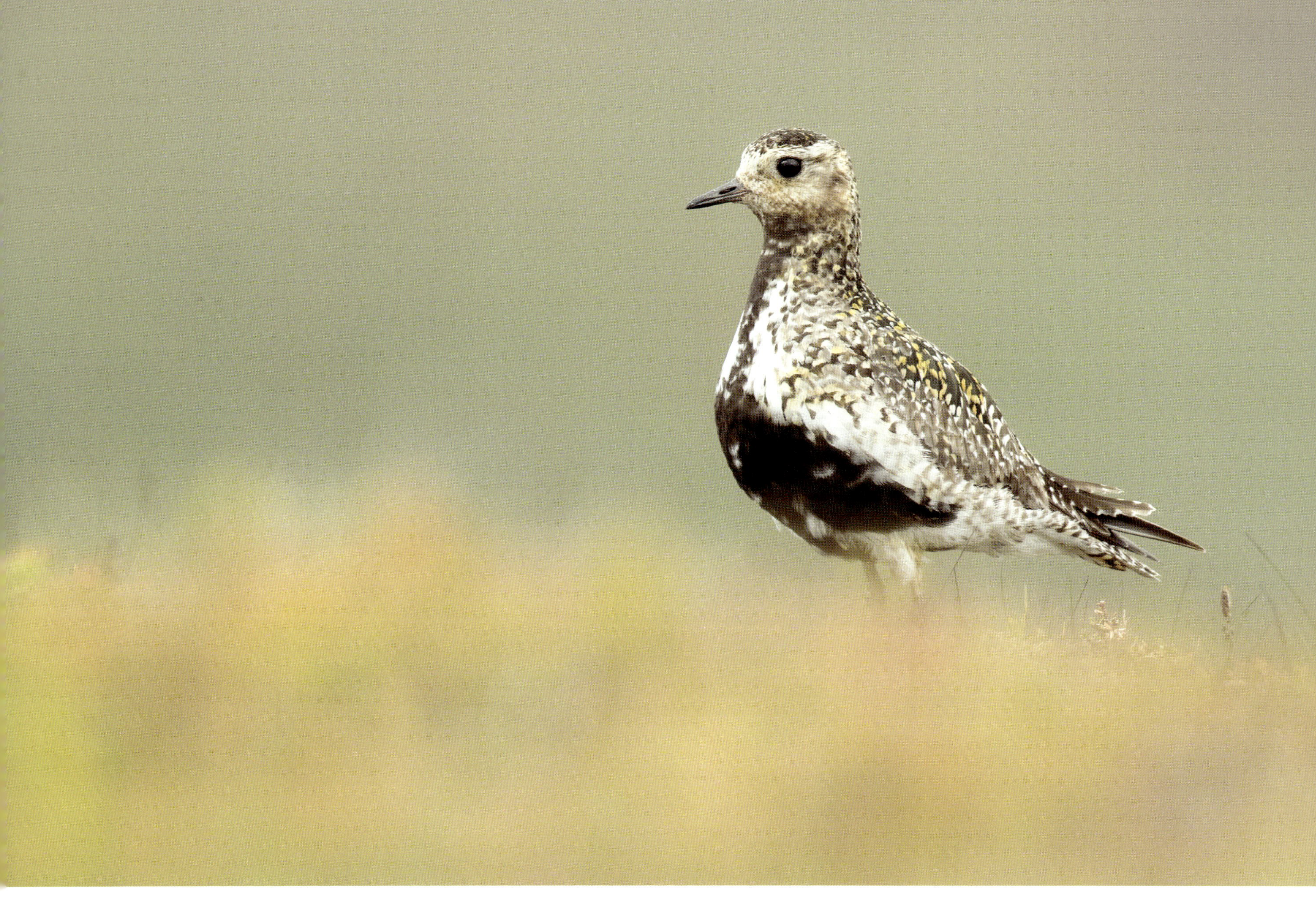

Golden Moor
Animal Portraits

Chris Hawes
Golden plover (*Pluvialis dominica*)
Cairngorms National Park, Scotland

Canon 1D X II with Canon 300mm f/2.8 II lens
& 2x teleconverter. 600mm; 1/500th second;
f/8; ISO 800.

I spent a day over the summer in the Cairngorms, 'bagging' a couple of Munros. As I often do on these hikes, I decided to add some weight to my backpack by taking my camera, hoping to encounter some wildlife. During a lunch break, I noticed the faint piping call of a golden plover nearby, and after some time I spotted its movement in the distance. While I was eating my sandwich, it gradually approached closer and closer. I abandoned my lunch, grabbed my camera, and lay down on the path to see if the bird would continue to approach and allow me to capture a few images. Sure enough, it appeared over a

tussock of moss and grass, posing beautifully against the backdrop of the distant hillside. It checked me out, seemed satisfied and then continued on its way as I returned to my sandwich, glad that, for once, my decision to bring my camera had paid off.

Parakeet
Habitat

Vai Meng Chan
Ring-necked parakeet
(*Psittacula krameri*)
Essex, England

GoPro Hero 10. 3mm; 1/640th second;
f/2.5; ISO 100.

This photo was taken with my GoPro.
For preparation, I took a picture of tree
bark and printed it on A3 paper. I used
this to wrap my 5m stand pole and my
GoPro. I placed the pole and camera
when the parakeet went out for food.
The most important thing is to respect
others and not disturb the wildlife.

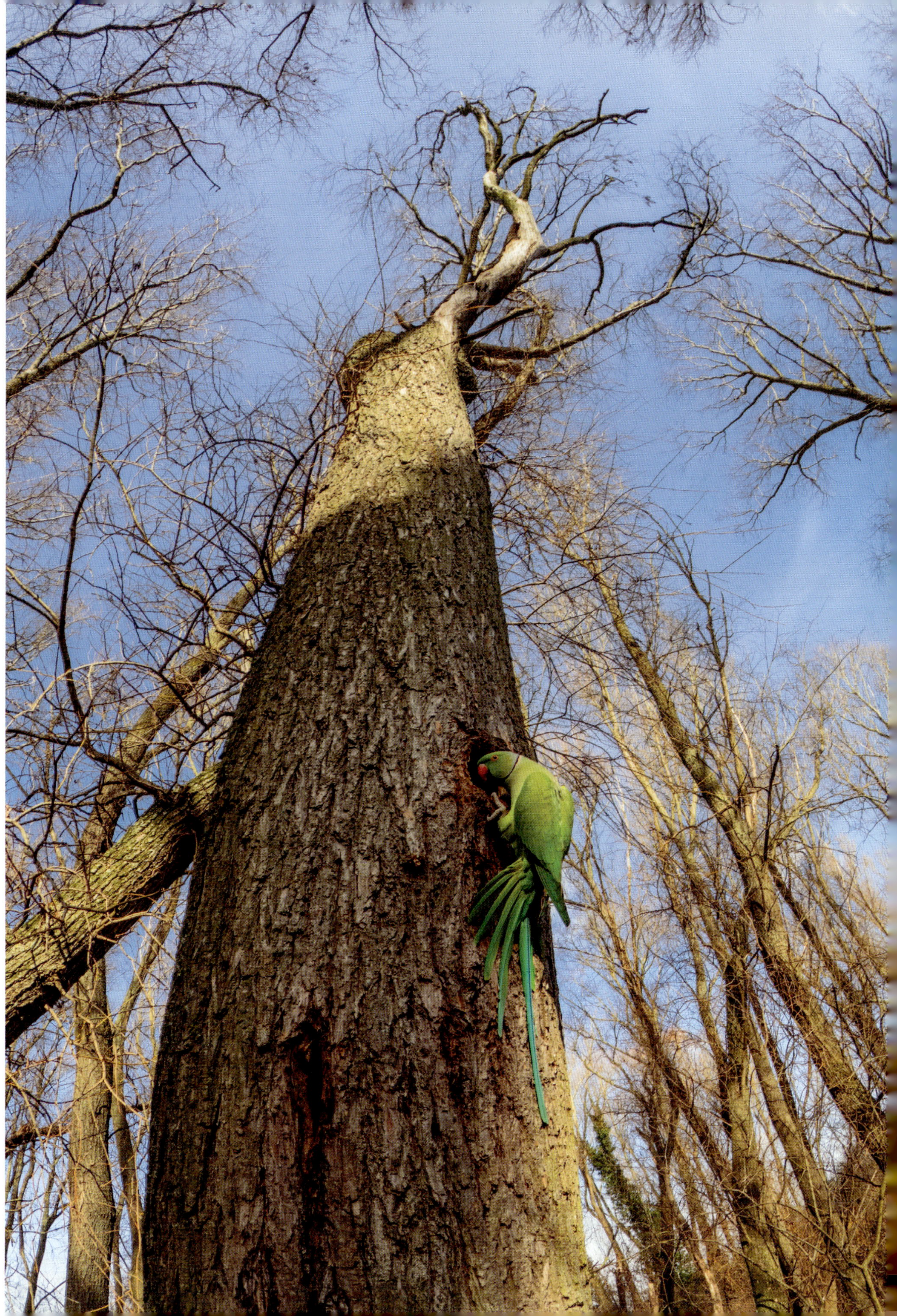

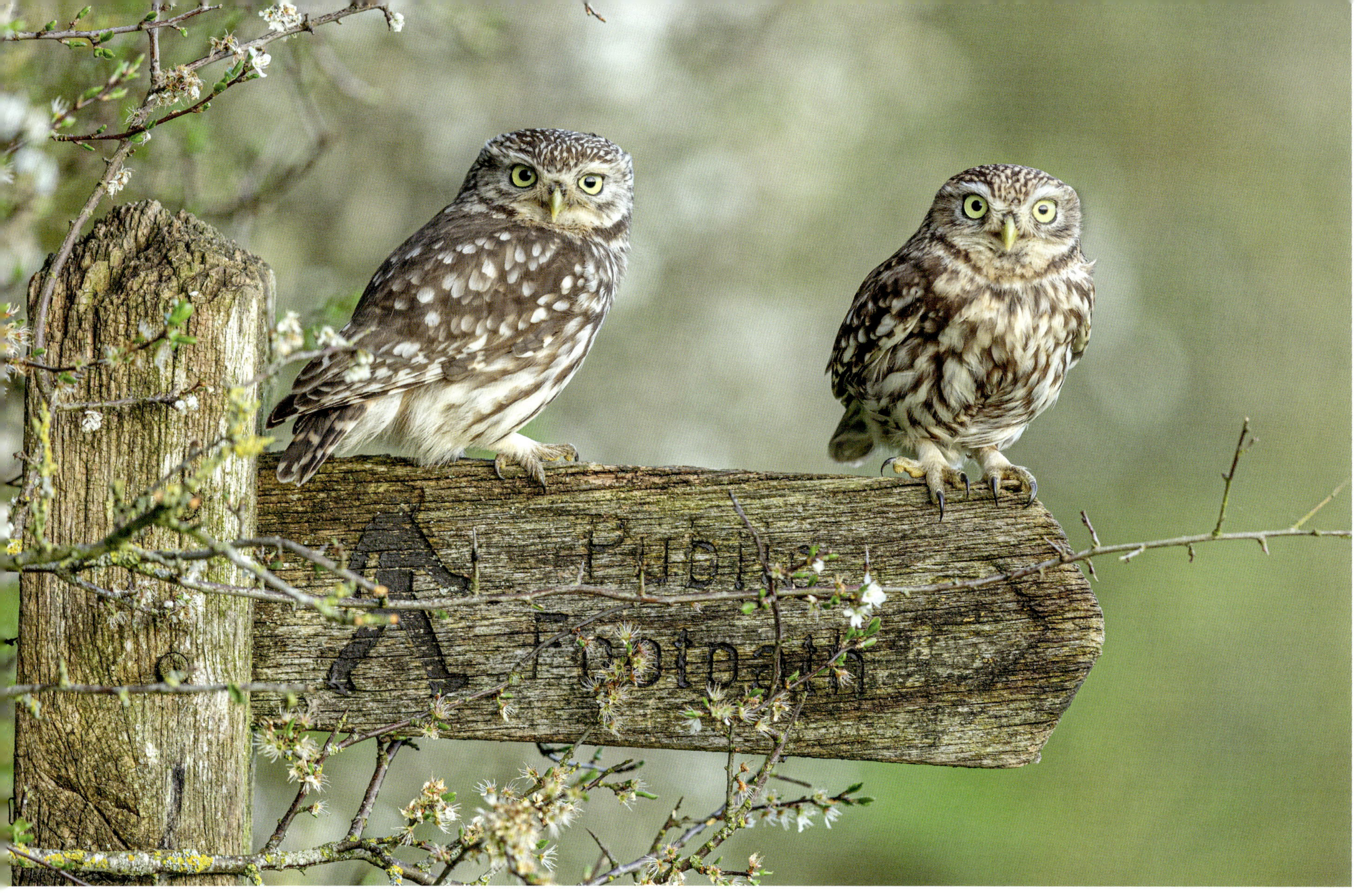

It Must Be a Sign
Animal Portraits

Philip Male
Little owl (*Athene noctua*)
Broad Town, Wiltshire, England

Canon EOS R3 with Canon 600mm f/4 II lens.
600mm; 1/250th second; f/4; ISO 3,200.

In 2020, a pair of little owls took up residence in one of my owl boxes. Sadly, both adults died; the male disappeared, and the female was hit by a vehicle. They partially raised three young. After speaking to the Owl Trust, they suggested putting out some cut-up meat to help them survive. I'm fairly certain that this male is one of the young from that year, as he is the most comfortable with me around the garden. He has been joined by the female on the right and now has three young of his own.

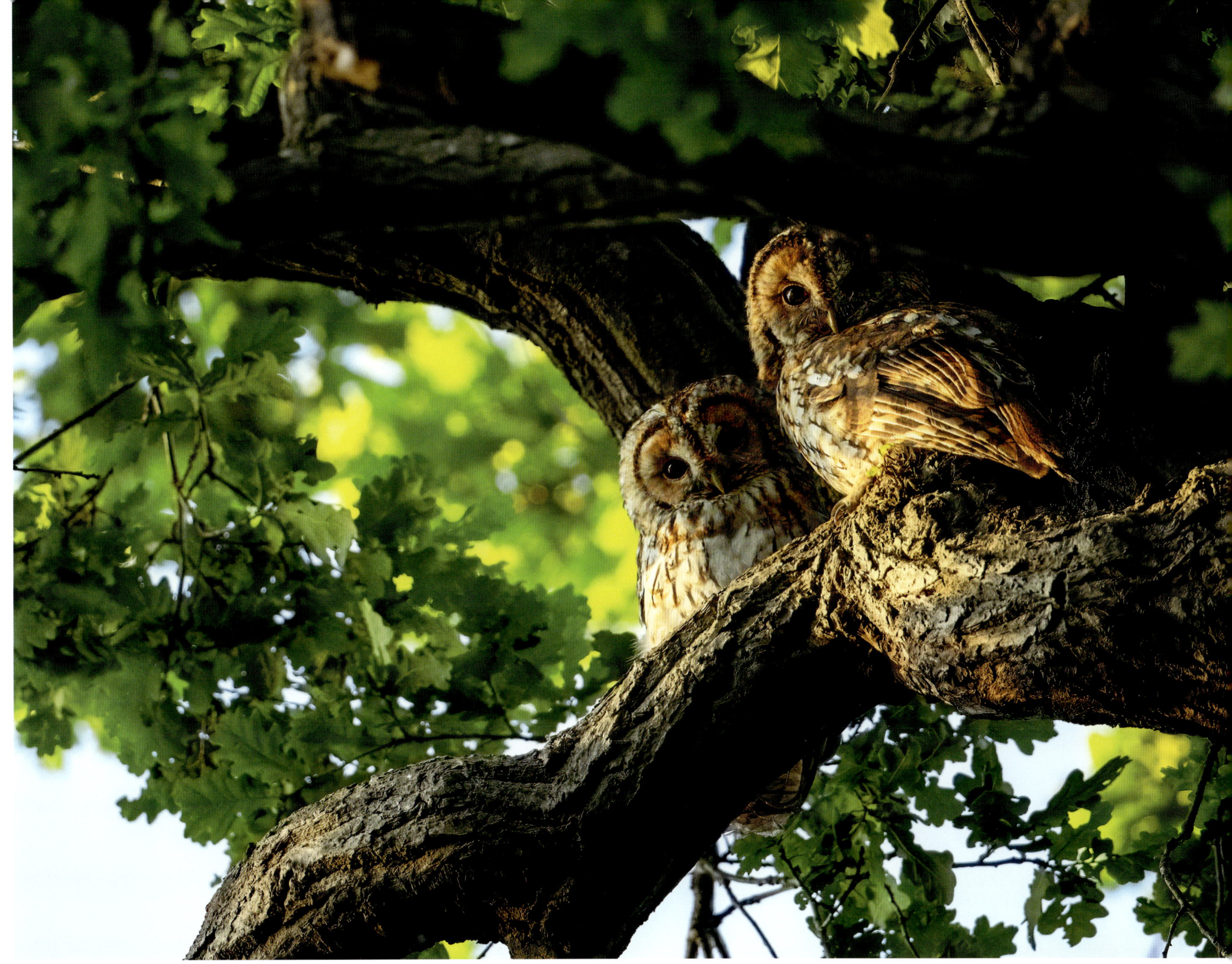

Lucky Dip
Animal Behaviour

Felix Belloin
Tawny owl (*Strix aluco*)
Richmond Park, London, England

Canon EOS 1D X III with Canon 500mm f/4 II lens.
500mm; 1/800th second; f/4; ISO 3,200.

After countless evenings spent scouting the treetops, I heard the distinctive call of a male tawny in the distance. A few minutes later, I spotted a male high up in an oak tree and set up for the shot. This was already a significant highlight of my photography career. Not wanting to disturb the owl, I didn't want to stay too long and decided to pack up after a few minutes.

As I was about to walk away, I couldn't believe my luck as a female landed right next to the male and started grooming him.

Pipefish Camouflage
Coast & Marine | Highly Commended

Shannon Moran
Broadnosed pipefish (*Syngnathus typhle*)
Helford, Cornwall, England

Olympus EM1 II with Olympus 60mm Macro lens.
60mm; 1/100th second; f/22; ISO 640.

Within the seagrass beds of the Helford Estuary, many pipefish species can be found. The hardest to spot is the broadnosed pipefish. They are often easier to find in the evenings under torchlight. These pipefish are incredibly well camouflaged. I only noticed this individual due to its large size compared to the surrounding seagrass blades.

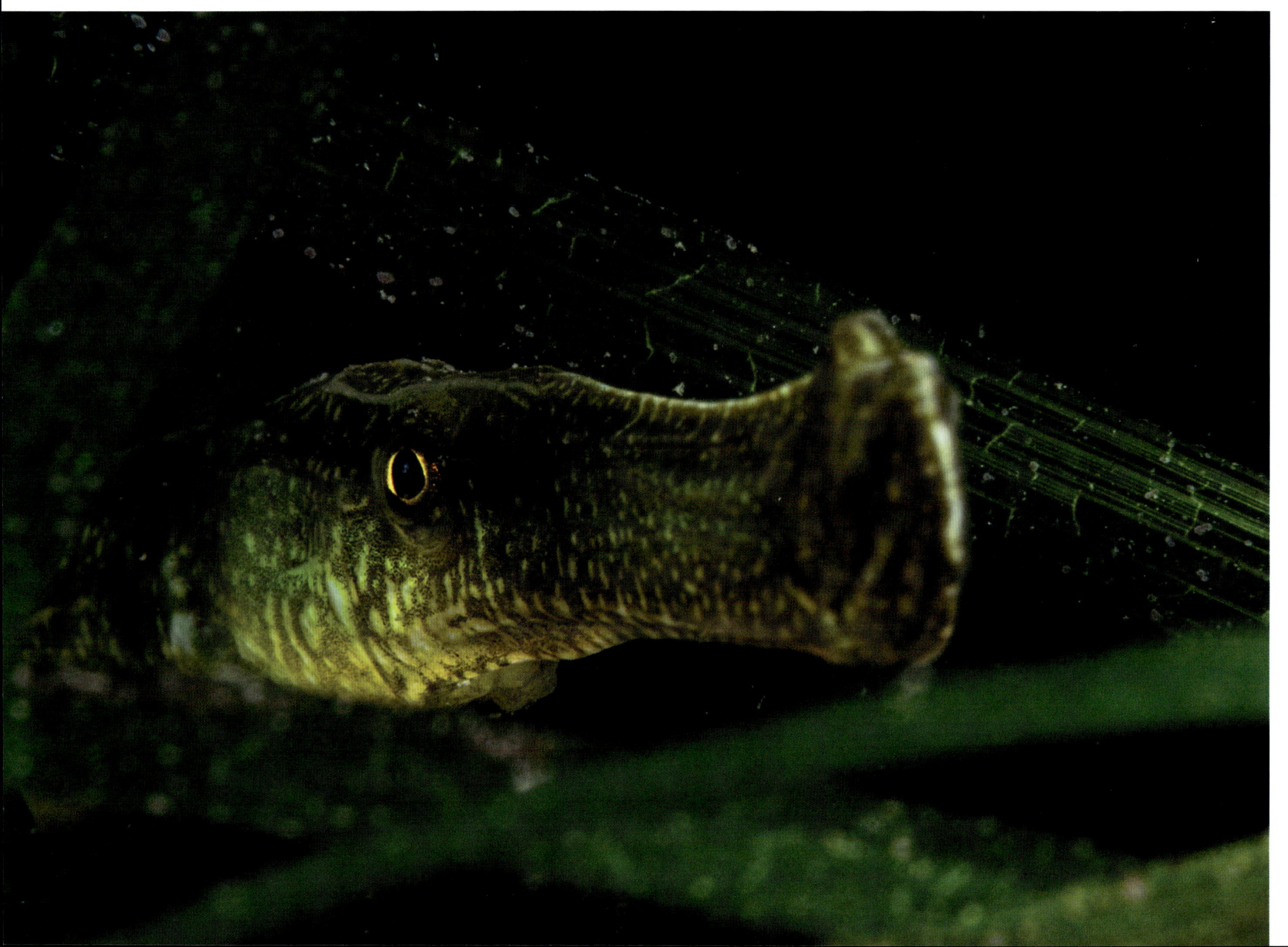

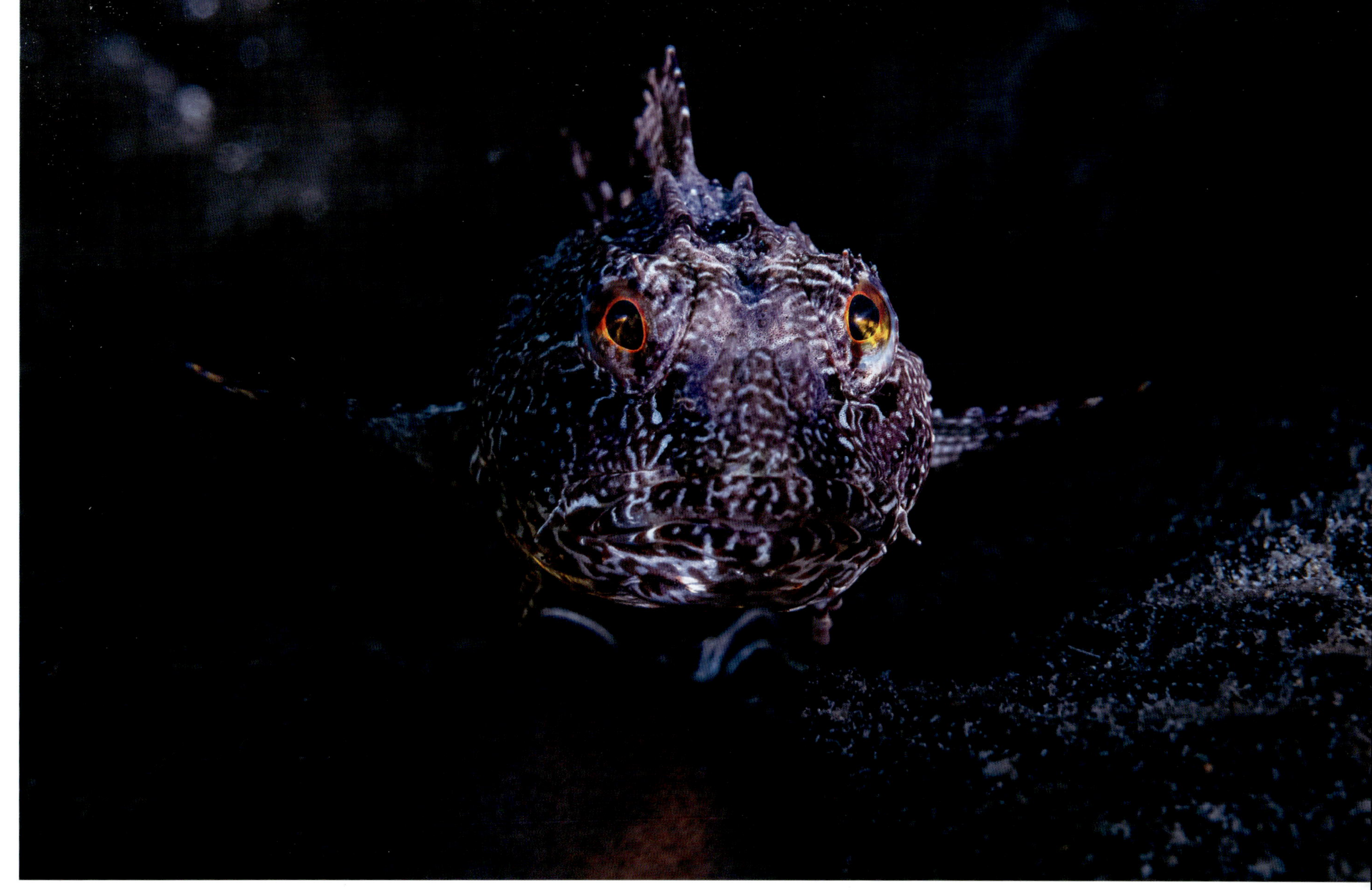

Sea Scorpion
Coast & Marine

Henley Spiers
Long-spined sea scorpion (*Taurulus bubalis*)
Shetland, Scotland

Nikon D850 with Nikon 60mm f/2.8 lens. 60mm;
1/200th second; f/16; ISO 400.

Living proof that British seas are far from drab and colourless: this long-spined sea scorpion has adopted a vivid purple shade as it seeks to blend into its environment. A skilled lie-in-wait predator, the sea scorpion relies on camouflage to lure its prey into a false sense of security.

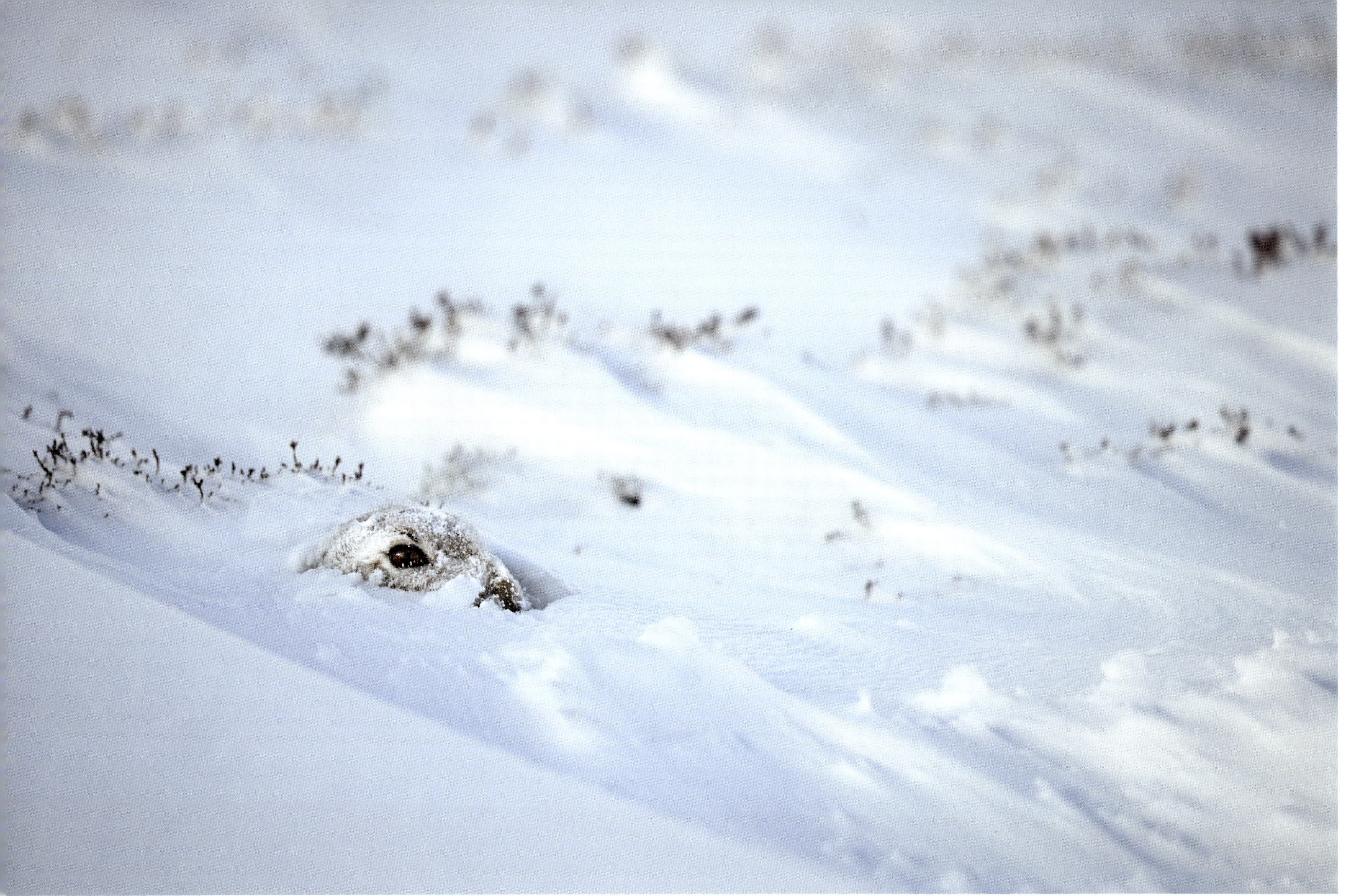

Snowed Under
Habitat

Simon Withyman
Mountain hare (*Lepus timidus*)
Cairngorms National Park, Scotland

Canon EOS R5 with Canon 500mm f/4 II lens.
500mm; 1/4,000th second; f/4; ISO 200.

The conditions were stormy, with high winds and snow battering me, along with a lot of spindrift obstructing my vision. As I waited patiently for the weather to calm, the hare, who was sitting just metres in front of me, became completely covered in snow. All of a sudden, everything settled, and visibility increased. Then, I noticed a tiny little head appear through the surface of the snow.

Seal Pup Bubble Bath
Animal Behaviour

Robin Lowry
Grey seal (*Halichoerus grypus*)
Winterton beach, Norfolk, England

Canon EOS R5 with Canon 600mm f/4 II lens.
600mm; 1/4,000th second; f/4; ISO 500.

While in Norfolk, I witnessed a special moment in nature. I saw a very young grey seal pup being led into the sea by its mother. The weather was surprisingly warm for the winter, which may have contributed to this behaviour. The windy conditions caused the sea to foam up like a bubble bath, which made the image almost monochrome. I was careful not to disturb the seals and used my Canon 600mm F4 lens handheld, dialling in a very fast shutter speed to stop any camera shake due to the wind buffeting the lens.

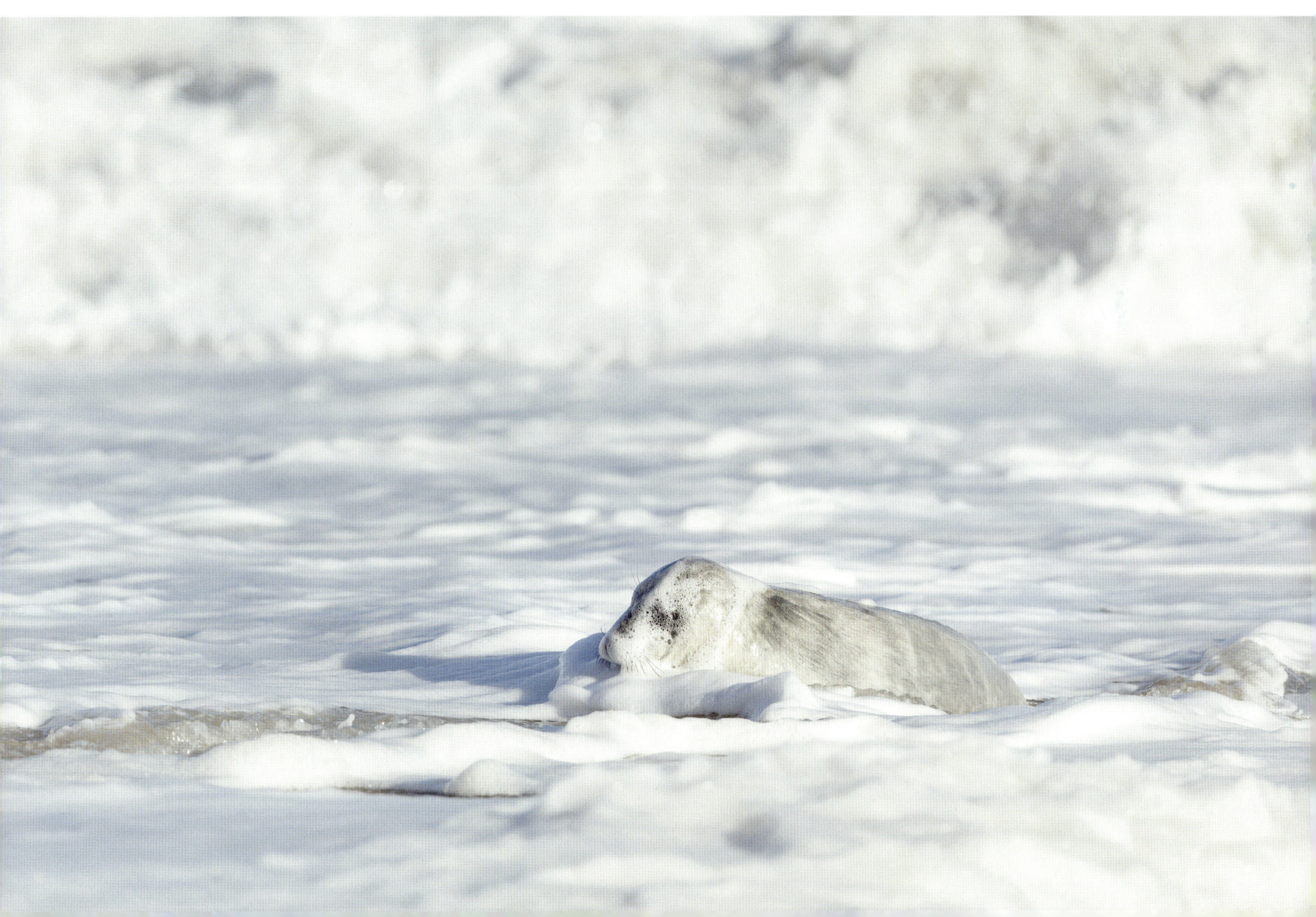

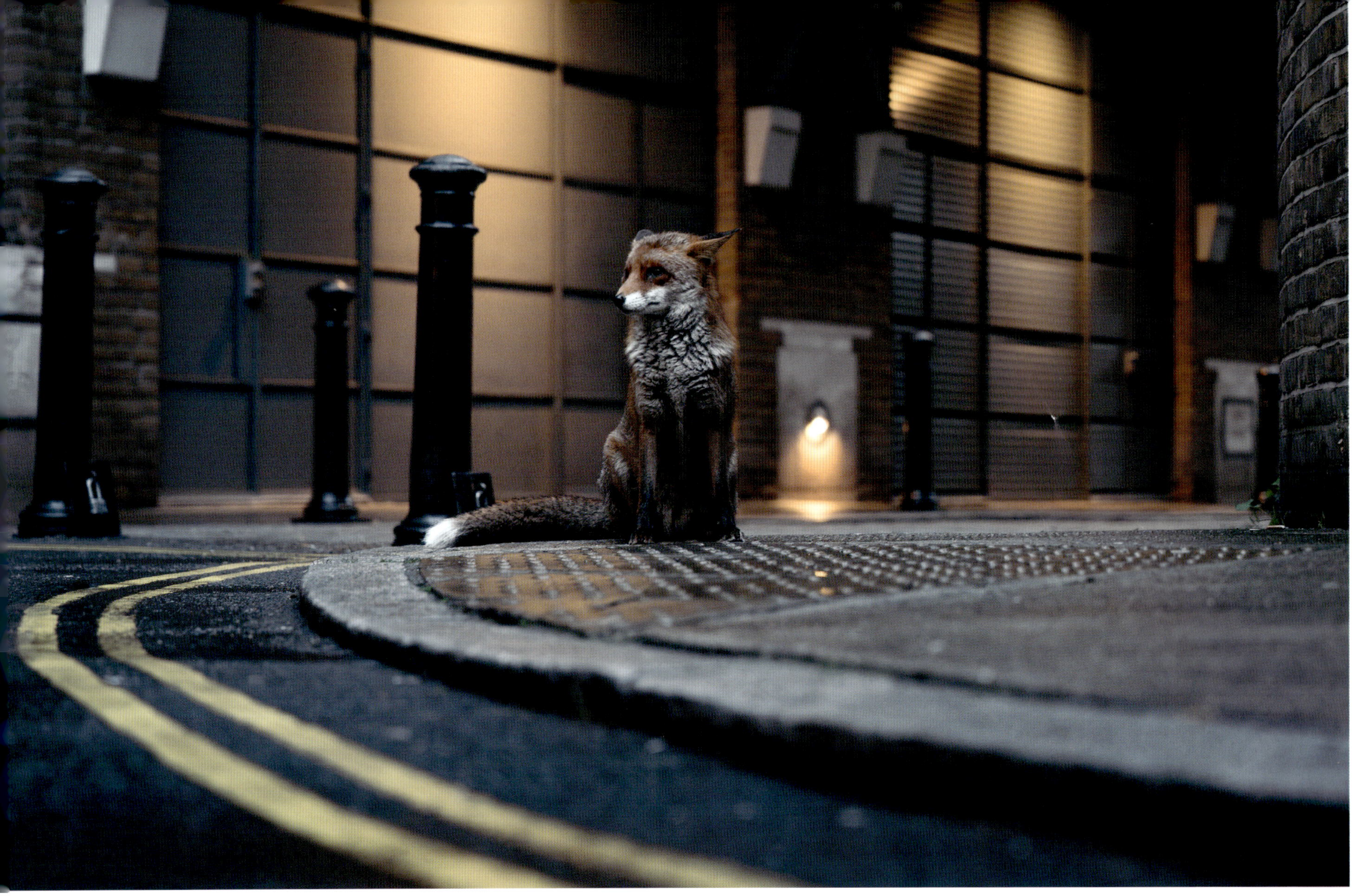

A Fox's Corner
Urban Wildlife

Oscar Lindsey
Red fox (*Vulpes vulpes*)
Shad Thames, London, England

Sony A7 III with Sony 24-700mm f/2.8 II lens.
70mm; 1/40th second; f/2.8; ISO 4,000.

I approached this fox cautiously at first, as I was
unsure of how it would react to my presence, but
was quickly surprised to discover it unfazed. The fox
can be seen innocently perched on the corner of a
road, with a curious and focused look on its face.
I later discovered that this fox was, in fact, a regular
visitor to this area of the city and could be easily
recognised by a distinctive scar above its right eye.
This initial interaction marked the beginning of a
series of encounters I had with this specific fox.

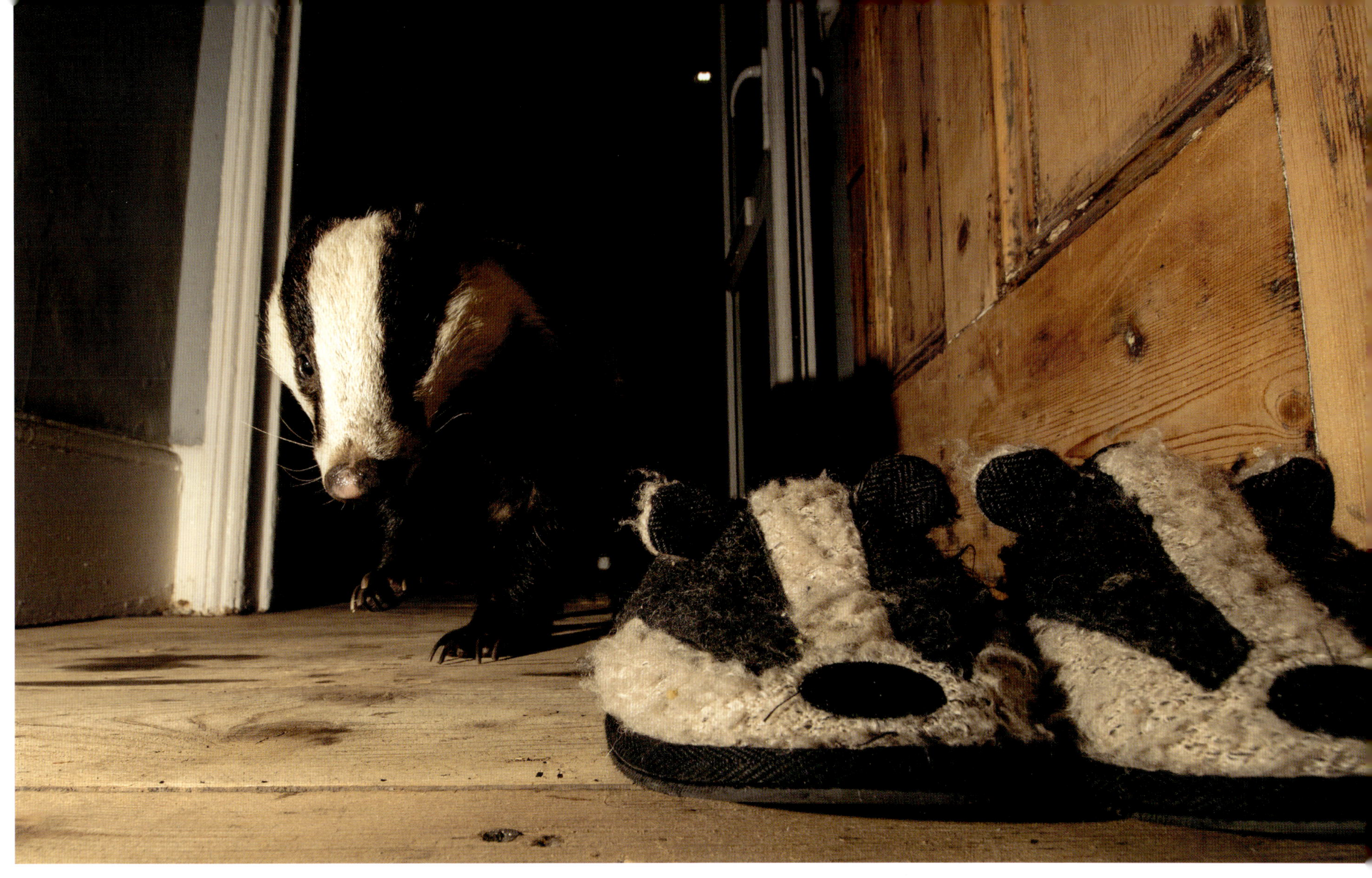

Paws for Thought
Urban Wildlife

Ian Wood
Badger (*Meles meles*)
St Leonards on Sea, East Sussex, England

Nikon D500 with Nikon 12-24mm f/4 lens.
12mm; 1/200th second; f/13; ISO 320.

In a hot spell, I had started leaving my front door open to get a breeze through the house, and I was amazed to see a badger come into the porch one night. My lovely partner had given me some badger slippers for Christmas, so I left them by the door and set up a home-made camera trap with a Nikon D500 and an off-camera flash on very low power. After about a week, this badger popped by and stopped in its tracks.

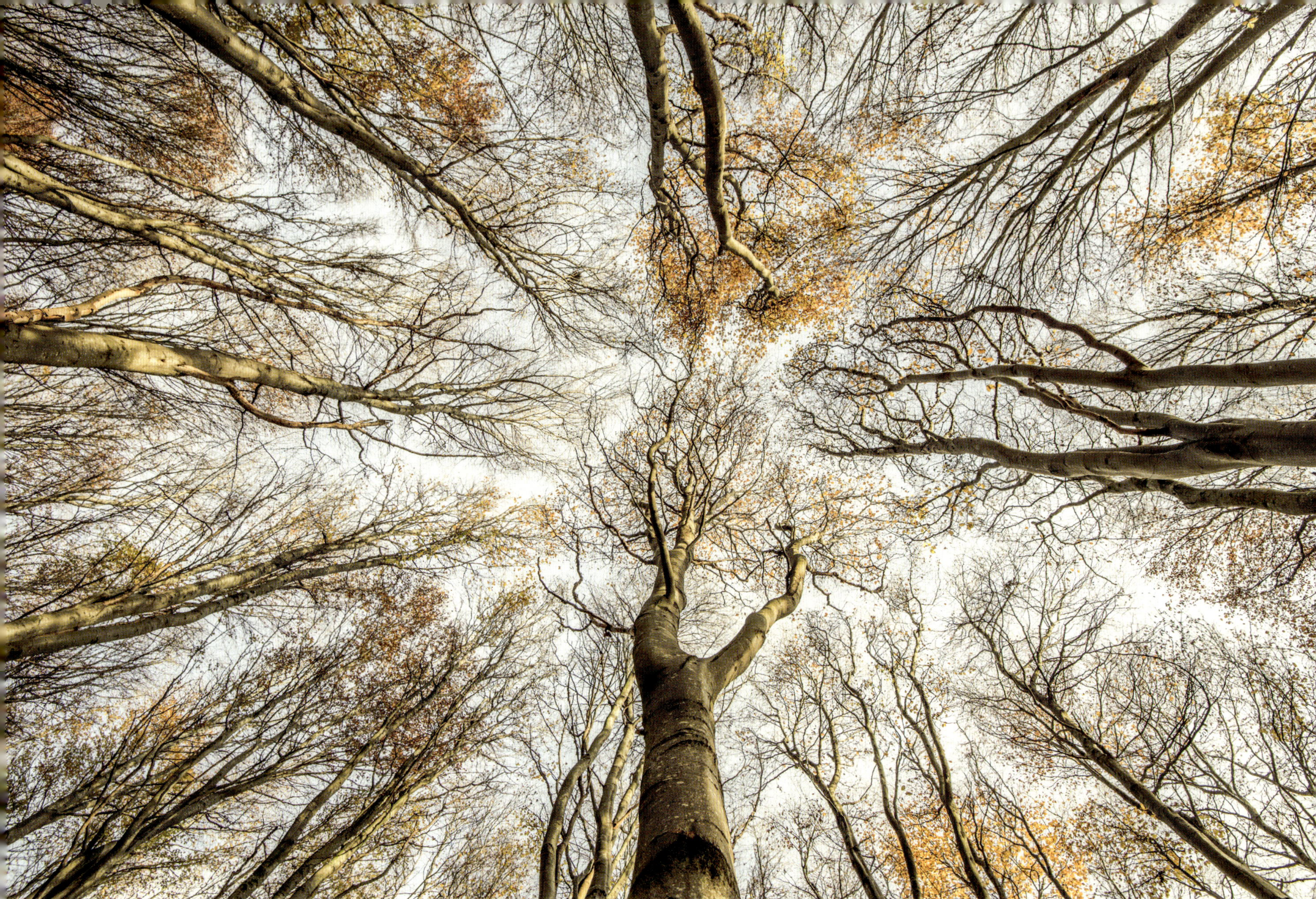

Beech for the Sky
Wild Woods | Winner

Graham Niven
Beech (*Fagus sylvatica*)
East Lothian, Scotland

Nikon D850 with Nikon 16-35mm f/4 lens.
16mm; 1/50th second; f/9; ISO 100.

Beech tree grove near Dunbar in East Lothian.
When the leaves are almost gone, the branches show
their 'canopy shyness' – a phenomenon observed
in many species of trees in which the crowns of
mature trees do not touch each other. In doing so,
the trees form a canopy that has channel-like gaps
which, when photographed from below, appear to
create an intricate network of channels between the
respective canopies. Besides the wondrous vision you
are afforded, it's also just a great excuse to lie down
in the forest.

Transcendent Light
Wild Woods

Stephen Davis
Savernake Forest, Wiltshire, England

Canon EOS 5D IV with Canon 70-300mm f/4-5.6 lens. 170mm; 1/15th second; f/16; ISO 100.

Savernake Forest is a former Royal hunting forest, particularly renowned for its ancient oak trees, some of which are up to a thousand years old. There are now extensive plantings of younger oak and beech trees among the older ones, dating back to about 70 years ago. The forest has a few shallow valleys that collect mist and fog during the winter. In favourable conditions, when the sun rises in the southeast through a low mist, you can experience extraordinary light. Such conditions are highly unpredictable, and capturing an image often relies on serendipity and reacting to the developing conditions. Thin mist like this often evaporates quickly with the warming sun.

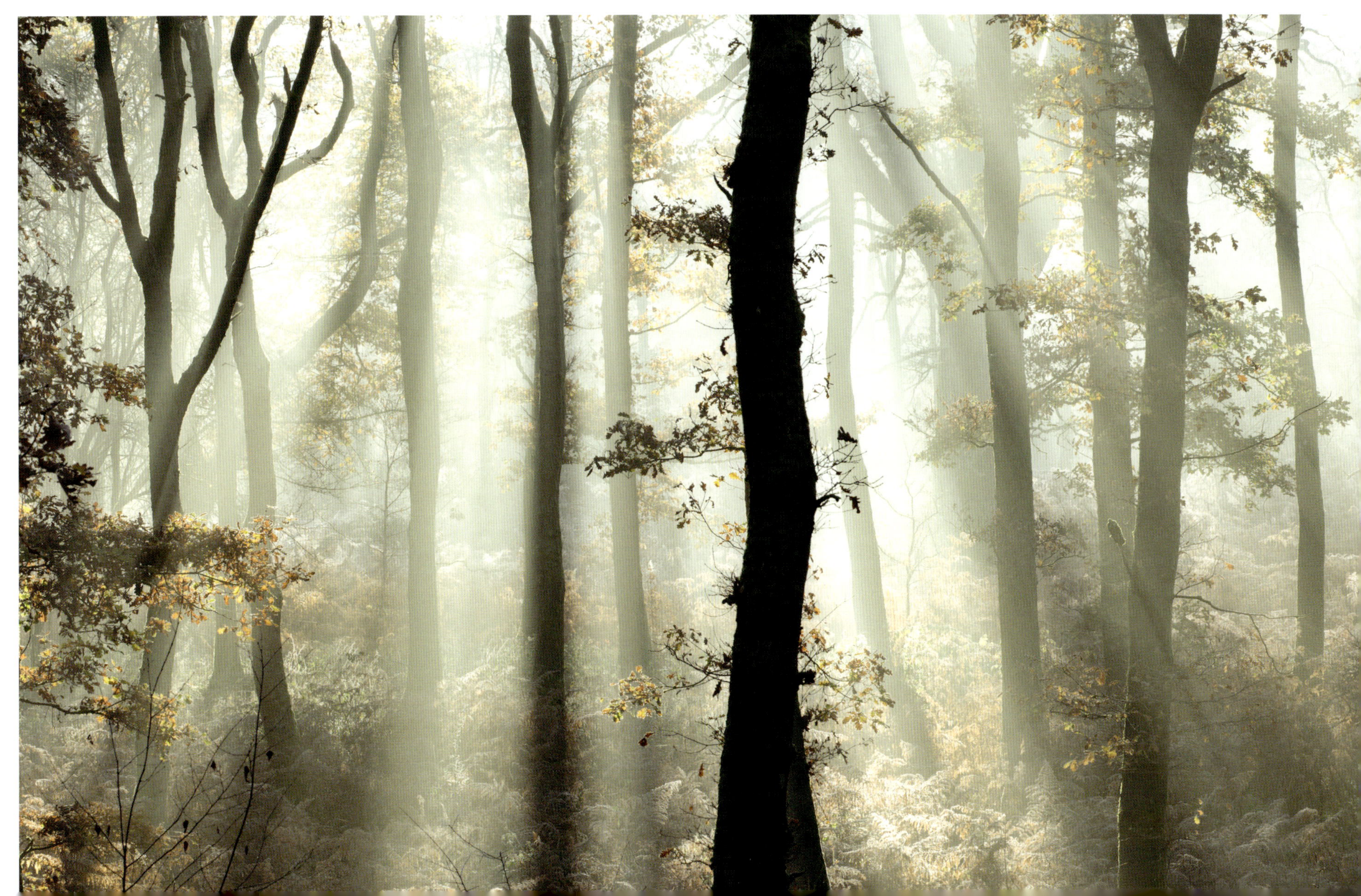

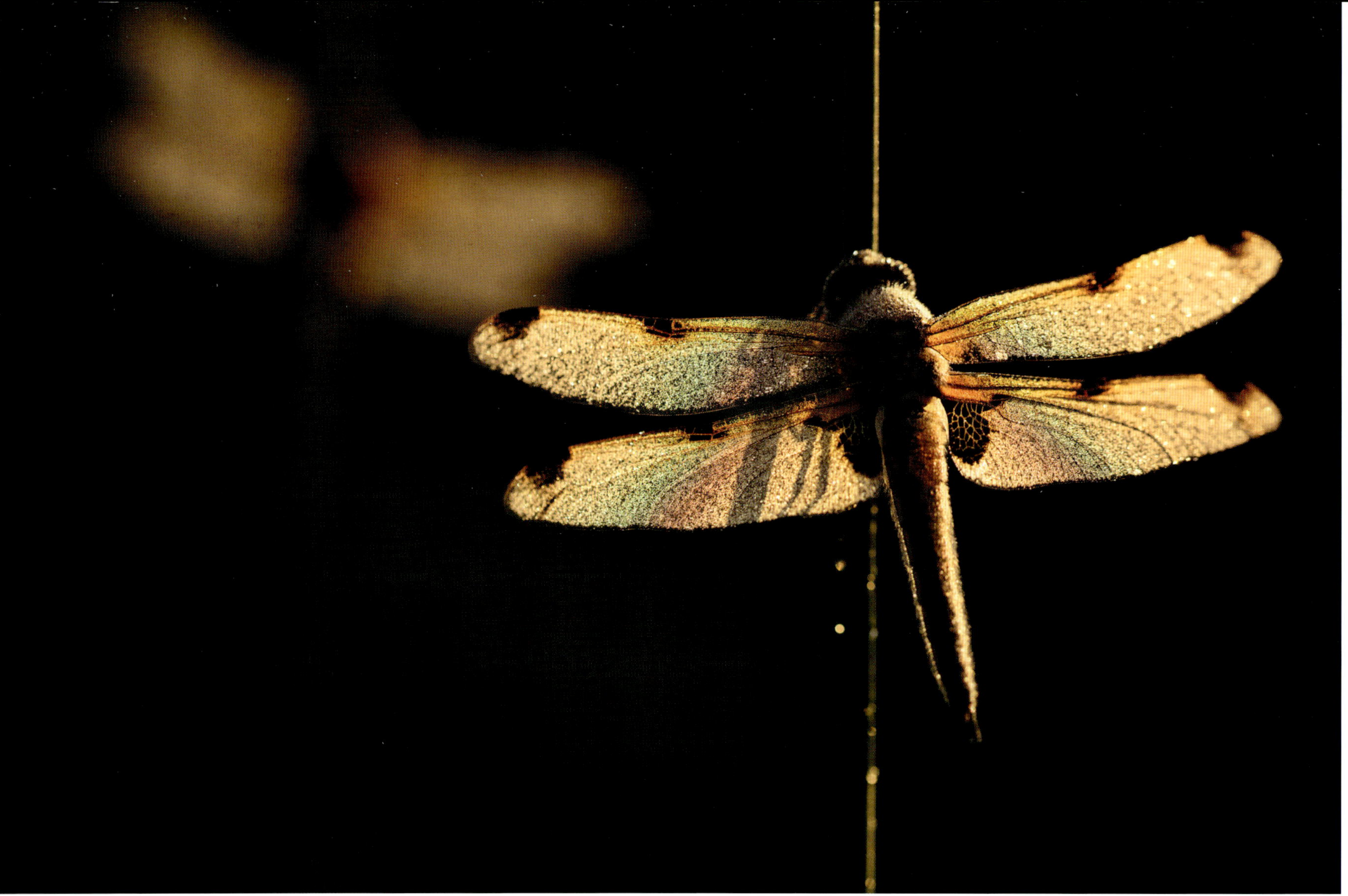

Reflection

Hidden Britain | Highly Commended

Clive Burns
Four-spotted chaser (*Libellula quadrimaculata*)
Ham Wall, Somerset, England

Nikon D850 with Sigma 105mm f/2.8 Macro lens.105mm; 1/1,600th second; f/5.6; ISO 800.

This image captures a roosting four-spotted chaser dragonfly at sunrise on the Somerset Levels. The desired effect was to have one dragonfly substantially in focus while having another dragonfly out of focus in the background. With a dark background and the early rays of sun illuminating the dragonflies, I achieved the desired effect, enhanced by the iridescent colours on the wings of the nearest dragonfly. I captured this image handheld, allowing for flexibility in exploring different compositions, rather than using a tripod.

Panes and Pearls ▶

Hidden Britain

Nick Clayton
Four-spotted chaser (*Libellula quadrimaculata*)
Upton Fen, Norfolk, England

Canon EOS 7D MII with Canon EF 180mm f/3.5 lens. 180mm; 1/8th second; f/16; ISO 800.

I was pleased to find this praenubila form of four-spotted chaser, which has dark smudges under the outermost spots of its wings. Since it was early morning, the light levels were low, resulting in slow shutter speeds. Therefore, I used a tripod with a remote release to keep my setup steady. Because this image was captured so early in the day, the dragonfly was covered in dew, resulting in beautiful little pearls settling around the perimeter. Intricate details of the wing panes can also be seen.

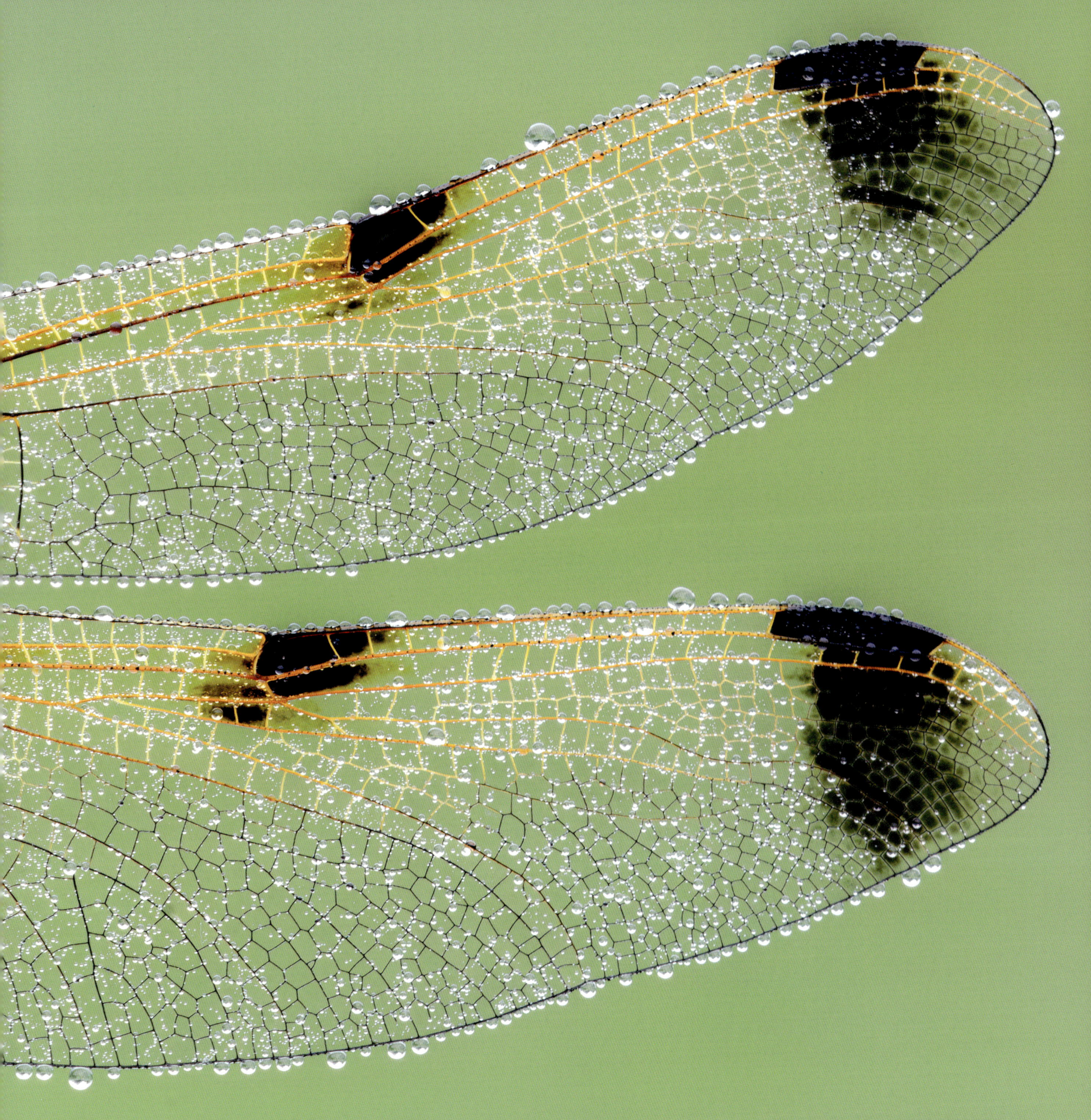

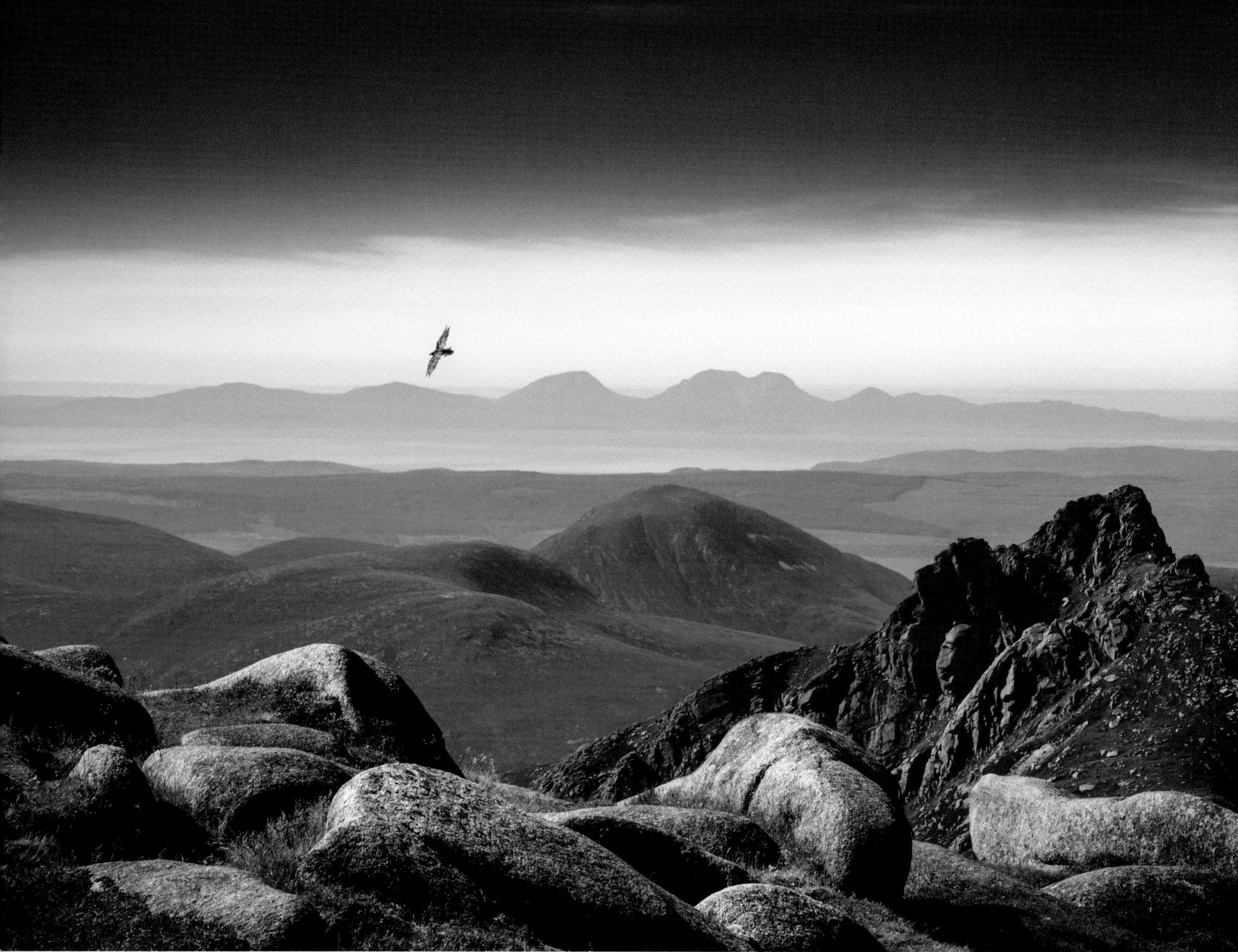

Raven Above Arran
Black & White | Winner

Robin Dodd
Raven (*Corvus corax*)
Isle of Arran, Scotland

Canon EOS R with Canon RF 24-105mm f/4 lens.
105mm; 1/320th second; f/14; ISO 400.

This is a shot from the top of Goatfell on the Isle of Arran, which is the highest mountain on the island. It was a lovely hike to the top on a bright summer afternoon after arriving by ferry a few hours before. When we reached the summit, it was deserted except for two ravens who seemed to dominate the peak. We sat for some time, observing these birds gliding over Arran just as gracefully as any bird of prey. It's a harsh yet beautiful world they inhabit. This image is in black and white and consists of two shots, focus stacked.

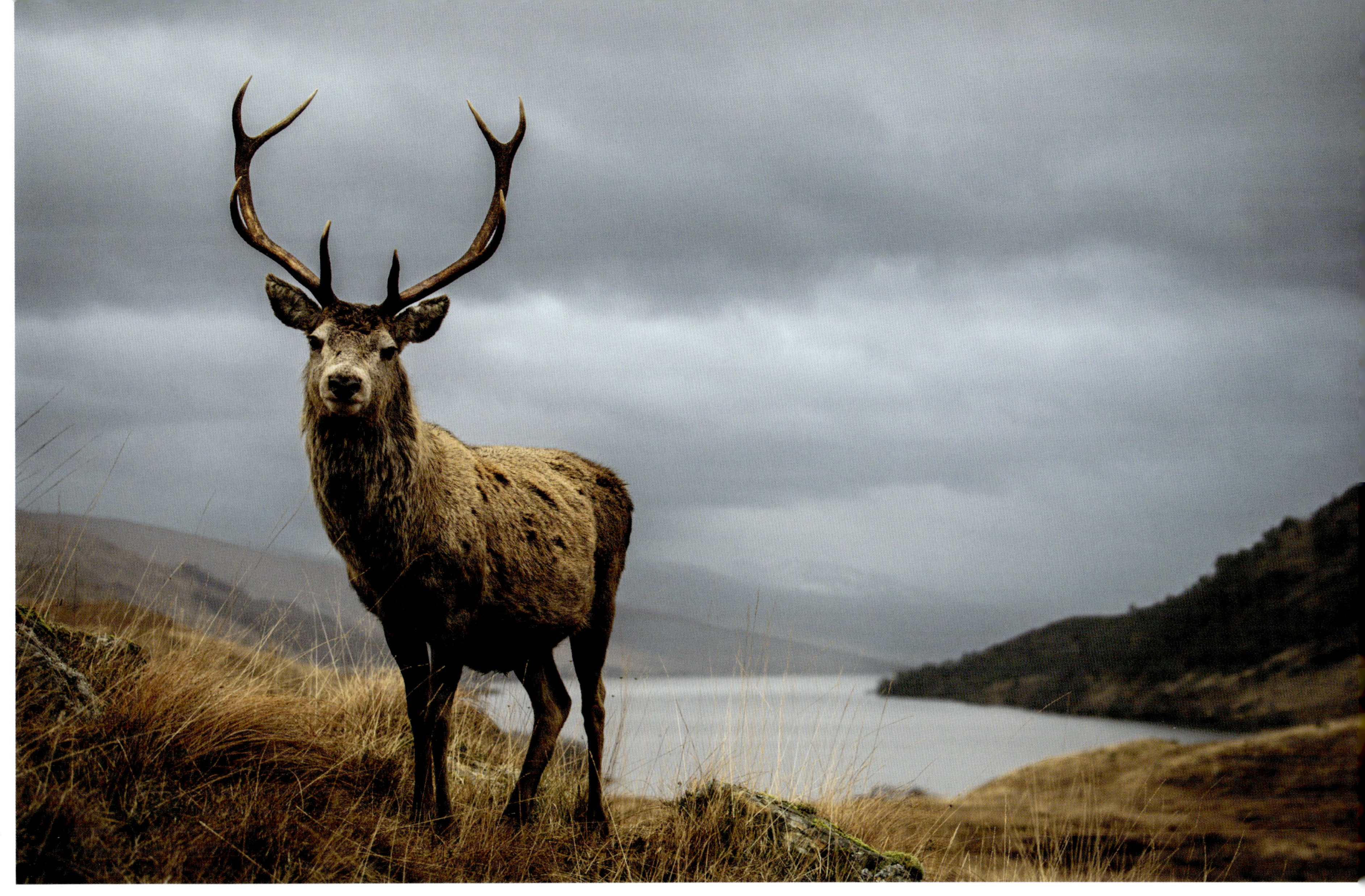

Proud Stag
Animal Portraits

Joshua Copping
Red deer (*Cervus elaphus*)
Western Highlands, Scotland

Nikon D850 with Nikon 70-200mm f/2.8 lens.
70mm; 1/200th second; f/4; ISO 125.

This image was captured in the Western Highlands of Scotland. Initially, I was using my telephoto lens to capture images of the distant red deer. However, as a small group of curious stags began to approach me, I switched to a lens with a shorter focal length to incorporate the stunning scenery, which included the mountains, a loch and dramatic clouds. In this shot, I successfully isolated a single stag in the frame, portraying it as a proud figure at the head of the glen.

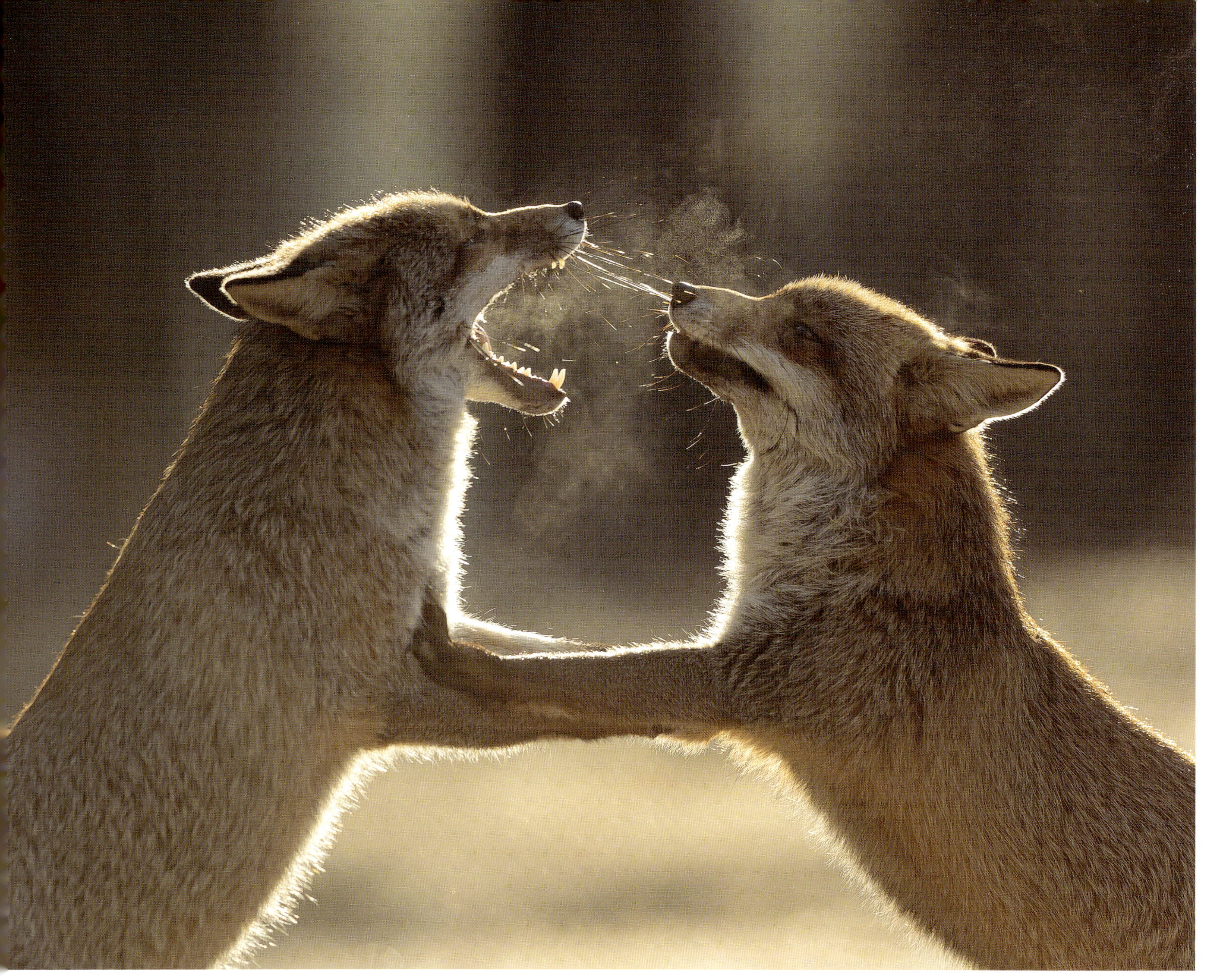

Vapour in the Environment
Animal Behaviour

Daniel Valverde Fernandez
Red fox (*Vulpes vulpes*)
Sherwood Pines Forest Park, England

Canon EOS R3 with Canon 300mm f/2.8 II lens.
300mm; 1/8,000th second; f/2.8; ISO 1,600.

In this image, we observe two specimens of red fox
interacting with each other during a cold dawn.
One of the foxes appears to be scolding the other,
and you can see the microdroplets of steam
being generated due to the cold environment
and the sunlight shining on them.

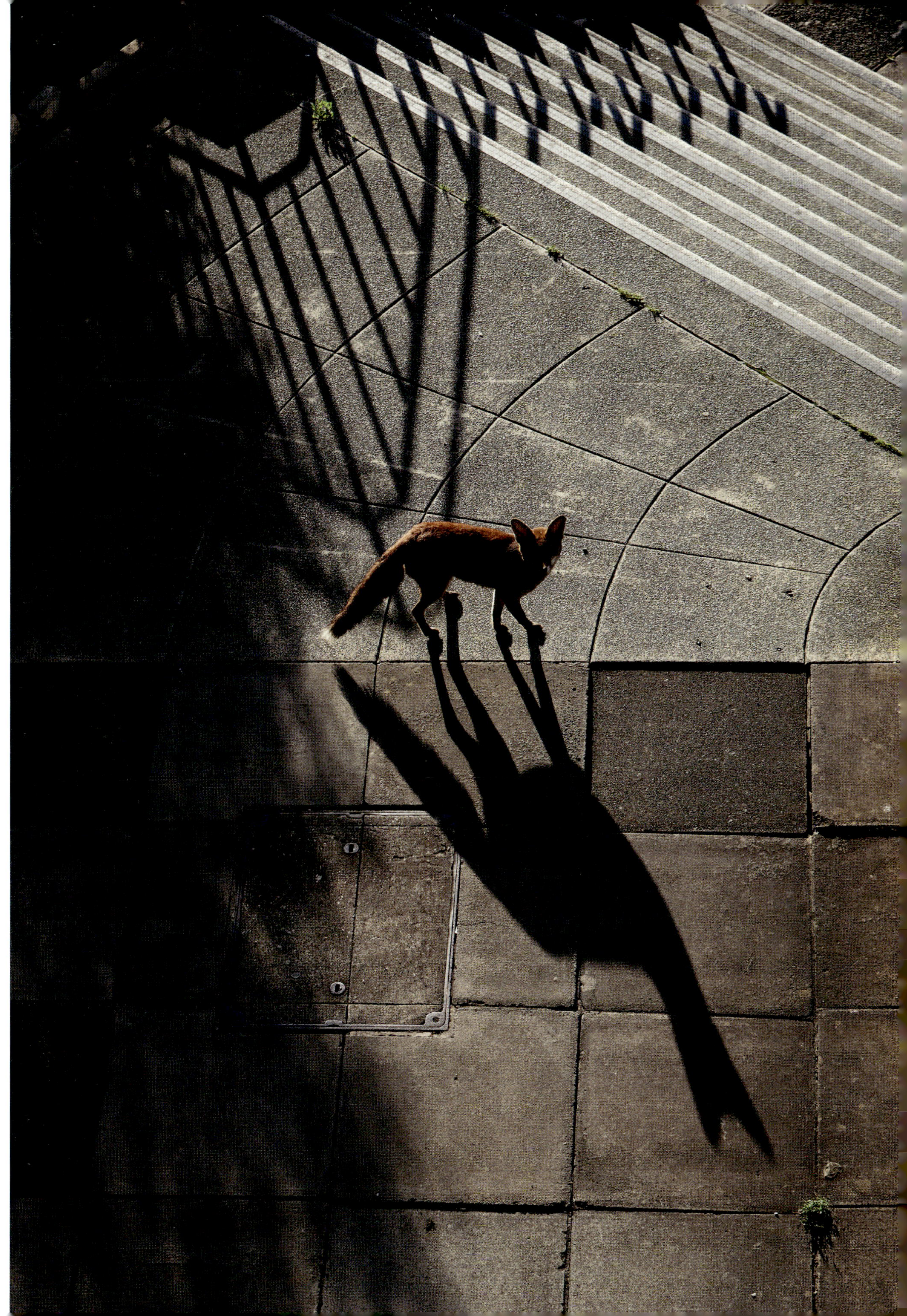

Casting Shadows
Urban Wildlife

Simon Withyman
Red fox (*Vulpes vulpes*)
Bristol, England

Canon EOS R5 with Canon 70-200mm
f/2.8 II lens. 75mm; 1/2,000th second;
f/4.5; ISO 400.

I had this image in my mind's eye for
a couple of years. Then, one day, the
stars aligned, and my furry subject
walked into the area at precisely the
right time of day for the shadows to
be long enough to create the image
I was looking for. To achieve the correct
perspective, I was looking down from a
high vantage point over some railings,
without the need for a drone.

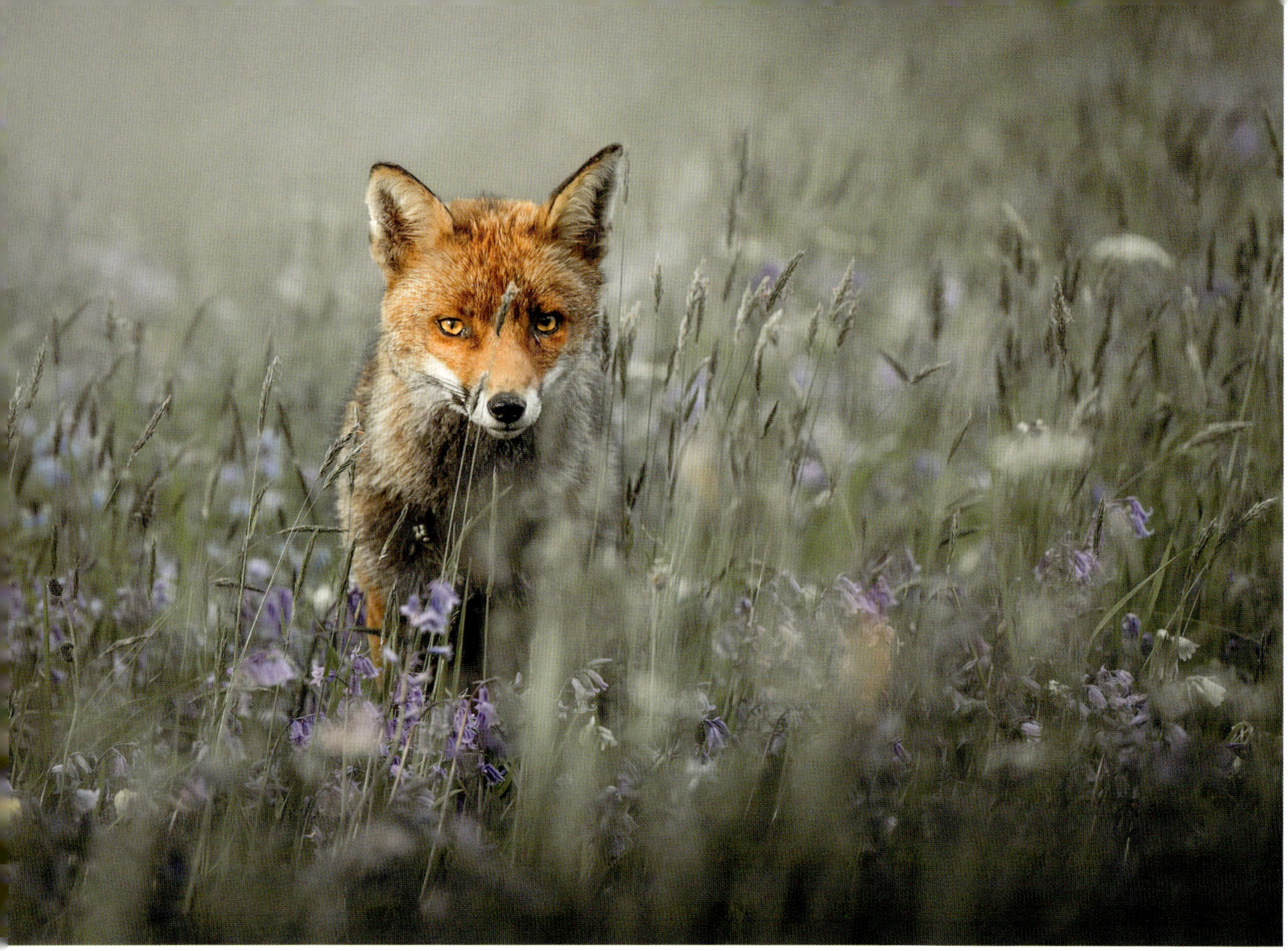

Hide & Peek
Animal Portraits

Pete Scott
Red fox (*Vulpes vulpes*)
Poole, England

Nikon Z 6 with Nikon 500mm f/5.6 lens. 500mm; 1/800th second; f/5.6; ISO 1,600.

I have been visiting and photographing this family of foxes for a few years, and had been planning this image for about three months, ever since the area around their den burst into colour with a carpet of crocuses. I knew bluebells and snowdrops would replace them soon, so I spent even more time in their company to make them feel comfortable with me around. Lying down on a well-trodden path, I got into position and waited, knowing they would have to come through the flowers.

A Fox in the Bluebells
Animal Portraits

Victor Soares
Red fox (*Vulpes vulpes*)
London, England

Canon EOS R6 with Canon 300mm f/2.8 II lens. 300mm; 1/400th second; f/5; ISO 500.

I photographed this stunning fox sitting in a small field of bluebells at a local park. The bluebells, a national symbol of truth and love, add their unmistakable colour and beauty to the image, but it was the look on the fox that caught my eye. Is this the shy fox that we usually encounter in our cities, giving a nervous grin as it turns to leave, or is this the cunning fox of legend and fairy tale that has just had a mischievous idea? I wonder...

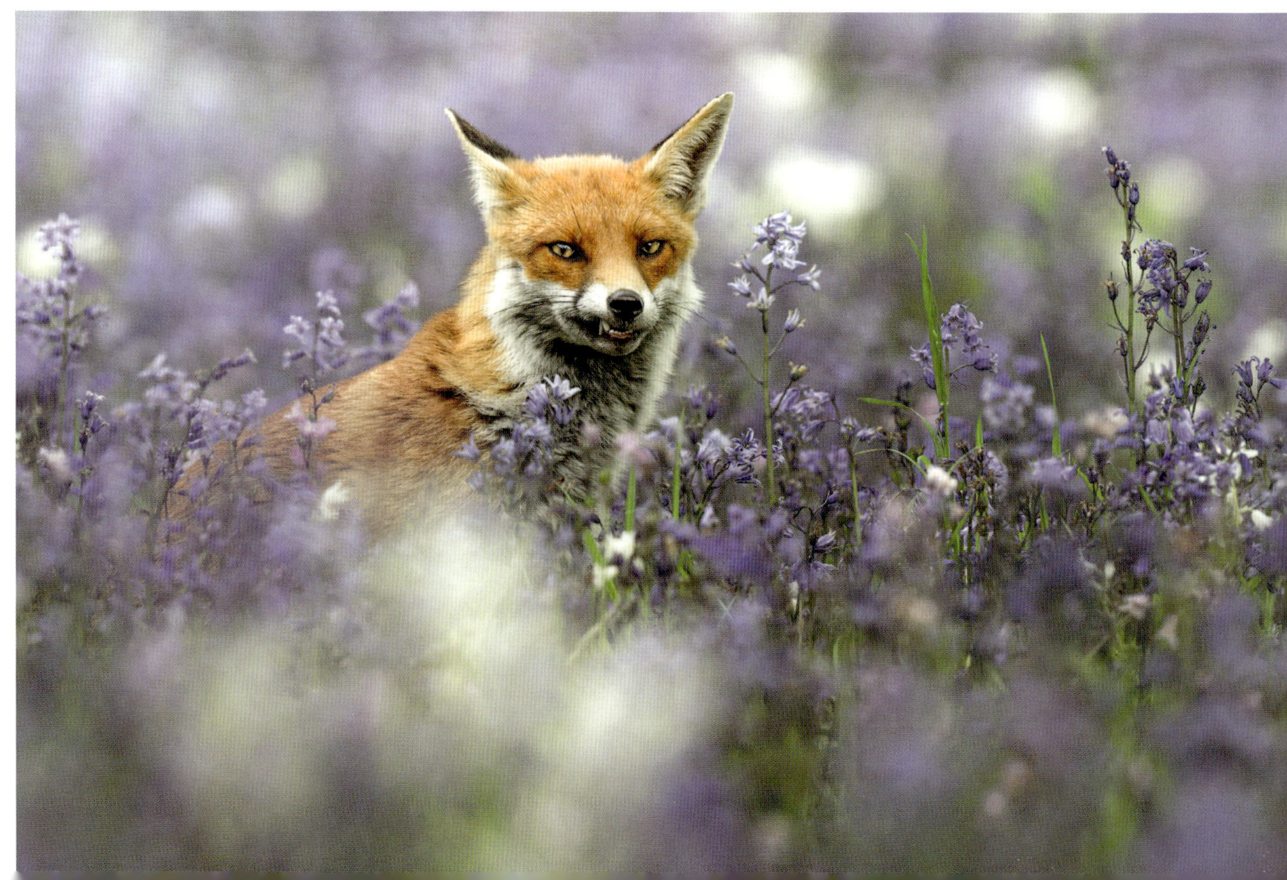

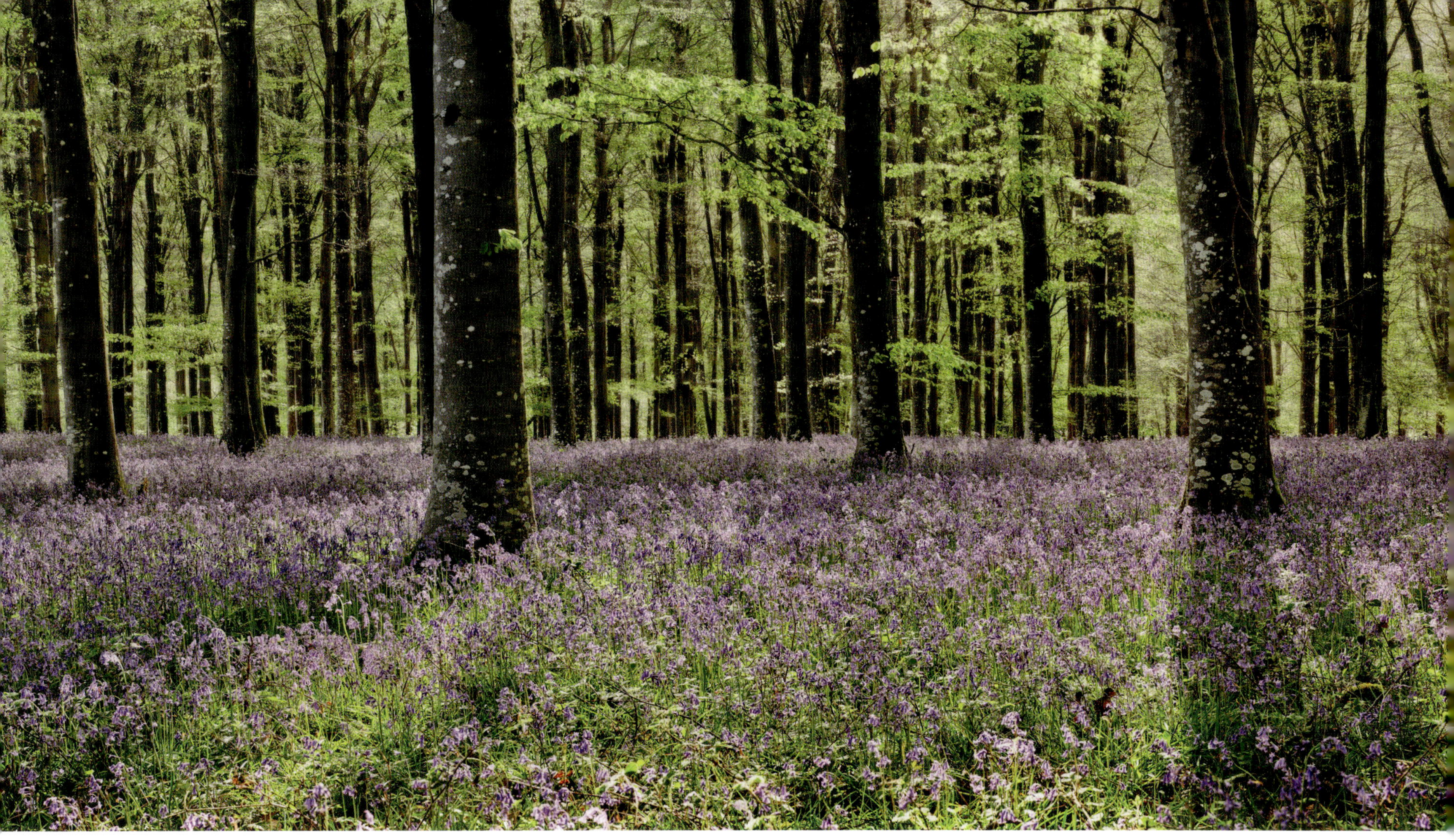

Enchanted Forest
Botanical Britain

Felix Belloin
Bluebell (*Hyacinthoides non-scripta*)
Dorset

Fujifilm GFX 100 with Fujifilm 110mm f/2 lens.
110mm; 1/6th second; f/9; ISO 100. Stitched
panorama.

Bluebell season in Dorset is one of my favourite times
of the year. I love wandering in ancient woodlands in
the hope of capturing the atmosphere of the place
with my camera. This year, I set myself the ambitious
goal of photographing one of my favourite spots in
the highest quality possible. Using my medium format
camera, an incredibly sharp prime lens, a levelled
base and a nodal rail to avoid parallax issues,
I photographed a three-tile panorama, with each tile
being focus stacked for front-to-back sharpness.
The result is a blend of all 81 102-megapixel files!

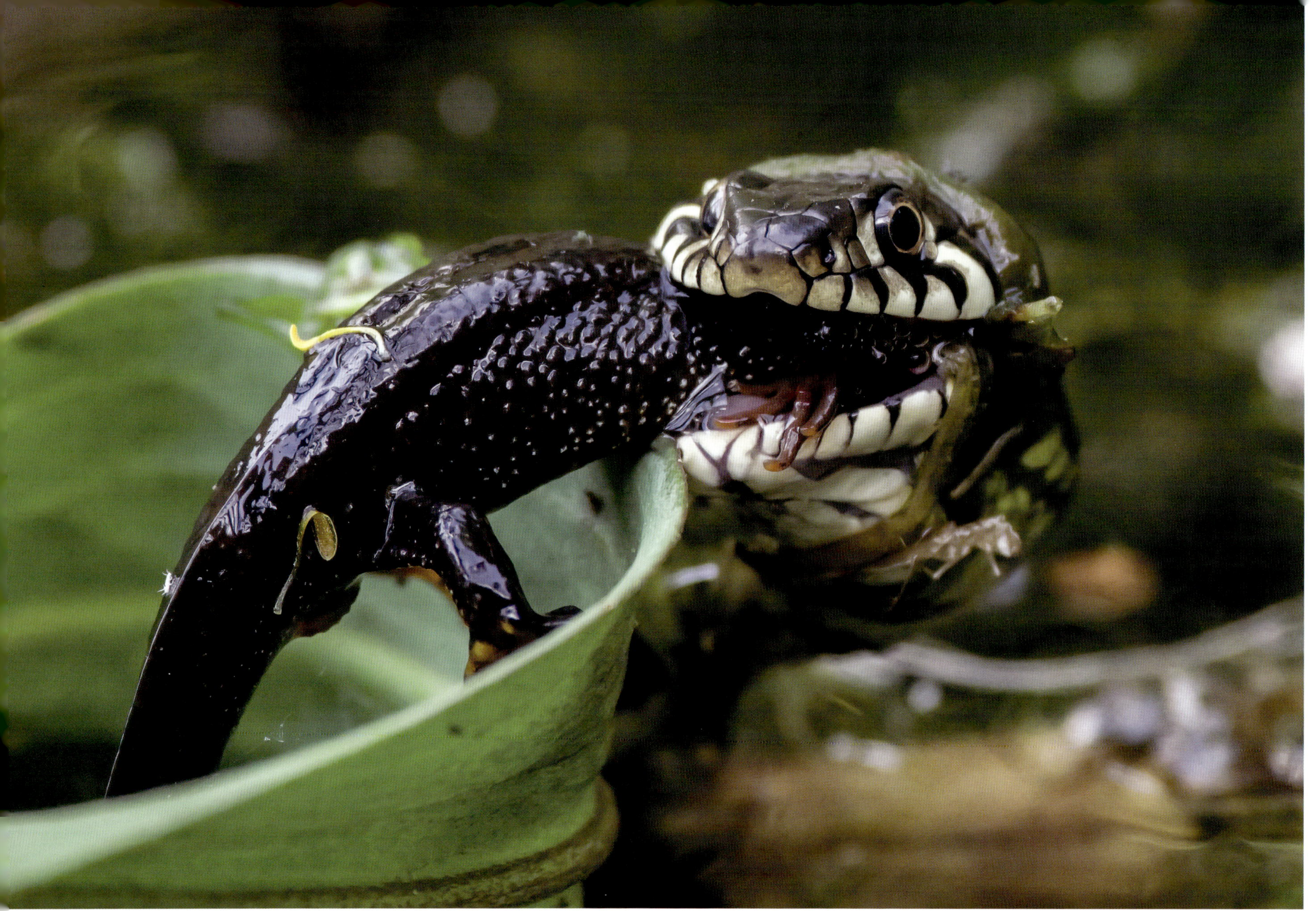

Grass Snake Eating Great Crested Newt
Animal Behaviour

Neil Phillips
Grass snake (*Natrix natrix*) and Great crested newt (*Triturus cristatus*)
Wat Tyler CP, Essex, England

Pentax K3 with Pentax-DA 300m f/4 lens. 300mm; 1/400th second; f/4.6; ISO 1,600.

I was demonstrating great crested newt eDNA tests to a small group when a grass snake decided to do a great crested newt survey of its own! I saw it dive down and suspected it would come up with a newt, so I got my camera ready, but was surprised when it came up with an adult great crested newt. I managed to get a shot through the vegetation of it halfway through swallowing its prey!

An Evening Meal
Hidden Britain | Highly Commended

Geraint Radford
Grey cross spider (*Larinioides sclopetarius*)
Swansea, Wales

Olympus OM1 with OM System 90mm f/3.5
Macro lens and Cygnustech Diffuser. 90mm;
1/800th second; f/16; ISO 320.

Exploring my local ponds brings me a lot of joy!
I often head out just before the sun sets to work with
beautiful lighting. On this day, I struggled to find
photo opportunities due to the wind. Luckily, I found
this grey cross spider, who had just caught a meal.
Shooting into the light meant that I couldn't see
through the viewfinder properly, but I managed to
capture this shot just before the magical light faded
away. This is a handheld, high-magnification image
using fill flash to balance the exposure.

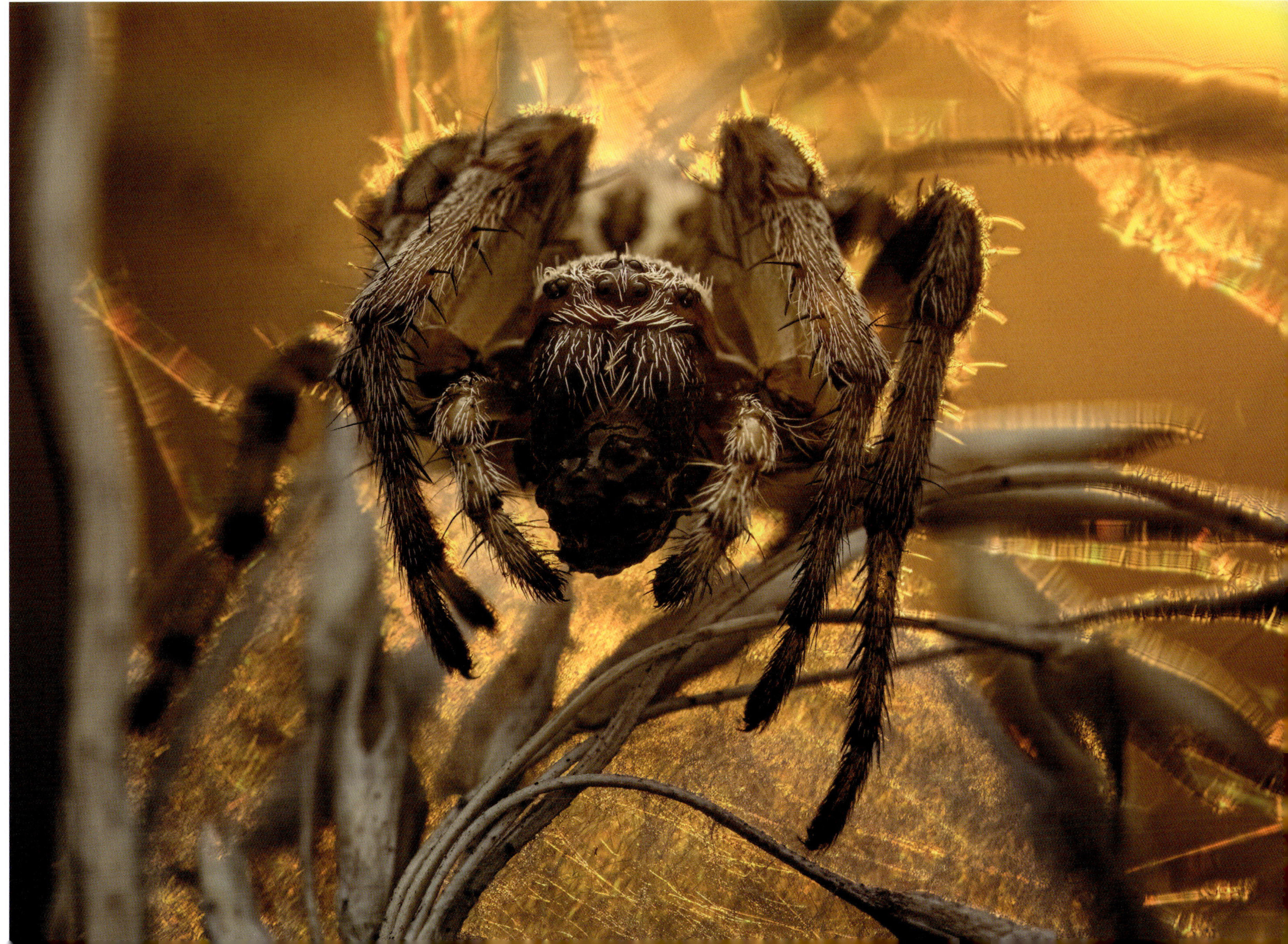

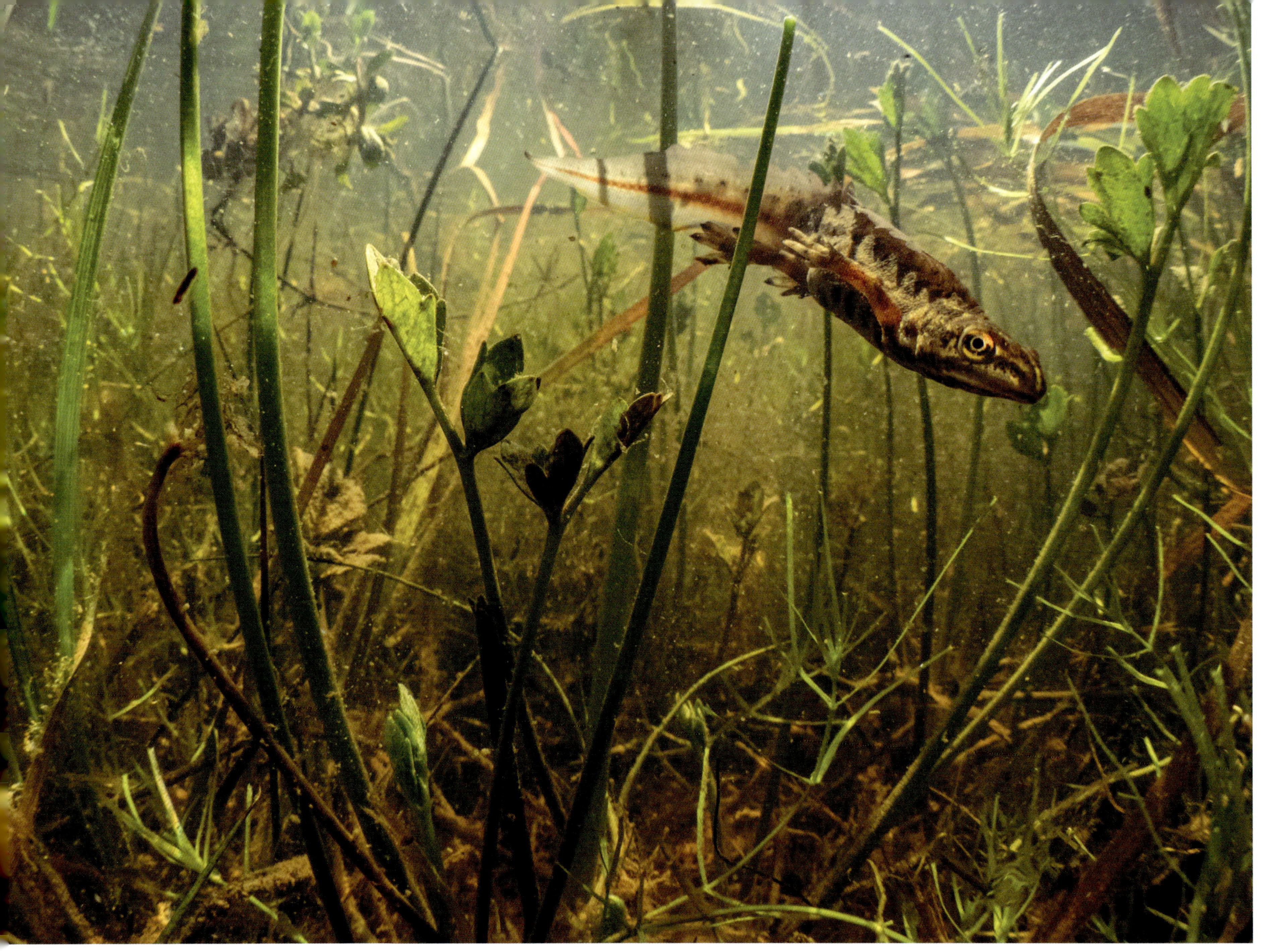

Smoothly Does It
Habitat | Highly Commended

Angus Andrew
Smooth newt (*Lissotriton vulgaris*)
Church Stretton, Shropshire, England

Olympus EM-1 with Lumix 8mm f/3.5 Fisheye lens.
8mm; 1/1,500th second; f/9.5; ISO 2,000.

This smooth newt was captured under licence and released early the next morning into a Shropshire pond. The camera, in its Nauticam underwater housing, is heavy and had to be carefully suspended at arm's reach to avoid disturbing the sediment. Strobes are too cumbersome for confined spaces and cause backscatter, but natural light levels are low. As soon as the newts touch the water, they bolt for cover, necessitating a shutter speed of at least 1/1000 sec. Such close focus creates depth of field limitations. Overall, this shot was backbreaking and awkward, pushing the Olympus EM1 to its limits. It took many releases and left me with very cold hands before I captured this image.

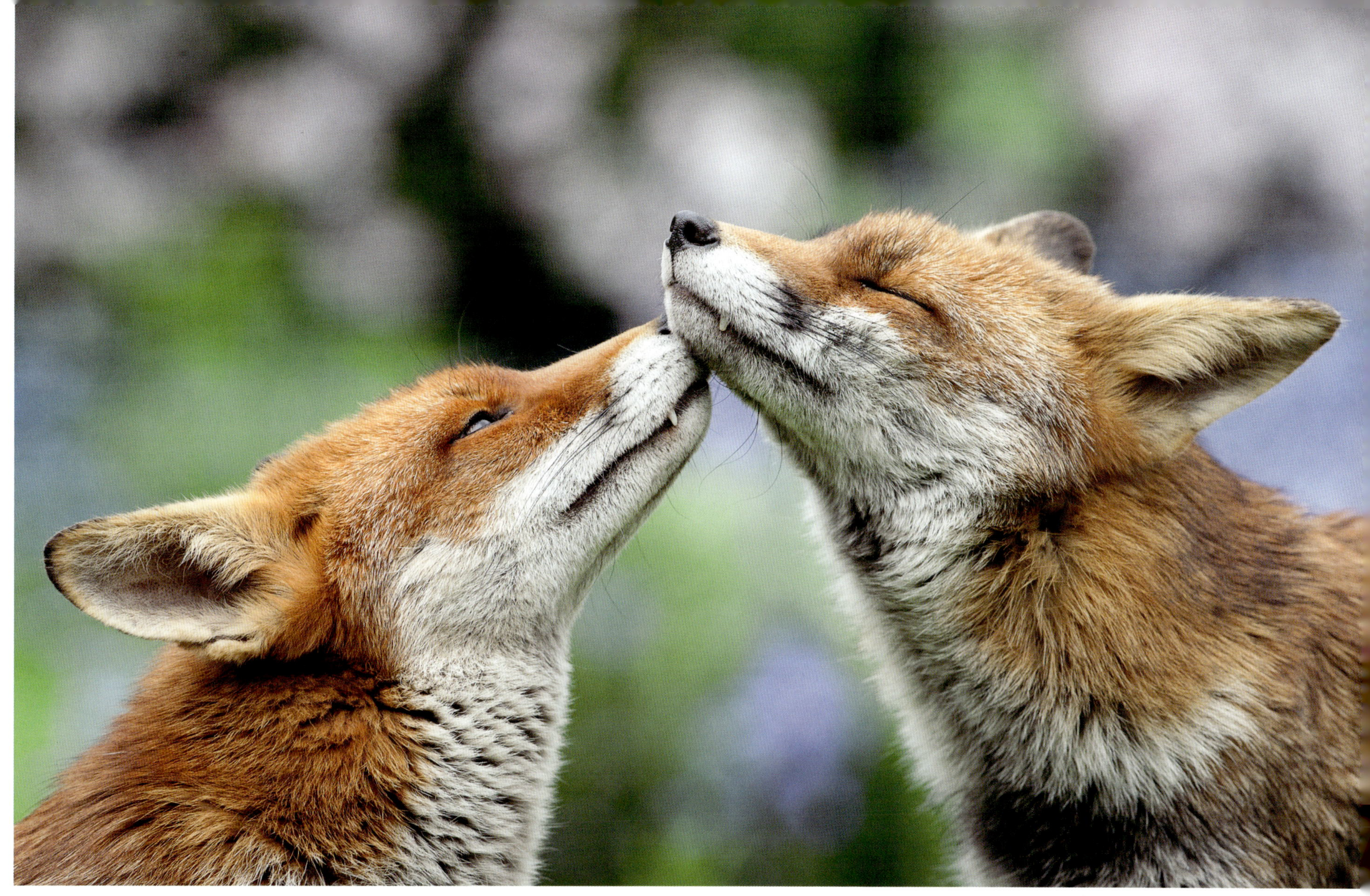

Affection

Animal Behaviour | Highly Commended

Lawrie Brailey

Red fox (*Vulpes vulpes*)
Merstham, Surrey, England

Nikon D3 with Nikon 300mm f/4 lens.
300mm; 1/1,000th second; f/6.3; ISO 1,600.

Although this may look like a greeting between a mated pair, these two red foxes are actually mother and daughter! The dominant vixen (on the right) is making preparations to give birth to a new litter, and she allowed one of her previous cubs to return to act as an auntie to the next generation. This image captures the moment they first greeted each other after months of being apart. With the benefit of hindsight, I'm not sure the youngster knew what she was getting into at the time!

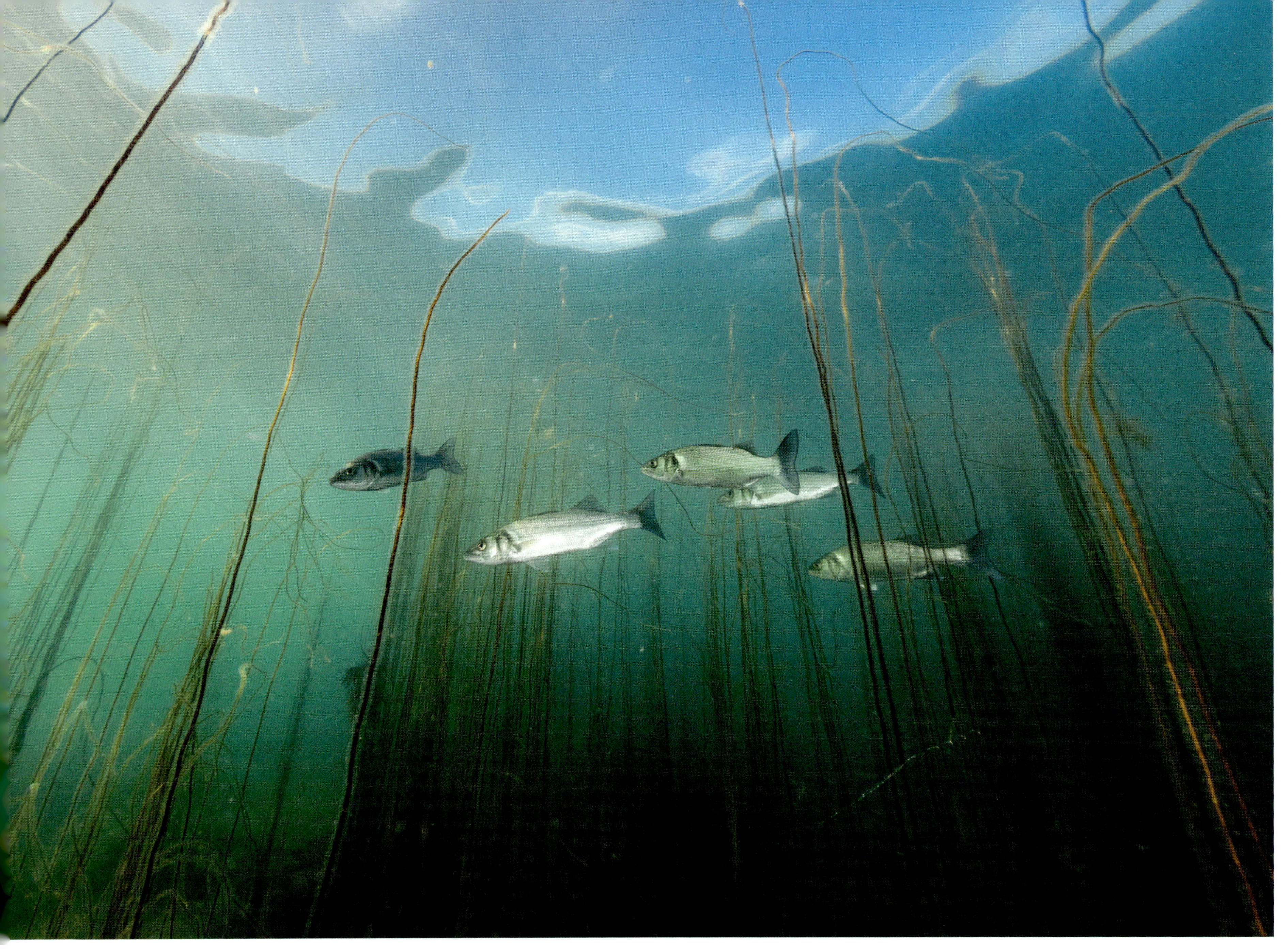

Bassworld
Habitat

Kirsty Andrews
Sea bass (*Dicentrarchus labrax*)
Porthkerris beach, Cornwall, England

Nikon D500 with Tokina 10-17mm f/3.5-4.5 lens.
10mm; 1/200th second; f/11; ISO 320.

On a beautiful August afternoon in Cornwall, while snorkelling amid the long seaweeds known as mermaid's tresses, I came across a shoal of bass, their scales glinting in the sunlight. Bass are irregularly spotted by divers, but they seemed to be less easily disturbed when snorkeling on this rocky beach and darting between the sunlit plants.

Stand Out from the Crowd
Coast & Marine

Billy Arthur
Brittle starfish (*Ophiothrix fragilis*) and Plumrose anemone (*Metridium senile*)
Lerwick Harbour, Shetland Islands, Scotland

Sony A7R II with Sony 28mm f/2 lens.
28mm; 1/200th second; f/14; ISO 800.

A lone plumose anemone amidst a bed of brittle stars. This slightly tidal site on the *Queen of Sweden* wreck in Lerwick Harbour means there will be plenty of food brought in on the tides to sustain this anemone and brittle stars. Plumose anemones are a common sight around Shetland, but the brittle star bed gave me the opportunity to capture them in a different environment.

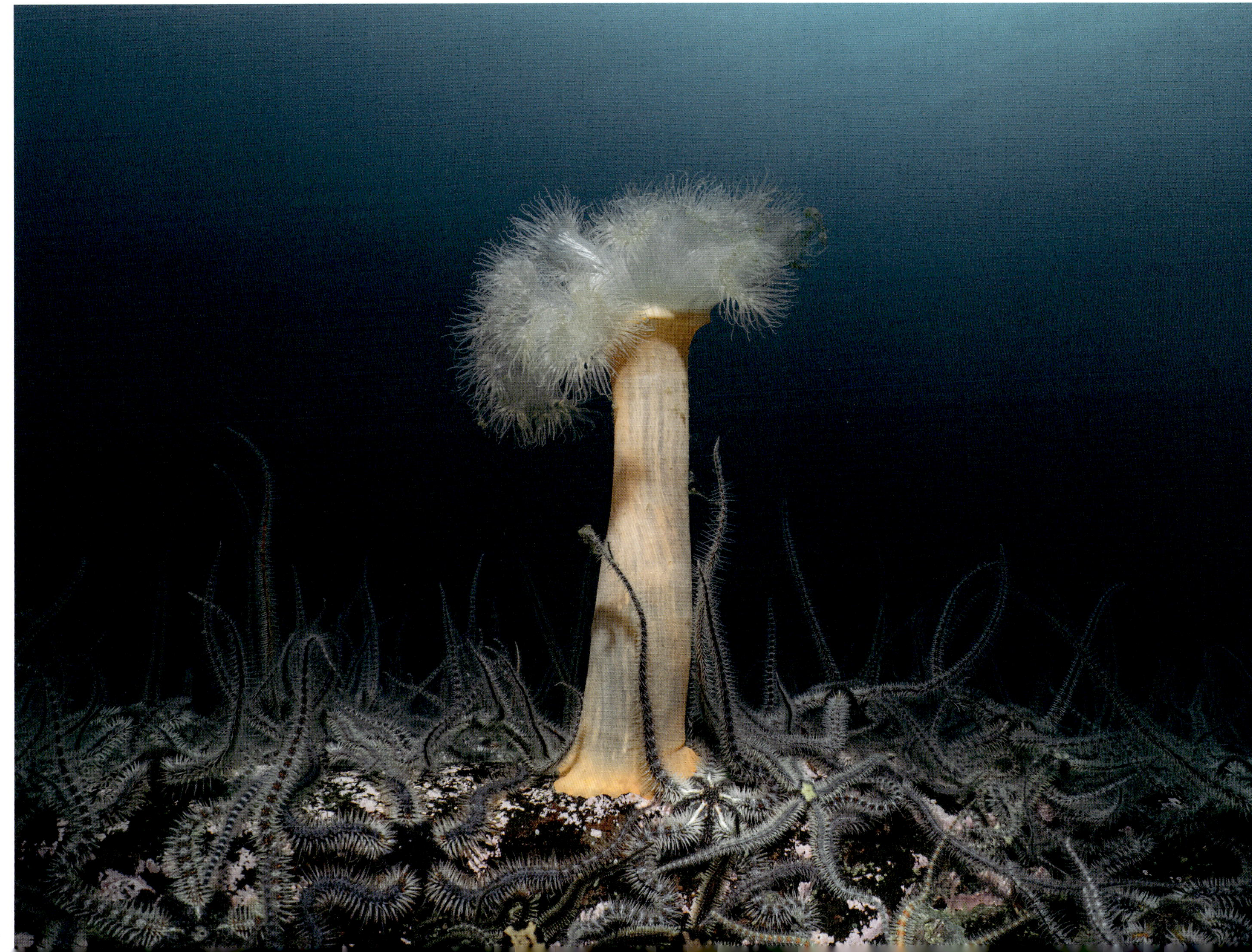

Fluo Cup Coral
Coast & Marine

James Lynott
Devonshire cup coral (*Caryophyllia smithii*)
Loch Dughaill, Scotland

Canon G7X Mark III with Fantasea UCL-900F
wet lens. 21mm; 1/100th second; f/8; ISO 400.

This image of a Devonshire cup coral was captured
during a fantastic wall dive in Loch Dughaill in April
2023. Many underwater species show incredible
fluorescence under blue/near-ultraviolet lights, and
out of all the species I have seen fluoresce in this way,
cup corals are one of the brightest. Light & Motion
Sola Nightsea lights and a barrier filter were used to
excite and view the fluorescence.

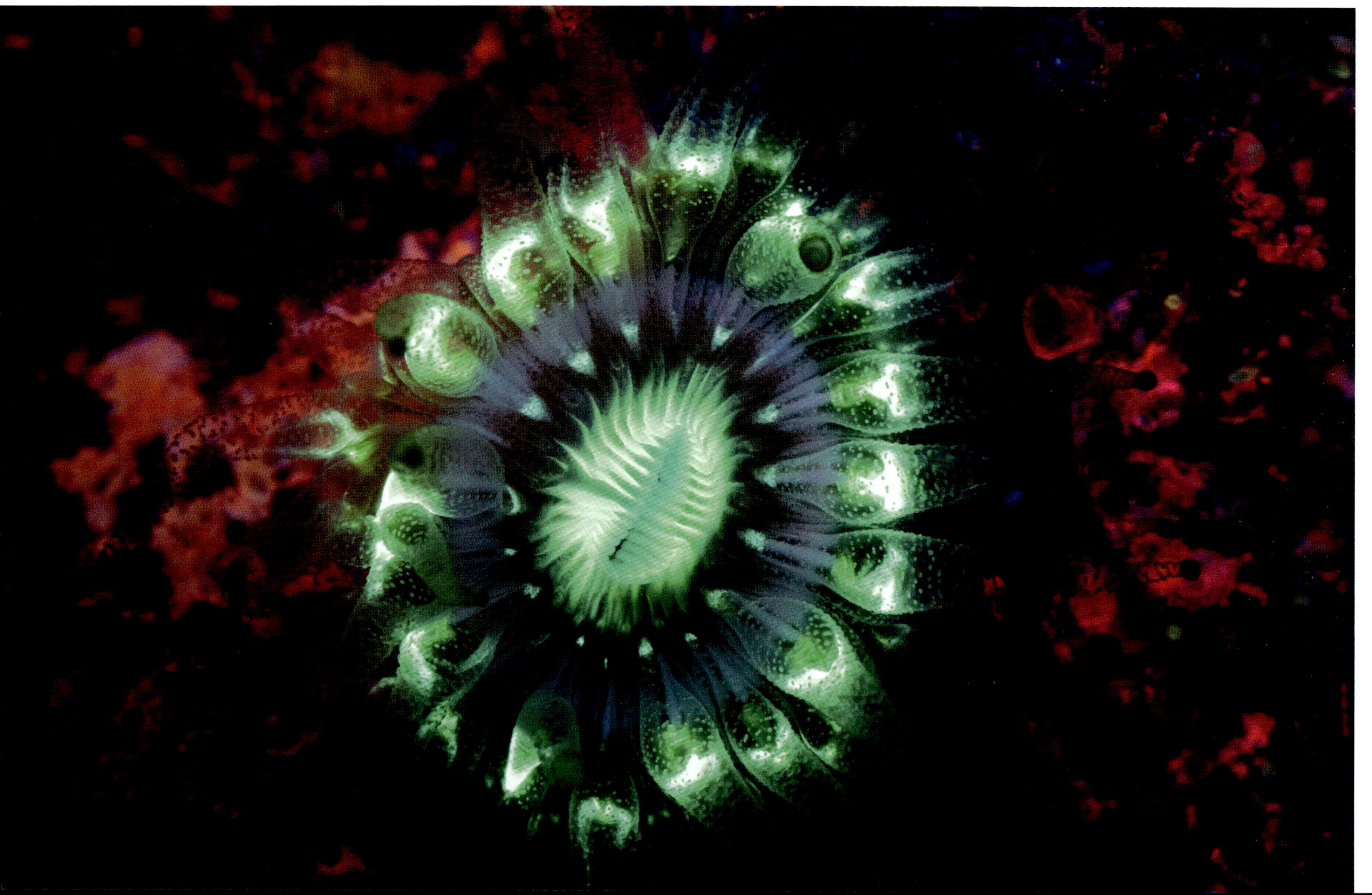

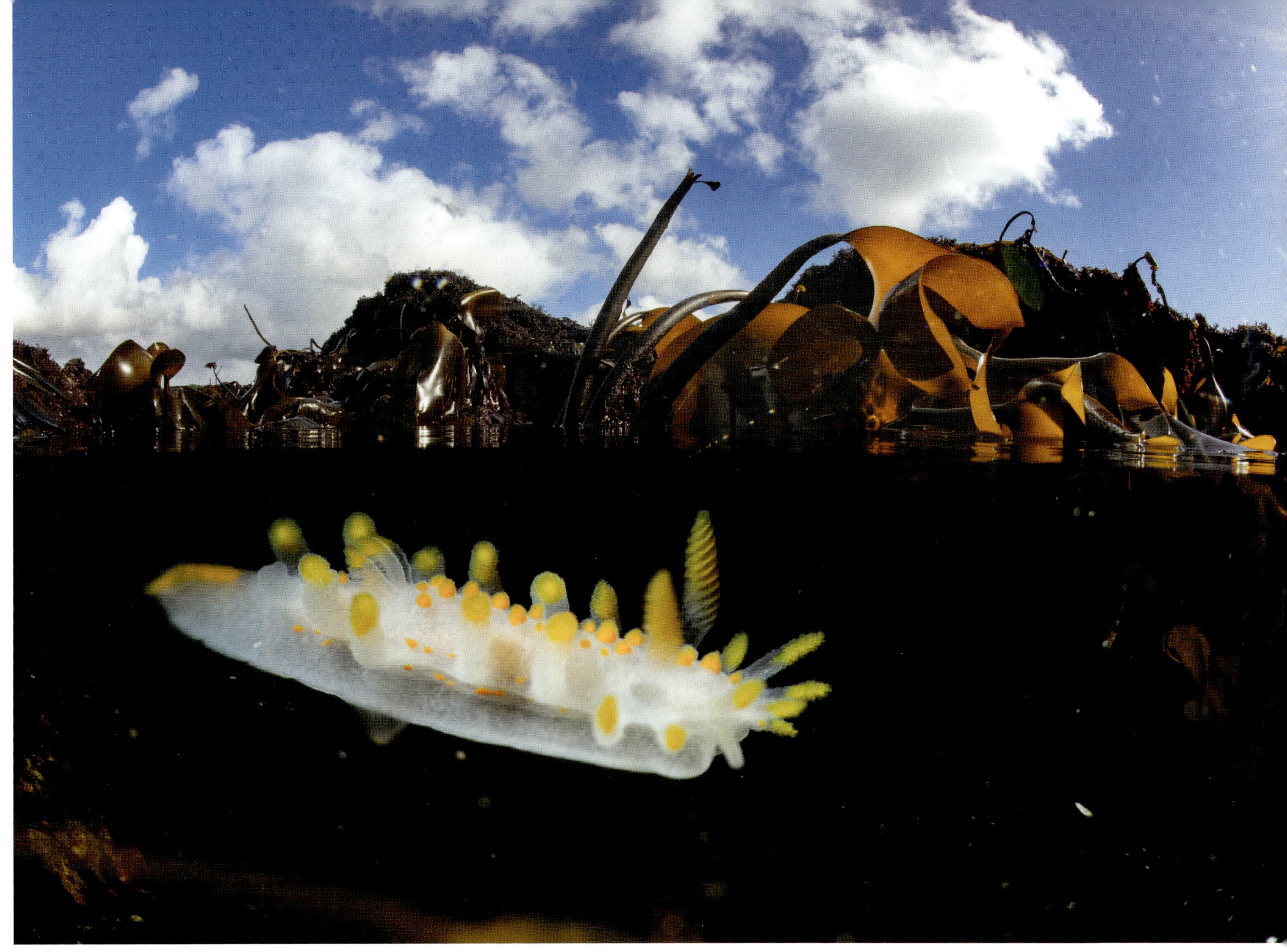

Shallow Water Sea Slug
Coast & Marine

Martin Stevens
Orange-clubbed sea slug (*Limacia clavigera*)
Falmouth, Cornwall, England

Olympus OM-D E-M5 Mark III with Olympus 60mm
f/2.8 Macro lens. 60mm; 1/250th second; f/11;
ISO 200.

An orange-clubbed sea slug on kelp; a common yet
beautiful and easily overlooked species due to its tiny
size (often just 1 cm). This is an in-camera double
exposure. The first exposure is a super macro shot of
the slug, which was crawling on kelp. It was taken
with a macro lens and diopter, along with a strobe
flash to create a dark background. The second shot
was taken at the same location and is a split shot
with a fisheye lens. It uses ambient light to capture
the topside of the lower shore, with the sky and kelp
protruding above the surface.

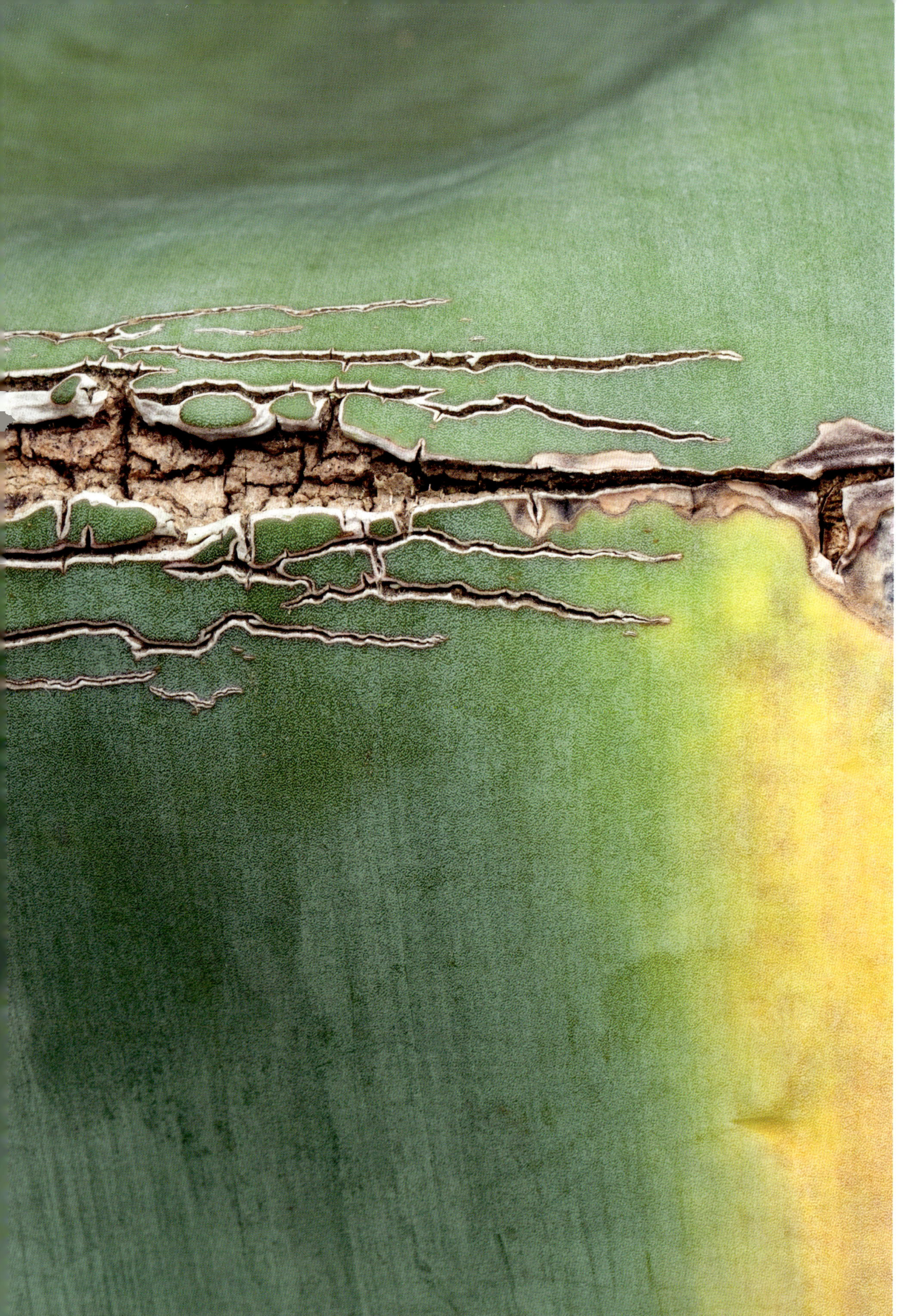

Plant Scars

Botanical Britain | Highly Commended

Tracy Calder
Agave (Asparagaceae)
Isle of Wight, Hampshire, England

Fujifilm X-T2 with Fujifilm 80mm f/2.8 Macro lens. 80mm; 1/12th second; f/20; ISO 200.

Many plants are allowed to self-regulate in 'self-maintaining communities' at Ventnor Botanic Garden. With minimal interference, these ecosystems attract 'companion organisms' such as parasites, fungi and rust – organisms that many gardeners try to discourage. Using the Ventnor Method, gardeners and volunteers are actively discouraged from removing leaf litter, damaged stems and fronds. Scars, gashes and evidence of decay are openly displayed – not hidden from view or suppressed. With everything out in the open, the healing process can begin.

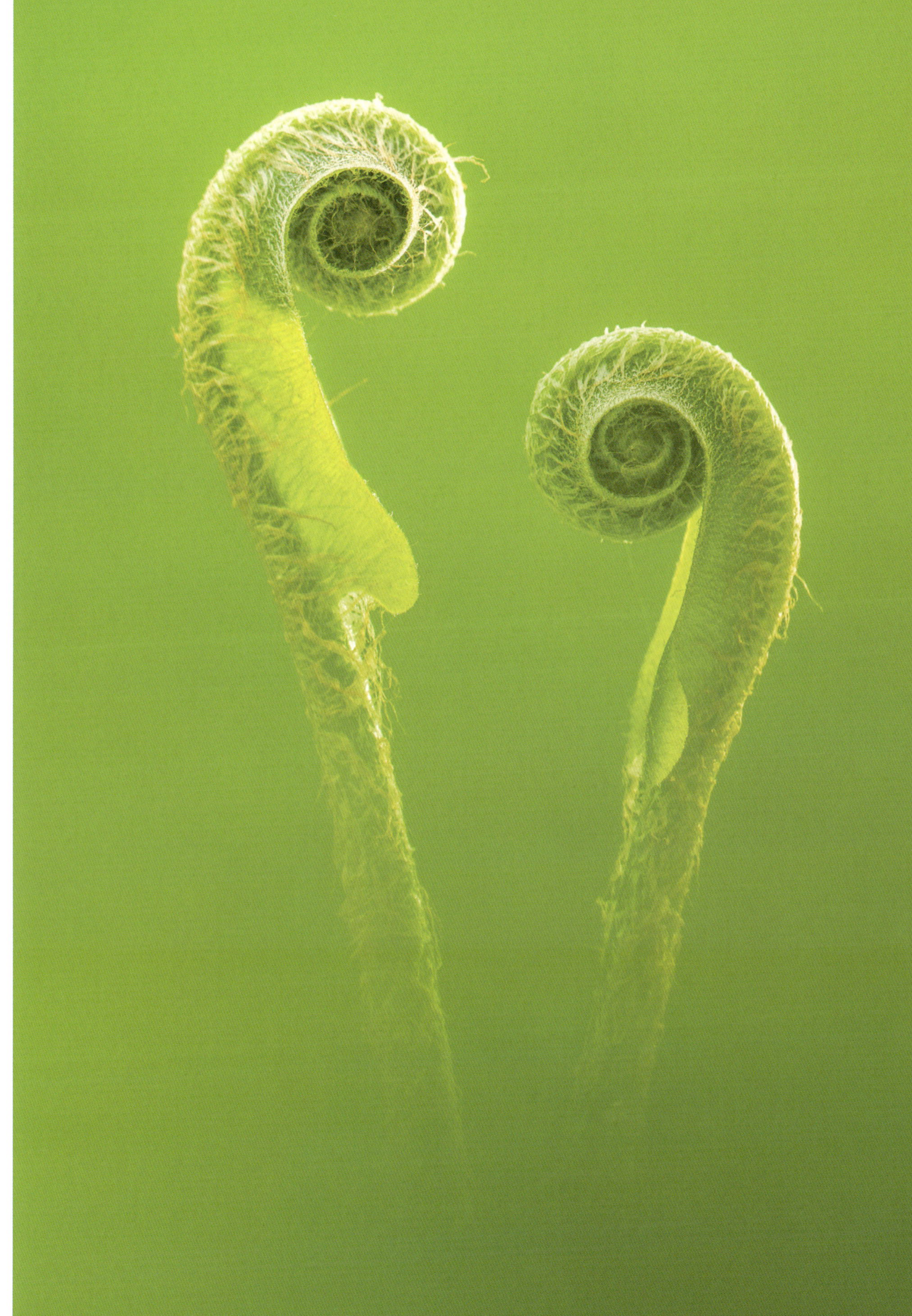

Hart's-tongue Ferns
Botanical Britain

Ross Hoddinott
Hart's-tongue fern (*Phyllitis scolopendrium*)
Broxwater, Cornwall, England

Nikon Z7 II and Nikon 200mm Micro lens. 200mm; 1/60th second; f/7.1; ISO 160.

I love the renewal of spring – there is so much vibrant, new life to photograph. I just can't resist unfurling ferns, and these two hart's-tongue ferns facing each other – growing on an old Cornish bank close to my home – caught my eye. I selected a low angle and a long focal length to isolate them from their surroundings and highlight their amazing shape.

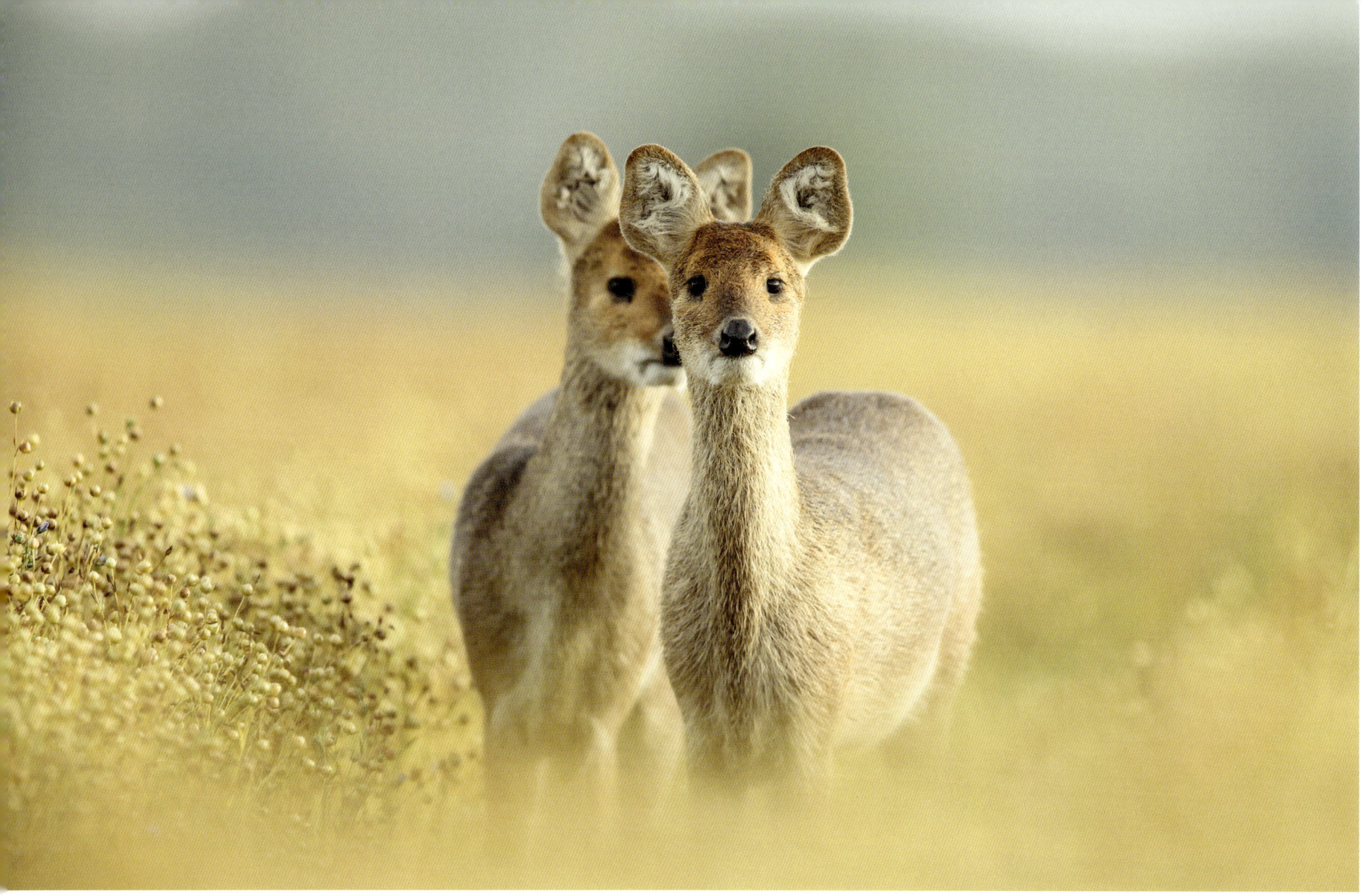

Teddy Bear Ears
Animal Portraits

Sarah Darnell
Chinese water deer (*Hydropotes inermis*)
Norfolk, England

Canon EOS 1D with Canon 600mm f/4 II lens
& 1.4x teleconverter. 840mm; 1/640th second;
f/5.6; ISO 1,250.

I had spent several mornings in the same spot
surrounded by the glorious gold linseed crop in
anticipation of photographing a fox. I saw a pair of
ears emerge, followed by a second pair and then a
third – round, fluffy ears, just like a teddy bear. I held
my breath until the approaching animals came within
identification range, and I was able to confirm that it
was a mother and two Chinese water deer fawns.
It was literally a breathtaking moment.

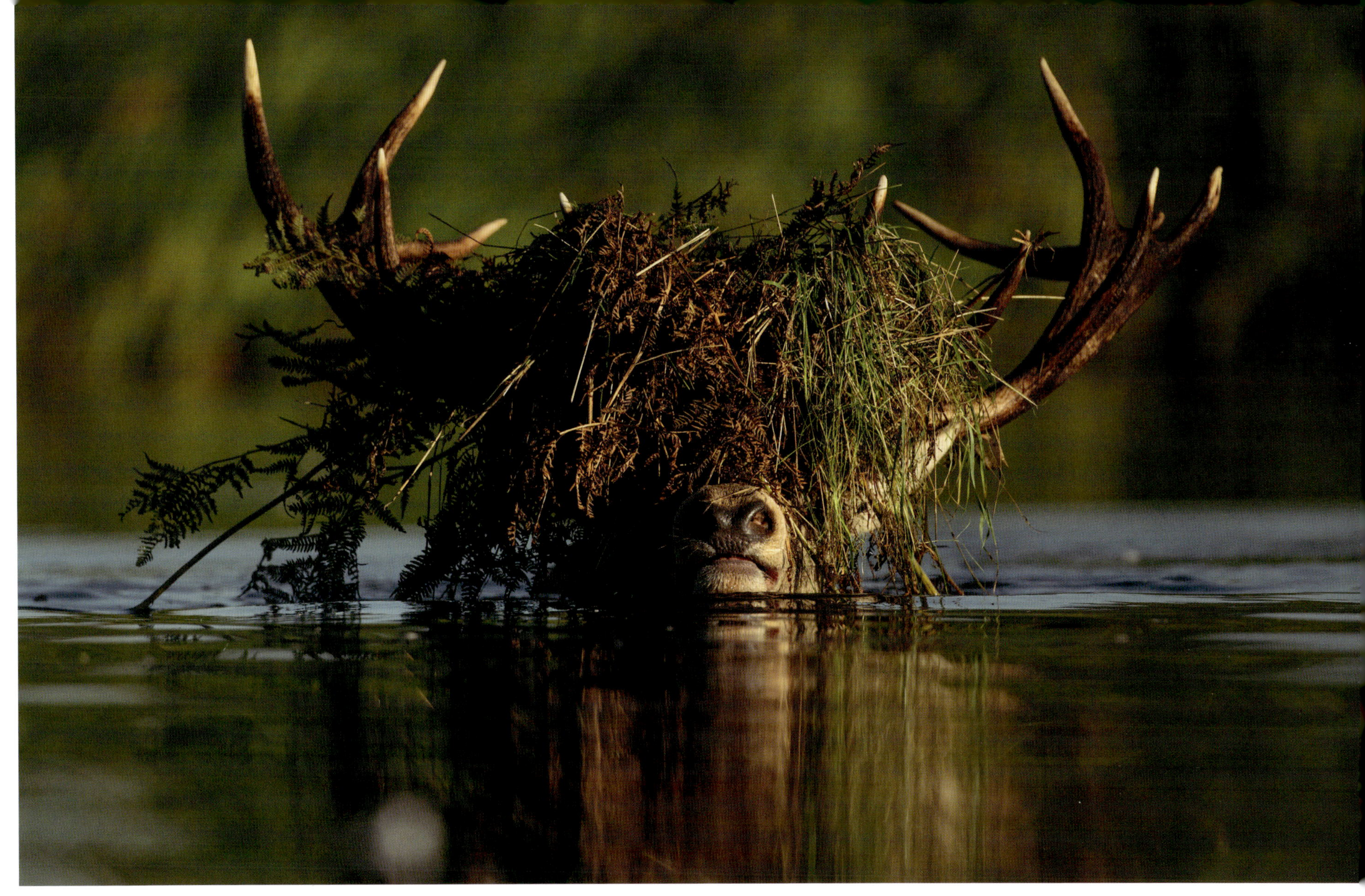

SAS Stag
Animal Portraits

Ben Andrew
Red deer (*Cervus elaphus*)
Bushy Park, London, England

Canon 5D IV with Canon 500mm f/4 lens.
500mm; 1/2,500th second; f/4; ISO 200.

I had been watching this red deer stag and another
thrashing about in some bracken during the peak
of the rutting season. Once their battle was over,
I stuck with this individual as it walked through more
bracken, adding vegetation to its antlers. Finally, it
submerged itself in a lake. It was incredibly low to the
water, so I also got down as low as I could to get this
unique perspective.

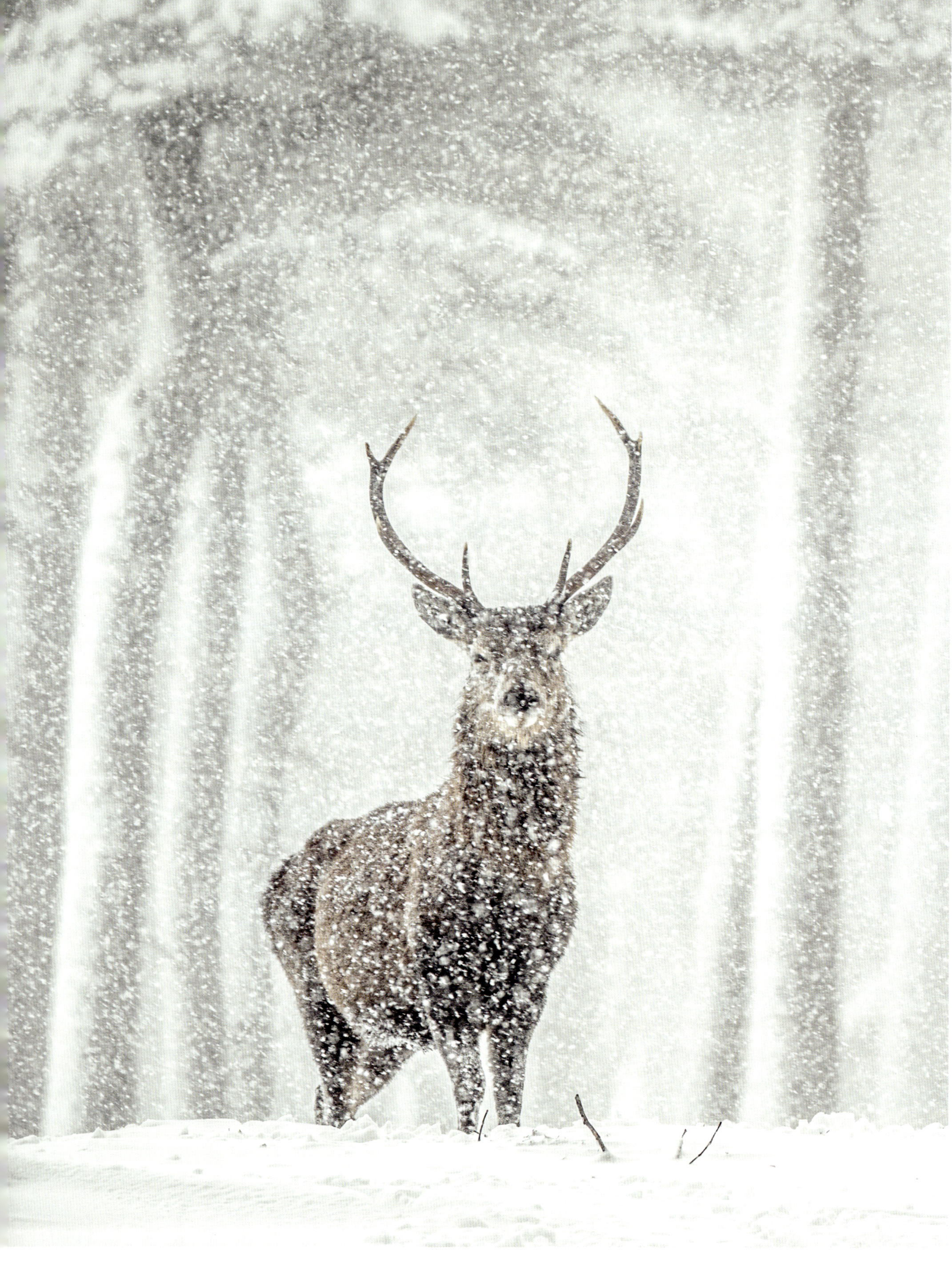

Stag in the Snow
Wild Woods

Michelle Coyle
Red deer (*Cervus elaphus*)
Cairngorms National Park, Scotland

Panasonic G9 with Leica 50-200mm
f/2.8-4 lens. 200mm; 1/500th
second; f/4; ISO 200.

Following a night of heavy snowfall,
I set out to try and photograph
one of my favourite animals, the
red deer. I reached the location,
a Caledonian pine forest in the
Cairngorms. Snow was still falling
heavily and blowing into my face,
making it quite difficult to see,
let alone focus the camera. It was
worth the wait, as this majestic stag
emerged from between the trees,
looking stunning in the snow. He
stood and watched briefly, just long
enough for me to capture a few
shots before he moved on.
A truly magical encounter in a
winter wonderland setting.

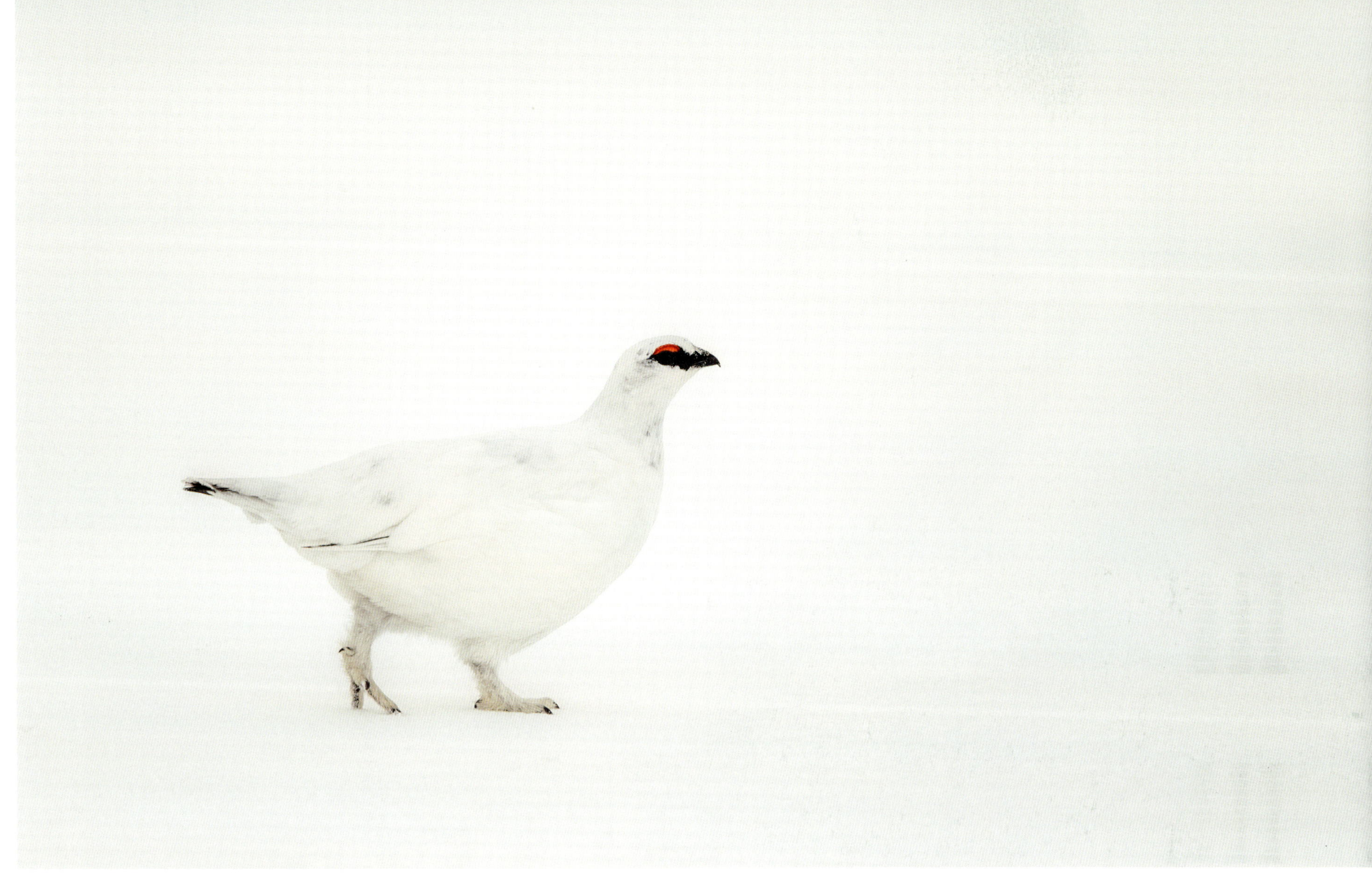

White Walker
Animal Portraits

Nick Clayton
Ptarmigan (*Lagopus muta*)
Cairngorms National Park, Scotland

Canon EOS 1D X with Canon 600mm f/4 II lens &
1.4x teleconverter. 840mm; 1/1,000th second;
f/5.6; ISO 800.

As I made my way up a mountain in the Cairngorms
National Park, the sun was shining with very little
cloud cover. It's amazing how the weather can quickly
change in these parts, and by the time I was up the
mountain photographing ptarmigan, I was in a snow
blizzard! This allowed me to obtain the image I had
visualised, which was of the white ptarmigan with a
pure white background with no distractions. The lack
of direct sunlight helped to show the image details
and the softness in the whites.

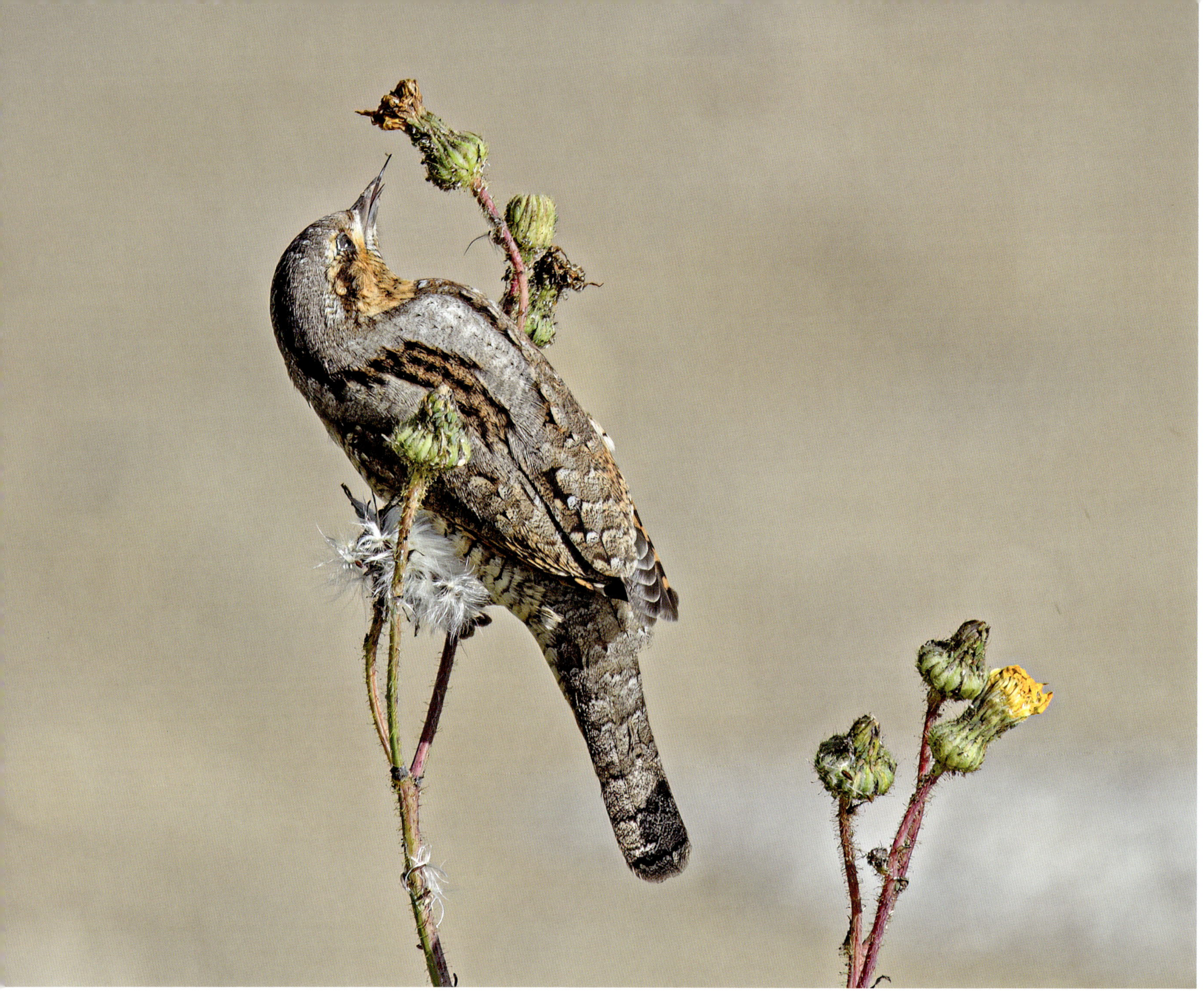

Eurasian Wryneck
Animal Portraits

Keith Allen
Eurasian wryneck (*Jynx torquilla*)
Spurn Point, Yorkshire, England

Nikon D500 with Nikon 300mm f/4 lens and 1.4x teleconverter. 300mm; 1/1250th second; f/5.6; ISO 200.

The wryneck was once a common bird in the UK but is now only a very occasional breeder and mainly seen on passage during autumn and spring migrations. I heard of a report of a wryneck showing very well at Spurn Point, a popular coastal migration spot, and saw this confiding bird feeding above the shoreline. Initially, the wryneck was low on the ground, probably hunting for its favourite food of ants, making any photography difficult. Fortunately, it perched up onto some vegetation and provided some great images as it extended its sticky tongue to feed on aphids.

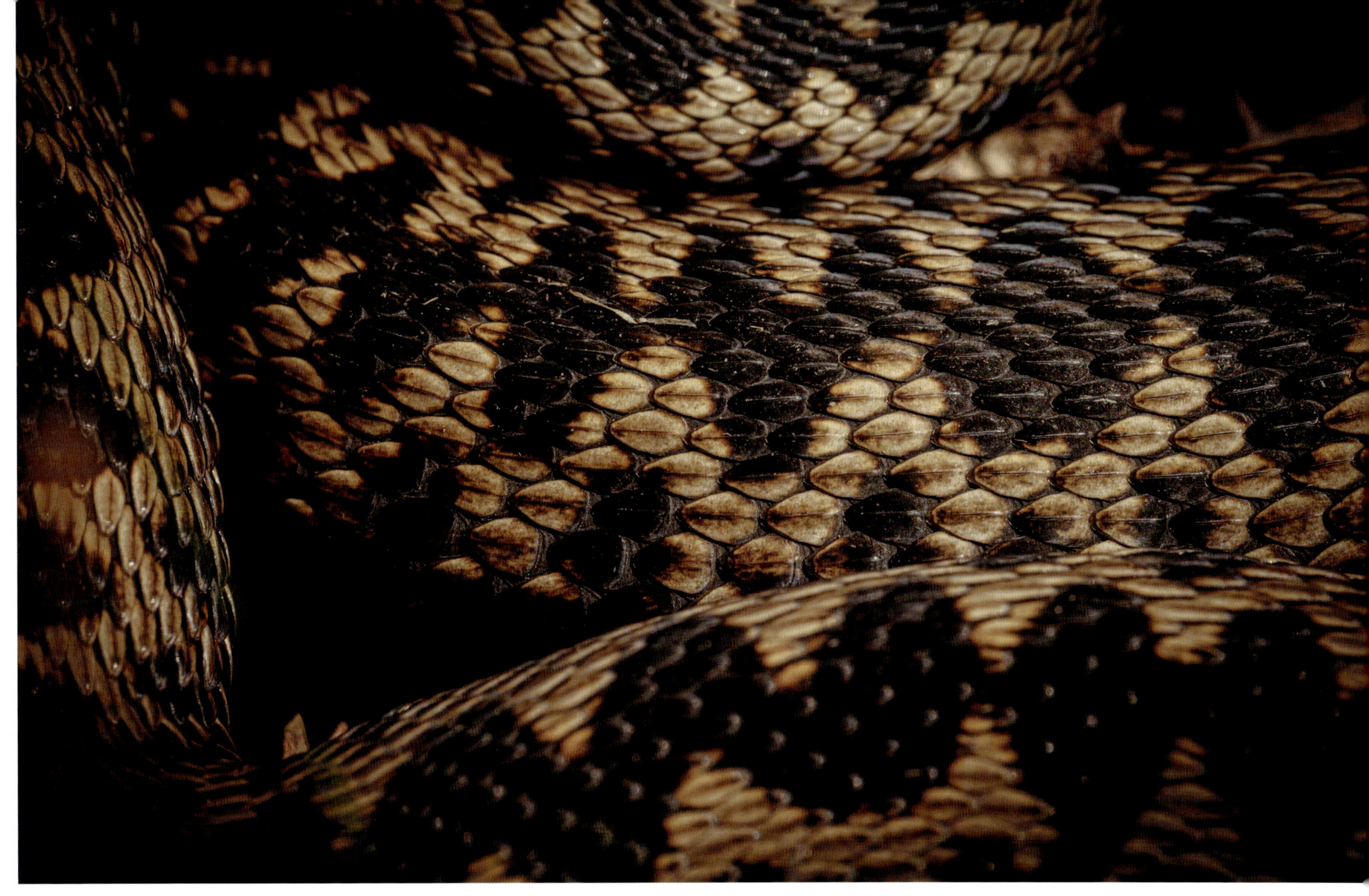

Diamonds and Gold
Hidden Britain | Highly Commended

William Harvey
Adder (*Vipera berus*)
Surrey, England

Canon R5 with Sigma 180mm f/2.8 lens.
180mm; 1/320th second; f/13; ISO 1,000.

I find the textures and patterns in an adder's scales very striking and wanted to create an almost abstract image that really focuses on the detail of these elements. Getting close enough to the adders to capture this detail can be challenging as they often flee at any sign of movement and repeated disturbance can be very detrimental to them. Having photographed adders at the same location for several years, I've come to know their regular basking spots, which means I'm able to anticipate where they may emerge and wait at those spots, which has helped me achieve close-up images such as this one.

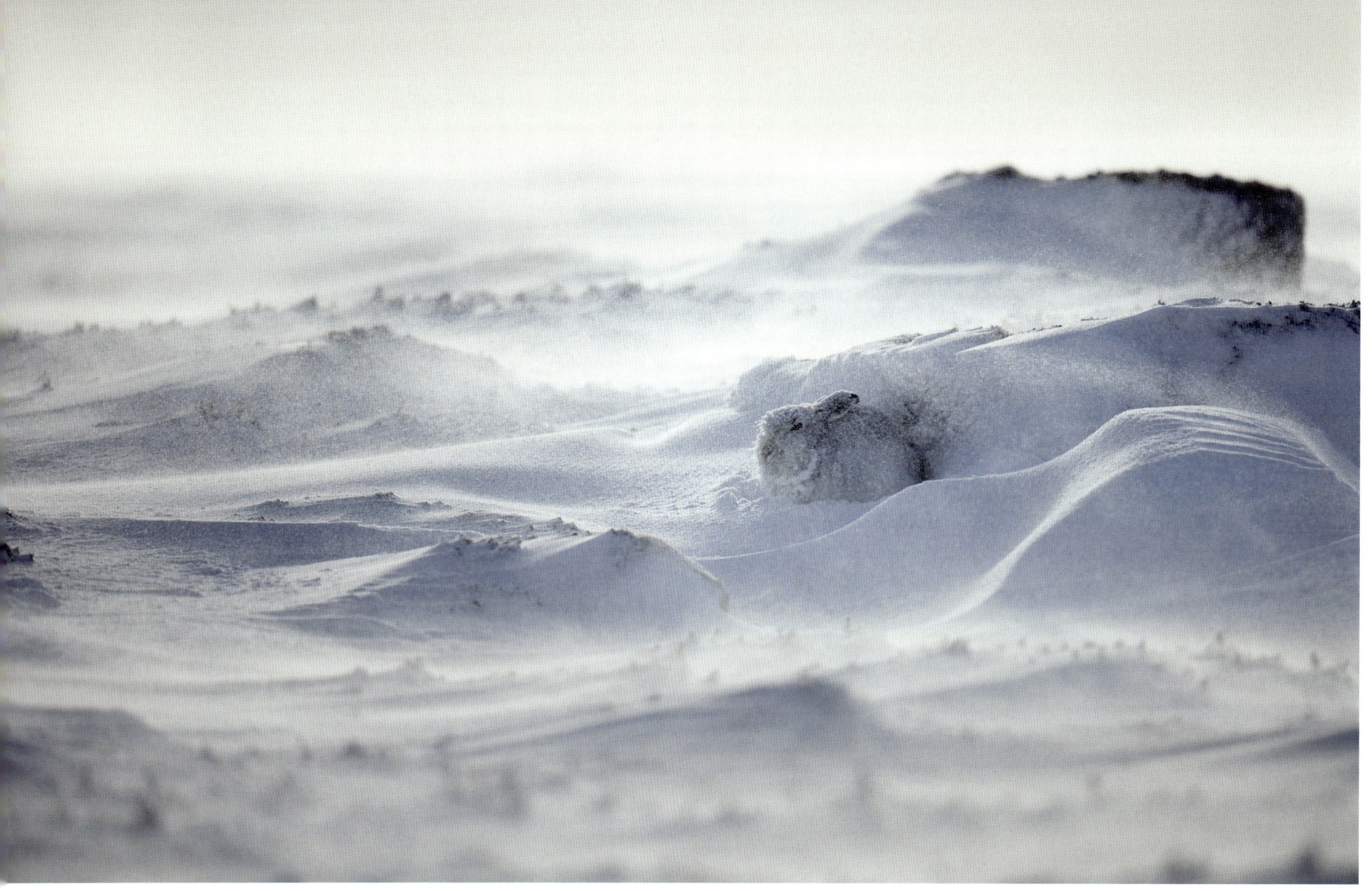

Toughing it Out
Habitat | Highly Commended

Simon Withyman
Mountain hare (*Lepus timidus*)
Cairngorms National Park, Scotland

Canon EOS R5 with Canon 500mm f/4 II lens.
500mm; 1/2,500th second; f/4; ISO 100.

The weather on this day was harsh, with high winds, lots of snow and strong spindrift creating some challenging but atmospheric conditions. As this was a mountain I was unfamiliar with, I kept my distance to avoid any disturbance and decided to incorporate the environment in the shot to make it as much of a focal point as the mountain hare itself.

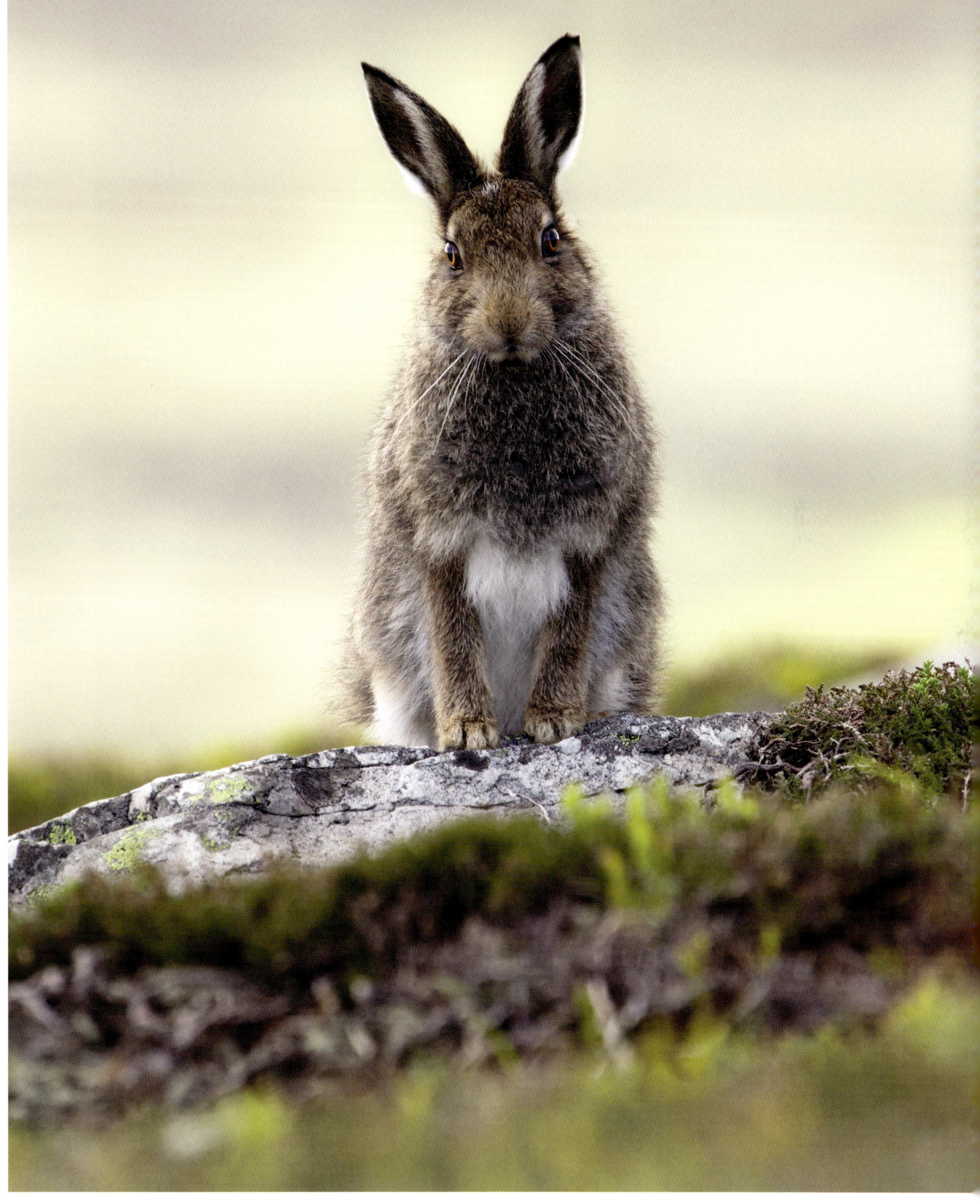

Young Mountain Hare Standing on a Rock
Animal Portraits

Michael Johnston
Mountain hare
(*Lepus timidus*)
Cairngorms National Park,
Scotland

Canon EOS R5 and Canon 100-400mm f/4.5-5.6 lens. 400mm; 1/800th second; f/7.1; ISO 500.

I spotted a couple of pairs of ears just over a rise while walking in the Cairngorms. I lay down, and soon a couple of grazing young mountain hares appeared. This one briefly stood on a rock as it approached before passing just to my right. I've been lucky to have had many close encounters with mountain hares, but I'm always surprised at how trusting they can be.

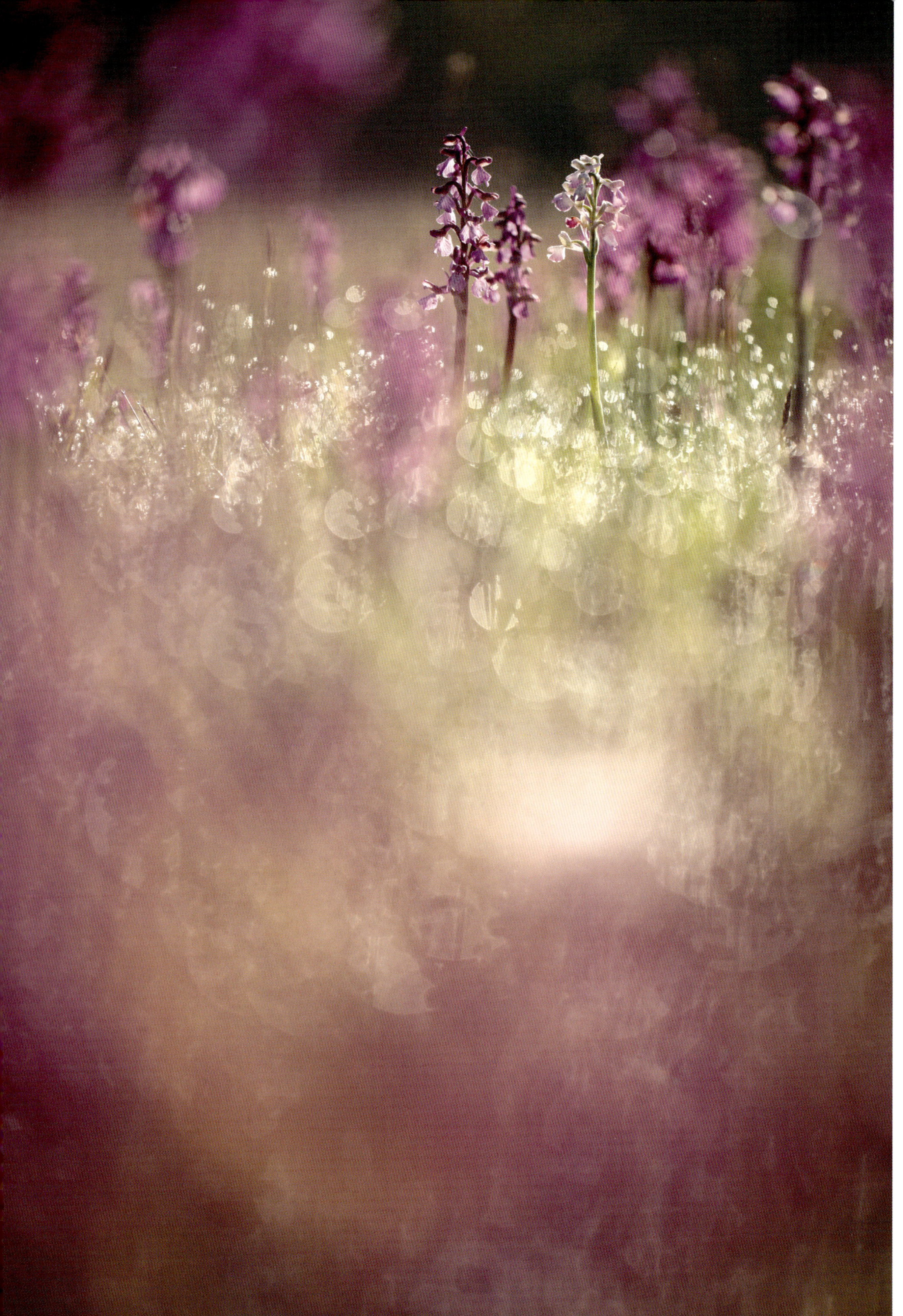

Purple Haze
Botanical Britain

Simon Carder
Green-winged orchid (*Anacamptis morio*)
Chew Valley Lake, Somerset, England

Canon EOS R5 with Sigma 180mm f/2.8 Macro lens. 180mm; 1/1,600th second; f/2.8; ISO 100.

Green-winged orchids flower in their thousands in a field near my home. This image was taken on a bright morning just after sunrise and highlights that while the majority of this species are a beautiful purple colour, every now and then there is a paler flower spike that provides a contrast and focal point. This image was taken by shooting through the orchids and into the sun to produce wonderful bokeh from the dew on the grass and a dreamy purple surround to the subject orchids.

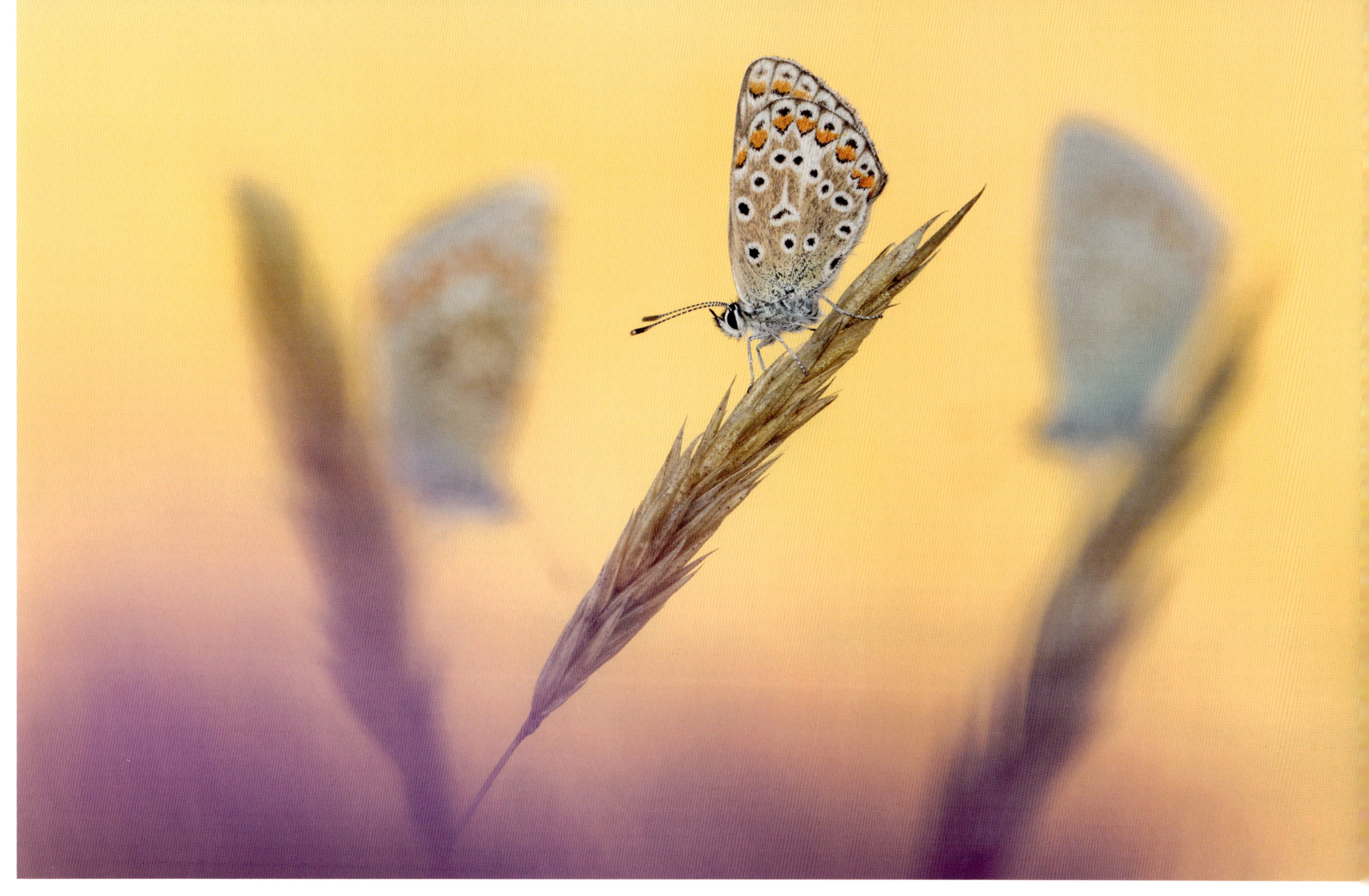

Three's a Crowd
Hidden Britain | Winner

Ross Hoddinott
Common blue butterflies (*Polyommatus icarus*)
Vealand Farm, Devon, England

Nikon D850 and Nikon 200mm f/4 Micro lens.
200mm; 1/100th second; f/16; ISO 640.

I think I have a slight addiction to photographing blue butterflies – I just love them! They are such beautiful little insects, and they enhance any wildflower meadow or garden they inhabit. Blues are quite social insects, and they can often be found roosting quite close together – or even on the same grass or flower. I found a dozen or so blues all resting close together one evening last summer. Using a shallow depth of field, I decided to 'frame' my subject with two out-of-focus butterflies to help add impact and context to my shot. The warm, evening light produced a vibrant natural background.

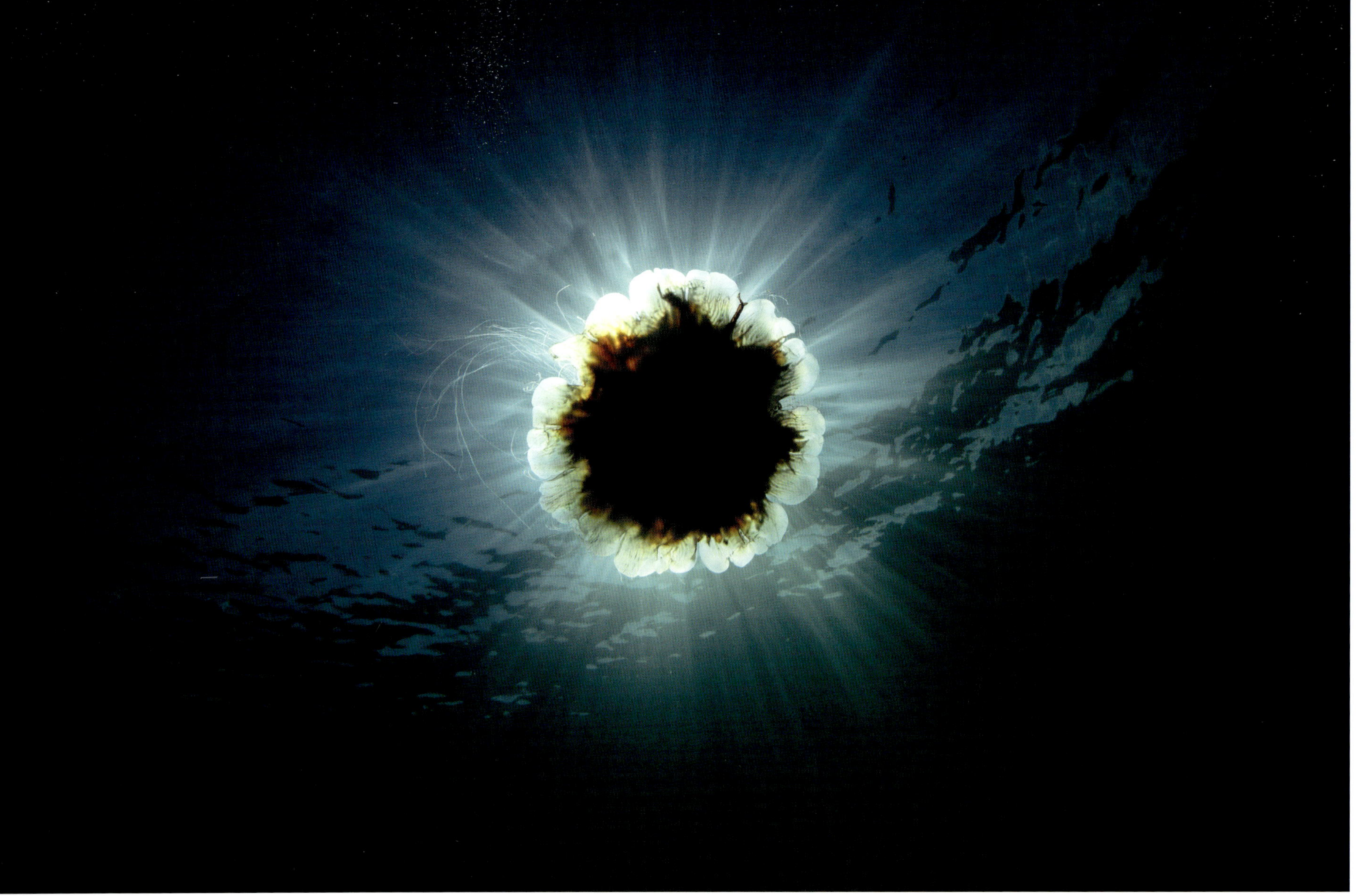

Lion in the Sun
Coast & Marine

Brian Matthews
Lion's mane jellyfish (*Cyanea capillata*)
Farne Islands, Northumberland, England

Canon EOS 5D IV with Canon 14mm f/2.8 II lens.
14mm; 1/1,000th second; f/14; ISO 100.

One of the largest jellyfish you can find in UK waters, these red giants are amazing to watch. I photographed this lion's mane jellyfish around the Farne Islands while looking for grey seals with the team from Billy Shiel's boats. Free diving below the jellyfish, I lined up the sun directly behind it to backlight the jellyfish as it passed above me.

Morning on the Reef
Coast & Marine

Martin Stevens
Compass jellyfish (*Chrysaora hysoscella*)
Falmouth, Cornwall, England

Olympus EM-5 III with Olympus 7-14mm f/2.8 lens.
7mm; 1/60th second; f/10; ISO 400.

First thing on a sunny morning, the golden light
is incomparable. In the summer, when the water
is often clear, compass jellyfish are found inshore
around Cornwall and the southwest. I got up early
specifically to photograph the jellyfish in the morning
light and captured this large individual with the
sun rays and sand eels in the background. Taken in
Falmouth Bay.

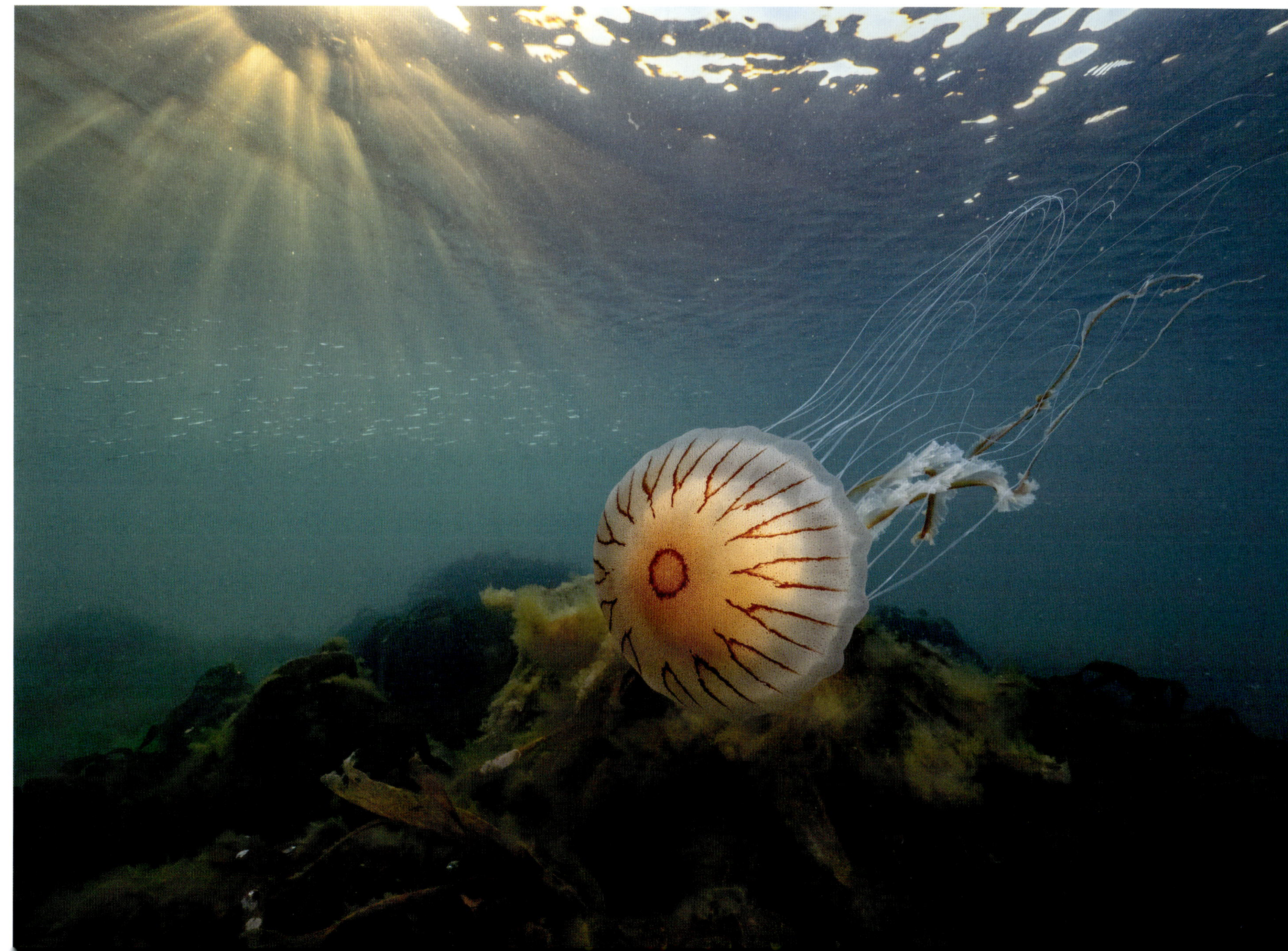

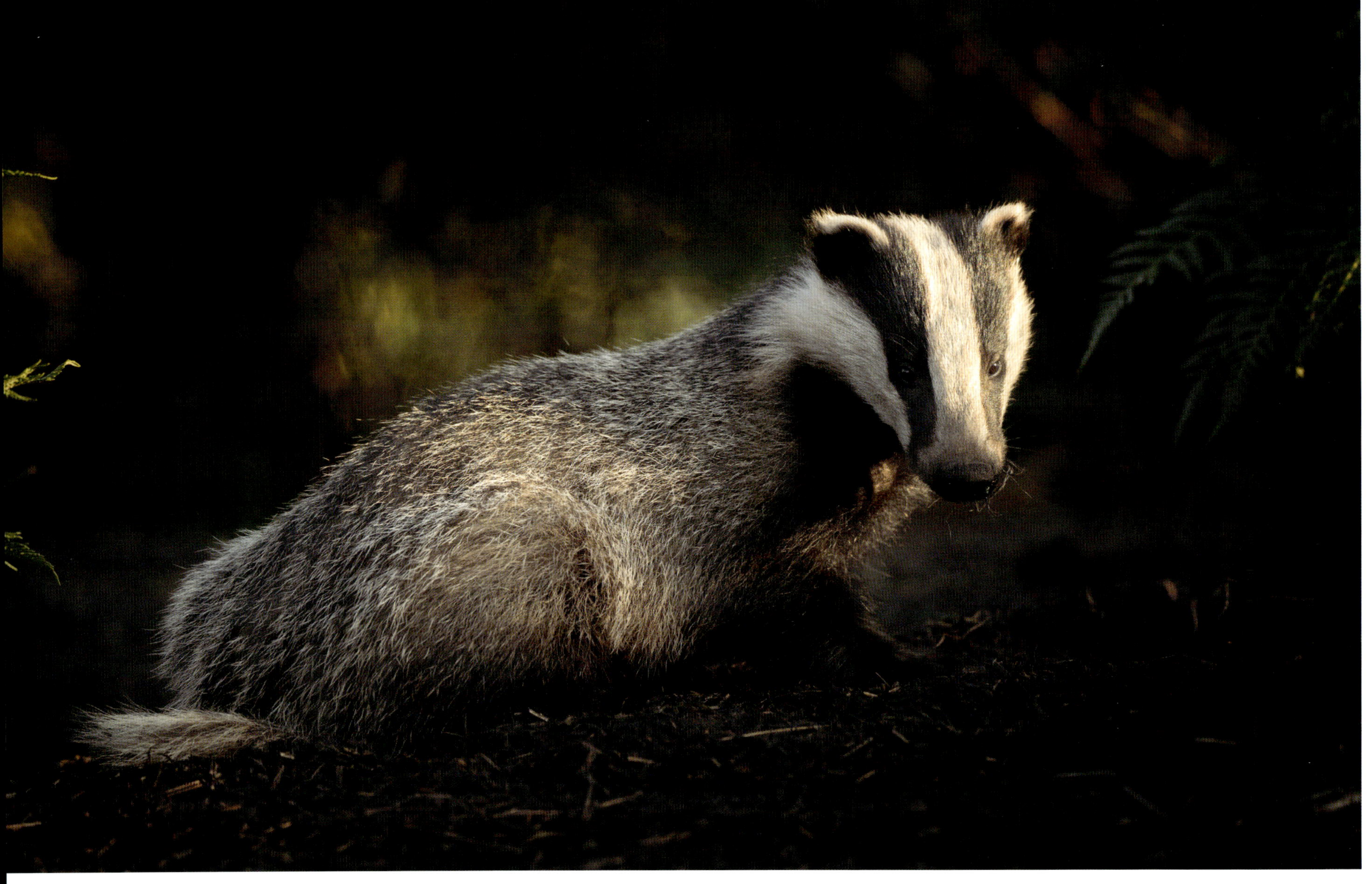

Sunlit Badger Cub
Animal Portraits

Francis Taylor
Badger (*Meles meles*)
Peak District National Park, England

Canon EOS 1D X Mark II with Canon 500mm f/4 II
lens. 500mm; 1/500th second; f/5.6; ISO 1,250.

A badger cub emerges from the sett in the last rays
of evening sunshine. This image was taken during
one exceptionally dry summer with no rain for weeks
on end. With no obvious water source around,
I visited several setts daily to put out water bowls.
I hope it helped!

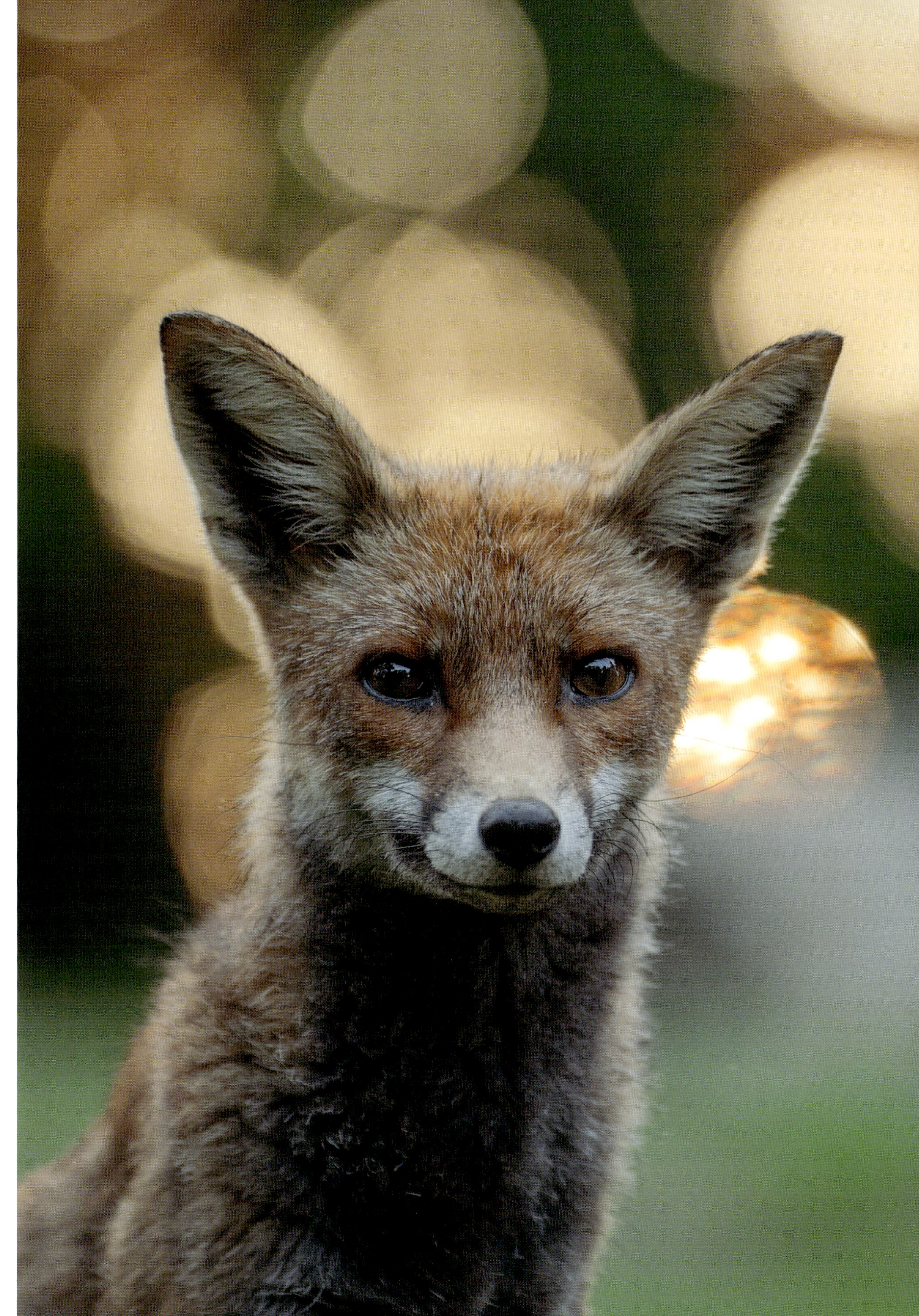

Vixen in Front of the Setting Sun
Animal Portraits

Dan Rushton
Red fox (*Vulpes vulpes*)
Dorset, England

Nikon D700 with Sigma 120-300mm
f/2.8 lens. 300mm; 1/400th second;
f/3.2; ISO 1,600.

One of the best things about working
locally is the opportunity to spend a lot
of time searching for the ideal lighting
conditions and the spots where it best
illuminates to create a beautiful bokeh
in the background of the shot. I have
been photographing a family group of
foxes in this graveyard close to home
for five years now. Over the last two or
three years, I have dedicated a lot of
time to finding areas that work well for
shooting into the sun as it begins to set,
often partially obscured by bushes and
trees. The results can be amazing and
vary throughout the year. Additionally,
having built a close bond with the foxes
helps immensely, as they usually spend
time in some of these areas, making it a
little too easy sometimes.

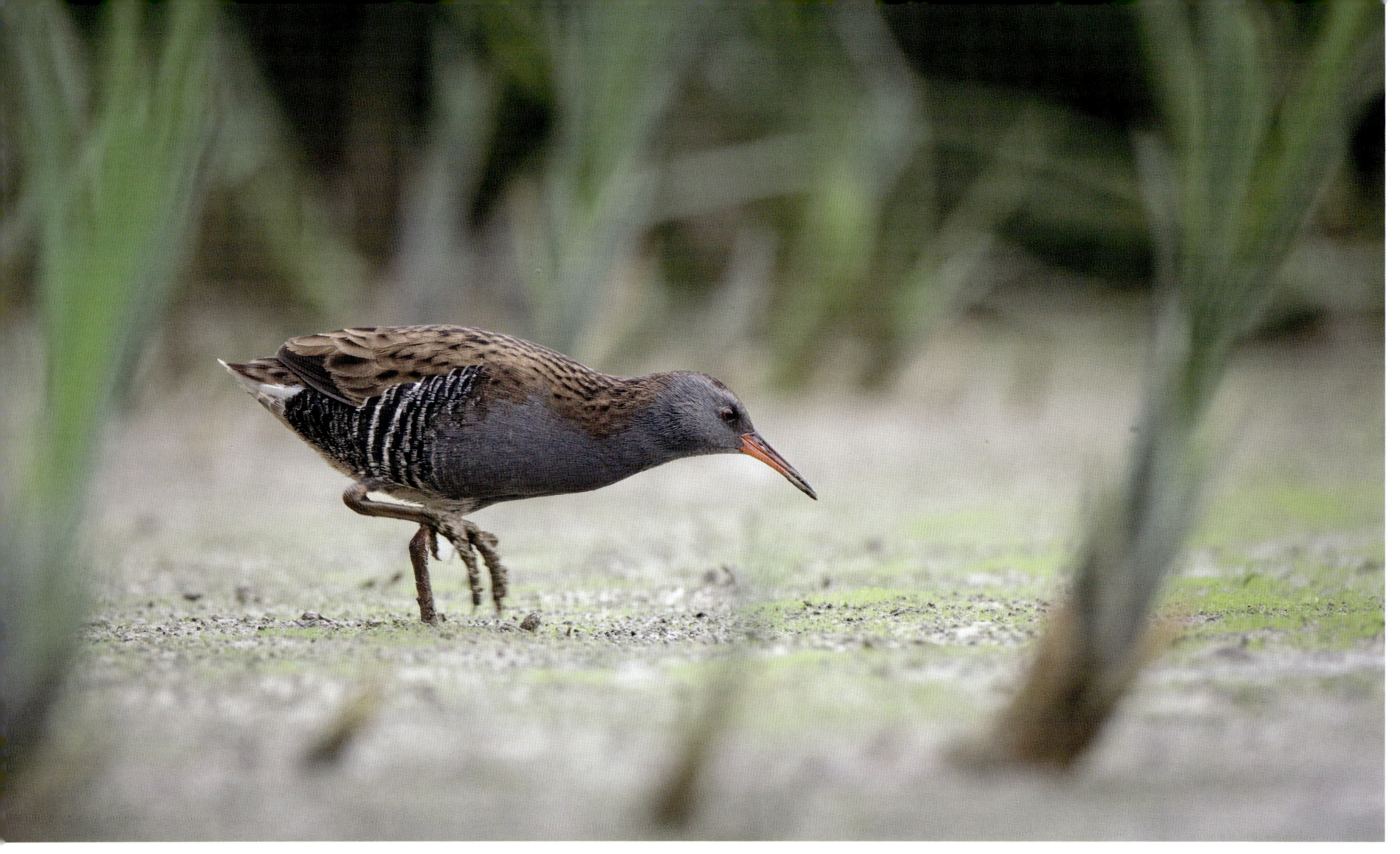

Water Rail Hunting in Reeds
Habitat

Martin Vaughan
Water rail (*Rallus aquaticus*)
Near Ibstock, Leicestershire, England

Canon EOS 1D X with Canon 500mm f/4 lens.
500mm; 1/640th second; f/5.6; ISO 3,200.

I had received permission to set up a small pop-up hide concealed within the reeds of a local reserve. My aim was to photograph snipe and green sandpipers from ground level. While in the hide, I heard the distinctive call of a water rail. I cautiously peered out and spotted the bird navigating through the reeds, delicately probing the mud for food. Capturing a clear view was challenging due to the dense vegetation, and the lighting conditions were quite low. However, I successfully captured this shot, which I'm pleased with as it showcases the water rail in its natural habitat.

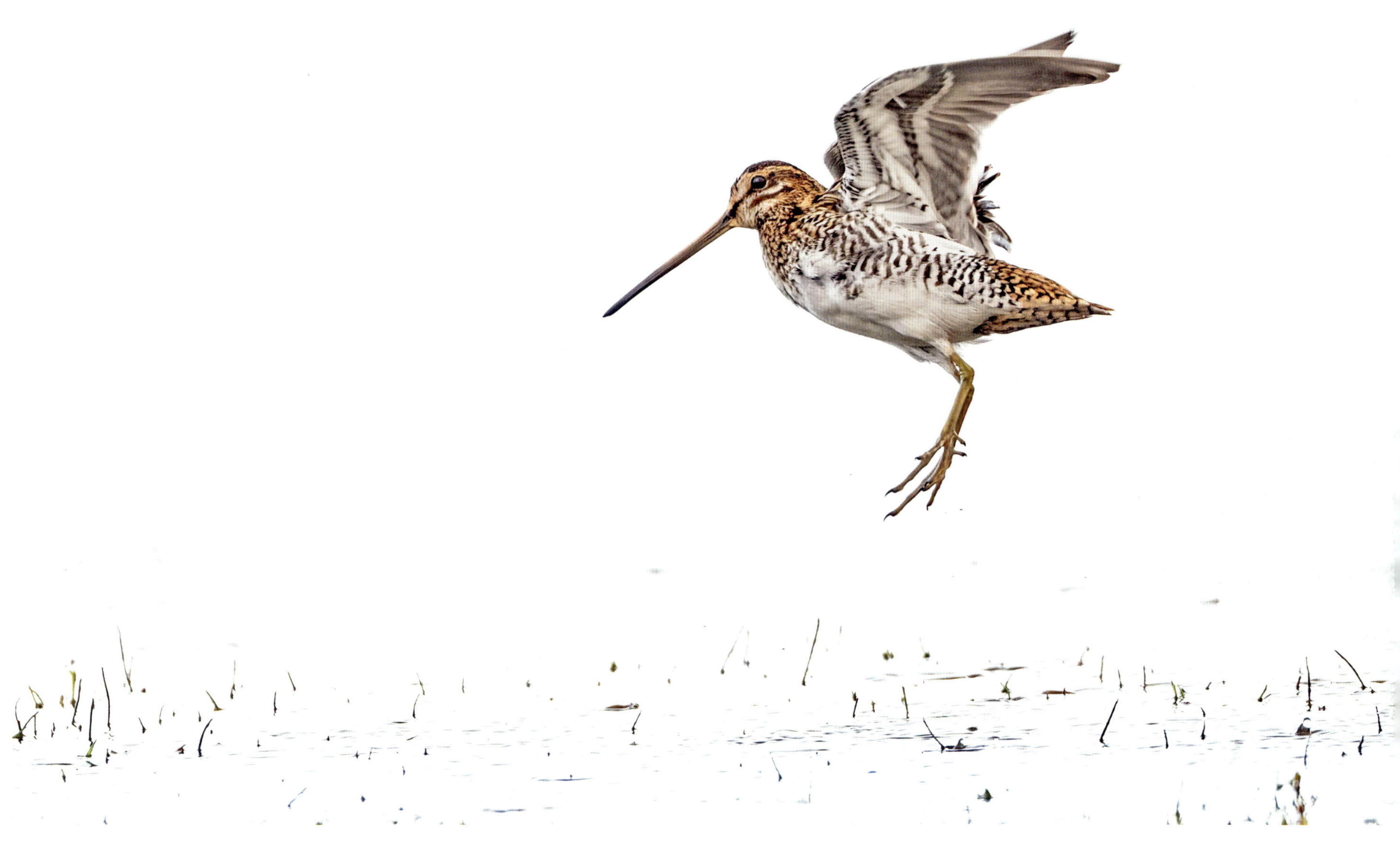

Snipe Jumping
Animal Behaviour

David Wolfenden
Snipe (*Gallinago gallinago*)
Musselburgh, Scotland

Canon EOS 1D X with Canon 500mm f/4 lens & 2x teleconverter. 1,000mm; 1/1,000th second; f/8; ISO 6,400.

I photographed this bird at Musselburgh Lagoons in Scotland. Although I had visited the site a number of times before, this was the first time I had seen a snipe. The bird was bathing at the edge of a lagoon, ducking down into the water and then rising and shaking itself. Suddenly, the bird flapped its wings and jumped into the air, presumably to help shed some water. Fortunately, I was in a good position to capture an image of this special moment.

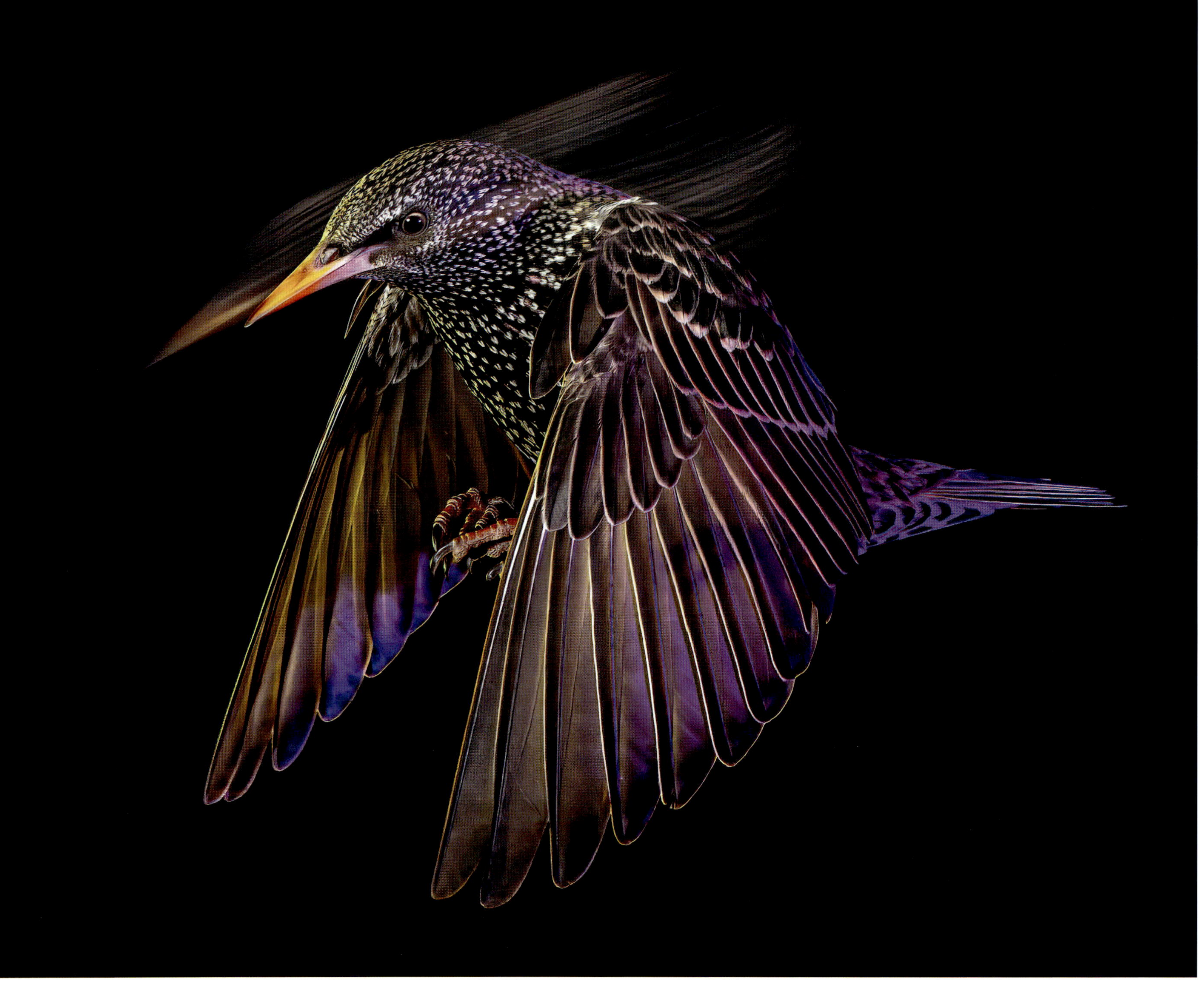

Starling at Night
Animal Portraits | Winner

Mark Williams
Common starling (*Sturnus vulgaris*)
Garden, Solihull, West Midlands, England

Canon 5D III with Canon 100-400mm f/4.5-5.6 lens.
200mm; 1/15th second; f/16; ISO 200.

I had been observing the birds in my garden as
they fed on sunflower seeds and peanuts from the
feeder for some time. I aimed to capture the sense
of movement and flight patterns in my images while
still preserving the fine details of the birds. To achieve
this, I used flash in rear curtain sync mode. Timing
was crucial, and I needed to carefully balance the
flash with the ambient light to record the starling's
trail at the beginning of the exposure, while a brief
burst of flash would freeze the bird in mid-flight.

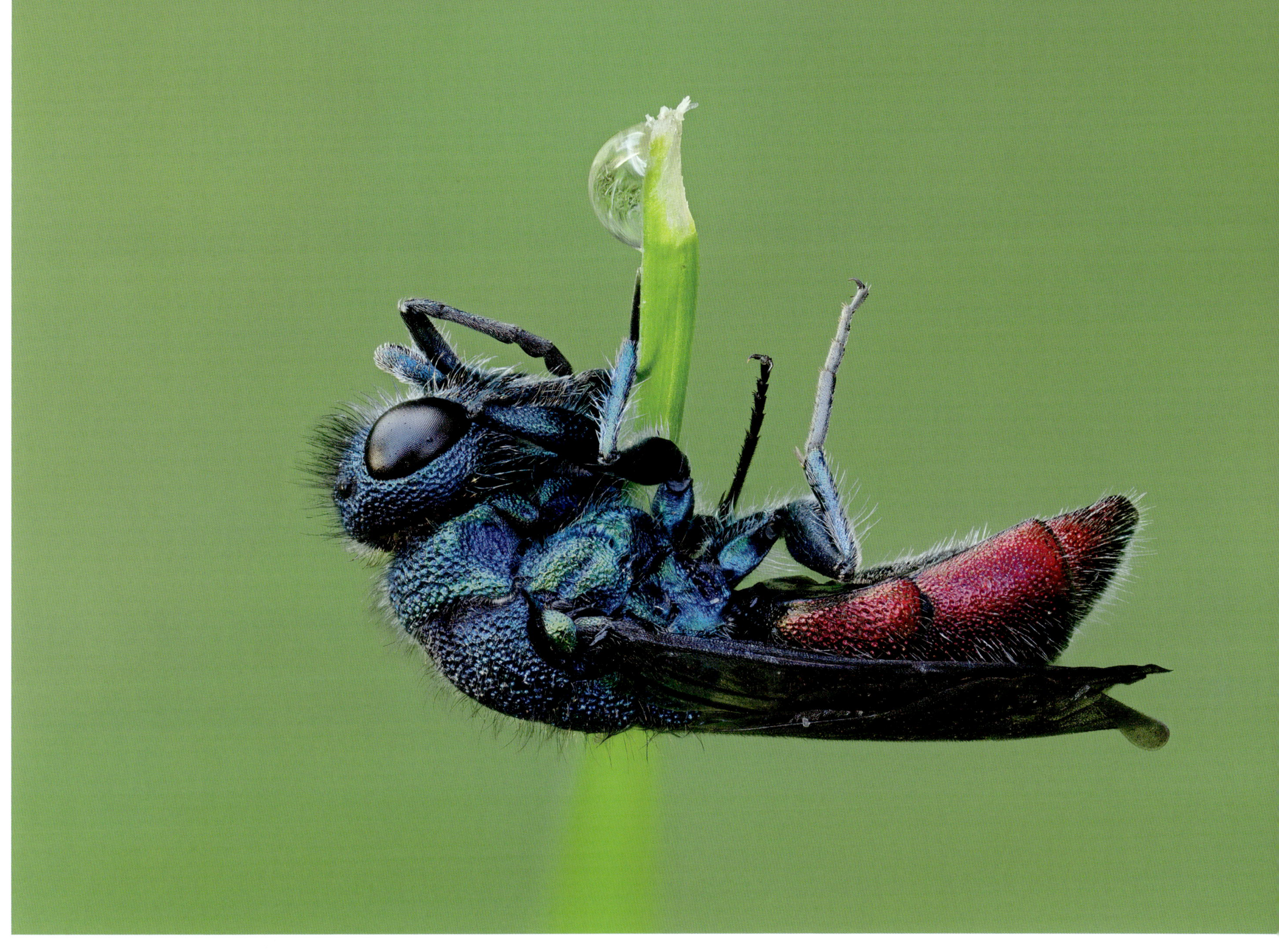

Cuckoo Wasp Sleeping
Hidden Britain | Highly Commended

Andy Sands
Cuckoo wasp (*Chrysis ignita*)
Hertfordshire, England

Olympus OM-1 with Olympus 90mm f/3.5 Macro lens. 90mm; 1/8th second; f/5.6; ISO 200.

I found this cuckoo wasp asleep in my garden, close to my bee hotels. I often see them inspecting the bamboo tubes and reed stems where they lay their eggs in the nests of various bees. Photographing the wasp was relatively easy as it was early morning and quite cool. I set up my Olympus OM1 with a 90mm macro lens on a Gitzo Explorer tripod and took 54 images using focus bracketing. Each image was shot at f/5.6, with a 1/8th-second exposure, ISO 200. The images were subsequently stacked with Zerene Stacker.

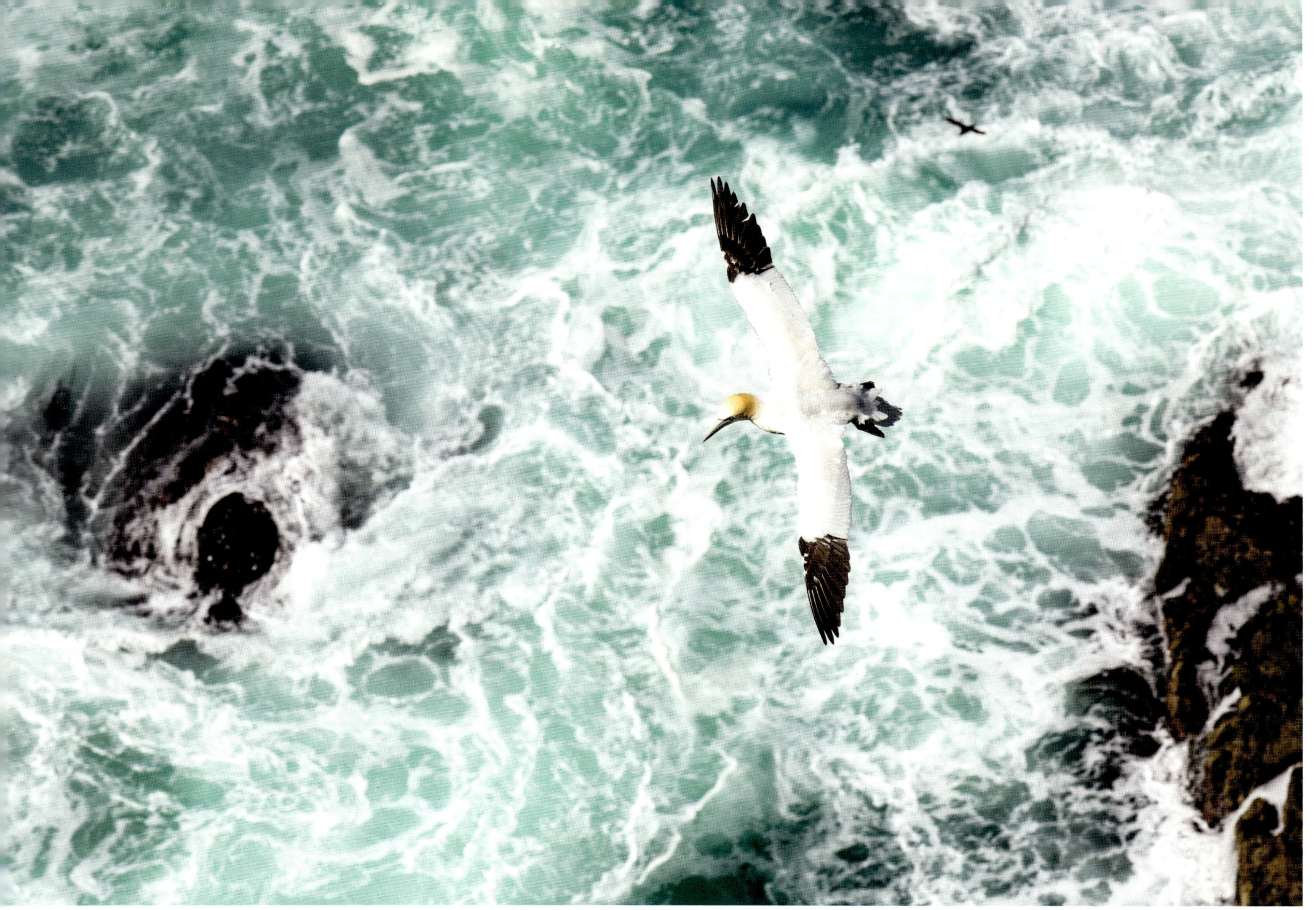

The Kraken Wakes
Coast & Marine

David Pressland
Northern gannet (*Morus bassanus*)
Hermaness NNR, Unst, Shetland, Scotland

Nikon D850 with Nikon 300mm f/4 lens.
300mm; 1/1,250th second; f/11; ISO 200.

Gannets are my absolute favourite birds and I never tire of photographing them. This one is soaring over the turbulent seas crashing on the rocks below at Hermaness, Shetland. The rock poking out of the water on the left looks to me like the eye of a huge sea monster – the Leviathan, or the Kraken in the John Wyndham novel.

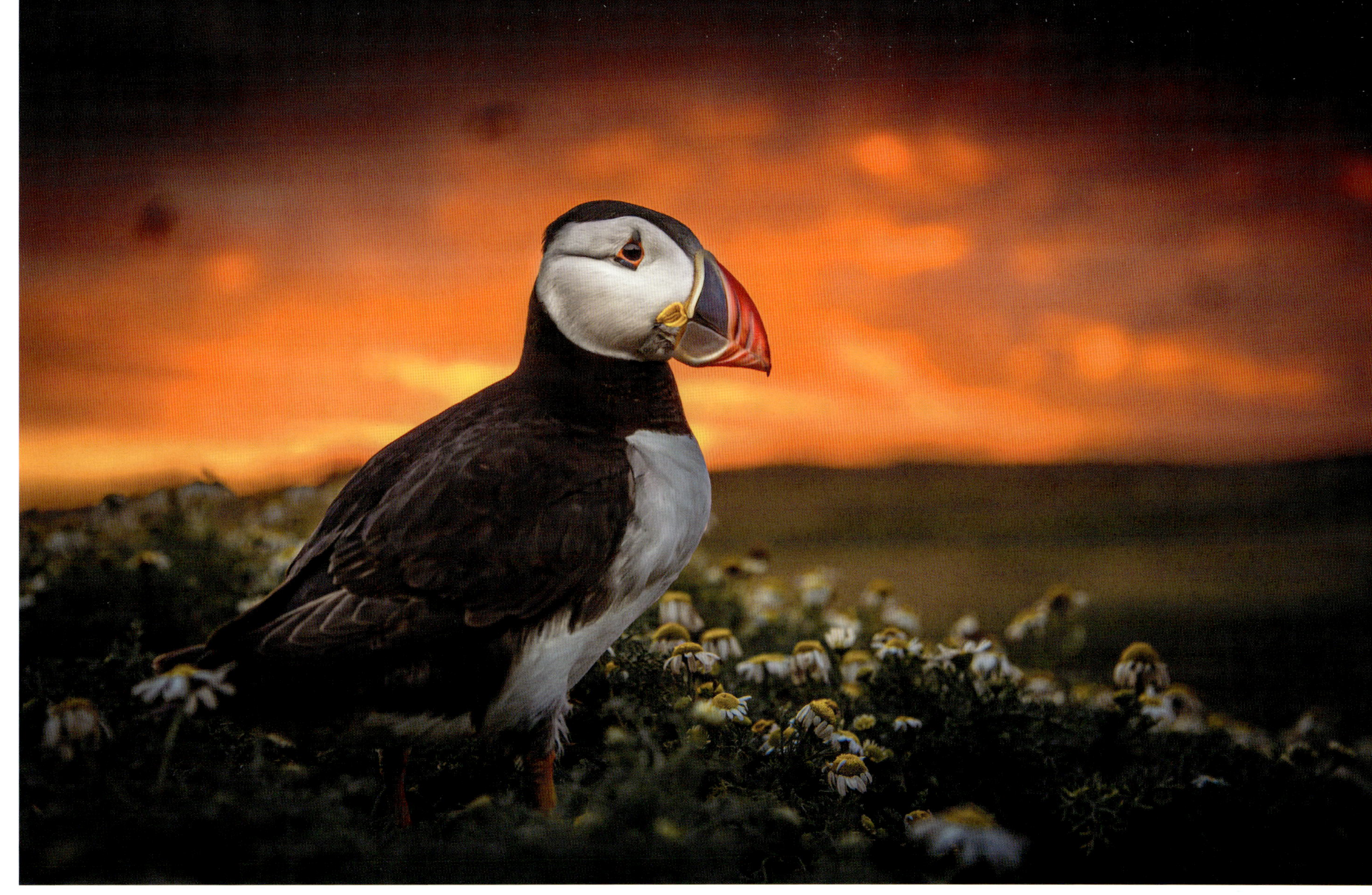

Night Watchman
Habitat

Philip Selby
Atlantic puffin (*Fratercula arctica*)
Skomer Island, Pembrokeshire, Wales

Canon 5D III with Canon 24-105mm f/4 lens.
58mm; 1/640th second; f/4; ISO 1,000.

Travelling with friends to the wonderful island of Skomer, off the Pembrokeshire coast, is an annual highlight, with multiple photographic opportunities and challenges abound. Staying overnight on the island brings the obvious opportunity to photograph at sunset. On this particular evening, we were blessed with the fiery sunset we all had hoped for. With the sun setting behind the cliff, I positioned myself with a shorter focal length lens to capture the puffin in the natural environment set against the last embers of colour in the sky.

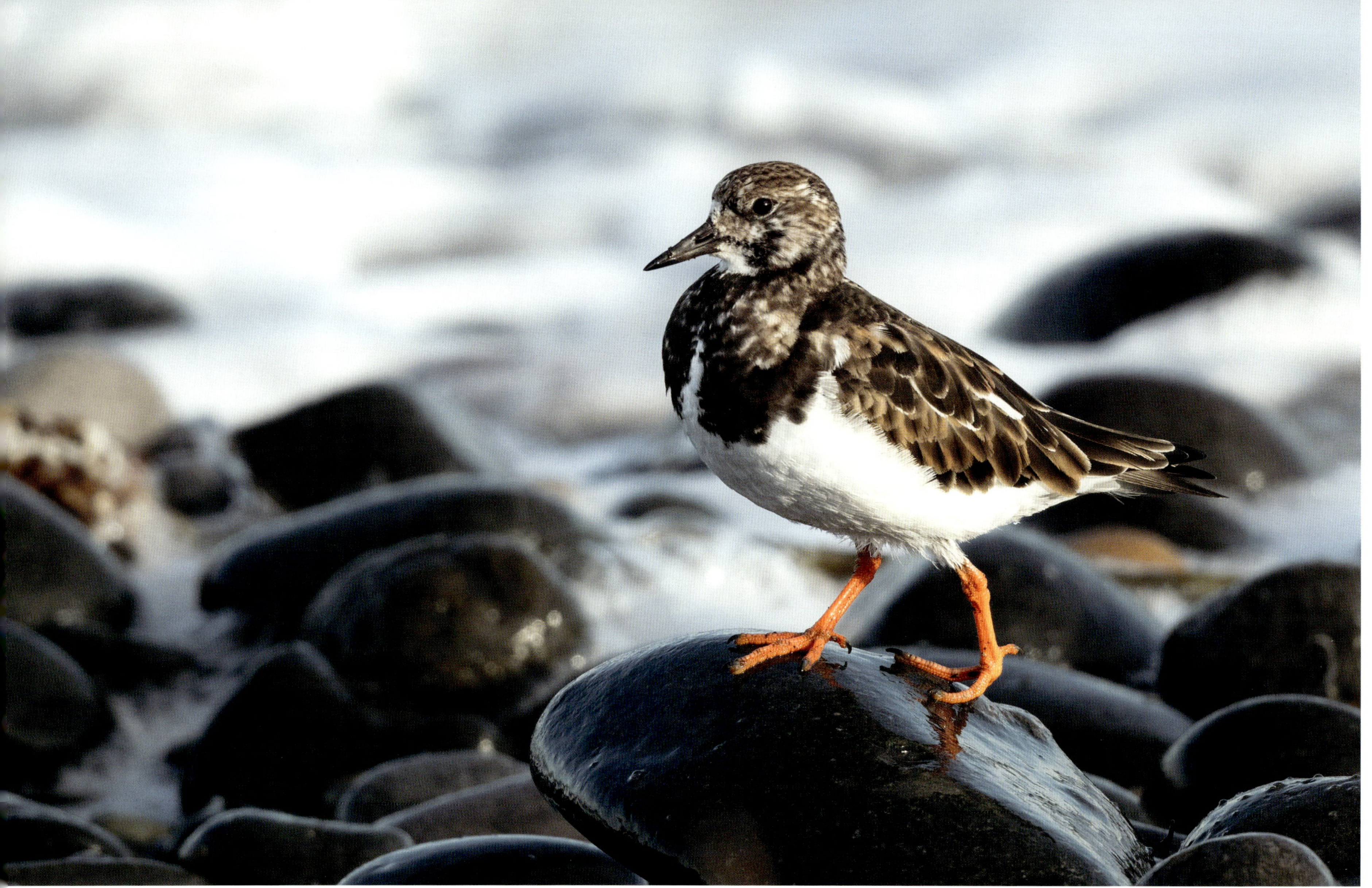

Winter Turnstone
Animal Portraits

Sarah Hanson
Ruddy turnstone (*Arenaria interpres*)
Northumberland, England

Nikon D500 with Nikon 500mm f/5.6 lens.
500mm; 1/1,250th second; f/5.6; ISO 450.

Coastal waders were the highlight of a winter trip to Northumberland. A mixed flock was having a last feed as sunset approached. I was able to get low on the shore to photograph them at the water's edge. This turnstone was very cooperative and showed perfect poise as it moved across the rocks.

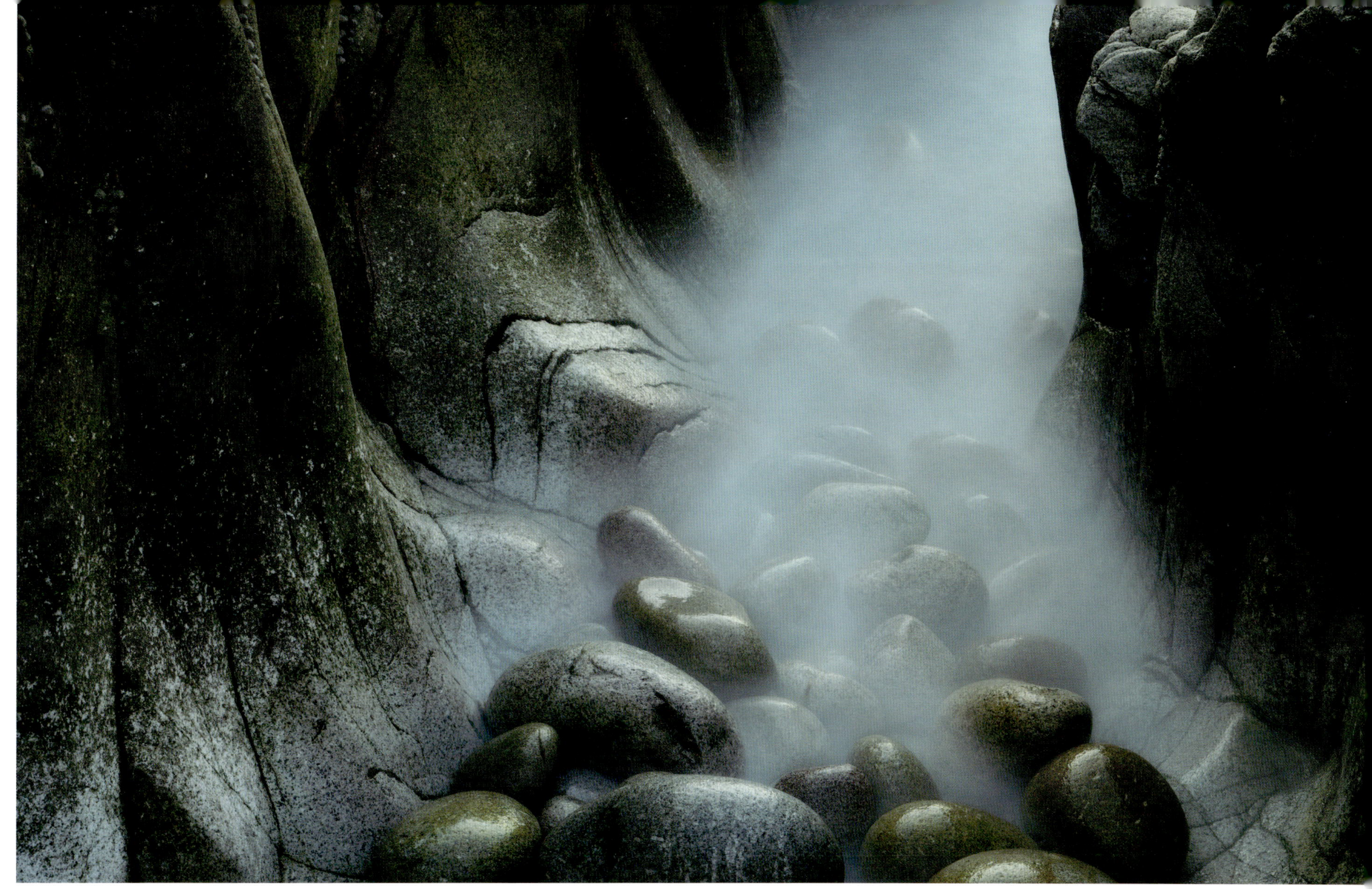

Time and Tide
Coast & Marine | Highly Commended

Jeremy Walker
Cornwall, England

Leica M10-R with Leica 50mm f/2 Summicron-M lens. 50mm; 42 seconds; f/4; ISO 100.

I was drawn to this location by the beautiful sculptural shapes and flowing forms in the rocks and boulders, but I couldn't find an image that pleased me until the tide started to rush into this small canyon. I only had the time to shoot a handful of exposures, each one lasting about 40 seconds, before the waves lapped at my feet and it was time to pack up and make a safe retreat.

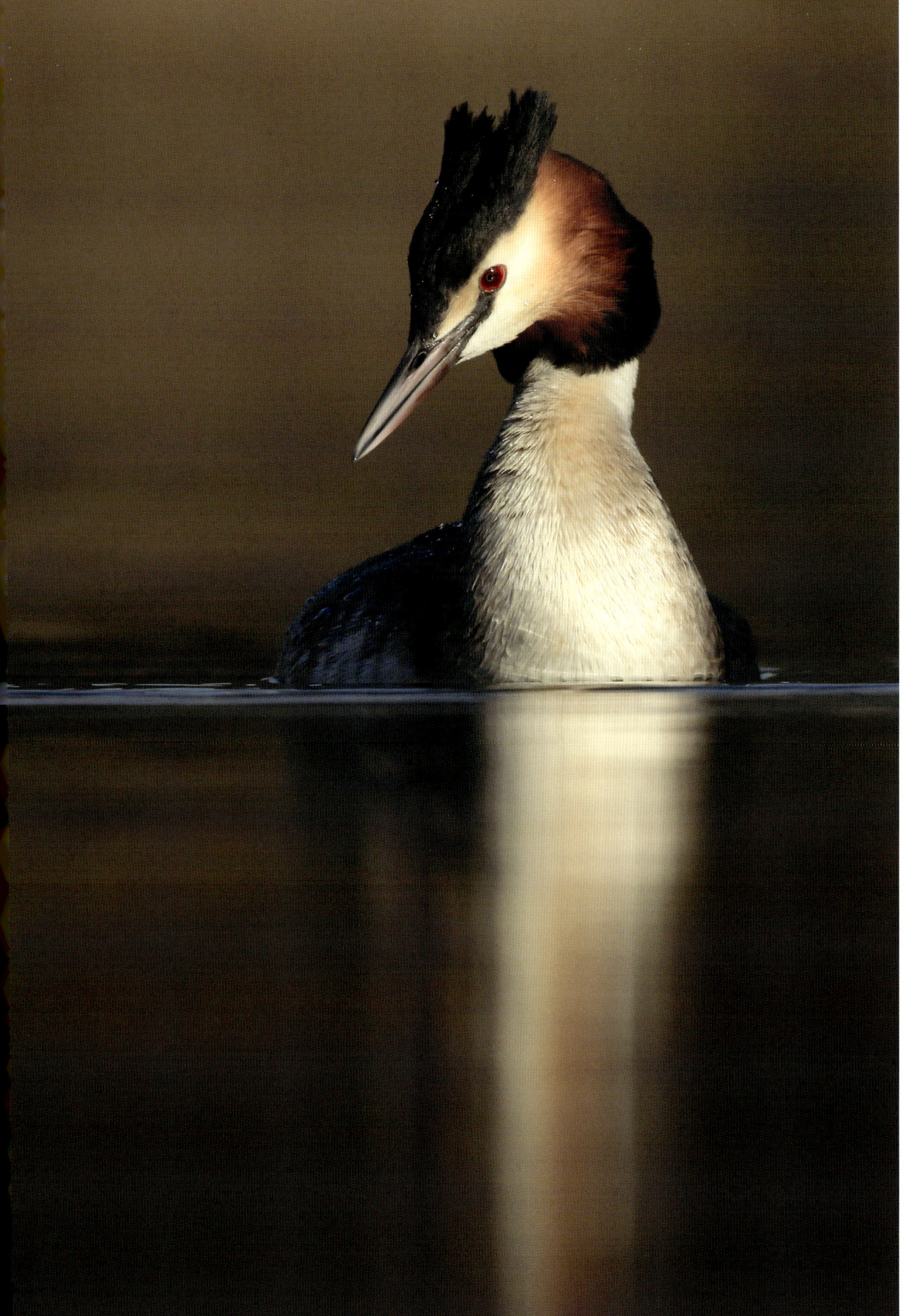

Reflective Grebe
Animal Portraits

Chris Hawes
Great crested grebe (*Podiceps cristatus*)
Cardiff, Wales

Canon 7D II with Canon 300mm f/2.8
II lens & 2x teleconverter. 600mm;
1/1,600th second; f/8; ISO 400.

Over several years, I observed the antics
of a population of great crested grebes
on this lake, and over time I believe
they became familiar with the strange
object with a camera lying on the shore.
At times, they would come very close,
allowing me to capture some intimate
portraits. I always felt very privileged
that they allowed me into their world,
becoming perfectly relaxed in my
presence just a few metres away. They
are stunningly beautiful birds with a
complex and elaborate set of courtship
behaviours. I hope that I have done
justice to them in some of my photos.

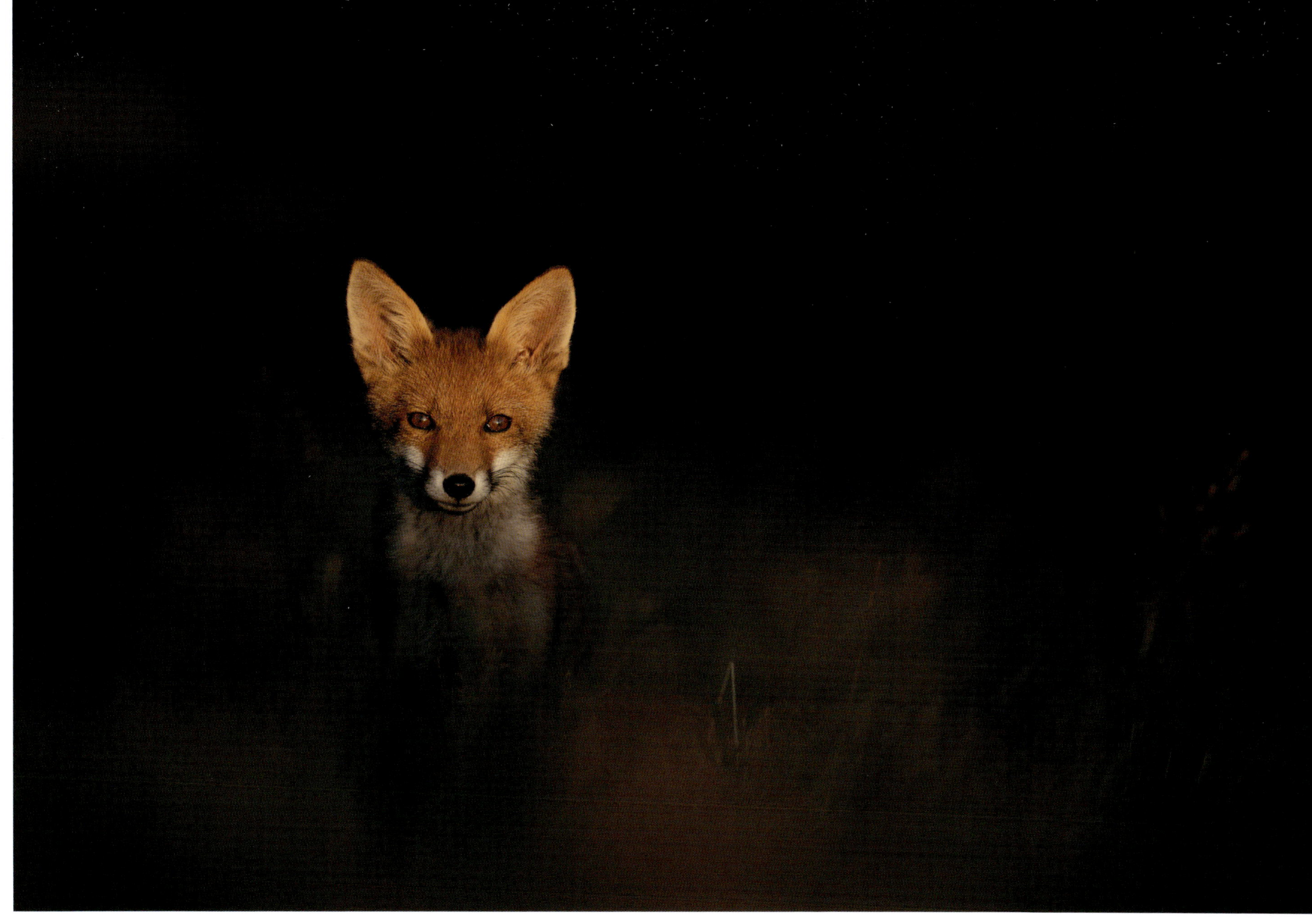

Last Light
Animal Portraits | Highly Commended

Andy Parkinson
Red fox (*Vulpes vulpes*)
Derbyshire, England

Nikon Z 9 with Nikon 600mm f/4 lens.
600mm; 1/1,250th second; f/4; ISO 400.

For many years, I have known that foxes den in this hidden corner of a quiet field. In 2022, the vixen had seven cubs, and for the first time I had the advantage of a silent, mirrorless shutter. At last, I could remain utterly silent, an unseen observer watching their everyday comings and goings. On this evening, this curious cub decided to venture a little closer to my hide, emerging into late evening sunlight as he did so.

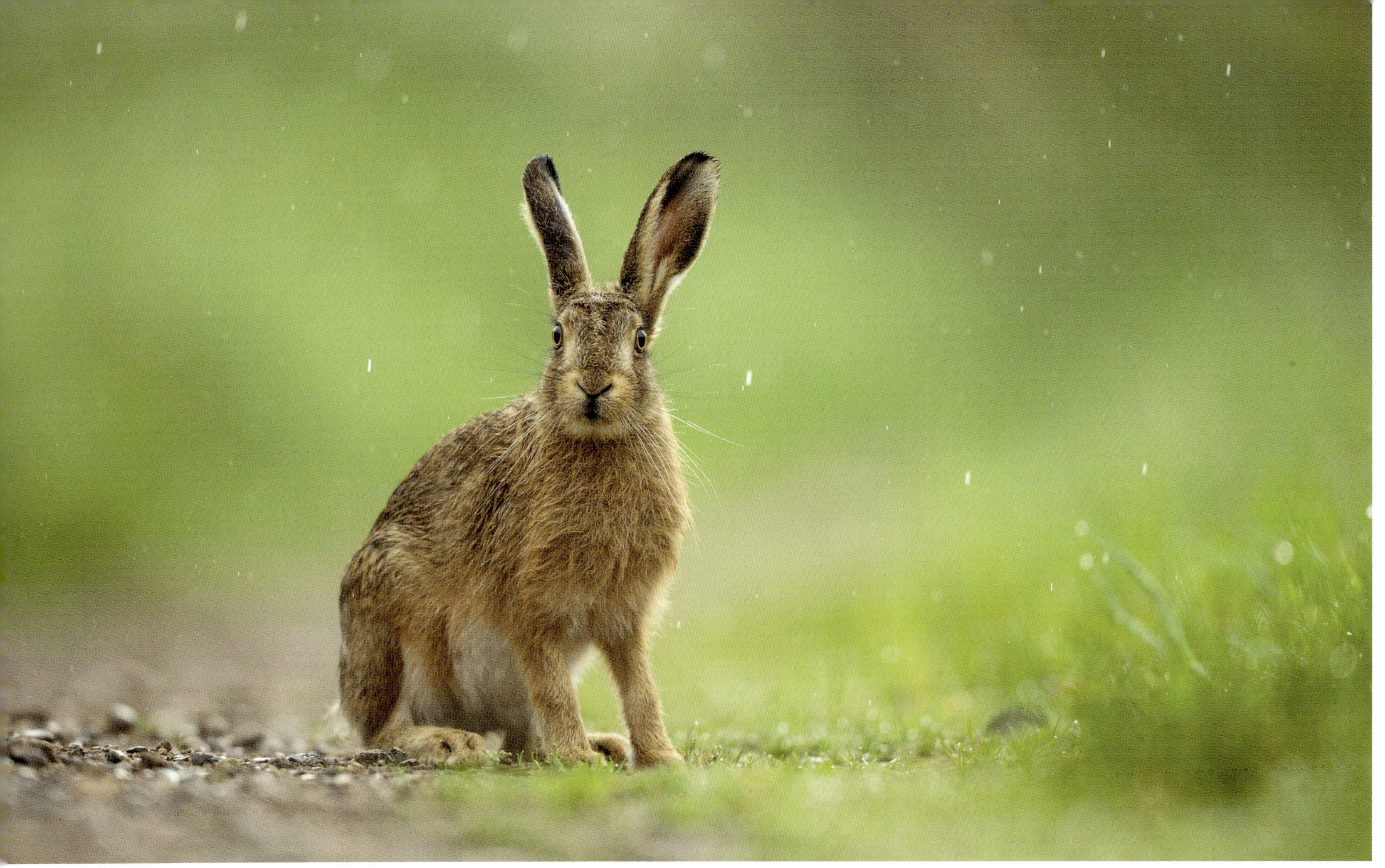

Hare in the Rain
Animal Portraits

Alastair Marsh
Brown hare (*Lepus europaeus*)
North Yorkshire, England

Canon EOS R3 with Canon 500mm f/4 lens.
500mm; 1/1,000th second; f/4; ISO 1,000.

I started photographing brown hares in 2019 after finding a small population not far from home in North Yorkshire. This developed into a bit of a project where I focus on watching and photographing them from late winter and into spring/early summer. I consider myself very lucky to have a healthy population within walking distance from home. I spend as much time as possible lying in wait on well-used 'runs' the hares use between fields at sunrise and sunset, trying my best to blend into the surroundings so as not to disturb these awesome animals.

Just a Nibble
Animal Portraits

Chris Hawes
Brown hare (*Lepus europaeus*)
Dumfries and Galloway, Scotland

Canon 1D X II with Canon 300mm f/2.8 II lens
& 1.4x teleconverter. 420mm; 1/800th second;
f/4; ISO 800.

I was photographing badgers at this location late
one evening in mid-summer. During a period of
waiting for the badgers to emerge from their sett, a
movement off to my right caught my attention, and
I spotted this brown hare making its way towards me
in the next field. I carefully shifted my position to give
myself a view through the fencing, and was delighted
when the hare stopped and began feeding on the
grass heads a short distance away. Although the
badgers later put in an appearance, this ended
up being my favourite photo of the session!

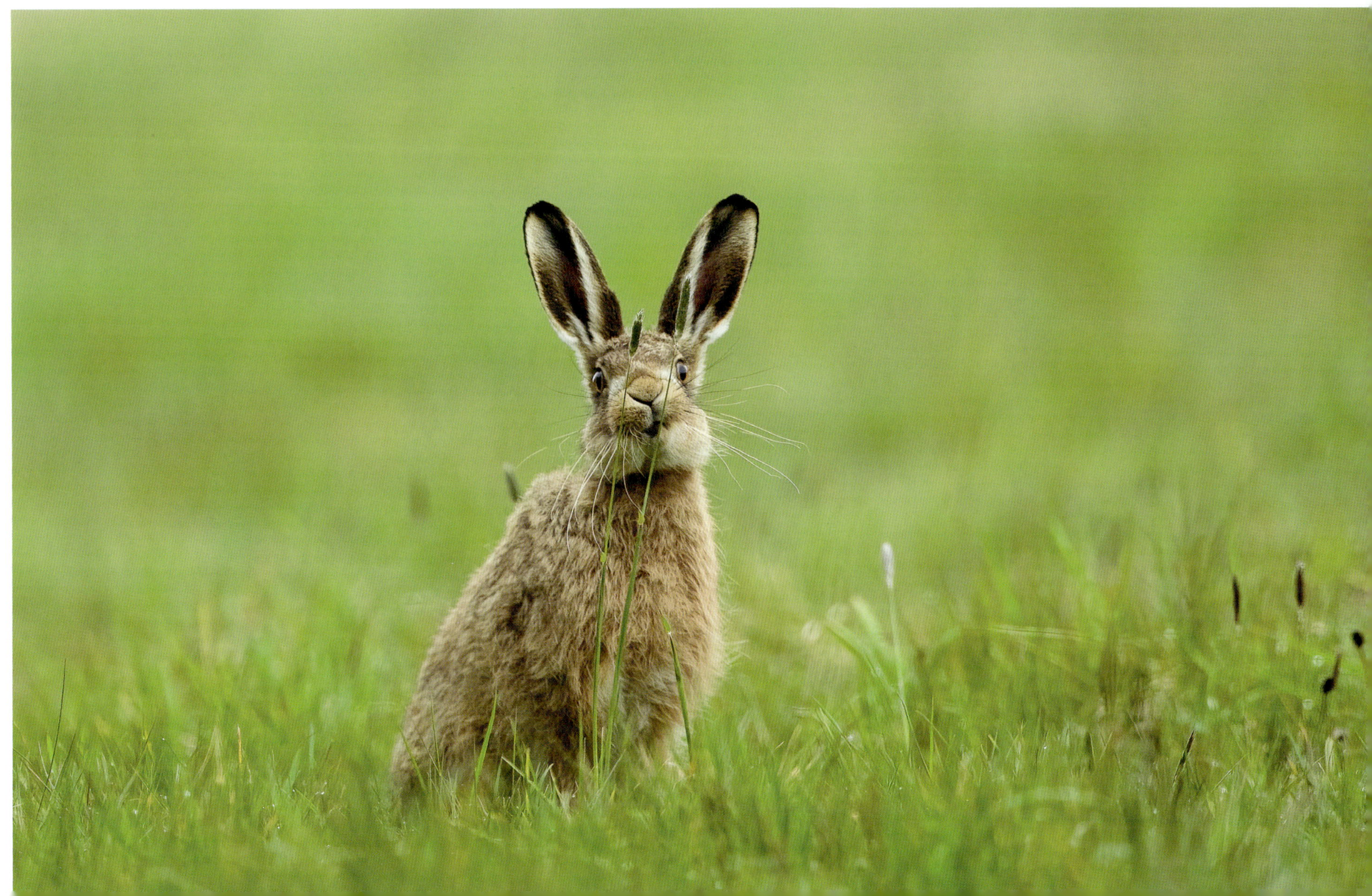

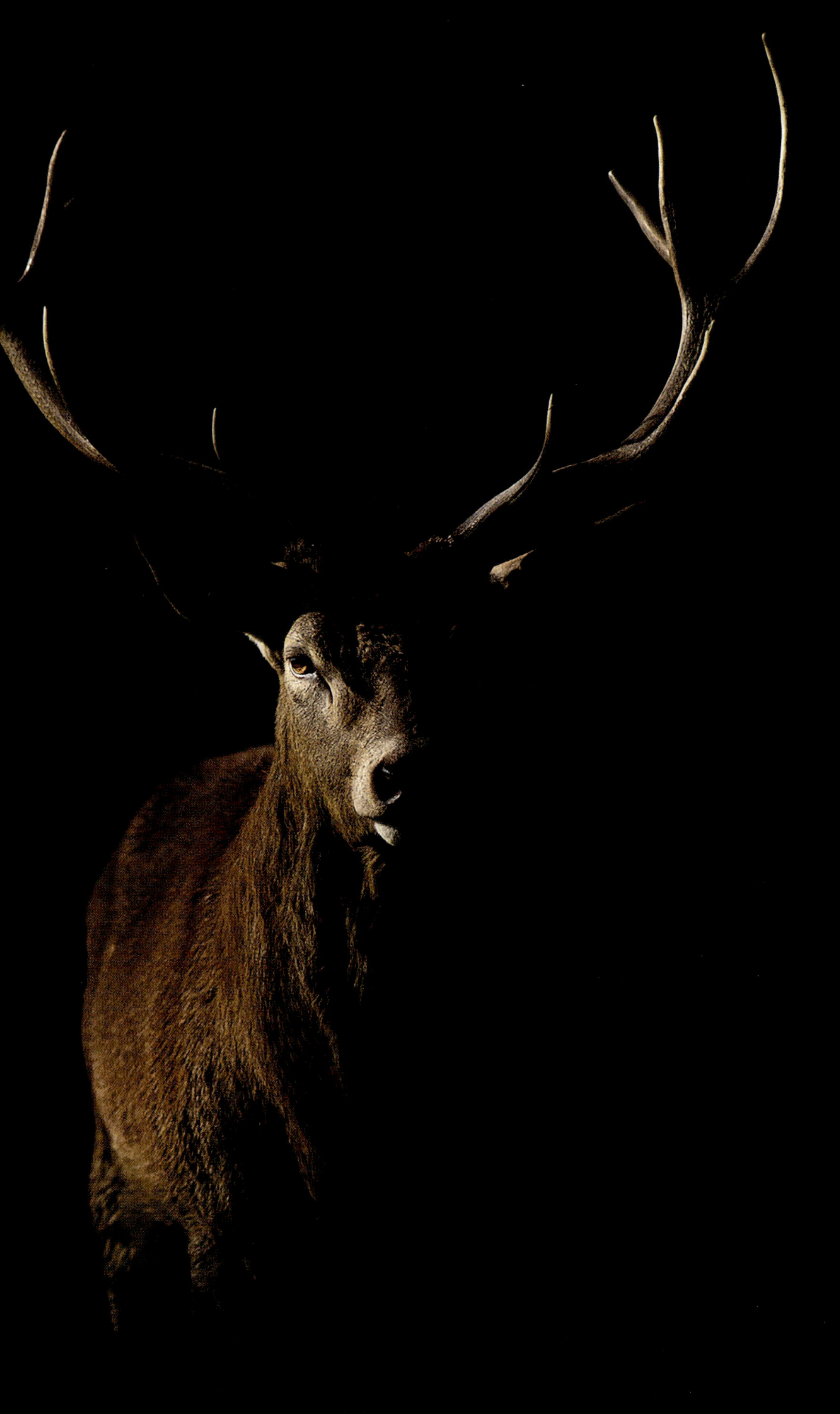

Majesty
Animal Portraits

Lawrie Brailey
Red deer (*Cervus elaphus*)
Richmond Park, London, England

Nikon D4 with Nikon 300mm f/2.8 lens & 1.4x teleconverter. 420mm; 1/8,000th second; f/4; ISO 200.

A red deer stag has got to be one of the most majestic things that UK wildlife has to offer. This one had just emerged victorious after a battle with another male, and as he turned to watch the challenger escape, he stepped right into a single shaft of midday light that had filtered between the trees to the left. By underexposing the image in-camera to only expose for the lit areas, the dark trees behind fell away to black, with the result almost looking like a studio-lit shot!

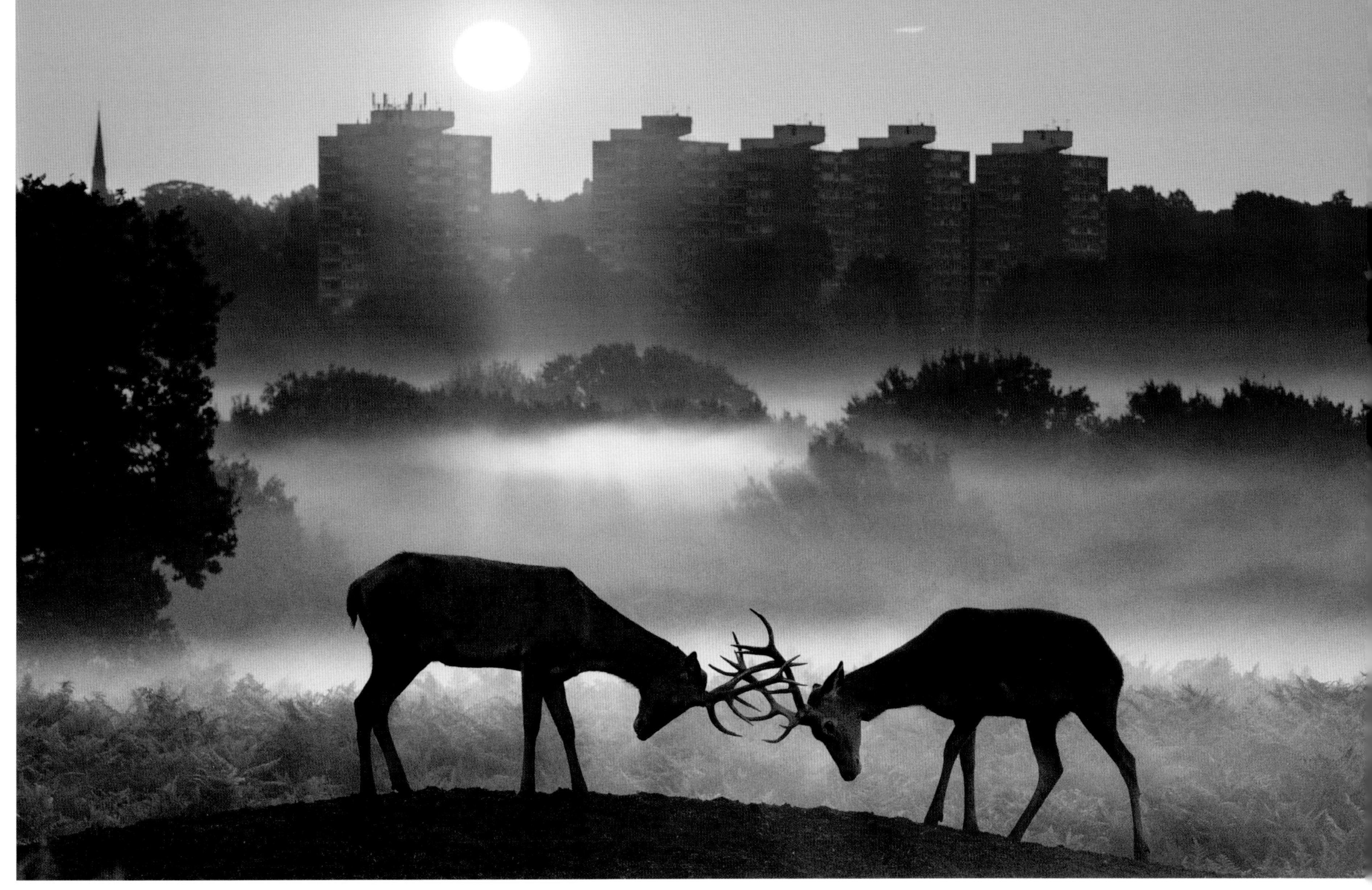

Urban Arena
Urban Wildlife

Daniel Langer
Red deer (*Cervus elaphus*)
Richmond Park, London, England

Fujifilm X-T2 with Fujifilm 100-400mm f/4.5-5.6 lens.
111mm; 1/1,000th second; f/8; ISO 2,000.

I noticed a small raised clearing in the bracken
with several juvenile red deer nearby, so I set up my
tripod facing the misty sunrise. It was very dark, and
I needed to increase the ISO significantly. The two
stags climbed onto the mound and locked antlers in a
training rut. I converted this blood-orange sunrise to
monochrome, as it creates an urban, gritty feel, like a
scene from a street fight, the deer entering the arena
under the spotlight of the sun, with the spectators
watching from the high-rises.

Hobby About to Strike a Mayfly
Animal Behaviour | Highly Commended

Richard Sheldrake
Eurasian hobby (*Falco subbuteo*)
Ripley, Surrey, England

Nikon D500 with Nikon 200-500mm f/5.6 lens.
410mm; 1/5,000th second; f/8; ISO 400.

This hobby was hunting mayflies voraciously for an hour, while I just stood, watched and photographed – quite an extraordinary experience. At one point along the River Wey, on one bank is the butterfly meadow, where the mayflies hatch, and on the other are some substantial oak trees which provided resting places for the hobby. It's a glorious hunt to watch, with the hobby climbing high, looping around, setting its sights on prey and swooping to grab the mayfly in its talons. The bird then eases up, pulls the wings off and eats the mayfly before climbing again to repeat the process.

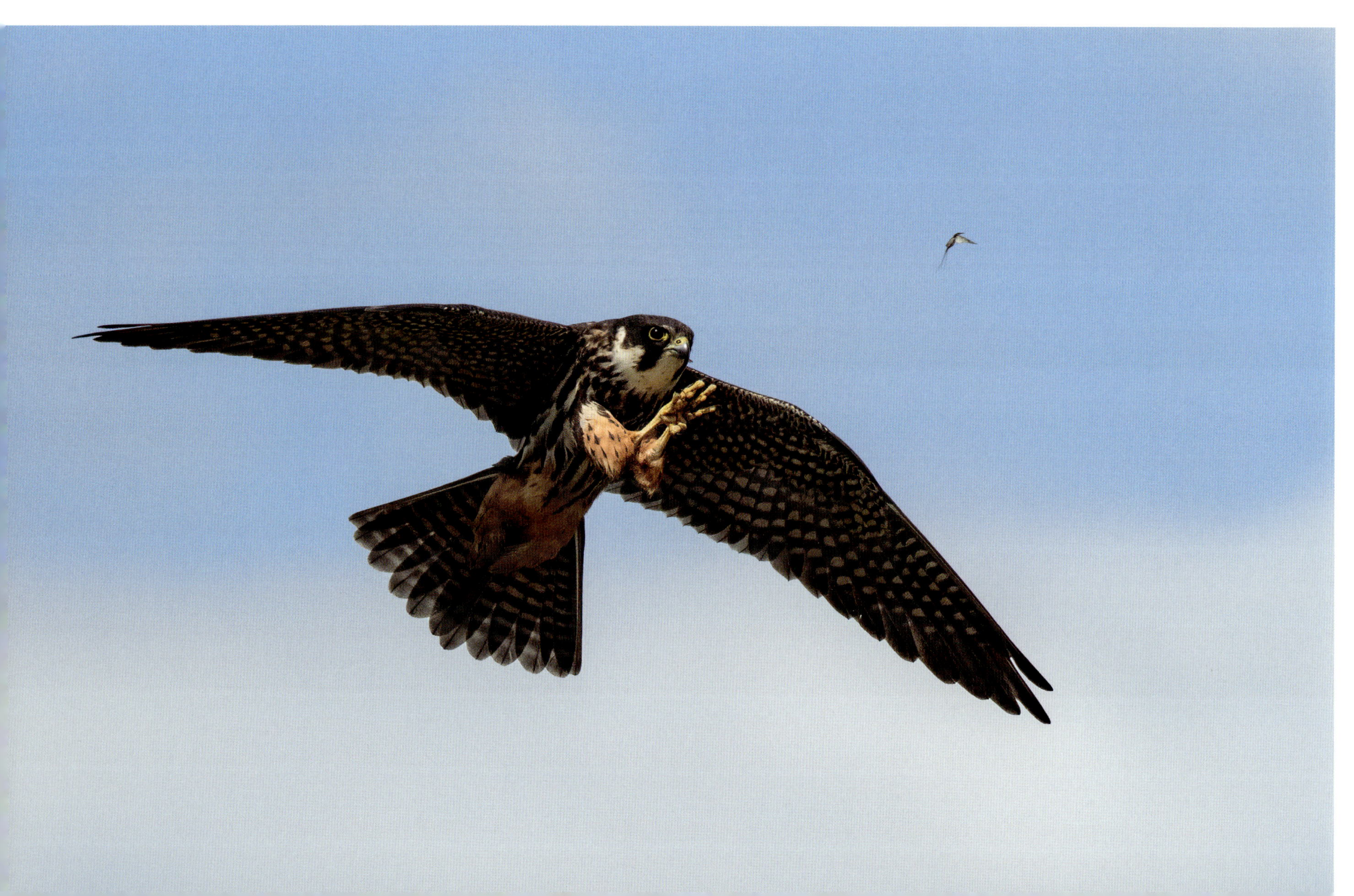

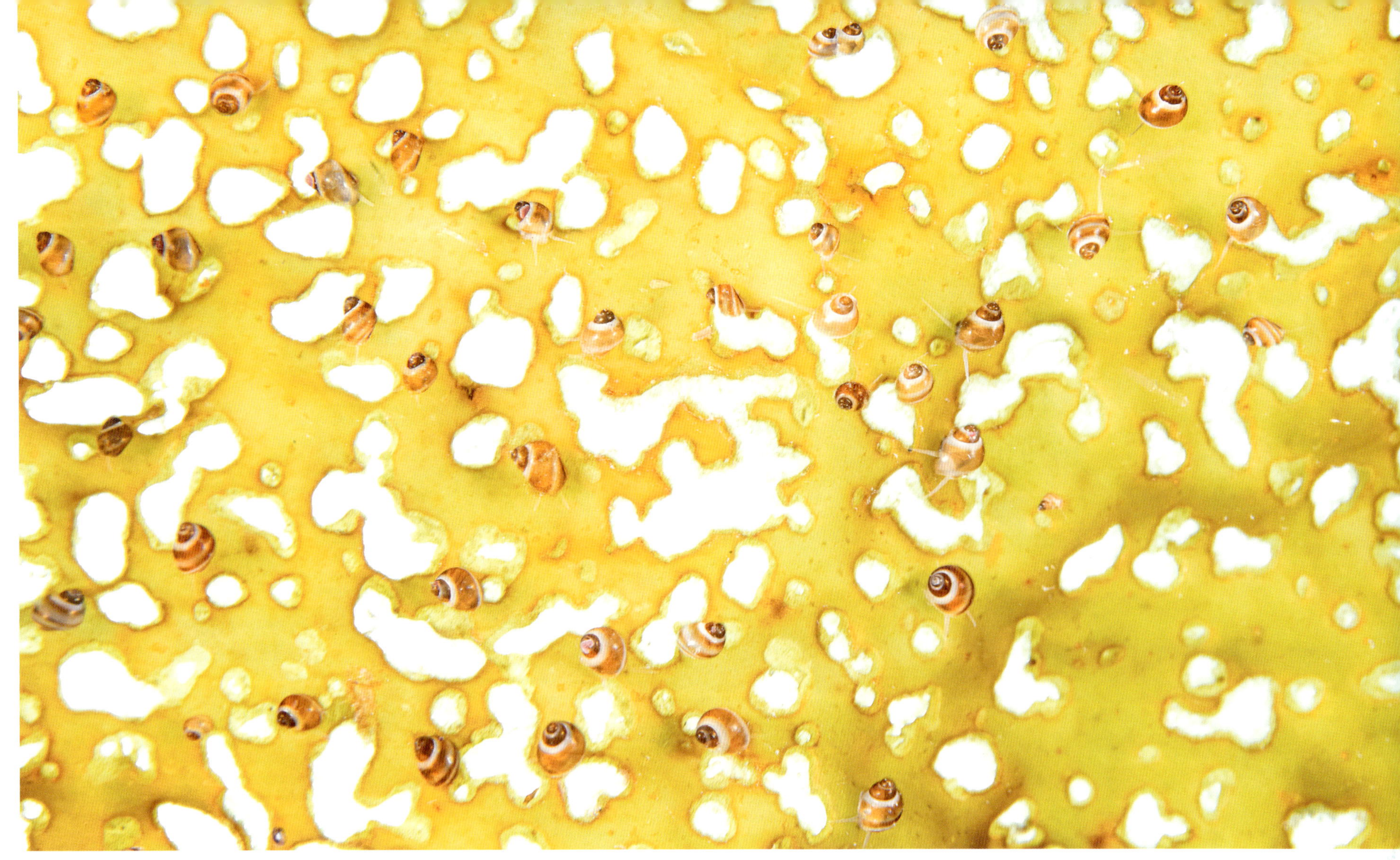

The Art of Eating
Coast & Marine

Henley Spiers
Sea snail (*Cingula trifasciata*)
Shetland, Scotland

Nikon D850 with Nikon 60mm f/2.8 lens. 60mm;
1/100th second; f/16; ISO 1,000.

Minute (4mm) sea snails create artful openings as
they feed on the underside of a kelp leaf. As it grows,
the kelp offers shelter, and as it decays, its seasonal
demise offers food to an array of animals.

During a dive in Shetland, at the northernmost tip
of Britain, I was captivated by the patterns created
by these snails and other creatures. This particular
arrangement seemed especially tastefully composed,
an easily overlooked example of the art of eating.
By overexposing and photographing straight up
towards the sky, each gap in the leaf is highlighted
in white, adding to the effect. The only challenge
with my creative strategy was that it required
a camera angle that could only be achieved by
shooting blindly. Holding my rig under the leaf and
hoping for the best, I would shoot, review and then
repeat, eventually settling on this frame as the most
satisfying.

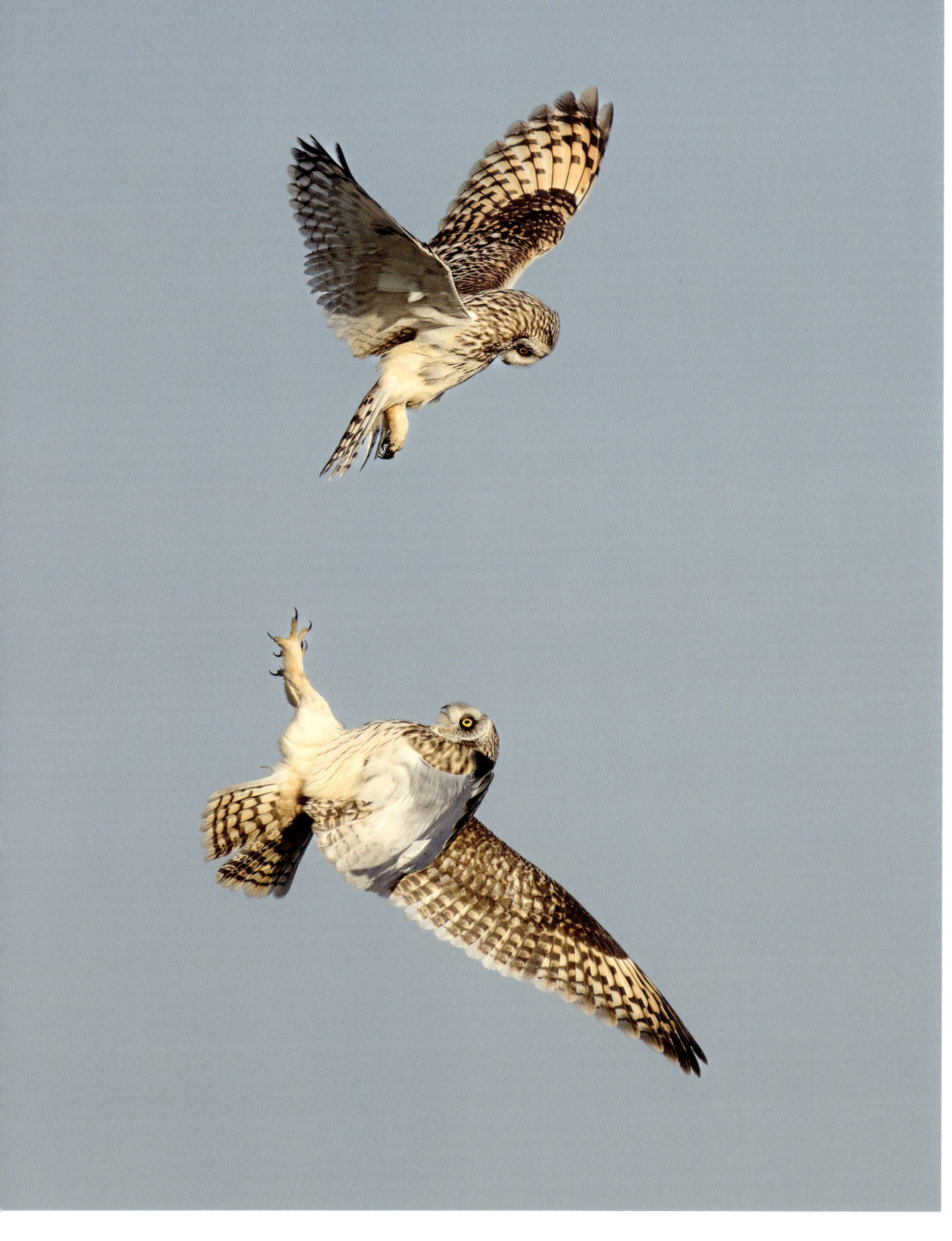

Incoming
Animal Behaviour

Sue Morris
Short-eared owl (*Asio flammeus*)
Farlington Marshes, Hampshire,
England

Canon EOS R5 with Canon
600mm f/4 III lens & 1.4x
teleconverter. 840mm; 1/2,500th
second; f/7.1; ISO 320.

After not seeing any short-eared
owls at my usual spots, I took a
chance very late in the season
to visit an area where they had
been seen. After a very long
wait, not knowing if they had
already moved on, two owls
lifted up from their roosting place
and performed a short aerial
display right in front of me in
the perfect evening light. As my
heart slowed back down, I hoped
that I had been able to capture
such an amazing sight and was
so thankful that I had made the
journey.

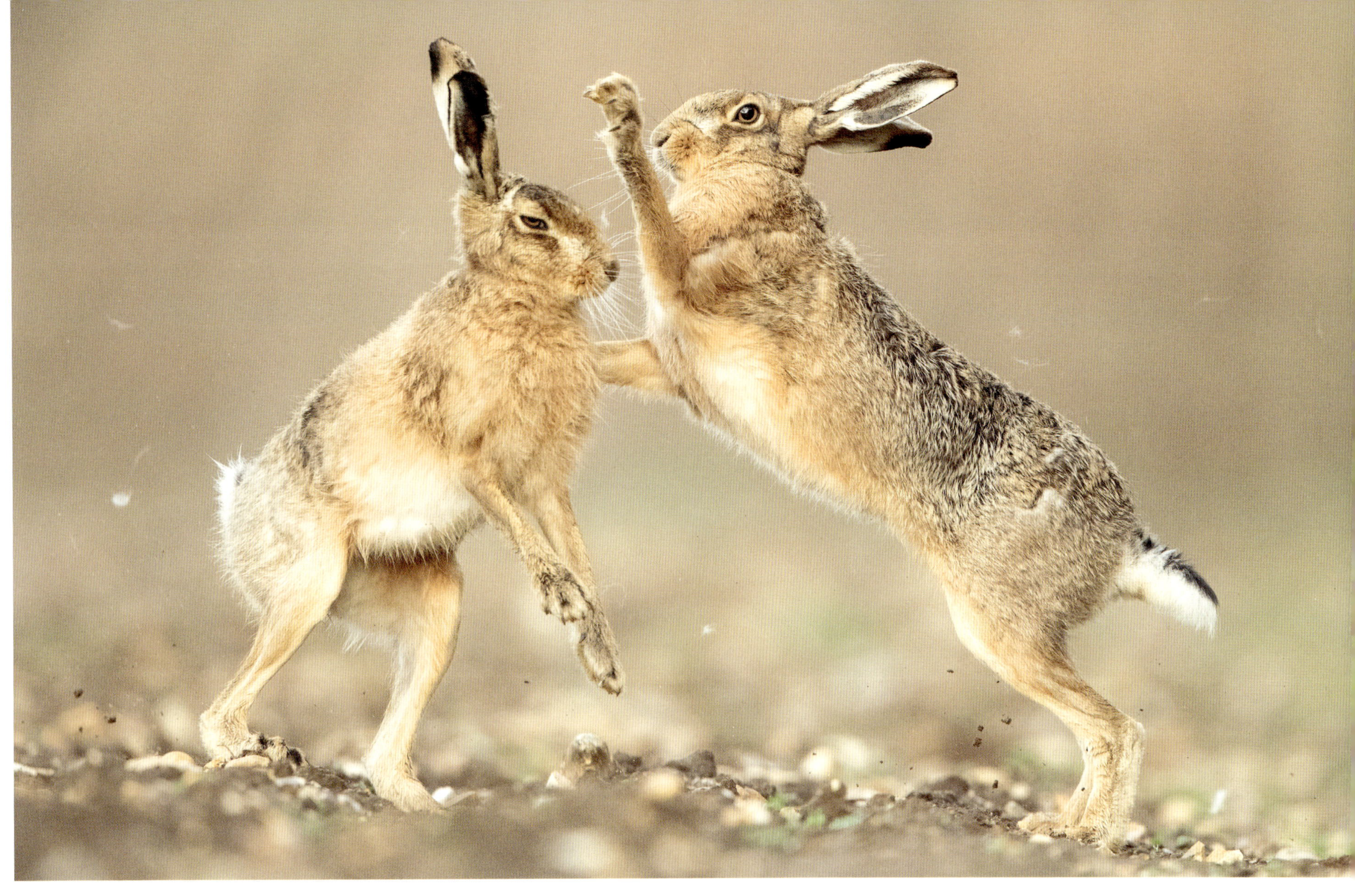

Boxing Clever
Animal Behaviour

Sarah Darnell
Brown hare (*Lepus europaeus*)
Norfolk, England

Canon EOS 1D X II with Canon 600mm f/4 II lens
& 1.4x teleconverter. 840mm; 1/3,200th second;
f/5.6; ISO 12,800.

Being in the right place at the right time to
photograph boxing hares has been a long-term
project. Usually, they pick the middle of the field, way
out of range, but this time they actually performed
right in front of me, catching me completely off
guard, and often too close for comfort. As their claws
made fur fly, grunts were audible, and the physical
effort involved left me even more appreciative of the
'survival of the fittest' instinct.

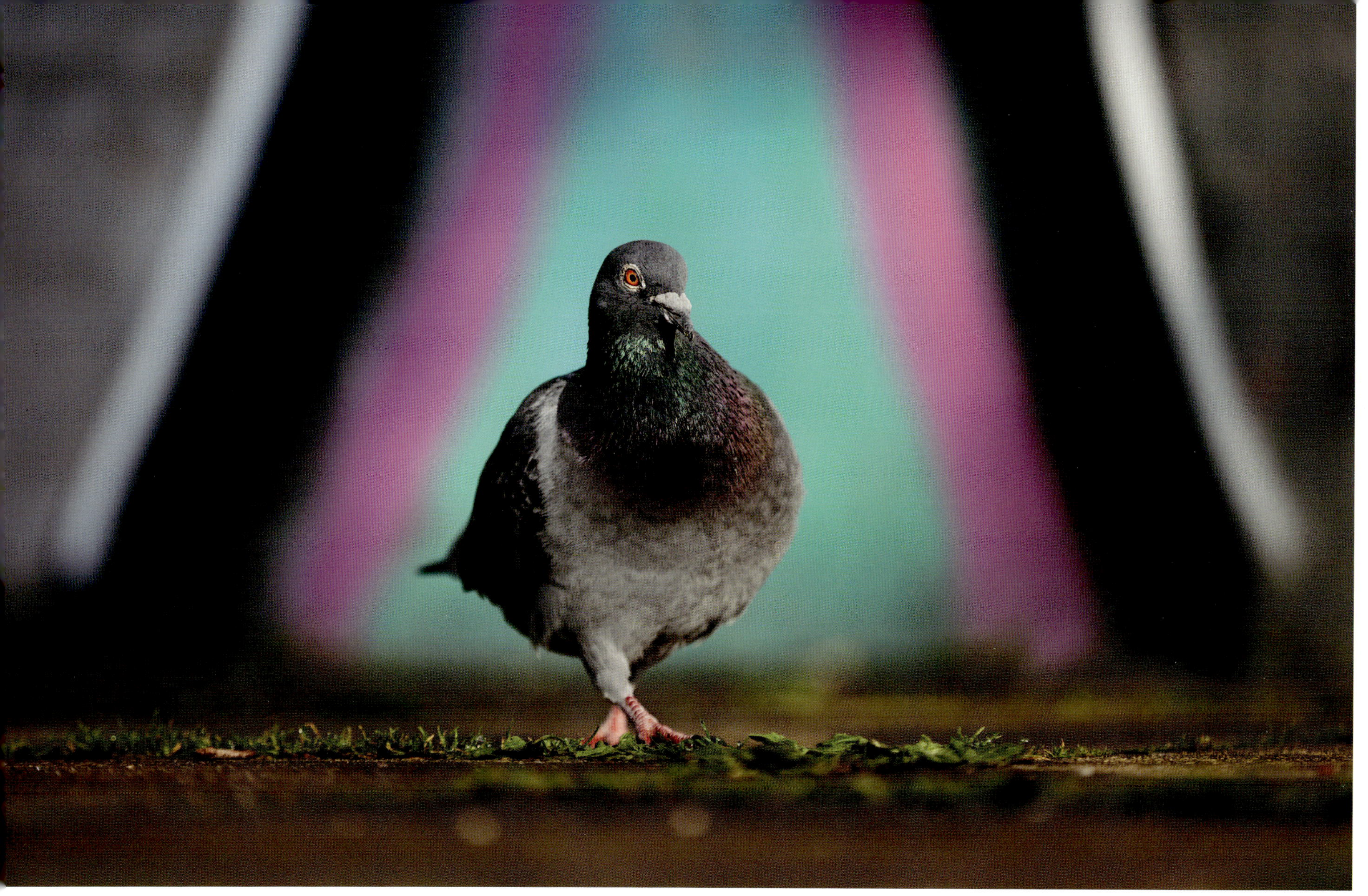

Strutting His Stuff
Urban Wildlife | Highly Commended

Simon Withyman
Rock dove (*Columba livia*)
Bristol, England

Canon EOS R5 with Canon 70-200mm f/2.8 II lens.
200mm; 1/3,200th second; f/2.8; ISO 160.

While waiting for some foxes, which failed to
turn up, I noticed some pigeons in front of some
nearby graffiti. I instantly noticed how the colours
complemented the pigeon's chest plumage and got
into a low position on the floor to take a handful of
photos as one of them came into frame.

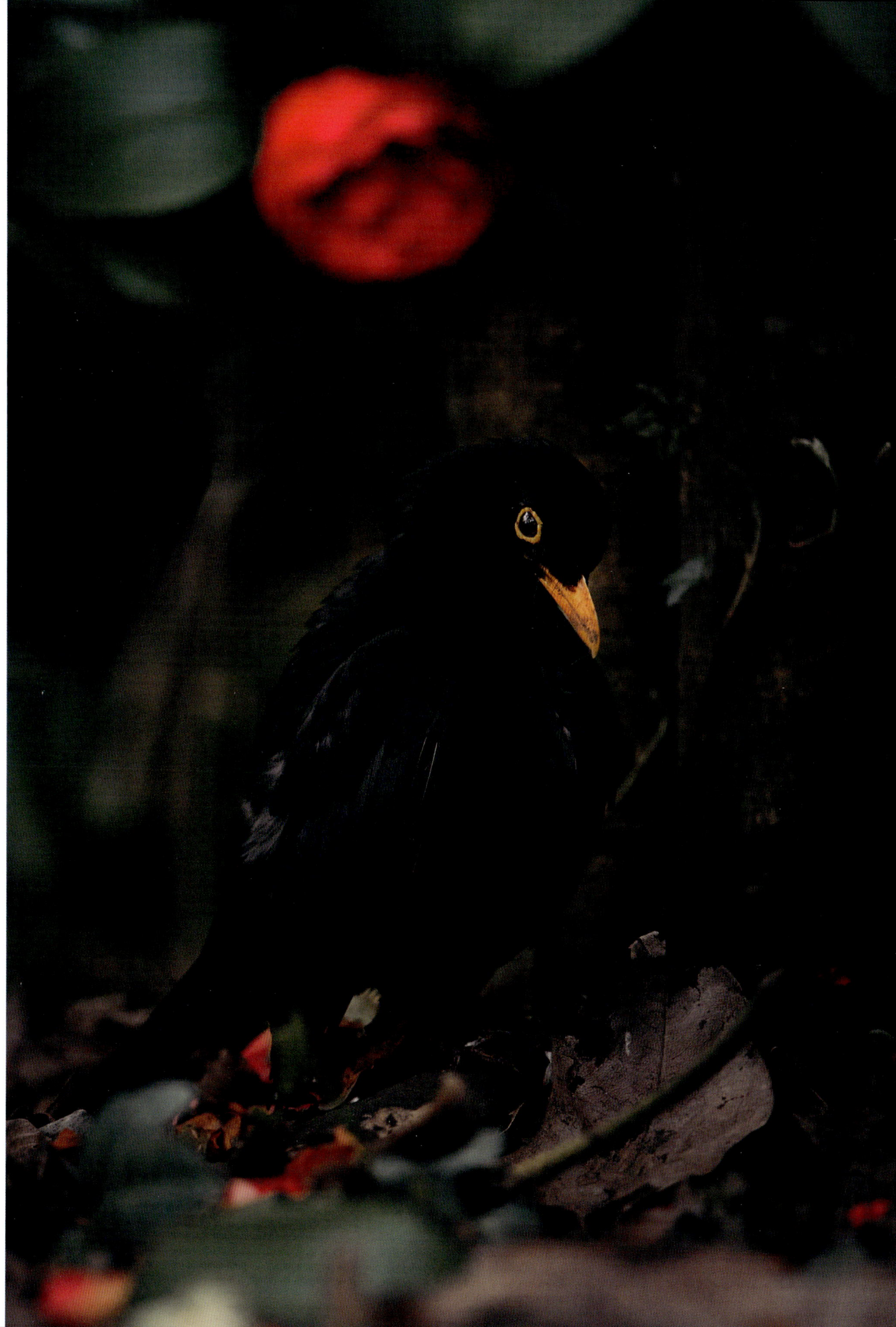

Regal
Animal Portraits

Alexander White
Blackbird (*Turdus merula*)
Cardiff, Wales

Nikon D7500 with Nikon 300mm f/4
lens. 300mm; 1/1250th second; f/4;
ISO 4000.

Cycling through my local park, I noticed
this blackbird rummaging through the
leaf litter of some camellia bushes.
I chose to sit with him for a while,
allowing him to become accustomed
to my presence. Over the course of
about an hour, I positioned myself so
that he was framed by the vivid red
of the flowering camellia. I lay in the
damp grass, and although I'd muddied
my clothes, I was rewarded with this
intimate portrait of a blackbird, striking
a majestic and regal pose.

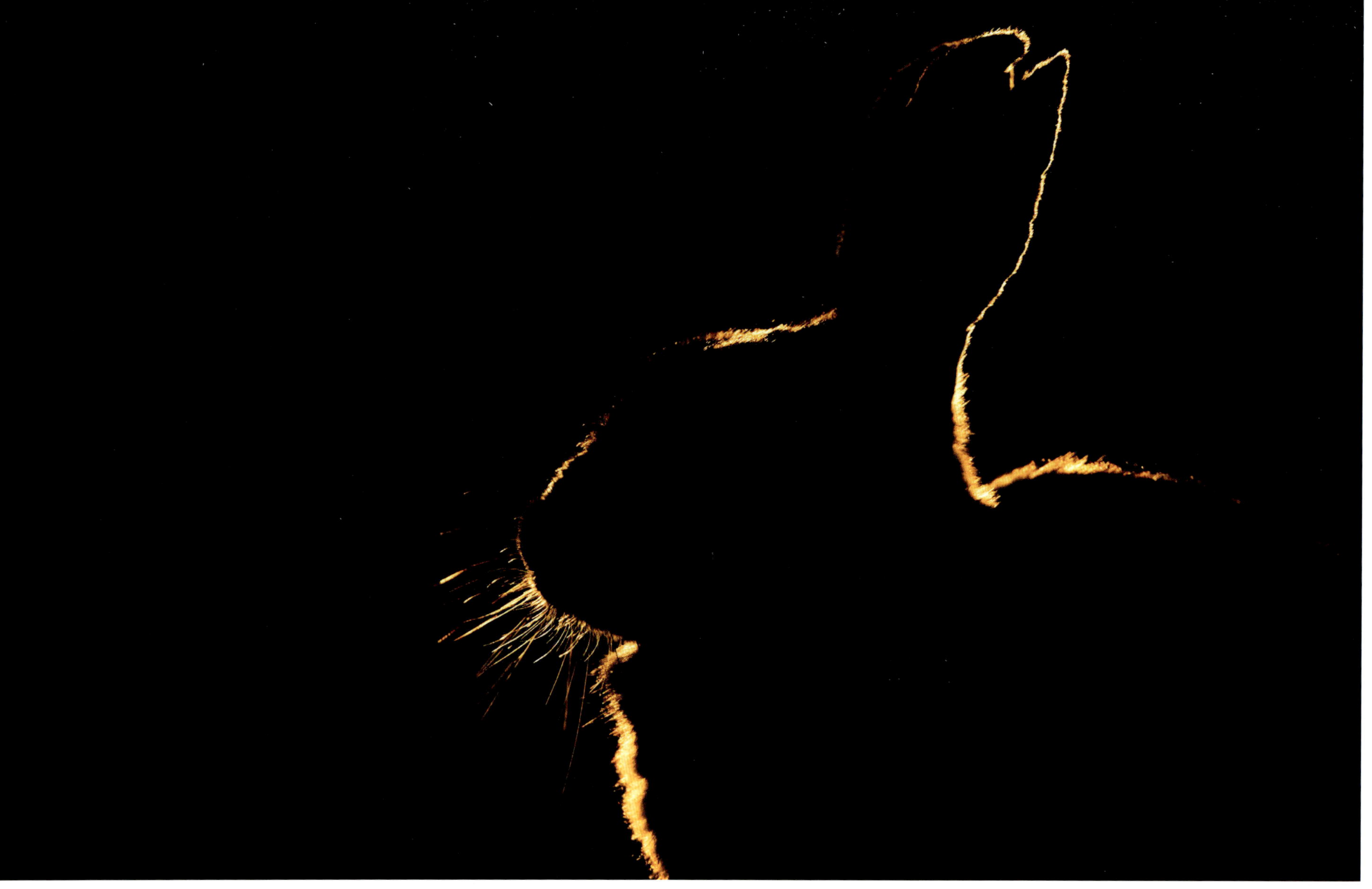

Backlit Bunny
Animal Portraits

Kevin Sawford
European rabbit (*Oryctolagus cuniculus*)
Suffolk, England

Canon EOS 1D X II with Canon 500mm f/4 lens
& 1.4x teleconverter. 700mm; 1/6,400th second;
f/5.6; ISO 400.

A rabbit enjoys the last rays of sunshine before the light fades for the evening. At this particular location, the rabbits can be tolerant of a close approach, so I was able to slowly get close enough to this individual to capture the rim lighting of the evening sun. By underexposing by a few stops, I could make the light stand out from the silhouette of the rabbit's head.

Badger in the Rain
Black & White

Jamie McDermaid

Badger (*Meles meles*)
Edinburgh, Scotland

Nikon D3100 with Nikon 18-55mm f/3.5-5.6 lens.
40mm; 1/200th second; f/10; ISO 400.

This image was obtained using a DSLR camera trap set up in my garden in Edinburgh during Lockdown 2020. This setup involved a DSLR, a flash and a PIR sensor, with a few peanuts used to tempt the badger into the right spot. After waiting a week or so for a night of heavy rain, a badger wandered in front of the setup. Eating some peanuts, it triggered the camera and the flash, lighting up the outline of the badger and the raindrops around it.

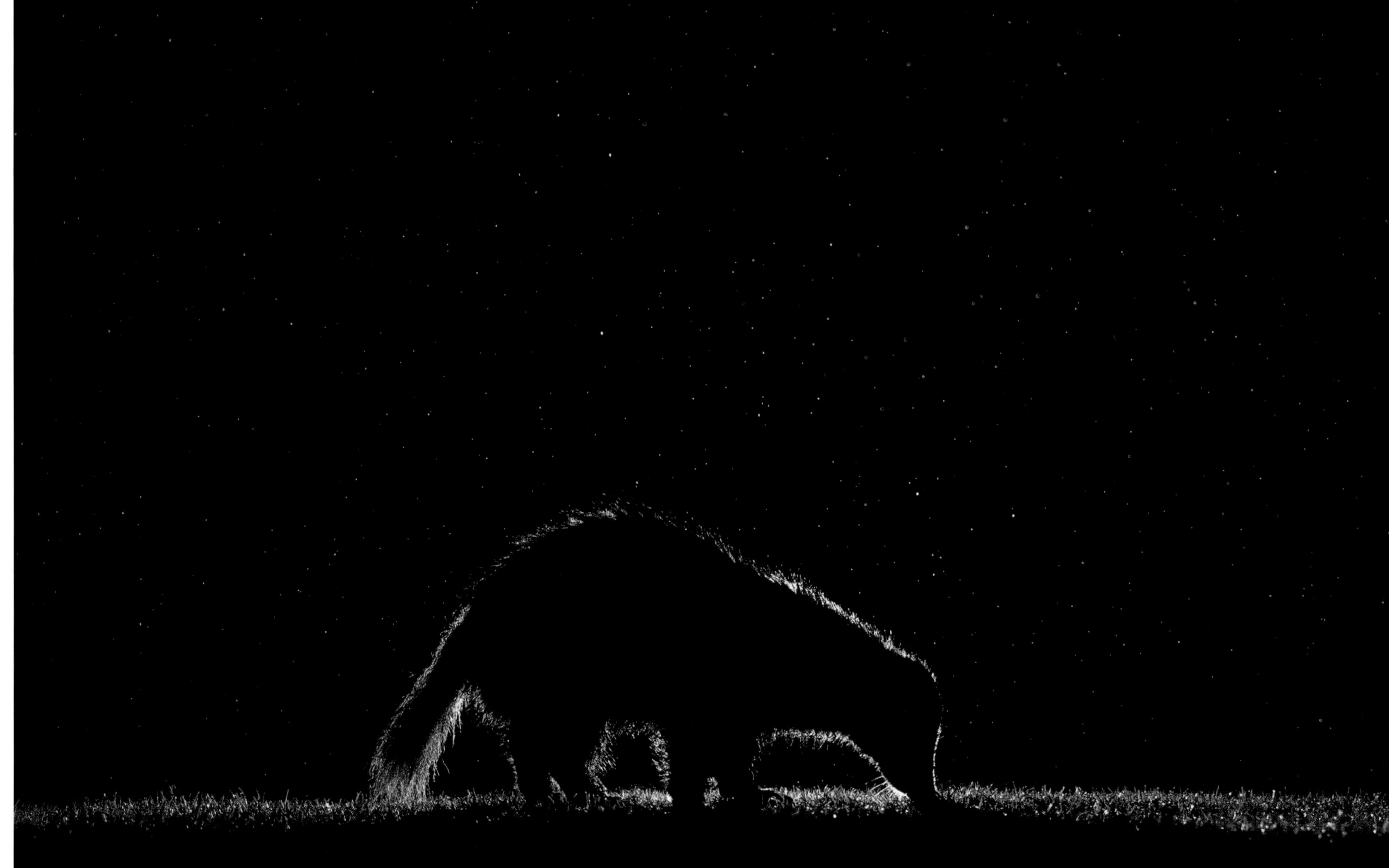

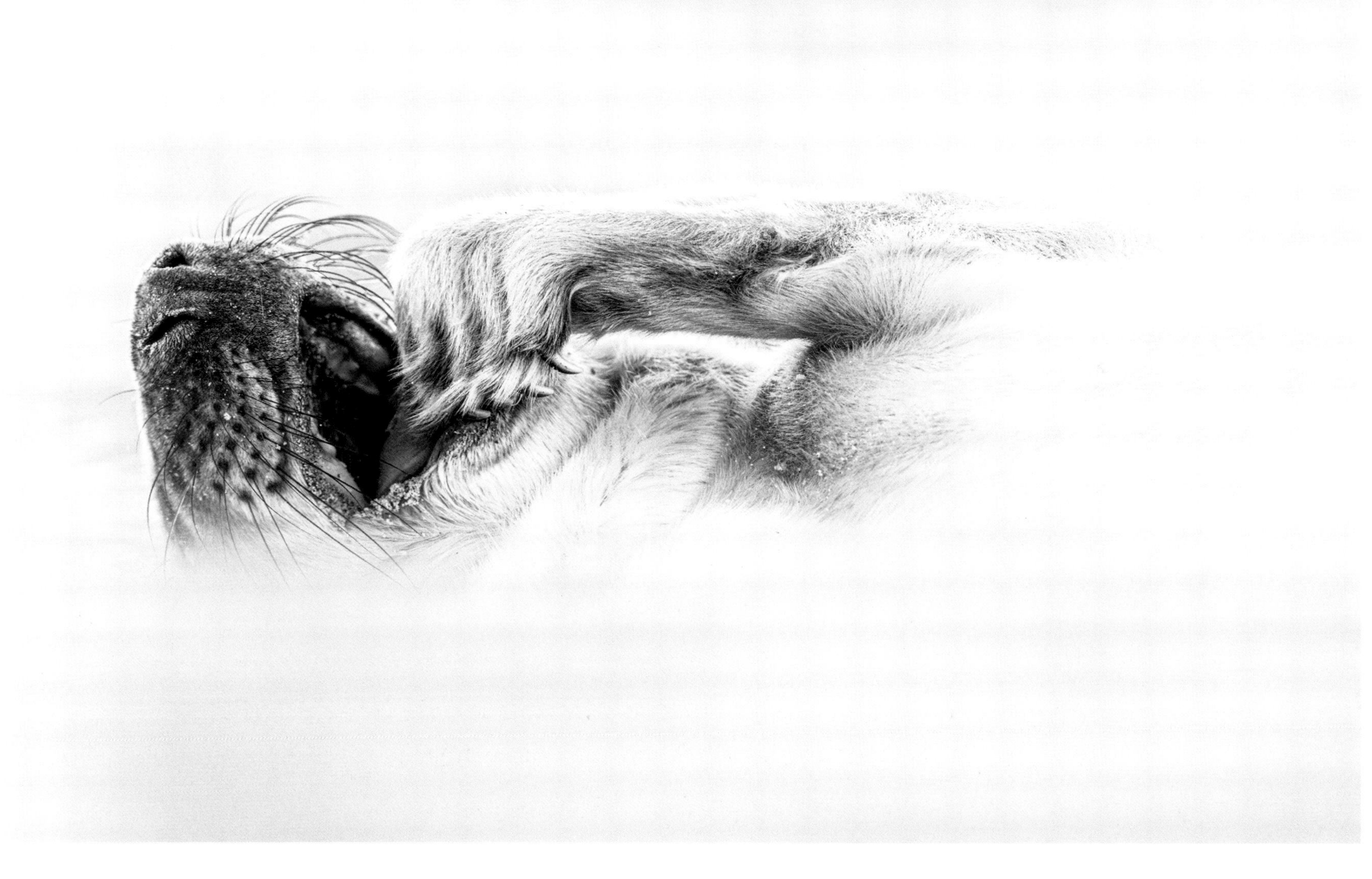

The Grey Yawn
Black & White

Robin Lowry
Grey seal (*Halichoerus grypus*)
Winterton beach, Norfolk, England

Canon EOS R5 with Canon 600mm f/4 II lens &
1.4x teleconverter. 840mm; 1/800th second; f/5.6;
ISO 800.

A yawning seal pup on its back conveys a sense of vulnerability and playfulness. I took advantage of the dull lighting conditions to capture this photograph. Utilising the soft light and positioning myself behind a sand dune created a blended foreground that added depth to this image. I knew at the time that a black and white conversion would create a dramatic feel while emphasising textures, shapes and contrast. Using my 600mm F4 wide open added to the isolation of the pup while keeping a safe distance.

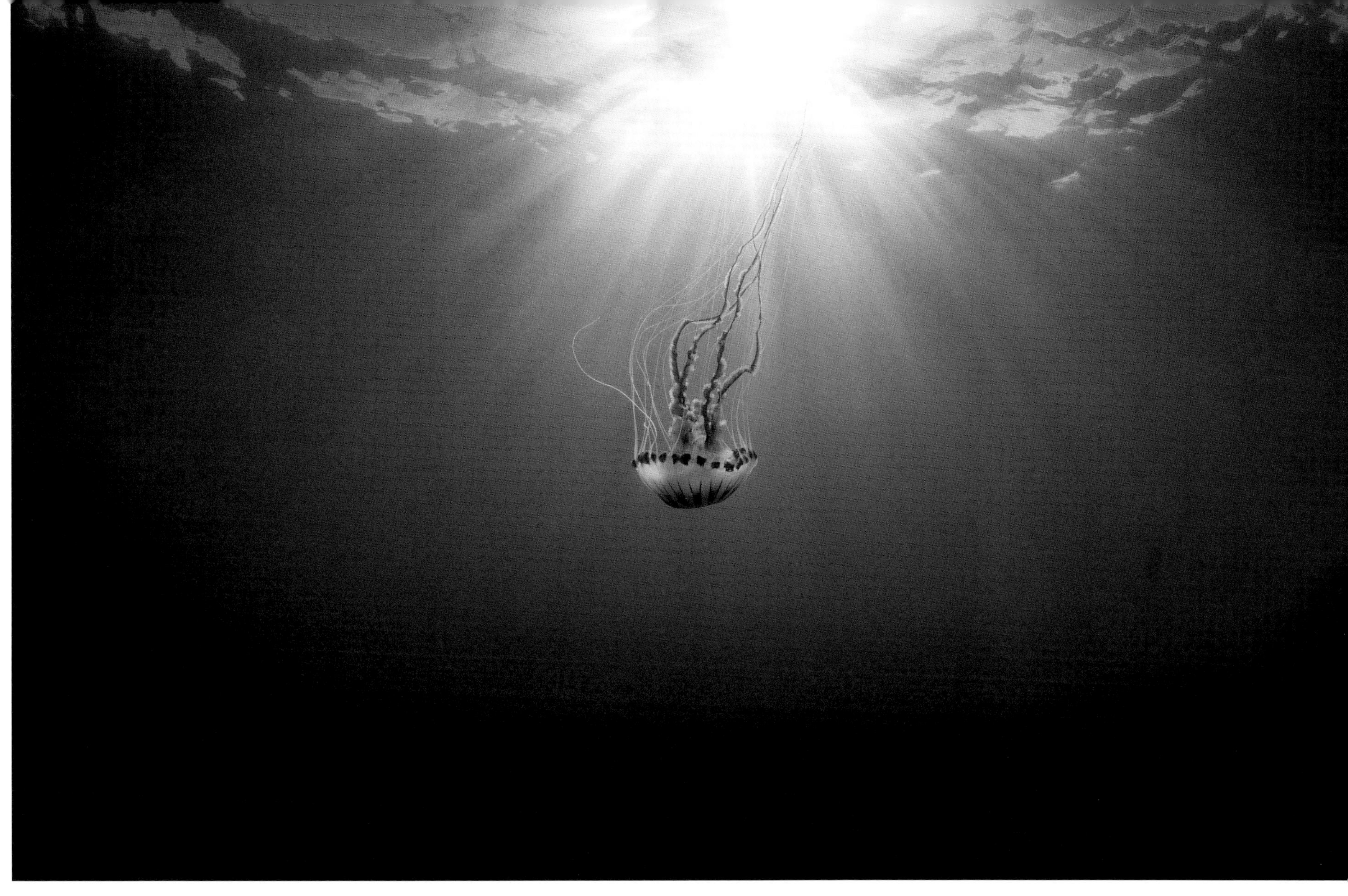

Abyss
Black & White | Highly Commended

Gina Goodman
Compass jellyfish (*Chrysaora hysoscella*)
Falmouth, Cornwall, England

Canon EOS R5 with Canon 8-15mm f/4 Fisheye lens.
15mm; 1/500th second; f/16; ISO 800.

In Cornwall, we're fortunate to witness a summer influx of jellyfish. It's my chance to experiment with new underwater photography techniques, sometimes even repurposing studio gear for underwater use. On this occasion, I embraced black and white photography.

To achieve a simple image with striking surface-to-depth contrast, I ventured away from rocky reefs and kelp patches, swimming into open water.

After encountering several jellyfish, some too small or damaged, I found one with sizeable dimensions and extended tentacles. I spent about an hour with it, capturing, reviewing, and refining my shots. As it slowly inverted, the image I envisioned began to take shape. I also experimented with high-speed sync, shooting at 1/500 for greater light control, especially near the surface.

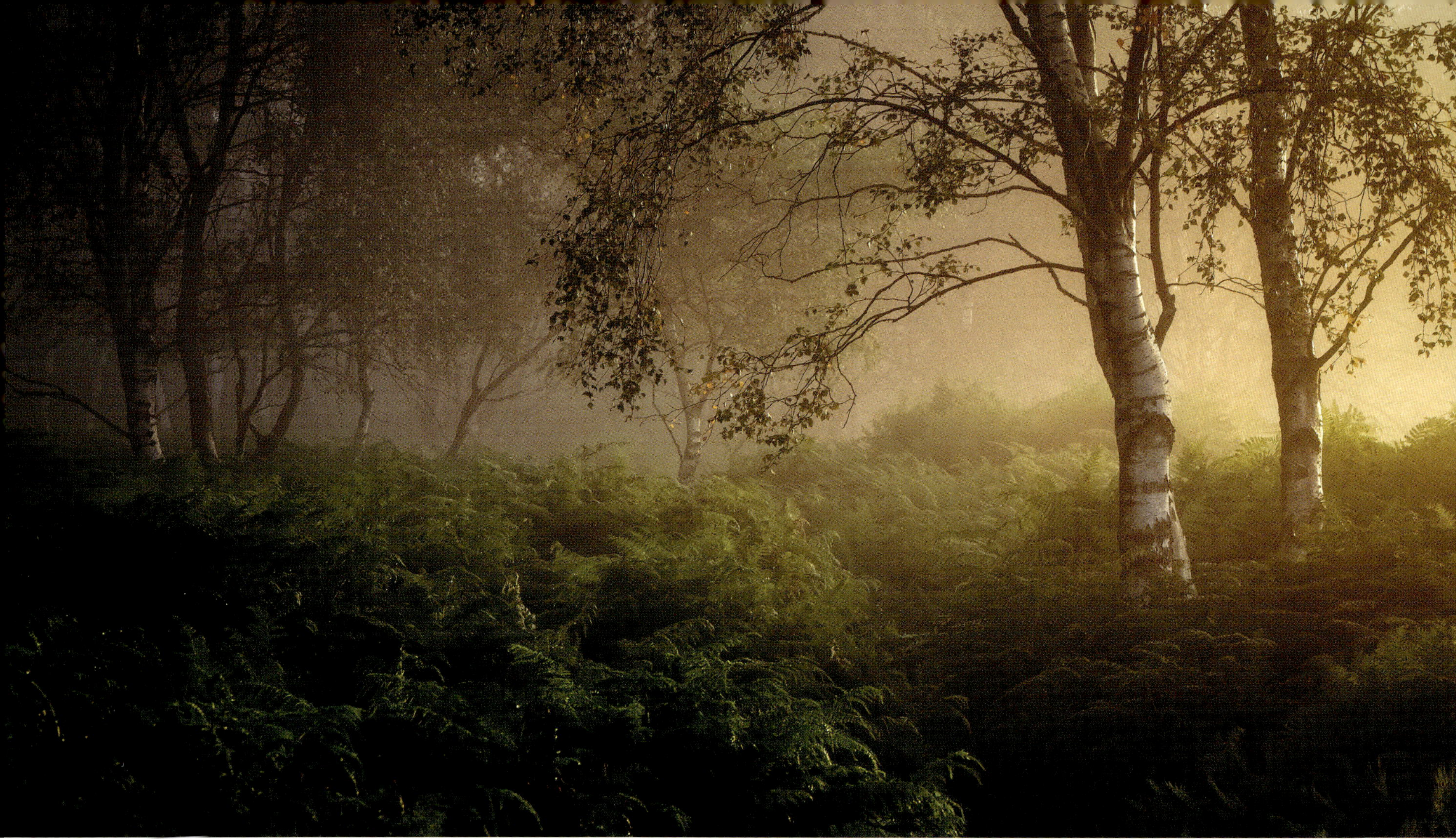

September Greens
Wild Woods

Verity Milligan
Surprise View, Peak District, England

Canon EOS R5 with Canon 28-70mm f/2 lens.
61mm; 1/125th second; f/9; ISO 100.

On the cusp of autumn, the silver birch woodland of Surprise View in the Peak District was bathed in the atmosphere created by the morning mist, enhanced by the light breaking through the canopy. I liked how the branches seemed to reach towards each other, with the woodland floor covered in bracken yet to show any sign of the season changing.

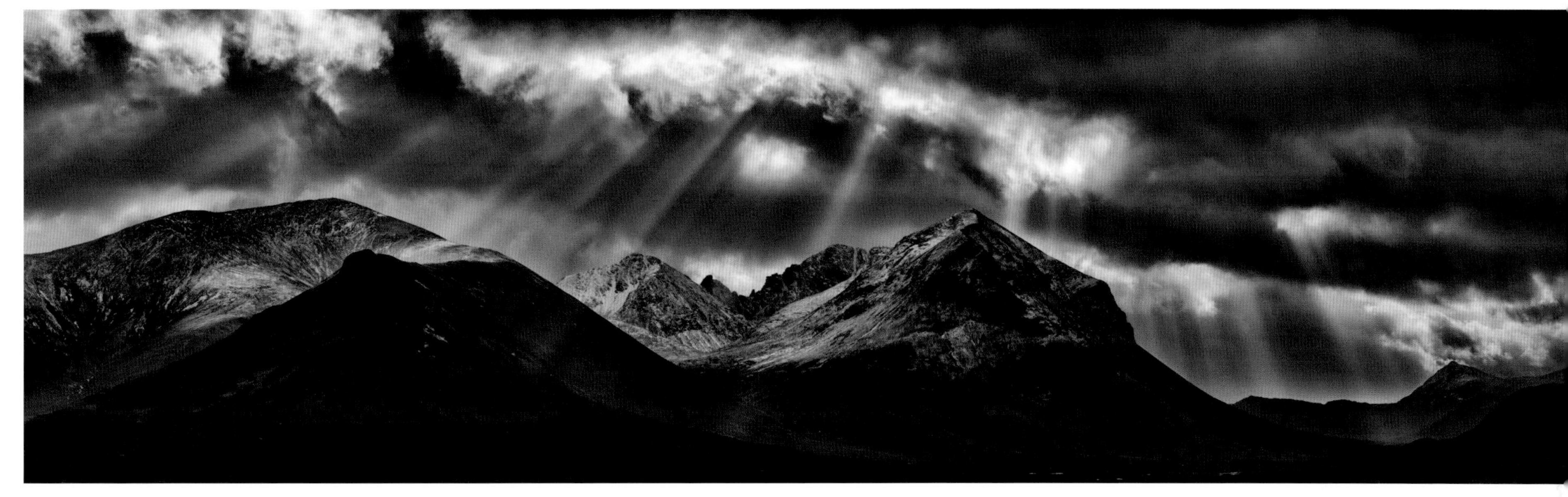

Clearing Storm on the Cuillin
Black & White | Highly Commended

Jeremy Walker
Cuillin Hills, Isle of Skye, Scotland

Nikon D810 with Nikon 70-200mm f/2.8 lens.
122mm; 1/640th second; f/8; ISO 64.

It was a day of enduring bitter winds and pelting hailstones. Tantalising glimpses of light vanished as quickly as they appeared. Eventually, the storm began to dissipate, and beams of light swept across the landscape like searchlights seeking the lost. The passing clouds and fleeting light allowed me to capture three frames, sufficient for a stitched panorama.

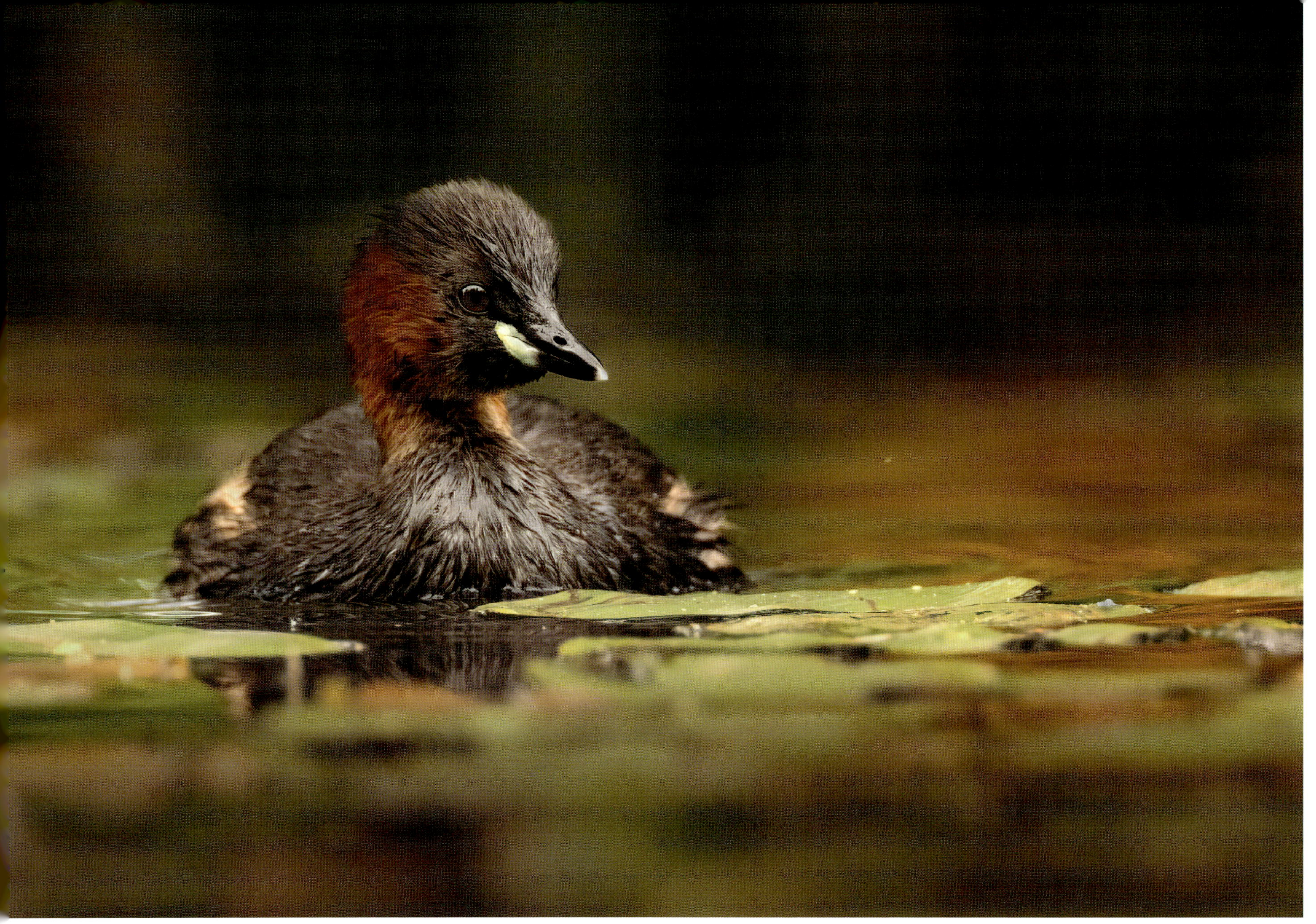

Little Grebe in the Lilies
Animal Portraits

Kirsten Asmussen
Little grebe (*Tachybaptus ruficollis*)
Peak District, England

Canon EOS R5 with Canon 400mm f/2.8 III lens &
2x teleconverter. 800mm; 1/500th second; f/5.6;
ISO 3,200.

I came across this little grebe on a canal in the Peak
District during the early morning hours. I was lying
flat along the water's edge, hoping to photograph
water voles. The voles were a no-show, but I was
nevertheless treated to some quality time with
this little bird as it fished between the water lilies.
Although it was initially quite skittish, it eventually
acclimated to my presence, allowing me to take a
few water-level portraits.

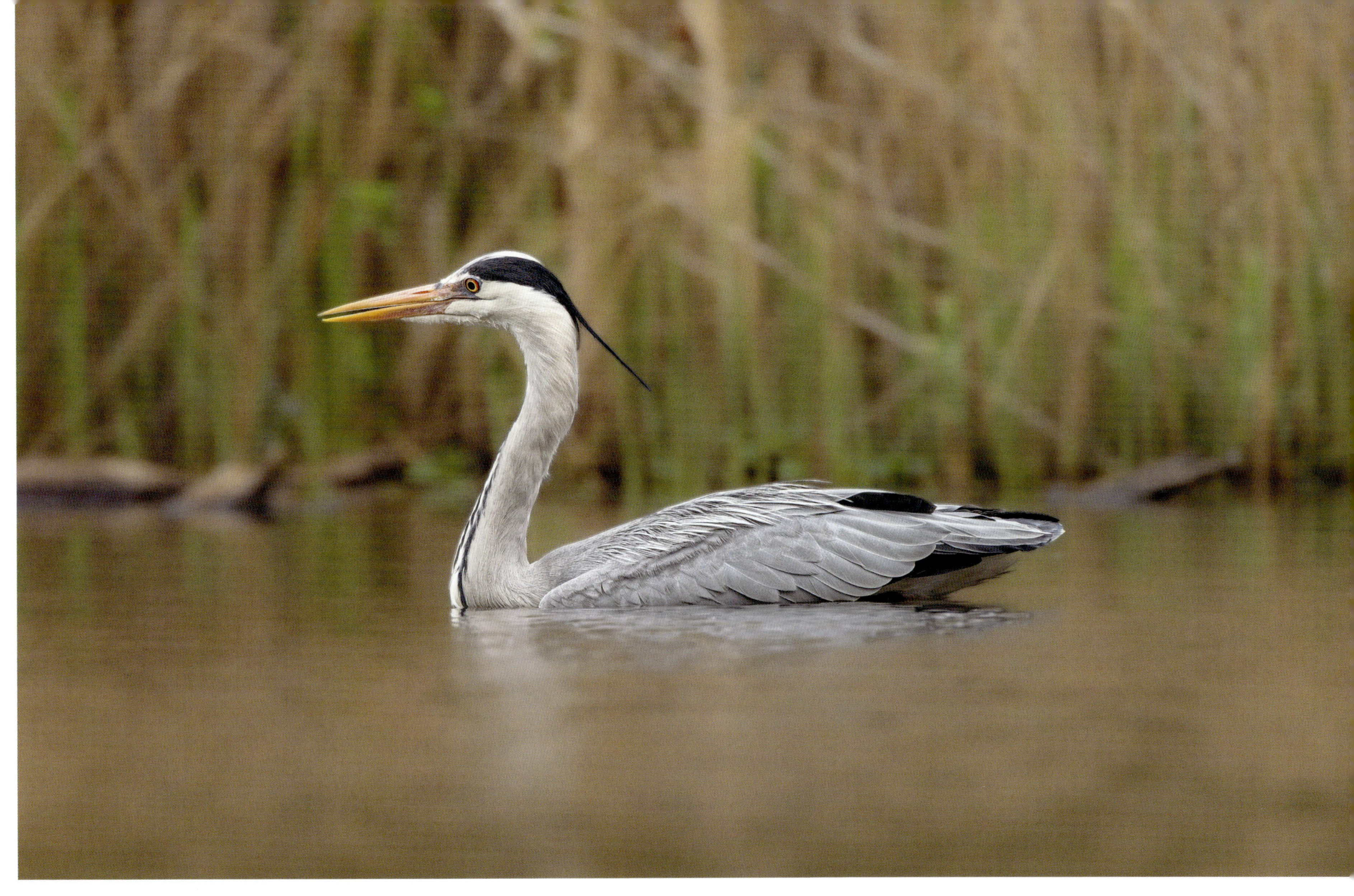

They Can Swim?
Animal Behaviour

Nathan Martin
Grey heron (*Ardea cinerea*)
Connaught Waters, Epping Forest, Essex, England

Canon EOS R5 with Canon RF 100-500mm f/4.5-7.1 lens. 500mm; 1/1,250th second; f/7.1; ISO 2,000.

Upon arrival, I spotted this grey heron straight away, perched on a fallen branch above the water, poised and ready. Doing my best not to startle it, it eventually took flight, and I thought my chance had gone, only for it to turn back and splash uncharacteristically straight into the water and start swimming on the surface. I'd never heard of them doing it, let alone seen it! I got as low to the water as I could to get my picture, then just sat and watched as it swam slowly, almost having a relaxing break from parenthood.

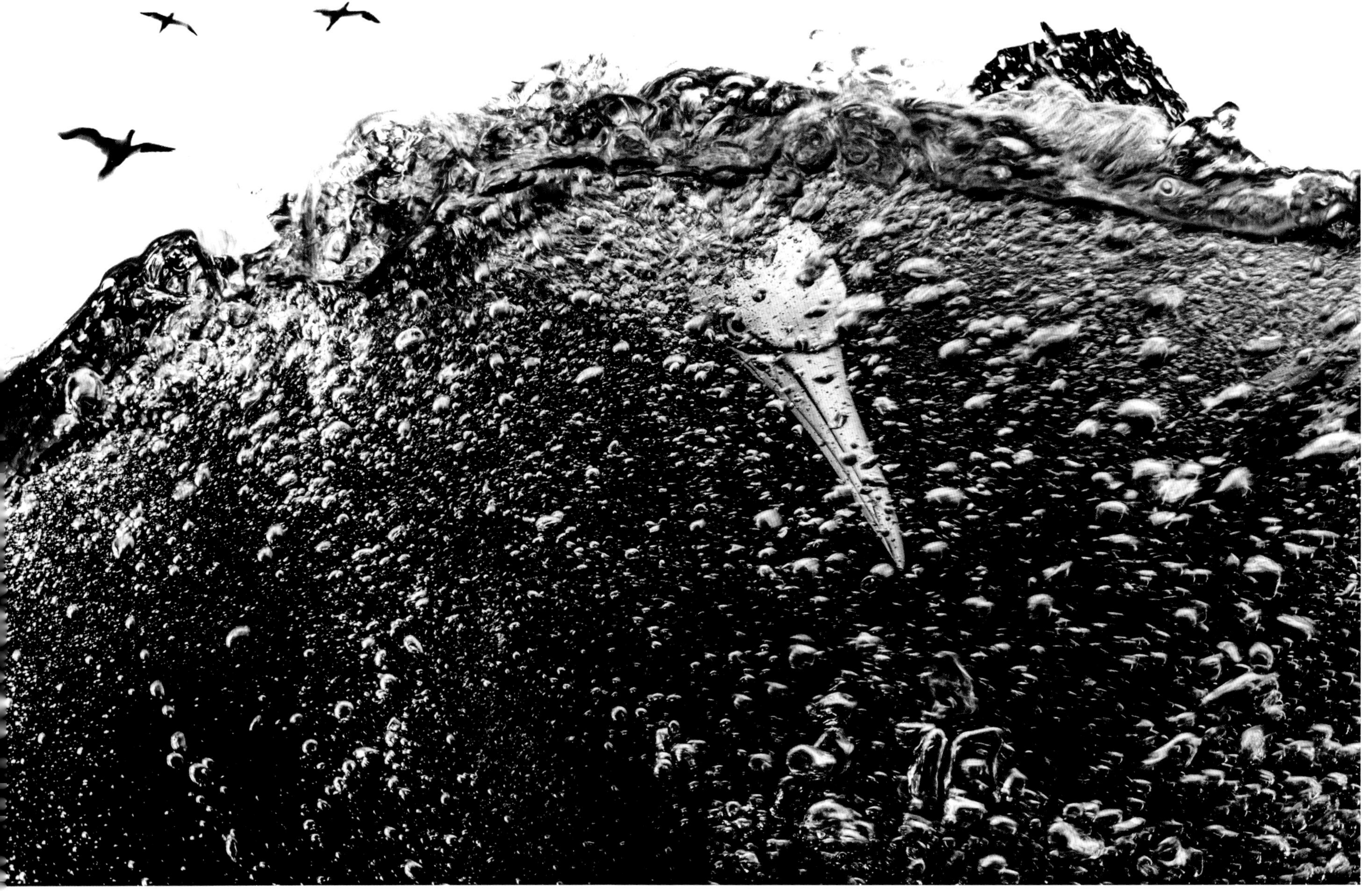

Through the Bubbles
Black & White | Highly Commended

Henley Spiers
Northern gannet (*Morus bassanus*)
Shetland, Scotland

Nikon D850 with Nikon 8-15mm f/3.5-4.5 lens.
15mm; 1/250th second; f/22; ISO 800.

A northern gannet stares through a cloud of bubbles, hidden yet unmistakable. The bubbles were created by gannets, Britain's largest seabirds, diving in pursuit of fish. The silhouettes in the sky complete the story. This image was captured using discarded fish as bait.

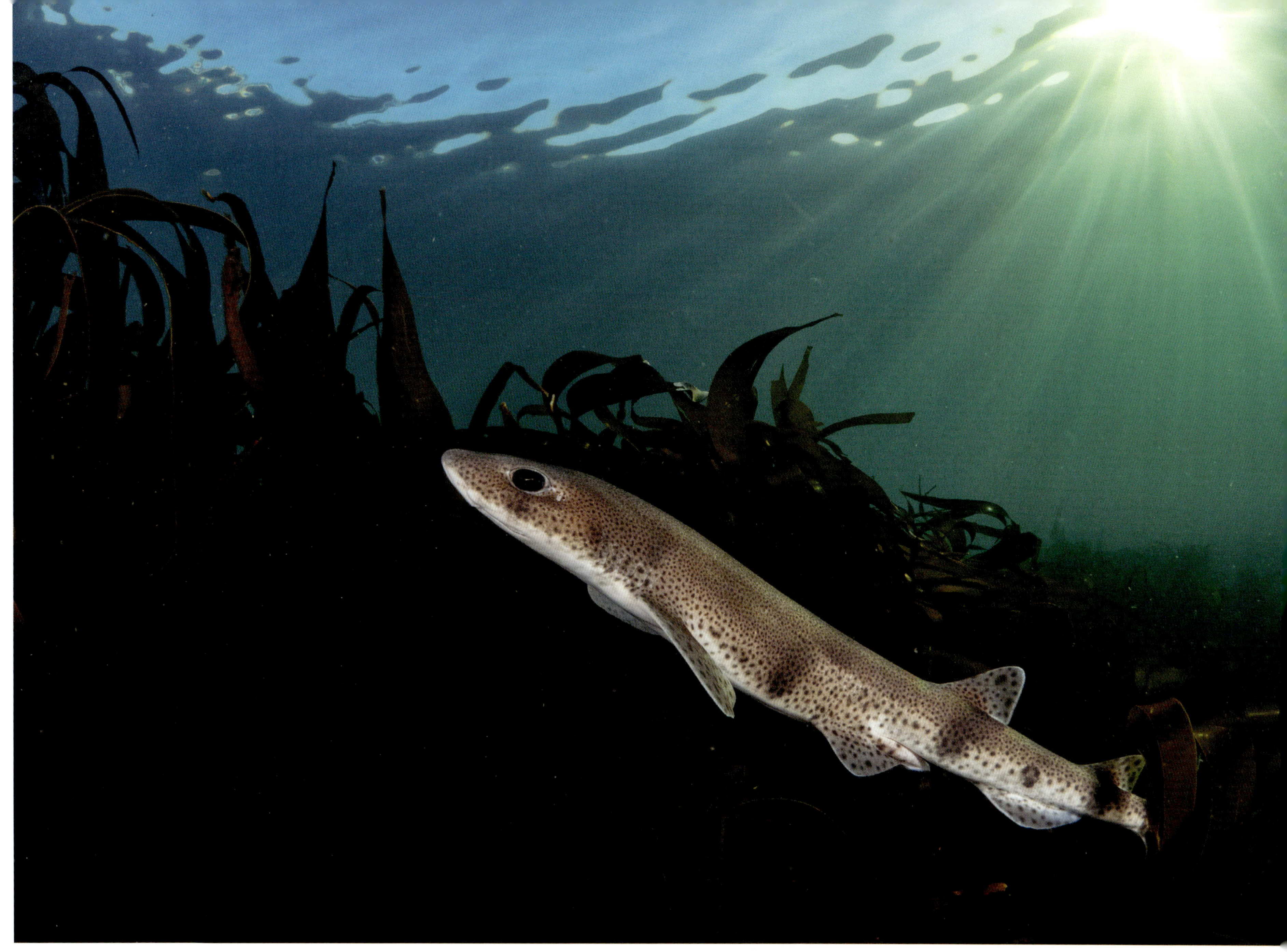

Catshark in the Morning Sunshine

Coast & Marine

Martin Stevens
Small-spotted catshark (*Scyliorhinus canicula*)
Falmouth, Cornwall, England

Olympus E-M5 III with Olympus 8mm f/1.8 Fisheye
lens. 8mm; 1/200th second; f/13; ISO 640.

Early morning in spring is a great time to spot
catsharks swimming around the rocky shore. On a
calm, sunny morning, I got up at sunrise and went to
my favourite location in Falmouth to observe them.
I had been trying for a while to photograph one
gliding over the kelp with the sunshine behind.
I was freediving to react quickly and anticipate where
to position myself, and I was lucky when one shark
swam right up and past me with the light behind.
I used two strobes on low power to illuminate the
shark against the dark kelp.

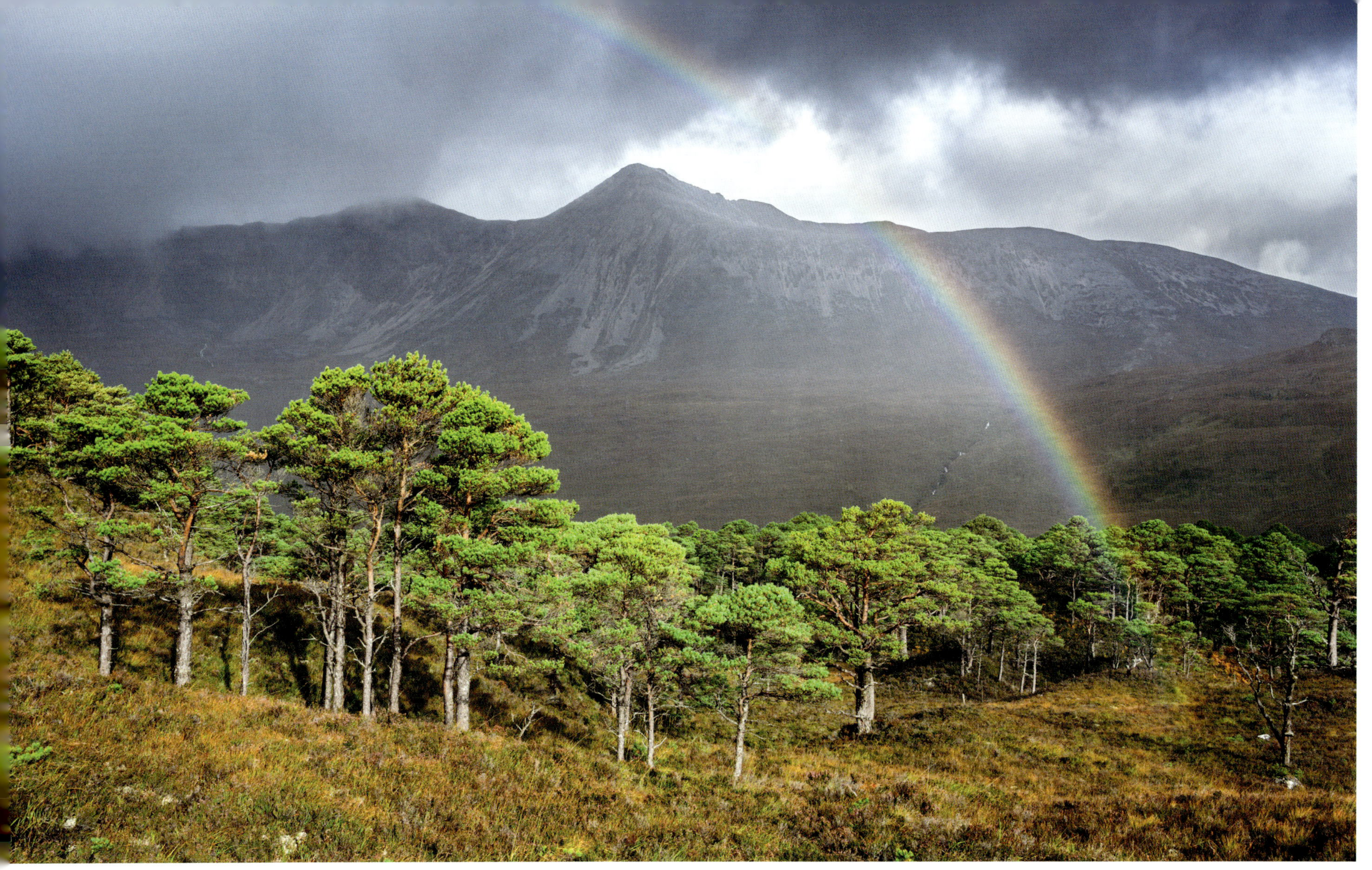

A Rainbow Over the Caledonian Forest
Wild Woods

James Roddie
Scots pine (*Pinus sylvestris*)
Torridon, Scotland

Nikon Z 7 with Nikon 24-70mm f/4 lens.
35mm; 1/40th second; f/10; ISO 125.

The fragments of Caledonian forest surrounding Beinn Eighe are undoubtedly some of the most spectacular woodlands in Scotland. A weather forecast for sunshine and showers looked promising for a day of photography, so I headed to a favourite location on a boggy hillside overlooking the woods. I had a long wait in heavy rain with no sign of any gaps in the cloud. I had almost given up when I was treated to this rainbow for just a few seconds, and the woods were briefly lit by a burst of sunshine.

Windswept Downy Birch
Wild Woods | Highly Commended

Michael Johnston
Downy birch (*Betula pubescens*)
Cairngorms National Park, Scotland

Canon EOS R5 with Canon 100-400mm f/4.5-5.6
lens. 124mm; 1.6 seconds; f/8; ISO 100.

After waiting in the rain, hoping for a break in the
clouds, I was rewarded with a spotlight of sun at
sunset that raced across the glen, briefly lighting
up these downy birches. The main tree is one of my
favourites in the area and is one of the last to lose
its leaves; there are even still a few green leaves on
one of the lower branches. It was very windy, and
I wanted to capture the movement in the trees, so
I used a filter to enable a slow shutter speed.

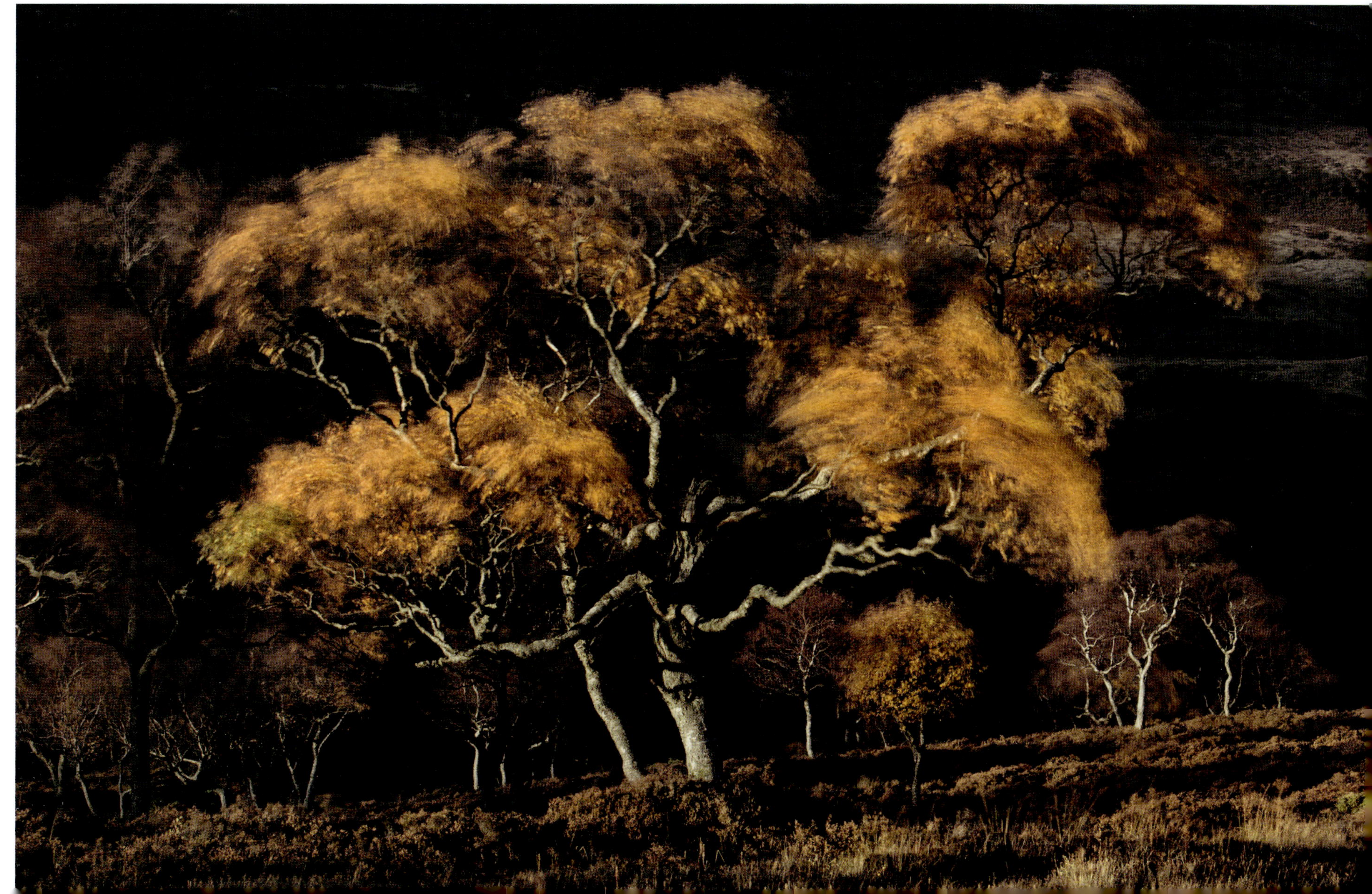

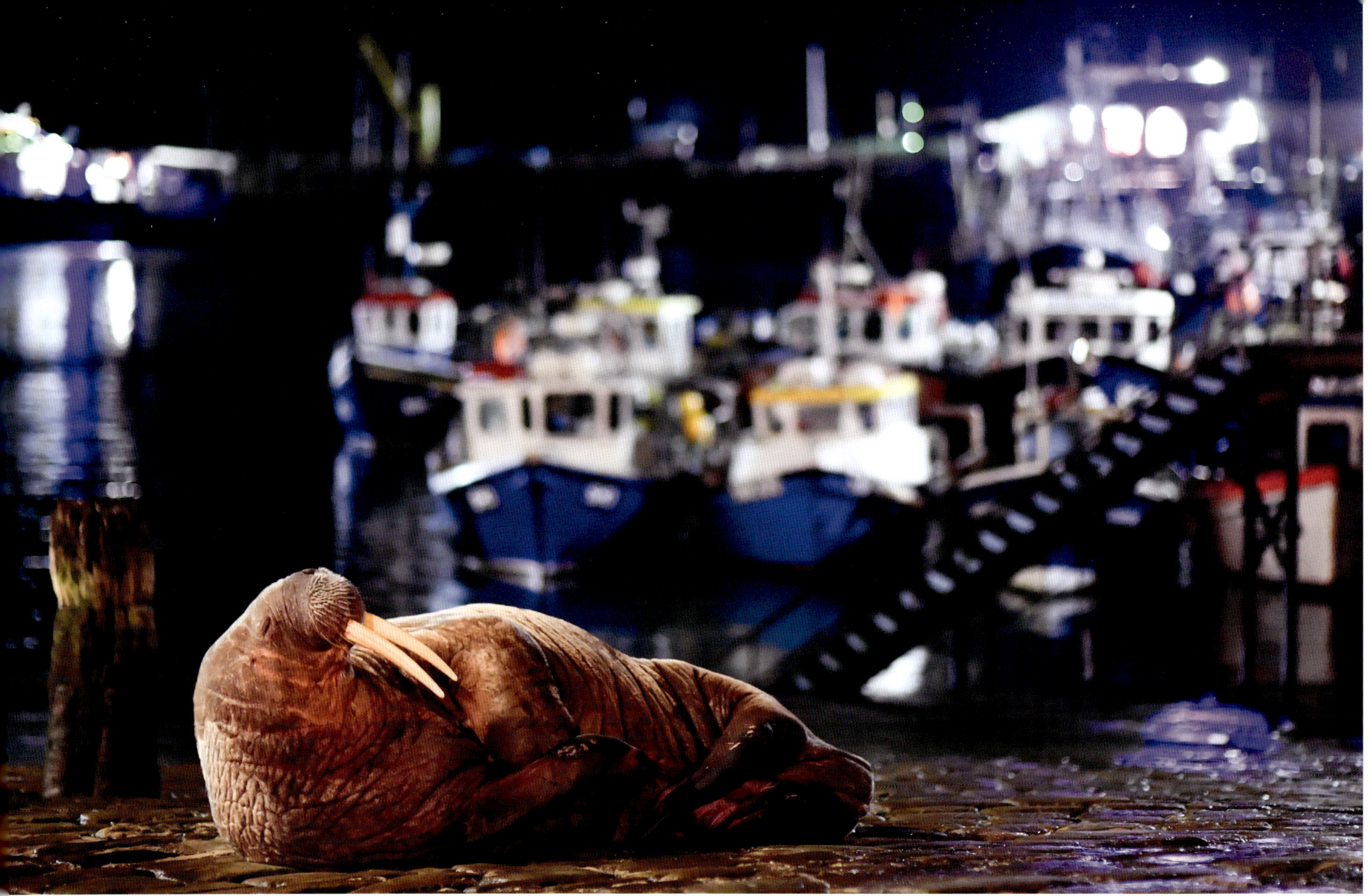

What's All the Fuss About?
Urban Wildlife | Runner-up

Will Palmer
Walrus (*Odobenus rosmarus*)
Scarborough, North Yorkshire, England

Nikon D5 with Sigma 85mm f/1.6 lens. 85mm;
1/80th second; f/1.6; ISO 6,400.

In this photograph, the Arctic walrus who had come
ashore to rest on the harbour slipway in Scarborough
has lifted its head as a car passed on Foreshore Road.
The image is lit by the streetlights to the left and
features the town's fishing boats in the background.
Despite being taken handheld at 1/80th of a second
at f/1.6, an ISO of 6400 was still needed to properly
expose Thor and the slipway at 2:28am.

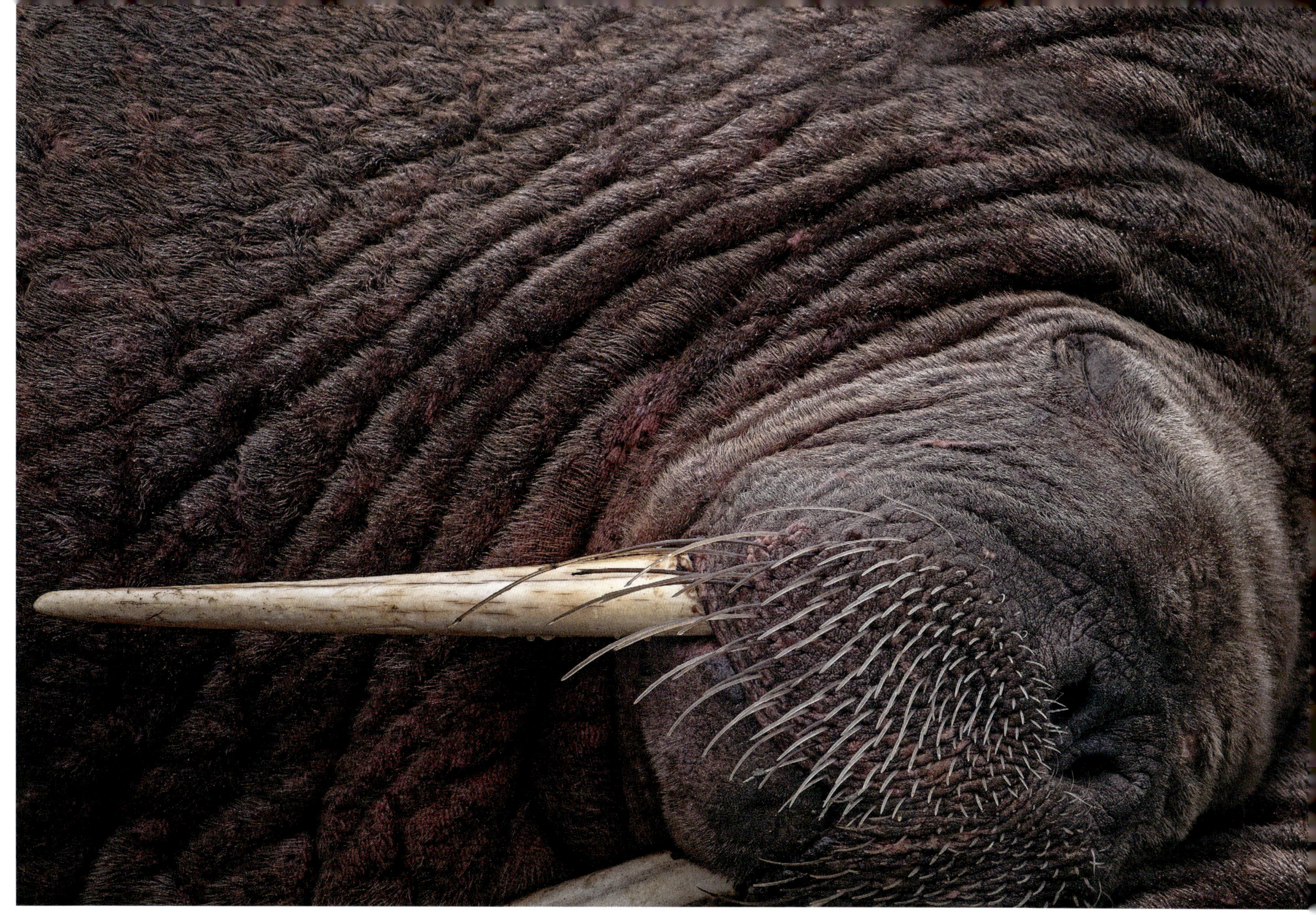

The Sleeping Giant
Animal Portraits

Rosie Dutton
Walrus (*Odobenus rosmarus*)
Scarborough, North Yorkshire, England

Nikon D810 with Nikon 200-500mm f/5.6 lens.
500mm; 1/320th second; f/5.6; ISO 800.

I was fortunate to be near Thor the walrus's location
when he arrived on Yorkshire's east coast on New
Year's Eve. Having never seen a walrus before,
I thought it would be the perfect opportunity to
witness this amazing animal. Thor was magnificent.
What stood out to me was his incredibly detailed
exterior: his blubber was thick and wrinkled, his
whiskers resembled plastic and his tusks bore the
marks of a well-travelled life. He was snoozing when
I photographed him. I used my 200-500mm lens
because, understandably, the crowds were kept at
a distance from him.

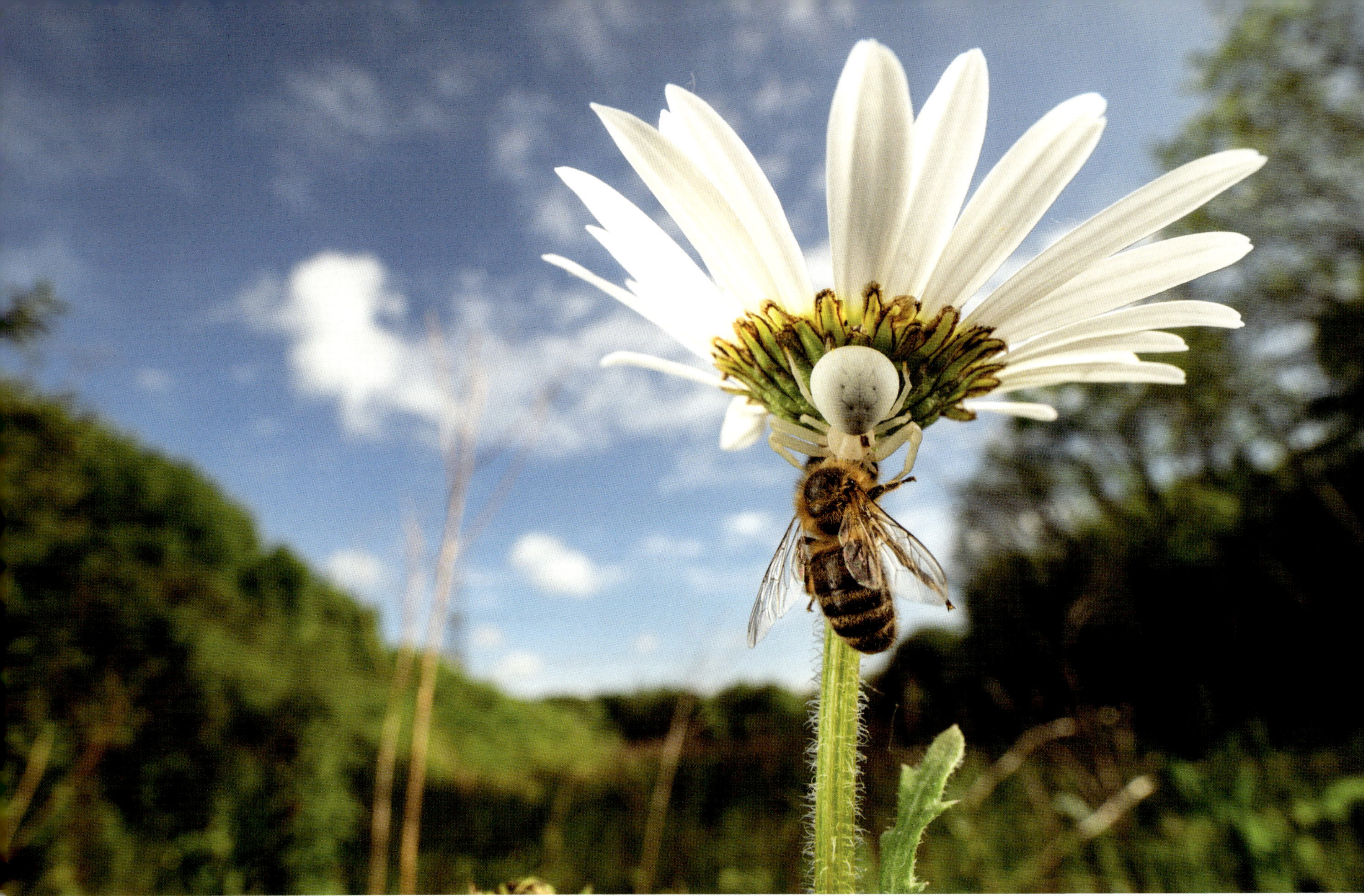

Daisy Danger
Hidden Britain | Runner-up

Lucien Harris
Flower crab spider (*Misumena vatia*) and
Honey bee (*Apis mellifera*)
Lee Mill, Devon, England

Nikon Z6 with Laowa 15mm f/4 Wide Angle 1:1
Macro lens. 15 mm; 1/125th second; f/16; ISO 100.

This photo was taken in a patch of land along the
A30 in Devon that has been left untouched for a
long time, making it a haven for wildflowers and the
wildlife that inhabits it. Using the Laowa wide-angle
macro lens, I aimed to capture this scene. While
walking, I came across a flower crab spider wrestling
with a bee on an ox-eye daisy. The light was behind
the subject, which backlit the flower nicely. However,
the spider itself was quite dark, so I used some
flashes and homemade flash diffusers to illuminate
it. This allowed me to capture the deadly strength of
these ambush predators.

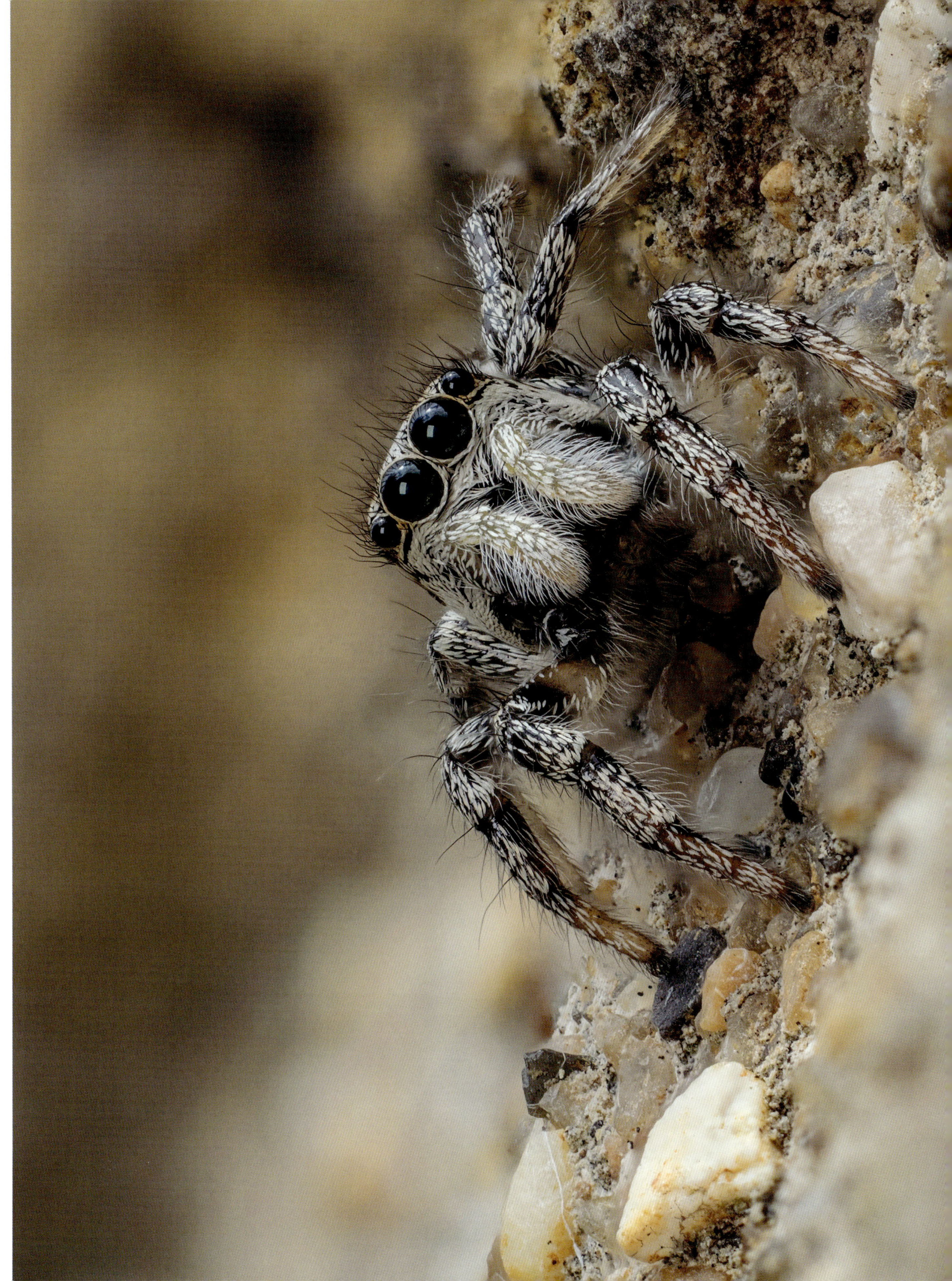

**Zebra Jumping Spider
on a Wall**
Hidden Britain

Neil Phillips
Zebra jumping spider
(*Salticus scenicus*)
Wat Tyler CP, Essex, England

Olympus EM1 MII with
Olympus 60mm f/2.8 Macro
lens. 60mm; 1/250th second;
f/4.5; ISO 250. Stacked.

This zebra jumping spider
appeared transfixed by my
camera, so I took advantage
and captured this stacked
image while resting my
camera on the wall. I achieved
this by using the focus
bracketing mode to take 77
shots in a matter of seconds,
and then stacked the images
on a PC afterwards.

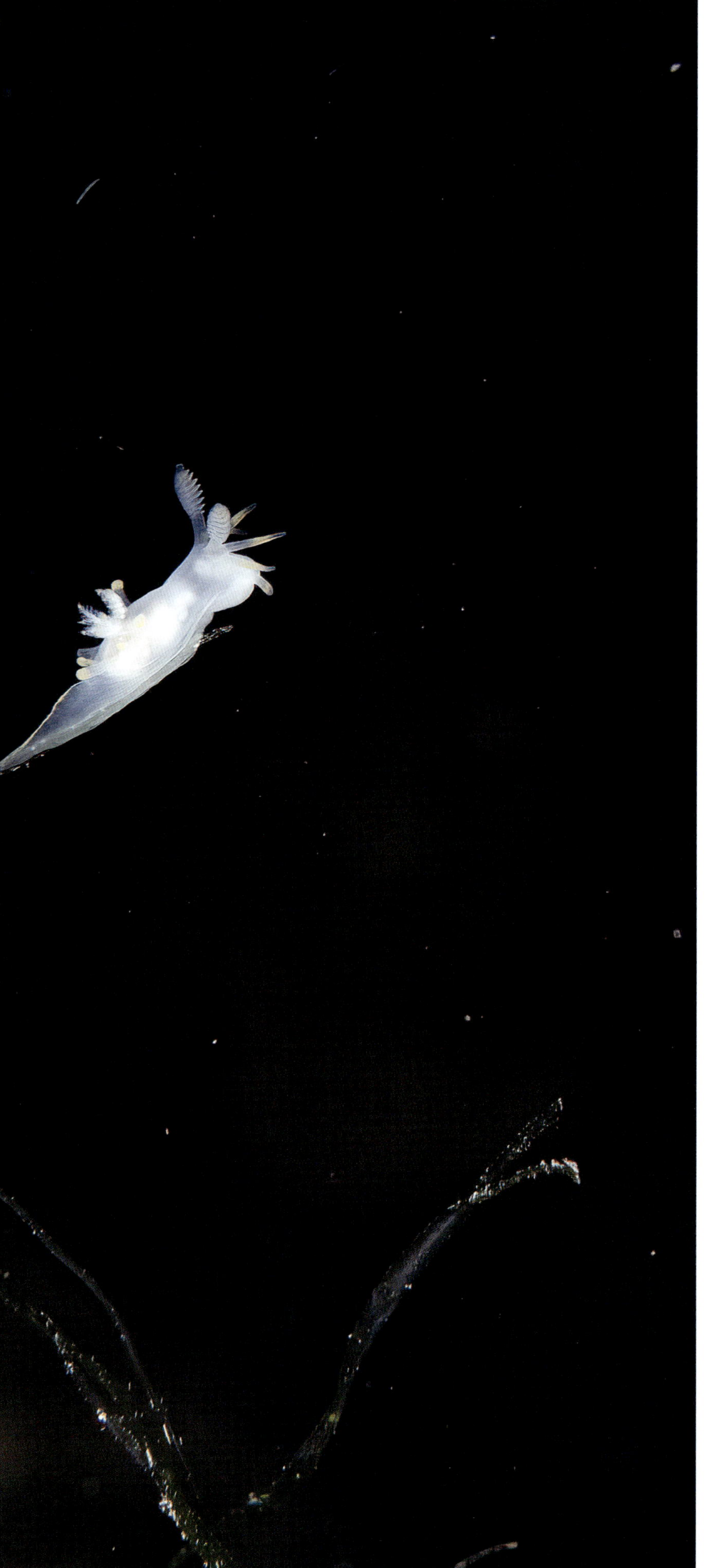

Hanging About
Coast & Marine

Paul Pettitt
Nudibranch (Nudibranchia)
Weymouth, England

Nikon D500 with Nikon 60mm f/2.8 lens. 60mm; 1/200th second; f/22; ISO 250.

This nudibranch was spotted and photographed in a small bay in Portland, Dorset. They can usually be found in large numbers early in the year at a depth of about four metres. This particular subject appeared to be reaching out for food. I used a Nikon D500 in a Nauticam housing with a 60mm lens and torch lighting.

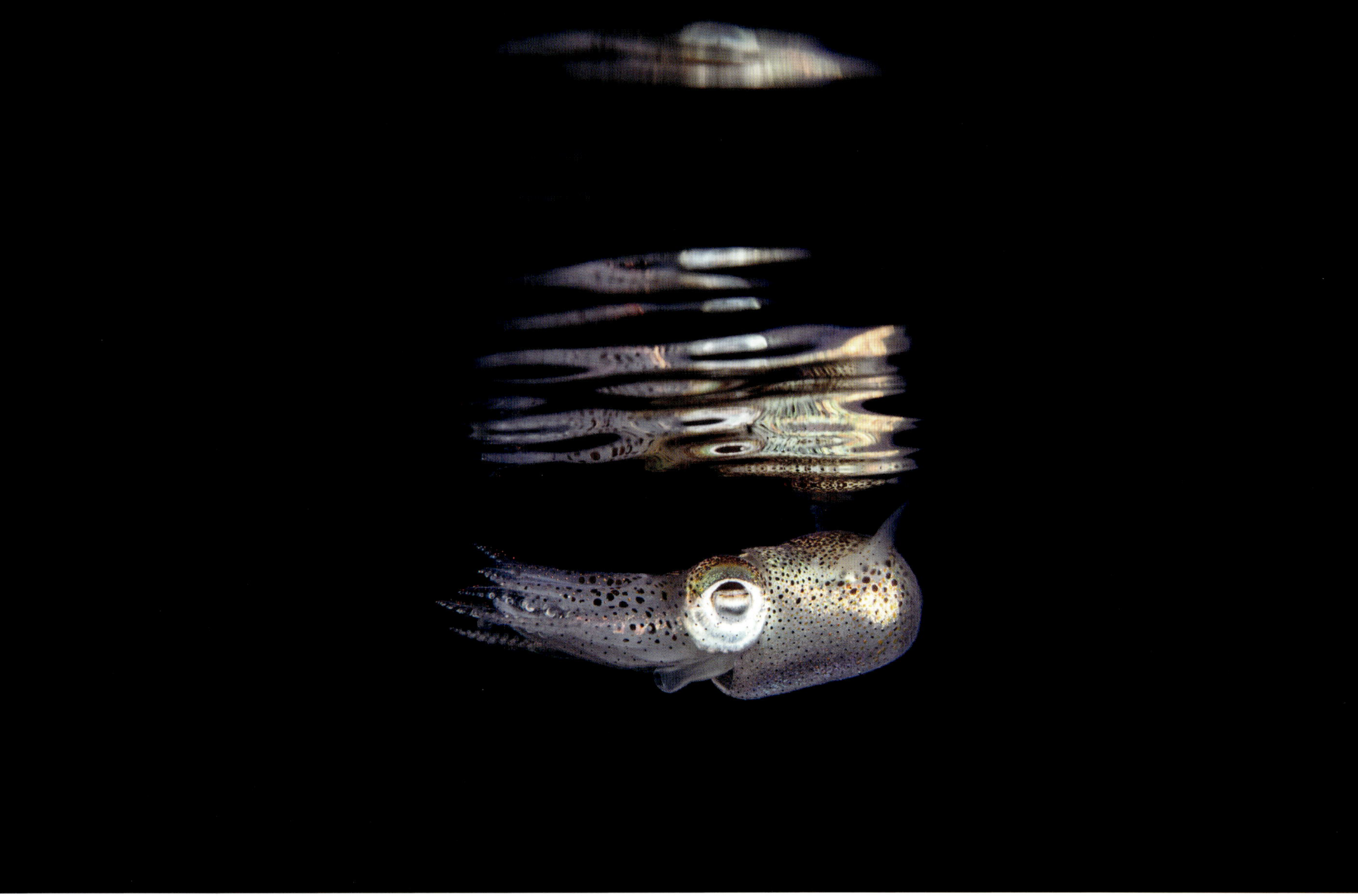

Surprise Encounter
Coast & Marine

Aaron Sanders
Bobtail squid (*Sepiola atlantica*)
Durgan Beach, Cornwall, England

Nikon D850 with Nikon 60mm f/2.8 lens.
60mm; 1/200th second; f/20; ISO 200.

Night diving is by far my favourite way to explore the ocean; the darkness conceals so many hidden wonders and otherworldly creatures. Just when you think you understand the workings of the underwater world at night, it will surprise you. Having previously believed bobtail squid to be shy and cautious, only venturing into the water column if necessary, I was left dumbfounded when this individual surprised us after a dive. This little bobtail cruised along at the surface, zooming around and putting on quite the show, making me rethink all my previous judgements of these animals' behaviour. The calm conditions enabled me to capture the squid's reflection as it jetted along below the surface.

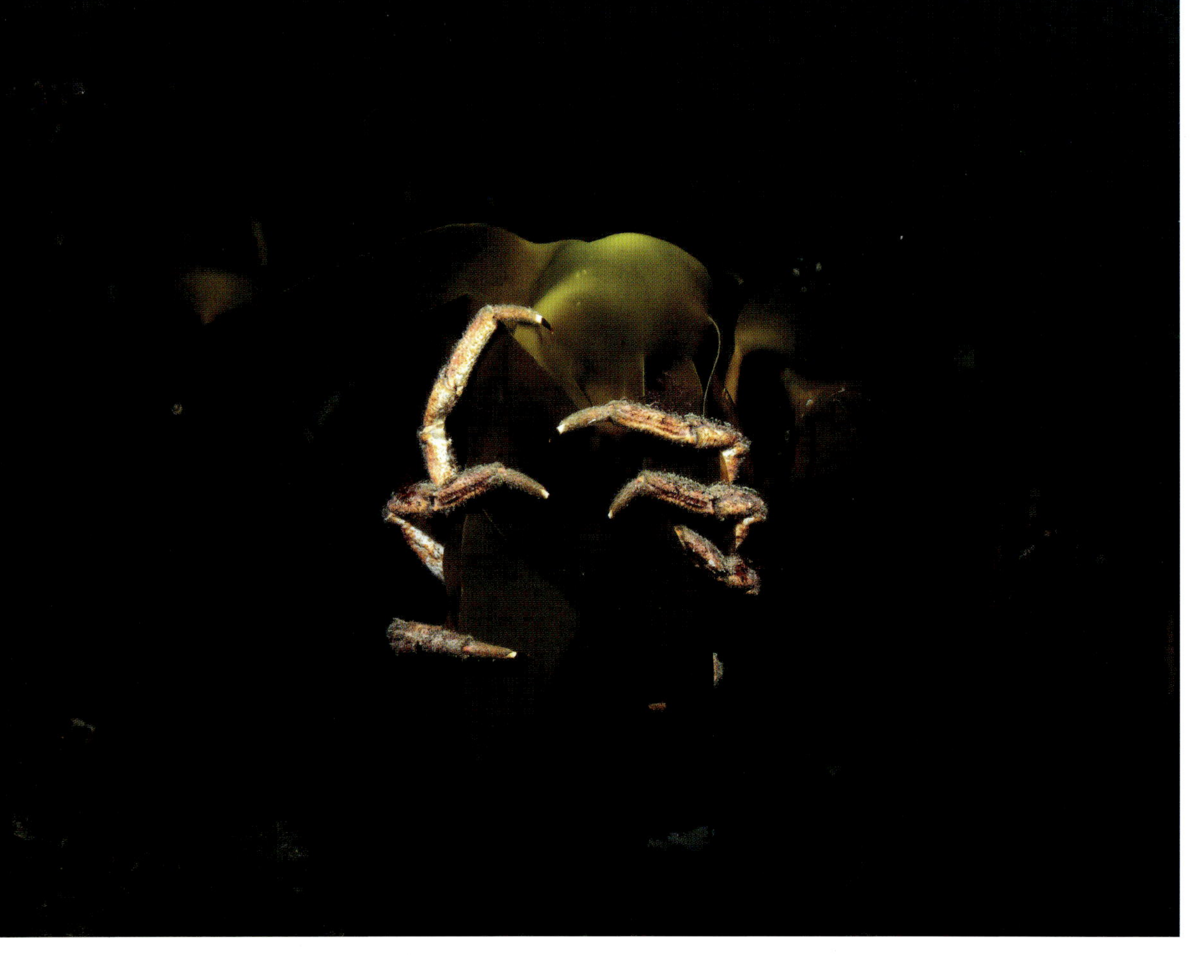

Clutching Kelp
Coast & Marine

George Turner
Great spider crab (*Hyas araneus*)
Silver Steps, Falmouth, England

Nikon D500 with Tokina Fisheye 10-17mm f/3.5-4.5 lens. 17mm; 1/160th second; f/13; ISO 400.

In the depths of the ocean, a spider crab clings to a strand of kelp. Lit from above, the tightly clutched mass of seaweed takes on a silky luminous-green hue, fading to a softer maroon shade towards the base of each ribbon. The crab's slender legs are closed in a tight embrace; its limbs resemble skeletal fingers, mottled with soft orange and red.

Wolf Spider Carrying Its Spiderlings
Animal Behaviour

Neil Phillips
Wolf spider (Lycosidae)
Harewood Dale, Yorkshire, England

Olympus EM1 MII with Olympus 60mm f/2.8 Macro lens. 60mm; 1/40th second; f/5.6; ISO 400. Stacked.

On some dry mud near a pond, I spotted some wolf spiders scampering about and noticed that this one was carrying newly hatched spiderlings. I managed to get close enough to fire off 62 images using the focus bracketing mode in a matter of seconds, which I stacked on the PC later to create this shot.

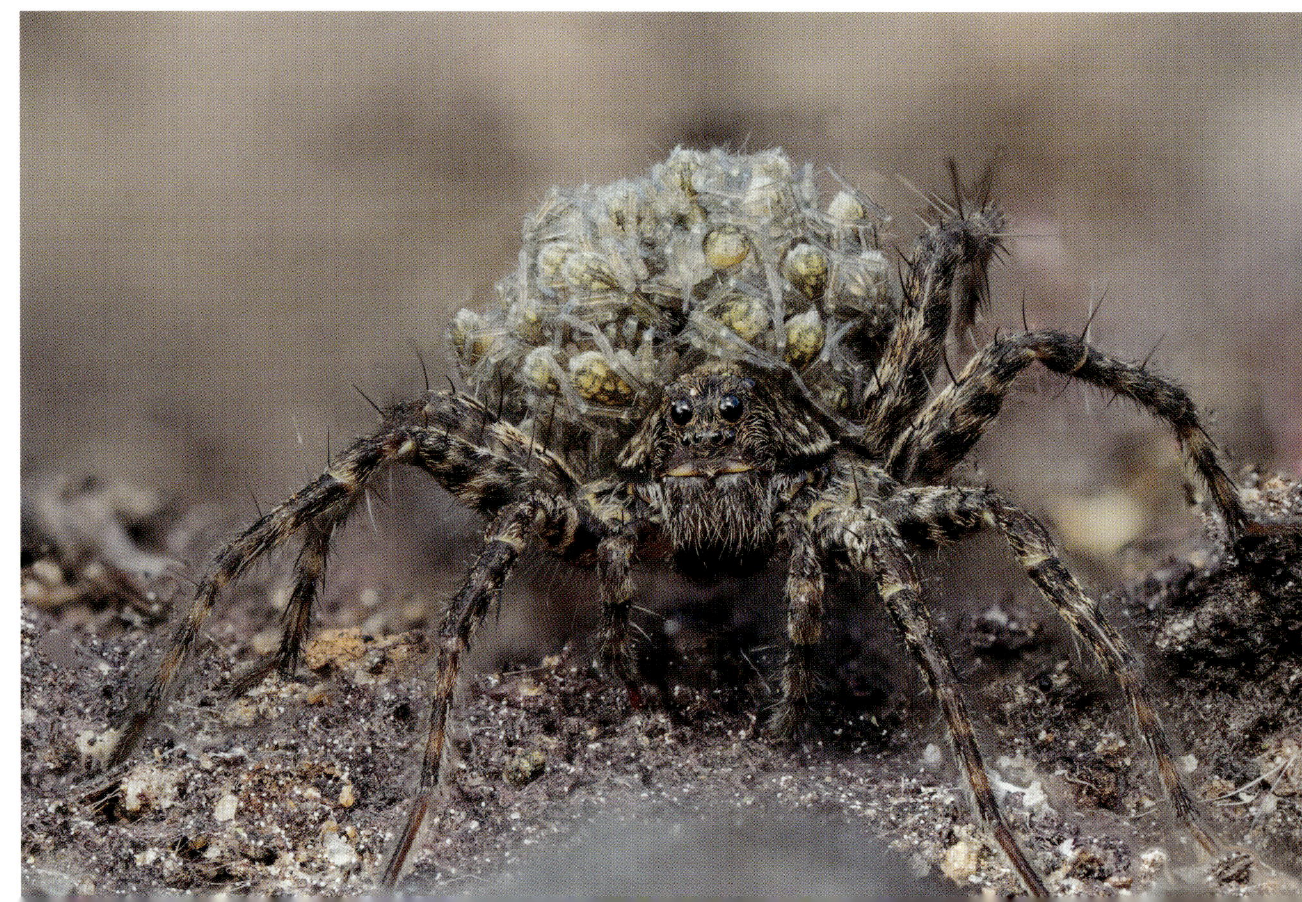

Nap Time
Hidden Britain

Geraint Radford
Bumblebee (*Bombus* sp.)
Port Talbot, Wales

OM System OM-1 with OM 90mm
f/3.5 Macro lens. 90mm; 1/100th
second; f/3.5; ISO 1,000.

Each winter, I eagerly await
the arrival of spring and the
emergence of flowers and insects
to photograph. On this day, I went
for a walk at a country park and
found some crocus flowers. The
bumblebees were hard at work!
This bee rested inside a flower, so
I began taking some photographs.
The evening light was fading, the
flowers were closing for the night
and the crocus closed around the
bee. I love how the bee has one leg
poking out, maybe to keep cool?
This shot is a stack of 30 images,
focused when the wind paused!

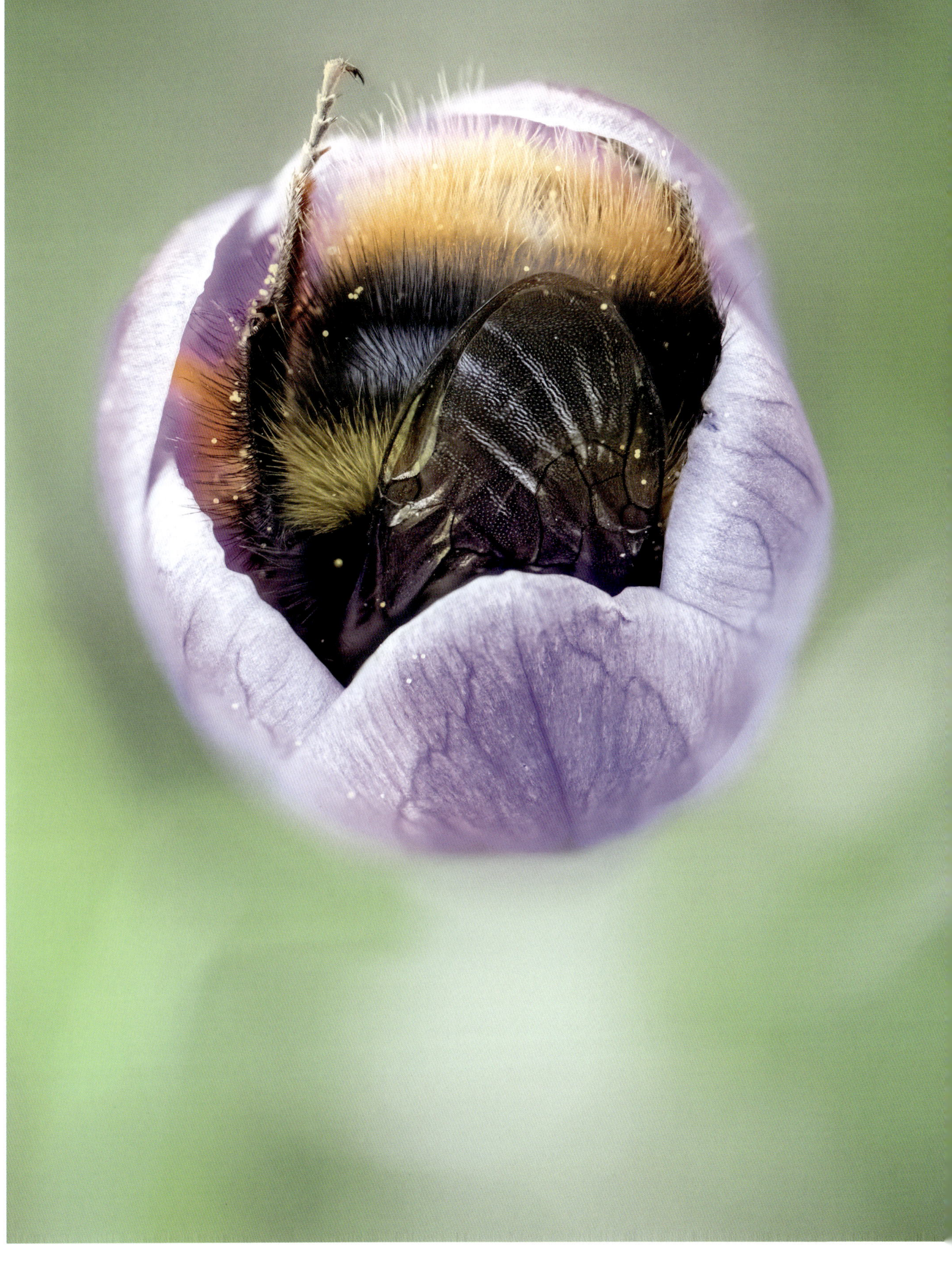

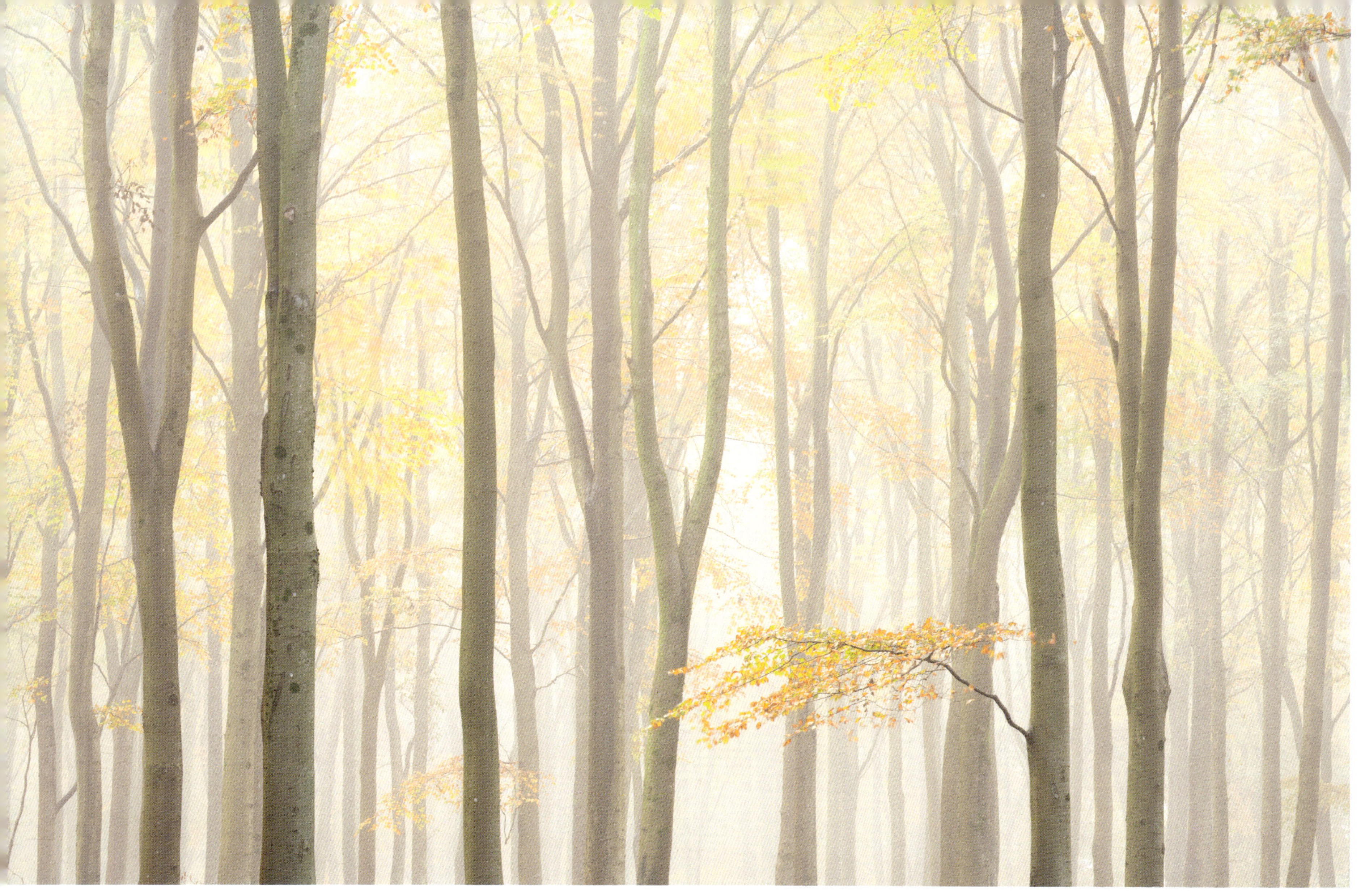

Golden Autumn
Wild Woods

Jeremy Walker
Marlborough, Wiltshire, England

Nikon D810 with Nikon 105mm f/2.8 lens.
105mm; 1 second; f/8; ISO 100.

A thick blanket of fog shrouded the forest when
I arrived. It was too thick, and everything seemed dull
and gloomy. It wasn't until well after sunrise that
soft golden light started to penetrate the woodland.
Conditions were perfect: the leaves were in the most
wonderful autumnal shades of orange, red and
yellow. The density of the fog was just right, not
too thick, not too thin, and there wasn't a breath
of wind. It is rare to get such perfect conditions,
making the early start well worth it.

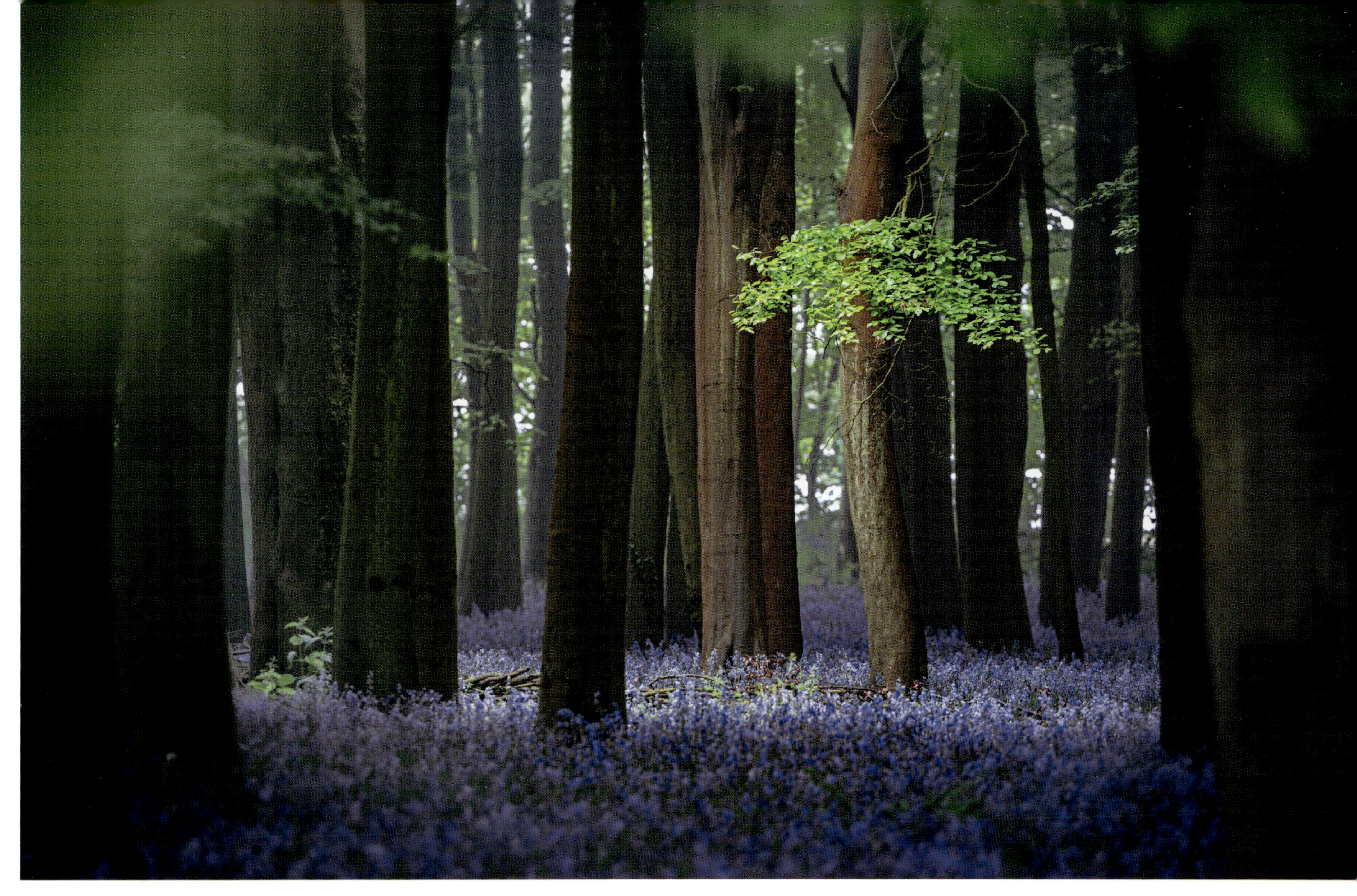

Spring Has Sprung
Wild Woods

Philip Selby
Beech (*Fagus sylvatica*)
Badbury Hill, Oxfordshire, England

Canon EOS 5D IV with Canon 100-400mm f/4.5-5.6
II lens. 321mm; 1/8th second; f/5.6; ISO 100.

Badbury Clump in Oxfordshire is an area of wonderful
beech woodland, carpeted with bluebells each spring.
Living locally, I am lucky enough to be able to visit
regularly, in varying weather. As is often the case,
the conditions don't always meet expectations, and
on this particular morning the fog forecasted soon
dissolved not long after arriving. Not giving up too
soon, I took a walk around the perimeter and spotted
a weak shaft of light breaking through the murk,
subtly highlighting a single branch of new, vibrant
foliage far into the woodland. I quickly set up and
changed to a longer telephoto zoom and was able to
capture a few images before the light ebbed away.

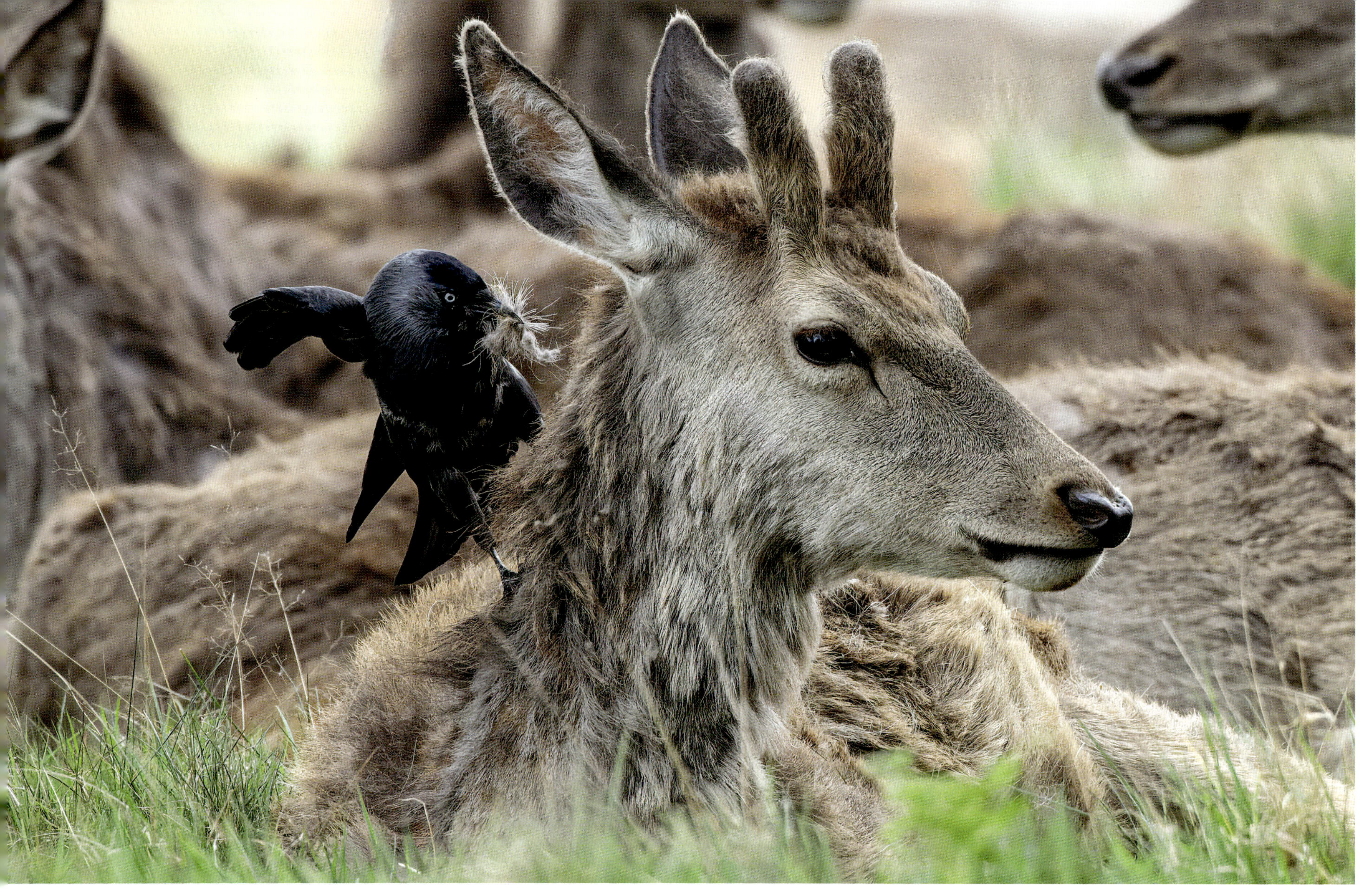

The Fur Thief
Animal Behaviour

Adam Ferry
Red deer (*Cervus elaphus*) and Jackdaw
(*Corvus monedula*)
Richmond Park, Richmond Upon Thames, England

Canon EOS R5 with Canon RF 100-500mm f/4.5-7.1
lens. 500mm; 1/3,200th second; f/7.1; ISO 5,000.

Walking through Richmond Park, I found a large herd
of red deer relaxing in an open field. Surrounding
these deer were large gatherings of jackdaws. Every
so often, a small group of jackdaws would swoop
down on an unsuspecting deer, land on them and
collect as much fur as they could carry in their beaks.
The deer shed their winter coats in April/May, which
coincides with the jackdaws nesting around April.
This picture was taken towards the end of April.
The shedding of the fur is perfect timing for the
jackdaws in the park to start collecting nesting
material.

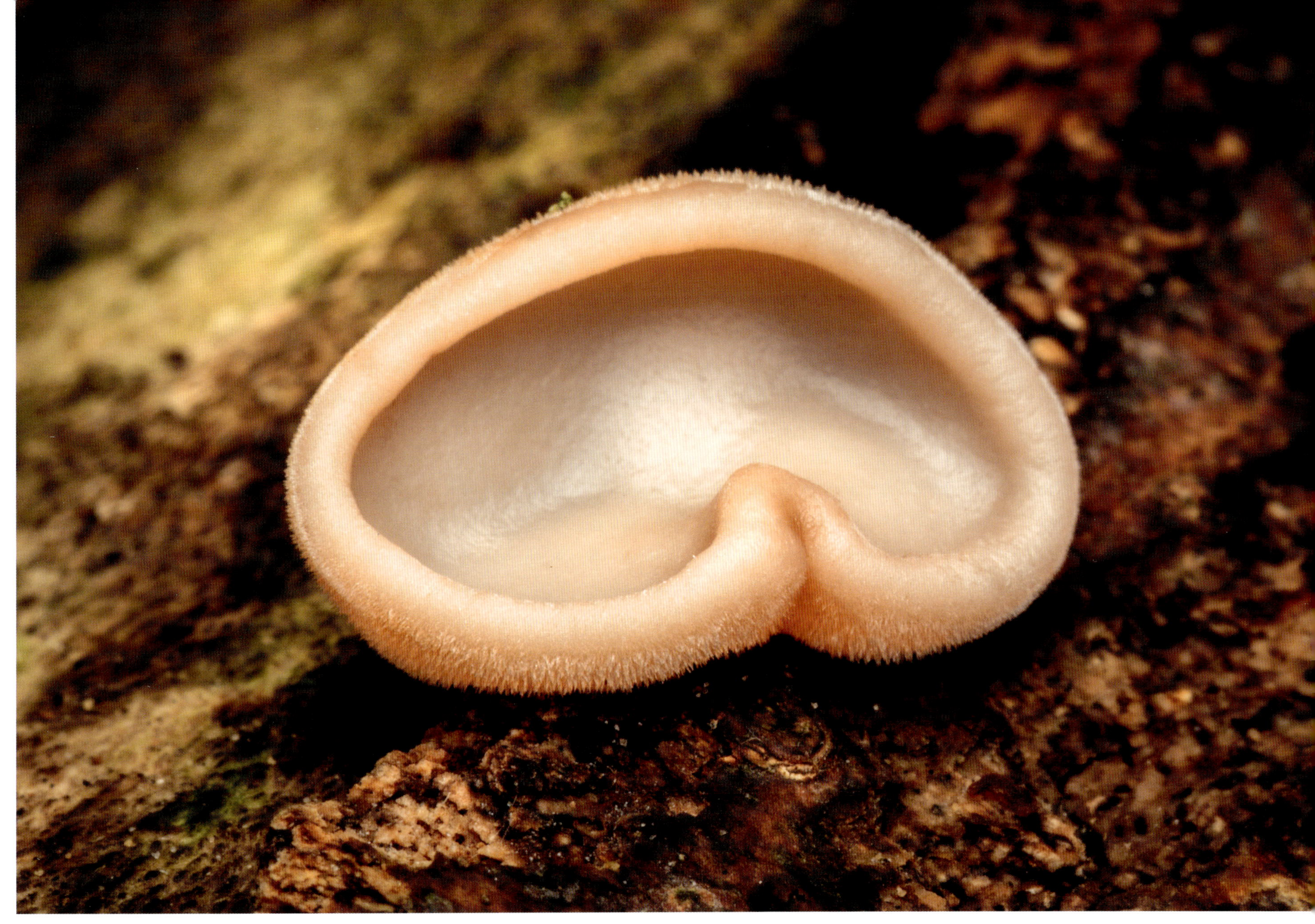

Can You Hear That?
Botanical Britain

Jimmy Reid
Jelly ear (*Auricularia auricula-judae*)
Bilston Glen, Scotland

Canon EOS 70D with Canon 100mm f/2.8 Macro
lens. 100mm; 1/200th second; f/20; ISO 100.

I found this mushroom while on a mushroom
hunt in my local woodland in Loanhead, Scotland.
I originally thought I had found an ear until I realised
it is actually a fungus called *Auricularia auricula-judae*, commonly known as Judas's ear or Jew's ear.
Quite a fitting name!

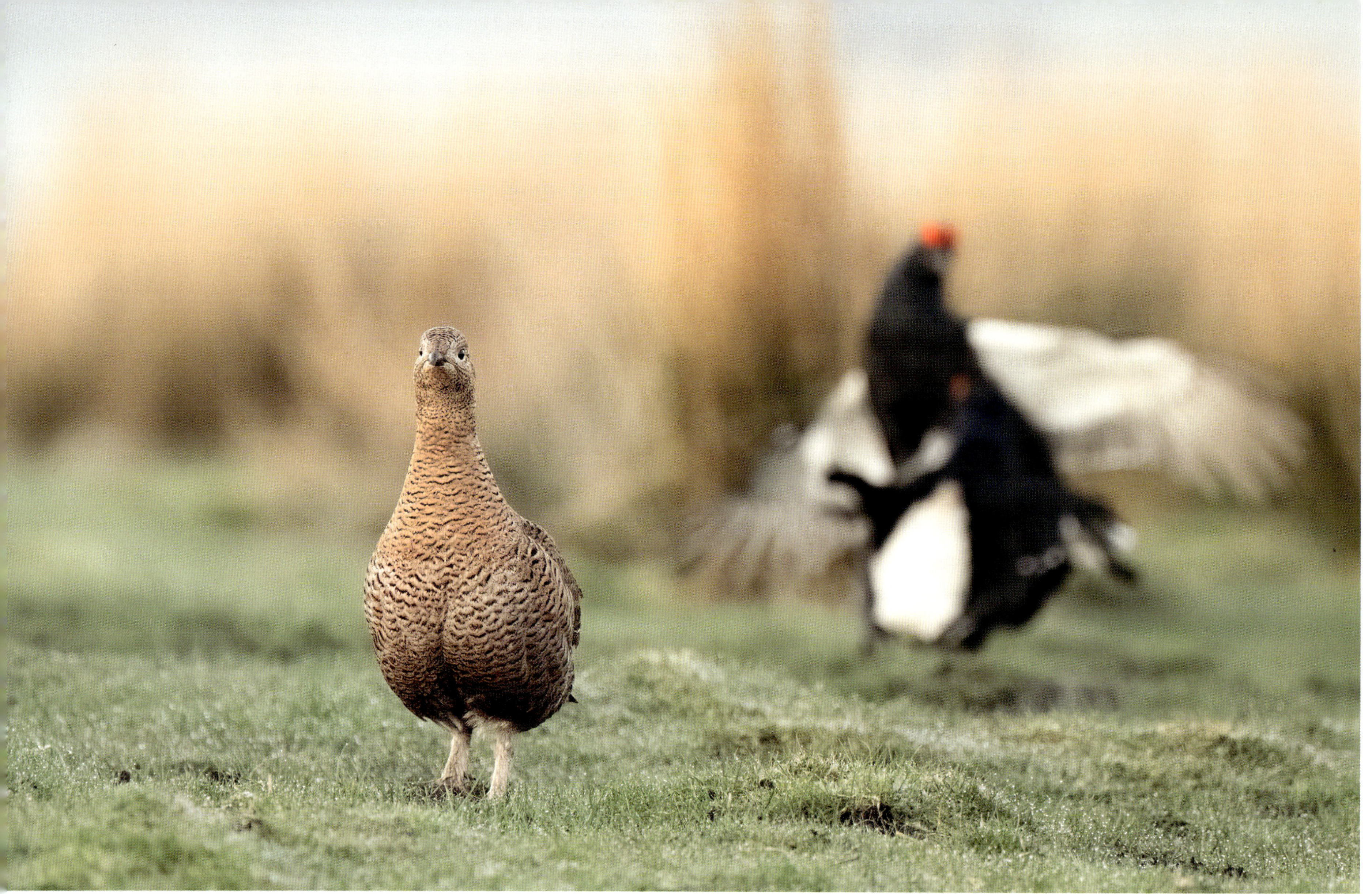

Pick of the Pack
Animal Behaviour

John Birch
Black grouse (*Tetrao tetrix*)
Appleby-in-Westmorland, Cumbria, England

Nikon Z 9 with Nikon 70-200mm f/2.8 lens &
1.4x teleconverter. 280mm; 1/800th second;
f/4; ISO 8,000.

Every April, the North Pennine hills come alive with
the cooing and rasping sounds of the black grouse
lek. Cock birds compete for the right to mate with
the female greyhen, which arrives before dawn.
They occasionally fight or display. If a greyhen visits,
they all significantly step up their performance. The
spectacle makes it well worth getting up very early
and sitting in a cramped tent hide. This shot shows
the greyhen waltzing through the lek, apparently
unimpressed by the fierce battle for her attention
behind her.

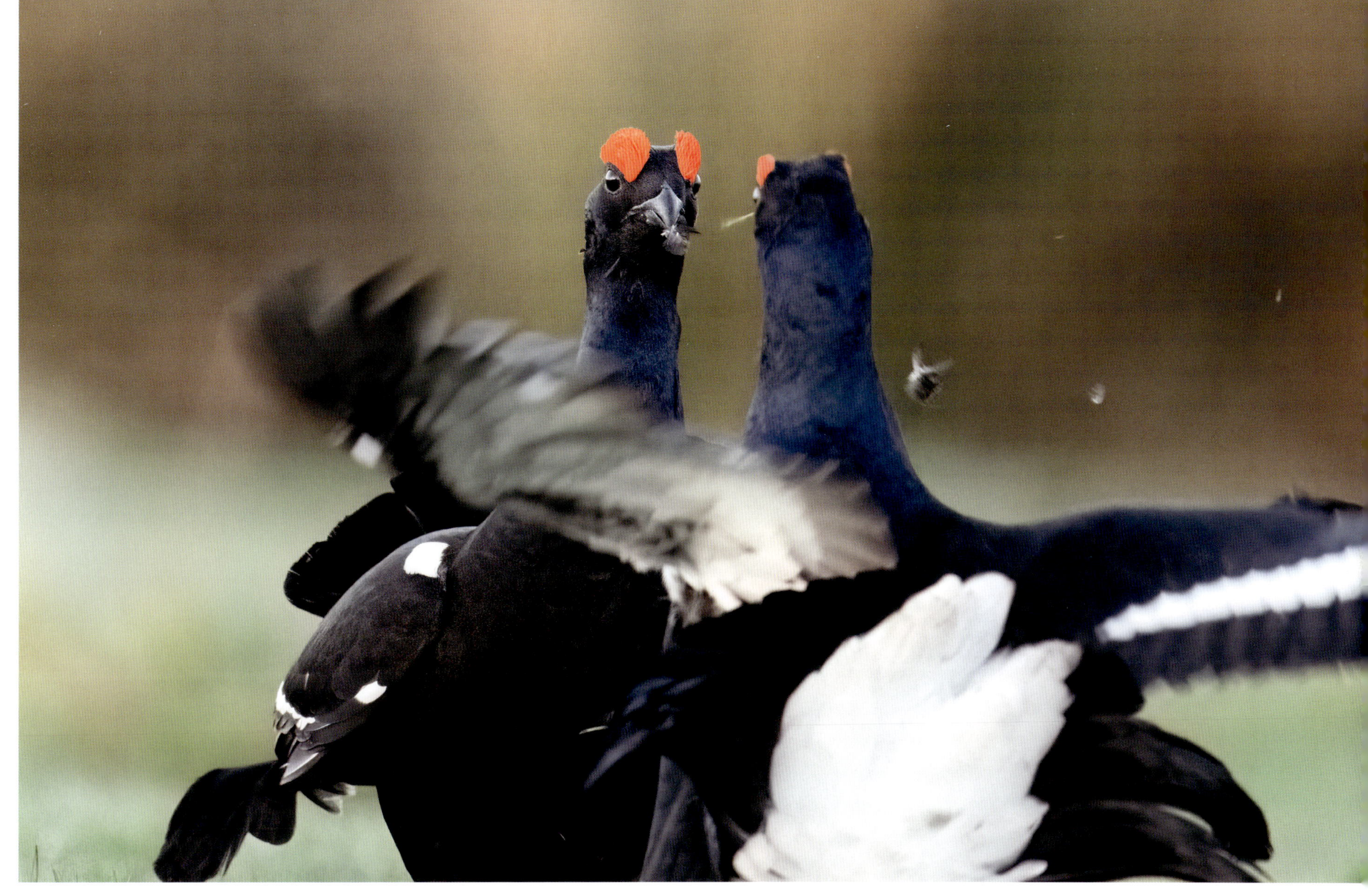

Black Grouse Lekking
Animal Behaviour

John Birch
Black grouse (*Tetrao tetrix*)
Appleby in Westmoreland, Cumbria, England

Nikon Z 9 with Nikon 800mm f/6.3 lens.
800mm; 1/500th second; f/6.3; ISO 25,600.

Every April, the North Pennine hills come alive with the cooing and rasping sound of the black grouse lek. Cock birds compete for the right to mate with the female greyhen arriving before dawn, occasionally fighting, or displaying. If a greyhen visits, they all significantly step up their performance. The spectacle makes it well worth getting up very early and sitting in a cramped tent hide. This shot shows two cock birds during a momentary pause during a fight, feathers still flying.

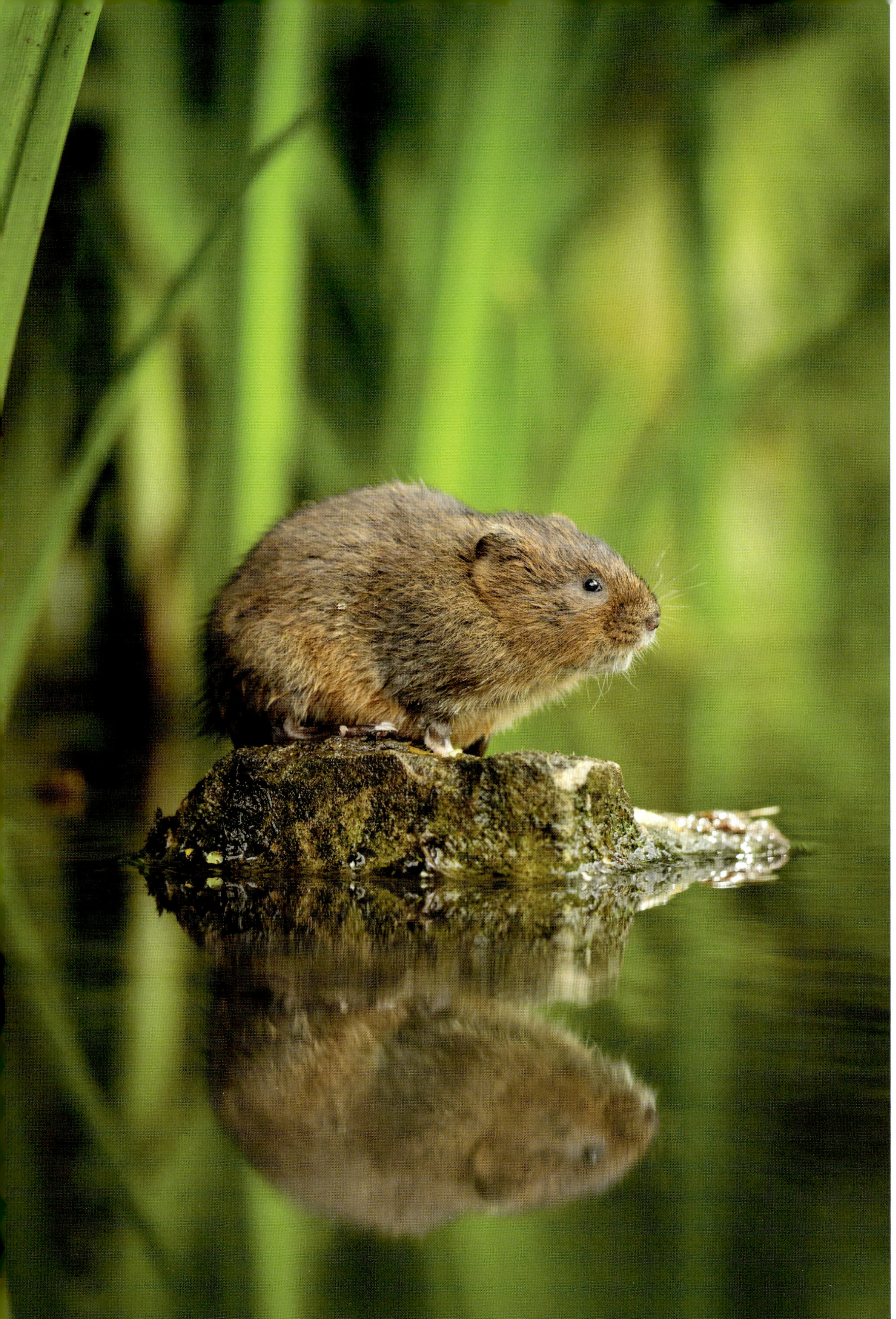

Water Vole Reflection
Animal Portraits

James Leyland
Water vole (*Arvicola amphibius*)
Dorset, England

Canon 1D X II with Canon 500mm f/4 II lens. 500mm; 1/320th second; f/4; ISO 1,000.

This photo was taken in June on private land in Dorset, using a Canon 1D X II and a Canon EF 500mm F4 II prime lens. The private land had a sunken hide next to a large pond, which was known to have water voles visiting. Some food was placed around the pond to attract the water voles, and then it was just a matter of waiting. After a few hours, I was rewarded when a water vole came within a few metres of the hide, where I was able to stay hidden and capture this photo.

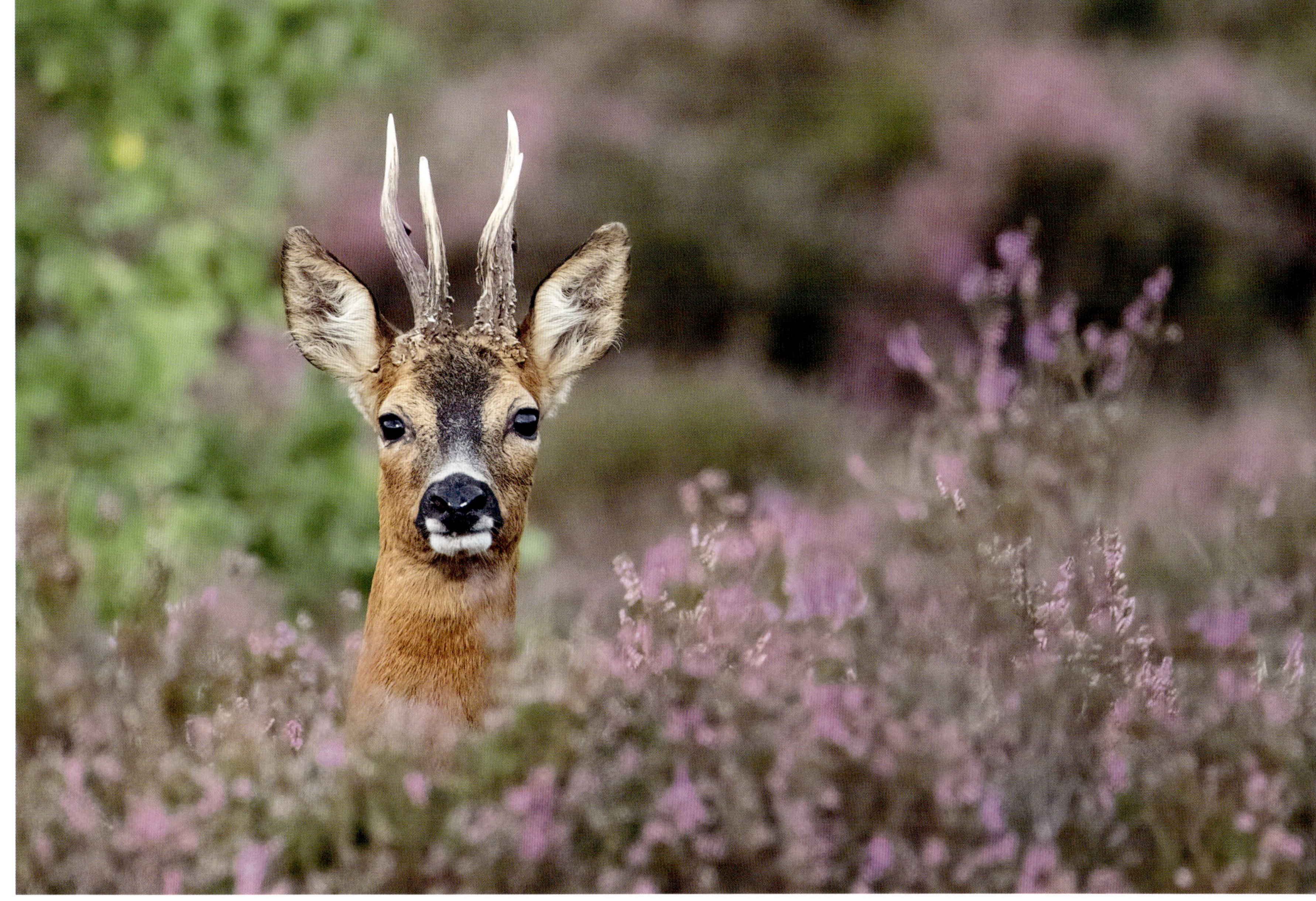

Heathland Buck
Habitat

Daniel Langer
Roe deer (*Capreolus capreolus*)
Surrey, England

Fujifilm X-T2 with Fujifilm 100-400mm f/4.5-5.6 lens.
400mm; 1/1,000th second; f/5.6; ISO 800.

I had visited this particular heathland with a friend who is an expert in deer behaviour. My plan was to capture a portrait photo of a roebuck among the heather. The purple colour complements the beauty of this elegant native species. In July and August, coinciding with the heathland blooms, males are solitary and roam large territories. So it was a matter of waiting, sitting hidden among the heather, with the camera mounted on a tripod, ready to swing the camera wherever a buck might emerge. And he did. He stared straight into my camera for five seconds, then he was gone.

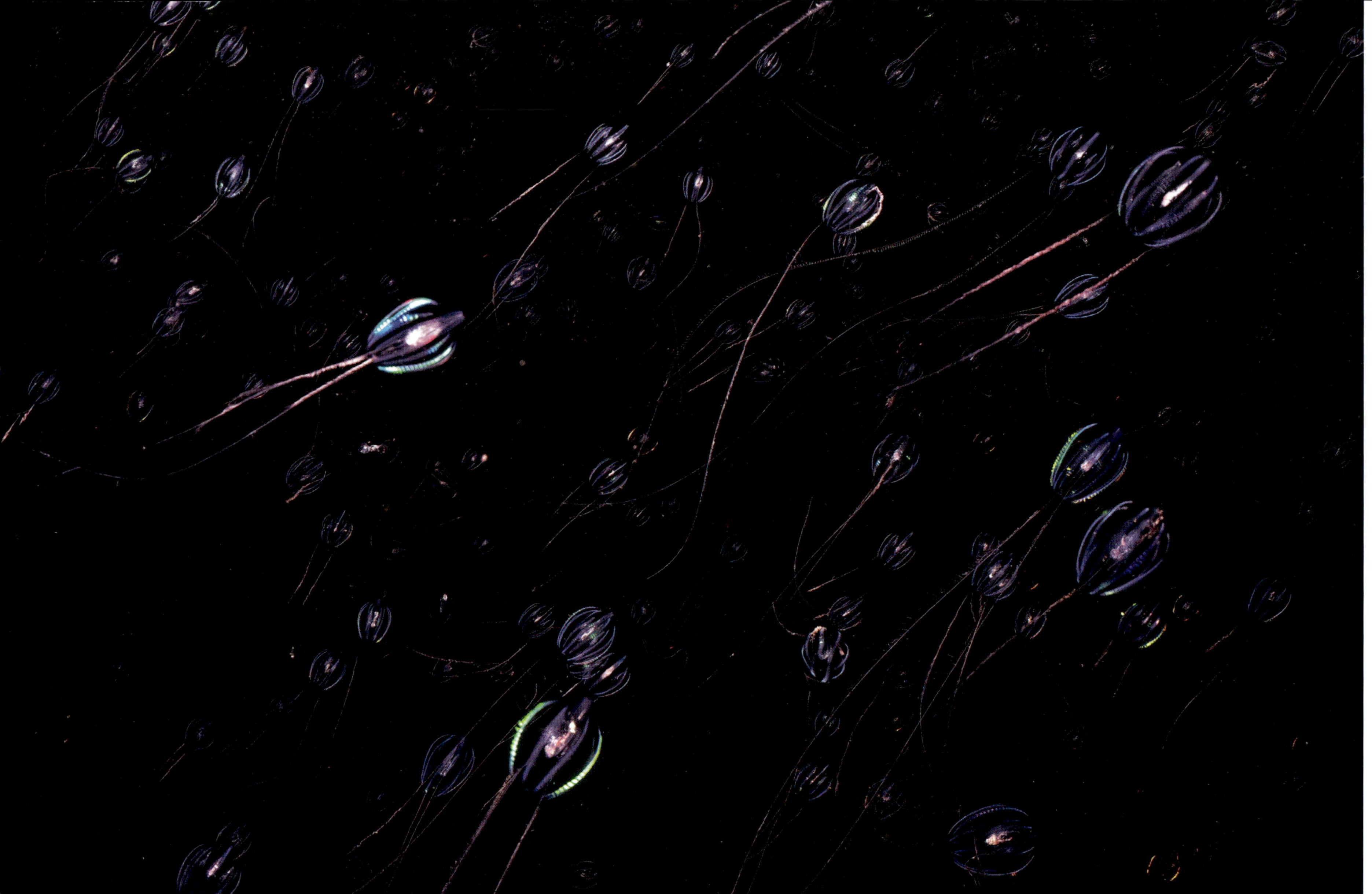

Galactic Gooseberries
Coast & Marine | Highly Commended

Billy Arthur
Sea gooseberry (*Pleurobrachia pileus*)
Orkney Islands, Scotland

Sony A7R III with Sony 28-60mm f/4-5.6 lens.
28mm; 1/160th second; f/16; ISO 250.

This dense group of sea gooseberries was great fun
to shoot. I used my underwater strobes and a narrow
aperture to try to reduce the amount of ambient light
and give the image a space-like feel.

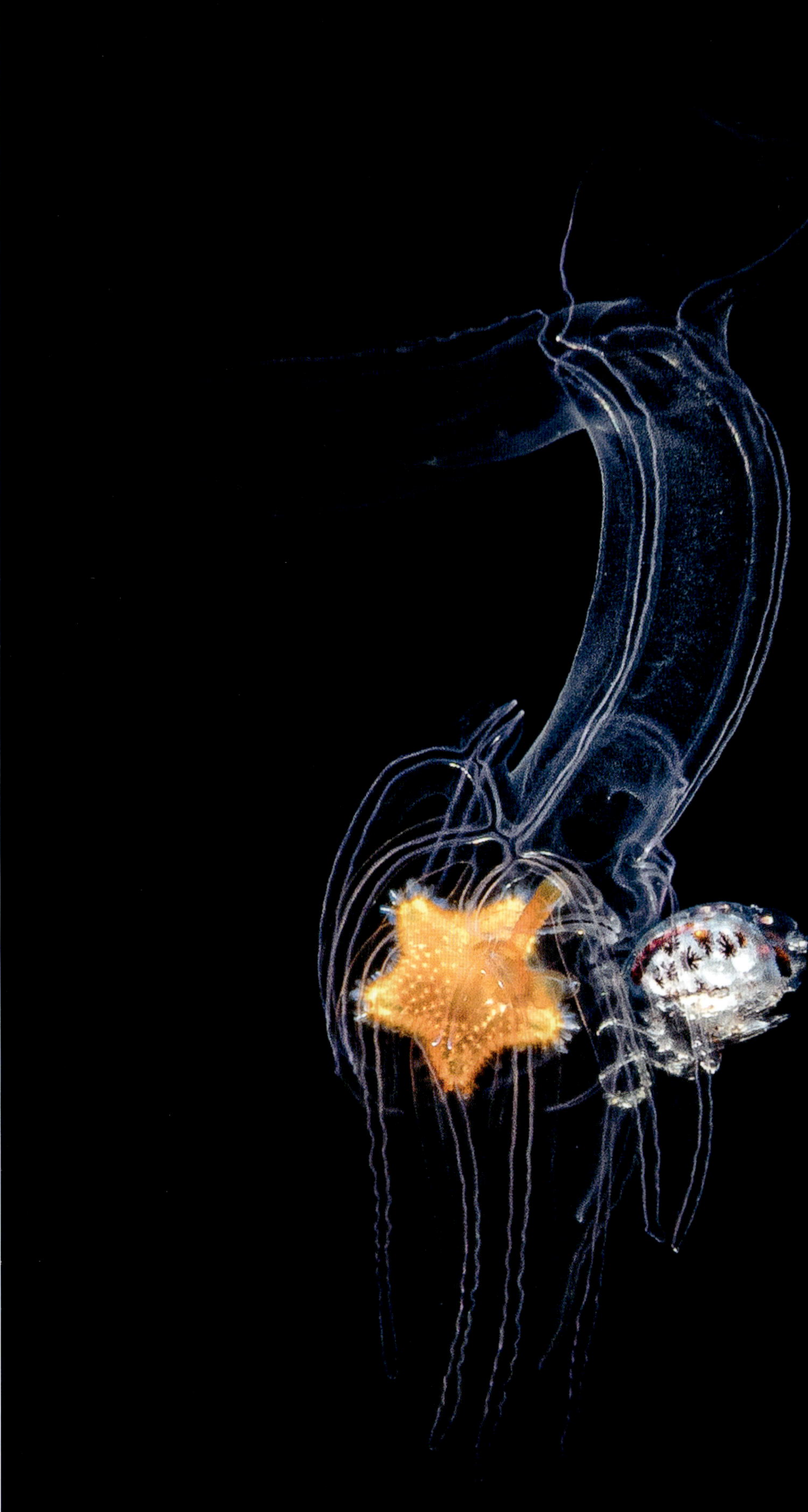

Star Rider
Coast & Marine

Kirsty Andrews
Starfish larva (Luidiidae) and Amphipod
(Hyperiidae)
North Rona, Scotland

Nikon D500 with Nikon 60mm f/2.8
lens. 60mm; 1/250th second; f/22;
ISO 250.

I saw this pair on a night dive off North
Rona, an uninhabited island in the
North Atlantic, 45 miles north of the
Outer Hebrides in Scotland. It was a
remote and exhilarating dive, simply
due to the location. The tiny amphipod,
a crustacean a few millimetres in size,
had hitched a ride on a juvenile starfish.
In this stage of its growth cycle, the
starfish propels itself through the water
by moving jelly-like appendages, which
it will later shed. The amphipod digs
in to make a convenient home and
feeding spot as it grabs passing food.

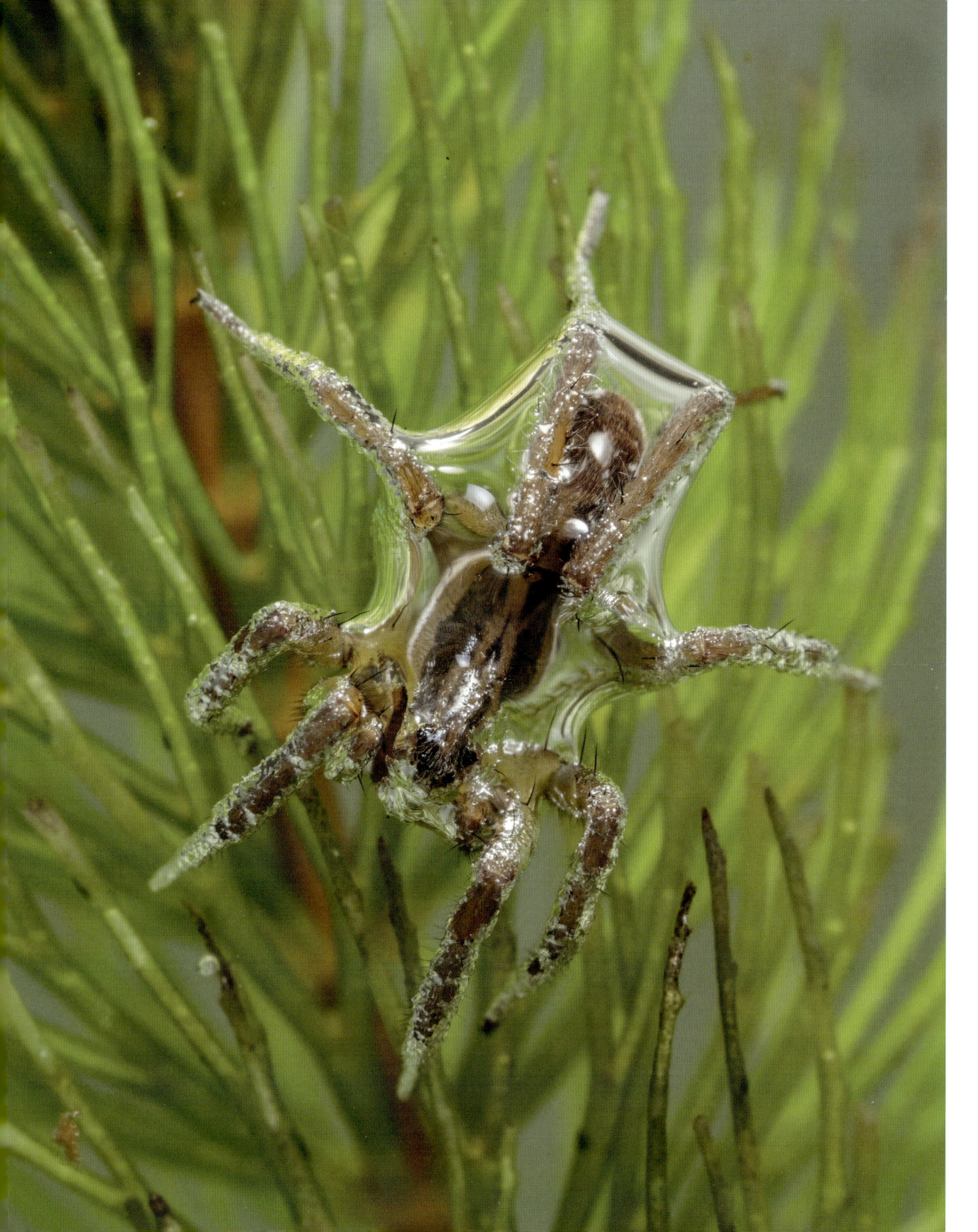

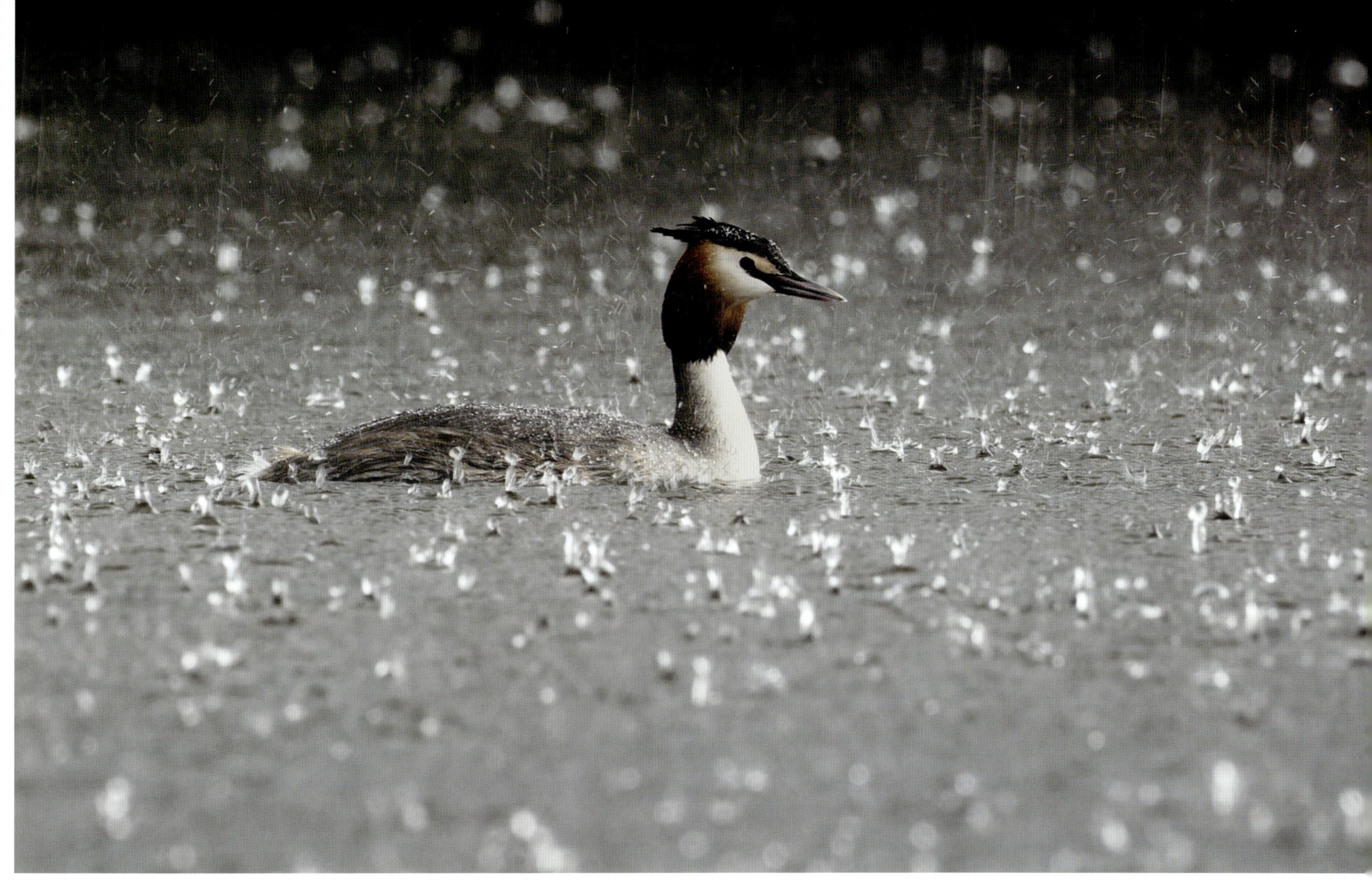

◀ **Pirate Otter Spider**
Animal Behaviour

Neil Phillips
Pirate otter spider (*Pirata piraticus*)
My garden in south Essex, England

Olympus E-M1 with Olympus 60mm f/2.8 Macro
lens. 60mm; 1/250th second; f/11; ISO 200.

While carrying out a pond survey, I caught this pirate
otter spider. I placed it in a photo aquarium with
some pond weed, and it proceeded to crawl down it.
In doing so, it trapped a bubble of air on the hairs on
its body and legs. This species can stay underwater
for an extended period of time, using the bubble as
both an air supply and a physical gill. It was released
afterwards.

Great Crested Grebe in Torrential Rain Storm
Habitat

Richard Sheldrake
Great crested grebe (*Podiceps cristatus*)
Verwood, Dorset, England

Nikon Z 9 with Nikon 500mm f/4 lens.
500mm; 1/100th second; f/9; ISO 400.

I had been photographing this lone great crested
grebe from a much lower position closer to the
water level. However, it swam away around a bank,
so I moved and was trying to get even lower when
this torrential rain hit, but it lasted only a matter of
seconds (thankfully). While I would have loved to get
down even lower, it just wasn't possible in that short
time. So, I took what I could, and I love the absolute
fury of those rain/haildrops splashing on the lake
surface. Of course, the grebe couldn't have cared less!

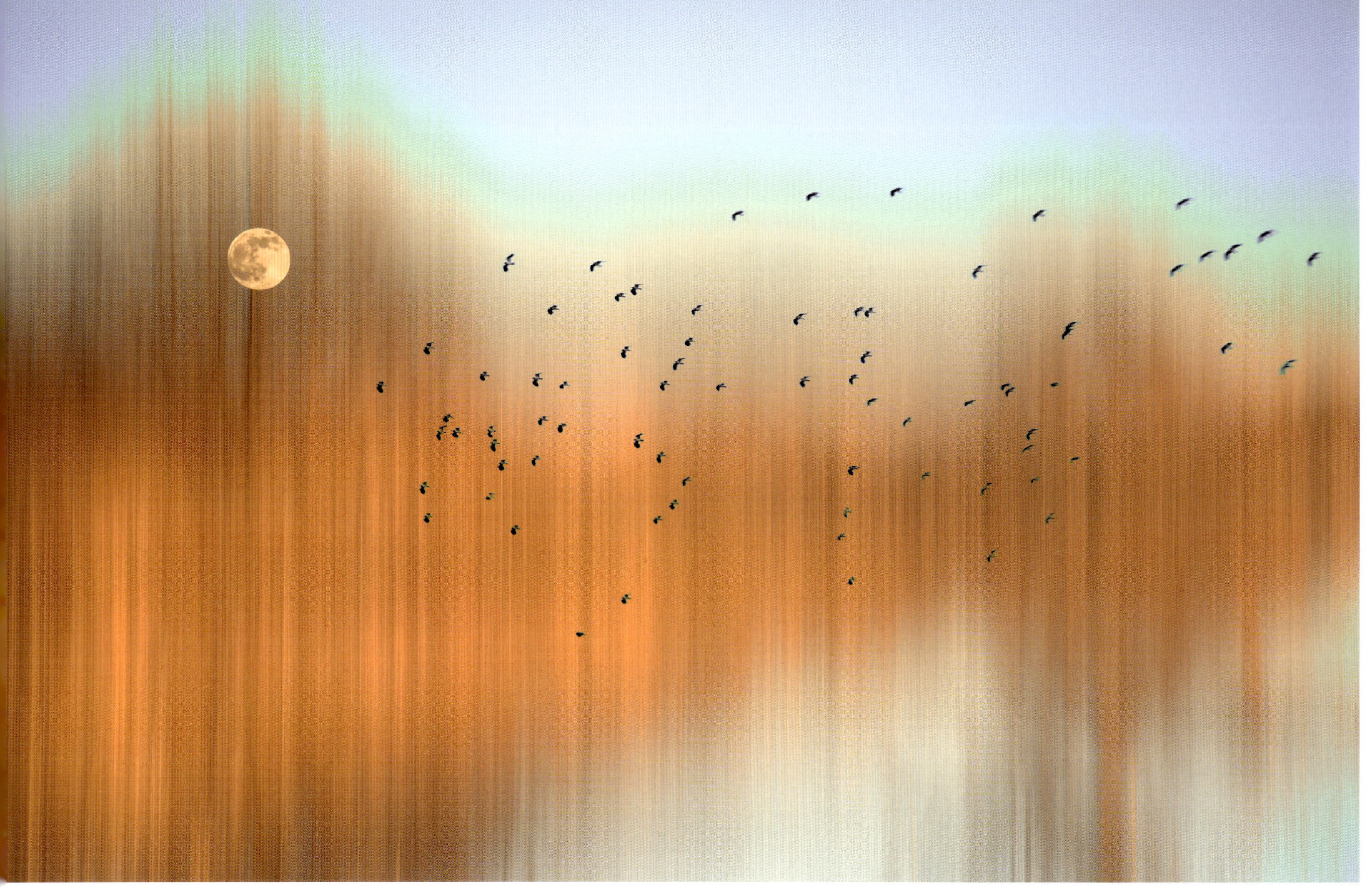

Dreamscape
Habitat

Simon Carder
Lapwing (*Vanellus vanellus*)
RSPB Ham Wall, England

Canon EOS R5 with Canon 70-200mm f/2.8 II lens.
200mm; 1/640th second; f/2.8; ISO 100.

This is a three-image, in-camera multiple exposure taken at RSPB Ham Wall in Somerset. I aimed to create an abstract image that conveys the essence of the Somerset Levels landscape and its wide-open spaces. The foundation of the image is the golden reeds in the late afternoon sun, which were captured using Intentional Camera Movement (ICM) to create blur. The lapwings and moon were overlaid on this to create the final image.

Single Snowdrop
Botanical Britain | Highly Commended

Ross Hoddinott
Snowdrop (*Galanthus nivalis*)
Broxwater, Cornwall, England

Nikon D850 with Nikon 200mm f/4 Micro lens.
200mm; 1/200th second; f/4.5; ISO 800.

I captured this delicate, nodding snowdrop late one evening in our little woodland. I lay on the ground to achieve a low, natural perspective. I carefully selected my angle to include the diffused setting sun in the frame and used my camera's multiple exposure mode to create a dreamy, soft-focus effect in-camera. I later processed the image with a cool blue hue.

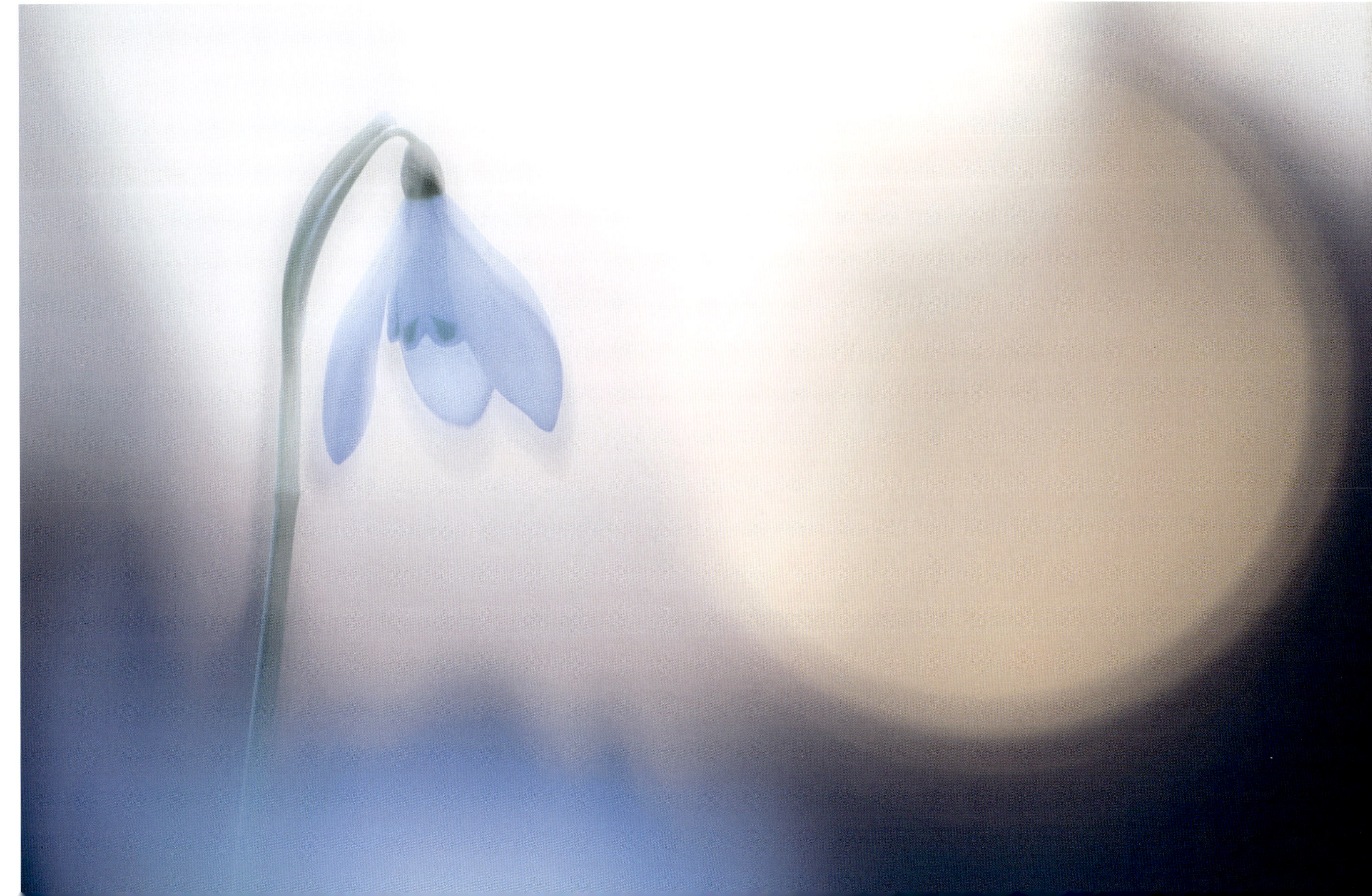

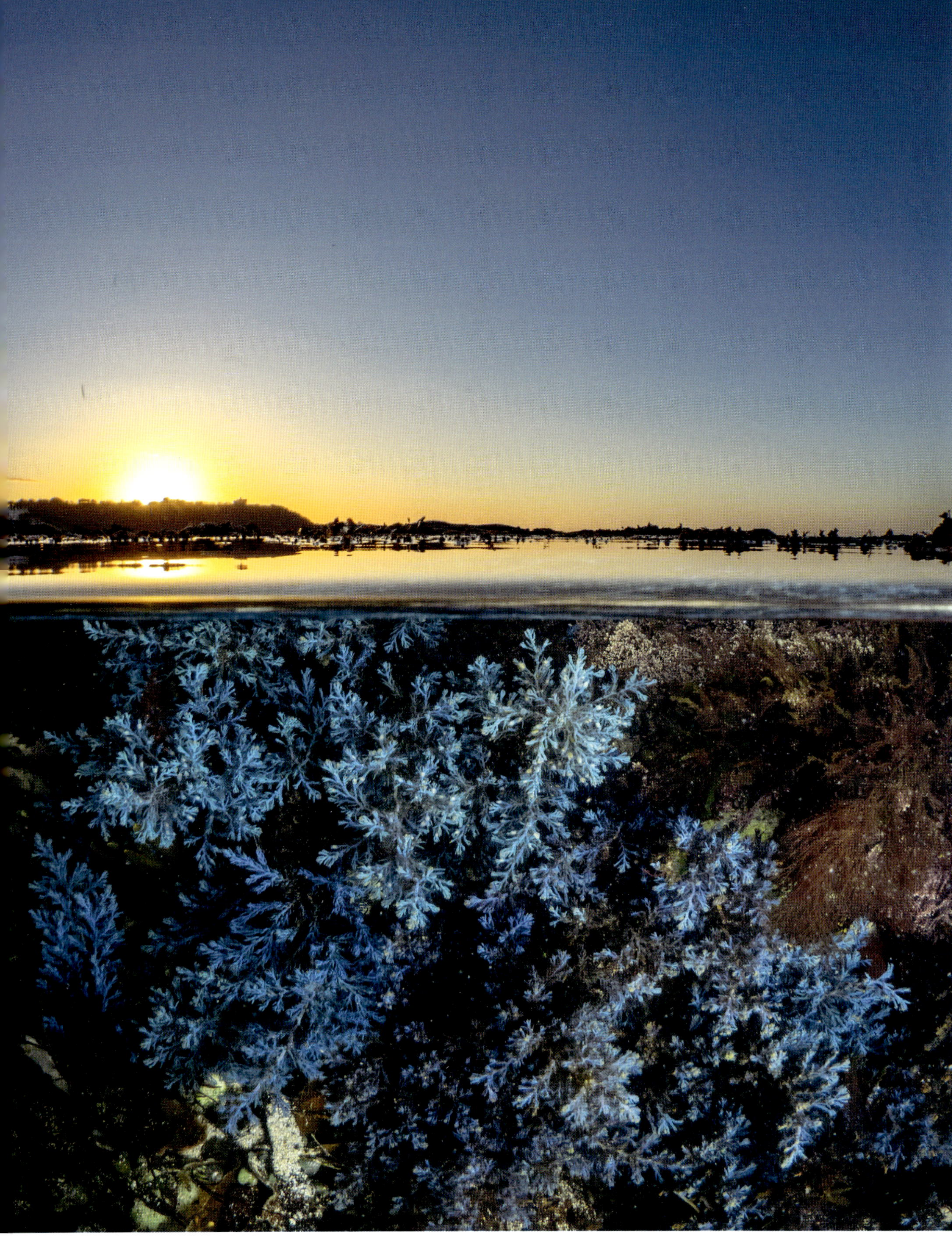

Rainbow at Dawn
Botanical Britain | Runner-up

Martin Stevens
Rainbow wrack (*Cystoseira tamariscifolia*)
Falmouth, Cornwall, England

Olympus E-M5 III with Olympus 8mm f/1.8 Fisheye lens. 8mm; 1/160th second; f/14; ISO 640.

I've had a mild obsession with rainbow wrack seaweed for years, with its spectacular iridescent blue colour. I'd taken many photos of it before, but I had long had in mind a split shot of it in a rock pool at sunrise. It required planning and luck because the seaweed only grows back in spring, being most colourful for a few weeks before the summer sun dulls its colour. I needed a low tide to expose the pools, in sync with sunrise – and a sunny morning! Fortunately, on one day it all came together. Taken with strobes on low power to light the seaweed.

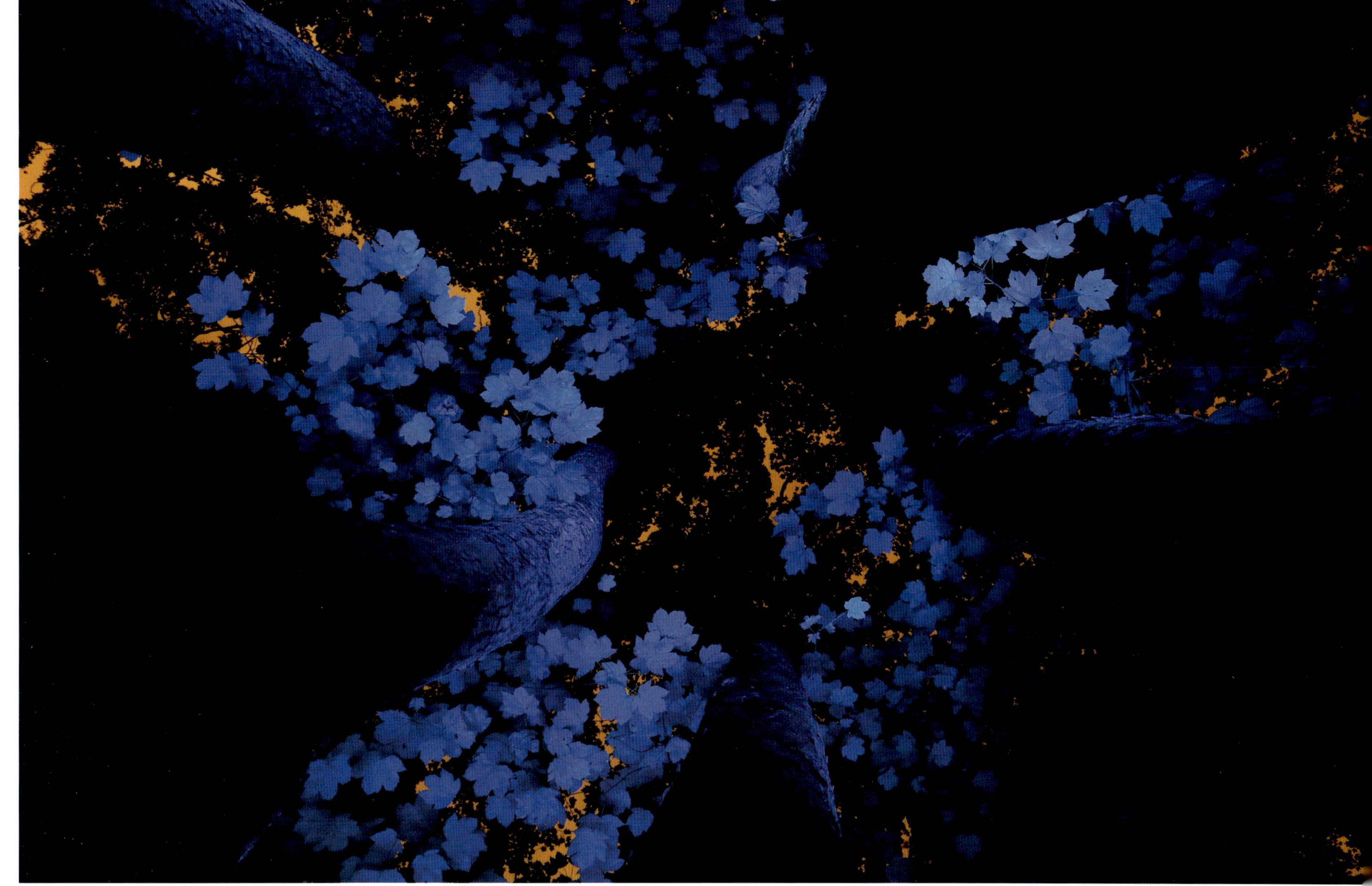

Blue Forest
Botanical Britain | Highly Commended

Ian Wade
Bristol, England

Canon 5D III with Canon 24-105mm f/4 lens.
24mm; 30 seconds; f/10; ISO 1,250.

I've been experimenting with different lighting techniques in my local woods for over six years. On this particular evening, I used a blue light to light-paint the tree canopy, set the shutter speed to 30 seconds and ran around the group of trees with the blue light facing up. The blue light created a beautiful effect, highlighting the intricate details of the tree branches and leaves. The long exposure also allowed me to capture the movement of the light as I ran through the trees. The result is a dreamy, ethereal image that captures the magic of the forest at night.

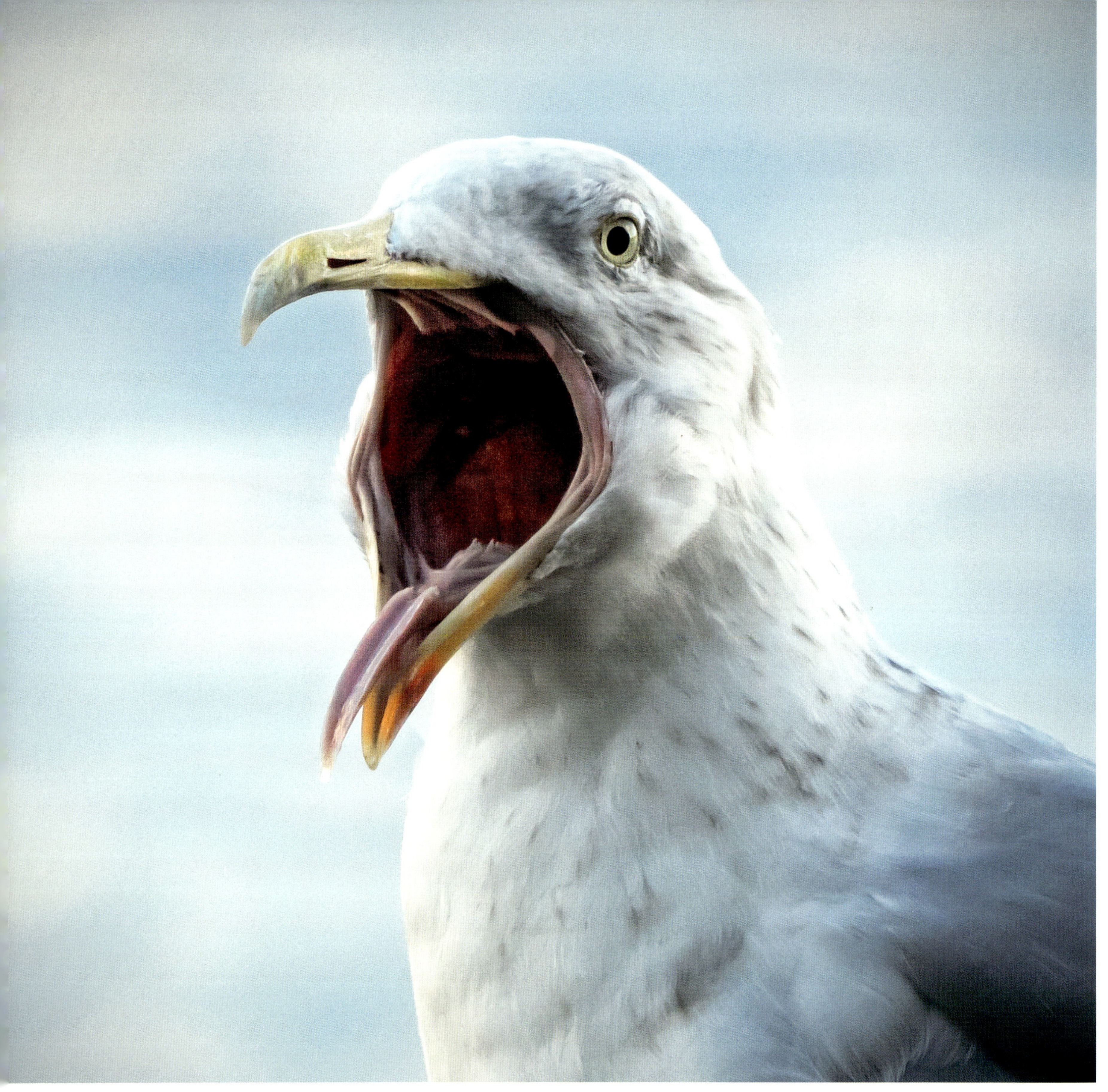

◀ **London Calling**
Animal Portraits

Robert Wilkinson
Herring gull (*Larus argentatus*)
Thames foreshore at Tower Bridge,
London, England

Olympus E-M5 II with Olympus
100-400mm f/5-6.3 lens. 400mm;
1/1,000th second; f/6.3; ISO 800.

I made eye contact with this herring
gull on the Thames Foreshore at Tower
Bridge on a chilly and overcast January
morning. She seemed unfazed by my
presence as she called urgently across
the river to another gull as if to coax
them over to the South Side, but to no
avail. There has long been a reluctance
for North Londoners to cross that
boundary.

Pheasant ▶
Animal Portraits

Weng Lee
Pheasant (*Phasianus colchicus*)
Cleatham, Kirton in Lindsey, England

Sony A1 with Sony 200-600mm f/5.6-
6.3 lens. 600mm; 1/800th second;
f/6.3; ISO 2,500.

Often, many pheasants come along
the field near Cleatham Hall. I got
permission to capture some wildlife
there, so I had been waiting for over
an hour for this pheasant to decide
to stand in front of me.

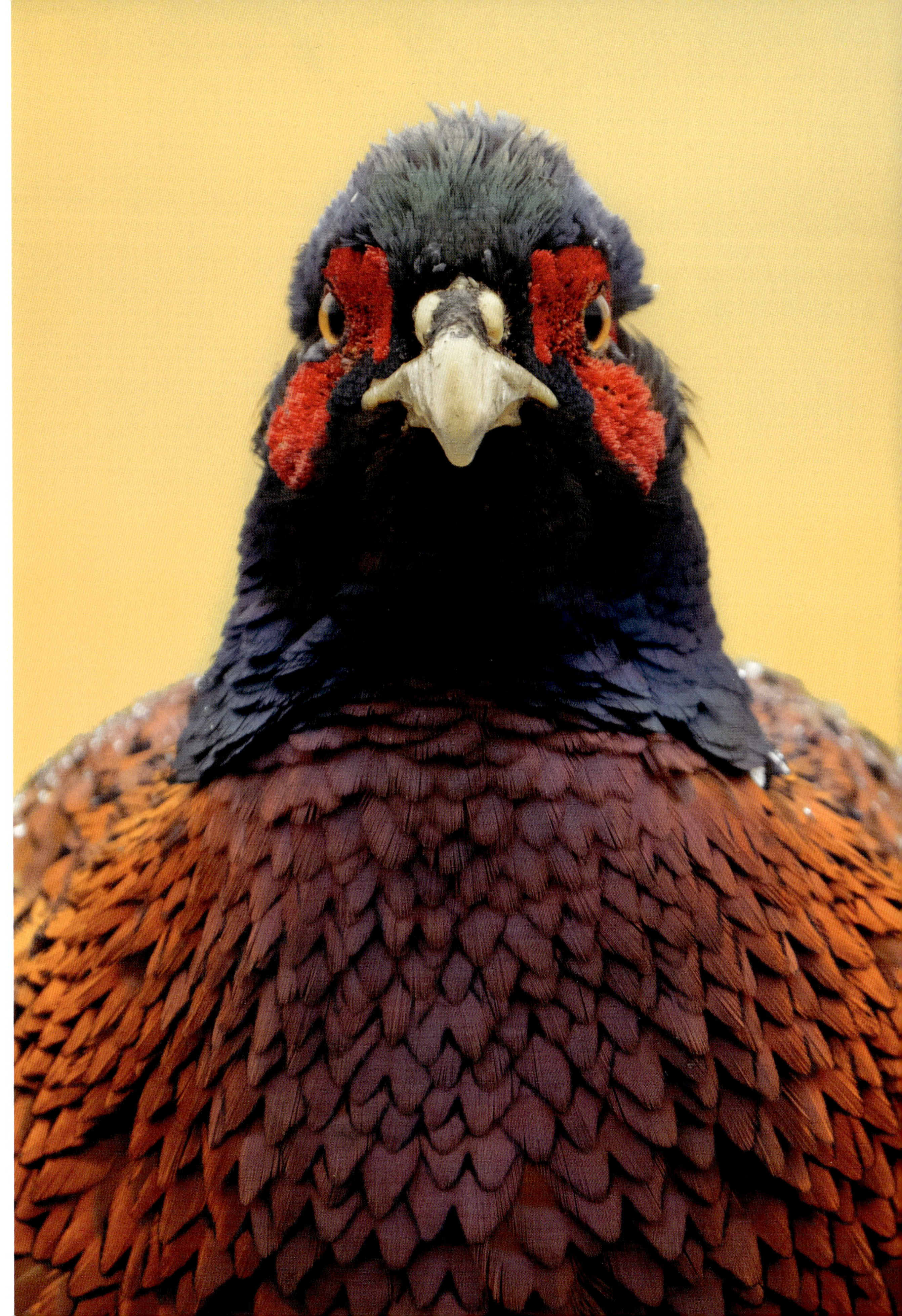

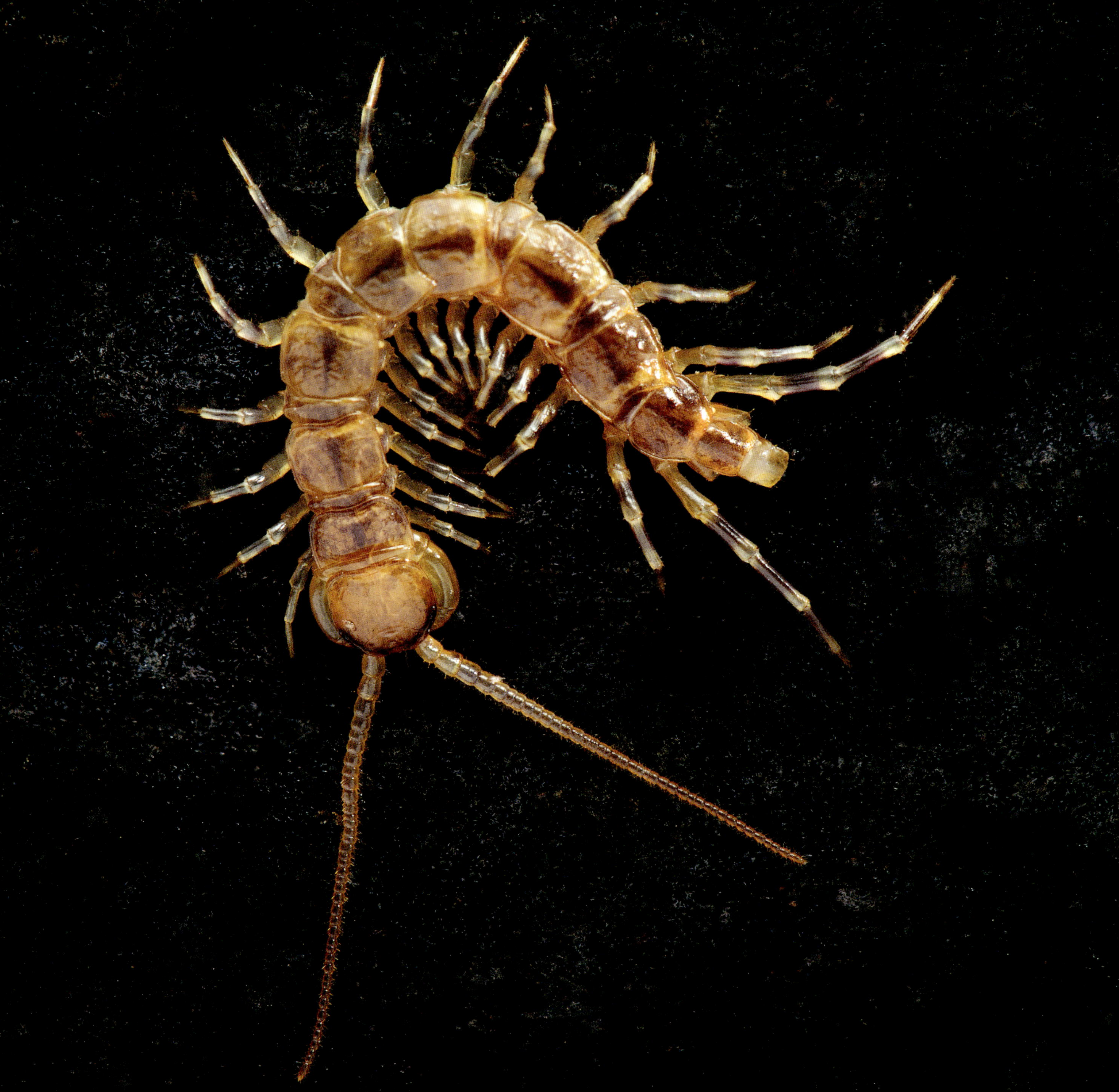

Chris Robbins
Brown centipede (*Lithobius forficatus*)
Devon, England

Canon 5D III with Canon 100mm f/2.8 Macro lens.
100mm; 1/160th second; f/8; ISO 100.

I was moving a pile of old roof slates at the bottom
of the garden and kept seeing various creatures
running out, but this centipede stayed dead still,
so I gently replaced the slate and went in to get my
camera and flash with a homemade diffuser. I was
pleased to find that the centipede was still in this
lovely curved position when I got back.

The Gaze ▶
Animal Portraits

Simon Withyman
Red fox (*Vulpes vulpes*)
Bristol, England

Canon EOS R5 with Canon 70-200mm f/2.8 II lens.
160mm; 1/1,250th second; f/5.6; ISO 125.

This young male fox was resting on some grass
in the early morning sun. He briefly looked straight
at the camera, and due to the side lighting, created
this dramatic portrait.

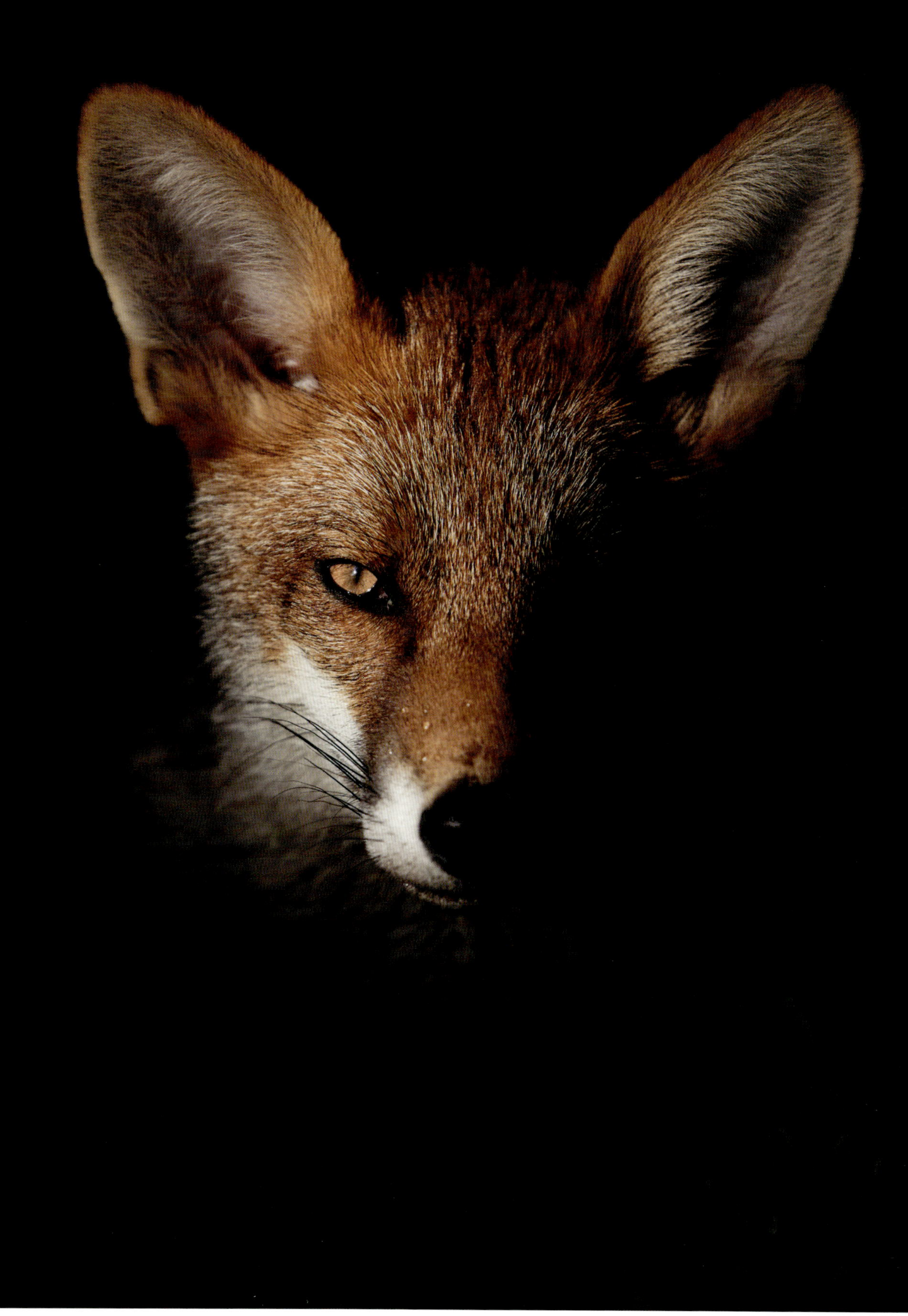

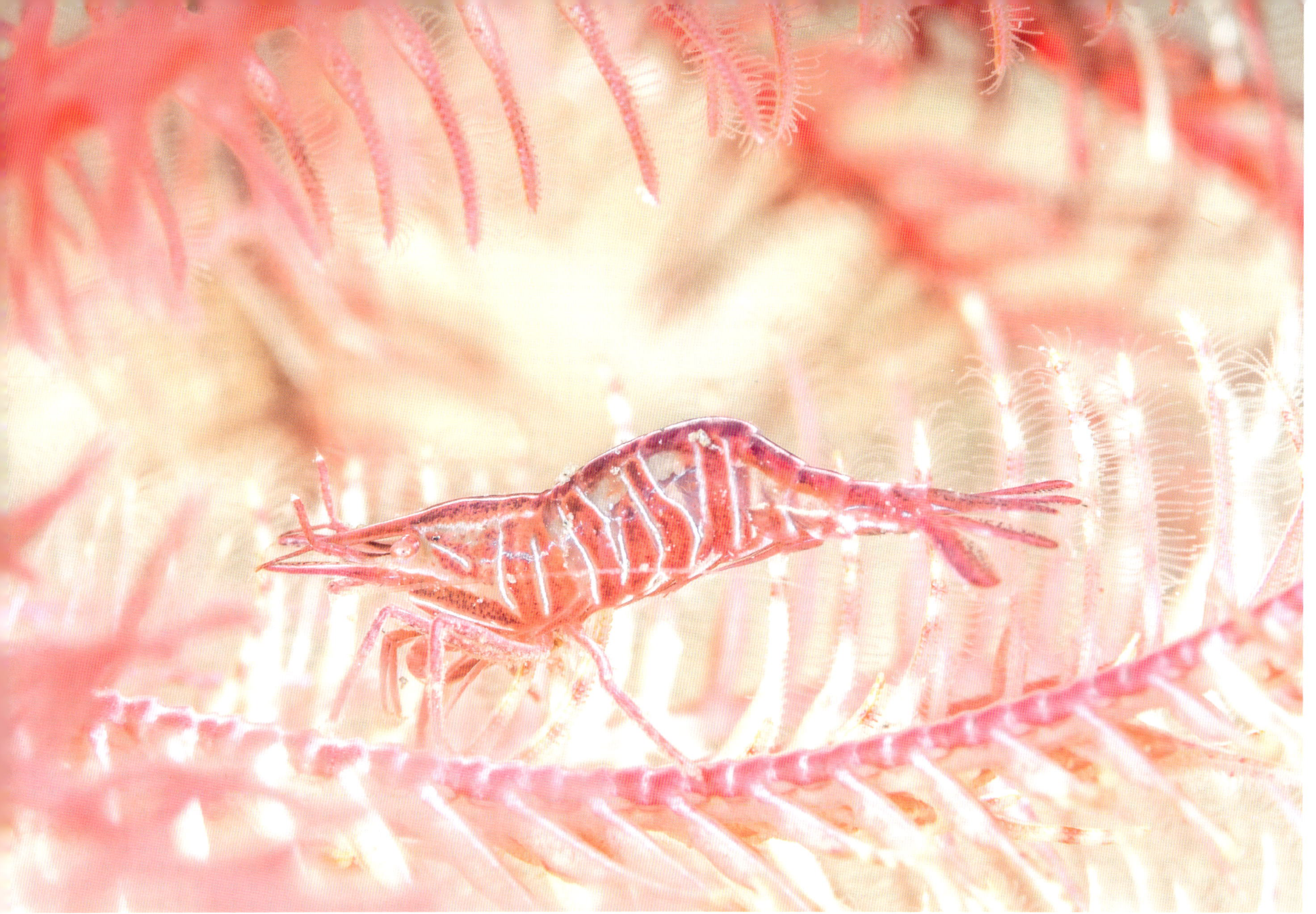

Camouflaged Crinoid Shrimp
Coast & Marine

Dan Bolt
Crinoid shrimp (*Hippolyte prideauxiana*)
Loch Duich, Scotland

Canon EOS R7 with Canon 100mm f/2.8 Macro lens.
100mm; 1/250th second; f/10; ISO 200.

Finding this elusive species (one that is both uncommon and very well camouflaged) is just the first part of photographing it. The second part is to wait until both it and its host crinoid (a featherstar) are relaxed so as to find a way through the crinoid's limbs to try to grab a few frames before they close up again. For this shot, I decided to use one strobe to light the foreground and one aimed at the white sand in the background to create the pleasing high-key look in this image.

Hermit Crab Atop an Orange Finger
Coast & Marine

Simon Temple
Hermit crab (Paguroidea) and Dead man's fingers
(*Alcyonium digitatum*)
Lochcarron, Ross and Cromarty, Scotland

Nikon D50 with Tamron 90mm f/2.8 lens.
90mm; 1/250th second; f/18; ISO 250.

A hermit crab sits atop an orange sponge amongst feeding polyps. The green/blue of the crab juxtaposes the orange of its background. I chose to shoot the crab off-centre to highlight the outline of the polyps to the right against a black background, adding more depth to the frame.

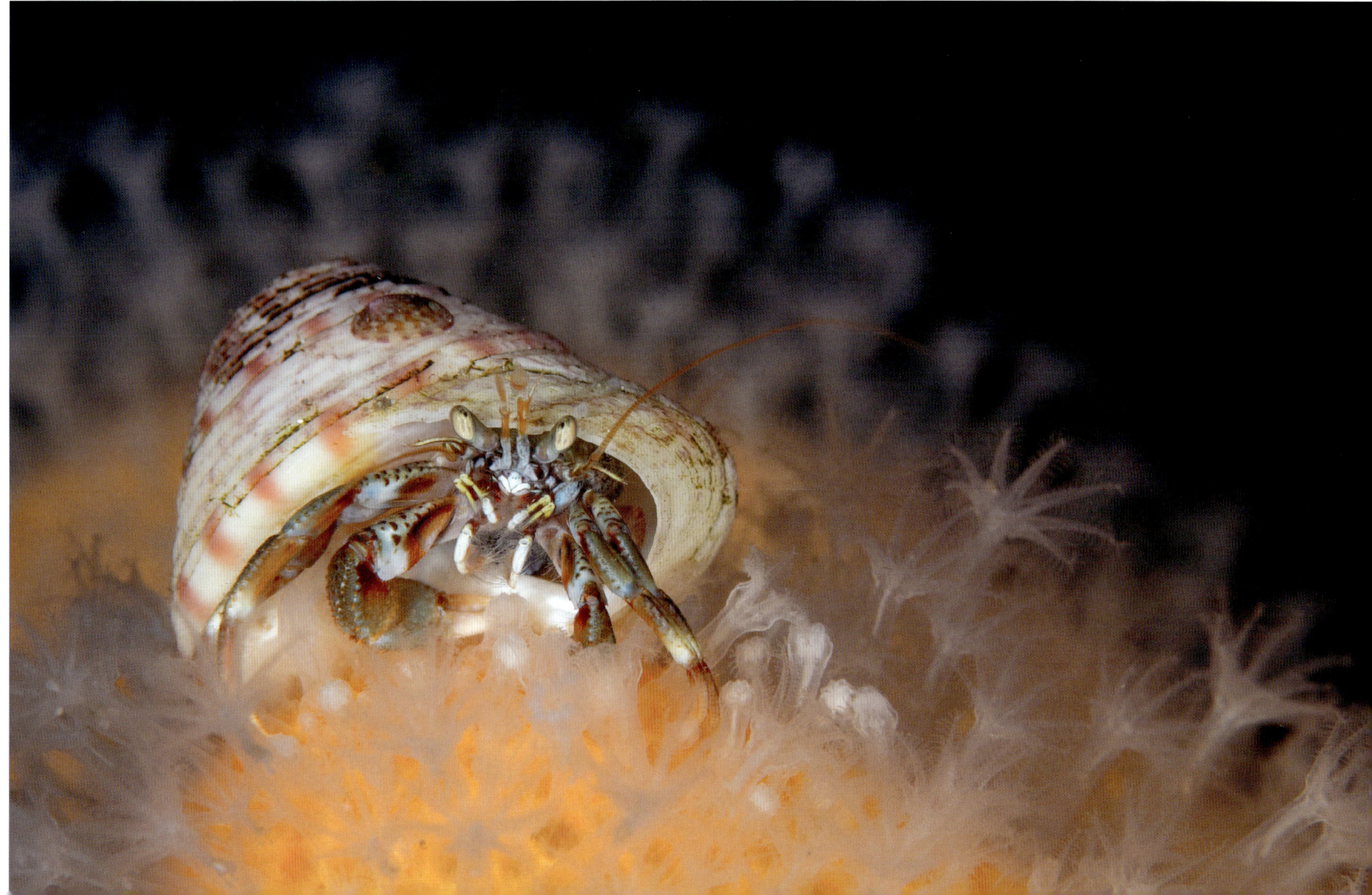

In the Pink
Animal Portraits

David Pressland
Guillemot (*Uria aalge*)
Flamborough Head, East Yorkshire, England

Nikon D750 with Nikon 300mm f/4 lens. 300mm;
1/1,250th second; f/5; ISO 200.

June is a busy month at Yorkshire's seabird colonies, and Flamborough Head is no exception. I was there to photograph auks in flight but couldn't resist the bright yellow gape of this guillemot perched on the cliff top, calling to its mate. I got down low and shot through the red campion flowers to produce the pink haze in the foreground.

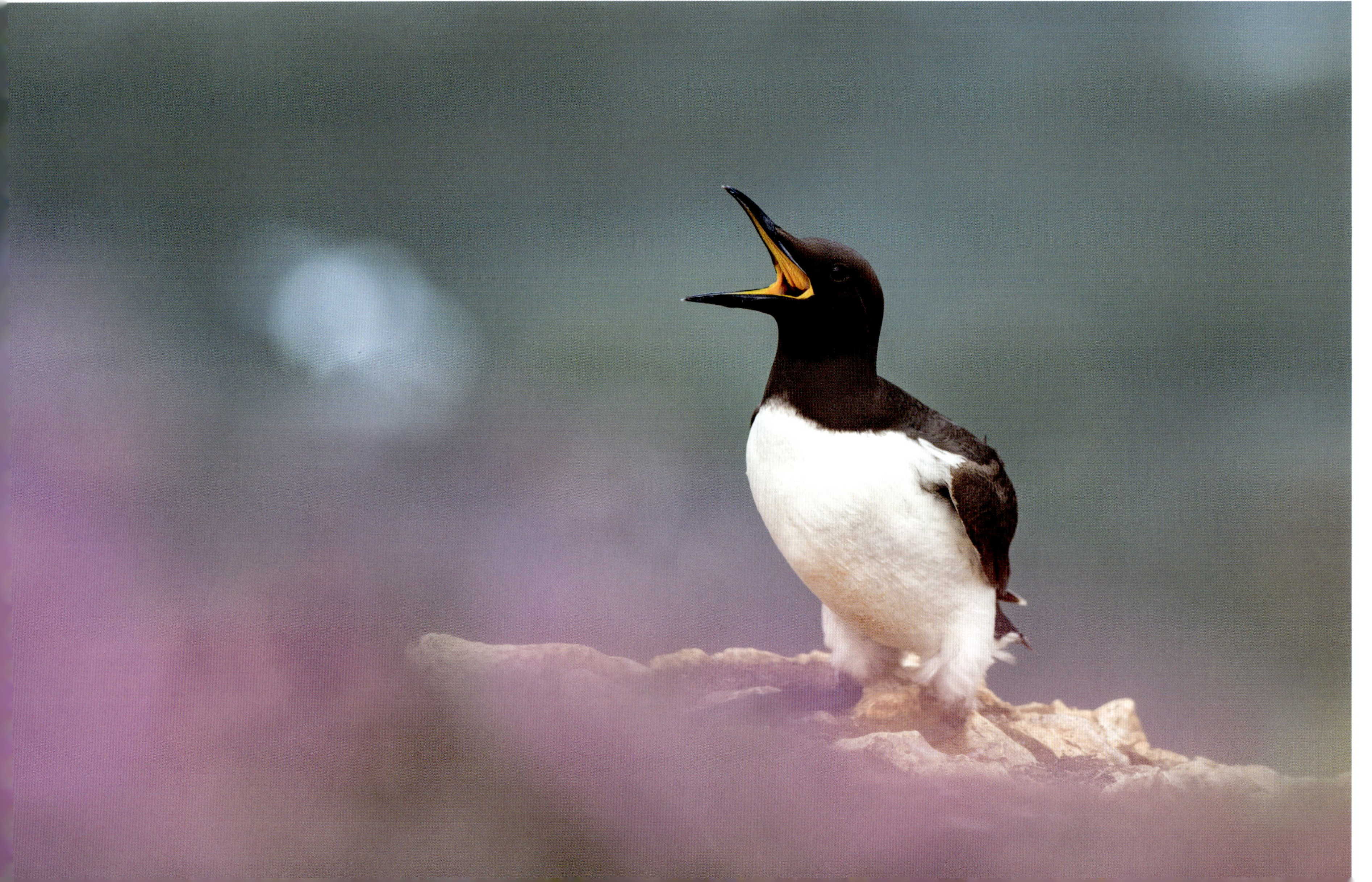

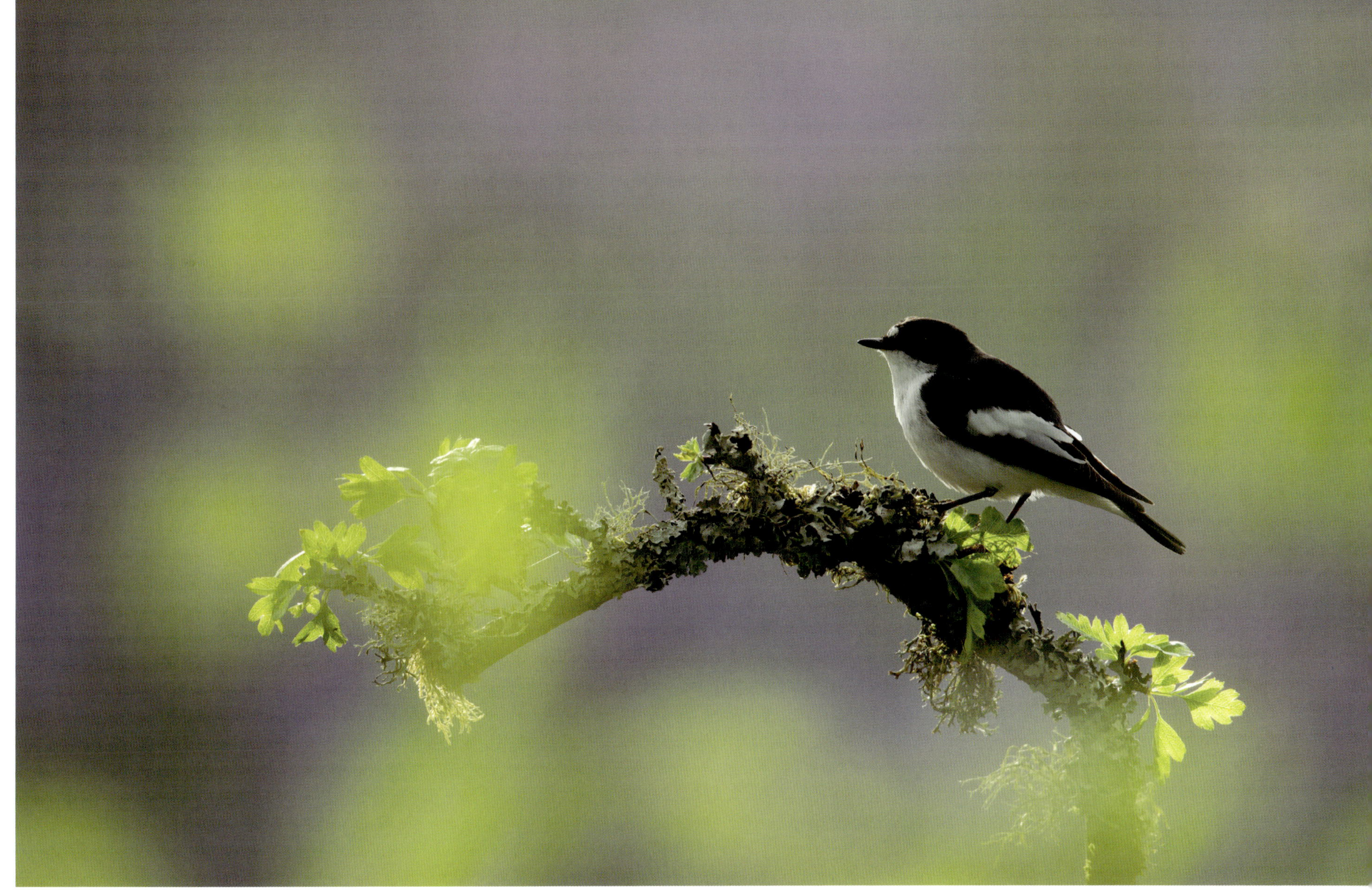

Pied Flycatcher
Wild Woods | Highly Commended

Danny Green
Pied flycatcher (*Ficedula hypoleuca*)
Dumfries and Galloway, Scotland

Canon 1D X II with Canon 500mm f/4 II lens.
500mm; 1/160th second; f/5.6; ISO 400.

I took this image in Dumfries and Galloway in May.
I think the pied flycatcher is one of our most beautiful
summer visitors. The wood that this pair of pied
flycatchers has chosen to rear their chicks was such
a special location.

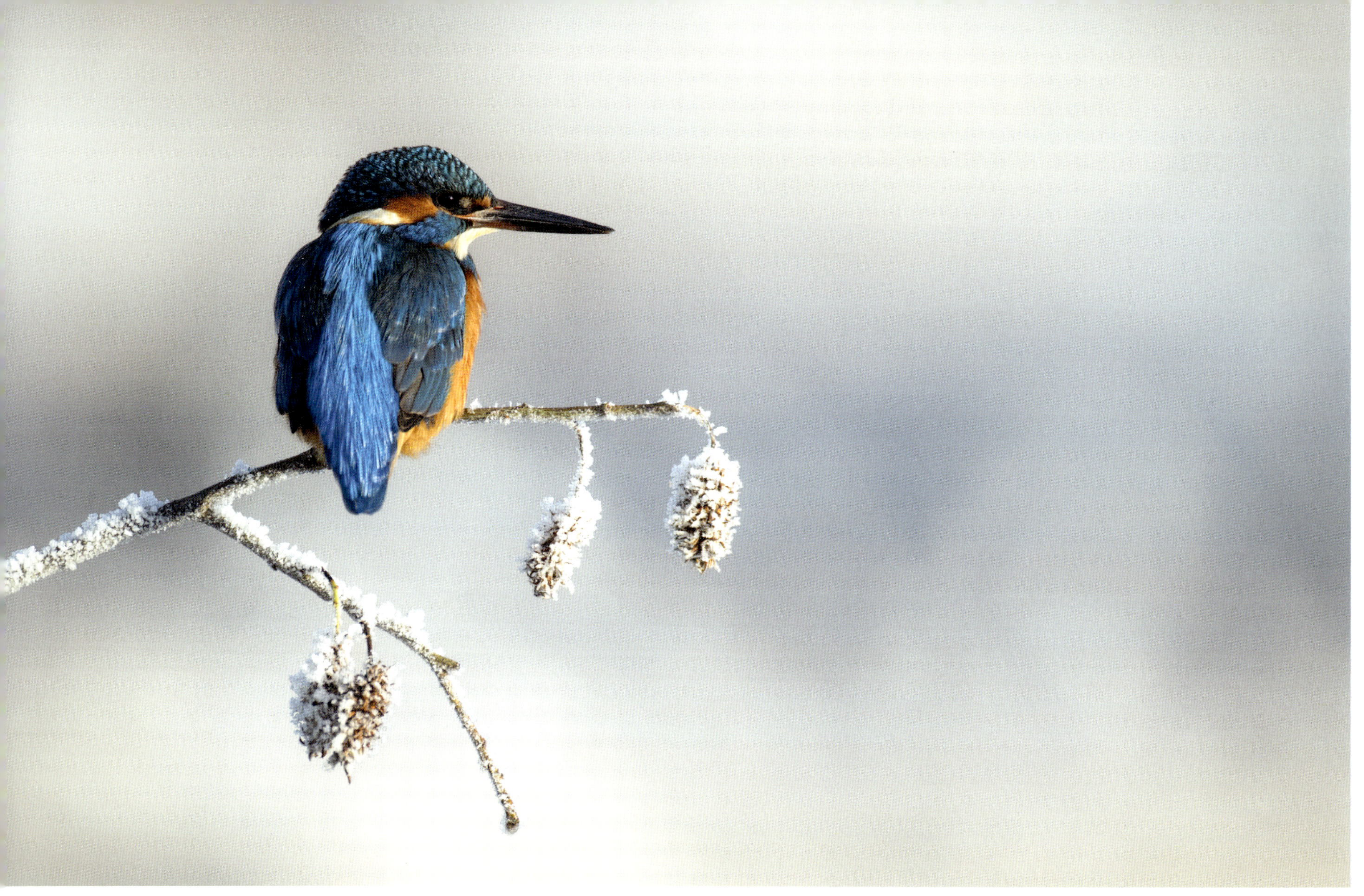

Cold King
Animal Portraits

Joshua Copping
Common kingfisher (*Alcedo atthis*)
Dumfries and Galloway, Scotland

Nikon Z9 with Nikon 500mm f/4 lens. 500mm;
1/400th second; f/4; ISO 125.

A common kingfisher in the frost on a mid-winter morning. I used a long focal length to isolate the bird and focus on the colour and detail in the feathers. The bright blue and orange of the bird stand out against the white, frosty background. I'm glad the bird arrived and sat where it did because throughout the day the frost began to melt, so any images wouldn't have been as striking.

Cold Tap
Animal Portraits

Sarah Darnell
Blue tit (*Cyanistes caeruleus*)
Norfolk, England

Canon EOS 1D X II with Canon 600mm
f/4 II lens & 1.4x teleconverter. 840mm;
1/800th second; f/5.6; ISO 6,400.

Not sure who was the coldest, me or
the blue tit, but it was a beautiful hoar
frost morning. I love the footprints in
the frost on the tap and the direct look
into the camera lens. Fortunately for
me, I could go back indoors into the
warm, but I filled up the bird feeders
before doing so, in the hope that this
little bird would get through the wintry
weather.

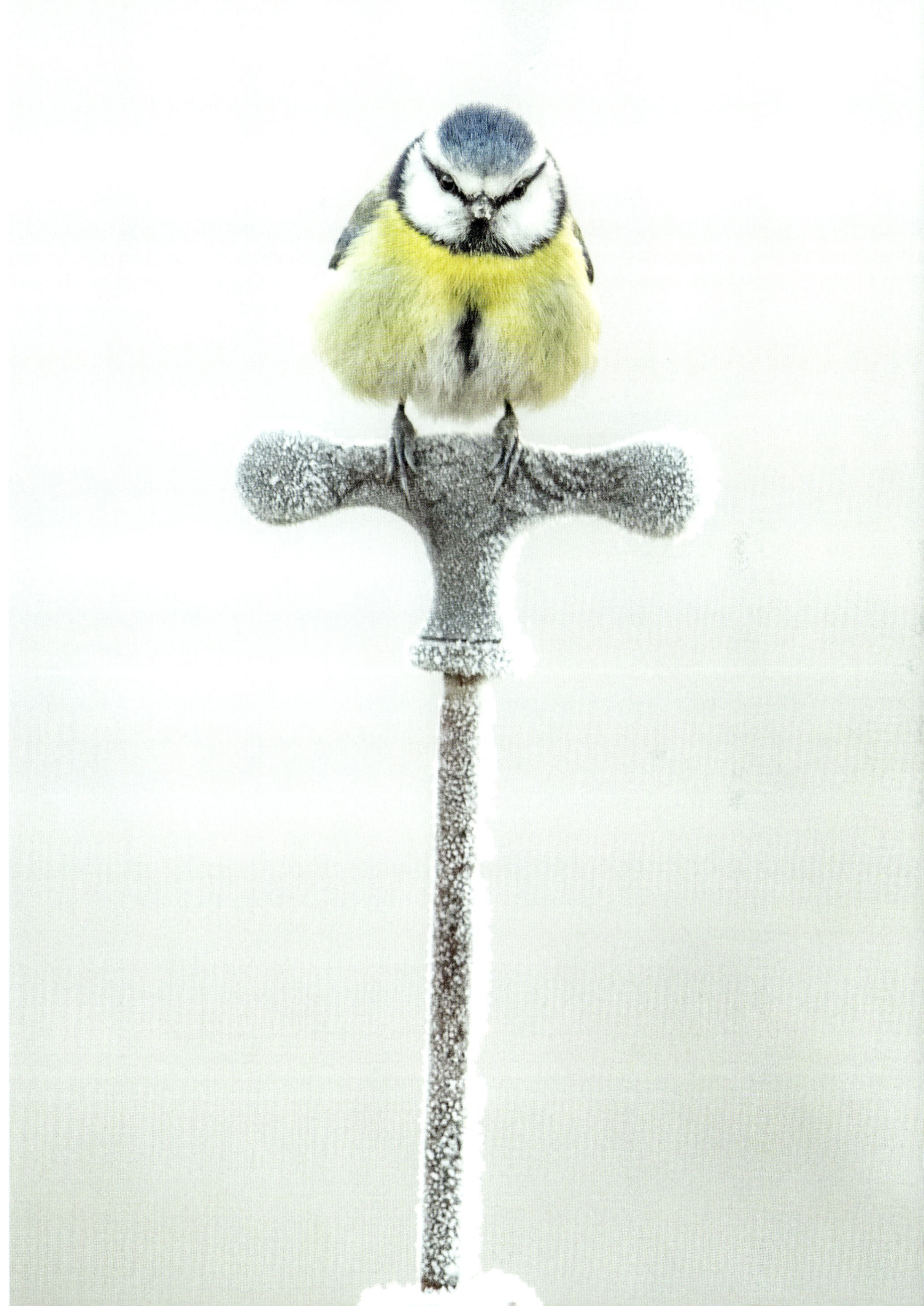

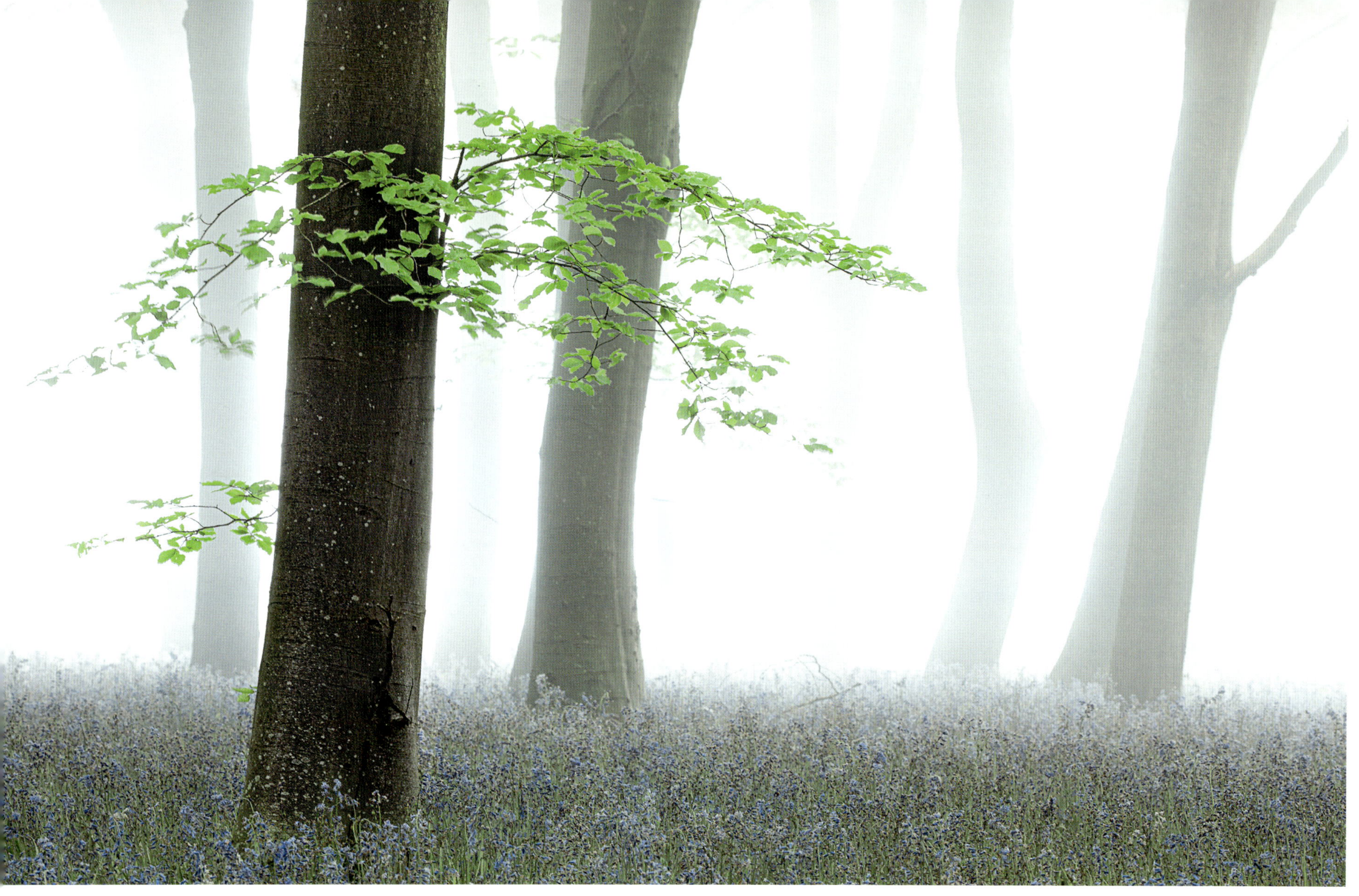

Into the Mist
Wild Woods | Runner-up

Philip Selby
Beech (*Fagus sylvatica*)
Badbury Hill, Oxfordshire, England

Canon 5D IV with Canon 100-400mm f/4.5-5.6 II
lens. 200mm; 1.6 seconds; f/14; ISO 100.

On the remains of an Iron Age hill fort on Badbury
Hill in Oxfordshire, Badbury Clump is an area of
wonderful beech woodland, carpeted in bluebells
each spring. Like most photographers during those
precious few weeks of spring, it's a time of anxious
weather forecast watching, hoping that atmospheric
weather conditions and schedules align. Luckily,
the woodland was shrouded in dense fog on this
particular morning, and the vibrant new beech leaves
and subtle hues of the bluebells added a contrasting
splash of colour to the otherwise monochromatic
scene.

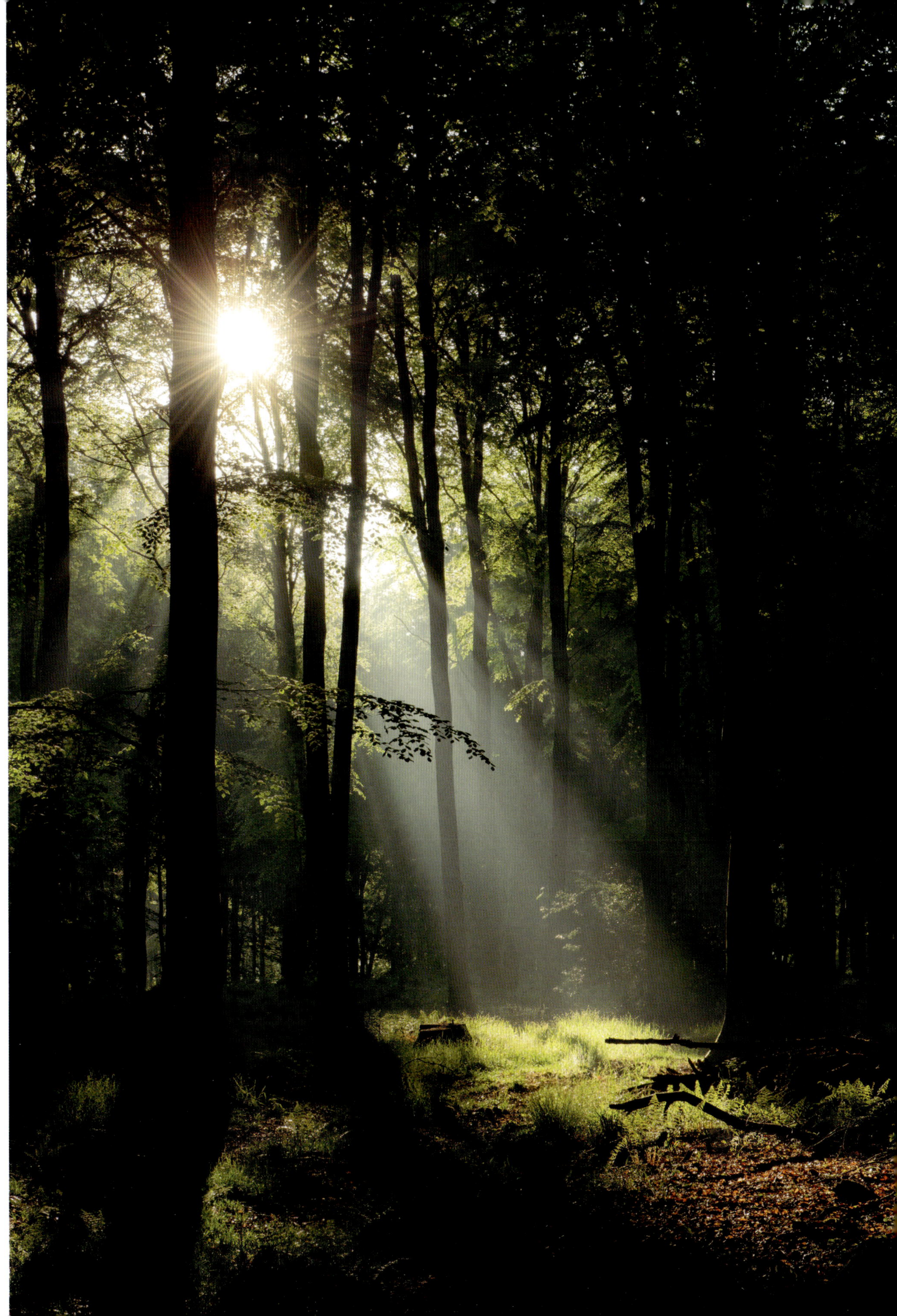

Morning Mist
Wild Woods

Lauren McIntyre
Micheldever Woods, Hampshire, England

Nikon D850 with Nikon 24-70mm f/2.8 lens. 70mm; 1/125th second; f/18; ISO 1,250.

I love being in the woods at sunrise as you never know what you're going to encounter. As the sun rose, it started to peek through the tree canopy and highlighted a thin layer of mist that hadn't left the forest floor yet. I liked how the sun shone down like a spotlight through the mist, highlighting the winding deer track. I composed the shot so that the deer track led you into the light and mist, as if it were a path to a mystical place.

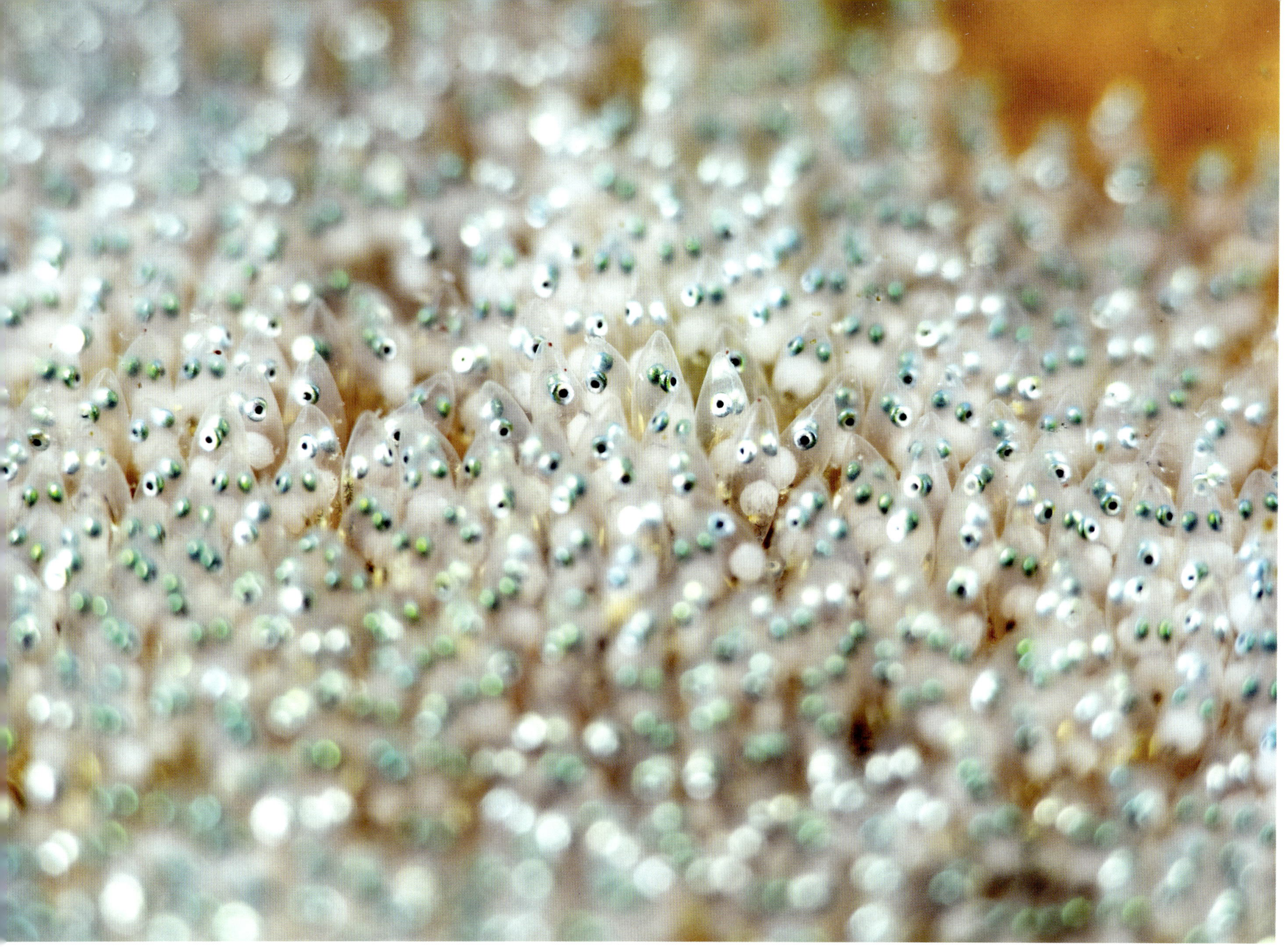

Sparkling Eyes
Coast & Marine

Martin Stevens
Rock goby (*Gobius paganellus*)
Falmouth, Cornwall, England

Olympus E-M5 III with Olympus 60mm f/2.8 Macro
lens. 60mm; 1/250th second; f/6.3; ISO 200.

Rock gobies are common fish found in rock pools,
laying their eggs in spring under and on rocks. I was
watching adult fish dart back and forth in a pool and
spotted their eggs on the side of an overhang on a
large rock. I managed to position my camera next
to the overhang and aimed it at the eggs to take
some photos. I used a macro lens with an additional
strong diopter to achieve this 'super macro' photo.
Two strobe flashes produced the reflection of the
fish eyes as bokeh with a shallow depth of field.

Conger Eel
Coast & Marine

Malcolm Nimmo
Conger eel (*Conger conger*)
Plymouth Sound, England

Nikon D7200 with Nikon 600mm f/2.8 lens.
60mm; 1/160th second; f/10; ISO 100.

One of my favourite dive sites is Firestone Bay in Plymouth Sound. The site is located at the mouth of the Tamar Estuary and influenced by strong tidal flows, leading to a biologically diverse and abundant ecosystem. The reef crevices host various species of fish, including this juvenile conger eel. The eel was peeping out of a small crevice just enough for me to capture a snooted image of its head.

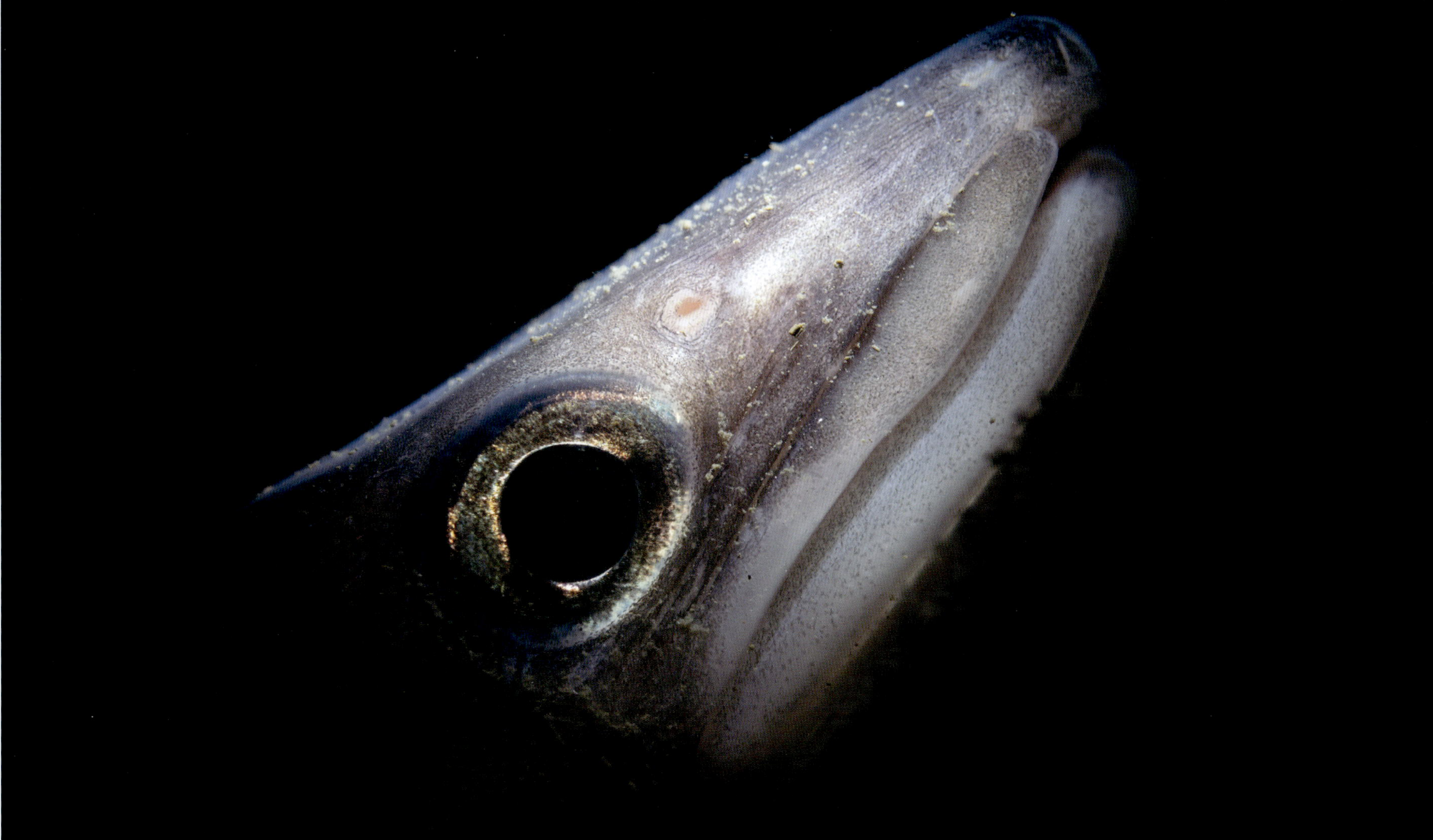

Deer Kiss
Animal Behaviour

Felix Belloin
Red deer (*Cervus elaphus*)
Richmond Park, London, England

Canon EOS 1D X III with Canon 500mm f/4 II lens.
500mm; 1/1,000th second; f/4; ISO 800.

I was out photographing stags in Richmond Park when I noticed this hind lying down in the dew-covered bracken. The sun filled the scene with golden backlight, and the dew almost sparkled in the foreground. I observed a young deer approaching the older hind, and as it got close, it rested its nose on her as if giving her a kiss. One frame later, the moment was over.

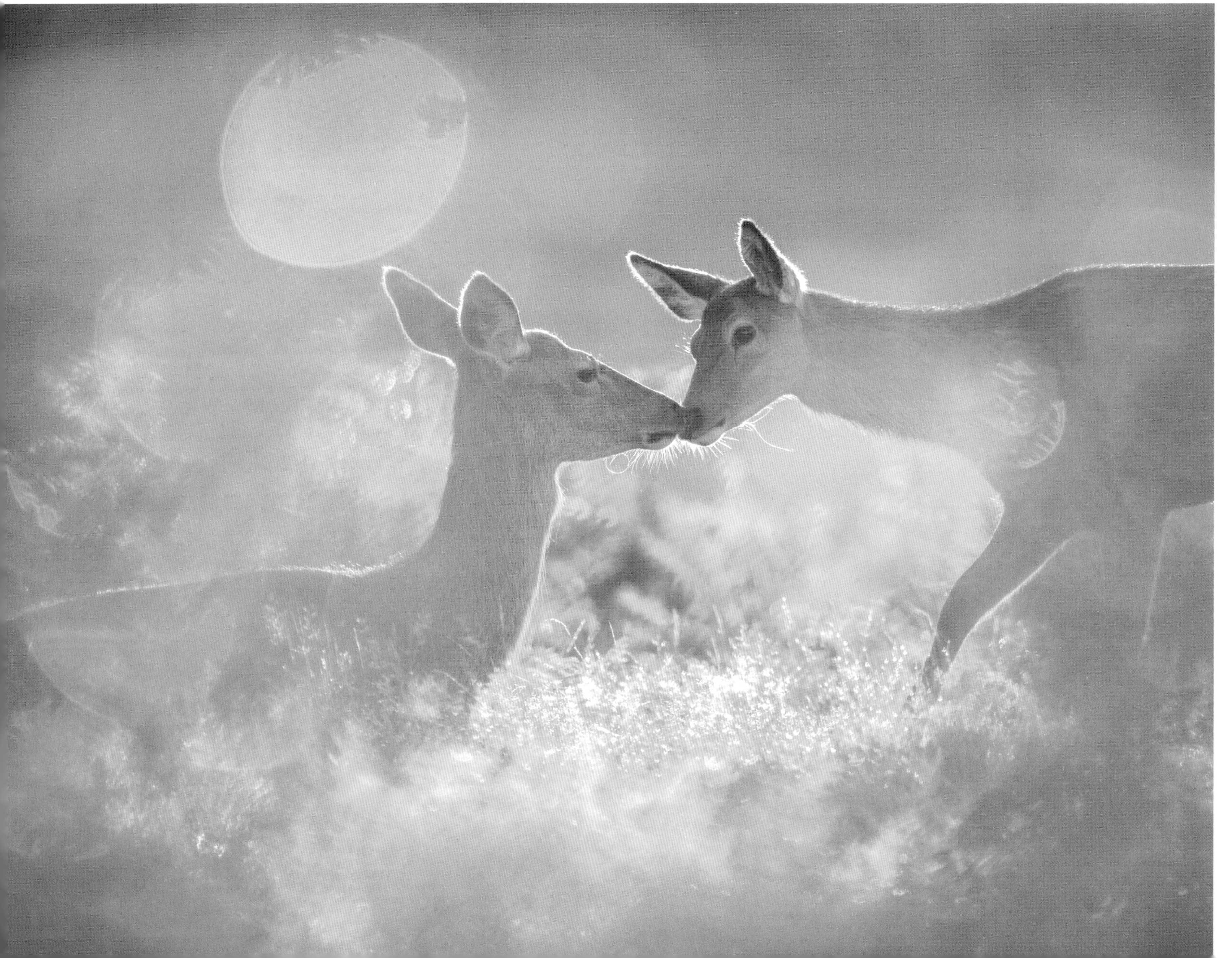

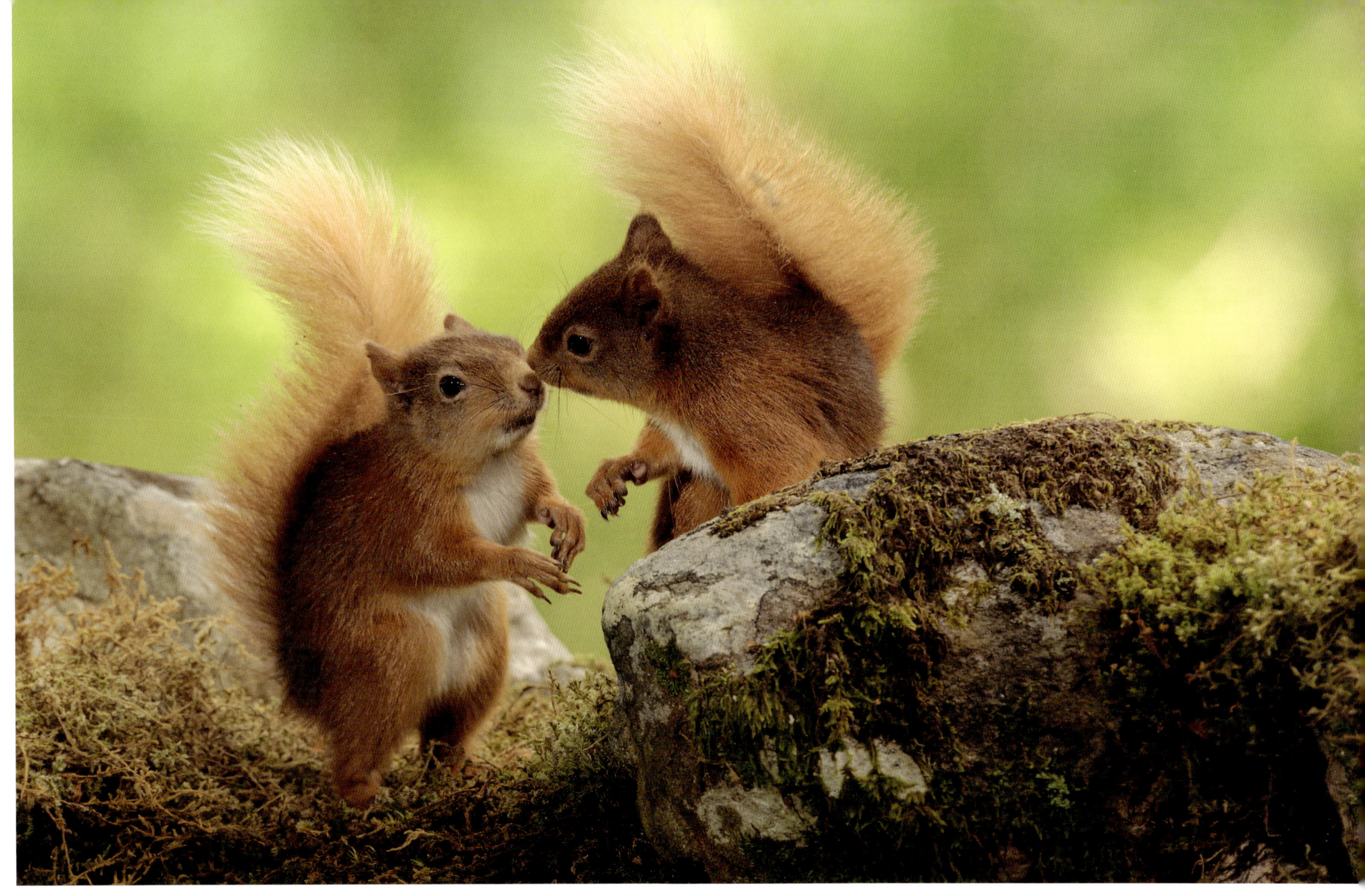

Father Daughter Time
Animal Behaviour

Keith Thorburn
Red squirrel (*Sciurus vulgaris*)
Mamores, Scotland

Nikon D780 with Sigma 150-600mm f/5-6.3 lens.
600mm; 1/125th second; f/9; ISO 800.

This moment was captured when the father and daughter were feeding on the hazelnuts I had put out on the wall, and the trigger just caught that moment when they were interacting with each other. As soon as I captured this image, I thought, 'Aww, that is so cute'.

Hyperspace

Coast & Marine | Highly Commended

Grace Bailey

Barrel jellyfish (*Rhizostoma pulmo*)
Jersey

Olympus TG-6. 4.5mm; 1/30th second; f/2.8;
ISO 100.

While ascending from a dive, I encountered a barrel jellyfish. This type of photography is rare, as these jellyfish only visit Jersey waters once a year. My local diving site often has particle-rich waters, leading to common backscatter in photos. Curious if backscatter could add an artistic touch, I tried an alternative angle for a creative effect. Though the side view was less than ideal, the photo surpassed my expectations.

This experience has motivated me to explore new photographic techniques. The appropriately named barrel jellyfish now appears poised to leap into a mysterious, low-key backdrop, evoking a sense of hyperspace. Taken in the afternoon sun, this shot was captured five metres below the surface using my Olympus camera without artificial lighting, as natural light produced the desired effect.

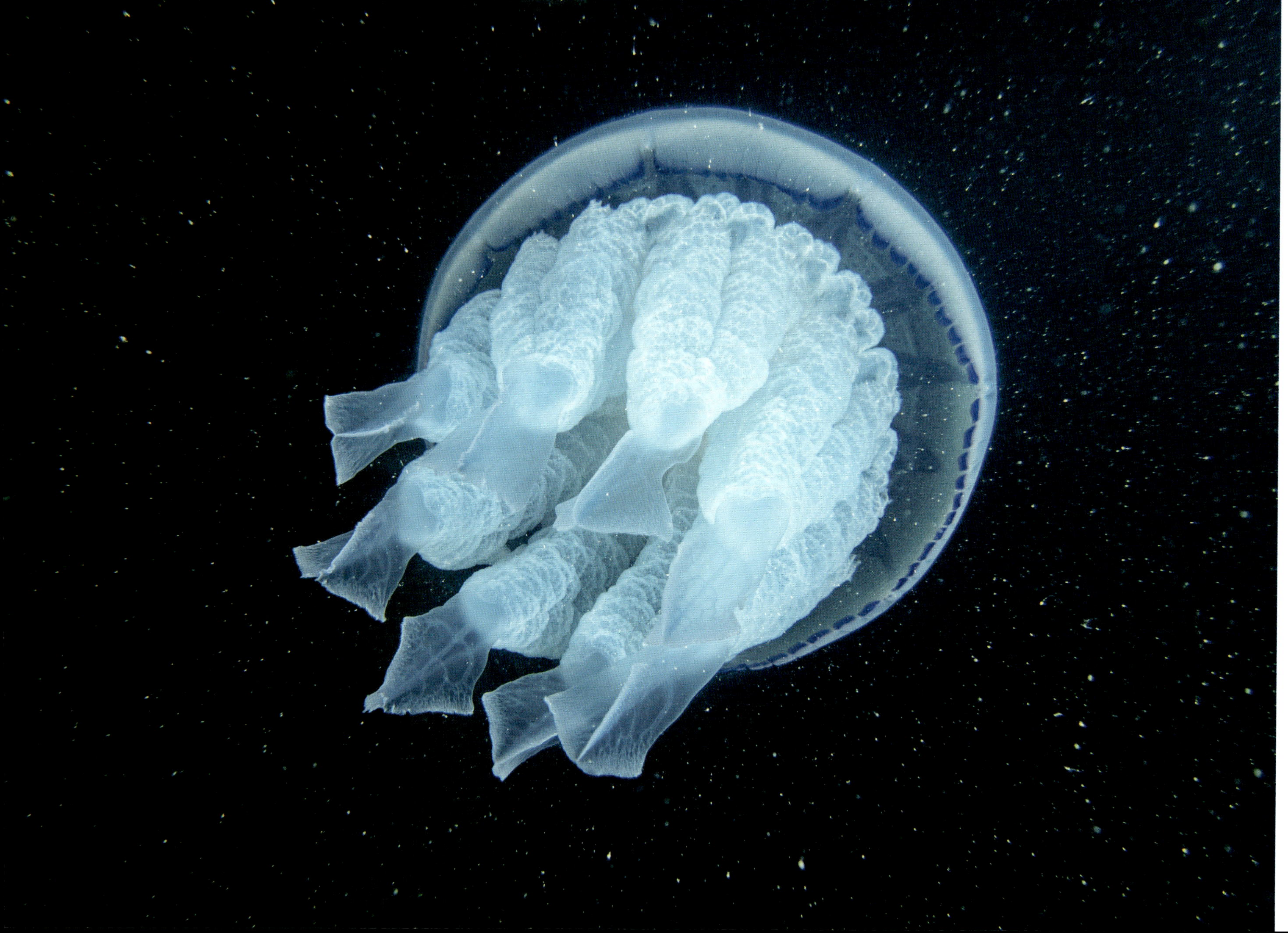

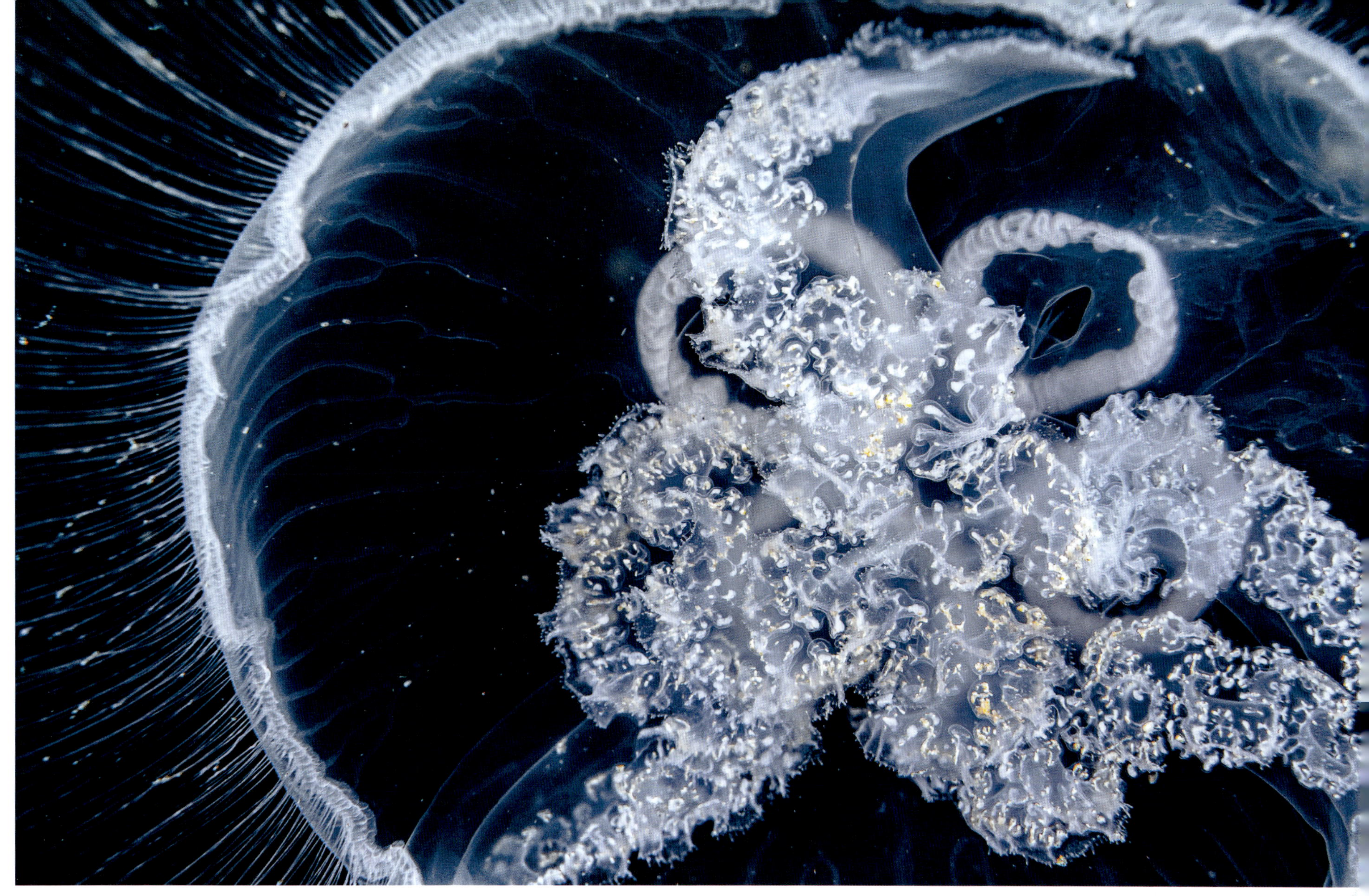

On the Moon
Coast & Marine

Henley Spiers
Moon jellyfish (*Aurelia aurita*)
Shetland, Scotland

Nikon D850 with Nikon 60mm f/2.8 lens.
60mm; 1/200th second; f/16; ISO 400.

During the summer months, moon jellyfish are abundant along the British coasts. Yet, within their profusion lies an exquisite beauty, as exemplified by this close-up of the underside.

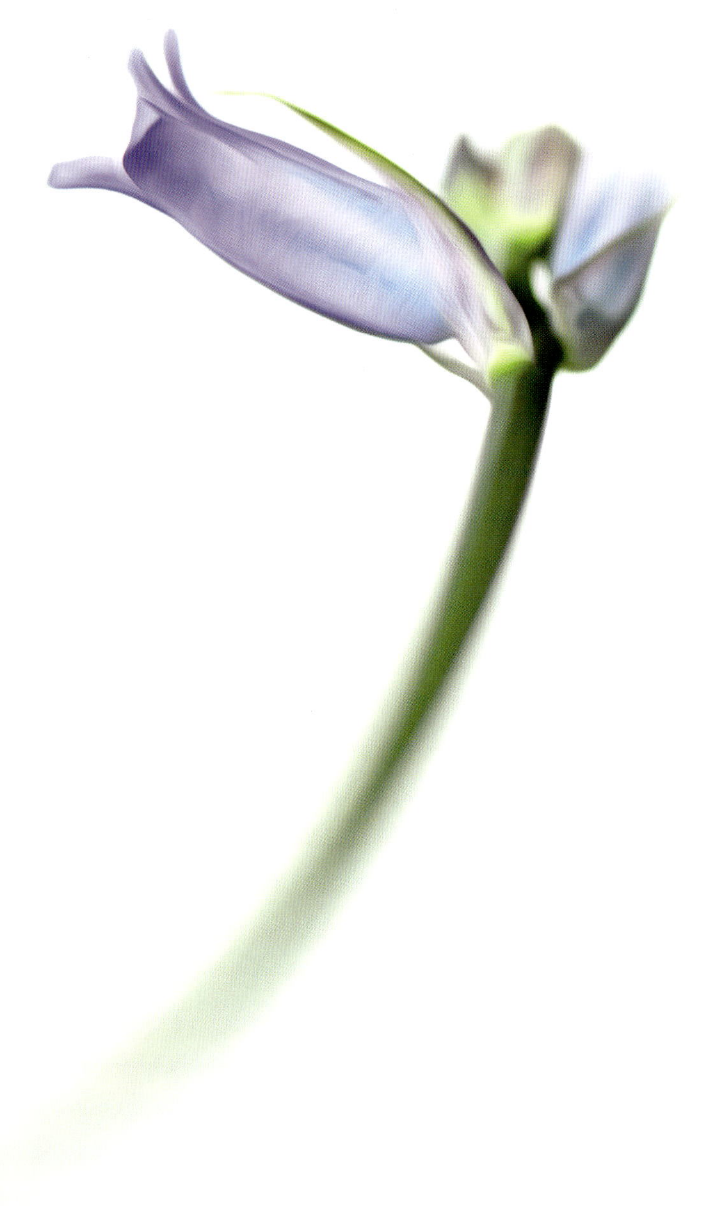

Solitude
Botanical Britain

Rachel Piper
Bluebell (*Hyacinthoides non-scripta*)
Hemel Hempstead, Hertfordshire,
England

Canon EOS 90D with Canon 60mm
f/2.8 Macro lens. 60mm; 1/1,000th
second; f/2.8; ISO 100.

I am often asked how I achieve plain
backgrounds when photographing
flowers. The answer is simple: I carry
pieces of card with me to place behind
my subjects. On this occasion, I felt that
white would highlight the beautifully
subtle colours of this bluebell.
To enhance the softness of the image,
I selected a very large aperture, and
I love the way the stem appears to
be floating out of the photograph.

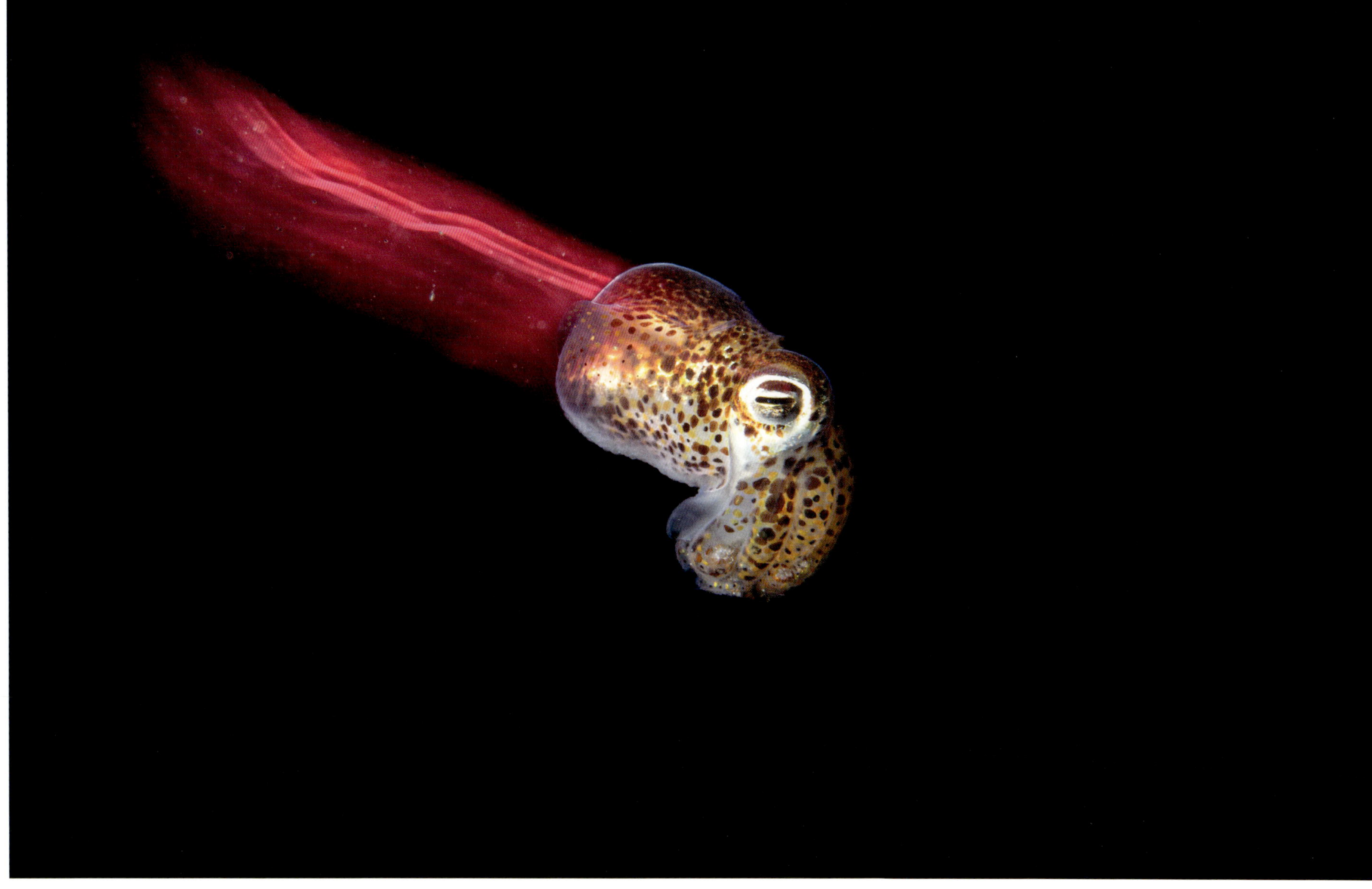

Liquid Light
Coast & Marine

Aaron Sanders
Bobtail squid (*Euprymna scolopes*)
Durgan Beach Cornwall, England

Nikon D850 with Nikon 60mm f/2.8 lens. 60mm;
1 second; f/22; ISO 250.

Under the cover of night, this little bobtail squid
emerged from the dark. Jetting around, moving
through the inky blackness as though it were one
with the water, it performed a beautiful display of
colour. Its iridescent skin changed from deep red to
a glowing golden yellow, standing out against the
black water like a star in the sky. Using a slow shutter
speed, I was able to capture its trail of motion as it
bobbed through the water. With a specific lighting
technique, I coloured the blurred motion pink.

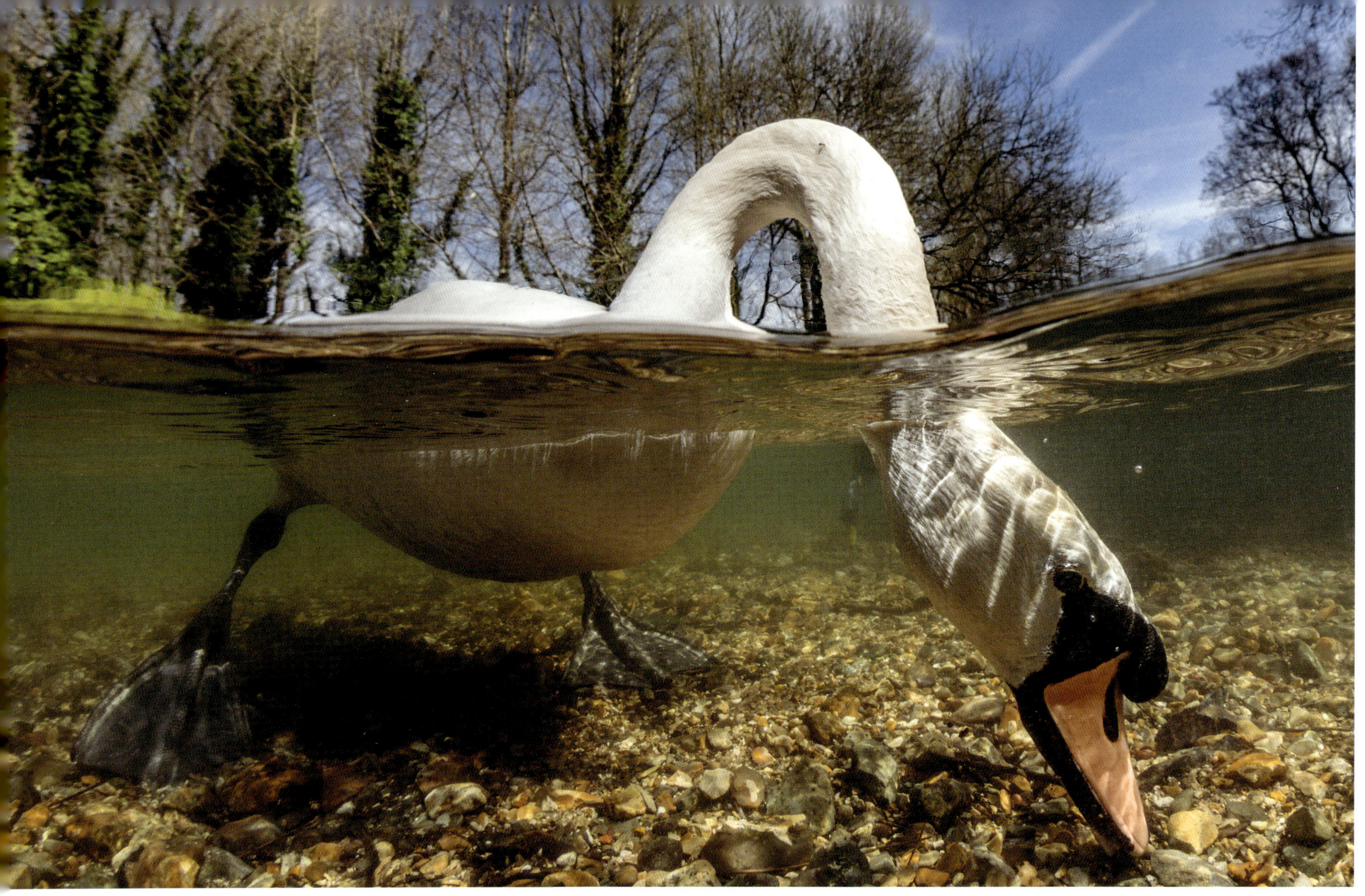

Submerged Swan
Animal Behaviour

Paul Colley
Mute swan (*Cygnus olor*)
River Anton at Goodworth Clatford, Hampshire, England

Nikon D4 with Sigma 15mm f/2.8 lens.
15mm; 1/250th second; f/16; ISO 640.

Like all water birds, swans have a life that is half in and half out of the water. This image seeks to portray both at once, as a mute swan foraged in the bed of the river Anton at Goodworth Clatford in Hampshire. I used bird seed to encourage the swan's natural behaviour and bring it close to a remotely-controlled Nikon D4 in a self-built underwater housing.

Andy Parkinson

Social Distancing
Animal Portraits

Mute swan (*Cygnus olor*)
Derbyshire, England

Nikon D6 with Nikon 200-400mm f/4 lens.
340mm; 1/2,000th second; f/5.6; ISO 1,600.

Captured in the height of the Covid pandemic, I had little alternative but to work close to home. Here, a mother swan leads her cygnets across a local lake, in a dawn-like scene, with each cygnet adhering strictly to government social distancing guidelines.

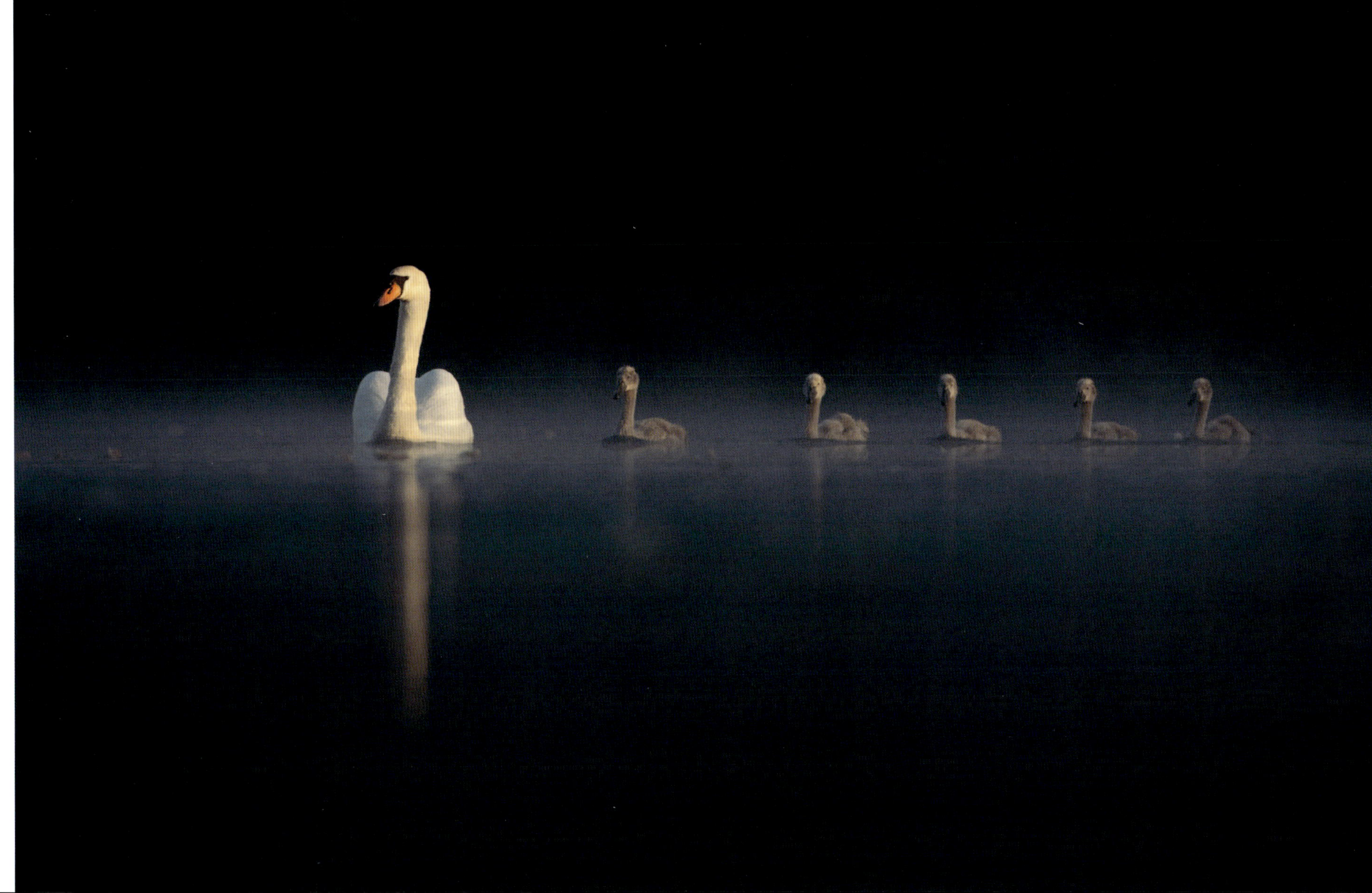

The Crop Thief
Habitat | Runner-up

Steven Allcock
Brown hare (*Lepus europaeus*)
Nantwich Cheshire, England

Canon EOS 7D with Sigma 150-500mm f/5-6.3 lens.
500mm; 1/400th second; f/6.3; ISO 400.

It was a pleasant spring evening, and I was spending
some time on recently obtained farmland permission
where I had observed good numbers of brown hares.
I stood at the edge of a crop field when I suddenly
noticed this small hare leveret down the tramline,
chewing on the crops. I approached slowly and
quietly, getting close enough to capture the image.
I got down low and fired a burst of shots.
I particularly like this one because of the facial
expression on the hare as it munches on the crop.

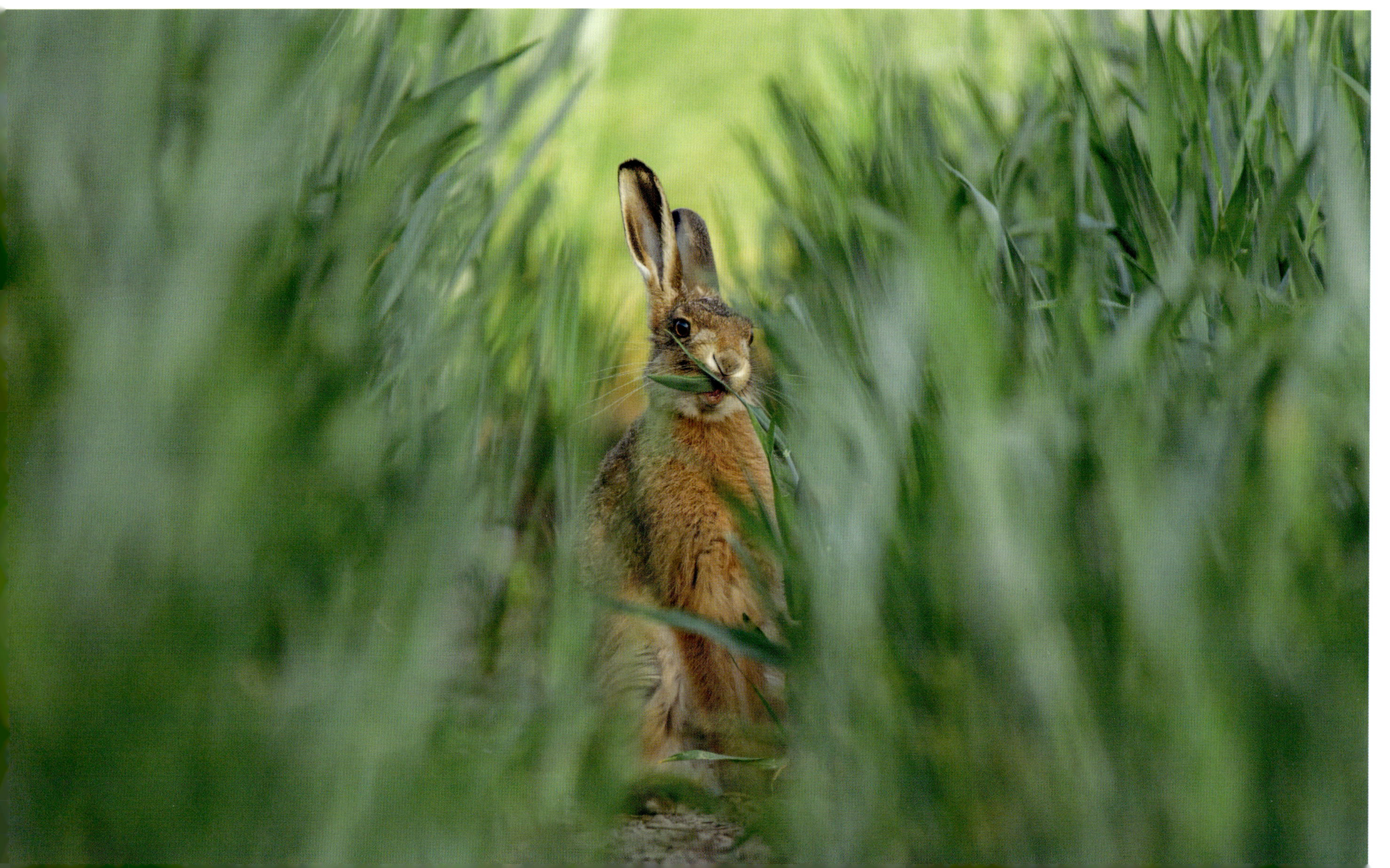

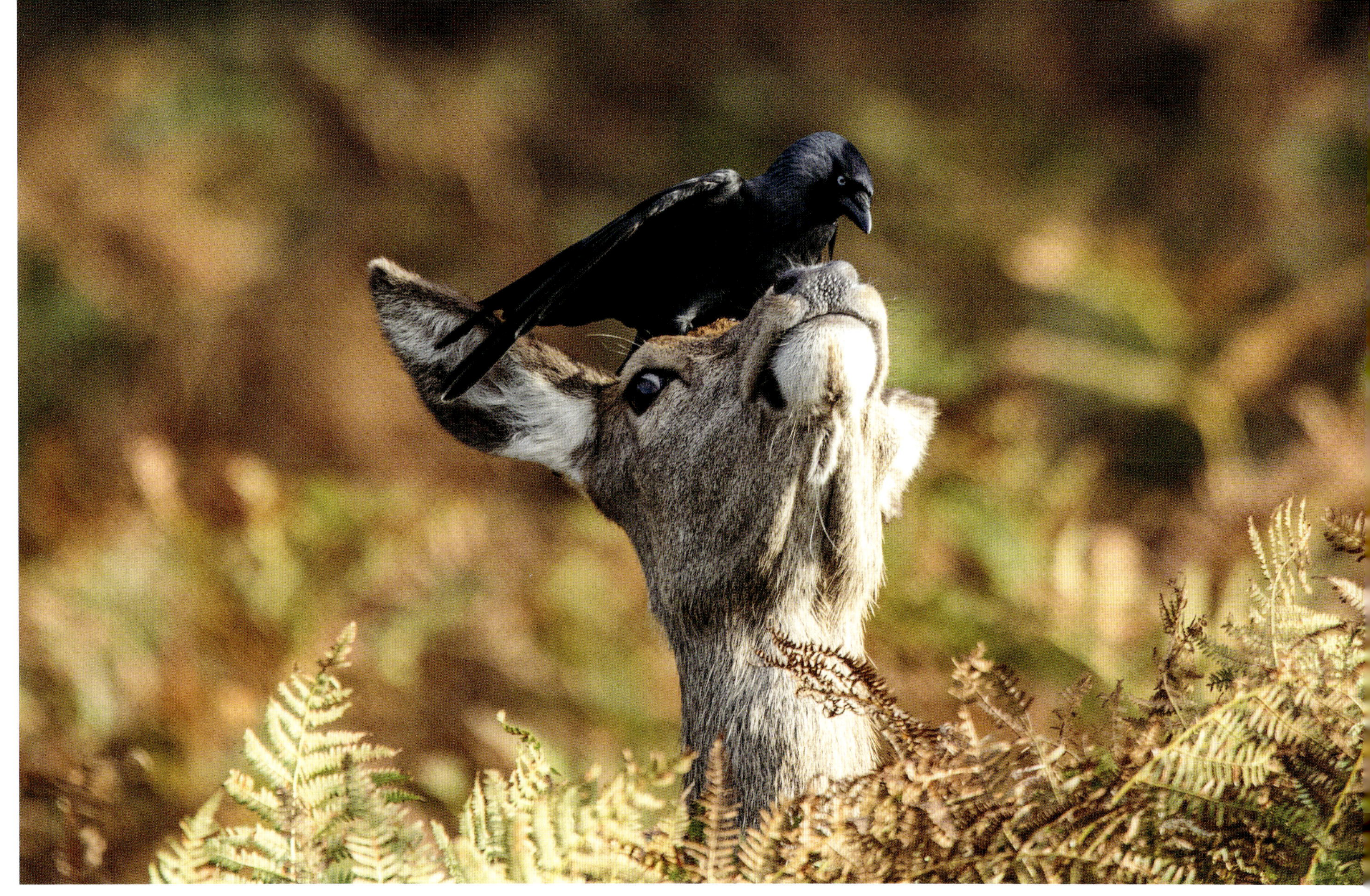

A Look for Help
Animal Behaviour

James Ball
Red deer (*Cervus elaphus*) and
Jackdaw (*Corvus monedula*)
Richmond Park, London, England

Canon 5D III with Sigma 150-600mm f/5.6-6.3 lens.
600mm; 1/1000th second; f/6.3; ISO 1000.

I was observing the interesting relationship between the many jackdaws and red deer in the park. The jackdaws were moving from deer to deer in search of an easy meal in the form of ticks, which are insects feeding on the deer. It was a win-win for both the bird and the mammal. I spotted an incoming jackdaw and managed to capture a few shots as it crash-landed on the very surprised doe's head. My favourite aspect of the image is the female red deer making eye contact with my camera lens and appearing to give a look of 'help!'

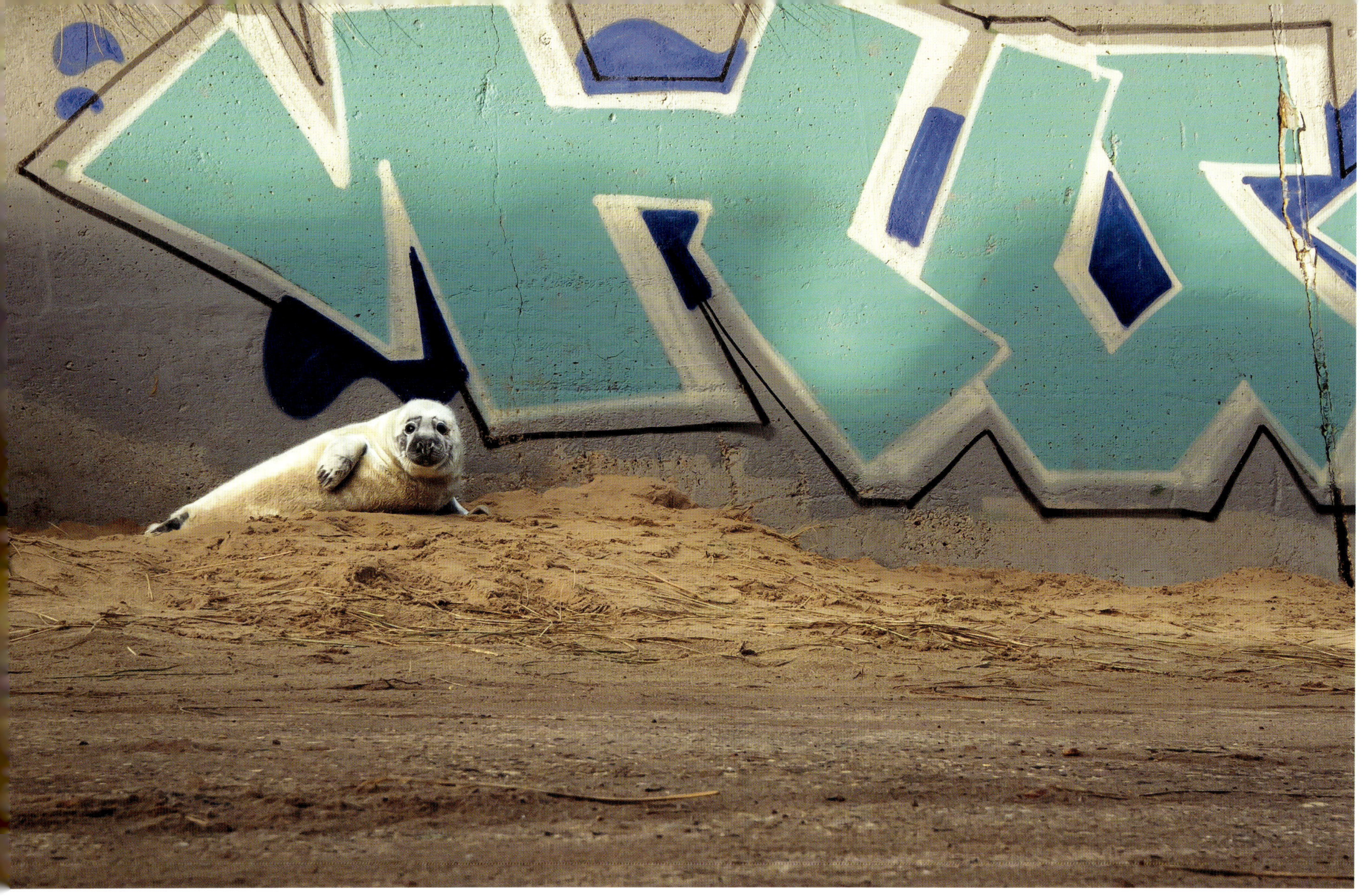

Juvenile Delinquent
Urban Wildlife

Ben Hancock-Smith
Grey seal (*Halichoerus grypus*)
Waxham, Norfolk, England

Nikon D500 with Sigma 10-20mm f/4-5.6 lens.
20mm; 1/500th second; f/8; ISO 450.

Walking down a path from the sand dunes to the beach, I spotted a grey seal pup lying next to a wall with some graffiti sprayed across it. I switched to my wide-angle lens to capture a shot of the guilty-looking pup with the paint-covered concrete wall in the background.

Sleepy Otter
Animal Portraits

Chris Bourne
Otter (*Lutra lutra*)
Shetland, Scotland

Canon EOS R5 with Canon RF 100-500mm f/4.5-7.1 lens. 500mm; 1/750th second; f/8; ISO 1,250.

We glimpsed an otter foraging in the far distance off the stormy shores of Yell, and anticipating where she might come ashore to rest from her labours, we just had time to get into position before she did just that. We were able to enjoy her company for an hour or more while she basked on a bed of seaweed under a weak sun. Upon waking, she continued on her way, foraging all the time, completely oblivious to our presence. A perfect wildlife encounter for all!

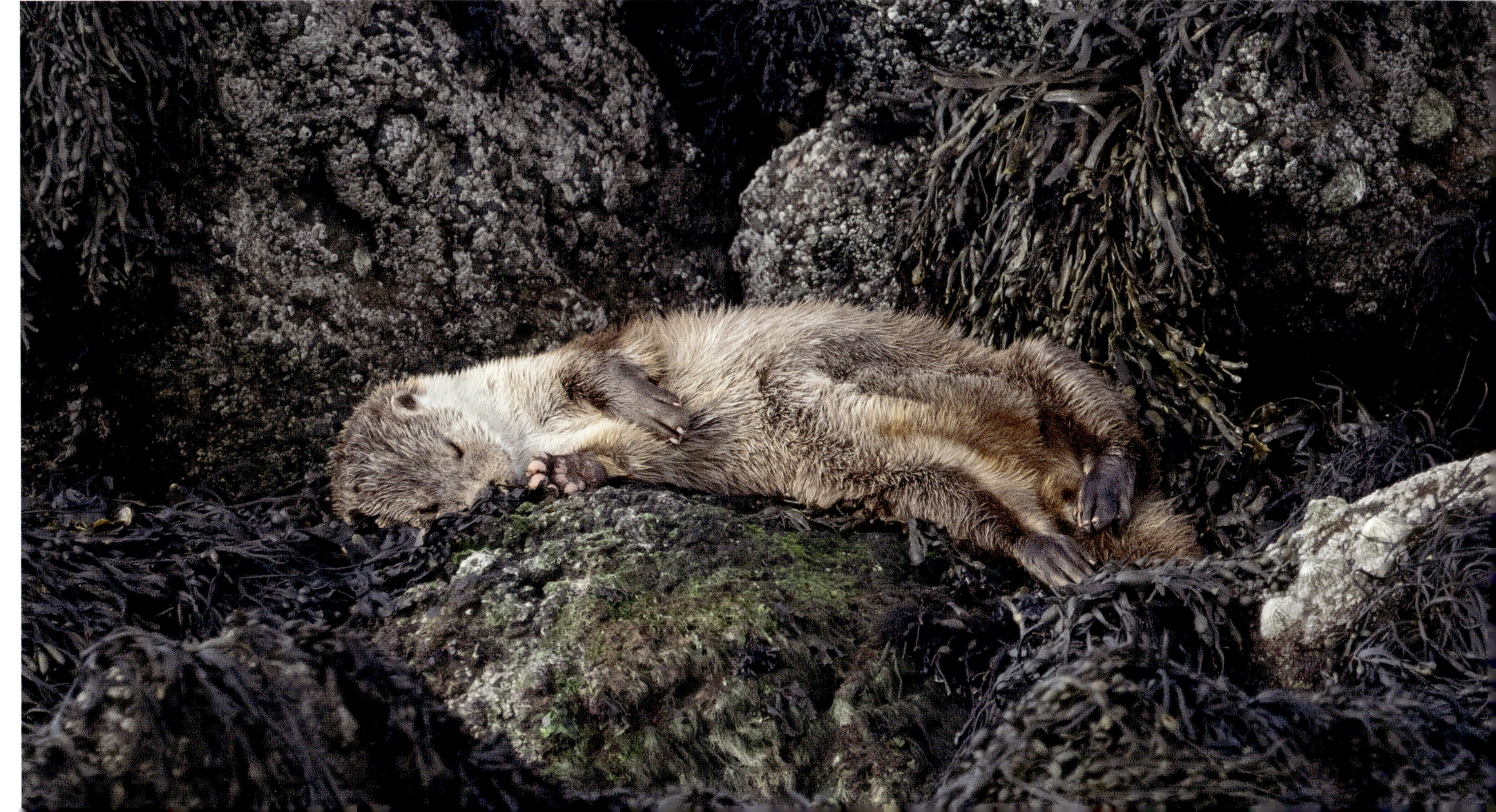

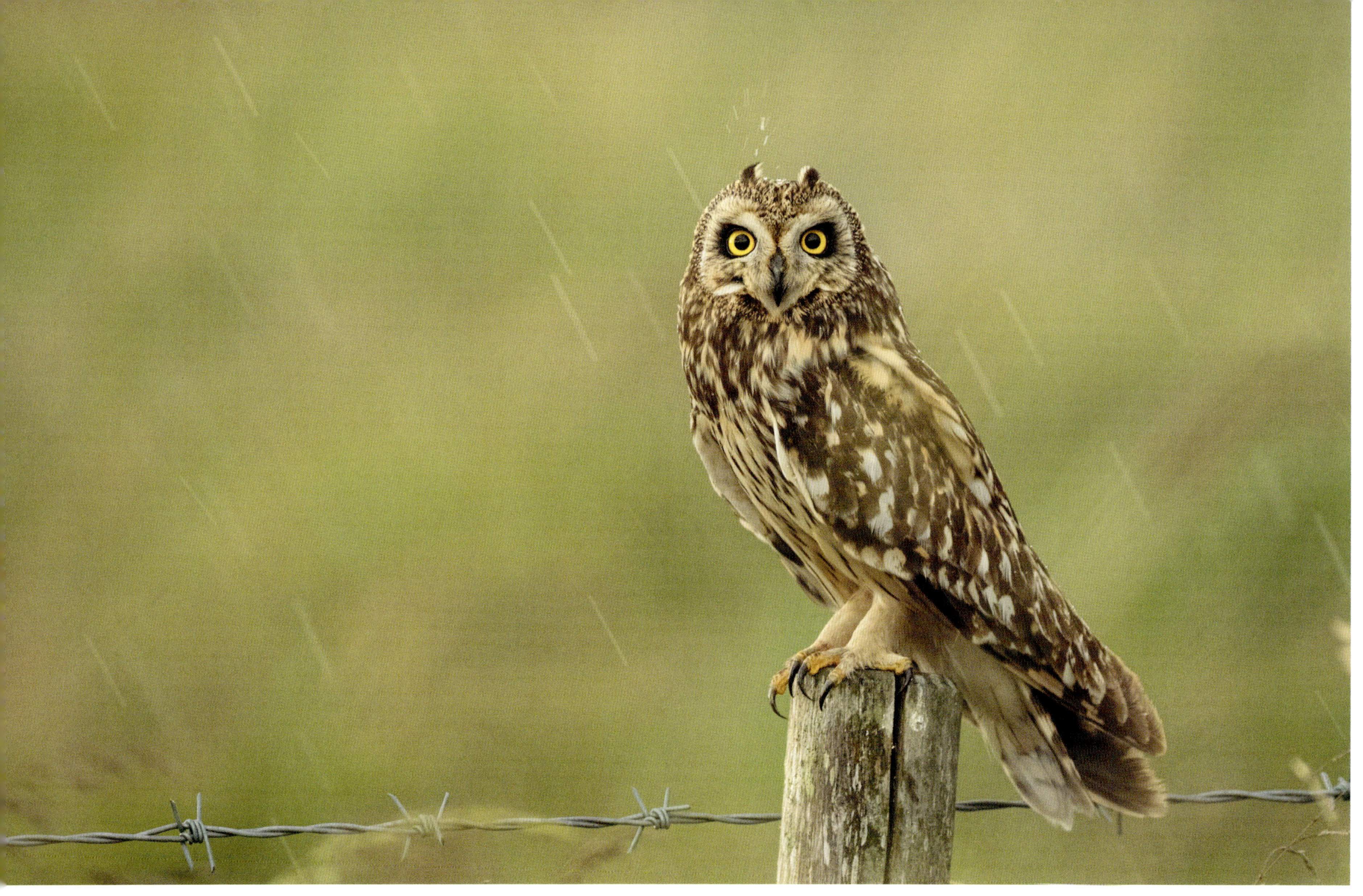

Summer Rain
Animal Portraits

Francis Taylor
Short-eared owl (*Asio flammeus*)
Peak District National Park, England

Canon EOS R5 with Canon 200-400mm f/4 lens &
1.4x teleconverter. 560mm; 1/200th second; f/5.6;
ISO 2,500.

Portrait of a short-eared owl perched on a fencepost
during a summer rain shower on the Eastern Moors
of the Peak District National Park. I had been
photographing these owls using my car as a hide
when this owl flew in and perched right next to me.

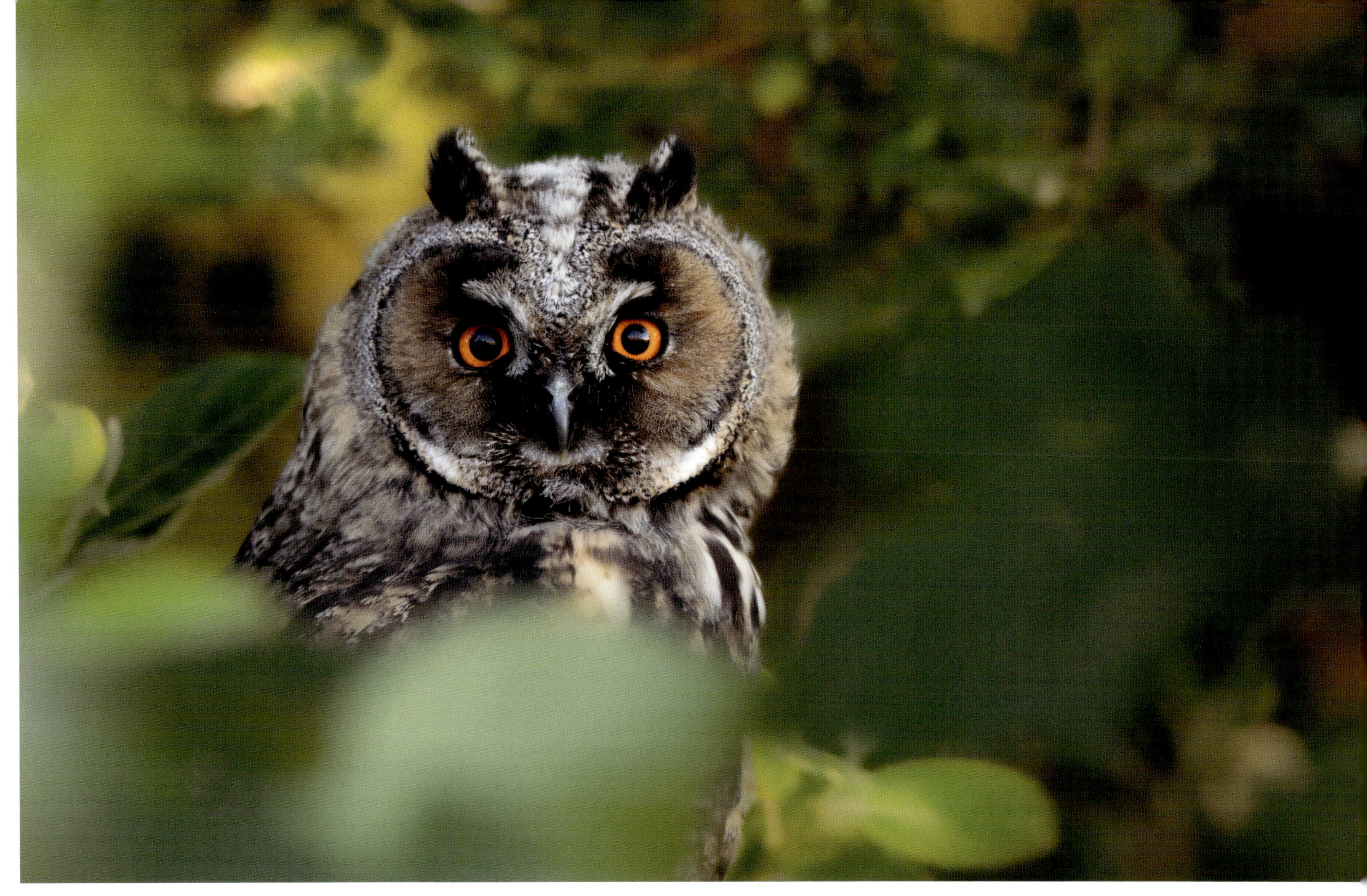

Long-eared Owl Portrait
Animal Portraits

Ben Harrott
Long-eared owl (*Asio otus*)
Saddleworth, England

Canon 80D with Tamron 150-600mm f/5-6.3 lens.
250mm; 1/200th second; f/5.6; ISO 800.

During a summer trip up to spot some mountain hares in the Peaks, I heard the unmistakable call of young long-eared owls coming from a small group of trees. I immediately headed over and could see an adolescent long-eared owl perched on the edge of the trees. I managed to sneak my way around, watching every footstep until I was looking directly at the owl who still had not seen me. If it wasn't for the camera shutter noise, it would've never had any idea, but after the first couple of shots, the youngster swivelled its head and looked me dead in the eye, which is when I was able to get this image.

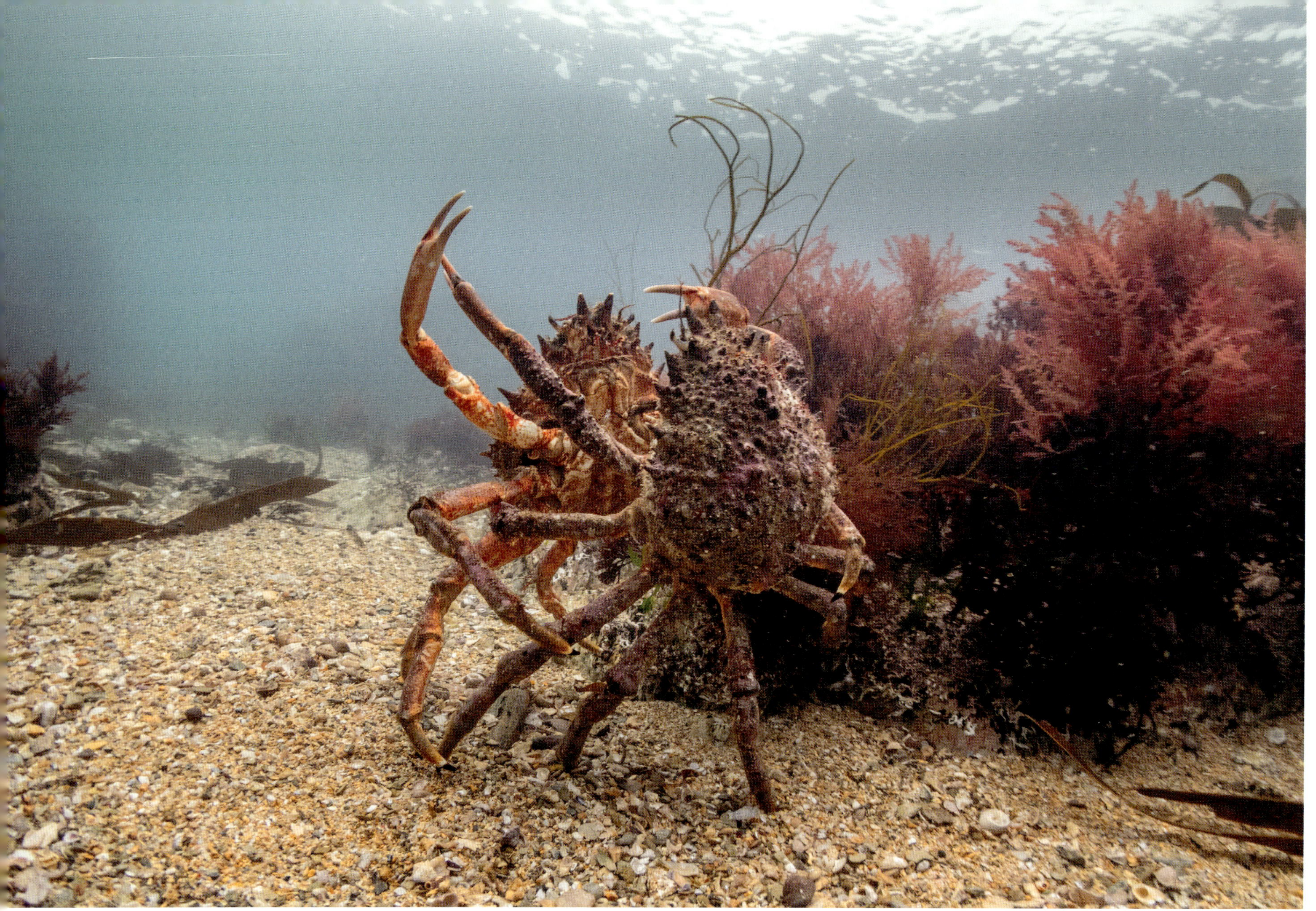

Fighting Crabs
Animal Behaviour

Martin Stevens
Spider crab (*Maja brachydactyla*)
Falmouth, Cornwall, England

Olympus E-M5 III with Olympus 7-14mm f/2.8 lens.
10mm; 1/60th second; f/7.1; ISO 400.

In spring, spider crabs return inshore from deeper
waters. These two females were not happy to see
one another, engaging in a grappling contest before
going their separate ways into the kelp forest.
I dived down and took a few photos before the
action ended.

Red Stags Boxing
Animal Behaviour

Calum Campbell
Red deer (*Cervus elaphus*)
Monadhliath Mountains, Scotland

Nikon D810 with Sigma 150-600mm f/5-6.3 lens.
320mm; 1/320th second; f/8; ISO 320.

Red deer stags cast their antlers every spring, which is nature's way of replacing any broken or damaged antlers. Additionally, as they mature, their antlers become bigger, stronger and heavier. The new antler is made of cartilaginous tissue and is supplied with blood vessels and nerves, protected by a velvet skin. It can grow at a rate of 1cm to 2cm per day. Since it is soft, it is easily damaged. During this time, stags will rear up on their hind legs and engage in boxing matches to establish dominance and protect the delicate new antler.

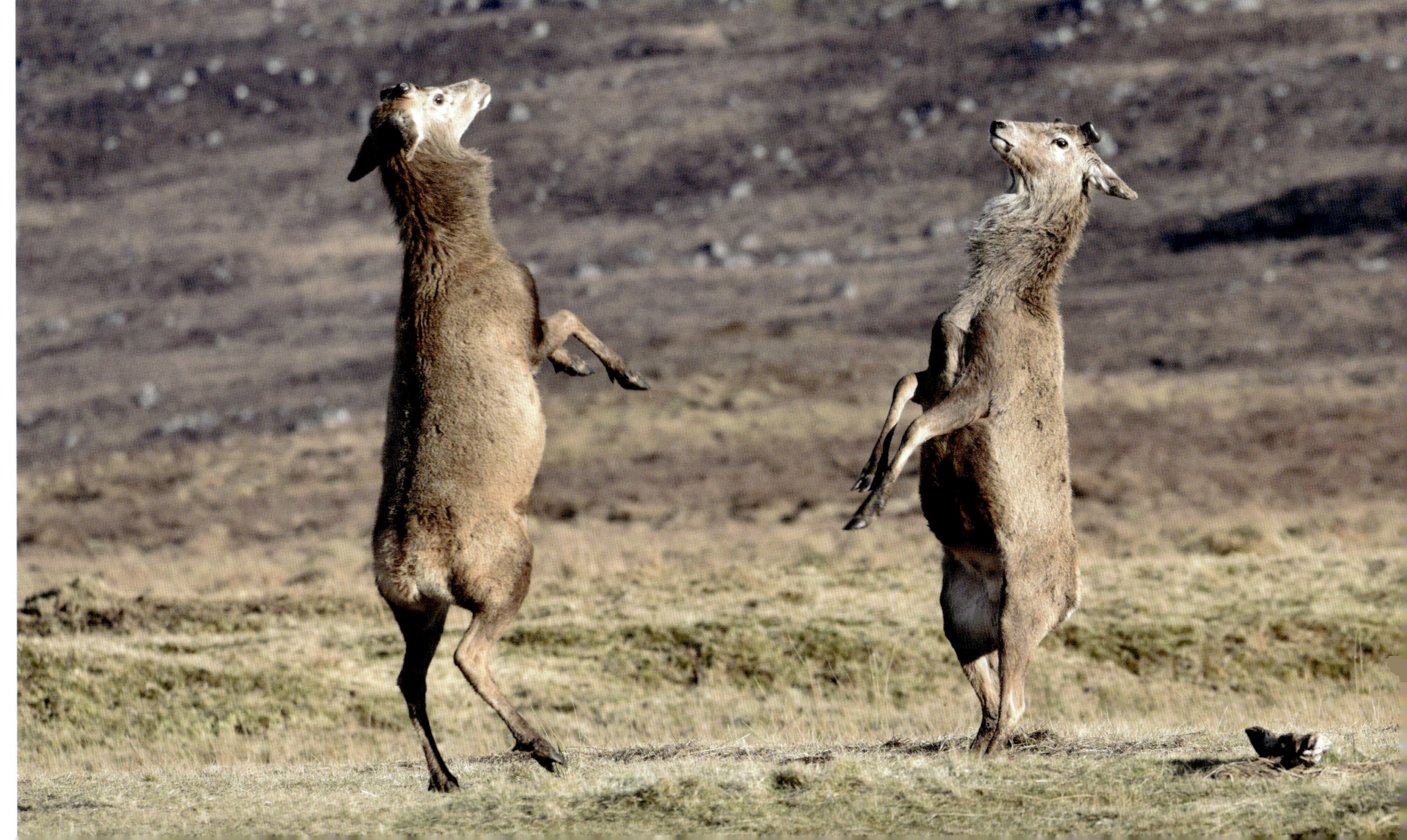

Eating Walls… It's a Bird Thing!
Animal Behaviour

Victor Soares
Rock Dove (*Columba livia*)
London, England

Canon EOS R6 with Canon 300mm f/2.8 II lens.
300mm; 1/500th second; f/2.8; ISO 800.

This feral pigeon displays a very peculiar behaviour that, while documented, is seldom seen or photographed. These birds are, in fact, acquiring grit for their gizzards to aid in digestion, or perhaps supplementing their calcium intake. The calcium obtained from limestone or cement is an important mineral that helps the birds produce strong and sturdy eggs. So, there's a rational explanation behind all of this, but it's still a peculiar sight and one that I was keen to document and share. I aimed to capture not only the bird's activity but also convey the texture, colour and contour of the wall, so I used a shallow depth of field to isolate the bird's antics.

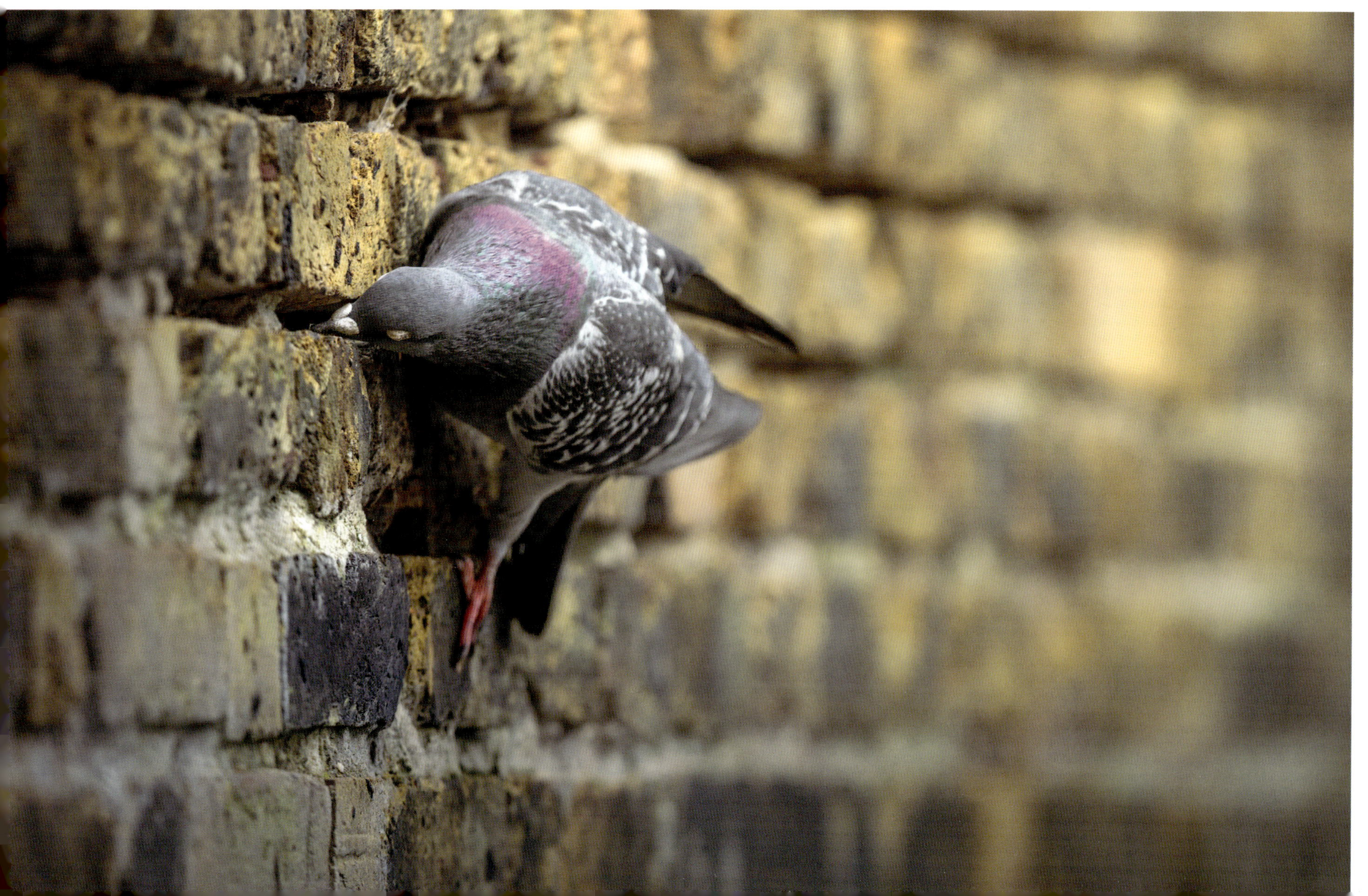

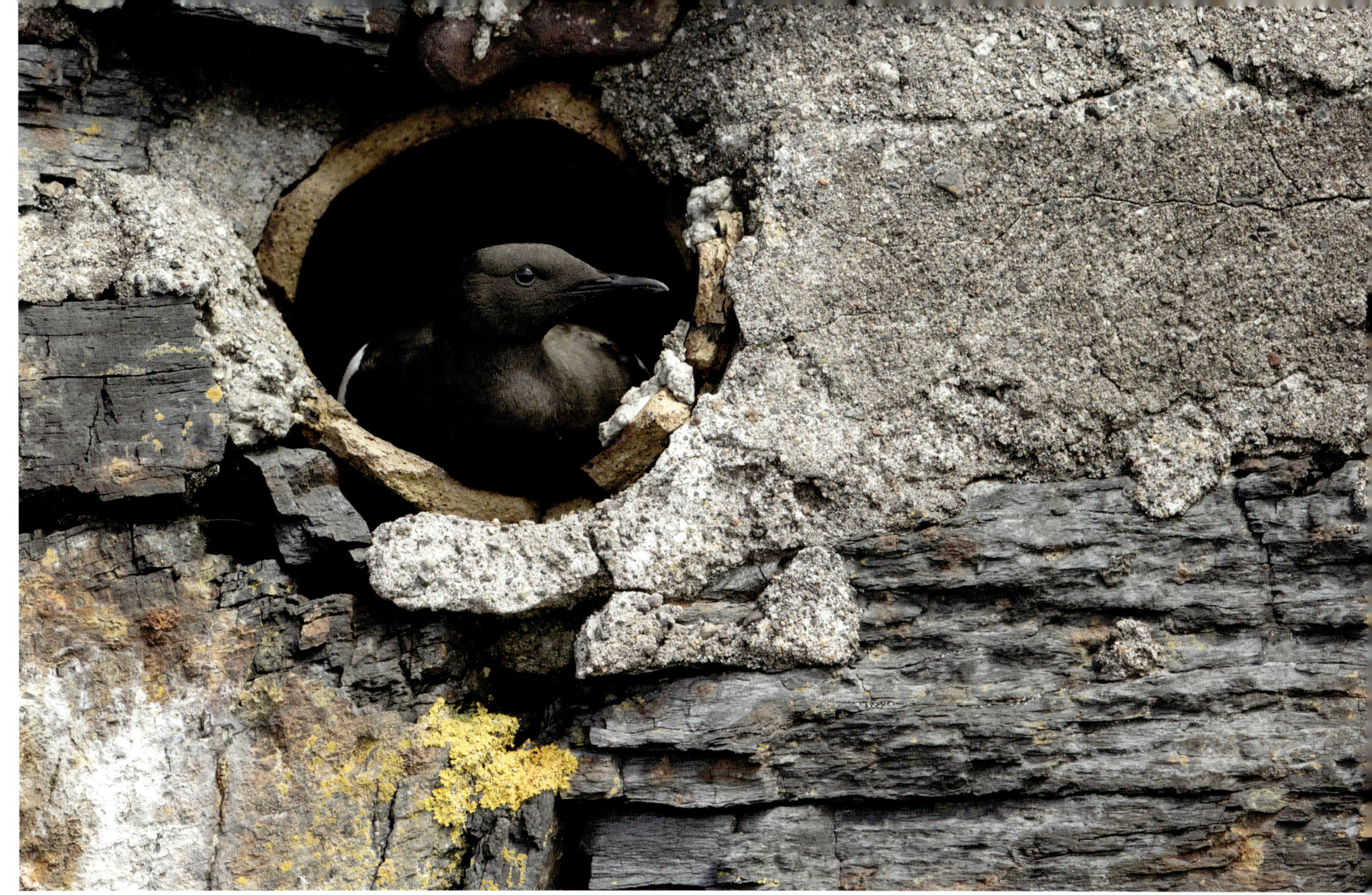

Pipe Dream
Animal Portraits

Daniel Trim
Black guillemot (*Cepphus grylle*)
Oban, Scotland

Canon EOS 5DS with Canon 500mm f/4 II lens.
500mm; 1/1,250th second; f/4.5; ISO 640.

Oban is famous for its urban black guillemots that breed in the harbour wall. The chattering and action are great to watch as passersby walk just feet away. At low tide, I was able to walk down to the shoreline and shoot back at the wall for a different perspective. This bird had chosen an especially nice spot to nest, so it was just a case of waiting for a nice pose and some flat light, as harsh light and black and white birds don't mix!

Stourhead Snow
Black & White

Jeremy Walker
Stourhead, Wiltshire, England

Nikon D810 with Zeiss 50mm f/1.4 lens.
50mm; 1/15th second; f/11; ISO 64.

I was on my way to another location when I found this scene. The forecasters had promised a dusting of snow, but within 20 minutes of travel, the snow was six inches deep, and the roads had not been ploughed or gritted. I then entered a bank of fog. Deciding it was unwise to drive any further, I safely parked up, happily right next to a footpath sign.

On following the path, I was greeted with a view of fog-shrouded, snow-covered trees. Three images were shot horizontally and then stitched in post-production to form the panorama.

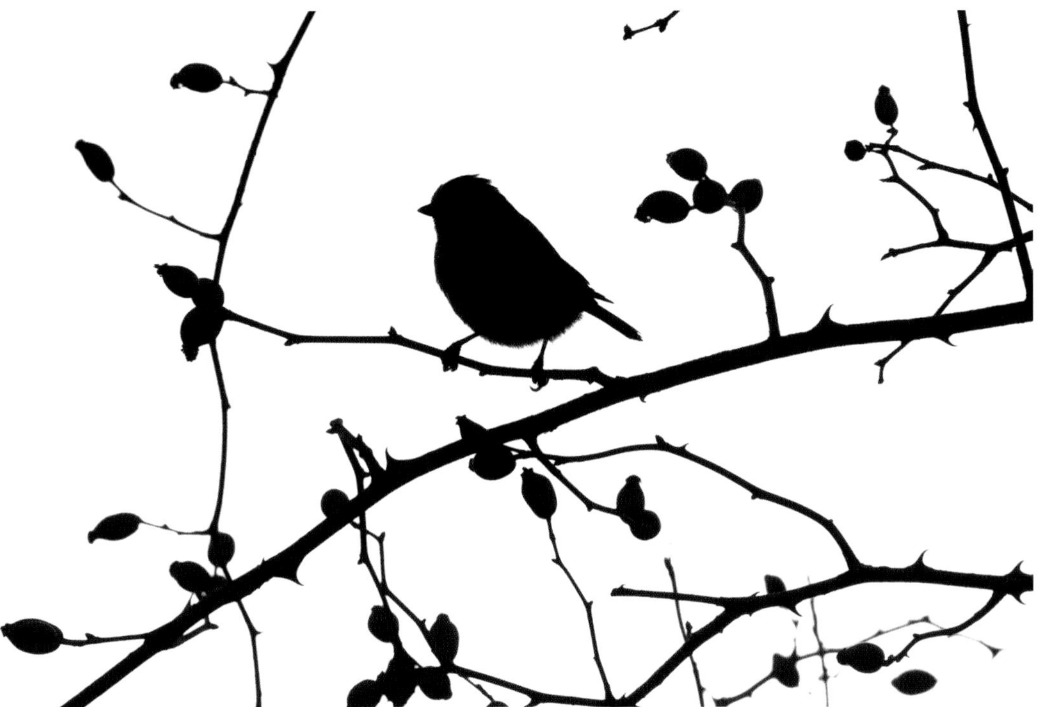

Blue Tit Amongst the Hips
Black & White

Matthew Wharf
Blue tit (*Cyanistes caeruleus*)
Bovey Tracey, Devon, England

Nikon D500 with Nikon 300mm f/2.8 lens.
300mm; 1/200th second; f/14; ISO 200.

I had been photographing birds in the garden all day and getting some nice portraits, but the light was now fading. I sat down near the bird feeders by the house and noticed that the blue tits and great tits waiting for their chance to feed were silhouetted in the old rose by the setting sun. I think it shows that even though it is not the best-maintained rose, it is of value to the birds and can look beautiful.

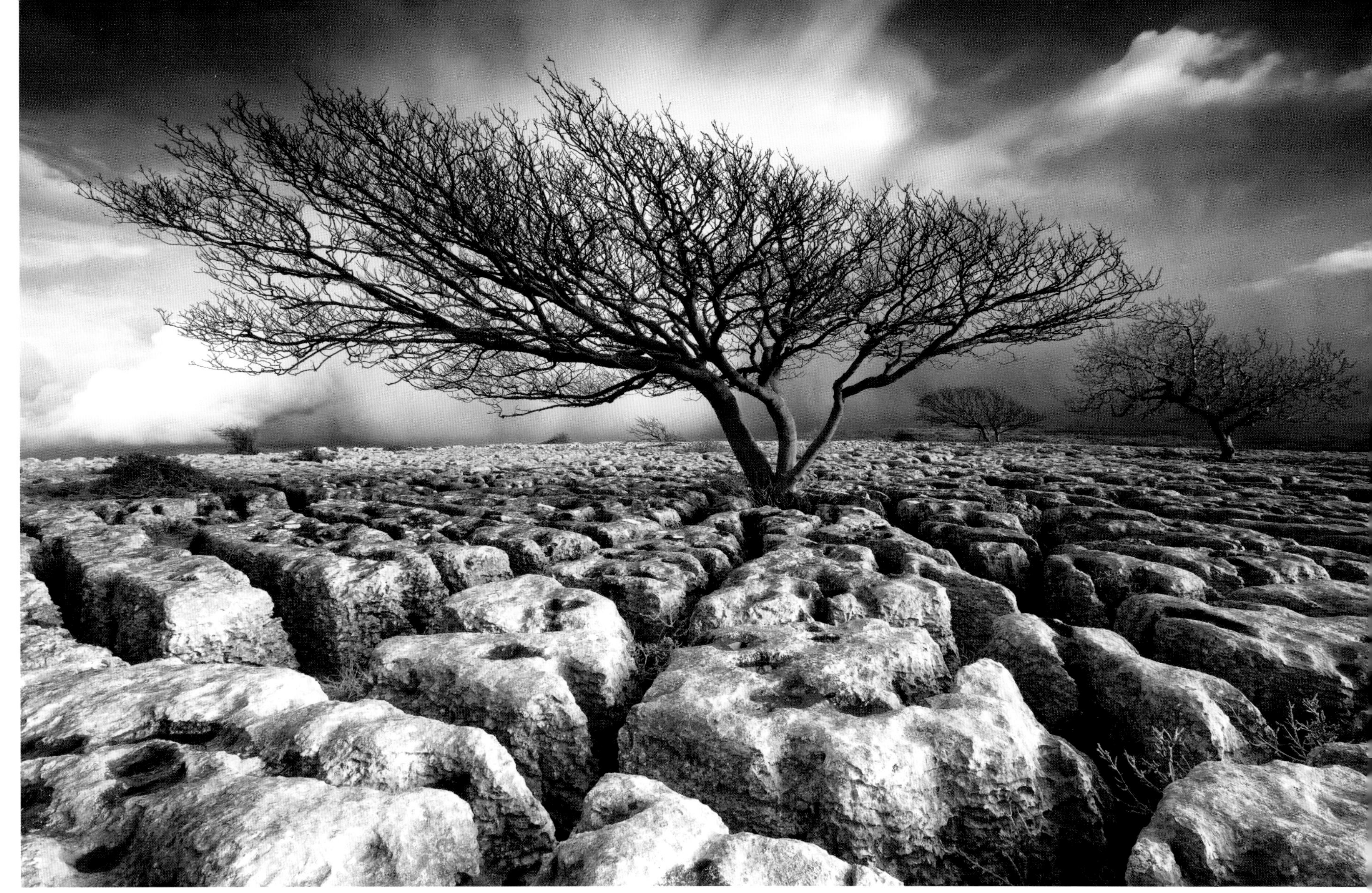

Defiance
Black & White | Highly Commended

Robin Goodlad
Farleton Fell, Cumbria, England

Nikon D800 with Nikon 17-35mm f/2.8 lens.
17mm; 1/5th second; f/18; ISO 100.

I love how even amongst a landscape of rock and relentless wind, these trees have found a way to survive on the limestone pavement of Whinberry Crag on Farleton Fell. The grikes eroded by water over the years created the perfect leading lines for the composition. I've visited this tree over the seasons, and it has become an old friend.

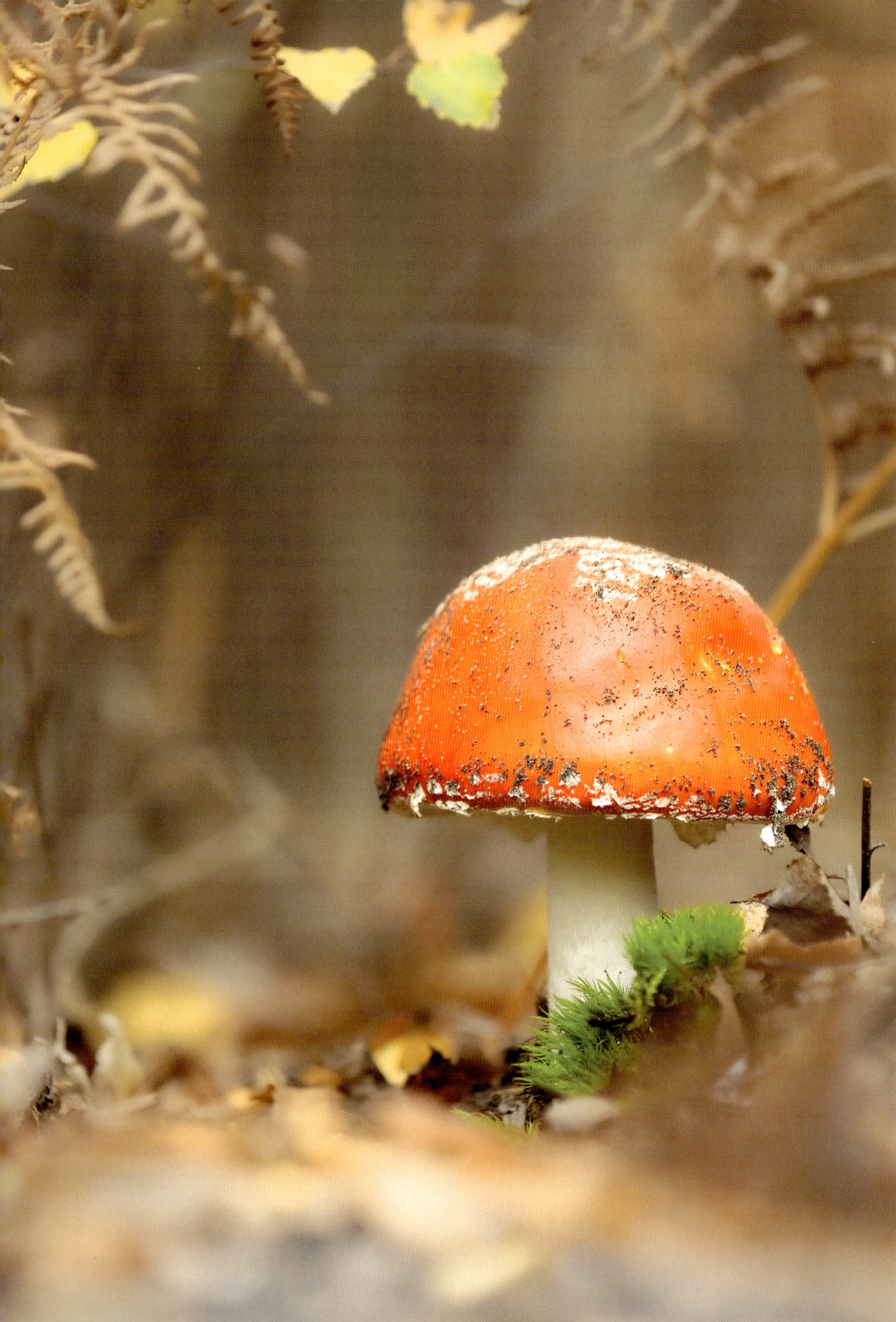

Fly Agaric Fairyland Portrait
Botanical Britain

Donna Samuels
Fly agaric (*Amanita muscaria*)
RSPB Sandy, England

Canon EOS R5 with Canon 70-200mm
f/2.8 III lens. 142mm; 1/160th second;
f/2.8; ISO 200.

Fairytale books are full of magical and
mystical mushrooms. November was a
good time to look, and I set out at RSPB
Sandy to find the beautiful fly agaric.
Despite extensive searching, I returned
to the car park empty-handed. Back at
the car, I spotted something red peering
through a glade of trees in a field
nearby and discovered the motherlode
of fly agarics – I had found the magical
spot! The photo was taken flat to
the ground to encompass the whole
structure and from a fairy's viewpoint
in the magical heathland setting.

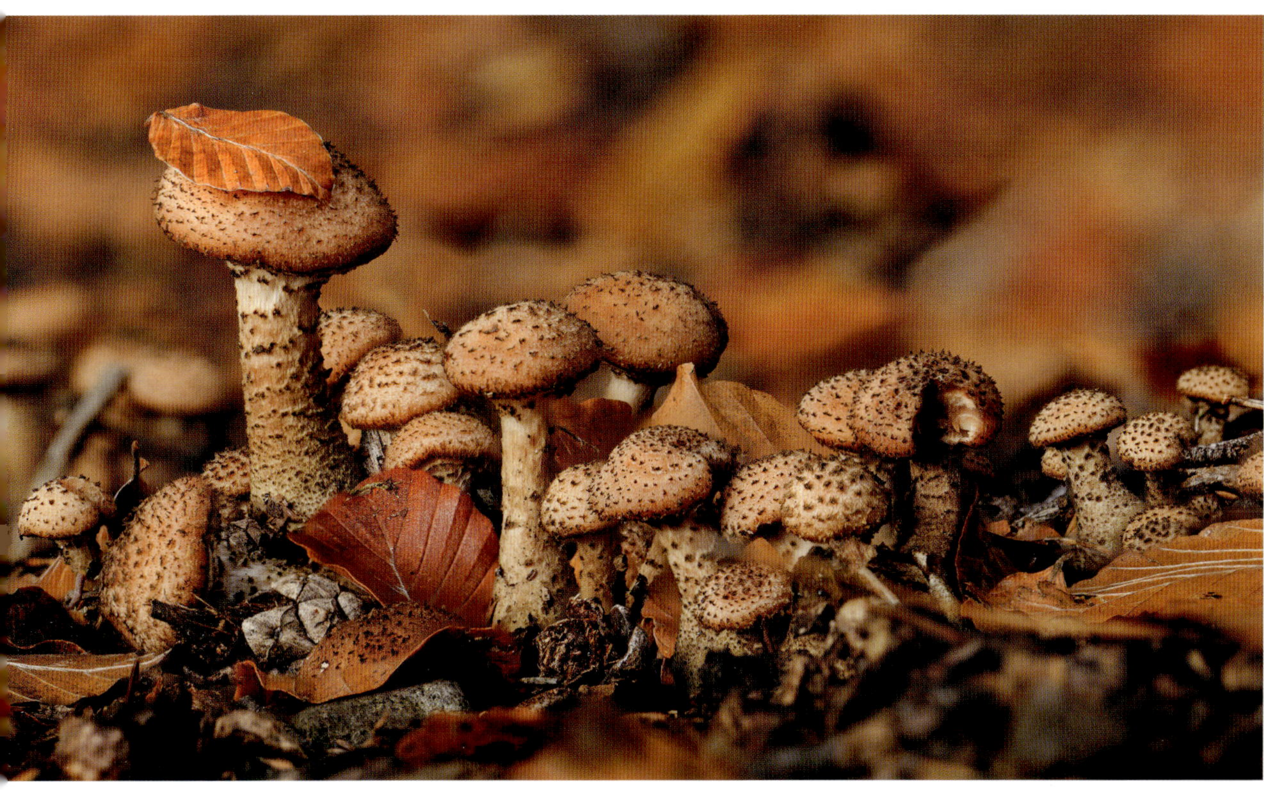

Fungi in a Beech Wood
Wild Woods

Wendy Ball
Fungi
Valley of the North Esk, Scotland

Canon EOS R5 + EF 100mm f2.8, Macro IS USM, Benro Tortoise tripod TTORO3C, focus stacked.

These prolific fungi were very well camouflaged among the autumnal gold of the fallen leaves in the spectacular Valley of the North Esk, Scotland. A weak parasite that enters the host through damaged bark or wounds, this slightly poisonous fungus can cause digestive upsets. This is a stacked image.

Beech Leaf and Mushroom
Wild Woods

Ross Hoddinott
Beech (*Fagus* sp.)
Bolderwood, the New Forest, Hampshire, England

Canon EOS R5 with Canon 100mm f/2.8 Macro lens. 100mm; 1/40th second; f/4.5; ISO 100.

This is a purely accidental photo. I was lying on the woodland floor photographing a small mushroom growing among the leaf litter, using a small LED device to create a backlit effect. While I was carefully removing a few distracting beech leaves from the frame, I noticed the shadow cast by my subject. I gently placed a leaf against the tiny mushroom and continued taking photos, but with the focus now on the shadow instead.

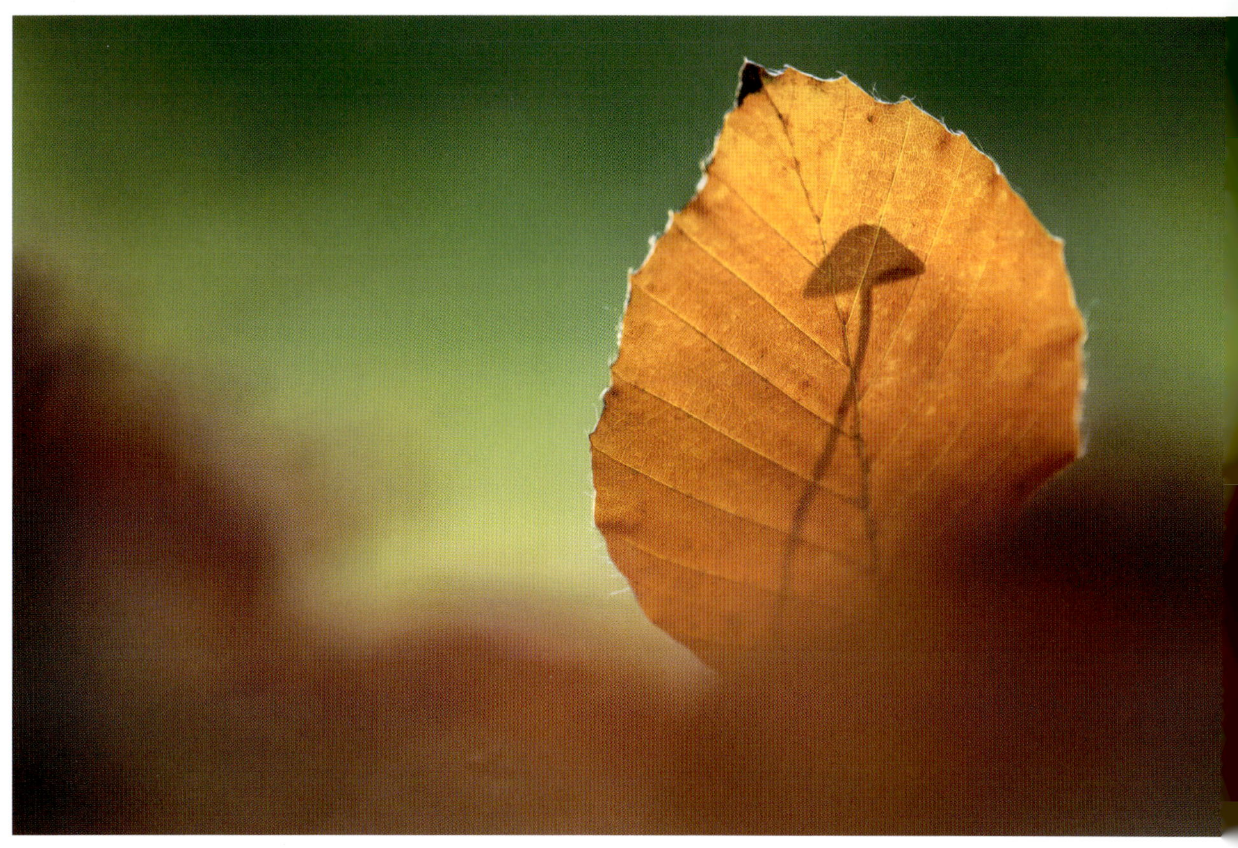

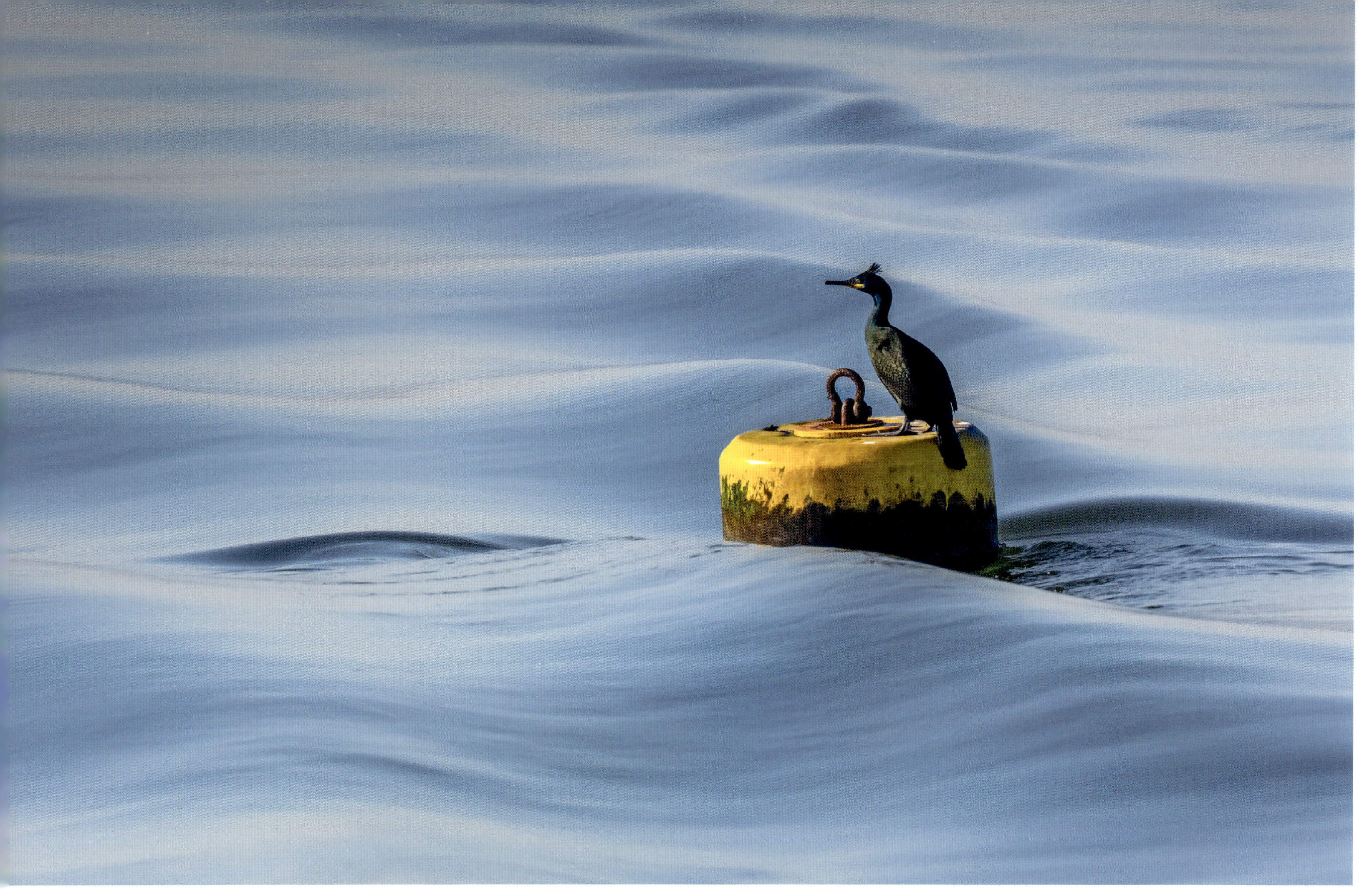

All at Sea
Habitat | Highly Commended

Robin Morrison
Shag (*Phalacrocorax aristotelis*)
Poole Harbour, Dorset, England

Canon EOS R7 with Canon 300mm f/2.8 II lens.
300mm; 1/1,600th second; f/8; ISOS 400.

This image of a shag on a mooring buoy in Poole Harbour was taken from a boat on a beautiful, calm and sunny February morning in 2023. The small, soft, smooth-looking waves were amazing. Standing at the back of the boat, it was possible to get as close as possible to the water level. The bird is in full breeding plumage, even displaying its crest, and seems to be enjoying the early morning sunshine.

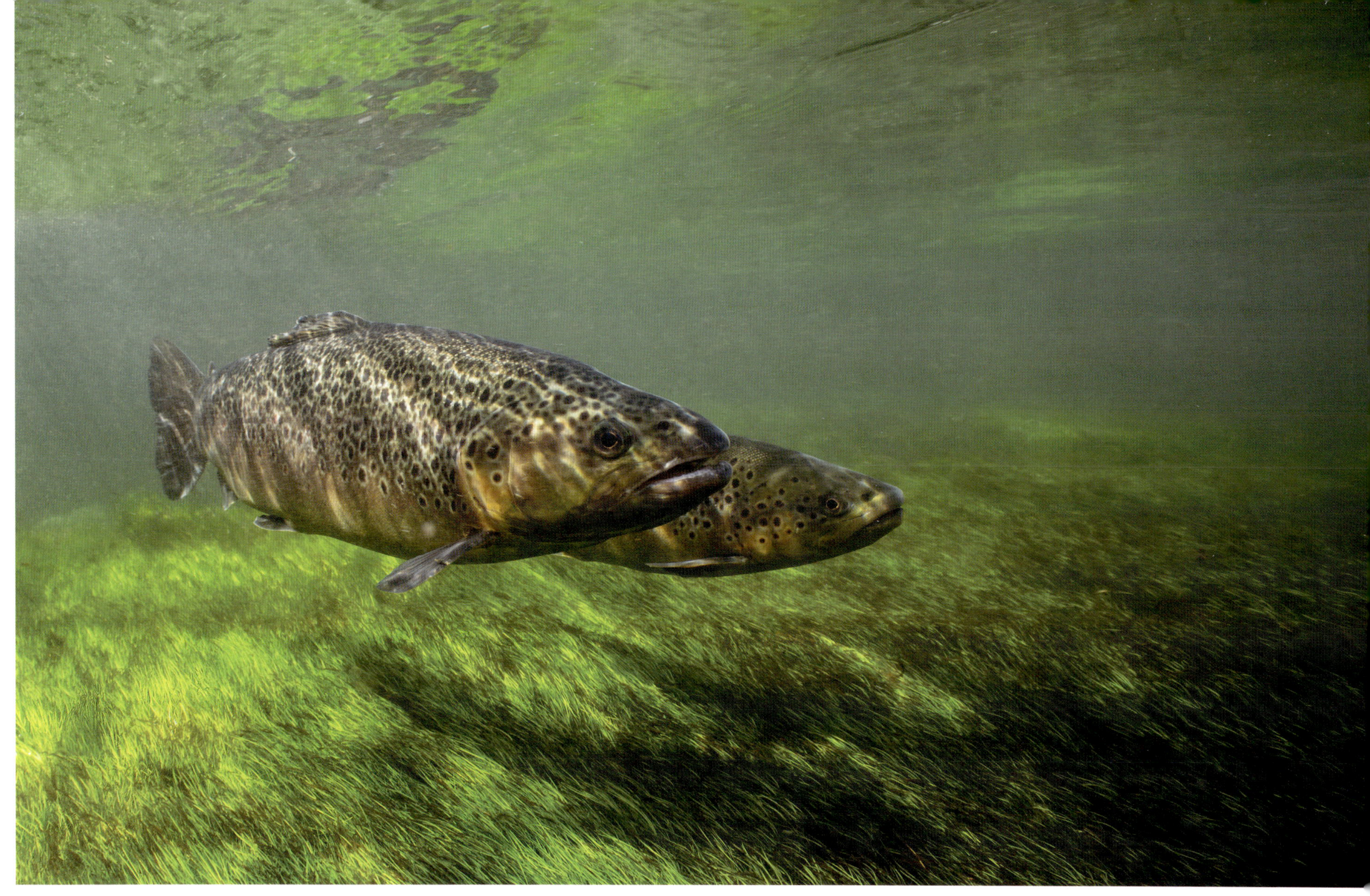

A Chalk Stream Under Threat
Habitat

Paul Colley
Brown trout (*Salmo trutta*)
River Test at Whitchurch Silk Mill, Hampshire, England

Nikon D4 with Nikon 28mm f/2.8 lens. 28mm; 1/200th second; f/10; ISO 360.

A pair of brown trout swim above a weed bed in the River Test at Whitchurch Silk Mill in Hampshire. The river is one of the UK's iconic chalk streams but is under constant threat from water company and farming pollution. Early indications of pollution are visible in this image, with the brown algae on the normally pristine weed bed most likely caused by excess phosphates in the water. If the weed is eventually choked by this, the vibrant insect life in it will suffer, and the whole food chain up to and beyond the trout will falter.

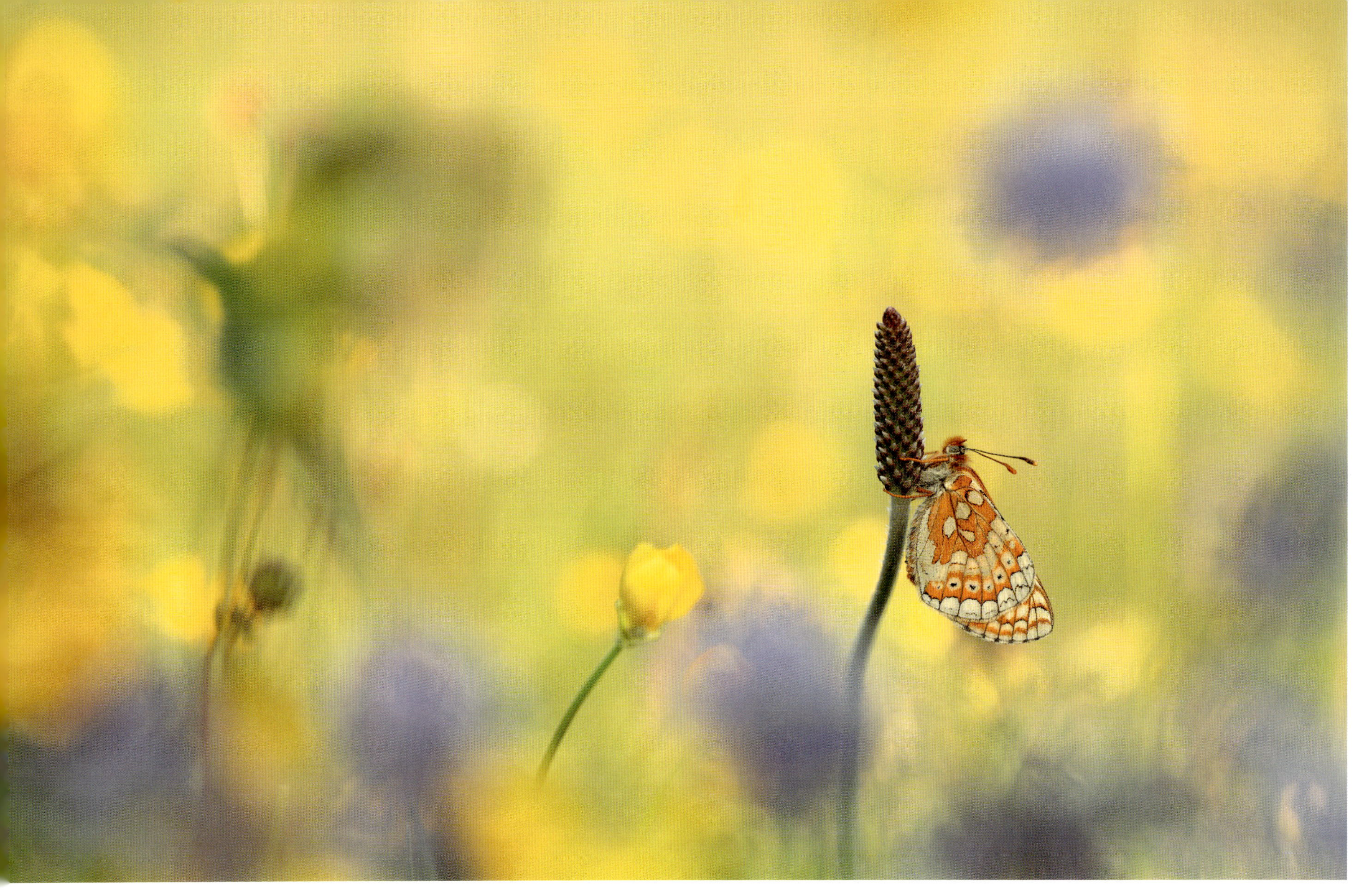

Marsh Fritillary
Hidden Britain

Daniel Callejo Rossi
Marsh fritillary (*Euphydryas aurinia*)
Cotley Hill, Wiltshire, England

Sony A7 IV with Sigma 105mm f/2.8 Macro lens.
105mm; 1/250th second; f/5.6; ISO 500.

It was a beautiful and sunny day spent on Cotley Hill looking for marsh fritillary butterflies. This year, most of the species appeared later in the spring than normal. This delay could have been caused by the cold weather affecting the food plants for most of the spring species, which were unable to feed and complete their life cycle. The butterflies were very active, and it wasn't until late in the afternoon that I was able to photograph these stunning creatures. There was a beautiful carpet of buttercups and small blue violet flowers that helped me frame the butterfly.

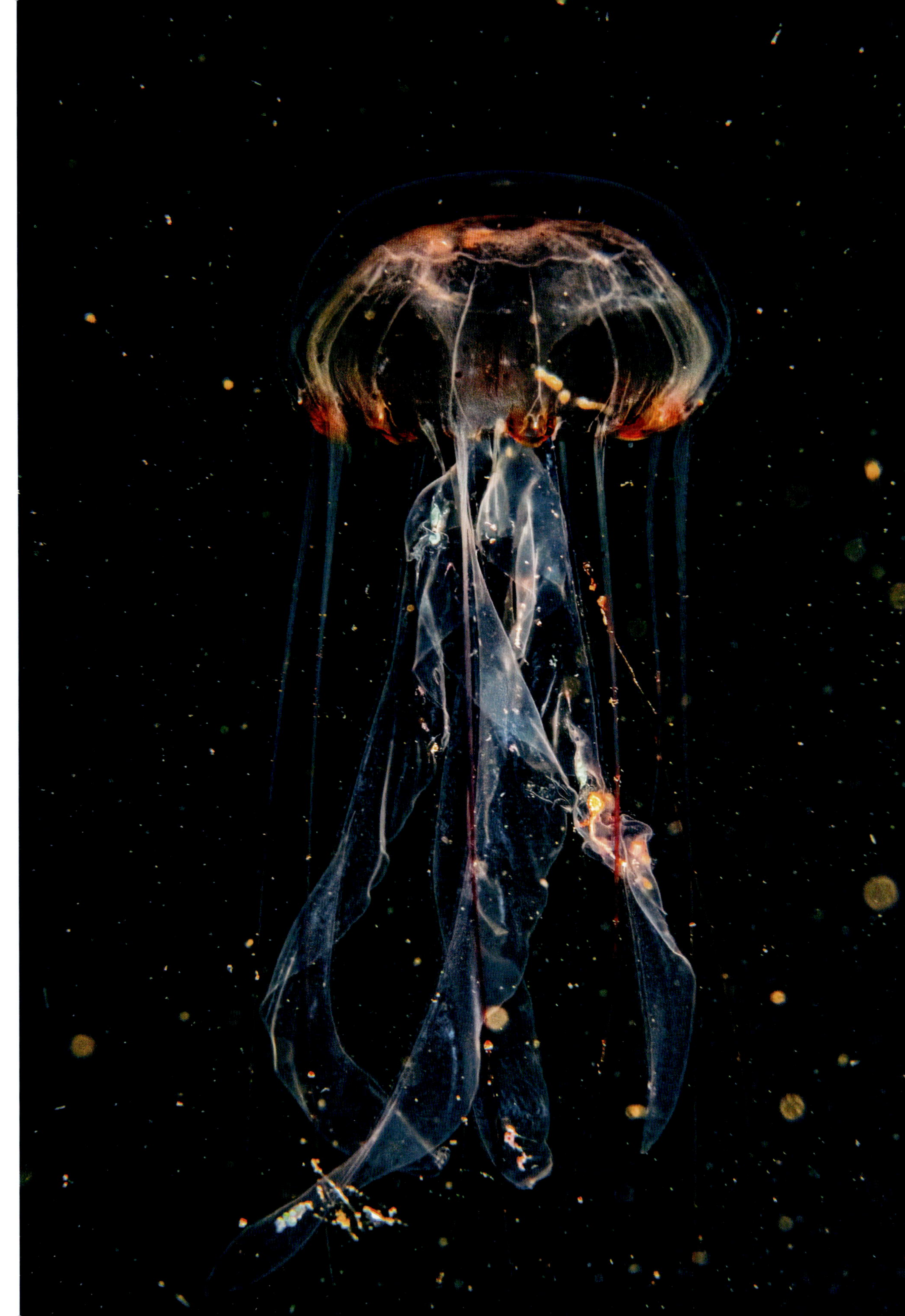

Plankton Heaven
Coast & Marine

Paul Pettitt
Compass jellyfish (*Chrysaora hysoscella*)
Chesil Beach, England

Nikon D500 with Nikon 105mm f/2.8.
105mm; 1/100th second; f/25; ISO
1250.

This compass jellyfish was floating
merrily along in a soup of plankton near
Chesil Cove. On this particular day, we
knew they would be present. The image
was taken at a depth of about four
metres on an early May evening. The
trick is not to spend too long with any
individual, as they tend to curl up into a
ball and lose their shape and lines.

Sunrise Hare
Animal Portraits | Runner-up

Spencer Burrows
Brown hare (*Lepus europaeus*)
Nottinghamshire, England

Nikon Z 9 with Nikon 800mm f/6.3 lens.
800mm; 1/3,200th second; f/6.3; ISO 2,000.

I'm fortunate enough to have access to a private farm and have spent a lot of time with brown hares over the past couple of years. During this time, I've invested many hours into developing fieldcraft and gaining a good understanding of their behaviour, allowing me to get close without disturbing the animal – hares are often skittish.

For this image, I lay low and silent in a spot of the field they tend to follow from the hedgerow. This hare was very relaxed and allowed me to capture some portraits as the sun was starting to rise over the field.

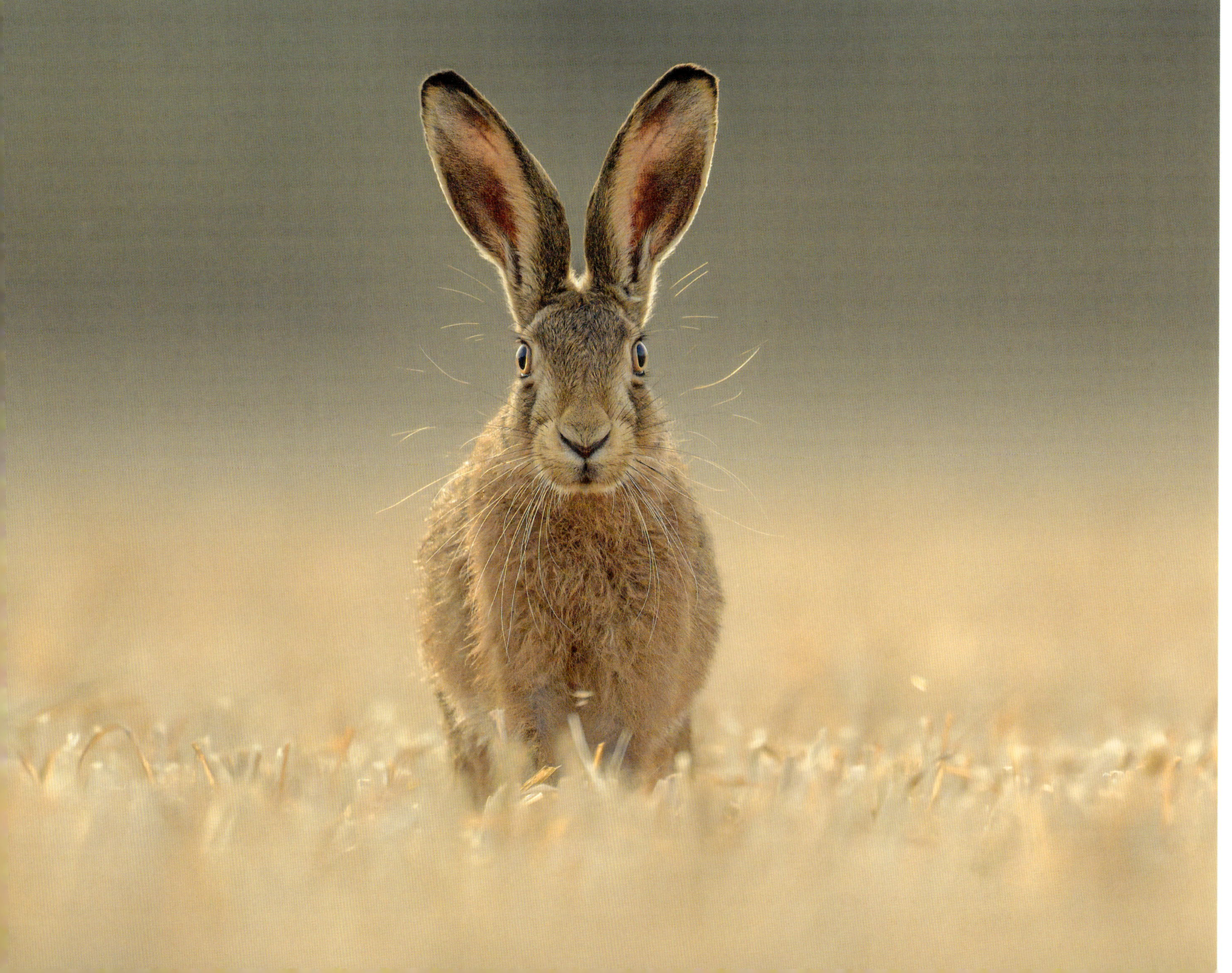

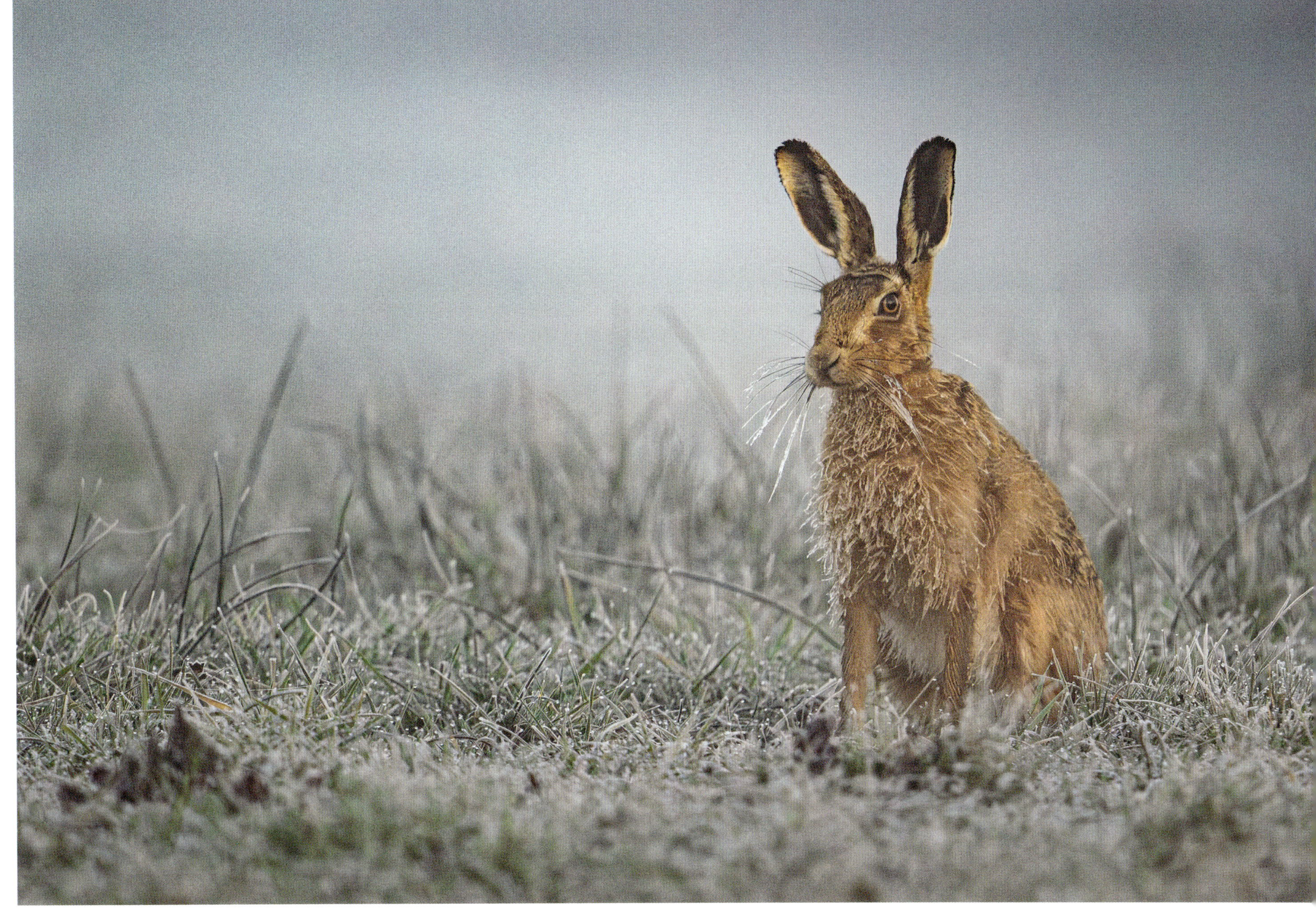

Frozen Hare
Habitat

Robin Morrison
Brown hare (*Lepus europaeus*)
Somerset Field, near Langport, England

Canon 1D X III with Canon 500mm f/4 II lens &
1.4x teleconverter. 700mm; 1/1,600th second;
f/5.6; ISO 2,500.

On a bitterly cold, frosty morning on a Somerset
moor, I chose to lie down on the edge of a field that
I knew had hares, hoping that one might pass by. The
fog made it impossible to see them, and suddenly this
one emerged with amazing frosted whiskers from the
mist. It heard the click from the camera and paused
briefly before walking by. Given the flat, low-light
conditions, I have boosted the colour slightly but
left the 'noisy' background, as it provides the misty
atmosphere of that low-light morning.

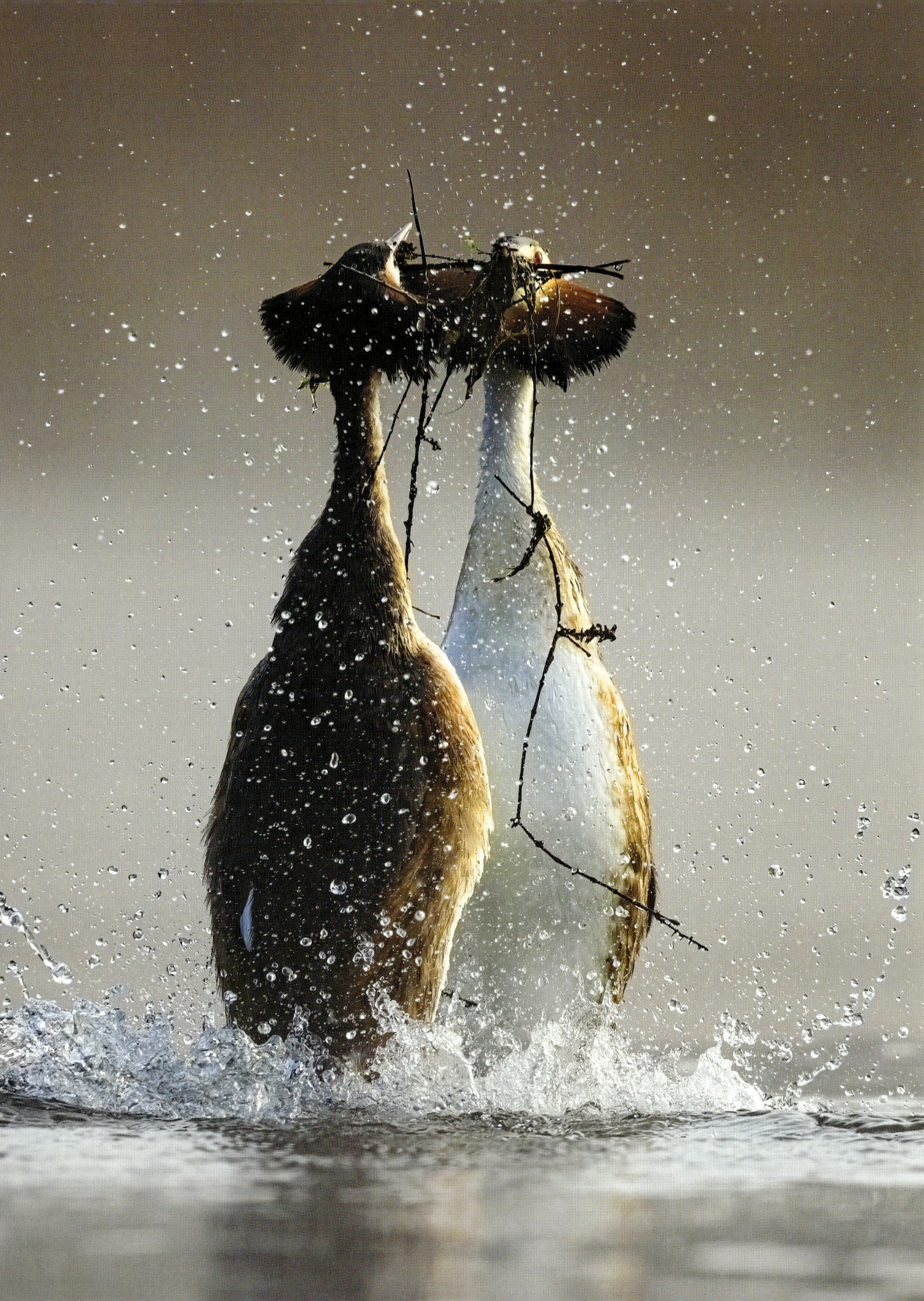

Weed Dancing at Dawn
Animal Behaviour

Stephen Rodger
Great crested grebe (*Podiceps cristatus*)
West Lothian Loch, Scotland

Canon EOS R5 with Canon 600mm f/4 II lens & 1.4x teleconverter. 840mm; 1/2,000th second; f/8; ISO 2,000.

Great crested grebes have a wonderfully dynamic and elegant courtship ritual, which is capped by the 'weed dance'. On this morning, the conditions were perfect, and the early morning light was still soft as it filtered through the dawn mist. Fortunately for me, the birds were close to where I was sitting, allowing me to clearly photograph their dance, while the mist reduced the far reed bank to a subtle orange hue.

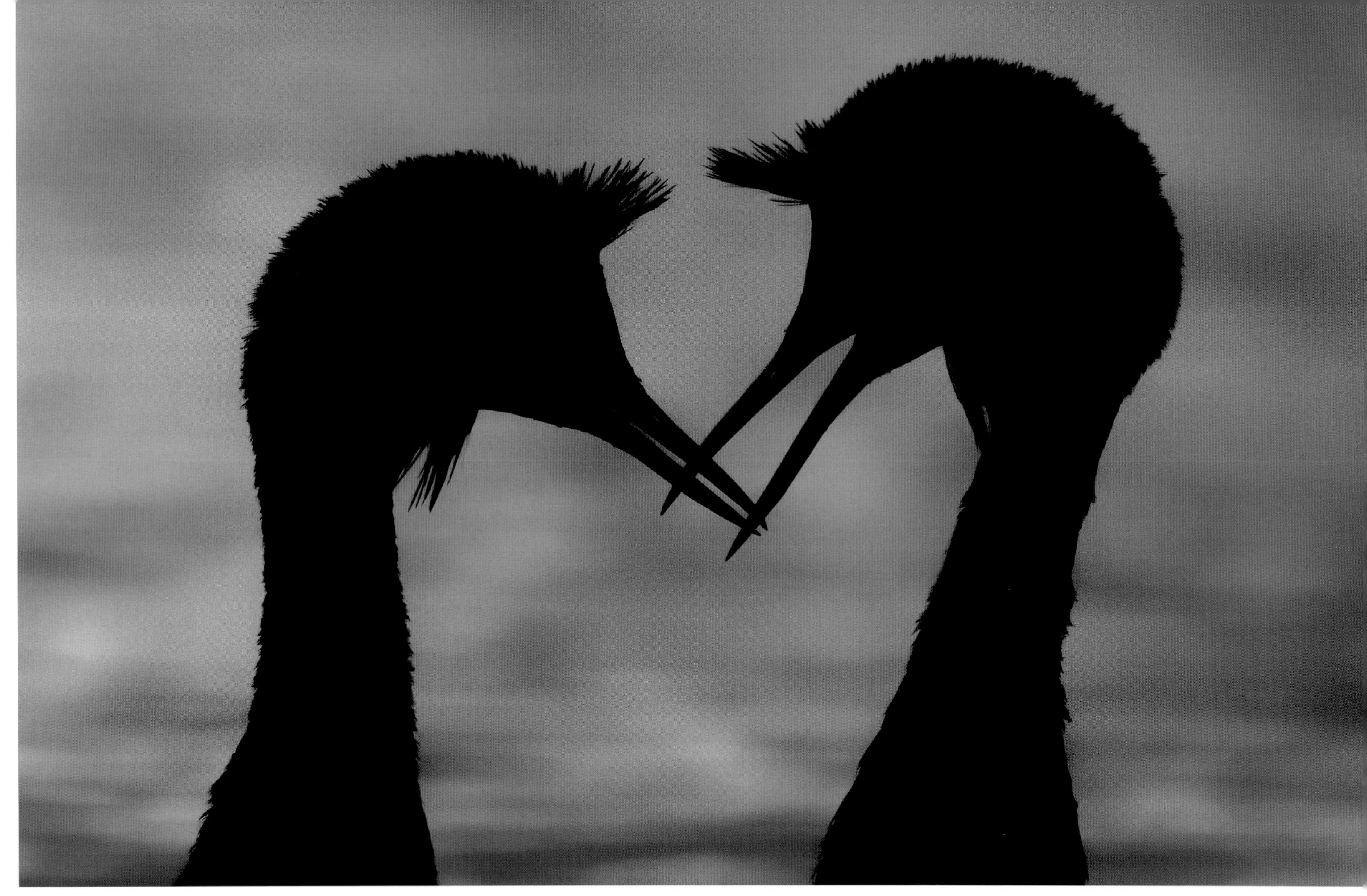

Dancing in the Dark
Animal Behaviour | Runner-up

Matthew Glover
Great crested grebe (*Podiceps cristatus*)
Killingworth, North Tyneside, England

Canon EOS R5 with Canon RF 100-500mm f/4.5-7.1
lens. 500mm; 1/1,000th second; f/7.1; ISO 8,000.

'Dancing in the Dark' portrays a pair of great
crested grebes engaged in their courtship ritual at
sunrise. This carefully choreographed dance serves
to strengthen their bonds during the mating season.
The photo was captured in the early hours on an
urban lake in North Tyneside – once a former mining
site, now thriving with wildlife, it hosts up to four
separate pairs of grebes, competing for territory and
displaying their flamboyant courtship style. Spending
considerable time with these birds, I've learned to
anticipate their courtship 'dances' and be prepared
to capture these beautiful moments.

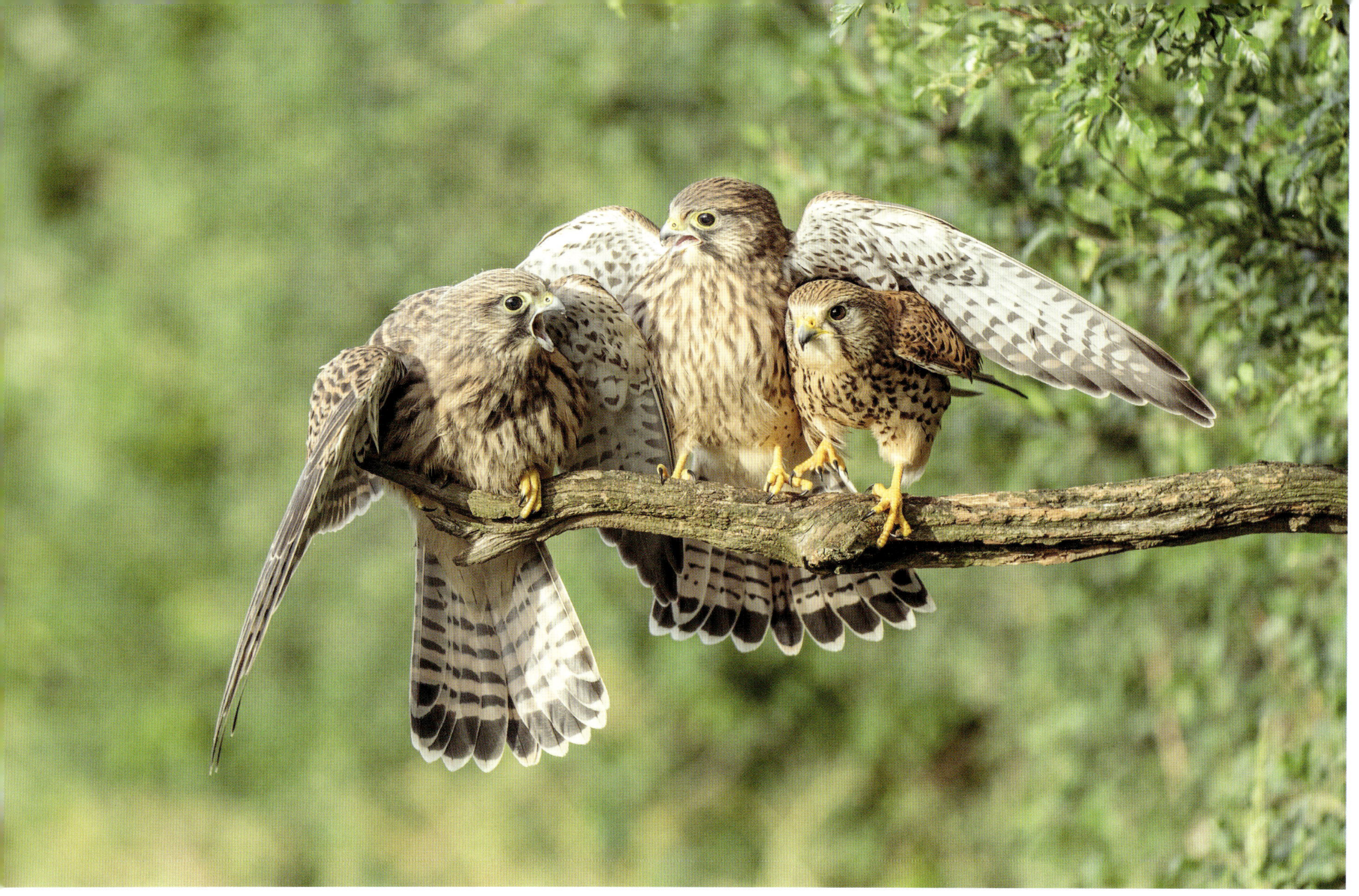

Three's a Crowd
Animal Portraits

Philip Male
Kestrel (*Falco tinnunculus*)
Broad Town, Wiltshire, England

Canon EOS R3 with Canon 100-400mm f/4.5-5.6 II
lens. 340mm; 1/1,250th second; f/5.6; ISO 2,000.

I'm fortunate to have a pair of kestrels nesting in an
old oak tree in the field behind my house. When the
youngsters began to fly, they would come to this old
branch and Mom (on the right) would arrive with
food for them. The female has grown remarkably
tolerant of me as I move around the garden. I provide
food for all the wild birds in the vicinity of the house
and occasionally offer tidbits from roadkill that I've
collected. This is primarily for the foxes, but she
has also come to take the occasional piece.

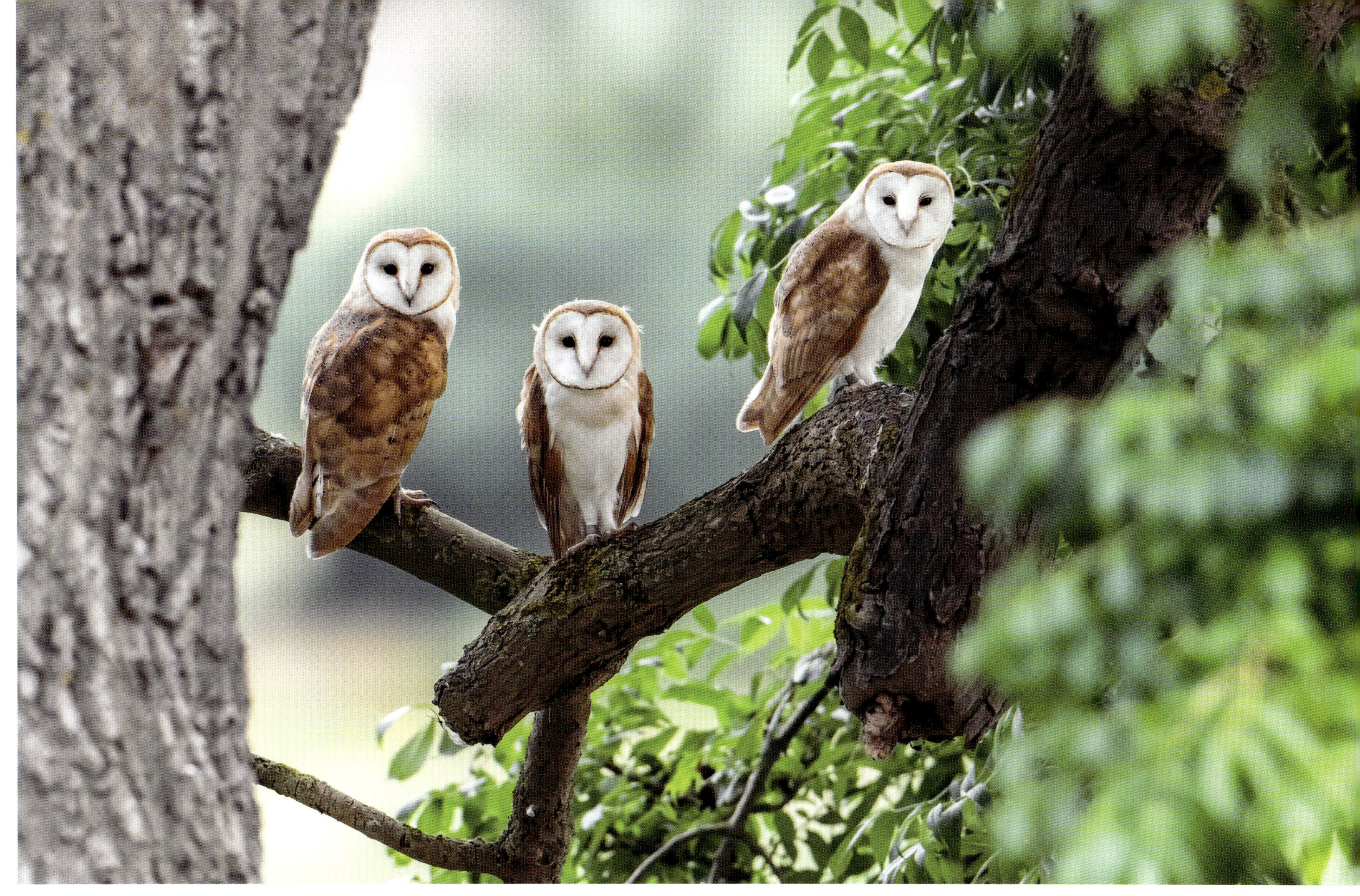

Three of a Kind
Animal Portraits

Charlotte Rhodes
Barn owl (*Tyto alba*)
Bank Island, near York, England

Canon EOS R5 with Canon RF 600mm f/4 lens
& 1.4x teleconverter. 840mm; 1/500th second;
f/8; ISO 5,000.

I headed to a local nature reserve before dawn,
knowing that barn owls had nested in an ash tree
the previous year, relatively close to the path. As I
wandered down the path, I could hear the distinctive
sound of a young owl calling for food and waited
patiently. After a short while, one, then two, then
three young barn owls came out to perch on the
branches and call impatiently for breakfast. This was
taken with a 840mm lens from some distance to
ensure the owls were not disturbed.

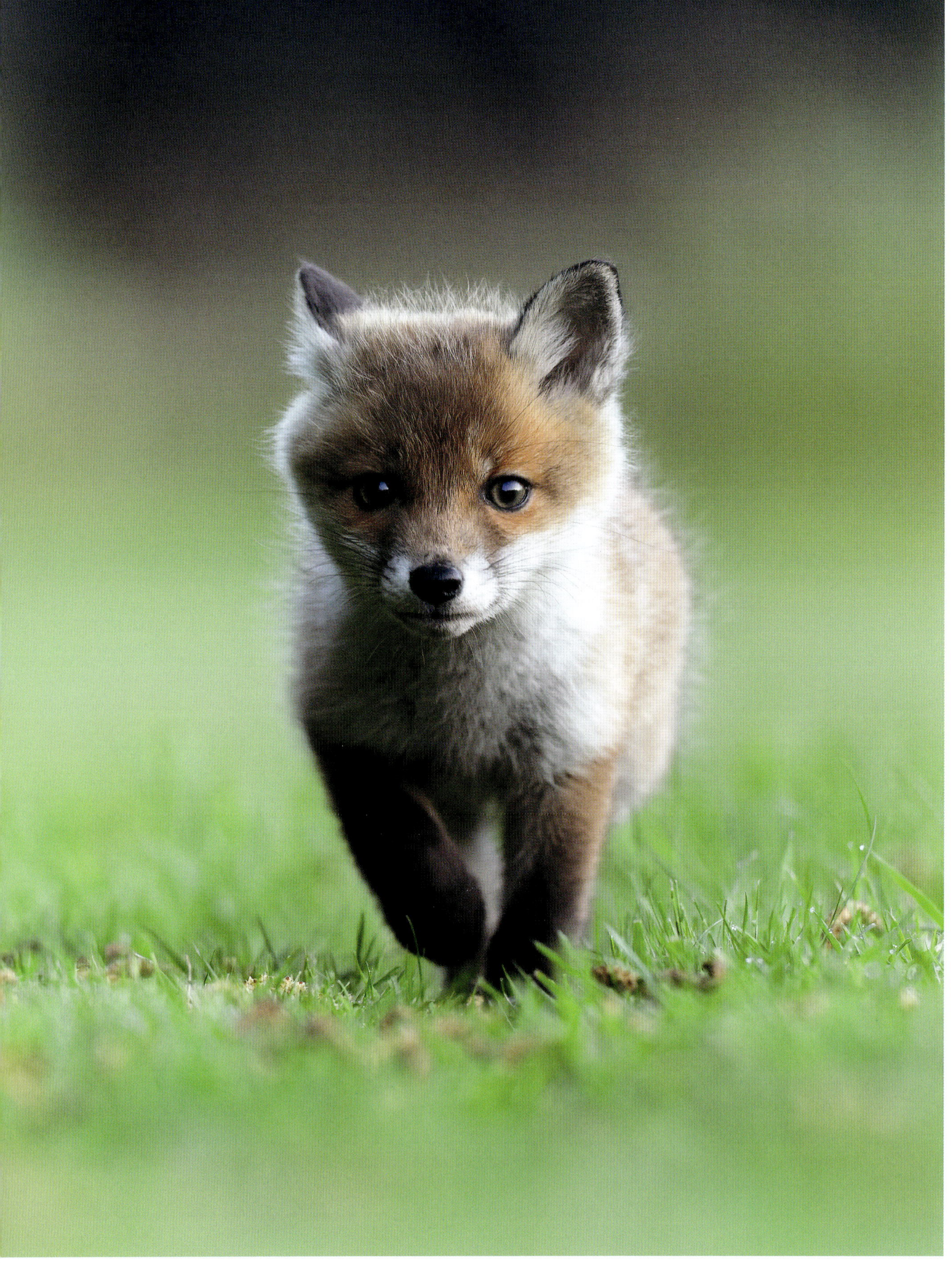

Stalking the Photographer
Animal Portraits

Ben Nicholson
Red fox (*Vulpes vulpes*)
Ripley, Surrey, England

Canon EOS R5 with Canon 500mm f/4 II lens. 500mm; 1/200th second; f/4; ISO 8,000.

For the first few weeks, the fox cubs stayed within the small wood; however, they began to venture out into the field. I crept out from the wood and positioned myself in the long grass, trying to stay hidden so as not to disturb them. They were like children being let loose on the world, chasing each other, oblivious to their surroundings. This allowed me to capture some close-up portraits.

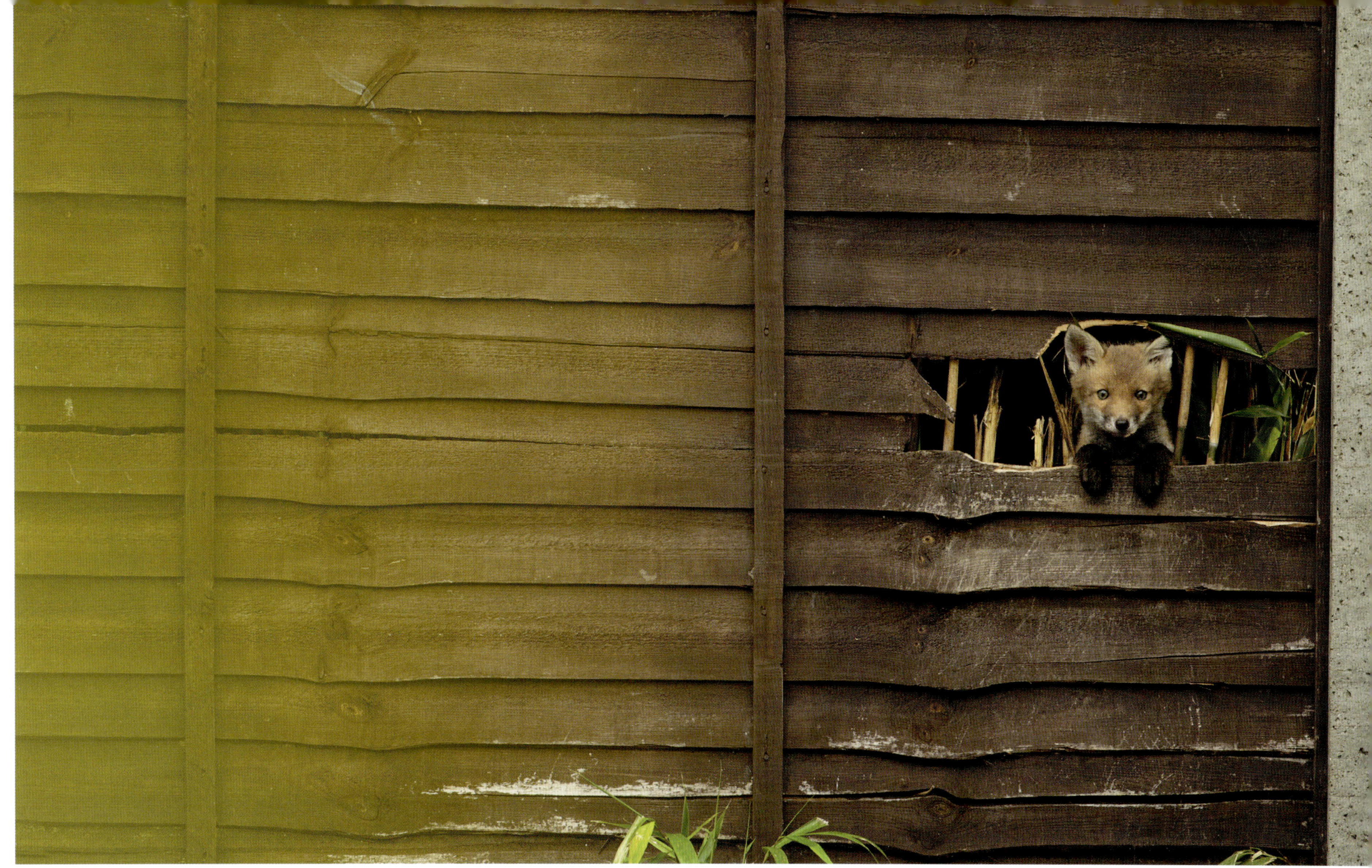

Fox Hole
Urban Wildlife

Ben Andrew
Red fox (*Vulpes vulpes*)
Bedford, England

Canon 5D IV with Canon 500mm f/4 lens.
500mm; 1/160th second; f/4.5; ISO 400.

I have a friend who regularly has foxes den under the decking in her garden. As the cubs get bolder, they start to explore more and more. There is a hole in the fence that they'd often jump through to access an area behind the garden. They often leapt through so quickly, but on this occasion one stopped and stared long enough for me to capture this cheeky shot!

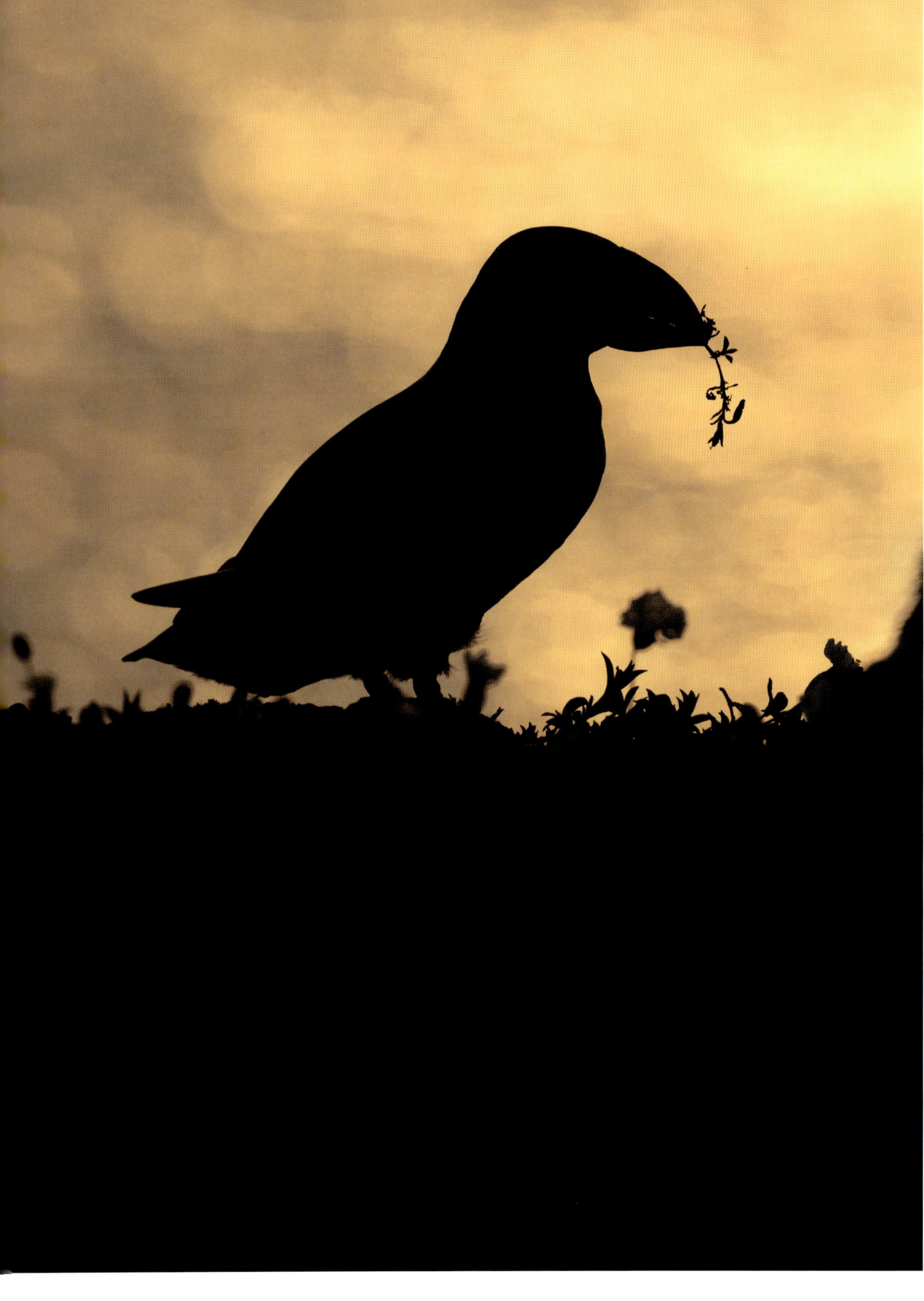

A Gift
Animal Portraits

Rosalie Smith
Atlantic puffin (*Fratercula arctica*)
Skomer Island, Pembrokeshire, Wales

Canon EOS R5 with Canon RF 100-500mm f/4.5-7.1 lens. 324mm; 1/400th second; f/7.1; ISO 100.

In the last light on Skomer Island, I sat waiting in hope for a puffin with foliage so that I could capture a silhouetted puffin clutching a precious flower gift in its beak. Puffins, like many other animals, engage in gift-giving behaviour as a way to strengthen social bonds and display affection. Captured just as the sun was dropping, it gave a beautiful backdrop for this captivating puffin courtship ritual.

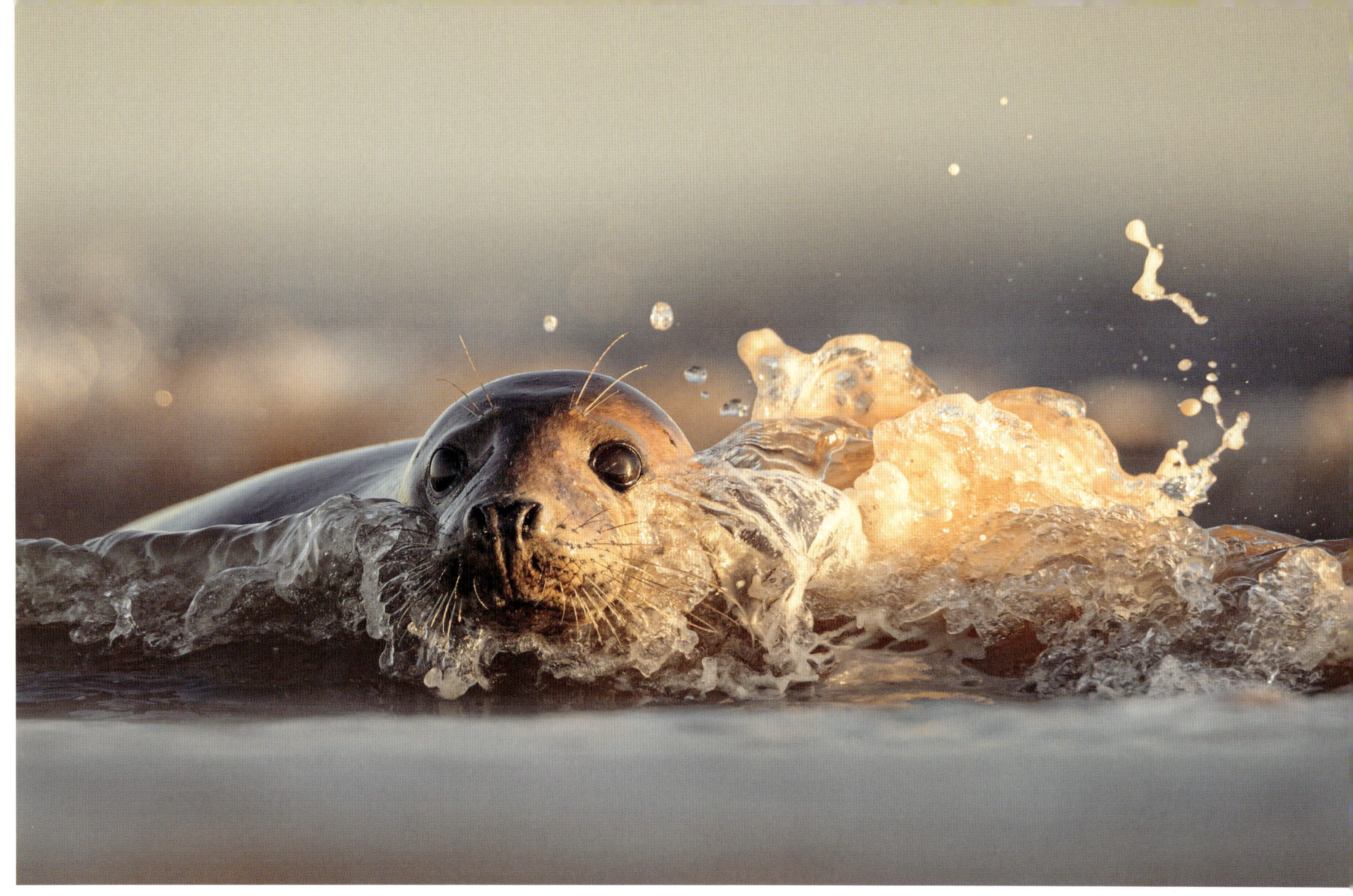

Seal in the Surf
Coast & Marine

Francis Taylor
Grey seal (*Halichoerus grypus*)
Lincolnshire, England

Canon EOS 1D X II with Canon 500mm f/4 II lens &
1.4x teleconverter. 700mm; 1/800th second; f/5.6;
ISO 500.

Some of my happiest wildlife-watching days have
been spent lying for hours on the shoreline, watching
the seals playing and socialising in the surf. Images
like this are all about timing, and here I was lucky
to catch the wave just as it crested around the seal,
illuminated by golden early morning sunshine.

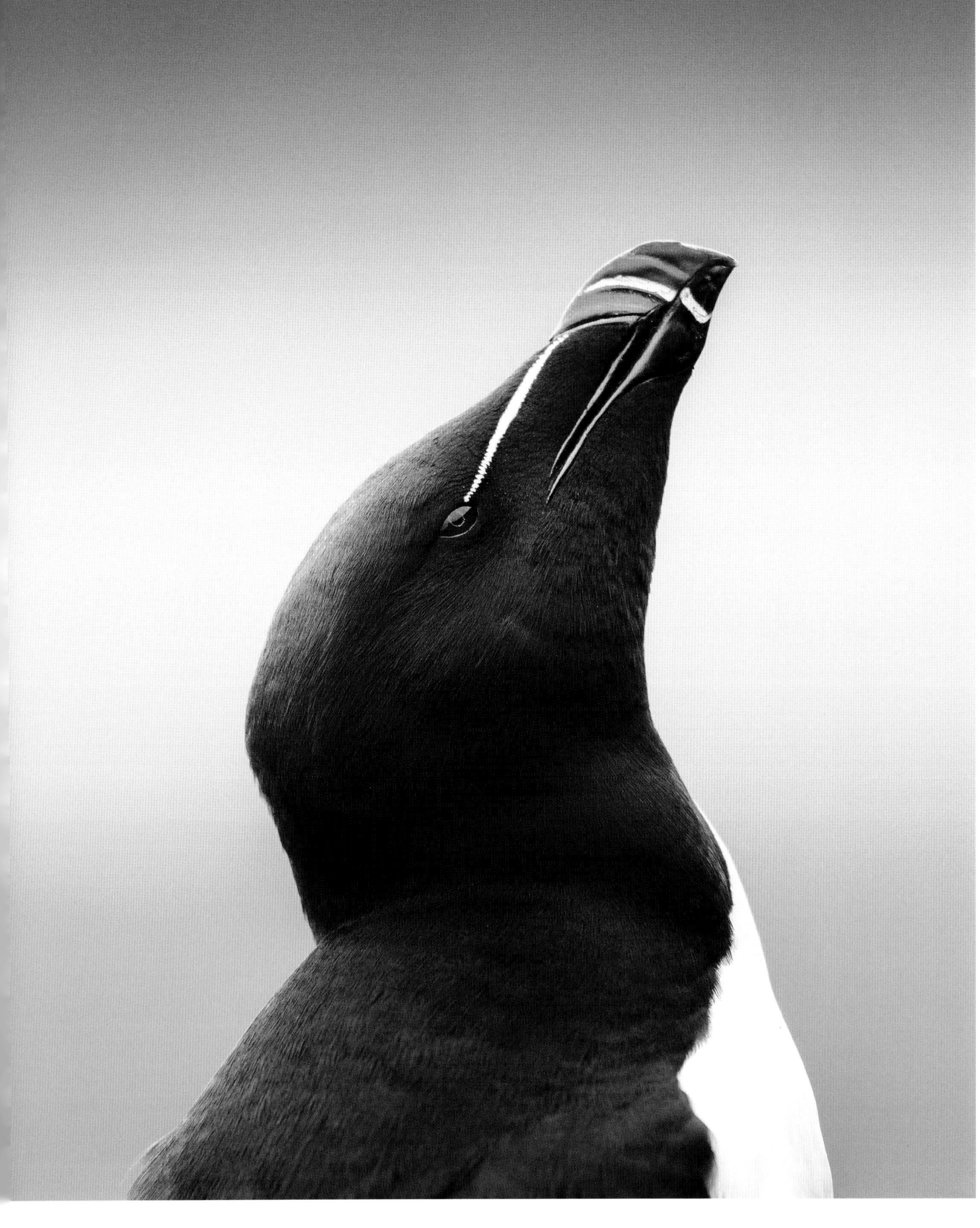

Drew Buckley
Razorbill (*Alca torda*)
Skomer Island,
Pembrokeshire, Wales

Canon EOS 1D X II with
Canon 500mm f/4 II lens &
1.4x teleconverter. 700mm;
1/800th second; f/5.6;
ISO 500.

While waiting for the
return boat on Skomer,
I noticed this razorbill
nesting on a nearby cliff
edge. Every now and
then, it would look up and
scour the skies for passing
gulls. Timing my image
when it was looking up,
the overcast conditions
helped to diffuse the light,
exposing the bird evenly.
Converting the image to
black and white helped the
subject pop even more.

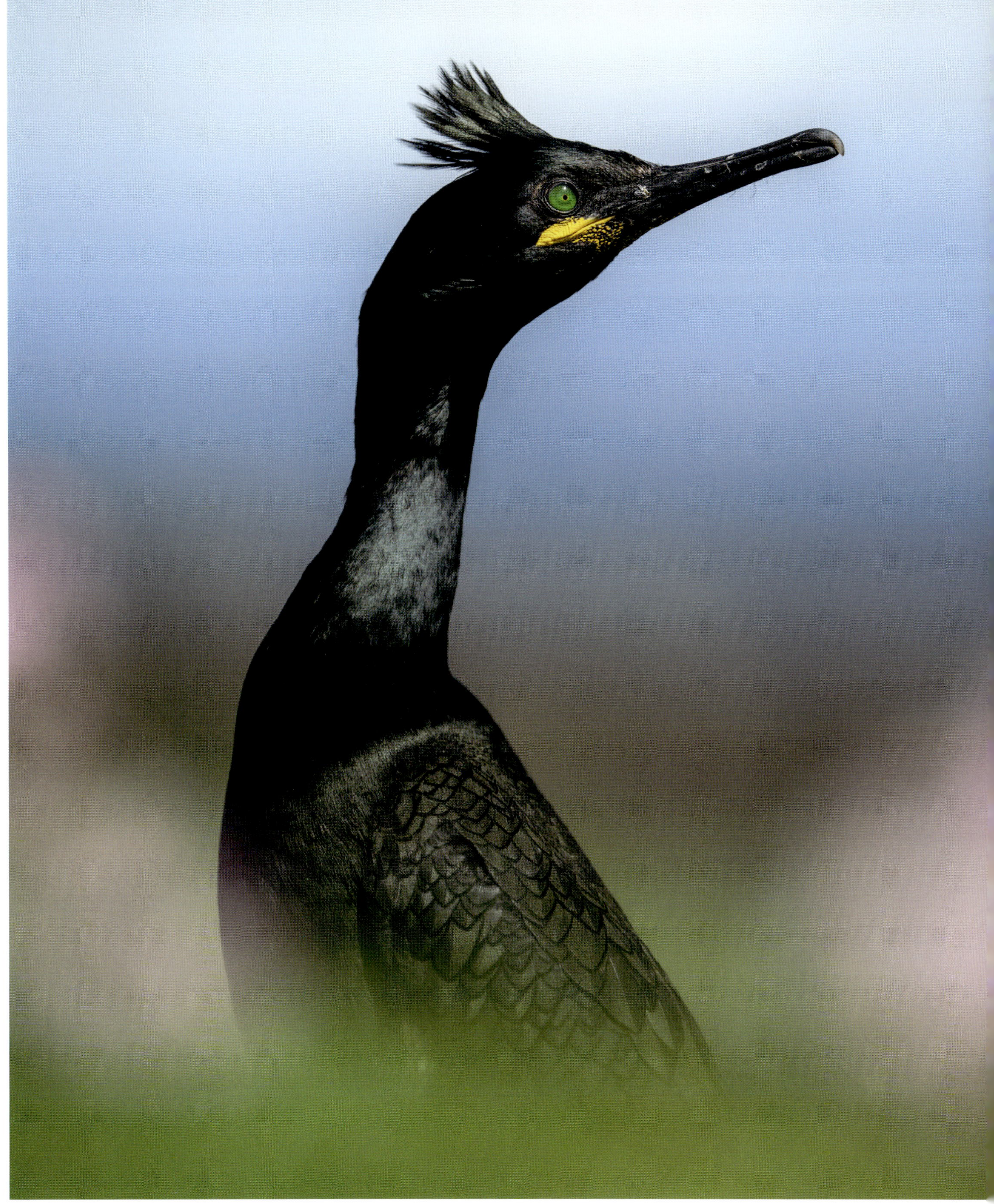

Joshua Copping
Shag (*Phalacrocorax aristotelis*)
Isle of Lunga, Scotland

Nikon Z9 with Nikon 500mm f/5.6 lens. 500mm; 1/640th second; f/5; ISO 80.

A European shag on the cliff tops of the Treshnish Isles, Scotland. Here, I used a 500mm lens to isolate this individual and capture detail in the feathers. The bright sun made the bird's iridescent plumage shine, and the wide aperture on my lens, low to the ground, created the soft blurred foreground from the grass and thrift.

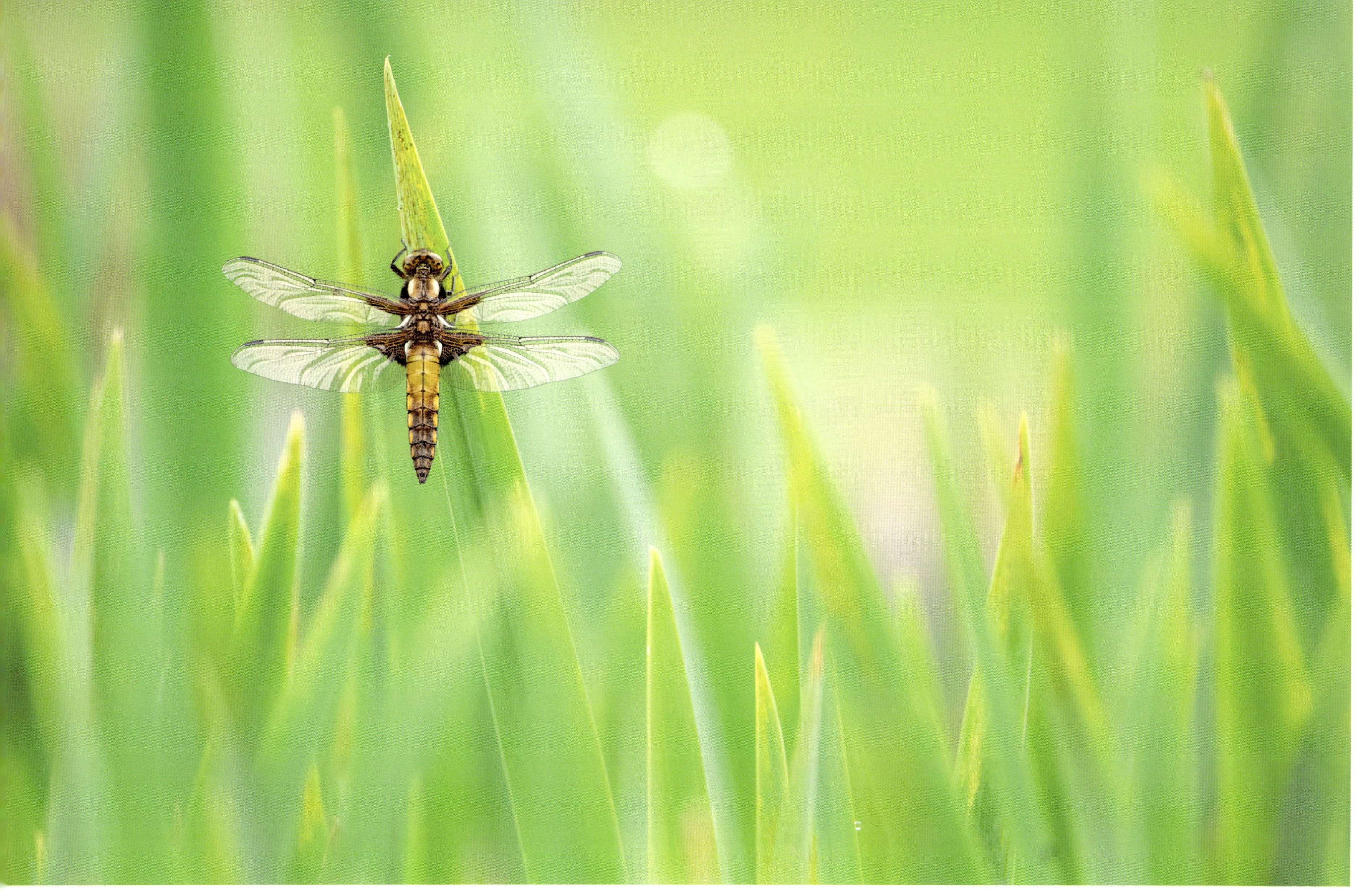

Teneral
Hidden Britain

Ross Hoddinott
Broad-bodied chaser dragonfly (*Libellula depressa*)
Broxwater, Cornwall, England

Nikon Z 7 II with Nikon 500mm f/5.6 lens.
500mm; 1/2,000th second; f/5.6; ISO 2,000.

We are lucky to have a few acres of land that we
have rewilded. We've planted trees and wildflowers
and created a couple of ponds which are alive with
damsels and dragonflies each spring and summer.
Broad-bodied chasers are among the first to emerge,
and I found this teneral resting among a group of
yellow iris. I decided to shoot from further away,
using a telephoto lens, to minimise disturbance and
capture a slightly more environmental perspective.

Roosting Brown Argus at Sunrise
Hidden Britain

Richard Sheldrake
Brown argus (*Aricia agestis*)
Martin Down, Wiltshire, England

Nikon Z 9 with Nikon 105mm f/2.8 lens.
105mm; 1/4,000th second; f/3.2; ISO 100.

Early morning roosting brown argus butterfly climbing a grass stem. I was specifically looking for roosting butterflies at Martin Down Nature Reserve, Hampshire, for sunrise, so I had been there early to find butterflies before the sun rose. I found this brown argus in a sheltered space and opted to shoot handheld against the sun to get this silhouette.

I shot this with the aperture wide open to make sure the sun was very large in the frame and quite close to the butterfly, enhancing its size relative to the orange sun.

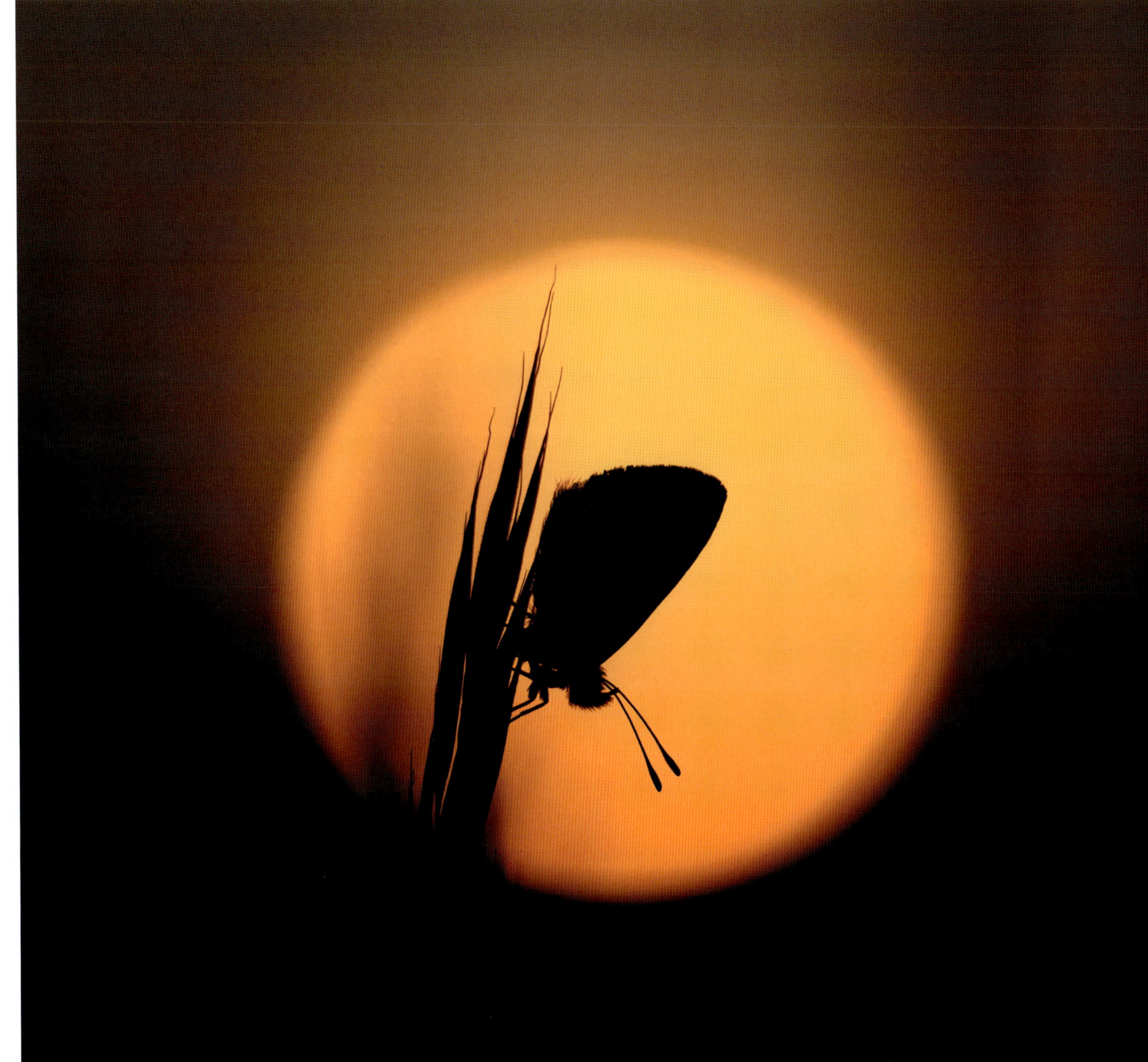

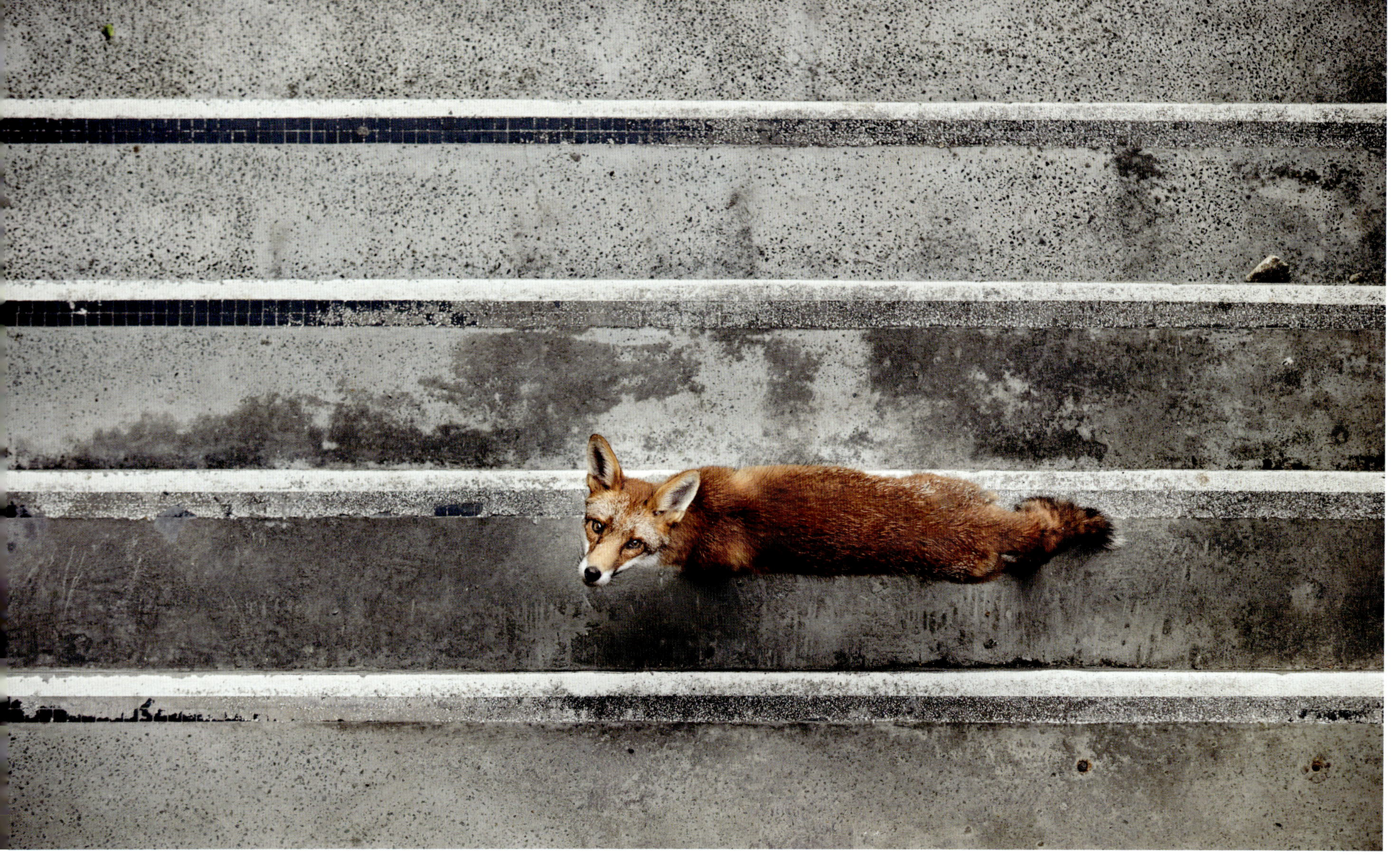

Line Up
Urban Wildlife

Simon Withyman
Red fox (*Vulpes vulpes*)
Bristol, England

Canon EOS R5 with Canon 70-200mm f/2.8 II lens.
105mm; 1/640th second; f/4; ISO 1,000.

I wanted to capture a different angle from what I was used to when photographing foxes while also showcasing their urban environment. I found a spot where I could safely lean over some railings, eliminating the need for a drone. One day, everything came together, and I was able to compose the image I had in mind, capturing enough of the rich texture of the concrete steps. The male fox noticed me and glanced up for a brief moment, looking directly at the camera.

Spring Nibbles
Animal Behaviour

Daniel Trim
Roe deer (*Capreolus capreolus*)
London Cemetery, England

Canon 5DS with Canon 500mm f/4 II lens.
500mm; 1/320th second; f/4; ISO 800.

As soon as the spring oak leaves unfurl, they are subjected to browsing pressure from deer, and although most are out of reach, a little leg up on the base of a headstone can make all the difference! I wanted to truly convey the story of where this roe deer called home, so I positioned myself in a way that two crucifix headstones filled the negative space of the frame.

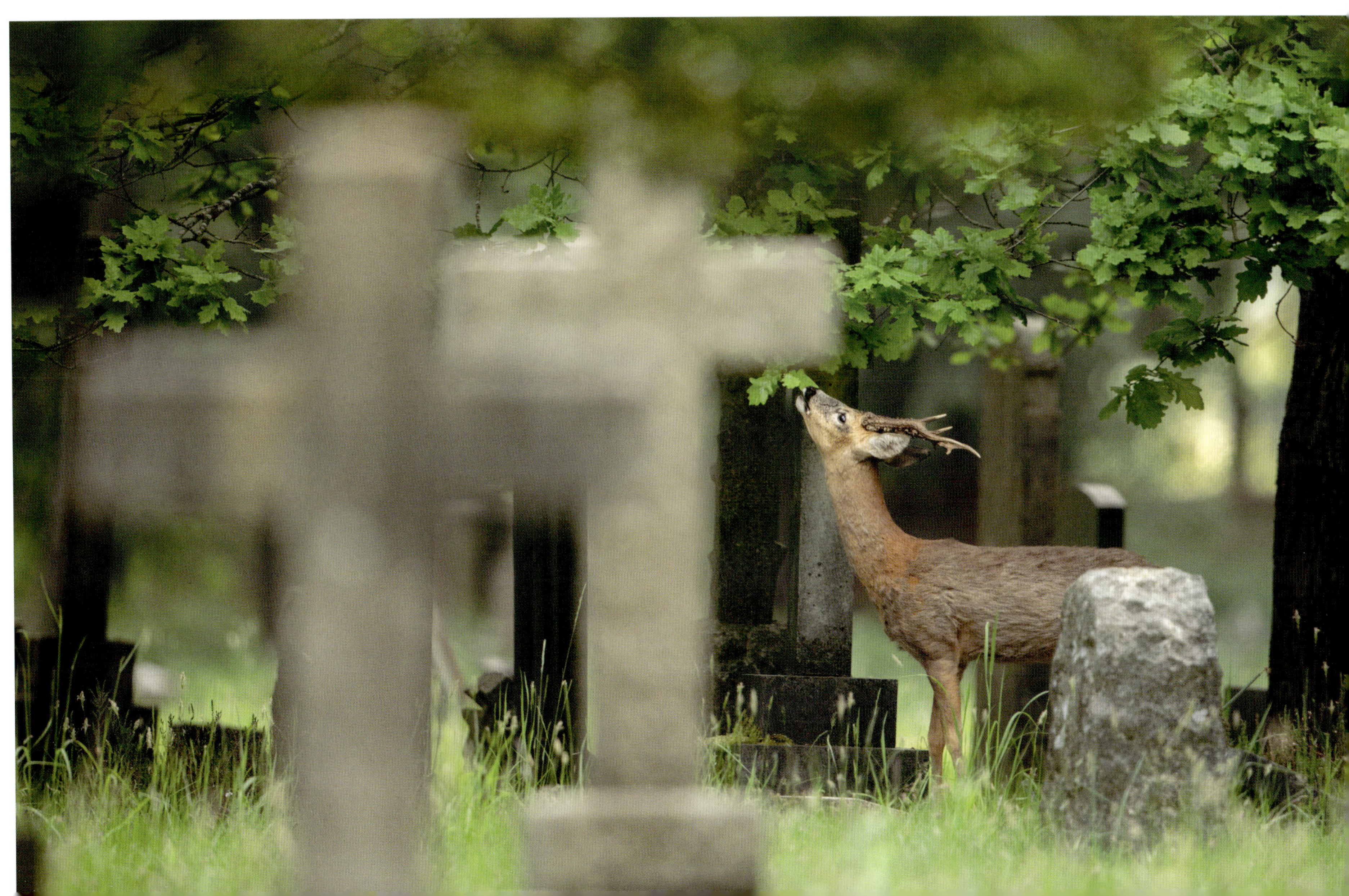

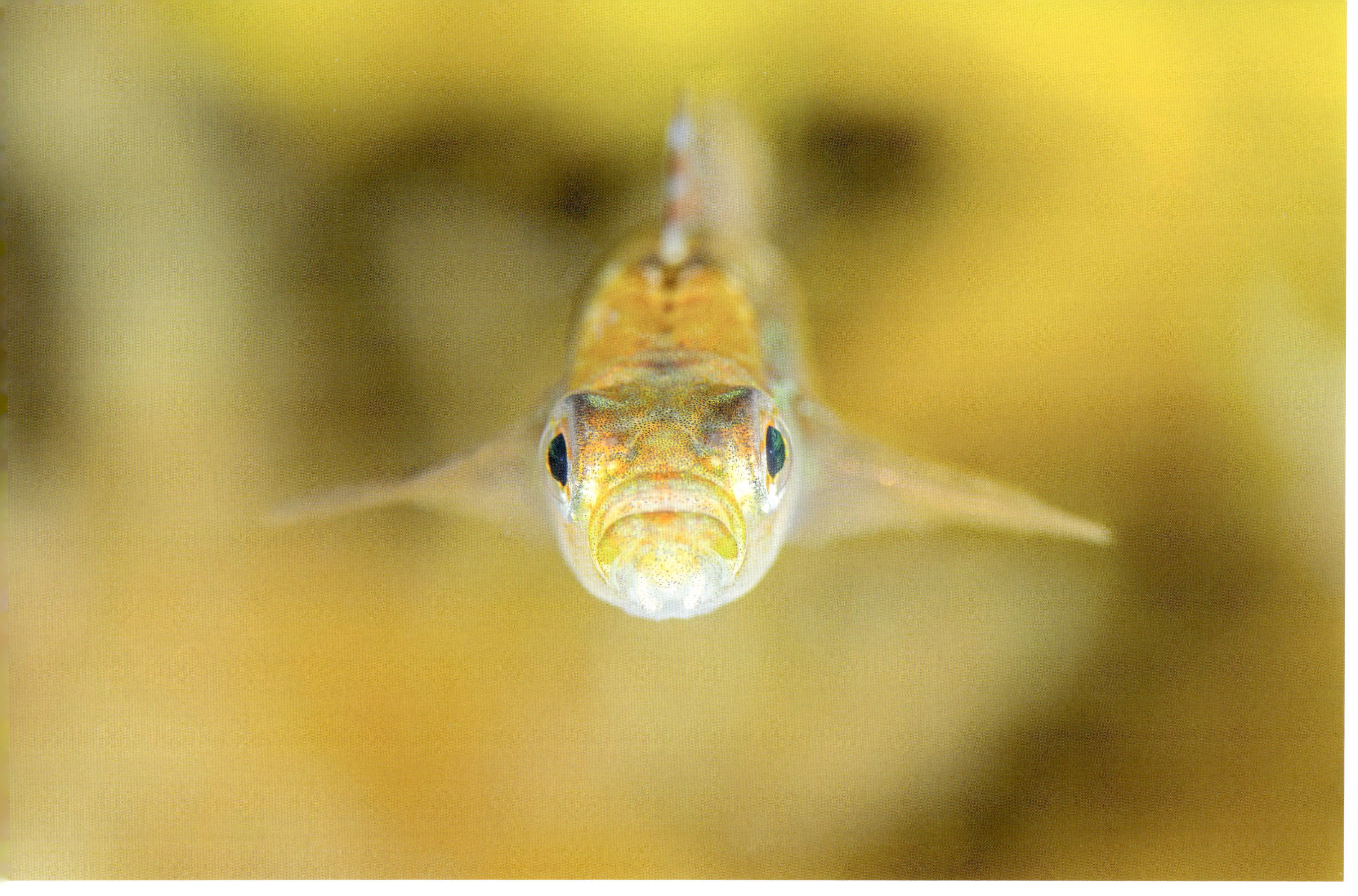

Two-Spotted Goby

Coast & Marine

Malcolm Nimmo

Two-spotted goby (*Gobiusculus flavescens*)
Isles of Scilly, England

Nikon D7200 with Nikon 85mm f/3.5 lens.
85mm; 1/125th second; f/11; ISO 100.

The two-spotted goby is often overlooked by
snorkelers and divers alike due to its relatively small
size. However, with closer inspection, they are very
colourful fish, particularly during the breeding season.
They make better subjects when photographed
head-on, although this can be challenging. The
best approach, as with most nature photography,
is to patiently wait and allow a subject to become
comfortable with your presence, then wait for an
opportunity.

Autumnal Frog
Animal Portraits

Kevin Sawford
Common frog (*Rana temporaria*)
Woolpit, Suffolk, England

Canon 1D X II with Canon 180mm f/3.5 Macro lens.
180mm; 1/320th second; f/4; ISO 1,600.

I found this common frog in our garden, wandering across some fallen autumn leaves. I saw the opportunity to capture a seasonal image. By lying down, I was able to shoot the frog at eye level and place it among the seasonal colours. Thankfully, as the weather was quite cool, the frog stayed in position, allowing me to take a few images before leaving it to go about its business.

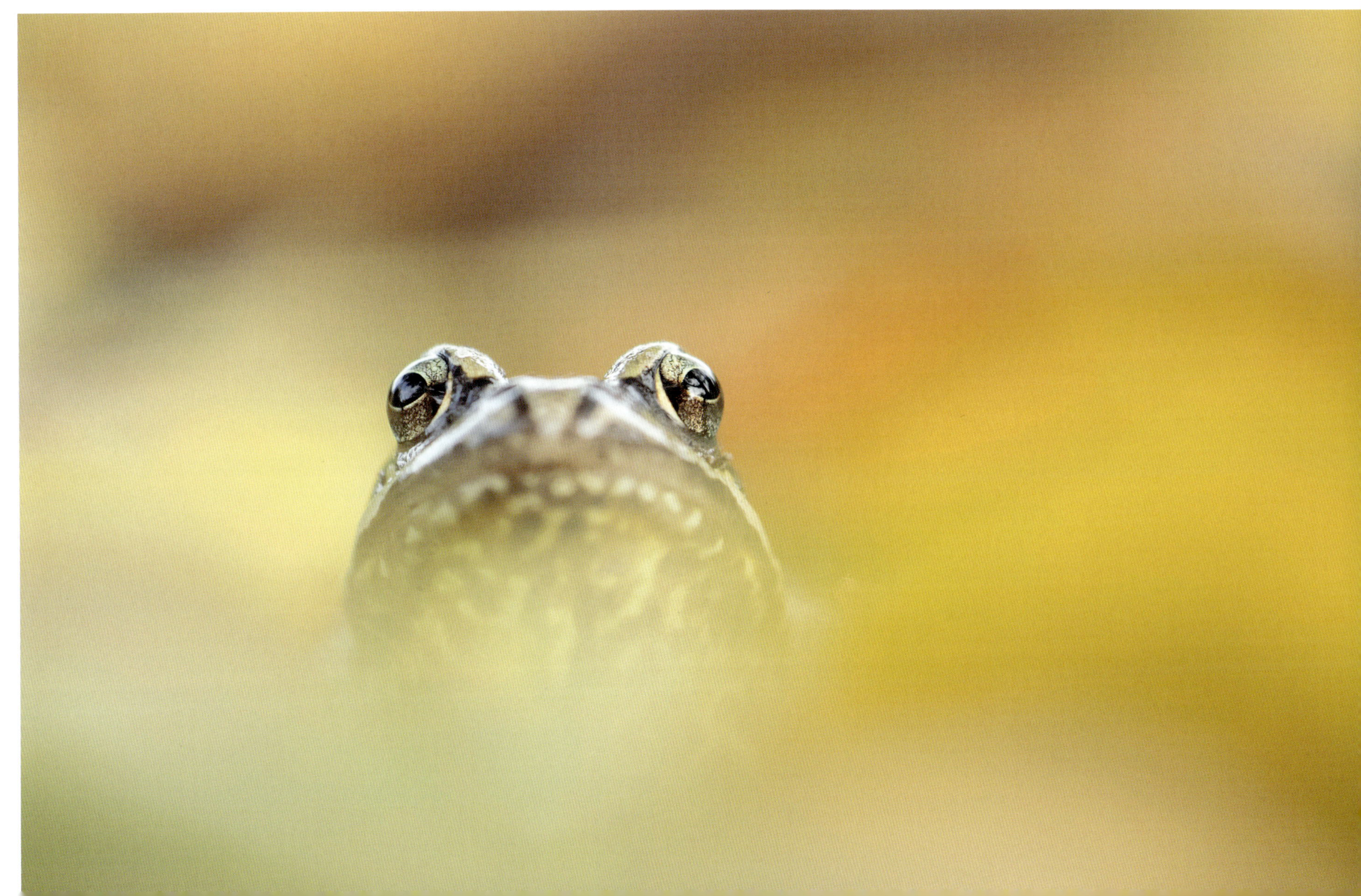

BRITISH SEASONS
THE KING'S QUARTERS

Ever since I saw a kingfisher by complete chance while walking our dog along a small village stream that meandered through farmland, I have been captivated by its beauty.

From that moment, I have always been interested in spending my spare time photographing the bird, with the kind permission of the farmer, of course. Over the following year, I sat hidden away for endless hours on the tranquil riverbank, watching the seasons change and the kingfisher come and go.

I wanted to capture the change in the seasons, not only with the kingfisher but also in the perches of the trees used by the kingfisher on the farmland. The transition includes the blossom of spring, the blossom turning into bright-colored summer fruits, the first frosts of autumn ravaging the fruits and, finally, the arrival of the bitter snows of winter.

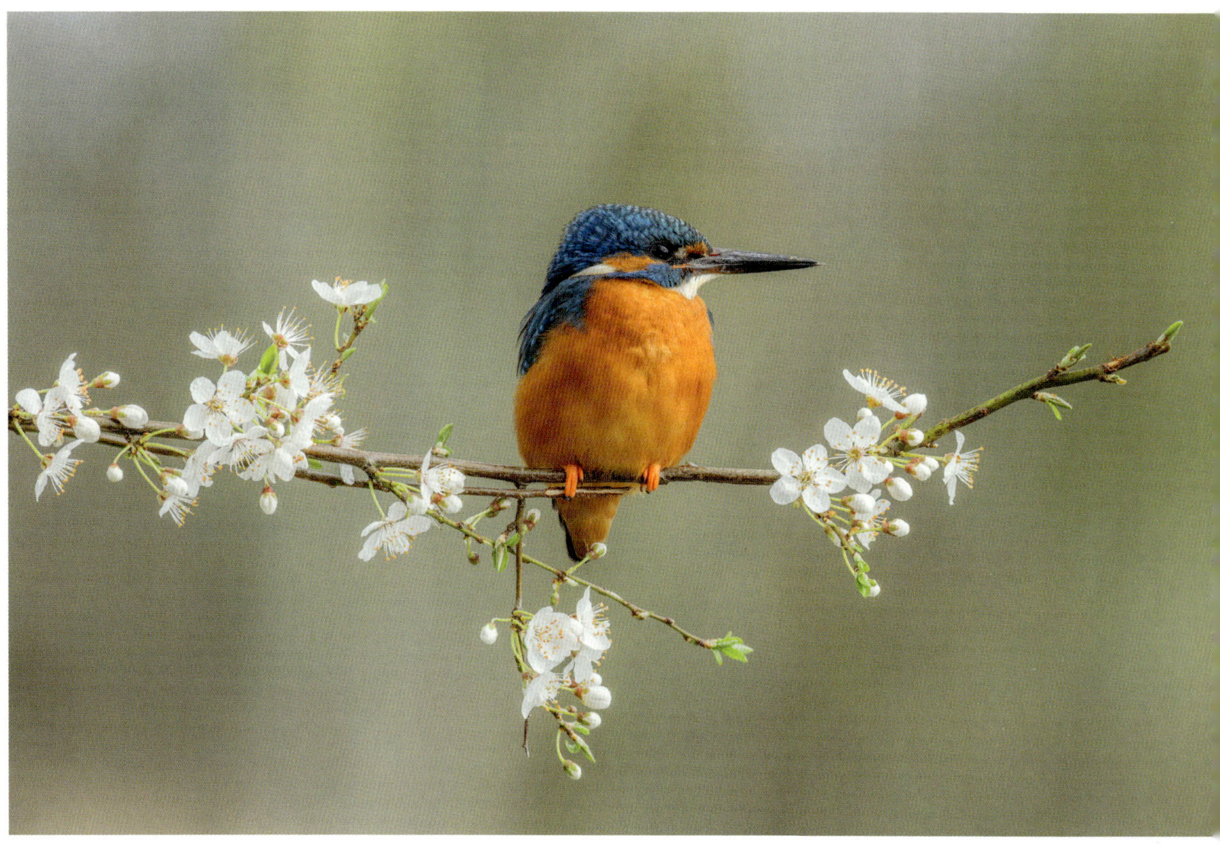

Spring
British Seasons | Winner

Warren Price
Common kingfisher (*Alcedo atthis*)
Bedfordshire, England

Canon EOS R5 with Canon 500mm f/4 lens. 500mm; 1/125th second; f/7.1; ISO 1,000.

Blossom is the true embodiment of springtime and represents the promises of new beginnings. I wanted to catch the start of the new spring season with the kingfisher amongst the blossom, an exciting time, as the kingfisher starts to search out its own territory and a partner for the fast-approaching breeding season.

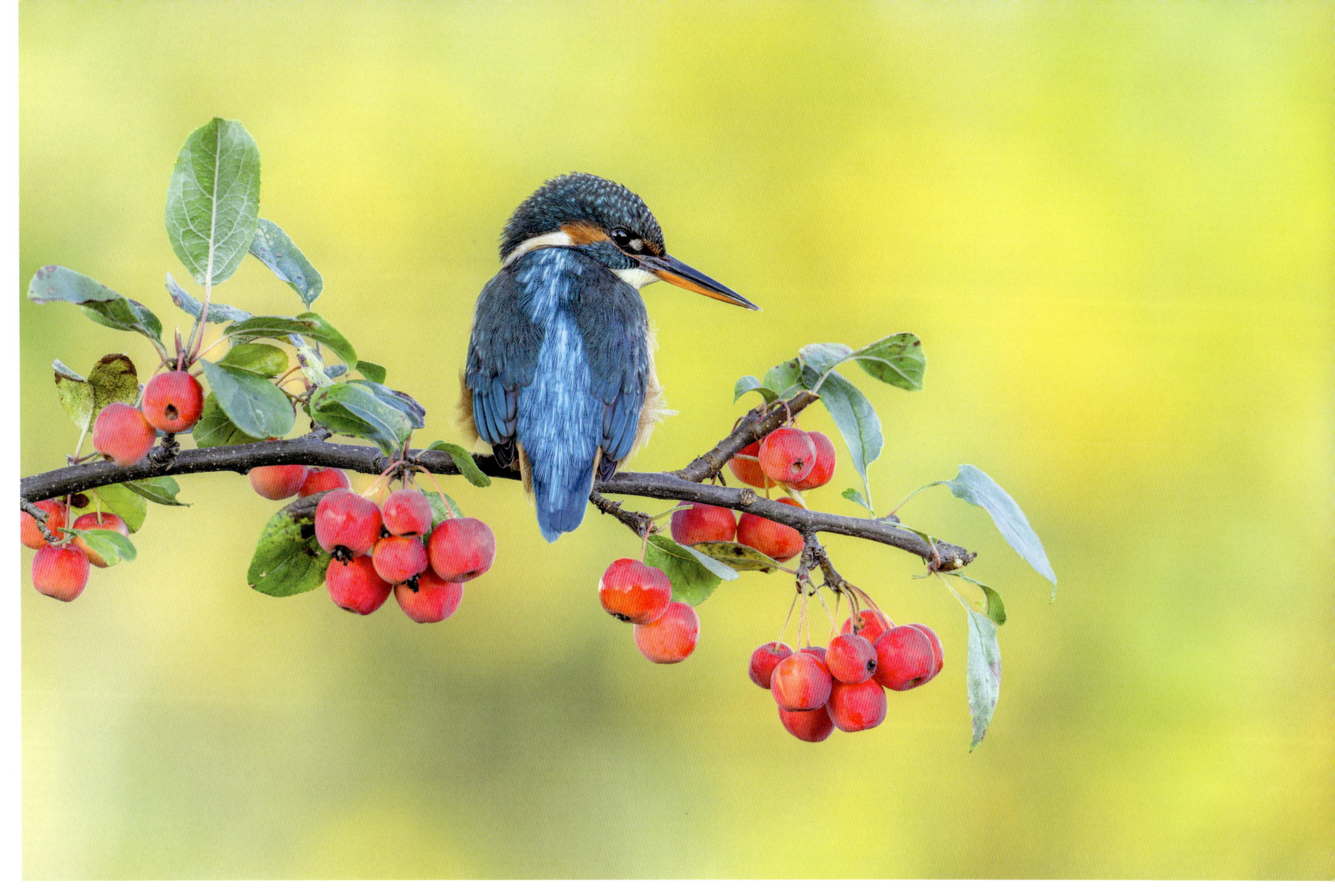

Summer
British Seasons | Winner

Warren Price
Common kingfisher (*Alcedo atthis*)
Bedfordshire, England

Canon EOS R5 with Canon 500mm f/4 lens.
500mm; 1/640th second; f/9; ISO 1,600.

The spring blossom has turned into vivid summer fruits, the days are long and warm and the riverbank is full of bright colours and activity. The kingfisher is perched amongst the summer fruits, taking a break from the hectic schedule of feeding its young, which is shared by both of the adult birds. If the summer is kind and food is plenty then the kingfishers will possibly raise several broods of young.

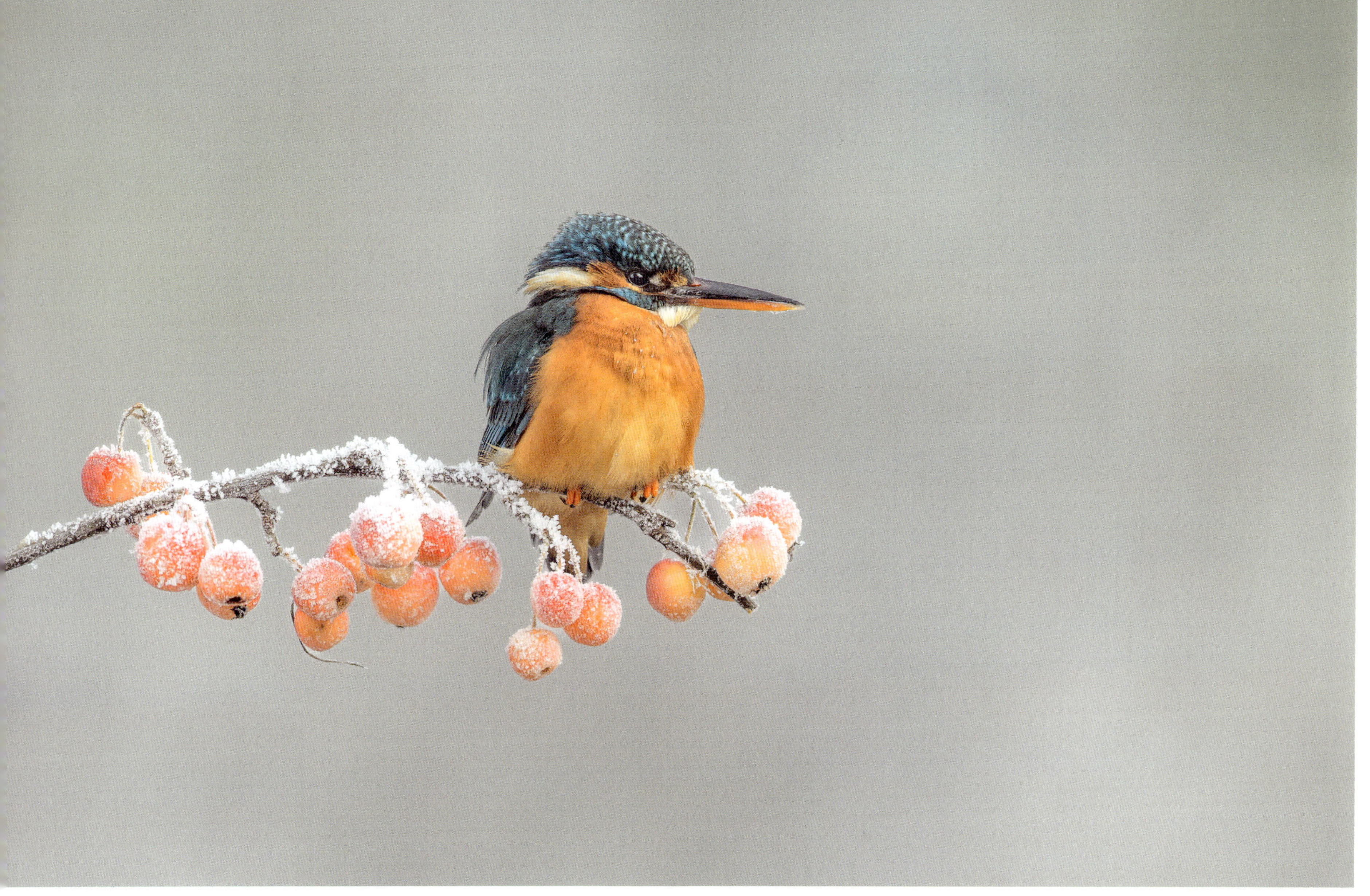

Autumn
British Seasons | Winner

Warren Price
Common kingfisher (*Alcedo atthis*)
Bedfordshire, England

Canon EOS R5 with Canon 500mm f/4 lens.
500mm; 1/200th second; f/6.3; ISO 1,000.

The first harsh frosts of autumn arrive, the summer fruits start to show signs of decay and the leaves are drained of their summer colours and dropping to the floor. Autum is the best time to watch kingfishers – they are more relaxed now the breeding season is over and are more visible from the riverbank, as the summer foliage has disappeared. They return to a more solitary existence now that the summer is over and the adult birds tend to do their own thing.

Winter
British Seasons | Winner

Warren Price
Common kingfisher (*Alcedo atthis*)
Bedfordshire, England

Canon EOS R5 with Canon 500mm f/4 lens.
500mm; 1/200th second; f/5.6; ISO 1,250.

In the bleak mid-winter, bitter temperatures arrive that bring the first heavy snowfall of the winter season. The remaining fruits are frozen solid and covered heavily by the snow. Prolonged freezing temperatures like this can be devasting to the kingfisher population – it's a genuine challenge of survival for the bird. The small stream starts to freeze and hunting becomes incredibly difficult as daytime temperatures struggle to rise above freezing.

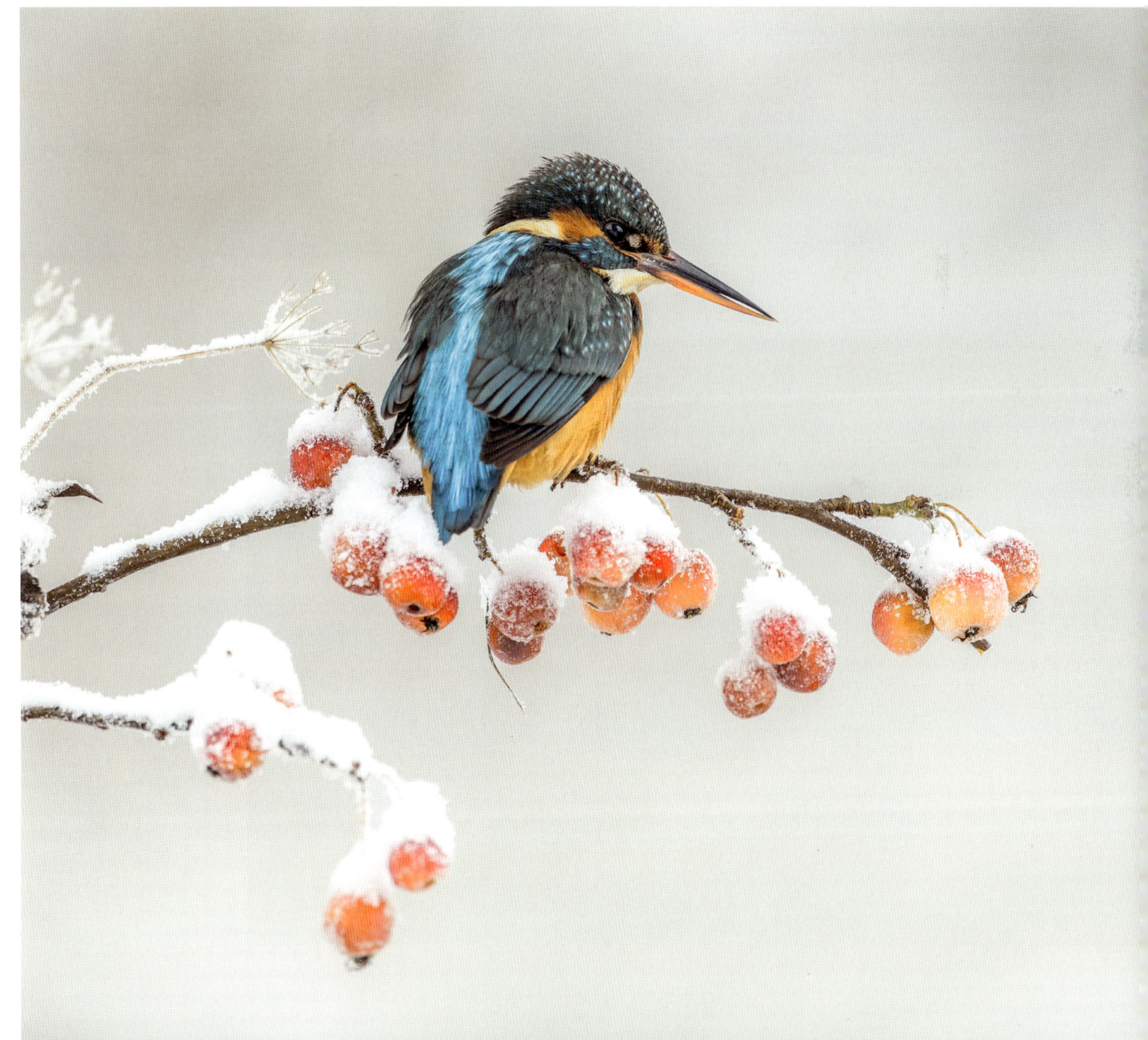

DOCUMENTARY SERIES

THE SHAME OF BRITAIN

Make no mistake, fox hunting in Britain is organised crime. Despite the ban on hunting with packs of hounds in England and Wales since 2005 (and in Scotland since 2002), more than 200 hunts continue to operate with relative impunity across Britain for eight months of the year.

Since the ban, hunts have claimed to engage in trail hunting, where a scent is dragged for hounds to follow. However, in 2021, a leaked webinar of hunt organisers revealed that trail hunting is being used as a smokescreen for illegal hunting. This brought fox hunting back into the public and political consciousness.

In the last 25 years, the fox population in Britain has fallen by almost half, thanks in part to persecution by hunts. But fox hunts also kill other wildlife, such as protected badgers. Despite a mountain of evidence and surveys showing that 85% of the public supports the ban, police forces have either turned a blind eye or, in many cases, enabled illegal hunting. This is why organised groups of volunteer activists, called saboteurs, or simply 'sabs' – who are teachers, lawyers, doctors, artists and postal workers in our communities – work tirelessly to gather legal evidence and stop hunts from killing wildlife.

This dedication to preserving life puts sabs in harm's way as violent hunt supporters threaten, intimidate and physically assault sabs to protect what they see as a right to hunt.

Despite the history of hunting in Britain, this is an original story that has not been told in depth by a photographer before, and it is one that is very rarely published. This is due to the dangers and difficulties involved in capturing the images and because of the power and reach of hunts within society. The photographer has been followed and assaulted in their pursuit of capturing this story, the purpose of which is to influence public awareness.

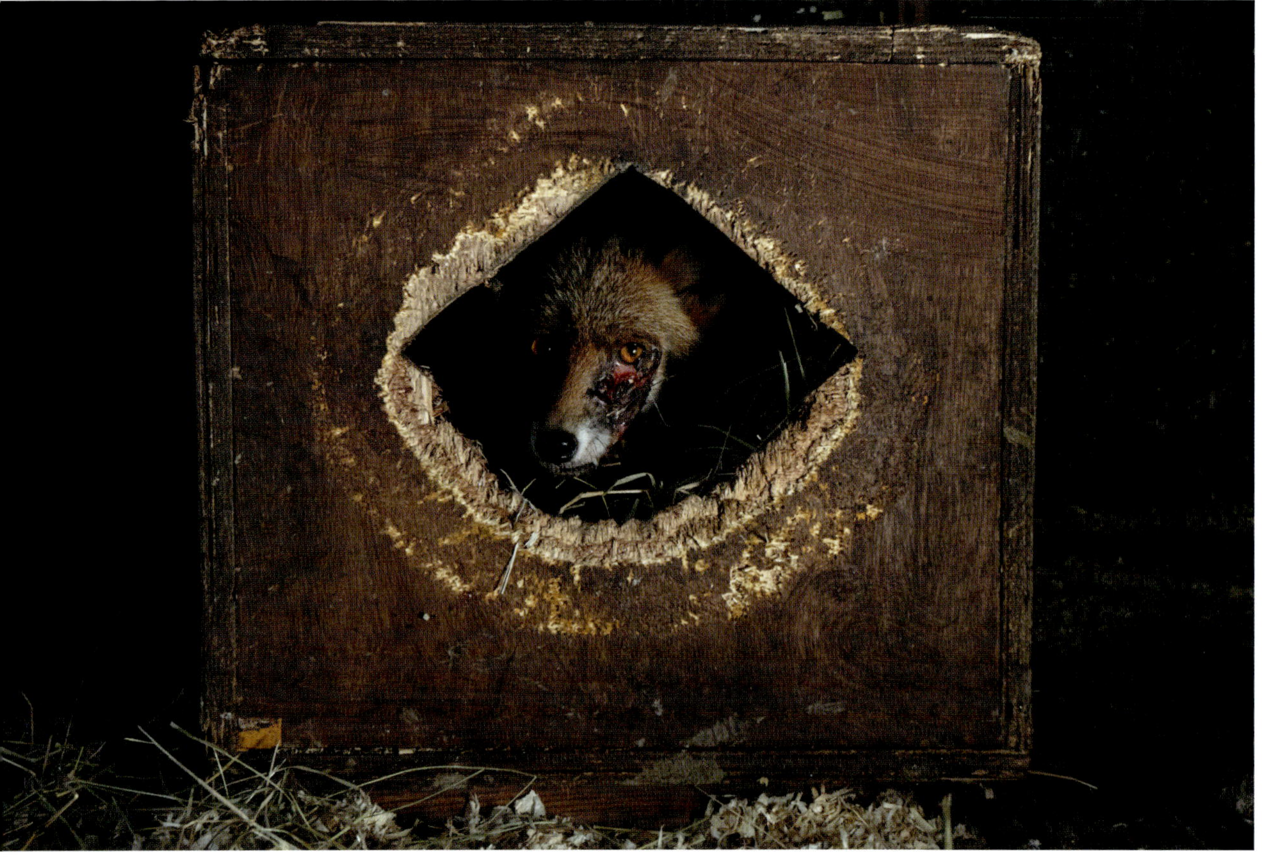

Survivor
Documentary Series | Winner

Neil Aldridge
Red Fox (*Vulpes vulpes*)

Canon EOS 5DS with Canon 16-35mm f/2.8 lens. 35mm; 1/100th second; f/9; ISO 640.

The terrible injuries suffered by this vixen were almost certainly inflicted by dogs, most likely terriers sent into a den to flush her out. Taken into care by a rehabilitation group in Kent, she was later released back into the wild, although with her teeth and eye left permanently exposed. This picture was part of Neil's nine-year project photographing the complex relationship the British have with the red fox. Hunting foxes with a pack of dogs has been illegal in England and Wales since 2005. Yet more than 200 hunts remain active, claiming to be trail hunting, where a scent trail is laid through the countryside for hounds to follow. Trail hunting can be used as a cover for illegal hunting, in which terriers are routinely used to flush out exhausted foxes that have taken refuge from the hounds underground.

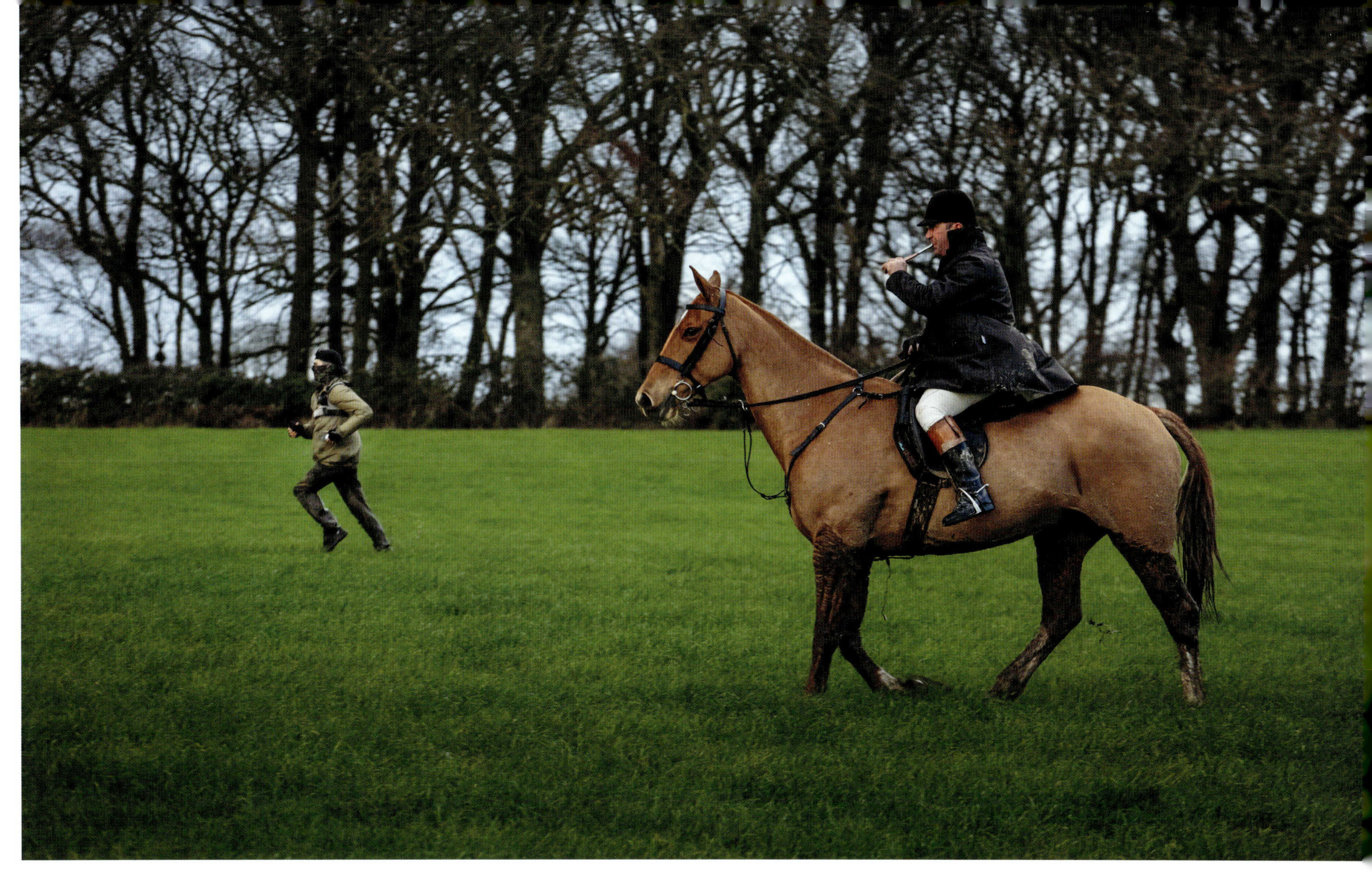

Shadowing the Hunt
Documentary Series | Winner

Neil Aldridge

Canon EOS 5DS with Canon 70-200mm f/4 lens. 200mm; 1/200th second; f/6.3; ISO 640.

A hunt saboteur, or sab, runs to keep up with the huntsman of a fox hunt in Devon. Sabs employ a range of tactics to track, monitor and foil hunts, and technology such as drones is helping to turn the tide in their favour. However, despite the intensity of keeping up with hounds and mounted riders on foot in wintry conditions in the British countryside, running sabs remain the best bet for gathering evidence of illegal hunting.

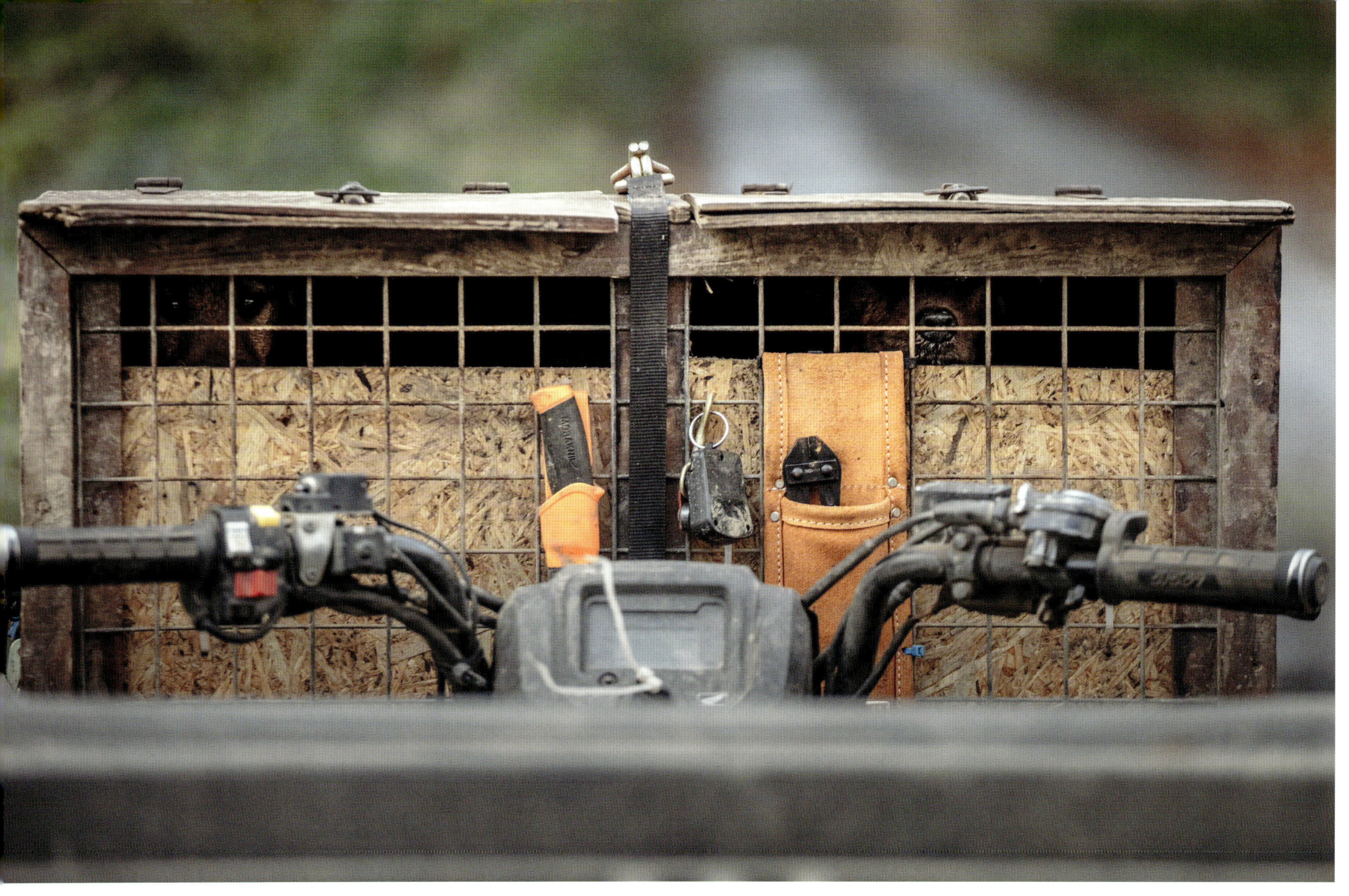

Hidden Terriers
Documentary Series | Winner

Neil Aldridge

Canon EOS 5DS with Canon 70-200mm f/4 lens.
159mm; 1/30th second; f/4; ISO 2,000.

Terrier dogs peer out from inside a dark crate
strapped to the front of a terrierman's quad bike in
southern England. Fox hunts employ one or more
terriermen, who use these small and fearless dogs
to send into fox dens and flush out exhausted foxes
that have tried to find safety underground from the
threat of the advancing hunt. It begs the question
that, if hunting foxes with hounds has been outlawed
in Britain and hunts are said to carry out trail hunting
where a scent is followed instead of a live fox, why
would a hunt require a terrierman and his dogs?
Hunts continue to operate illegally across Britain
on a daily basis and target other wildlife, such as
badgers, and the terriermen are often the aggressors,
protecting what they see as their right to hunt.

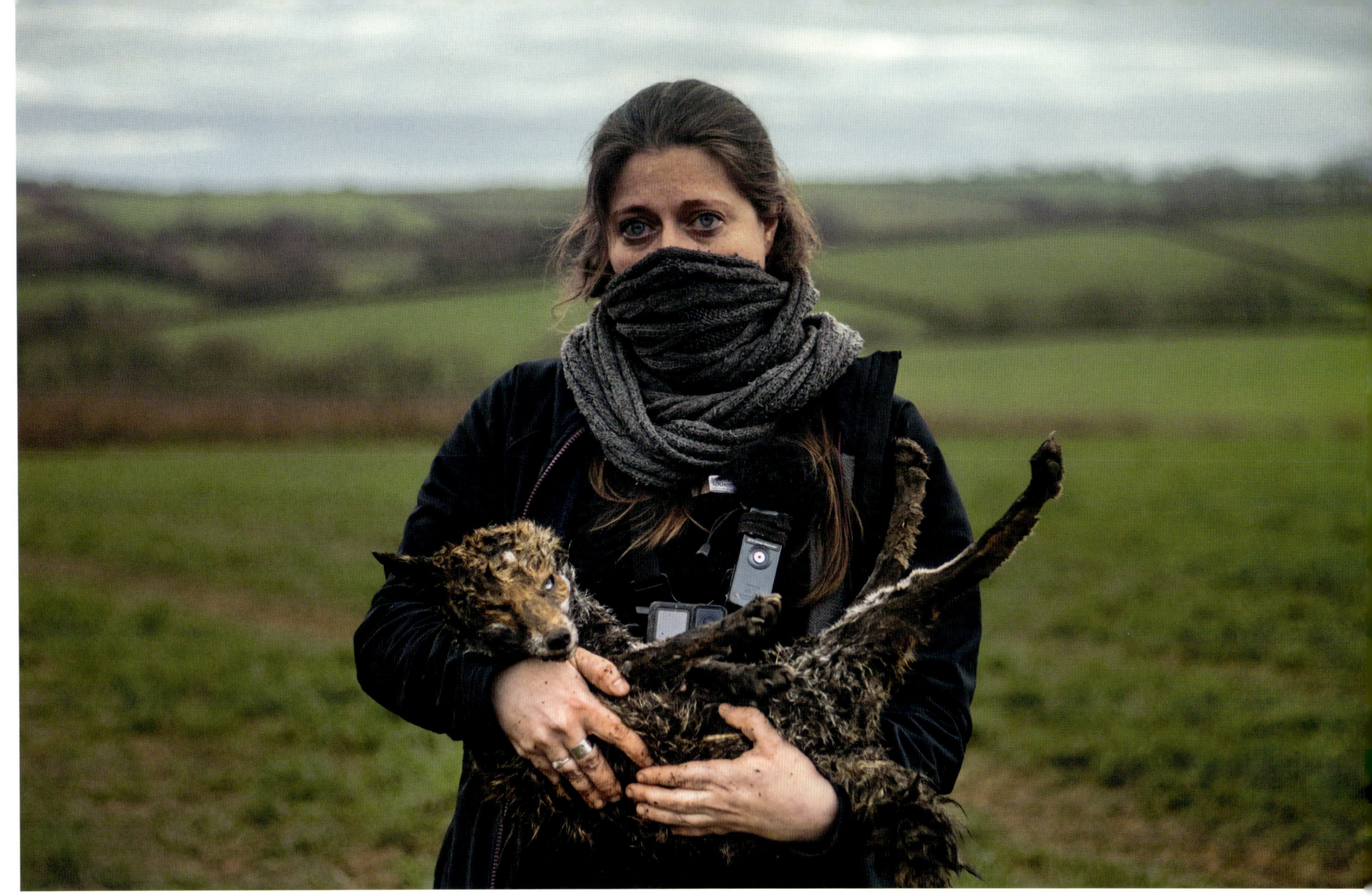

Gone But Not Forgotten
Documentary Series | Winner

Neil Aldridge

Panasonic GH6 with Canon EF 50mm f/1.8 II.
35mm; 1/500th; f/1.6; ISO 320.

Fox numbers in Britain have been driven down by nearly 50% in 25 years, partly due to the presence of more than 200 actively hunting hunts across the countryside. In this photo, a hunt saboteur cradles a female fox killed by the hounds of the Stevenstone Hunt in Devon in February 2023, and there is a possibility that she might have been pregnant by that time. Just like with every fox recovered by the saboteurs, this one was buried with respect in a local woodland. Each fox's death serves as motivation for the saboteurs to continue putting pressure on the hunts.

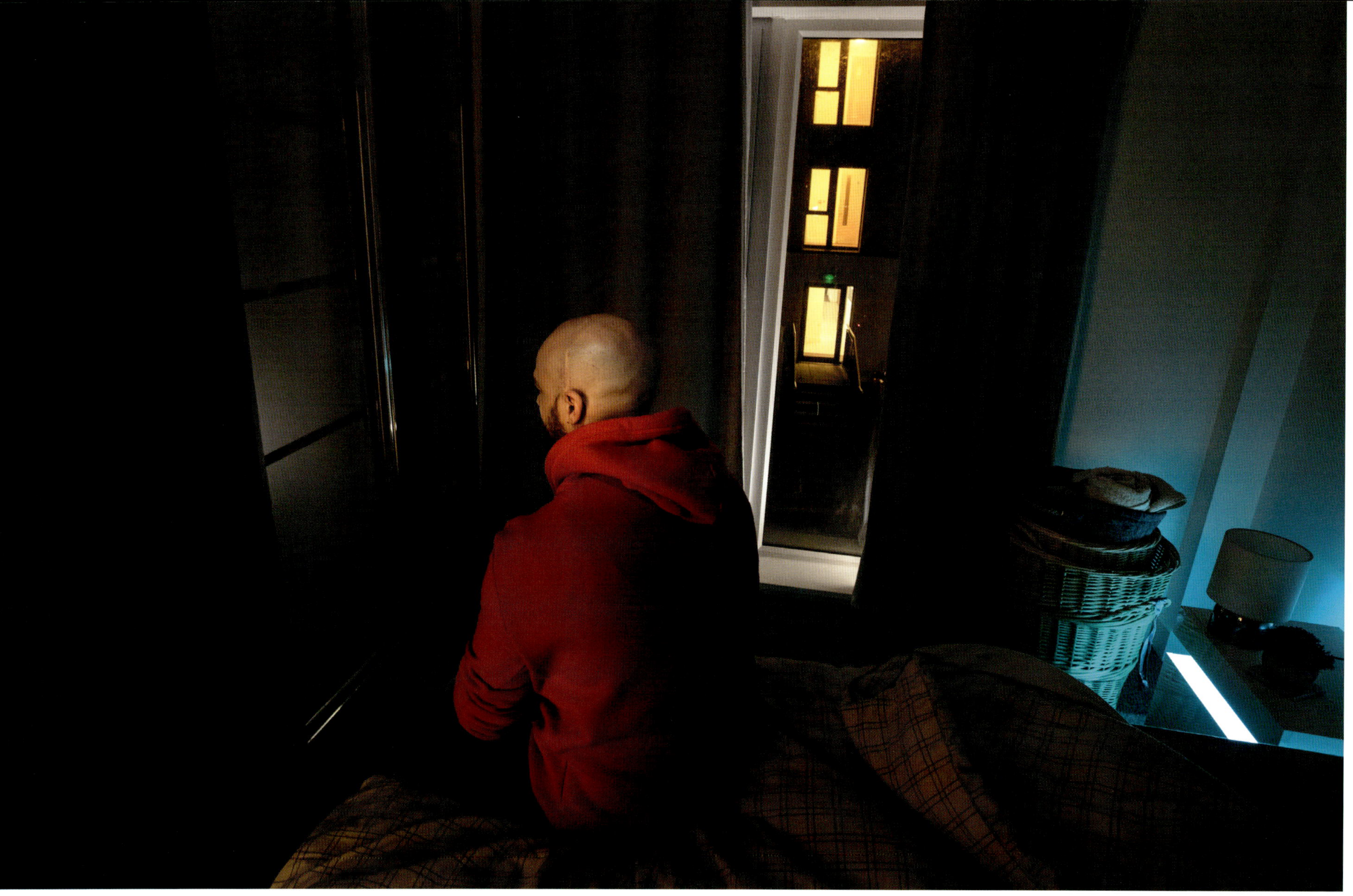

Scarred for Life

Documentary Series | Winner

Neil Aldridge

Canon EOS 5DS with Canon 16-35mm f/2.8 lens.
18mm; 0.6 seconds; f/7.1; ISO 320.

A former hunt saboteur bears visible scars from reconstructive surgery after sustaining fractures to his skull and eye socket in an attack by a huntsman. Similar to many other cases involving assaults on saboteurs, even with video evidence of the attack, the huntsman was not prosecuted and continues to participate in hunting. Throughout Britain, sabs face weekly assaults involving knives, fists, horses and vehicles during the extended hunting season.

A Dying Tradition
Documentary Series | Winner

Neil Aldridge

Canon EOS 5DS with Canon 70-200mm f/2.8 lens.
80mm; 1/250th second; f/13; ISO 400.

A police officer stands between protesters and
the Berkeley Hunt on Thornbury High Street,
Gloucestershire, on Boxing Day, 2022. Hunting foxes
with dogs was banned in England in 2005, and 85%
of the public – and, crucially, 80% of the rural public
– supports the ban. Yet, hunts remain defiant and are
supported by influential individuals in the legal and
political system.

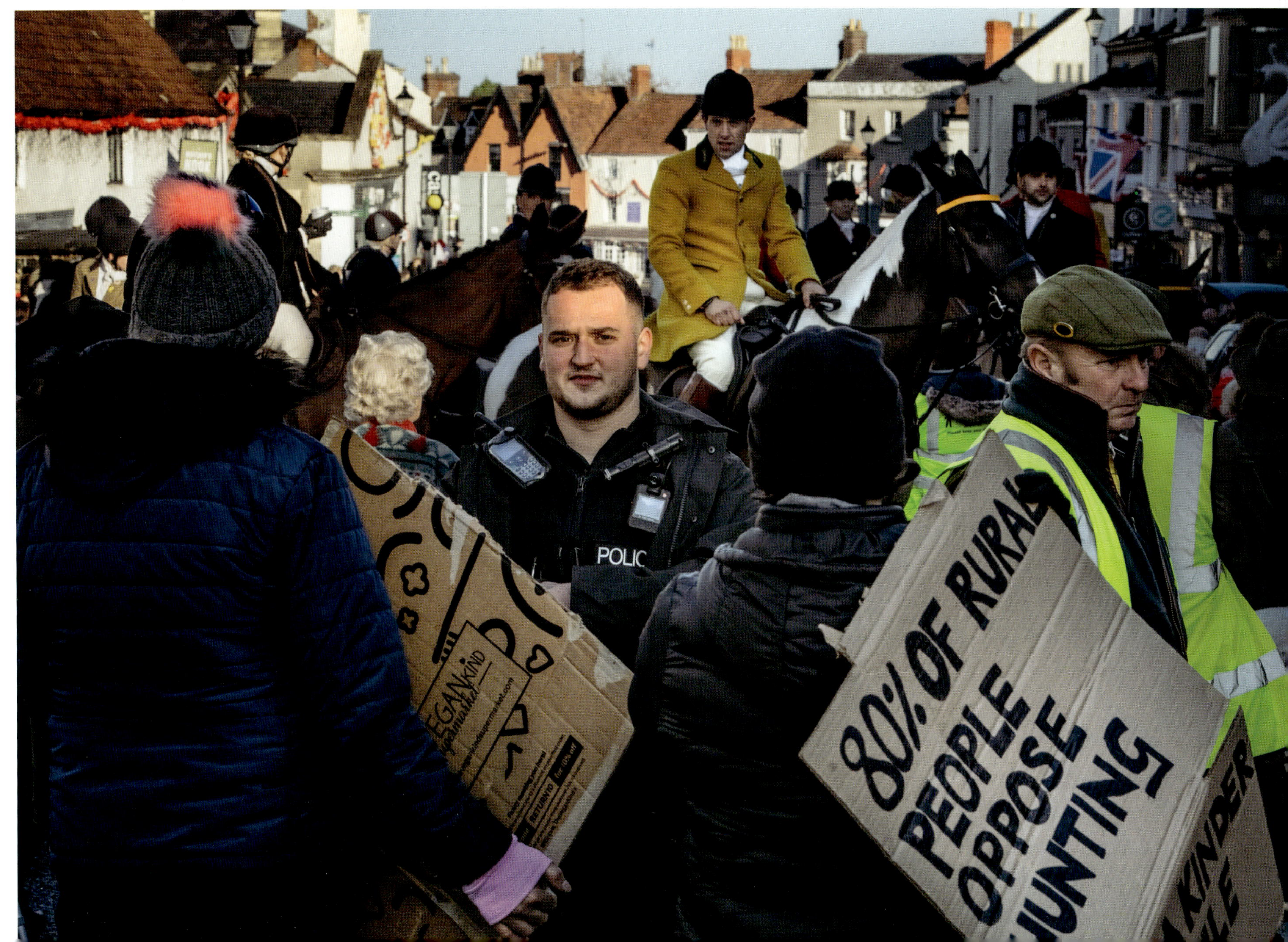

VEGANkind
thveganknd.supermarket.com

80% OF RURAL
PEOPLE
OPPOSE
HUNTING

KINDER

RSPB YOUNG BRITISH WILDLIFE PHOTOGRAPHER OF THE YEAR
FOREWORD BY CAZZ JONES

As editor of the amazing RSPB youth publications, I get to enjoy the privilege of being able to work with and witness the never-ending talents of our incredibly switched-on and passionate young people.

Whether they are aspiring young writers, artists, visionaries, campaigners or, in this case, photographers, to see the world through their eyes gives me much hope for the future. It is our job, as adults, to nurture their passions, aide them on their mission to create a world richer in wildlife and, most importantly of all, we must acknowledge that their voice matters, for it speaks with the truth and authenticity needed to bring about real change.

A huge congratulations from all of us at the RSPB – we see you, we support you – and never give up hope. Together we'll turn the tide on the climate and nature crisis, one photograph, one vision, one voice at a time.

I've been inspired by your creativity and conversations about the lengths you go to capture the 'perfect shot!' in an effort to bring the beauty of the natural world and its subsequent plight into our homes, so I thought I'd finish with a little poem to say thanks.

'Waiting patiently, not moving an inch, subject walks into frame, it's perfect – pinch!

Steady now, don't make a sound, paws are frozen on the ground.

Snap and click, a few more for luck, check the pictures… heart is stuck!

Exhale and breathe, feelings of delight! The perfect picture now in sight.

I may be young, but I see so clear, that nature needs us to have no fear.

What difference can I make? I get so frustrated! Nature laws now abated.

But one snap at a time, people look up with a glance, I realise we've still got a chance!

For we are one with nature, separate we cannot exist – let's stop adding to the red list.

I may be young, but in my heart I know – it'll take everyone for the seeds to grow.'

Cazz Jones
Supporter Publications Manager and Editor of the RSPB Youth Magazines: *Wild Times, Wild Explorer* and *Wingbeat.*

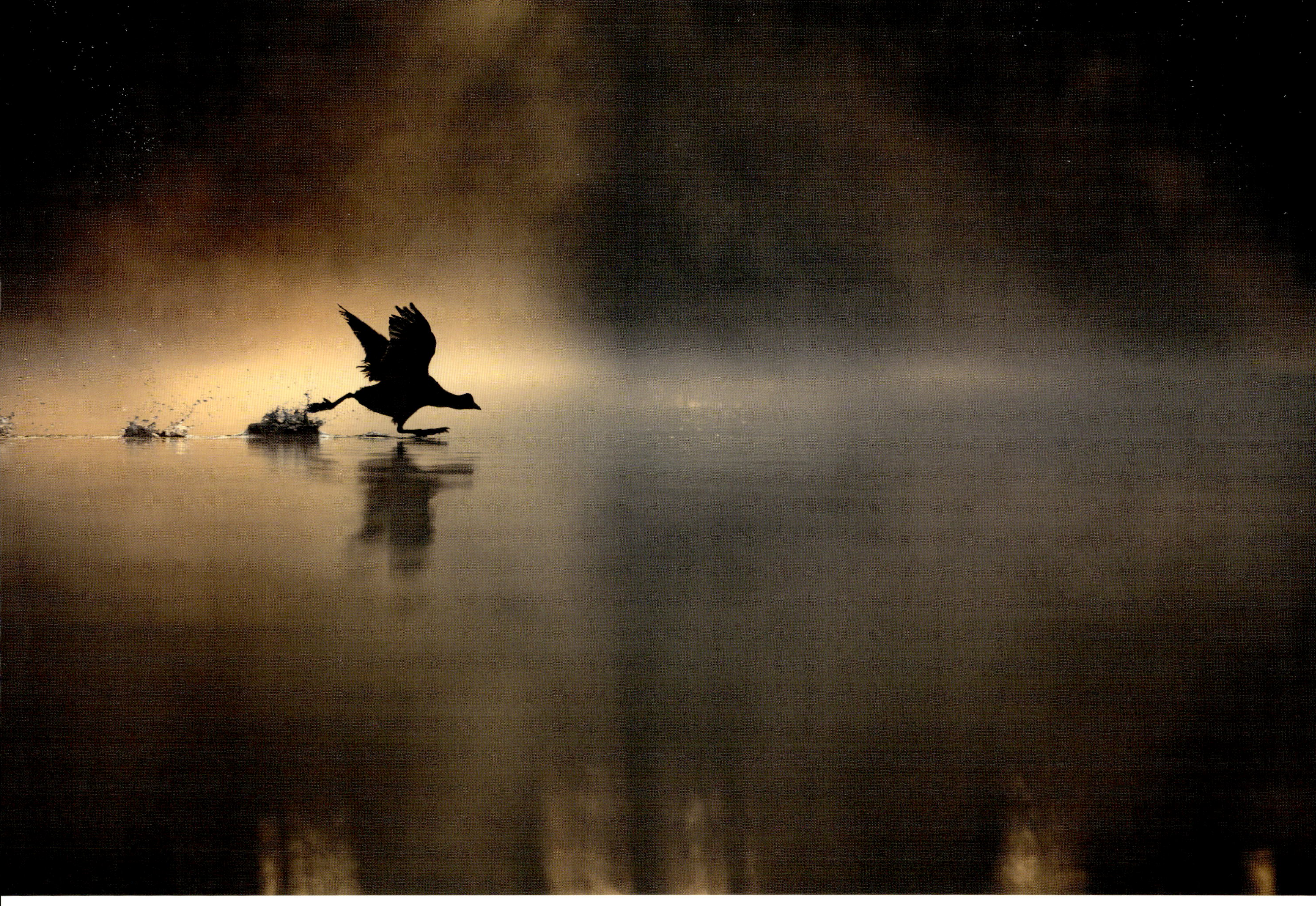

Running on Water
RSPB Young British Wildlife Photographer of
the Year 2023 and 15-17 Years Winner

Max Wood
Coot (*Fulica atra*)
Frensham Little Pond, Surrey, England

Canon EOS 6D with Canon 70-200mm f/2.8 II lens
& 2x teleconverter. 400mm; 1/1,250th second; f/5.6;
ISO 400.

I woke up at 4:45am with the hope of capturing
backlit waterfowl images at Frensham Pond in Surrey.
I lay down at the edge of the pond and waited
for the birds to become active. As the morning
progressed, rays of sunlight began to shine through
trees along the edge of the pond, creating spotlights
in the morning mist. This created a beautiful
atmosphere, which I aimed to capture in my images.
This coot was fleeing a fight, running across the
water to take flight through the mist and rays
of light.

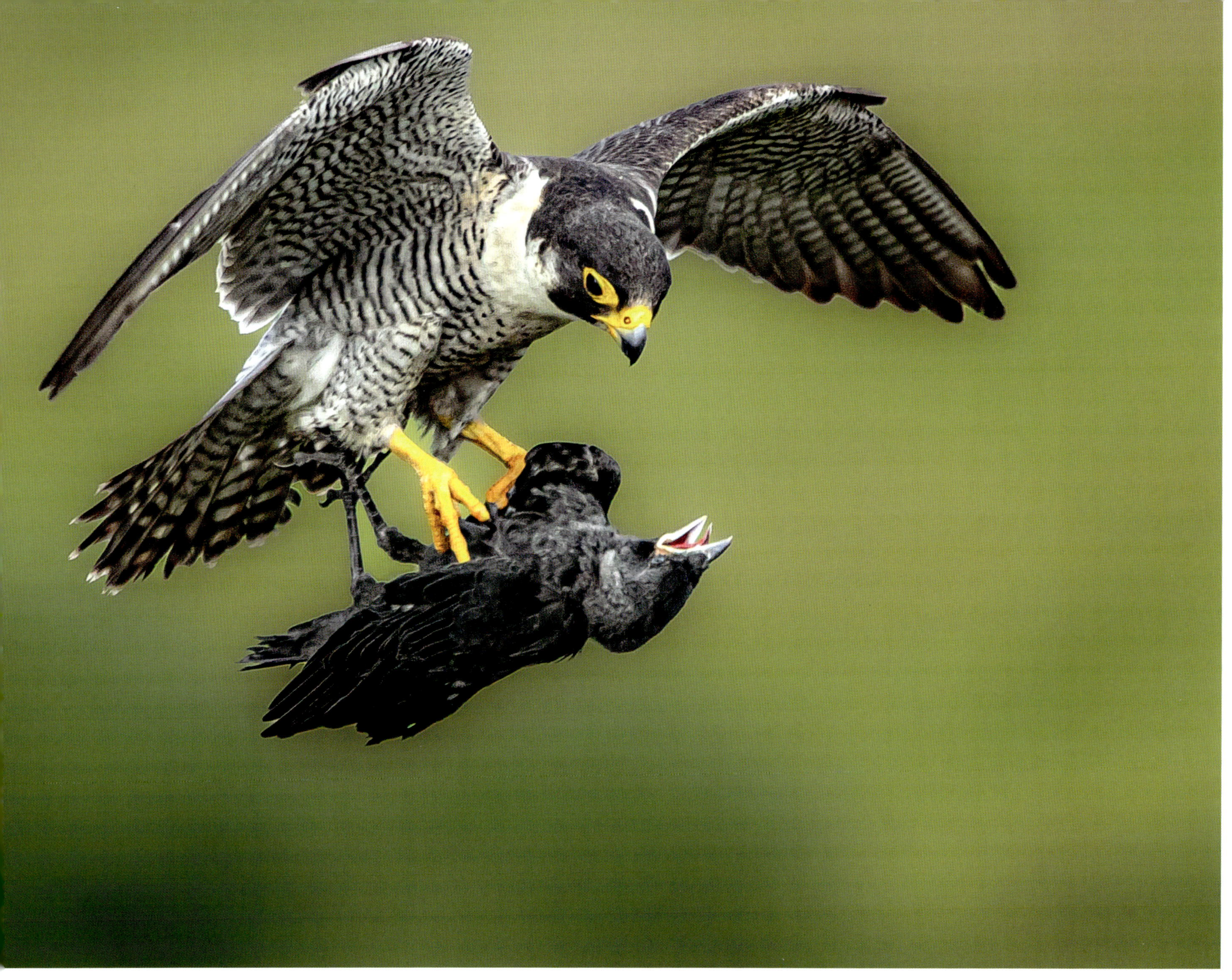

Death Stare
15-17 years | Runner-up

James Pearson
Peregrine falcon (*Falco peregrinus*)
East Sussex, England

Canon EOS 7D II with Sigma 150-600mm f/5-6.3
lens. 600mm; 1/2,000th second; f/6.3; ISO 400.

Some days, I've been up at this spot from dawn to
dusk without taking a single photo. But on days like
this, my luck would pay off. Not five minutes after
I arrived, the male peregrine swooped down on an
unsuspecting jackdaw. It circled back around and
passed right by where I was standing to encourage
the chicks to fly up and snatch it from his talons.

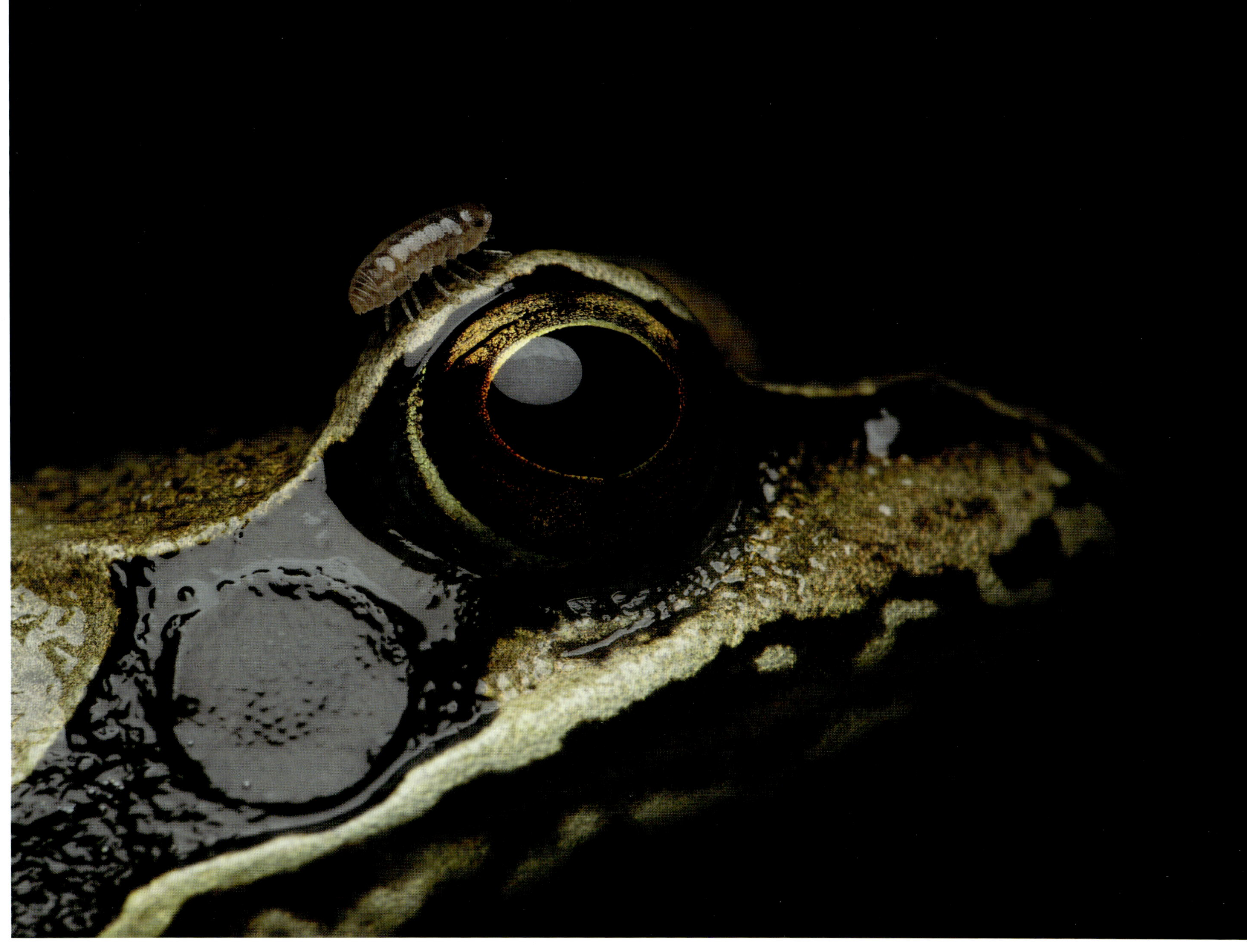

Predator Meets Prey
15-17 years | Highly Commended

Max Wood
Common frog (*Rana temporaria*)
Farnham, Surrey, England

Canon EOS 6D with Canon 100mm f/2.8 Macro lens.
100mm; 1/180th second; f/20; ISO 160.

While searching my garden for macro photography subjects, out of the corner of my eye I saw this common frog hopping around in some leaf litter. I laid down to get some photos of its beautiful and intricate eyes when a brave woodlouse crawled up its back and onto the bridge of its eye. Before long, the woodlouse was brushed off by the frog, narrowly missing out on being eaten.

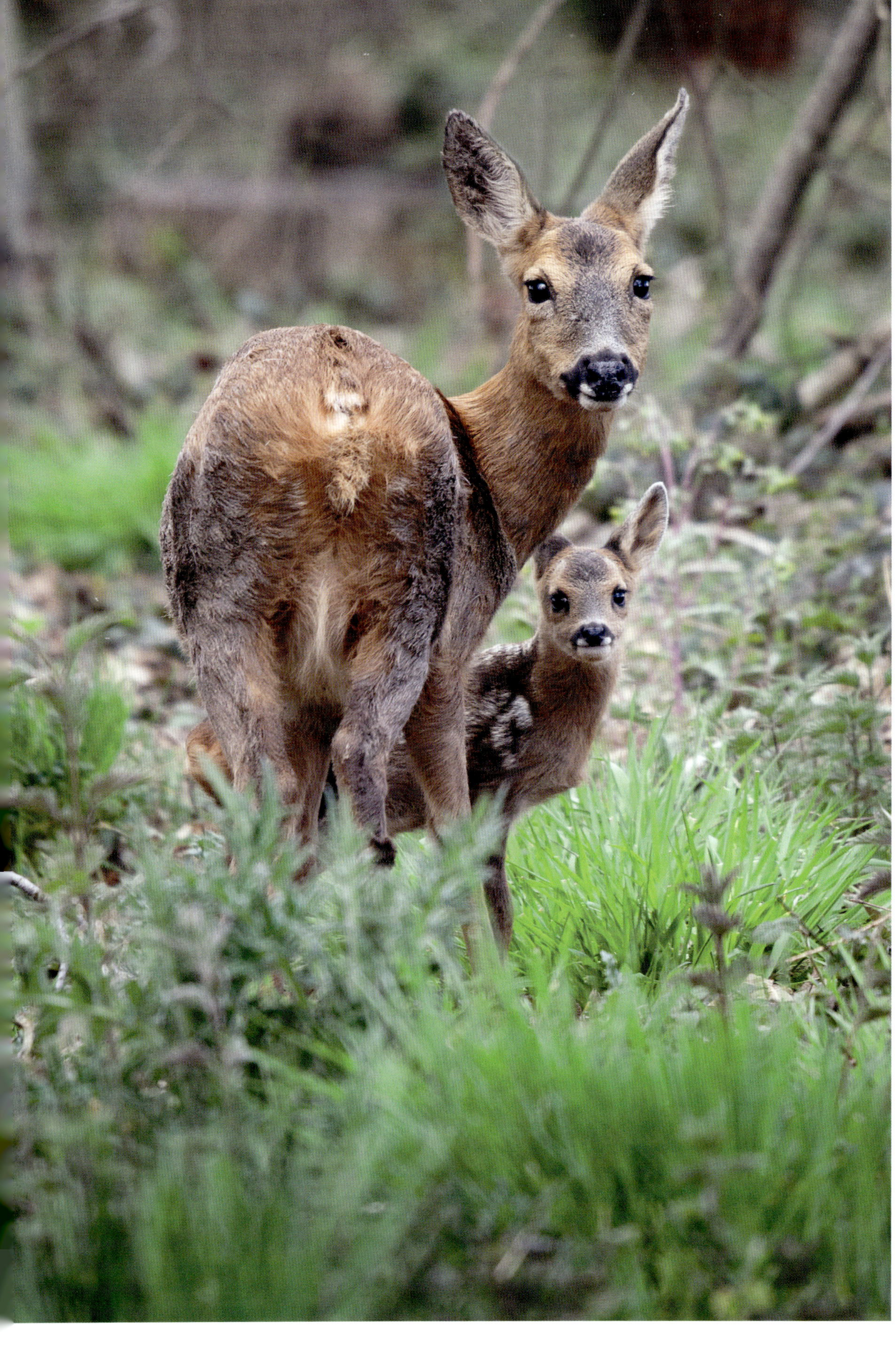

Mother and Fawn
12-14 years | Winner

Felix Walker-Nix
Roe deer (*Capreolus capreolus*)
Sherfield on Loddon, England

Canon EOS 5D II with Sigma 100-400mm f/5-6.3 lens. 400mm; 1/320th second; f/6.3; ISO 800.

Walking through the woods, I spotted this roe doe grazing the foliage. Slowly, I crept towards her, careful not to startle her. To my delight, when she turned round, I saw a small fawn staring back at me! Keeping quiet, I raised the camera to take some photos, then swiftly left so I didn't disturb the young fawn and mother any longer. It was an incredible experience to see a 'humbug' patterned fawn before it loses its spots, and it was a magical experience to get so close.

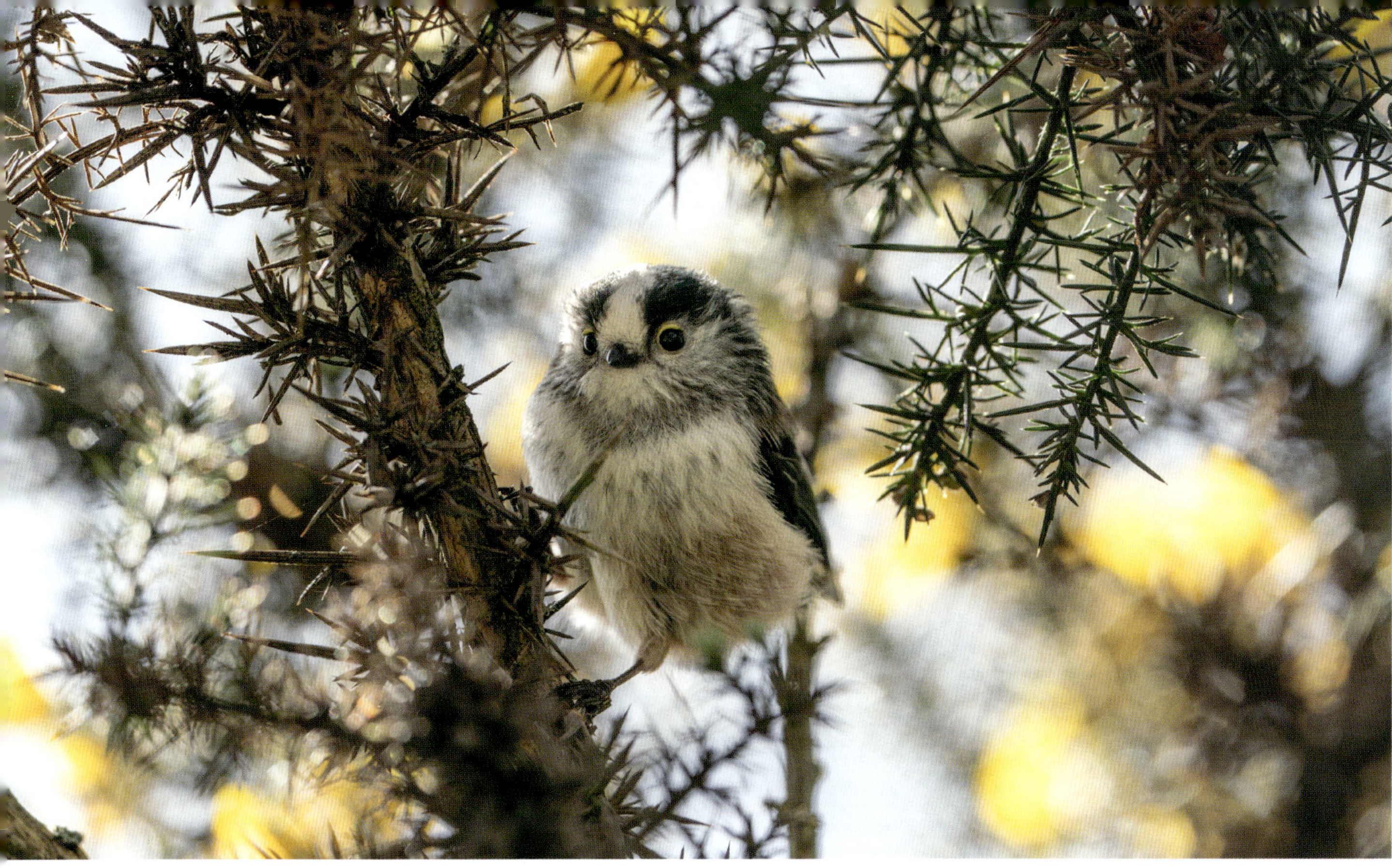

Male Banded Demoiselle
12-14 years | Highly Commended

William Lambourne
Banded demoiselle
(*Calopteryx splendens*)
Whixall Moss, Shropshire, England

Nikon D7000 with Sigma 150-500mm f/5-6.3 lens. 380mm; 1/250th second; f/9; ISO 320.

I was walking alongside a stretch of the Shropshire and Union Canal when I noticed a large 'cloud' of banded demoiselles flying around some hogweed. I singled out this male and isolated it against the dark background of trees. I positioned my camera so it was side-lit, highlighting all the details on its body.

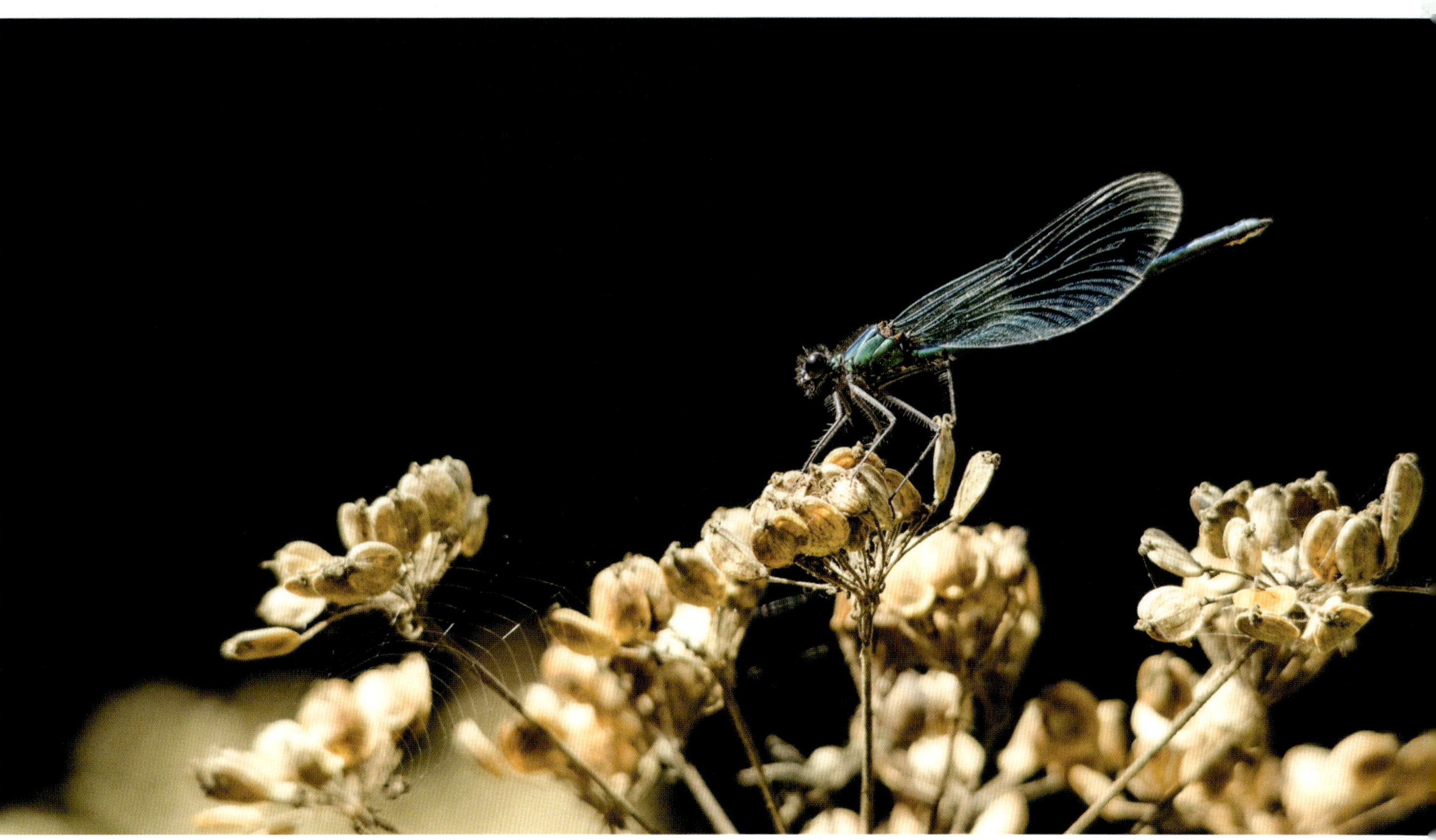

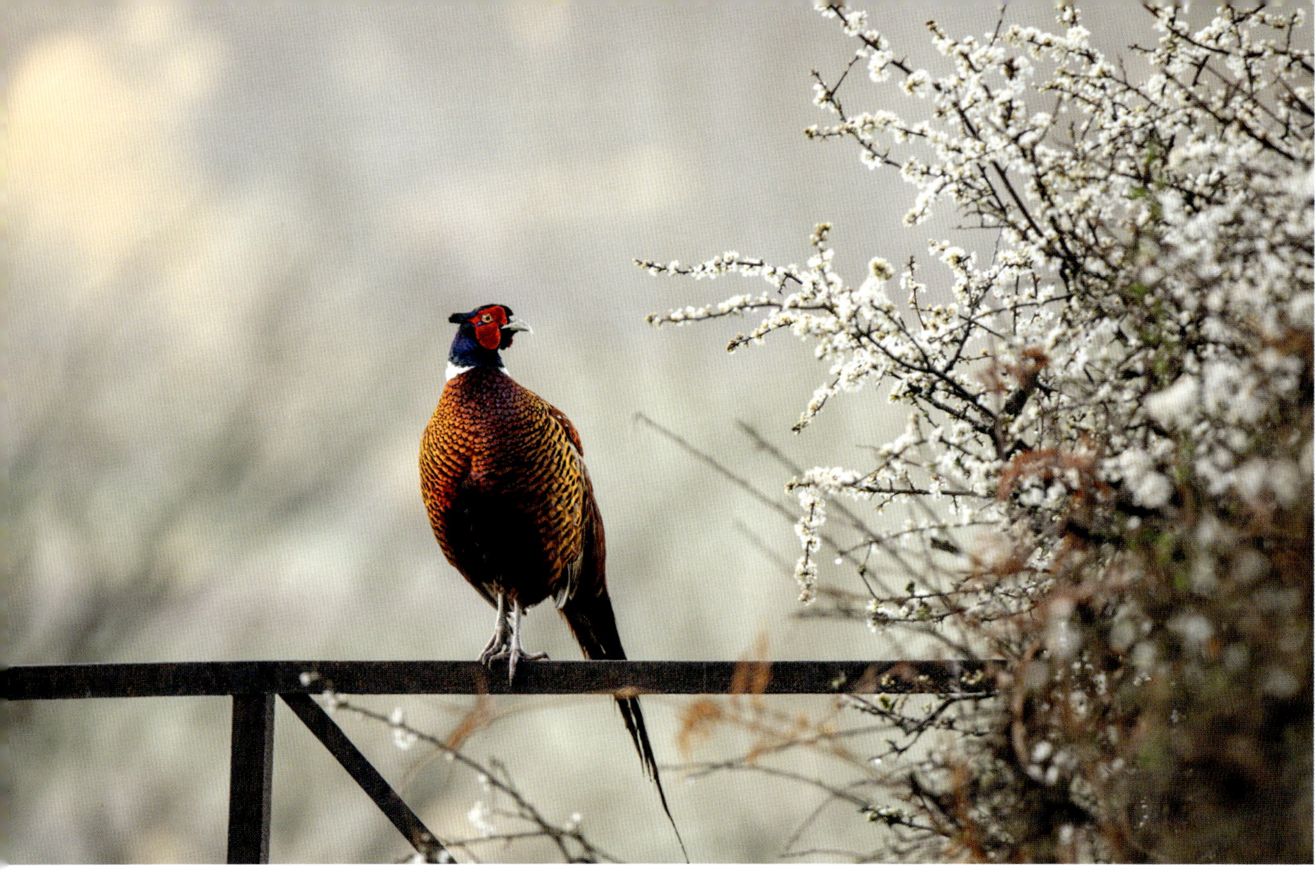

Palmate Newt
11 and under | Runner-up

Wilbur King
Palmate newt (*Lissotriton helveticus*)
Devon, England

Canon 5D III with Canon 100mm f/2.8 Macro lens. 100mm; 1/160th second; f/11; ISO 100.

When I stay at my grandparents' house, I always like to catch newts in the pond. So, my grandad and I decided to set up the fish tank so we could photograph one. It was a wet day, so we set up two flash guns and positioned them above and to the side to give the impression of natural sunlight.

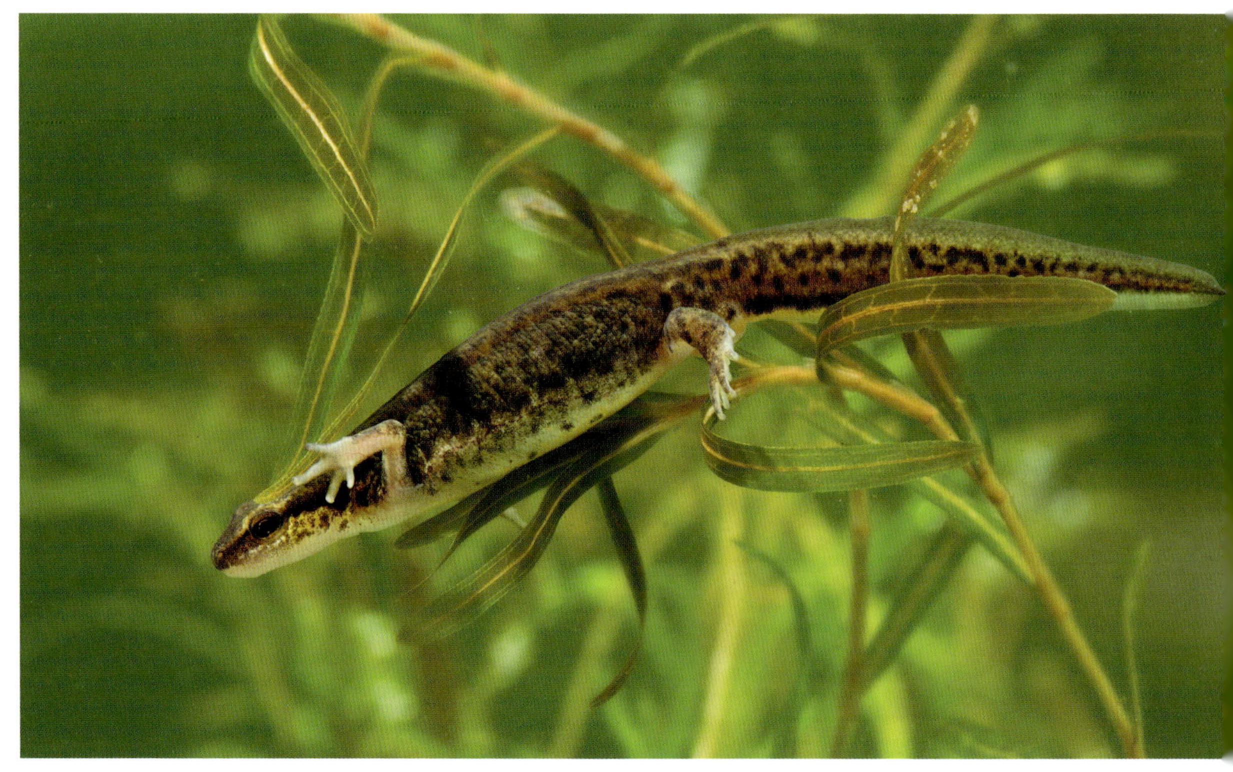

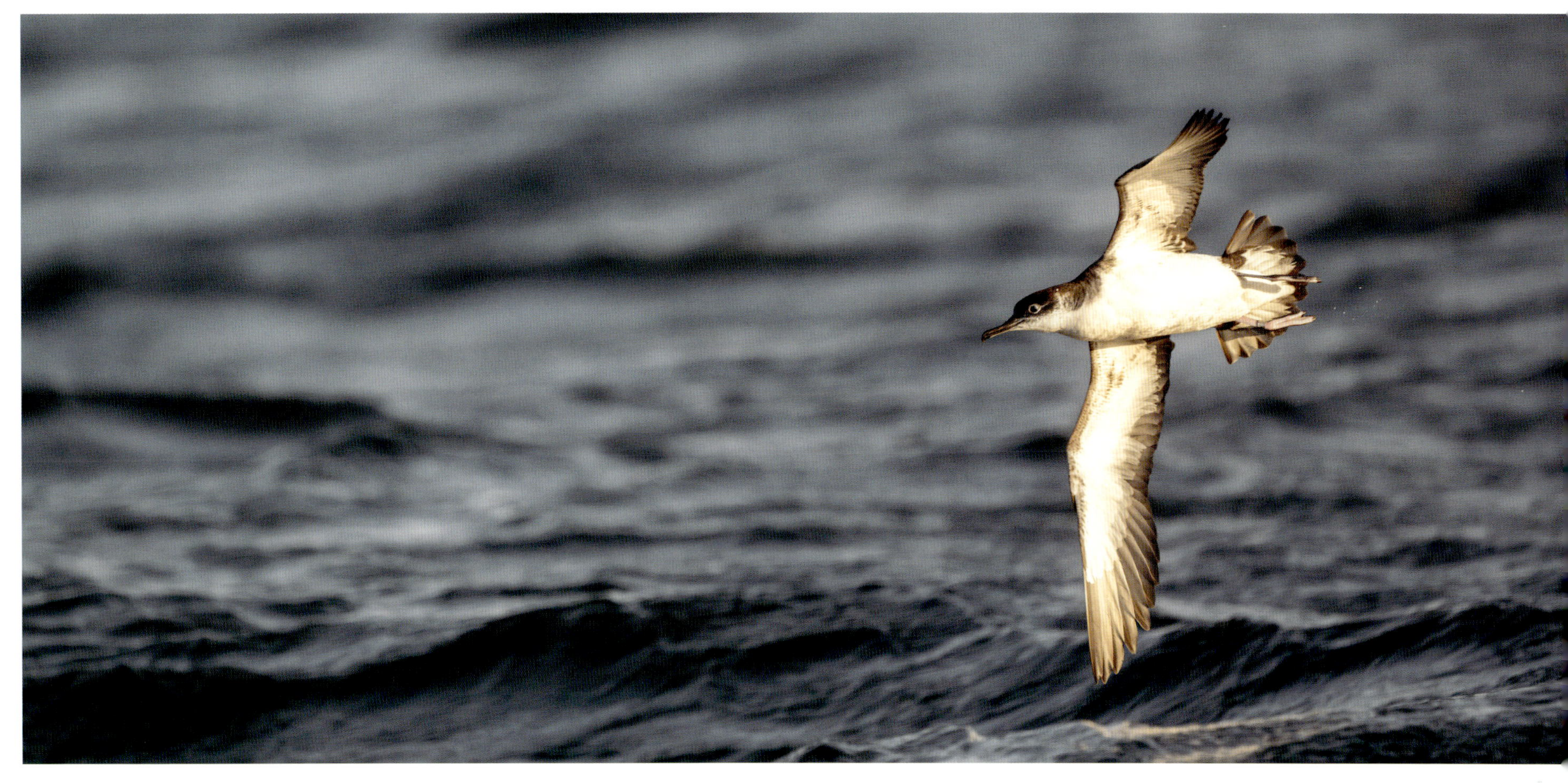

Shear De-light

11 and under | Highly Commended

Jamie Smart
Manx shearwater (*Puffinus puffinus*)
Pembrokeshire, Wales

Nikon Z 9 with Nikon 800mm f/6.3 lens. 800mm;
1/2,500th second; f/6.3; ISO 2,800.

I was given a trip to Skomer Island as a Christmas present last year. Sadly, it was cancelled last minute due to poor weather. We booked an evening trip around the island instead, and I'm pleased to say I wasn't disappointed. I was eager to see some Manx shearwaters, but the captain said it was unlikely as it wasn't quite dark enough for their return to land yet. Just as the boat was making a turn back to shore, I spotted a raft of around eight Manxies in the distance. Using my long lens and trying my best to steady myself on a lollopy boat, I managed this photo just before they flew away into the sunset. Even the captain was impressed!

INDEX